FORTRESS AMERICA

The Forts That Defended America 1600 to the Present

J. E. Kaufmann
and
H. W. Kaufmann

Illustrated by Tomasz Idzikowski

DA CAPO PRESS
A Member of the Perseus Books Group

To our parents and Leo

Cataloging-in-Publication data for this book is available from the Library of Congress.

ISBN 0-306-81294-0   623.1973

Unless otherwise indicated, all illustrations by Tomasz Idzikowski.

Published by Da Capo Press
A Member of the Perseus Books Group
http://www.dacapopress.com

Da Capo Press books are available at special discounts for bulk purchases in the U.S. by corporations, institutions, and other organizations. For more information, please contact the Special Markets Department at the Perseus Books Group, 11 Cambridge Center, Cambridge, MA 02142, or call (800)255-1514 or (617) 252-5298, or email special.markets@perseusbooks.com.

1 2 3 4 5 6 7 8 9-08 07 06 05 04

Printed in the United States of America.

CONTENTS

Sidebars

Maps

ACKNOWLEDGEMENTS

We would like to thank all those who helped us in the preparation of this work. Many of those who helped are members of SITEO, an international research organization devoted to fortifications and artillery (SITEO can be found on the internet through most search engines). A number of these people are also members of the British Fortress Study Group and the American Coast Defense Study Group. Hopefully, we have not forgotten anyone on the following list. The main area of their contribution is in parenthesis. * denotes those who contributed considerable information:

Prof. Felix Almarez* (Spanish Presidios), Reginaldo Bacchi* (Brazilian fortifications), Emerson Woods Baker II (Engineer Romer & New England forts), Ismael Barba (Spanish engineers), Andy Bennett (photos), John Bennett** (information and photos of Hawaiian fortifications), Mark Berhow** (modern American fortifications), Charles Bogart* (photos and information on sea mines), Gerry Borden (forts in British Columbia), Judith Bowman (curator, U.S. Army Museum of Hawaii, information on steel "pillboxes"), Jack Buckmeir (information on small fortifications of the northwest in World War II), Henry Cary (Canadian forts), Brian Chin** (forts of San Francisco), Tom Clinard (Governor's Island), Bob Cromwell (NPS Ranger, Fort Vancouver), Diana K. Depew* (supervisory park ranger, Colonial Yorktown National Historical Park), Clayton Donnell* (photos and Fort Delaware), Martin Dwyer* (photos and HECP), Whit Edwards (Oklahoma Historical Society, Fort Gibson), Pierre Etcheto* (Plans), William Gaines (information on Hawaiian fortifications), Prof. John Hancock (Fort Ancient and other Indian sites), Rick Hatcher* (NPS Ranger, Fort Sumter), Susan Hoskinson (director of Fort Vasquez Museum), David Johnson** (Casemate Museum of Fort Monroe), Talley Kirkland (NSP Ranger, Fort Pulaski), David Kirchner* (Hawaii and coast defenses), Robert E. L. Krick (historian) and the staff at the Richmond National Battlefield (Richmond/Petersburg battlefields), Michelle C. Lewis* (director at Fort Pike, documents), Sandra Lowry* (NPS librarian at Fort Laramie), Chris Morgan (director of Fort Gibson Historic Site), Prof. Narciso Menocal (Havana), Dennis Mroczkowski (Director of Casemate Museum of Fort Monroe), Roberto Mundo* (drawings), Patrick Paternostro (service manager, information on bunkers at Hoover Dam), Marco Ramerini (Portugese and Dutch fortifications in America), David Rankine (Canadian forts and Fort Henry), Sony Reisch (superintendent Fort Phil Kearny), Nick Reveliotty (internet sites), Charlie Robbins (documents and contacts), Andy Rohde (information and photos of bunkers in the northwest), Dan Rowbottom** (photos and NW fortifications), Nuno Rubim (Brazilian forts), CSM Daniel Sebby (California Center for Military History, information on California's defenses), David A. Simmons** (associate editor of Timeline; forts of Anthony Wayne), R. Hugh Simmons (Fort Delaware Society), Bolling Smith* (photos), Ron and Barbara Stoetzel** (photos of forts in NY, PA, & Canada), Lee Unterborn** (loan of books and research), Juan Vasques (Spanish military forces), Joan Wahl (Fort Hall, Idaho), Joseph C. Walack (manager of Island County Historical Museum, Coupeville; Alexander's Blockhouse), Dr. Richard Walding (magnetic loops), Newton Warzecha (plans for Presido La Bahia), John Weaver (3rd System forts), Larry S. Wilson (DEW Line stations), and Robert C. Wilson (curator Fort Phil Kearny, drawings), Harold Wright (information and map of St. John's defenses).

We would also like to thank David Johnson at the Casemate Museum for helping with gathering data and David Simmons for his articles and the sidebar he prepared. Also we thank Michelle Rodriguez, librarian at Palo Alto College, for helping us to obtain materials through ILL. Finally, we would like to mention some of the authors of the many articles in the Coast Defense Study Groups journal that are noted in the text that are a unique reference source. These authors included Mark Berhow, Charles Bogart, William Gaines, Dale Manuel, Bolling Smith, and Glenn Willford.

Many of the measurements and other data for fortifications in the United States are taken from the *Encyclopedia of Historic Forts: The Military, Pioneer, and Trading Posts of the United States* by Robert B. Robert (1988, New York: Macmillan Publishing). In a number of cases, this data has been taken from other secondary sources and some primary sources that are listed in the bibliography.

Please refer to the bibliography for sources that will provide more detail and illustrations not included in this introductory work. Those interested in American fortifications shoould contact: The Coast Defense Study Group at www.cdsg.org and the Council of Abandoned Military Posts at P.O. Box 1151, Fort Myer, VA 22211.

PROLOGUE

Fortified sites existed in the Americas long before the arrival of Europeans. During the pre-Colombian era the Native Americans did not have coastal defenses, but they did build fortifications throughout the two continents. In North America, some of the most famous fortified sites are those built by the Pueblo Indians of the Southwest who lived in fortified communities. In the northeastern part of the United States, the Iroquois built circular forts with timber stockades similar to those of the Europeans. Many sites of the Mississippi Valley, such as Etowah, also show vestiges of wooden stockades and towers. However, the most impressive pre-Colombian fortifications were encountered by the Spanish. Only thirty years after the arrival of Columbus, Hernán Cortez landed on the coast of Mexico and encountered several impressive fortified sites, such as the one at TLAXCALA, which he compared favorably to the city of Granada in Spain. He concluded his operations against the Aztecs in one of the largest siege operations to take place in the Americas. The Aztec capital city of TENOCHITLÁN was a virtual fortress. Built on islands accessed by defended causeways, it was one of the most interesting defensive positions ever created in the Americas. The battle to take this fortress on the lake in 1521 involved over 100,000 combatants. No other battle in the Americas involved such numbers until the American Civil War.

The Spanish Crown built a system of forts and fortresses to protect its ports in the Americas from piracy. The first Spanish fortifications were crude stockades like the one Columbus left behind on Hispañola on his first journey to America, at the settlement of La Navidad. Although Columbus found this fort in ruins on his return, the island of Hispañola—known then as Santo Domingo—became the first base of operations for Spain. Before Cortez sailed for Mexico, early in the sixteenth century, the Spanish moved their main base of operations to Cuba. From that point on, stone fortifications in the form of castillos, fortalezas, or fortins were built at almost every major Spanish port in the Americas. The most important fortress positions were established at Havana, San Juan (Puerto Rico), Vera Cruz (Mexico), and Cartagena (Colombia).

During the next three centuries, each one of these fortified forts would be put under siege or attacked. They represented the largest fortification complexes in the Americas until the French built a formidable fortress at Louisbourg in the eighteenth century, which proved less successful than the Spanish fortresses. The Spanish also built a number of other fortified sites of masonry with relatively modern designs in places such as Campeche, Portobello, Panama City, Santa Marta, Maracaibo, Puerto Cabello, Arraya, and Santiago. All were initially designed to protect the ports from European raiders. CASTILLO SAN MARCOS was built on the Florida coast to protect the return route to Spain.

Presidio La Bahia

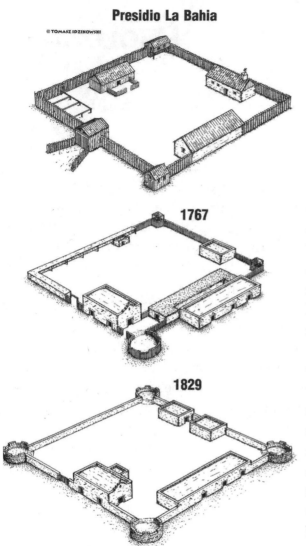

© TOMASZ IDZIKOWSKI

1767

1829

When English Sea Dogs, like Sir Francis Drake, and Dutch raiders struck at the west coast of the Americas, the Spanish responded by fortifying the ports in that area with masonry fortifications. Thus were born the complexes at Valdivia, Concepción, and Callao with its CASTILLO REAL FELIPE—the largest fort on the west coast—and Acapulco. Further north, on the Mexican coast, the port of San Blas was fortified in readiness for the exploration and settlement of the California coast. The major Spanish fortifications in both North and South America tended to be coastal positions. One the exceptions was the inland FORT IMMACULATA on the San Juan River in Nicaragua, built to block the water route to Granada.

To advance and secure the landward frontier, a line of presidios was established along the northern frontier of New Spain (modern-day Mexico). The first presidios were mostly small castle-like positions built of adobe rather than stone. In the seventeenth and eighteenth century, as the Spanish moved north toward the Rio Grande and then further north, they built a line of PRESIDIOS that began at ADAES and LA BAHIA (at Goliad) in eastern Texas, near French Louisiana, and stretched westward into Arizona. Although this line was not solid and more than one of the presidios had to be abandoned, it was the first defensive line of fortifications in the Americas. Usually built of adobe and sometimes stone, these presidios were generally square and were surrounded by a wall. Sometimes the buildings of the presidios formed the outside walls. The Dutch, English, and French laid claim to those islands of the West Indies that had been neglected by the Spanish. The forts, whether earthen and timber or stone, proved of limited value on these islands.

Masonry coastal fortifications in the style of Vauban's First System were found throughout the Spanish, Portuguese, and French empires in South and Middle America during the sixteenth, seventeenth, and early eighteenth centuries. In the remainder of North America (north of the Spanish empire), however, the fortifications were generally made of wood and seldom became impressive before the latter part of the eighteenth cen-

The First European Fortified Site in North America

The first European settlement in North America was a Viking outpost founded by Icelander Leif Erikson around 1000 A.D. First mention of this outpost was made in the Vinland Sagas, which were orally transmitted for over a century before they were committed to parchment in the early twelfth century. Long thought to be the fruit of fanciful imagination, these sagas were proven correct when the remains of a Norse settlement were found at L'ANSE AUX MEADOWS, in Newfoundland in 1961.

The settlement, named STRAUMFJORD by the Norse, consisted of three large longhouses and associated buildings, probably built for the crews of three vessels. The three Viking crews, which included women, wintered at l'Anse aux Meadows and dispersed in the summer to explore further south along the American coast where they trapped animals for fur, collected wood and grapes, and occasionally traded and even fought with the natives.

According to the sagas, Straumfjord was occupied at two or three different times, by different expeditions, for periods of a few years. During one of the expeditions, they traded milk and milk products with the natives. However, Karlsefni, one of the Norse leaders, "had a palisade built around his farm, where they prepared to defend themselves." After the last expedition, the site was abandoned, apparently because the Vikings did not have the manpower necessary to establish a permanent colony in America.

Source: Fitzhugh, William W. and Elisabeth I. Ward, *The Vikings, the North Atlantic Saga*, Smithsonian Institution Press, Washington.

tury. Most of these fortifications were built for inland defense and were involved in considerable combat. The defenses of the British Thirteen Colonies and New France and Louisiana evolved from simple stockades to more complex forts during the seventeenth and eighteenth centuries. The strategy and outcome of the French and Indian War, the American Revolution, and the War of 1812 were based heavily on these fortifications. To a degree, the same is true of the American Civil War, but after the War of 1812, the emphasis shifted mainly toward coastal fortifications until the end of World War II for most of the Americas.

After World War II, a radical new type of fortification and defensive system emerged. Lookouts no longer scanned the horizon from blockhouses or towers attached to forts. Instead, new warning systems relied mainly on electronic equipment, in many cases located far from the fortifications and forming warning lines with no defenses. The new concrete fortifications, usually of a subterranean type, no longer had the purpose of defending a coastline or holding a vital piece of territory. Instead, many of them protected weapons of mass destruction that could obliterate an enemy's homeland far away from the fortresses concrete walls.

Native American Fortifications

Fortifications were by no means a new notion in North America when the European colonists started building their fortified settlements on the East Coast in the sixteenth century. Although archaeological evidence of the earliest palisades has not yet come to light, it is very likely that they appeared about the time the Indians abandoned a nomadic lifestyle for a settled village life based on the cultivation of Meso-American plants like corn and squash. By 800 B.C., large fortified settlements associated with the Adena culture appeared in Ohio and Kentucky. The Adena village was a large settlement that included various earthen ceremonial mounds and was enclosed by a square earthen wall with rounded corners.

The Adena culture was followed by the Hopewell culture (100 B.C.– 400 A.D.), which was also characterized by ceremonial mounds and earthworks. One of the most impressive Hopewell sites was FORT ANCIENT, located on a 235-foot bluff on the Little Miami River and surrounded by earth-and-stone walls. Curiously, sections of the wall were lined with internal, rather than external ditches. Although archaeologists at the site claim the wall had no defensive purposes, it is baffling to think that the villagers spent so much time and effort on erecting a wall around their village simply for esthetic or religious purposes. Further research and analysis will shed more light on the function of the Fort Ancient wall.

The southern Hopewell culture evolved into the Mississippian, which flourished between 500 A.D. and 1500 and was characterized by elaborate mound building. Some of the best-known sites of this culture are Cahokia and Etowah, which consisted of large central settlements surrounded by satellite villages. The large settlements were surrounded by elaborate wooden fortifications.

CAHOKIA (700–1400 A.D.) was contemporary with the castleß and fortified cities of medieval Europe. It covered almost six square miles and had a population of about twenty thousand people. Its central section was surrounded by a two-mile long, tall stockade with evenly spaced bastions that projected in front of the curtain wall, allowing the defenders to cover the walls with arrows. Some sections of the wall appear to have been hastily built. The original stockade is dated at around 1100 A.D. and seems to have been rebuilt three times during the following two hundred years. Archaeologists working on the site estimate that it might have required fifteen to twenty thousand oak and hickory logs, one foot in diameter, to build the twenty-foot wall. It is thought that the wall was covered with a layer of clay to prevent the enemy from burning it down.

The site of ETOWAH (950–1450 A.D.), located at the confluence of the Etowah River and Pumpkinwine Creek near Cartersville, was also a large stockaded settlement with ceremonial mounds and pyramids. Like Cahokia, it was surrounded by sattelite villages, still occupied by the Creeks at the time of the Hernando de Soto expedition. Benjamin Hawkins, an Indian agent, reported in the eighteenth century that "Creek legends tell of palisaded, compact towns." Hawkins himself observed that the Creek settlements he had visited were "well fenced with fine stocks of cattle, horses and hogs surrounded by fields of corn, rice and potatoes." This indicates that the Mississippian tradition of building fortified settlements had persisted well into colonial times.

Many of the nations of the Eastern Woodlands also built well-defended, stockaded settlements when the Europeans arrived. According to Samuel de Champlain, the Iroquois village he attacked was "enclosed with four good palisades of logs of wood interlaced, so that there was not more than half a foot of opening between any two. These palisades were thirty feet high, and had galleries after the fashion of a parapet, which were furnished with pieces of wood set double ... They were near a pond, where the water never failed. There were a good many gutters, one placed between each pair of loopholes, by which water was poured outside, and they had water inside, under cover, to extinguish fire. This is their method of fortification and of defence, and they are stronger that the villages of the Attigouantans."

In the southwestern United States, there is also abundant evidence of fortified villages. However, whereas the materials of choice were earth and wood in the Mississippi Valley and the Eastern Woodlands, in this semi-arid zone the material was stone. According to archae-ologist Stephen LeBlanc, the people of the Southwest began moving their villages from the valley and canyon floors to higher, more easily defended locations around 1200 A.D., a period that coincided with increasing drought and famine. Fierce competition for arable land and water led to armed conflict. Fortified sites, like MESA VERDE, sprouted on easily defended bluffs and cliffs. When villages stayed in the valley, the houses were built in tiers around a central plaza, in a circle, semicircle, or rectangle. Doorways and openings faced the plaza, while the back walls formed a solid curtain wall, thicker than the interior walls. The defenders were able to shoot at their enemy from the rooftops. If possible, the village encompassed a spring to supply the villagers with water; if not, cisterns were dug to collect rainwater. In the Zuni area, many sites included one or more masonry towers that might have served as lookouts or refuges of last-resort.

Example of a defensive tower at Mesa Verde, Colorado.

New France 1750s

Based on map by Jean Baptiste Nolin

Ft Beausejour
Port Dauphin
Isle Royale
Louisbourg
Ft S. Jean
Port Royal
Port de Toulouse
outh
C. de Sable

Chapter 1

New France and Louisiana

Early Settlement

WHEN THE SPANISH CLAIMED THE NEW WORLD and divided it with the Portuguese in the 1490s, the French were the only European power in a position to counter their claims. But the Americas did not hold much appeal for the French until the Italian John Cabot (Giovanni Cabotto) made two exploratory voyages along the North American coast from what is now Maryland to Baffin Island on behalf of England late in the 1490s. His discovery of excellent fishing banks stimulated some interest of the French king, Francis I, who sent his own Italian mariner, Giovanni da Verazzano, to explore the region in 1525. Verazzano's voyage along the North American coast from Carolina to Newfoundland would be the basis for future French claims, just as Cabot's journey served as a basis for English claims.

Francis I commissioned Jacques Cartier to lead another expedition in 1534. Cartier, who sailed along the Gulf of St. Lawrence, thought that great waterway might provide a northwestern passage through the Americas. But the French would not begin to settle in the region until the next century.

In 1604, an expedition that included a small number of settlers and Samuel de Champlain, a royal geographer who mapped the coast, set out for Canada. The leader of the expedition set up a settlement and built a fort of earth and palisades on the island of Sainte Croix, which proved unsuccessful because its poor location left it exposed to the elements. The site was abandoned after the first brutal winter and some of the survivors moved to another island on the Bay of Fundy, where, under the leadership of Champlain, they established the settlement of Port Royal (now Annapolis) in 1605. Located in western Nova Scotia, Port Royal became the first French colony in Acadia, an area that would eventually be heavily contested in the struggle between France and

13

England. According to Leslie Hannon, author of *Forts of Canada*, Champlain is credited with the construction of the HABITATION because, being the expedition's cartographer, he was the only one with the skill to draw up the plan. In addition, he was familiar with the designs of late medieval-type fortifications built in small farms and hamlets in northern France. His Habitation was essentially a rectangular enclosure with high walls that served to defend the settlers. According to drawings of the period, it included a square corner bastion, which was little more than a platform outside the fort's walls that mounted four bronze cannons to protect the harbor. The high walls of the enclosure were actually formed by the buildings and their upper levels included small windows or embrasures for muskets. Access was through a single narrow entrance protected by a projecting flanking palisade reminiscent of a bastion with a platform for the defenders. A ditch partially encircled the position and the buildings that formed the Habitation included quarters, storage, a bakery, and all other necessary facilities.

In 1607, the colony was abandoned and was not reestablished until 1610. In 1613, an English expedition from Jamestown sailed into the bay, raided Port Royal, destroyed the Habitation and took the prisoners back to Virginia, which claimed the land of Acadia. In 1621, King James granted the land to a Scot and the first settlers arrived from Scotland in 1629 and founded CHARLES FORT, located about five hundred yards above the old site of Champlain's Habitation. By the time the war between the French and English ended, the Scottish settlers were removed and Acadia was returned to France by virtue of the treaty of 1632. The Scots reluctantly departed, destroying everything in their wake including their small fort. The French built an earthen fort on a new site several miles away. However, this did not end the strife in Acadia. Charles de La Tour built FORT LA TOUR (also known by other names such as FORT MARTIGON and FORT ST. JEAN) at the site of present-day St. John, on the river of the same name. Port Royal and its fort changed hands several times during the period between 1632 and 1690.

French influence extended down the coast to Penobscot Bay in modern-day Maine, where the French claimed the land north of the Kennebec River. In 1635, they drove out merchants from the English Plymouth colony, which had operated a post there for several years. They then constructed a square fort of stone and earth with four corner bastions named FORT PENTAGOËT. Some of the stone used for the walls included slate from Brittany that was carried over as ship's ballast. It is believed that the walls were 60 feet in length and 16 feet thick at the base, tapering off to 6 feet at the top. Archaeological evidence shows that the 1670 plan exaggerates the size by 40 percent. According to archaeologist Alaric Faulkner, this was a ruse practiced by some administrators to impress the king. One can only guess how many other plans of small forts had similar distortions. The fort included a stone barracks, a two-floor magazine, and a chapel placed over the entrance. The fort mounted twelve cannons, the largest of which were a pair of 8-pdrs. The fort changed hands several times until 1722, when the British leveled it.

In 1608, Champlain founded a post at the site of present-day QUEBEC, on a peninsula

Port Royal Habitation

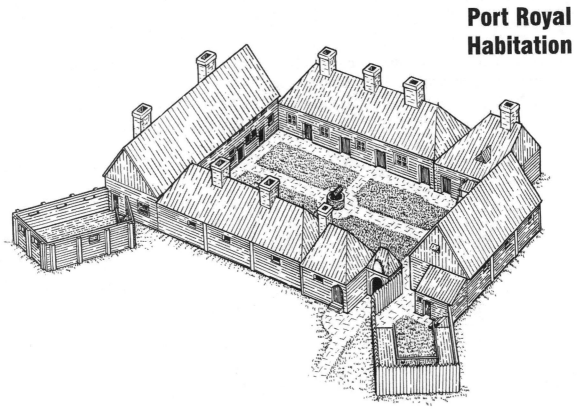

© **TOMASZ IDZIKOWSKI**

formed by the St. Charles River, and protected terrain by cliffs along the St. Lawrence River. During the seventeenth century, the defenses of Quebec remained unremarkable, despite the fact that the city served as the key to New France. Initially, in 1608, Champlain built another Habitation, more medieval in appearance than the one at Port Royal. Quebec, at this time, was a fortified trading post consisting of a series of buildings inside curtain walls that also formed the walls of the Habitation on the banks of the St. Lawrence. Its small size did not allow it to take advantage of the natural defensive features in the vicinity. The first Habitation on the site included three two-story buildings with walls made of a wooden palisade, the whole surrounded by a ditch. Outside the walls, Champlain added a "boulevard," a low bastion-like position for artillery placed in front of the walls of a medieval castle in Europe. The first settlers did not arrive until 1617 and by the early 1620s, the population still numbered fewer than a hundred souls, almost half of whom resided in the Habitation. In 1620, Champlain began work on FORT ST. LOUIS on nearby cliffs overlooking the lower city and replaced the Habitation. In 1623, Governor Champlain created a second Habitation that included small towers. He also had to incorporate in the defenses of Quebec some of the permanent structures of the city, including churches, to serve as redoubts and places to protect artillery batteries.

When an English fleet showed up in 1629, both Quebec's fortifications and its garrison, consisting of fewer than two dozen men, were physically too weak to put up a defense. Champlain was compelled to surrender his starving garrison and was taken prisoner by the British. He returned to Quebec in 1633, after the city was returned to the French. He brought with him several hundred more colonists. During his absence, the English had improved Fort St. Louis, but the second Habitation had burned down. Charles Huault de Montmagny soon replaced Champlain as governor and turned Fort St. Louis into a stone structure with four towers in the 1640s. As the town grew along its peninsular position between the 1640s and 1665, the French governors of New France set up new defensive works to protect it.

After King William's War ended in 1697 when Port Royal was returned to them, the French decided to build a new fort to defend the port. The fort would be instrumental in repelling English attacks on Port Royal once in 1704 and twice in 1707 during Queen Ann's War. However, in 1710, a force of three thousand British colonials and over three thousand Redcoats finally succeeded in taking the fort and town, which had been isolated from outside support since 1707. The English renamed the fort of Port Royal as FORT ANN. In 1711, a French force returned to put the fort under siege, but when their cannons failed to arrive, they had to give up and retreat. The Treaty of Ütrecht of 1713 awarded Port Royal to the British and the region became known as Nova Scotia, in honor of the Scots who first attempted to settle there.

Fortifying Quebec and Access to the Mouth of the St. Lawrence

The fall of Port Royal during King William's War had galvanized the governor of New France to fortify QUEBEC adequately in the 1690s. The upper city of Quebec, though less vulnerable to attacks from the sea than the lower city because of its location on an elevated plateau, remained exposed on its landward side. In 1690, Governor de Frontenac ordered the erection of an earth and timber fortification to seal off the peninsula, thus blocking the approach from the landward side. However, the 1690 works were only of a temporary nature. In 1693, before the conclusion of King William's War, eleven redoubts linked by an earthwork enceinte that included revetted palisades spanned the peninsula and protected Quebec. Josué DuBois Berthelot de Beaucours, the engineer responsible for this work, was clearly influenced by Vauban's First System, a rather simple but effective system of fortifications based on geometric design.

After the war, the engineer Levasseur de Néré was commissioned to create a second enceinte in 1700. By this time, some work had already been done on the defenses of the lower town, including the construction of the Royal Battery in 1691. To the west of Quebec, over ninety yards from the shore, stood Cape Diamond whose steep slope required only artillery batteries to control the river. Although the modernization and completion of the defenses was far from finished in the early 1720s, the French Navy minister, Jean-Fréderic Phélypeaux, Conte de Maurepas (1723 to 1749), concluded that the resources allotted to the defenses of New France should be diverted to the con-

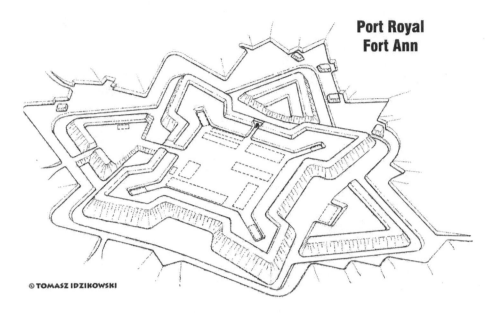

**Port Royal
Fort Ann**

© TOMASZ IDZIKOWSKI

struction of a fortress at Louisbourg on Isle Royale (Cape Breton Island) and to the fortification of Montreal. Thus, the fortification of Quebec remained incomplete.

Even though military engineer Gaspard-Joseph Chaussegros de Léry urged new construction projects for the fortifications of Quebec during the first half of the eighteenth century, his advice was disregarded. It was decided that Montreal, Louisbourg, and the forts on the Richelieu/Lake Champlain route should form the first and only line of defense of the capital and the heart of New France on the banks of the St. Lawrence. After doing some work at Quebec, de Léry moved to Montreal, called Ville Marie prior to 1700. In 1717, he began replacing the wooden palisade encircling the city with masonry walls.

When the French ceded Newfoundland to the British, access to the mouth of the St. Lawrence was left wide open and the French fishermen in the area lost the protection of a military base. As a result, the island of Isle Royale acquired new significance and French settlers were dispatched to Havre à L'Anglois (English Port), which was renamed Port Saint-Louis. The group included about 150 settlers and soldiers, including Major L'Hermitte, the engineer responsible for planning the fortifications of Port Saint-Louis (renamed Louisbourg in 1719) in 1713. St. Peter's Island, now renamed Port Toulouse, and St. Anne's, which became Port Dauphin, each received a fort.

In a book entitled *Louisbourg*, J. S. McLennan mentions that when Governor Vaudreuil arrived at Port Saint-Louis (Louisbourg) in 1714, he rejected L'Hermitte's plans to create a series of forts. Instead, he wanted to fortify the entire position, turning Louisbourg into a fortress. However, this ambitious plan would be difficult to carry out since there was no lime for mortar or building stone available in the immediate vicinity and the governor brought no funds to launch the operation. Louisbourg was selected as the site for the new fortress because it was closer to the fishing grounds and offered ice-free anchorage. The drawback was that it was not the easiest position on the island to fortify.

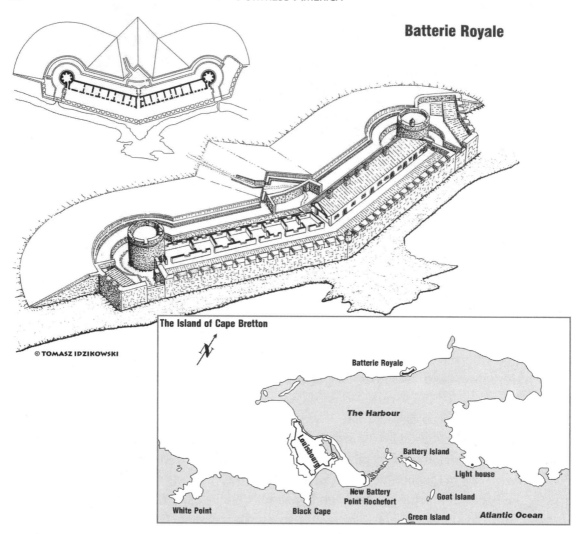

Batterie Royale

The Island of Cape Bretton

© TOMASZ IDZIKOWSKI

Batterie Royale

The Harbour

Louisbourg

Battery Island

Light house

New Battery
Point Rochefort

Goat Island

White Point   Black Cape   Green Island   Atlantic Ocean

When pirates became a threat in the region in 1721, LOUISBOURG boasted a population of about a thousand souls, but it was still poorly fortified. Only about a dozen cannons protected the harbor. The garrison consisted of eight *compagnies franches de la marine*, but, unlike others formed in America as colonial units, most consisted of enlisted men who came from France and returned home when their six years of duty were up. Until the main fortifications were completed, the Batterie Royale—known as the Grand Battery by the English—was the main defensive position.

The fortifications for Louisbourg, planned since 1714, were finally completed in 1738. The landward or west side was protected by the Princess Demi-Bastion, which was connected by a curtain wall to the Queen's Bastion, which, in turn, led to the King's Bastion, which stood on a slight rise and was fully enclosed. This bastion was also known as the Citadel because it housed the governor's palace (the largest building in Louisbourg) and had its own fortified entrance. From the King's Bastion, the curtain wall descended to the Dauphin Bastion adjacent to the Dauphin Gate, the main entrance into Louisbourg. A moat and a counterscarp with a covered way and glacis completed these

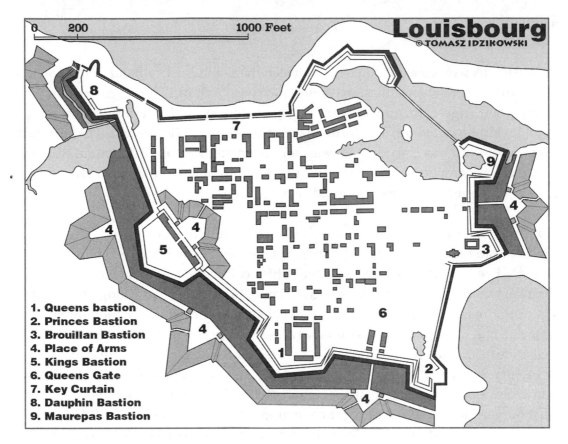

Louisbourg
©TOMASZ IDZIKOWSKI

0   200   1000 Feet

1. Queens bastion
2. Princes Bastion
3. Brouillan Bastion
4. Place of Arms
5. Kings Bastion
6. Queens Gate
7. Key Curtain
8. Dauphin Bastion
9. Maurepas Bastion

landward positions. Although it was declared complete by 1738, additional improvements were made on the fortress at a later date. Beyond the walls lay a bog or marsh punctuated by some low hillocks, which the engineers believed was too soggy to allow the enemy to move his artillery close enough to bombard the defenses. The walls continued around the city harbor and seaward sides. On the harbor side of the Dauphin Bastion, the curtain ran to a point northeast of the city on the opposite side of a pond that bordered the city. There, a battery position, Battery La Grave, was set up. From there, a bridge bisected the pond, crossing to the east side of the city where it met the Maurepas Bastion, which had a small pond in its center. This bastion was connected by a curtain to the Brouillan Bastion. Between these two bastions was the Maurepas Gate. All these features were fronted by a moat, counterscarp, and glacis since they faced a small peninsula with headlands and a beach where an enemy could land. From the Brouillan Bastion (named for the governor) the curtain led back to the Prince's Bastion. The curtains surrounding the city were generally lower in height than those on the landward defenses. On the walls and bastions encircling the city there were firing positions for up to 148 cannons. The docks were located on the harbor side, along the curtain wall on the north side of the city, between the Dauphin Bastion and the large pond. A boom was stretched from the vicinity of the Dauphin Gate across the water to the area where the shoreline bulged out to the northeast of the docks. The entrance to the harbor area was a little less than a mile wide. It was defended by the Island Battery that stood on an island almost in the middle. Between this island and Louisbourg there were shoals. The deep channel for ships ran between them and the headland to the northeast called North Cape where a masonry lighthouse was built in 1734.

The second largest structure in Louisbourg was the hospital, one of the grandest facilities of its kind in America. The fortified complex also included arsenals and barracks. However, duty in this isolated post was not rewarding because the climate was harsh and the only distraction available was liquor. With so much idle time on its hands, the garrison of Louisbourg soon acquired a reputation for drunkenness and mutinous behavior.

Until 1744, when a new war began with Great Britain, the fortress of Louisbourg not only served to protect the fishing grounds, Quebec, and French interests in the area, but also served as an outlet for trade with the British colonies despite the mercantile policy of France. When King George's War was declared, the fortress had enough foodstuffs in its storerooms to last a mere three weeks. William Shirley, the governor of Massachusetts, prepared an expedition against Louisbourg in 1745. With William Pepperell at its head, the invasion force of over three thousand troops, mostly militia, sailed out in fifty transport ships and a few warships, including a 60-gun man of war. Meanwhile, Louis du Chambon, governor of Isle Royale, prepared the defenses of Louisbourg which consisted of eight companies of marines, about four hundred men. They were reinforced by a couple of companies of Swiss mercenaries and about fourteen hundred militia, bringing the total to about two thousand men.

Pepperell's troops landed on the island's rocky beaches of Gabarus Bay on April 25, 1745, despite icy conditions. The French abandoned the Batterie Royale, and within a few days the New Englanders were laying siege to Louisbourg. The French defenders, running low on ammunition, surrendered on June 17. The victors took over the fortress and began repairing the damaged fortifications, and, as can be expected, renamed the bastions. After taking control of the fortress of Louisbourg, the British naval commander hoisted the French flag at the entrance to the harbor to lure French merchant ships into a trap. In October 1748, the war ended with the Treaty of Aix-la-Chapelle and Louisbourg and Cape Breton Island returned to the French in exchange for the lost British territory in India. The British, realizing they had given up a particularly important base in Nova Scotia, began the construction of their own fortress at Halifax. In 1749, a few months after the war, the British sent 2,500 settlers to populate the new stronghold that was to rival Louisbourg.

The fall of Fortress Louisbourg in 1745 left Quebec exposed and Governor Beauharnois took matters in his own hands, directing the construction of a masonry enceinte for the city. He took up de Léry's old plans from 1716 and incorporated the older enceintes in the new work. The governor also ordered the new enceinte to be placed further to the west on the land front, allowing room for future expansion of the city. Some sections, including the covered way, were not completed, but when the final war broke out in the 1750s, the city had an adequate set of fortifications.

Forts of the Great Lakes Wilderness

Although the fortress of Louisbourg is the focus of much attention because it guarded the gateway into New France, a number of other forts also played a significant role in the defense of New France in the eighteenth century. In the west, the French began to gain control of the Great Lakes region. The jumping off point for the expansion westward was Fort Frontenac, built in 1673 on the northeastern end of Lake Ontario, on the site of an Indian village at modern-day Kingston. As Canadians and Jesuits moved westward and a new fur-trading region was opened, the fort overflowed with furs for export to Europe and supplies to support the western outposts. A 1685 map shows that the fort had three corner-bastions, the two largest of which were on the landward side. Apparently there was no curtain wall facing Lake Ontario. The fort sealed a small peninsula and it also had a large barracks. Fort Frontenac not only served as a gateway to the west, but also protected the approaches down the St. Lawrence toward Montreal.

The governor, Jacques-René de Brisa Denonville, thought to use Fort Frontenac to keep the Iroquois from crossing the St. Lawrence and raiding the lands of his Indian allies. However, the fort failed to block the Iroquois raids. Finally in 1687, the exasperated governor led a 3,000-man expedition against the Iroquois from the vicinity of Fort Frontenac. After a hard-won victory, Denonville withdrew. Undaunted, the Iroquois struck back, placing Fort Frontenac under siege throughout the winter. Disease took its toll on the defenders, wiping out most of the troops at Fort Frontenac and at the outpost Denonville had built on the Niagara after his campaign. After the siege, he evacuated both forts and returned to Montreal. In 1689, the Iroquois launched a major raid, massacring on their way the inhabitants of Lachine (La Chine), a settlement near Montreal. In 1693, Governor de Frontenac reoccupied the fort bearing his name and repaired it, contemplating a new offensive against the Iroquois. In 1696, he led an expeditionary force across the lake, into western New York to crush the Iroquois. At this time, Fort Frontenac was manned by a garrison of 110 men and was armed with as many as sixty cannons and sixteen mortars. It remained a key post throughout the French and Indian War.

One of the most important posts in the west was established at the portage between the Great Lakes of Erie and Ontario. This post later became Fort Niagara, near the famous Niagara Falls. La Salle, recognizing the importance of the place during the previous century, had set up the first stockade fort with a warehouse in that location. He called it Fort Condé. This original structure left much to be desired as a defensive position and was abandoned in 1679 and later burned by the Senecas. After his campaign against the Iroquois in the summer of 1687, Denonville moved to Niagara and built a stockade with four corner bastions, which he named Fort Denonville. The garrison he left in the fort found itself isolated that winter and surrounded by hostile Iroquois. After the Senecas and disease struck, eighty men died. The following spring, the garrison pulled down the fort and departed.

Fort Niagara, New York. A view from the river of the French Castle or "House of Peace" from 1726. The Bake House is next to it. Photo courtesy of Don Stoetzel.

The French did not return to the area with intentions of establishing a base until 1701, when they built a new fort at the site of Detroit. In 1720, a French trader named Louis Joncaire was sent to negotiate with the Iroquois for permission to build a trading post at Niagara. The site selected was located below the escarpment. The trading post, given the lofty name of Magazin Royal, consisted of little more than a stockade and a cabin, but drew the displeasure of the British nonetheless.

In 1725, Joncaire reached an agreement with the Indians to build a more permanent structure, and in June 1726, Chaussegros de Léry arrived with French ships to build a new fort on the site of Denonville's old one. In order not to alarm the Indians, de Léry had to make it appear not to be a fort. With this in mind, he built a large stone house surrounded by a stockade. It was not until about the nineteenth century that it was referred to as the FRENCH CASTLE, but for many years it was the only structure at FORT NIAGARA. It was called "the House of Peace" to mislead the Iroquois and was designed to look like a trading post. The construction of the fort lasted until the end of the year. The position consisted of three levels, the uppermost of which included casemate positions for artillery. Granite for the construction of the French Castle was brought from the vicinity of Fort Frontenac. To prevent damage from fire, de Léry did not use wooden partitions, using instead stone for the walls as well as the floors. The ground floor included a powder magazine, guardroom, store rooms and even a bakery. There was also a well inside the building. The second floor housed quarters for about thirty soldiers and a chapel. Machicolations, so typical of medieval castles, were built to reinforce the defenses. The back of the structure overlooked Lake Ontario. The cannons arrived by ship the next year and were moved into the building under the cloak of secrecy to keep the Indians from realizing that the upper floor was actually a series of casemated positions for weapons concealed by a wooden roof. (The term casemate is used very loosely here.) Additional work was done in 1727 and the fort was assigned a garrison of a hundred men. During King George's War the garrison dwindled to as few as thirty men.

FORT ROUILLE, also known as FORT TORONTO, was built in 1750 to strengthen the link between Fort Frontenac and Fort Niagara. It was rather small and only had a garrison of about ten men since it was mainly a trading post. FORT LA GALETTE, built on the St. Lawrence about halfway between Montreal and Lake Ontario, strengthened the French line of 1749. It consisted of a masonry redoubt with five cannons and a palisade enclosure. After it was burned down in a Mohawk raid, it was rebuilt in 1750 as a square fort with four corner bastions and a moat.

Not to be outdone by the French, the British moved into the Lake Ontario area (in western New York) in 1727. They built FORT OSWEGO to challenge French control of the lake. During King George's War in the 1740s, Iroquois neutrality protected FORT NIAGARA, but the French replaced the old stockade and added more buildings, thus ending the illusion that the position was only a trading post. In 1750, a small fort, consisting of little more than a stockade, was built less than two miles behind Niagara Falls and named FORT LITTLE NIAGARA. Meanwhile, as the next major war loomed like dark clouds on the horizon, Fort Niagara was falling into disrepair. In November 1755, Captain Francois Pouchot, an engineer, arrived with five companies in tow. Since France was again at war with Great Britain, Pouchot would spend the next four years improving and repairing the defenses of Fort Niagara. New oak palisades replaced the rotting ones and a moat was dug across the landward front. While the northern walls ran along Lake Ontario, the southern walls were near the banks of the Niagara River. Most of the cape or peninsula-like position at the mouth of the Niagara River was occupied by the fort when Pouchot finished. He added bastions and even placed a large earthen ravelin in front of the timber section of the curtain. Pouchot built a main entrance with a drawbridge, flanked by the Dauphin Battery and called it the Gateway of Five Nations, no doubt in honor of the Iroquois who were still neutral. Additional buildings of wood and stone were built inside the fort for stores, magazines, quarters, etc. At the beginning of the French and Indian War, Pouchot received additional cannons taken from General Braddocks' column after its defeat at the hands of French forces.

Fort Niagara proved an excellent base for extending and securing the French hold on the Mississippi and Ohio valleys. French authority was administered through a series of mostly small forts, serving mainly as trading posts established on the rivers and lakes to control the lines of communications all the way to the French foothold on the Gulf Coast. Some of these forts had been established earlier in the eighteenth century and a number of them after King George's War.

Beyond the Great Lakes, Pierre La Vérendrey established FORT ST. CHARLES on Magnussen Island on the Angle River by Lake of the Woods in 1732. A year earlier, FORT ST. PIERRE had been built on Rainy Lake to control access to Lake of the Woods and Fort St. Charles. Both forts served as a gateway into Manitoba from the waterways feeding into Lake Superior. Fort St. Charles was a rectangular shaped palisaded fort, only 100 feet long and 60 feet wide that blended into the heavily wooded region. Beyond Fort St. Charles, at the end of the Winnipeg River, stood FORT MAUREPAS (1734) which led to Lake Winnipeg and the Red River. FORT ROUGE (1735) was built near modern-day Winnepeg where the Assiniboine River meets the Red River. FORT BOURBON (1741) was located at the other end of Lake Winnipeg on the Saskatchewan River. Together with FORT DAUPHIN, these small, fortified trading outposts were linked by the same system of waterways encircling the Winnipeg lake region. Like other forts west of the Mississippi, a shortage of troops resulted in the abandonment of these posts during the French and Indian War in the 1750s.

The Jesuits, like the missionaries in New Spain, had also built their own fortified missions as they expanded French control through the Great Lakes region to the west in the seventeenth century. The Jesuit mission of STE. MARIE built in Huron territory in 1644 is representative of these religious outposts. It consisted of a rather large palisade with some stone bastions and a few blockhouse-like towers. It stood on the banks of the Wye River in Ontario until another Iroquois invasion forced the Jesuits to move to a new location and eventually evacuate Huron territory altogether. When they returned, the Jesuits established new missions in modern-day Michigan.

While La Salle journeyed south toward the Ohio River, Louis Jolliet, a French trader, had set off to explore more of the Great Lakes. The French military were close on their heels to protect them and other traders. A company of French troops built FORT DE BUADE, also known as the first FORT MICHILIMACKINAC, as an addition to the existing Jesuit mission of Marquette in the late 1670s. FORT ST. JOSEPH was built in 1686 by Daniel Duluth near modern-day Port Huron north of Detroit. This palisade fort was destroyed in 1688 and its fifty troops moved up to Fort de Buade. The area was abandoned in the late 1690s because the fur trade had created a glut on the market. Despite the demands of fashion fueled by the court of Louis XIV, the surplus was driving prices down. The French abandoned the area of Michilimackinac in the 1690s.

In 1701, after abandoning Fort de Buade, which he had commanded between 1694 and 1697, Antoine de la Mothe Cadillac established FORT PONTCHARTRAIN (later known as FORT DETROIT) at the site of modern-day Detroit, which he also commanded for several years. The location was ideal for controlling the route between Lake Erie and Lake Huron. In 1713, Cadillac, the founder of Detroit, left the area to become governor of Louisiana. In 1712, when the First Fox War erupted, the fort was besieged by the Fox and their allies and rescued by native American allies of the French: the Ottawa, the Huron and their associates. The Fox were driven into Wisconsin and sued for peace in

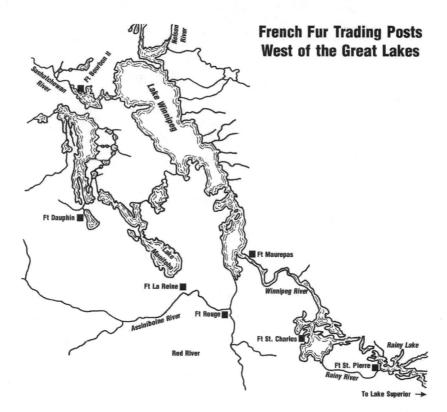

French Fur Trading Posts West of the Great Lakes

1716. At the time, Fort Pontchartrain was essentially a square palisade with sides about 200 feet long with four corner bastions. It was not expanded until the 1750s.

Detroit and the other forts in the western Great Lakes area were established at the beginning of the eighteenth century and remained in service, although they were even more remote from Montreal than Fort Niagara. When the glut of furs dissipated in 1715, French traders and soldiers returned to the straits and built a new FORT MICHILI-MACKINAC on the other side of the straits with palisades and four corner bastions, which were completed by 1720. This allowed the French to maintain control of the straits and the fur trade in the Upper Great Lakes. Because of its location, the fort was not heavily defended and held only six cannons. Most of the smaller forts had few if any cannons at all since they were generally intended for defense against Native Americans. Bruce Grant points out in *American Forts* that all the cannons were light because they had to be hauled to the forts by canoe. In addition, heavy cannons were unnecessary since the defenders did not have to face European armies or anticipate a typical Vauban-type siege.

Even though Fort Denonville on the Niagara was abandoned in the seventeenth century because of its isolated position, the French simply bypassed the area to reach Detroit. FORT ST. JOSEPH, established in 1697 near a Jesuit mission (the site of present-day Niles near Lake Michigan), controlled the portage between the St. Joseph and Kankakee Rivers. It began as a small stockade, but expanded during the next half century because of the heavy amount of trade with the locals and soon metamorphosed from an isolated post to an important economic center.

FORT LA BAYE (renamed by the British FORT EDWARD AUGUSTUS) was built at Green Bay,

Wisconsin, in 1684 by Nicholas Perrot, who traded with the Sioux and developed the lead mines. It too was as a small fort and trading post that soon grew into a bustling center of commerce. The old wooden fort had deteriorated when the Fox declared war on the French. As a result, it had to be rebuilt in 1717 when it was renamed FORT ST. FRANCIS. The fort was destroyed during the Second Fox War, which began in 1728. The French returned to the area the next year and rebuilt the fort in 1733. The Winnebago, allies of the French, also built a fort on an island near Green Bay where they were besieged by the Fox until the French sent reinforcements.

The French also built several other forts in modern-day Wisconsin, Michigan, and Illinois. In addition to FORT ST. JOSEPH (1683) at the site of Chicago, they erected FORT CRÈVE-COEUR, near Peoria on the Illinois River. Founded by La Salle in 1680, this fort was destroyed when its garrison mutinied. A few other forts left by La Salle in Illinois and Indiana proved equally unsuccessful.

Further to the west, on the backwaters of the Mississippi in Minnesota, René Boucher established FORT BEAUCHARNOIS in 1727 to trade with the Sioux, a small, square, log palisade typical of most French forts in the Great Lakes and Upper Mississippi region. This first venture was not too successful since the Sioux drove the French out by the next year. However, the traders returned several years later and put up a new fort around 1750, but lack of manpower forced the French to again evacuate during the French and Indian War.

The Lower Mississippi and Gulf Coast Forts

On the Lower Mississippi and the Gulf Coast, the French began expanding their Louisiana colony northward, up the great river and along other rivers leading into modern-day Alabama. After La Salle's exploration of the Lower Mississippi and his failure on the Texas coast, the French sent Pierre le Moyne d'Iberville to establish a series of forts along the Gulf Coast. At the time of d'Iberville's expedition, dominated by French Canadians, France no longer presented a serious challenge to Spanish claims. The French strategy was to dominate the Ohio Valley, the Mississippi Basin, and the Gulf coast in order to keep the English Atlantic colonies in North America hemmed in.

D'Iberville led an expedition to the Bay of Biloxi in 1699 and established FORT MAUREPAS (also known as FORT BILOXI) on the east side of the bay. Like most French forts, it was made of timber and included four bastions complete with loopholes and a surrounding ditch. Two of the bastions were built of logs and included a platform for positions on the upper level. The logs were squared, thus providing a better fit and more solid construction, whereas in a typical palisade or stockade this procedure was not followed. Since these bastions were the strongest positions, they were placed at diagonally opposite corners. According to d'Iberville, the other two bastions were constructed like the stockades, with the heavy timbers placed vertically. Since it was a coastal fort, Fort Maurepas was armed with twelve pieces of artillery and was strong enough to resist

standard European weapons. The curtain
walls consisted of a double row of logs inserted vertically to add strength. Outworks
included an additional timber stockade with
redans around the fort. D'Iberville set out
from the Gulf Coast in February 1700, sailing up the Mississippi to establish another
fort. Meanwhile, his brother, Jean Baptiste
Le Moyne de Bienville, took command of
the eighty-man garrison when the commandant of Fort Maurepas died. He abandoned
Fort Maurepas in December 1700 because
the government considered the area too
insalubrious for a colony to flourish. The
garrison moved to the vicinity of modern-
day Mobile, where it established a new fort and colony.

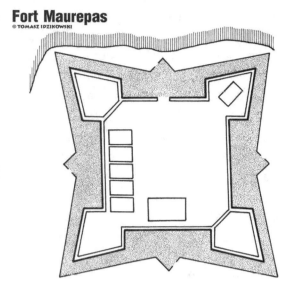

Fort Maurepas
© TOMASZ IDZIKOWSKI

At the end of 1720, the governor of Louisiana would send his chief engineer, Pierre le
Blond de la Tour, to found a new fort at the Bay of Biloxi. Le Blond de la Tour prepared
plans for an impressive, rectangular fort with four bastions, ravelins, counterscarps, and
a covered way named FORT ST. LOUIS. Workers cleared a glacis, but in 1722, the French
government decided to abandon the project.

When Bienville arrived at Mobile Bay from Fort Maurepas with his men, he established a new fort on Twenty-Seven Mile Bluff on the Mobile River. The fort, named FORT
LOUIS in 1702, was built on a similar pattern as Fort Maurepas. Unfortunately, it and the
settlement surrounding it suffered from flooding. Consequently, the colony was moved
once again and a new fort was built in 1711. Several years later, the new fort had to be
rebuilt and was renamed FORT CONDÉ in 1720. The construction of Fort Condé required
a relatively large labor force, since masonry ramparts replaced the old wooden structure. The renovated fort included four bastions, a demi-lune, a moat, a counterscarp, a
covered way, and a glacis built in true Vauban style. This brick fort, bristling with cannons, was the strongest French bastion in the Louisiana territory. Like the other French
positions along the Gulf Coast, its mission was to control the mouth of the Mississippi.

Earlier, in February 1700, d'Iberville had founded FORT DE LA BOULAYE west of Fort
Maurepas, about fifty miles from the mouth of the Mississippi. This fort, also known as
FORT IBERVILLE and FORT LOUISIANA, was the first French fort in Louisiana. It stood on the
east bank of the river and was little more than a large, square, two-level blockhouse of
cypress logs, 28 feet by 28 feet in length. The position was enclosed by a 12-foot-wide
moat. The battlements of its roof sported machicoulis. It mounted six cannons, two of
which were 18-pdrs. The fort was not far from the site known as Bâton Rouge, named for
the local boundary marker consisting of a blood-painted stick set up by two tribes. The

French used this area as a portage for linking the Mississippi to the Gulf of Mexico by using rivers and lakes to access Lake Borgne and the Gulf. Traveling down the Mississippi, into its bird-foot mouth was considered impractical at the time, and the Lake Borgne link was preferred. D'Iberville went to France in 1703, leaving the fort garrisoned by only eighteen men who had to abandon it in 1707 or 1711 in the face of hostility on the part of local tribes.

After establishing Mobile, Bienville departed several years later at the head of another west-bound expedition. In 1718, he founded NEW ORLEANS, which replaced Mobile as the capital of the Louisiana territory. Pierre le Blond de la Tour proceeded to lay out the city in a manner typical of eighteenth-century Europe. However, the walls of the city, instead of being built as planned, consisted for many years only of partially completed wooden palisades that offered little protection. The planned moat was also unrealized, leaving the 'crescent city' to rely on the surrounding Lake Pontchartrain, Mississippi River, and bayous for its defenses. The city of New Orleans was also established to serve as the main port for cargo carried down the Mississippi and replaced Baton Rouge up river as the key portage to the Gulf of Mexico. Cargo traveled down the Mississippi to New Orleans and from there it was carried over Lake Pontchartrain to Lake Borgne resulting in a much shorter portage than the previous one at Baton Rouge. By 1722, New Orleans had become the governor's capital. It was not until 1729 that the administration improved the position by creating a stronger palisade that included blockhouses. Although the planned moat was not completed, the city was relatively secure.

The French Fort Condé in Mobile, Alabama. Built early in the 1700s, this brick fort was considered the strongest French bastion in the Louisiana Territory.

To protect the frontier with New Spain, a site was selected on the Red River at Natchitoches. In 1714, a French Canadian, Louis Antoine Juchereau de St. Denis, on his way to New Spain from Mobile, encountered an Indian village where he built two huts. He left behind supplies and troops to guard them with instructions to erect a fortified position. This outpost was reinforced in 1716 when a forty-man company of *Franches de la Marine* (French marine militia) was sent there as a check against Spanish expansion. The fort, named FORT ST. JEAN BAPTISTE DES NATCHITOCHES, mounted four small cannons. It soon became a trading center for the Spanish, French, and Indians. In 1719, its garrison was sent to eject the Spanish from their presidio at Los Adaes during a brief conflict with Spain. When St. Denis was appointed as its commander in 1722, the fort saw little action until the Natchez Indians rose up against the French and placed it under siege in 1729. In 1733, new plans were drawn up to improve the fort at Natchitoches. The renovations included a pine-log palisade of double the normal thickness and an inner set of stakes to seal gaps and reinforce the outer wall. Small corner bastions and a single entrance gate were also added. The buildings within the enclosure included a church, the commander's house, a magazine, a warehouse, a large barracks, a guardhouse, and several other structures. The post was held and garrisoned until the French were defeated in the French and Indian War.

While Fort Jean Baptiste des Natchitoches protected the Spanish frontier, FORT TOULOUSE was founded in 1714 or 1717 by Governor Bienville at the junction of the Coosa and Tallapoosa Rivers in Alabama to protect the Louisiana territory from British incursions toward Mobile from the colony of Georgia. Le Blond de la Tour supervised the construction of Fort Toulouse, which, when finished, consisted of log curtains and four corner bastions which mounted two cannons each. It soon became a trading outpost with the Creeks, who had invited the French into the area because of their hatred of the English. The first garrison totaled thirty men, but over the years the number varied from twenty to fifty French marines. The harsh, isolated conditions, which bred boredom among the soldiers, coupled with supply shortages, led to a mutiny in 1722. The commander, Captain Marchand, was killed and the mutineers plundered the fort's remaining stores. The situation deteriorated to the point that the remaining French officers asked the local Indians to capture the deserters who were shipped back to Mobile where many were executed. It was not until 1740 that a few of the fort's soldiers were allowed to bring their wives from Mobile. As the wood deteriorated in the warm, humid climate, the fort had to be rebuilt in 1750. At the end of the French and Indian War, Fort Toulouse passed into British hands, but the Native American tribes refused to allow the Redcoats to garrison it so that over the next decade the unattended fort simply rotted away.

In 1735, Governor Bienville ordered the construction of FORT TOMBÉCHÉE in Alabama, at the confluence of the Tombigbee and Black Warrior Rivers in the tribal lands of the Chickasaw and Choctaw, both enemies of the British. This fort was another timber palisade in a modified square shape with one bastion and two demi-bastions at the corners. Each of the demi-bastions rested on a river bank while the fourth corner needed no bastion since it was protected by a steep slope at the junction of the two rivers.

Further up the Mississippi, well beyond Baton Rouge, Governor Bienville ordered the construction of a fort and trading post on the bluffs on the eastern bank of the river in 1716 at a place that later became known as Natchez. The Natchez Indians even helped build the fort, which was named FORT ROSALIE. This palisaded fort, in the shape of an irregular pentagon was surrounded by a moat and included a bastion made from thick planks. In 1729, when the Natchez Indians joined by the Yazoos revolted against the French, the fort became the scene of a massacre. After 250 soldiers and civilians were killed, the alarm spread through many of the French communities along the Mississippi. The French took six months to put down the uprising. Fort Rosalie was rebuilt in 1730, but as the years passed it was not maintained and turned into ruins.

An expedition headed by Pierre, Duque de Broisbraint, and sent from New Orleans in search of minerals erected FORT DE CHARTRES in 1720 a few miles from Prairie de Rochefort (Illinois) on the Mississippi. The French found that from this site they could dominate the Fox Indians who had been raiding the area around Green Bay. The fort consisted of a palisade made of squared logs with two corner bastions diagonally opposite from each other. It was replaced in 1725 because it suffered heavily from flooding. The new timber fort had four corner bastions and was located further from the Mississippi. Early in 1740, Governor Vaudreuil reinforced the garrisons in the Illinois region and ordered the rebuilding of Fort de Chartres. The fort continued to decay until, in 1747, after years of indecision, the government decided to build a new stone fort near the old site. Francois Saucier, the engineer in charge, began the work in 1752 and did not complete it until 1760. When it was finished, the fort had stone walls 2 feet thick and 15 feet to 18 feet high. Two large bastions were placed on either side of the entrance gate house and the curtain walls included firing embrasures and loopholes. Several large stone buildings stood inside the fort. Its troop capacity, although never maintained, was for four hundred men. It was one of the largest and most impressive forts in the Mississippi Valley and served as an administrative center between 1720 and 1763.

In 1738, the French built FORT ST. FRANCIS, an advanced position on the Mississippi located near modern-day Helena, Arkansas, on the border between Chickasaw and Choctaw territory. From there, the French could campaign against the Chickasaw, allies of the British. Fort St. Francis was nearing completion in 1739 when the French engineers decided that another location further up the river, at the site of modern-day Memphis, on the Fourth Chickasaw Bluff, would be a better location.

This new fort, called FORT ASSUMPTION, was completed in a few months during the summer of 1739, and was cut right into the bluff, which was 56 feet high. According to John Harris, author of *Old Mobile to Fort Assumption* the French workers began at the base of the bluff, cutting a wide shelf about 140 feet long into the face of the bluff. From the back of the shelf, they cut an upward slope, and then excavated another shelf. They continued in this way until they completed seven shelves and seven slopes that ended at the top of the bluff. Harris estimates that each shelf was 8 feet high. The fort consisted of a wooden palisade, which was widest at the foot of the bluff where it included two half-bastions. At the top of the bluff, the fort extended eastward with a wall that included three bastions. The fort provided a convenient halfway point between Fort Chartres and the Gulf, but its main purpose was to wage war upon the Chickasaw. When the campaign ended in 1740, the French abandoned and destroyed both Fort Assumption and Fort St. Francis.

Further west of the Mississippi, the French expanded into the prairies where many of the tribes were more hostile and less interested in trade. They maintained FORT DE CAVAGINAL (1745) about a mile or so from modern-day Fort Leavenworth (Kansas) until their defeat in the French and Indian War. A few other posts in this region, such as FORT ORLÉANS (1723) near modern-day Jefferson City (Missouri) on the Missouri River, were built to check the expansion of New Spain. Fort Orléans was abandoned in 1729 because too many of its soldiers were lost in the volatile region.

Unlike the Spanish, the French did not create any defensive lines of forts along this frontier with the Plains Indians. In fact, the French favored positions placed in echelon along communication routes (mostly the rivers) over linear defenses because the rough, mostly mountainous or hilly terrain of New France was covered with heavy forests with few trails.

The Acadia and Lake Champlain/Richelieu River Corridor

As the French spread along the Mississippi and its tributaries and along the Gulf Coast to contain British colonial expansion, the core of New France had to improve its defenses for the next major conflict. The already exposed mouth of the St. Lawrence had to be defended more securely as this river represented the most vital artery for the survival of the colony. In addition, the approaches to Quebec from New England also had to be defended more efficiently. But priority in this area had to be given to the creation of strong defenses along the valley formed by Lake Champlain and the Richelieu River.

Louisbourg was still the main bastion protecting the mouth of the St. Lawrence at the time of the French and Indian War. The loss of Acadia forced the French to create a few additional defensive positions to protect the modern-day province of New Brunswick from British advances out of Maine and Nova Scotia. The mission fell to the forts of St. Jean and Gaspereau. FORT ST. JEAN, also known as FORT MARTIGNON, had been built in the late 1640s on the mouth of the St. John River and later served as the main administrative center for St. John. By 1672, the fort had deteriorated so badly that it had to be restored by Sieur de Martignon, the son-in-law of La Tour. By 1700, a new fort had to be built since the old one was beyond repair. This new fort lasted for a number of years, but had to be replaced in 1749 with the new fort of Menagouche. In 1755, FORT MENAGOUCHE was abandoned as the British advanced. A few years later, the British built their own fort on the site.

FORT GASPEREAU was built at the mouth of the Gaspereau River on the Bay Verte in

1751. Located only 68 feet from the river, it consisted of a square with 114-foot-long sides. A two-level pentagonal blockhouse made of vertical timbers stood on each of its corners. The upper level overhung the lower by two feet. Its overhang served as machicoulis to protect the base of the position. The upper level also had embrasures for cannons. The curtain walls of the fort consisted of a palisade made of two rows of stakes and included a firing step. The spoil from its seven-foot-deep moat was used at the base of the palisade. A glacis was cleared around the fort. At the time of the French and Indian War, Fort Gaspereau mounted about a dozen cannons. The garrison of Fort Gaspereau consisted of a captain and 150 marines. After a short two-week siege and the surrender of Fort Beauséjour in June 1755, the situation at Fort Gaspereau became untenable and it was abandoned.

In 1751, months before construction began on Fort Gaspereau, French troops under Lieutenant Joseph Gaspard de Léry, son of Gaspard de Léry, built FORT BEAUSÉJOUR on the other side of the Isthmus of Chignecto (the south side) about twenty-five miles away, near an outlet to the Bay of Fundy. This pentagonal fort consisted of a palisade of heavy logs about 18 feet high with five corner bastions. The barracks and the officers's quarters were located behind two of the curtain walls. A storage building stood behind two of the other walls and the entrance was located in the remaining curtain wall. A well was located in one of the bastions and the powder magazine in another one. Each bastion had two gun platforms and embrasures for the cannons. A demi-lune lay in front of the entrance and a moat surrounded the entire fort. In 1752, the fort was strengthened with earth and timber placed behind the walls and a glacis was created outside the moat.

When the Missaquash River had become the unofficial boundary between French Acadia and British Nova Scotia, the British had built FORT LAWRENCE, across the river from Fort Beauséjour. Of the two forts, Fort Beauséjour was located at the best position, so when they took it, the British decided to keep it in service, renaming it FORT CUMBERLAND, and making some changes. A stone curtain wall replaced the palisade between two of the bastions and new barracks were built against two of the other curtain walls. A stone casement was erected against the curtain wall that had the old entrance used by the French.

The best and most direct overland route into the heart of New France was the lake route and the Richelieu River. There, the French had to extend a line of fortifications southward to prevent an invasion force out of New York from using this route. After the Regiment de Carignan-Saliäres arrived in 1665, its companies built five forts along the Richelieu in order to protect the French colonists in the area from raiding bands of Iroquois. Captain Jacques Chambly built FORT ST. LOUIS (later known as FORT CHAMBLY), which occupied a position below the falls of the Richelieu River and controlled the portages. The fort was a square wooden stockade 144 feet on each side with walls up to 20 feet high. The other four forts were FORT SAUREL near the St Lawrence River, FORT SAINTE-THERESE, FORT SAINT-JEAN, and FORT STE. ANNE up the Richelieu from Chambly's

Forts were generally named after places (exact site or town, regions or countries), people (leaders, notable personalities, the person responsible for the fort, or even a group of people) or sometimes a characteristic of the area or the fort. For instance, Fort Carillon (sound of chimes) was named for the sound of the falling water of Lake George where it emptied into an inlet to Lake Champlain. A few names did not represent anything of significance. In colonial America it was quite common to find forts named after the king or a past king. The French named quite a number of forts St. Louis after Louis IX and others in honor of King Louis the XIV. They also gave forts the name of the saint on whose feast day the construction of the fort began or ended. Thus, the first fort at Chambly was called Fort St. Louis because it was dedicated on that saint's day. Some forts received the names of the ministers of the navy and colonies. Thus, Fort Pontchartrain was named in honor of Louis de Pontchartrain and his son Jérôme Phélypeaux, Count of Pontchartrain, who served in that position in the last part of the seventeenth century. Fort Maurepas was named after the son of Jérôme de Pontchartrain, Jean-Fréderic Phélypeaux, Count of Maurepas, who replaced him in 1699. Fort Rosalie, on the other hand, was named for the wife of Maurepas.

Name changes usually occurred when another nation took over a fort, or when a fort was rebuilt after having deteriorated. Confusion often arises in historical sources when two or more forts bore the same name. Equally confusing is the fact that one and the same fort is referred to by different names in historical documents and references.

fort. Captain Saurel built FORT SAUREL (Fort Sorel) on the site of the old Fort Richelieu, at the mouth of the Richelieu River. The governor launched a first expedition against the Iroquois from Fort Chambly in December and a second one from the small post of Fort Ste. Anne in October 1666. Unable to deal with the French regulars or their forts, the Iroquois finally cried peace in 1667. Fort Ste. Anne, only 144 feet by 96 feet in size and located on Ile La Motte, was used by both French and English forces even after it was abandoned by the French in 1670. It stood at the end of the chain of forts built along the Richelieu and gave the French a foothold on Lake Champlain because of its location on an island at the northern end of the lake.

In 1690, FORT CHAMBLY was beyond repair and was replaced in February with a new wooden fort that lasted until 1702, when it accidentally burned down and was quickly rebuilt. This new fort no longer served as protection from the Iroquois, who had finally been forced to the peace table, but from British invaders from New York. While the fort was being rebuilt, Governor de Frontenac launched raids south into New York. However, after he withdrew, the English began their advance up the waterways, and in March they attacked Fort Chambly. After the English forces failed to take Montreal and Phips's unsuccessful expedition against Quebec, the Richelieu valley enjoyed a period of relative calm in the shelter of its forts. The only dangers were the ever-present Iroquois bands.

During Queen Ann's War, Governor Vaudreuil directed the construction of a stone fort at Chambly. The work on the new FORT CHAMBLY was accomplished between 1709 and 1711 under the supervision of the chief engineer of New France, Josué Dubois Berthelot de Beaucours. All the previous forts at Chambly had been built on the same site and were of similar size, except for the second, which was the smallest, and they all had four corner bastions. The stone fort was named FORT PONTCHARTAIN, but eventually reverted back to being called Fort Chambly. Its four corner bastions were tower-bastions since they were four-stories high and dominated the three-story high curtain walls. Each of the tower bastions included embrasures for cannons on three levels, loopholes for handguns, and a sentry box projecting from the outer corner. The curtain walls sported loopholes for handguns on two levels and the entrance was protected by a bretèche. This massive stone structure, because of its high foundation, looked more like a castle than an eighteenth-century fort. In 1720, Engineer de Léry surveyed the site and added a large platform for artillery on the north curtain wall facing the river. By 1735, as the French main defenses moved toward Lake Champlain, Fort Chambly lost its importance and was manned by a garrison of only thirty-five men.

In the 1730s, the governor of New France pushed the colony's defenses deeper into the Lake Champlain region. In 1731, Governor-General Marquis de Beaucharnois ordered the construction of a square fort at Crown Point. The small fort, with sides 100 feet long, accommodated a garrison of thirty men. In 1732, French troops rebuilt the small English wooden stockade fort at Chimney Island, across from Crown Point. In 1734, work began on a permanent fort at Crown Point. The design and execution of the masonry fort are attributed to de Léry. Construction was concluded in November 1737, when the fort was named for Frédéric de Maurepas. It was the most impressive French fortification on the main invasion route. FORT FRÉDÉRIC was in the shape of an irregular quadrangle that included a large four-story redoubt at one

Walls of the stone Fort Chambly built between 1709 and 1711 to replace the wooden fort along the Richelieu River. Photo courtesy of Don Stoetzel.

corner and had three large arrow-shaped corner bastions, each with a sentry box at the corner. In the corner where the redoubt or citadel was located were three smaller bastions linking the curtain walls. The citadel mounted twenty cannons on 12-foot-thick walls. The citadel's entrance was accessed by a drawbridge spanning a small moat in front of the structure. Each of the four floors of the redoubt were partitioned into four rooms that housed the commander, a magazine, the troops, and a bakery.

Peter Kalam, a Swedish botanist who visited the fort during the eighteenth century, wrote one of the best contemporary descriptions of Fort Frédéric. He reported that the fort's curtain walls, about 120 feet long and up to 18 feet tall, were built of black lime slate quarried about half a mile from the site. The total length of each side, including the large bastions, measured about 280 feet. The impressive gatehouse was located on the north side of the fort because the enemy was expected to come from the south. The gatehouse included a drawbridge over the small square dry moat, which led to an iron portcullis. Its lower floor included the guards's quarters and its higher floor housed a hospital. The interior of the fort included wooden quarters and other buildings as well as a church. The fort's garrison consisted of 120 men and its armament numbered about sixty cannons. A fortified stone windmill with stout thick walls that mounted a few small cannons on the upper floor and served as a defensive position was built to the south of the fort in 1740. In 1745, during King George's War, the French used Fort Frédéric as a base for launching raids into New York. In 1746, several raids were launched against British Fort Number Four in New Hampshire from Fort Frédéric. Vaudreuil personally led an expedition into Massachusetts from there also. However, the British colonial forces made no serious attempt to take this fort that blocked the gateway into New France.

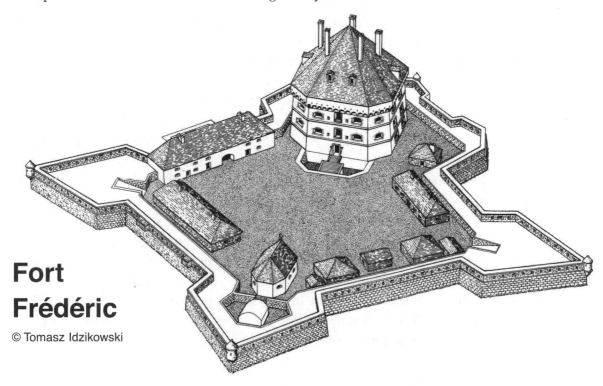

Fort Frédéric

© Tomasz Idzikowski

Fortified Road to the Ohio Valley

As the French moved up the Ohio Valley from the Mississippi and from Lake Erie, they secured their claim to the region with forts. Conflict arose when some of these forts were located in territory also claimed by several of the British thirteen colonies. Thus, the British merchants established in the Ohio Valley at the fortified Miami village of PICKAWILLANY, about 150 miles south of Detroit on the Miami River, were taken prisoner and the fortified village was destroyed in June 1752.

In 1753, the newly arrived Governor Duquesne ordered the construction of a line of forts that went from Lake Erie to the confluence of the Allegheny and Monongahela Rivers, at the site of modern-day Pittsburgh. In February 1753, Lieutenant Charles Deschamps de Boishébert set out from Montreal with 250 men to begin work on the new forts. Because of the icy conditions, he traveled overland, taking the long route via Fort Frontenac, Fort Toronto, and Fort Niagara. He also had to bypass the British fort at Oswego on the eastern side of Lake Ontario. He then moved on to establish a foothold on the southern shore of Lake Erie.

In May 1753, Captain François Le Mercier arrived at the site picked by de Boishébert to direct the construction of FORT PRESQU'ISLE on Lake Erie. He placed the fort atop a cliff (at the site of present-day Erie) so it could control the portage into the Ohio country. Each side of the fort, including the four corner-bastions, was about 120 feet long. The courtain walls were built of squared logs laid horizontally and reached a height of about 12 to 15 feet. Since there was no wall-walk, the curtains were hardly more than an obstacle, as the defenders were only able to fight from the bastions, which mounted light cannons. The fort dominated the portage from this site to a tributary of the Allegheny River, where a second fort was built.

In June 1753, Le Mercier sent Pierre-Paul de la Malgue de Marin with a large group of marines and militia to begin work on FORT DE LA RIVIÄRE AU BOEUF or FORT LE BOEUF (located at present-day Waterford), at the southern end of the portage. Like Fort Presqu'Isle, it was laid out as a square-shaped bastioned fort. A plan drawn late in the French and Indian War by Lieutenant Thomas Hutchins shows that the walls of the fort were formed by the back walls of two-story barracks. Only the arrow-shaped bastions constituted the main defensive positions. As the portage road became the main supply road, the constant heavy traffic made it almost impassable. Almost 25 percent of the men (over five hundred) succumbed to disease and the harsh conditions in the swampy region where they worked on the forts and a wagon road linking the two forts.

Further south at the Indian town of Venango (modern-day Franklin) where the small tributary river from Le Boeuf met the Allegheny, a third fort, FORT MACHAULT, was built by Lieutenant Michel de la Chauvignerie in August 1753. According to Hutchins's drawings, it was similar to Fort Le Boeuf, except for the fact that one of its sides and part of another appear to be formed by a stockade instead of barracks. However, this plan represented the fort that was rebuilt in 1757. Fort Machault was rectangular with a stockade rising to about 13 feet. Surrounding hills dominated the fort on both the east and west.

In mid-April 1754, a small force of Virginians under Lieutenant John Frazier had been fortifying the position at the point where the Monongahela and Allegheny Rivers merge into the Ohio, known as the Forks of the Ohio, when a large French contingent forced it to withdraw. François Le Mercier soon began construction of FORT DUQUESNE on the same site. The problem with this site was that it was subject to flooding, as became apparent in 1757 when an inundation inflicted major damage on the fort. Since time and resources were limited, Le Mercier built the walls, bastions, and parts of bastions that faced the rivers with simple stockades that included loopholes for small arms. How similar the layout of the fort was to the plan sent to Paris is still a matter of speculation. According to the plan, the fort was surrounded by a moat and had a counterscarp that included a covered way from which the soldiers could take up firing positions. The curtain walls were about 80 feet long. The total length of each side, including bastions, was about 155 feet. The fort's landward walls and bastions were much sturdier than those facing the rivers because this was the most likely direction of attack. They consisted of two walls built of squared logs stacked horizontally, placed about 10 feet apart and linked by cross-timbers holding them in place. The area between the walls was filled with earth, which acted like a shock absorber against cannon balls striking the walls. This crib-type construction was used in both the Old and New World in important non-masonry forts and dates back to ancient times. In the eighteenth century, it allowed fortifications to resist artillery. Atop these heavy walls were platforms and firing embrasures for cannons. The fort did not cover enough area to hold a large garrison and a stockaded camp was later built outside the fort to accommodate more troops.

The military value of a fort is based not only on its actual strength, but also on the enemy's perception of its strength. Since most of the French forts, especially those in the region of the Great Lakes and Ohio River Valley, were located in the wilderness, British opinion of their strength was important in determining England's strategy in the event of war. Of course, the French could not know how the British perceived their positions. There are documents, however, which give us an indication of what the British knew, or thought they knew, about the French defenses in October 1754. Much of their intelligence was based on an account given to Lord Halifax by John Deievre, who was captured by the French in 1749 and managed to escape. According to Deievre, the French forts in the Ohio region were rather weak and most had no artillery. British intelligence sources placed the total strength of the French in the Ohio region at 1,500 regulars supported by up to 600 Ottawa Indians. Essentially, British intelligence was as much in the dark about French positions as about the wilderness they sought to occupy.

17th Century North America

© TOMASZ IDZIKOWSKI

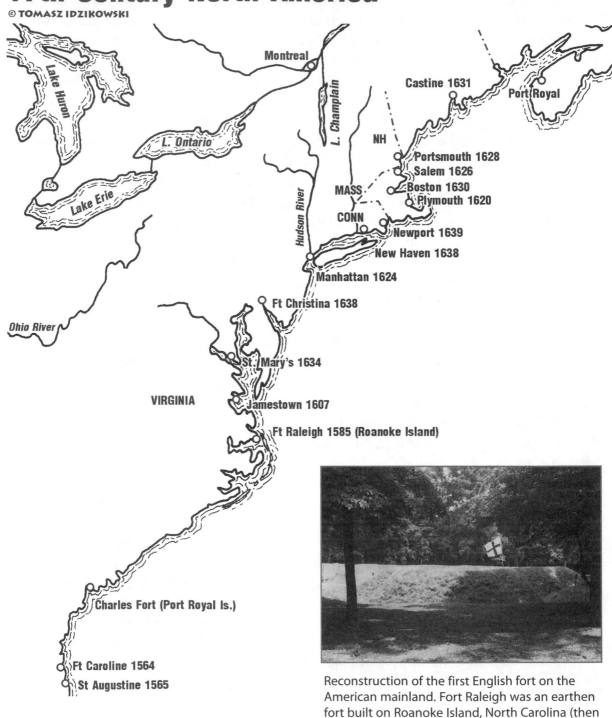

Montreal

Castine 1631

Port Royal

L. Champlain

Lake Huron

L. Ontario

NH

Portsmouth 1628

Salem 1626

Boston 1630

Plymouth 1620

MASS

Lake Erie

CONN

Newport 1639

New Haven 1638

Hudson River

Manhattan 1624

Ft Christina 1638

Ohio River

St. Mary's 1634

VIRGINIA

Jamestown 1607

Ft Raleigh 1585 (Roanoke Island)

Charles Fort (Port Royal Is.)

Ft Caroline 1564

St Augustine 1565

Reconstruction of the first English fort on the American mainland. Fort Raleigh was an earthen fort built on Roanoke Island, North Carolina (then referred to as the Virginia Colony).

Chapter 2

THE BRITISH IN NORTH AMERICA

IN 1585, SIR WALTER RALEIGH ESTABLISHED the first English colony in what he called Virginia, on the north end of Roanoke Island. When the colony was set up in July 1585, Governor Ralph Lane built a small fort made of earthworks close to the coastline. The settlers built their homes near the fort. (This fort was similar to another one Ralph Lane had built before reaching Roanoke when the expedition had landed in Puerto Rico to resupply. The fort in Puerto Rico represents the first English fortification in America. Although it was destroyed on the expedition's departure, a surviving drawing shows that it consisted of a simple square trace, one side of which rested against the beach. It had three bastions on the landward facing walls.)

Unfortunately, no drawings remain of FORT RALEIGH at Roanoke, but archaeological evidence indicates that it did not have a regular square trace. It was more or less star shaped with salients (sometimes incorrectly called redans) along the sides, which were about 50 feet in length. Apparently, one corner included a small bastion. The colony was short-lived because the colonists took to stealing food from the Indians, which soon resulted in open warfare. In June 1586, when Sir Francis Drake sailed in with a large raiding fleet, supplies had not arrived from England. Therefore, Sir Francis took the surviving colonists, barely over a hundred souls, back to England, leaving a party of fifteen men to hold the site. The supply ship arrived after they departed. In 1587, Raleigh sent a new group of a hundred and fifty colonists back to Roanoke with John White. The fifteen men left at the site of Fort Raleigh had gone by the time the new colonists arrived in July. In August, the colonists sent White back to England to get supplies. However, war with Spain broke out about that time and White was not able to return for three long years. When White finally returned in August 1590, he found all the houses had

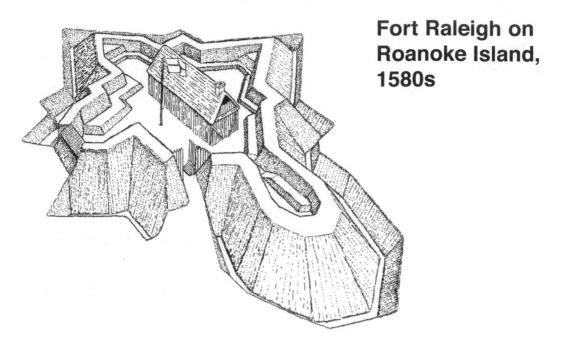

Fort Raleigh on Roanoke Island, 1580s

been pulled down. All that remained was a palisade, but there was no trace of the Lost Colony. The last news of the colonists came from the Spanish who had sailed from St. Augustine to reconnoiter the area and had determined that the colony and fort were so weak it was not worth their effort to remove them.

The English made no further attempt to settle the region until the next century. By this time, the Netherlands and France were also staking their claims on the fringes of the Spanish empire, in what was considered the rump end of the Americas in the sixteenth century.

In 1606, the British crown patent authorized the creation of the London Company and the Plymouth Company, founded by two groups of English merchants, formed for settlement of the new lands. The London Company was the first to found a successful colony. In the spring of 1607, it dispatched three ships with settlers who established Jamestown by the month of June. At the same time, the Plymouth Company set up a colony in Maine on the Sagadahoc River. A fort, probably similar to the one at Jamestown, was built there as well. The settler's buildings were enclosed within. However, by February 1608 that colony had failed, probably because their effort at colonization had coincided with one of the worst droughts the North American continent had witnessed in seven hundred years. It was not until November 1620 that the Plymouth Company managed to establish its first successful colony founded by the Pilgrims in Massachusetts.

While the two English companies were setting up their settlements far apart from each other, the Dutch entered the picture. The Dutch East Indies Company hired the Englishman Henry Hudson to search for a northwest passage to the Far East where a treasure in spices awaited. Hudson discovered what would be called the Hudson River and sailed as far as modern-day Albany, establishing a Dutch claim to the area in 1609. Next, the Dutchman Adrian Block landed in Manhattan in 1613 and founded FORT NASSAU, later renamed FORT ORANGE, well up the Hudson River near the future site of Albany. Thirteen merchants carried on trade from Fort Orange until the new Dutch West Indies Company entered the scene in 1621 and bought them out. In 1624, the company sent colonists to establish New Netherlands on the island of Manhattan. This move effectively separated the two English regions of Virginia and New England.

Early English Colonization: The Southern Colonies

Although there are some unresolved questions about the settlement of JAMESTOWN and its location in a swampy area up the James River, information about the problems faced by the early settlement and its fort is not lacking. In May 1607, three ships bearing a hundred and five settlers entered the Chesapeake Bay and turned up the James River where they selected a rather swampy site about sixty miles from the sea. This location offered concealment from the Spanish and other Europeans. However, by 1611 the Spanish had identified the location and even captured one of the colonists.

The local Algonquin tribes, who had formed the Powhatan Confederation killed some of the English colonists as soon as they entered the Chesapeake. This first encounter with the Powhatans, inspired the colonists to immediately build a fort. The construction took over a month. The result was FORT JAMES, a triangular stockade with three rounded bastions for the few available cannons. The main entrance was located in the center of the wall facing the river. Smaller entrances were also placed next to each bastion. A dry moat completely surrounded the fort. According to the archaeologists in charge of the reconstruction of the site today, the spoil was used to support the stockade and the area behind the wall was built up so the men could stand on an earthen platform and fire over the 15-foot-high walls. The village was set up inside the area enclosed by the fort. The side facing the river was 420 feet in length and the other sides were 300 feet each. Several hundred more settlers joined the founders of Jamestown. However, a fire destroyed the first fort and another had to be built.

Across from Fort James, on the south side of the river, on a marshy piece of land to the east of Jamestown, was a smaller work called the HOG ISLAND FORT, which served to protect the river approach against a possible Spanish raid and defend a hog farm as well.

In 1609, another fort was built on the south side of the James River about two miles up a creek near present-day Surry. This small position, named SMITH'S FORT after John Smith, served to protect the property of John Rolf, the man who turned tobacco into a commercial crop for the colony.

In the same year, Captain Smith sent Captain Francis West up the James River. West built FORT WEST on an island near the "Falls," the site of present-day Richmond. However, the Native Americans in the area were hostile and soon forced the English to

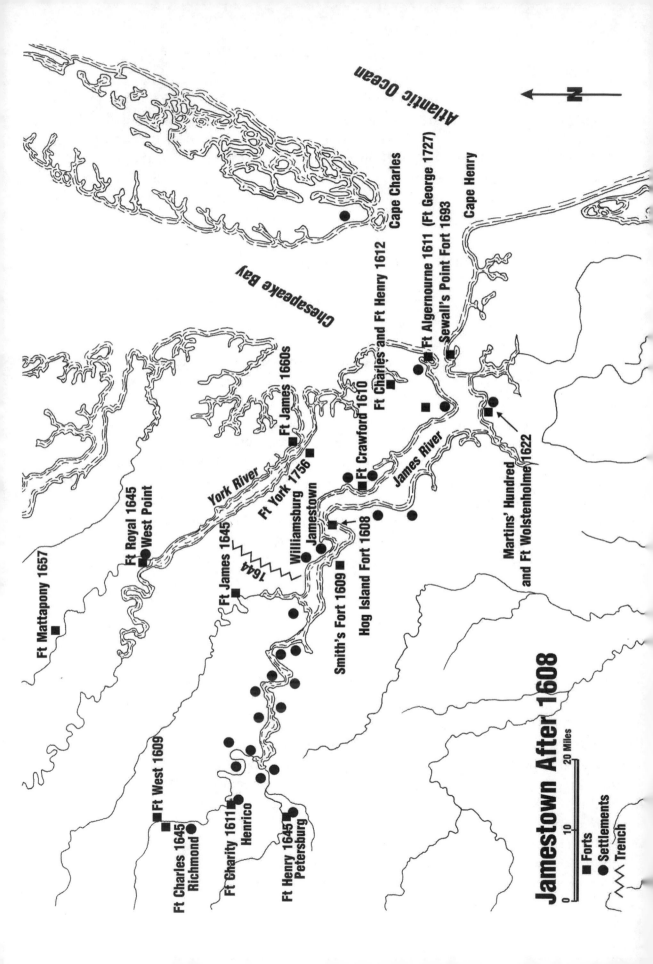

Jamestown After 1608

Atlantic Ocean

Chesapeake Bay

Cape Charles

Ft Charles and Ft Henry 1612

Ft Algernourne 1611 (Ft George 1727)
Sewall's Point Fort 1693
Cape Henry

Ft Crawford 1610

James River

York River

Ft James 1660s

Ft York 1756
Williamsburg
Jamestown

Martins' Hundred
and Ft Wolstenholme 1622

Smith's Fort 1609

Hog Island Fort 1608

1644

Ft Royal 1645
West Point

Ft James 1645

Ft Mattapony 1657

Ft West 1609

Ft Charles 1645
Richmond

Ft Charity 1611
Henrico

Ft Henry 1645
Petersburg

■ Forts
● Settlements
∧∧∧ Trench

0   10   20 Miles

N

The fort at Jamestown

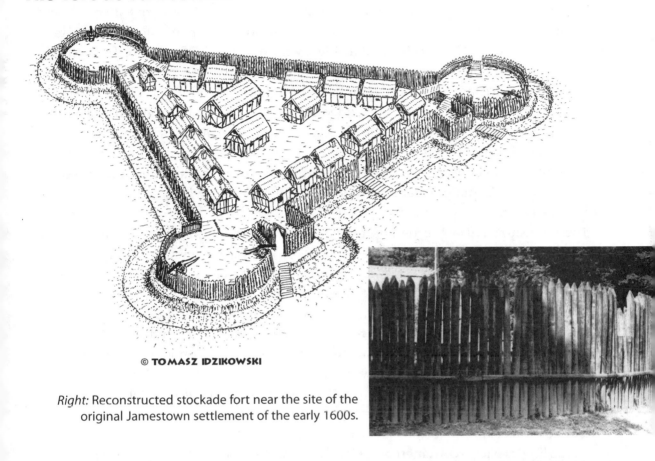

© **TOMASZ IDZIKOWSKI**

Right: Reconstructed stockade fort near the site of the original Jamestown settlement of the early 1600s.

abandon the site until 1611. At that time, Sir Thomas Dale, also a professional soldier, sent several hundred men back up the James with the mission of establishing a new town, named Henrico, on the site of an Indian village ten miles from present-day Richmond. They quickly erected FORT CHARITY at this site and four other forts nearby. The objective was to abandon the dismal location of Jamestown and occupy the new site, but the Indian uprising of 1622 resulted in the complete destruction of Henrico.

The English colonists, more so than the French and Spanish, had a flare for irritating the native populations. As a result of these strained relations, the local tribes rose against the English in 1622, almost destroying the Virginia colony, its settlements, and its small forts. After a year of hostilities, peace was arranged between the English colonists and the Indians. The arrival of new settlers swelled the population of the colony, and as the village expanded, the Jamestown fort fell into disuse and disappeared in time.

In 1633, the colonists attempted to seal the lower part of the Peninsula by extending a palisade across it. The wooden wall, which was to run from College Creek on the James River to Queen's Creek on the York River. The wall was to be extended to swallow up additional Indian lands. Details of this fortification are not well known since the discovery and first excavations of the remains only began in the 1990s. The archaeological evidence shows that the position consisted of a ditch and an earthwork with a palisade that cut across the peninsula with complete disregard for the terrain, often failing to take best advantage of it. The trench was 3 to 4 feet wide and 1 to 1.5 feet deep. The palisade had to be replaced in 1644 because of deterioration and expansion of the settlements.

The Indian uprising of 1644 gave another serious jolt to the Virginia colonists, but the Lower Peninsula was rather well-defended by this time. After this incident, Governor Berkeley ordered the construction of more forts along several rivers. Soon more wood and earthen fortifications began to appear. A second FORT JAMES was built on the Chickahominy River near Lanexa. At the mouth of the Appomattox River near present-day Petersburg, Captain Abraham Wood built FORT HENRY, which held a garrison of only ten soldiers.

The Englishmen also returned up the James River, passing the ruins of Henrico and advancing to the vicinity of the former site of Fort West, where they built FORT CHARLES in 1645. At the same time, FORT ROYAL was built on the Mattaponi River near West Point. In 1657, about twenty miles up the Mattaponi River near Walkerton, future governor Edward Digges built FORT MATTAPONY, which was eventually leveled in 1677. Other forts of the same period fell into ruins on their own due to the high humidity of the region. FORT MANASKIN was built on the Pamunkey River in 1660 as a frontier position and may have even been garrisoned by friendly Indians. A third FORT JAMES was built in the 1660s at Tyndall's Point across from Yorktown. The English hold on the Tidewater, the coastal plain of Virginia, was finally firmly established against the native population, but now had to be protected from incursions by pirates and other Europeans.

According to Richard Weinert and Colonel Robert Arthur, authors of *Defenders of the Chesapeake*, early in the colonization of Virginia, Captain John Smith, a professional soldier and erstwhile leader of the colony, decided that Point Comfort, at modern-day Hampton Roads, was an excellent site for a fort that would command the entrance to the James River. In the fall of 1609, Captain James Davis arrived from England at the head of a contingent of only sixteen men to act upon Smith's advice. Davis's force, augmented by about two dozen men from Jamestown, was placed under the command of Captain Ratecliffe. At Point Comfort, they built FORT ALGERNON, which began as an earthwork, and by 1611 consisted of a stockade with a magazine and barracks and mounted seven heavy cannons. A drawing at the Fort Monroe Casemate Museum in Fort Monroe, Virginia, shows that the fort was triangular and had an arrow-shaped bastion on the apex facing the sea. The Chesapeake lay on one side of the fort and Mill Creek on the other. A stockade with a continuous earthen platform ran along all the walls and accommodated six cannons.

Between 1611 and 1612, Thomas Gates built FORT CHARLES and FORT HENRY on the Hampton Creek, at the site of present-day Hampton. These two small stockades helped protect the position at Point Comfort from the hostile native population. When

Ratecliffe was killed by the Indians, Davis took command of Fort Algernon as well as Fort Henry and Fort Charles. These two forts were garrisoned, abandoned, and then reoccupied by Davis who manned them with barely a dozen men. Davis had to rebuild Fort Algernon in May 1612 after it accidentally burned down earlier that year. During the next few years, all these forts deteriorated to the point of being ineffective. A new fort was completed at Point Comfort in 1632 and soon additional forts followed. The colonists levied a special tax by forcing all passing ships to stop and pay. This situation continued for a number of years as long as the fort needed repairs. The tax was not repealed until the fort lost its defensive value.

During the Second Anglo-Dutch War in the 1660s, there were virtually no significant fortifications in the Virginia colony. In 1667, the colonial government authorized work on several new forts including one at Point Comfort. Before construction began, however, the Dutch raided the area. As a result, Colonel Leonard Yeo was directed to set up a fortified artillery position of eight cannons at Point Comfort. Unfortunately, a major storm destroyed all the fortifications that had been completed and the point remained without effective fortifications for several more years. By the end of the century, most of Virginia's forts were again in ruins.

More settlers had arrived in the 1640s and established themselves opposite Point Comfort, on the other side of the mouth of the James. As a result of the Anglo-Dutch Wars, they built a small fort in 1673, probably a stockade, at the site where the port and town of Norfolk were established in 1680.

The War of Spanish Succession brought a renewed interest in creating defenses for Virginia, especially around Hampton Roads. In 1711, the governor of Virginia mounted a number of cannons at Point Comfort, Yorktown, and Jamestown in timber and earth fortifications. The work on a masonry fort at Old Point Comfort (the "Old" part of the name was not added until the twentieth century) was completed in 1736. The fortification, named FORT GEORGE, consisted of a set of double brick walls, approximately 16 feet apart, in the typical criblike fashion. The space between the two walls was filled with sand. According to Colonel Arthur, the construction of the fort presented several weak points. These impressive looking brick walls were only 27 inches thick, which, even at that time, was considered too thin to prevent a major breach from just a few hits. In addition, most double walls were usually filled with dirt, gravel, and materials more coarse than sand in order to provide some adhesion and prevent the filling from spilling out in case of a breach in the outer wall. In 1749 a hurricane struck the Chesapeake, destroying the fort. Thus during the Seven Years War, Virginia was left with no significant fortifications to protect its coast. The situation did not change until the end of the American Revolution.

Inland, the colonists continued to drive the native population from their lands. In order to maintain their conquests they had constantly to maintain protection along their

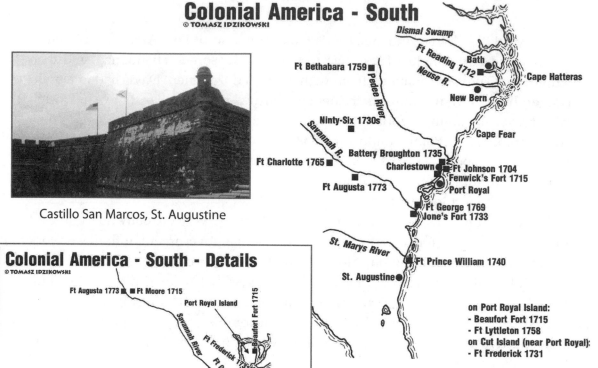

Colonial America - South
© TOMASZ IDZIKOWSKI

Dismal Swamp

Ft Bethabara 1759 ■

Ft Reading 1712 ■ Bath

Neuse R.

Cape Hatteras

New Bern

Pedee River

Cape Fear

Ninty-Six 1730s

Savannah R.

Battery Broughton 1735

Ft Charlotte 1765 ■

Charlestown ■ Ft Johnson 1704

■ Fenwick's Fort 1715

Ft Augusta 1773 ■

Port Royal

■ Ft George 1769

■ Jone's Fort 1733

St. Marys River

■ Ft Prince William 1740

St. Augustine ●

on Port Royal Island:
- Beaufort Fort 1715
- Ft Lyttleton 1758
on Cut Island (near Port Royal):
- Ft Frederick 1731

Castillo San Marcos, St. Augustine

Colonial America - South - Details
© TOMASZ IDZIKOWSKI

Ft Augusta 1773 ■ ■ Ft Moore 1715

Port Royal Island

Beaufort Fort 1715

Savannah River

Ft Frederick 1731

Ft George 1769

Savannah ●

Jone's Fort 1733 ■

Ogeechee River

Ft Argyle 1733 ■

Altamaha River

Ft Barrington 1751 ■

Darien (Ft Darien 1736) ●

Carr's Fort ■

St. Simon Island
Ft St. Frederick 1736

Cumberland Island
Ft St. Andrews 1736
Ft Prince William 1740

St. Marys River

Akenfonogo Swamp

new frontiers. They built a number of stockades and blockhouses on the new plantations and farms, most of which were not very impressive for the seventeenth century. As the Virginia colony had expanded during the latter part of the century, other settlements had appeared to the north. George Calvert, Lord Baltimore, was awarded the right to establish a proprietary colony north of the Potomac River in what became Maryland. His son took control of the operation. The first two small ships with Catholic colonists landed in 1634. The new settlers purchased land from the Indians and founded a settlement called St. Mary's on a peninsula formed by a tributary of the Potomac River. They also built FORT AT ST. MARY'S CITY on this easily defended peninsula. The fort, built in a month, consisted of a square palisade about 120 yards in length with four corner blockhouses. Built as a defense against the Indians, it had enough space to accommodate most of the colonists.

Early in the 1630s on the Chesapeake, on lands granted to Calvert, Captain William Claiborne from Virginia established FORT KENT and a trading post known as FORT CRAYFORD on Kent Island, across from modern-day Annapolis. Lord Baltimore drove

Claiborne from Kent Island after a skirmish in 1635. At the time of the English Civil War in 1644, Calvert's Catholic colony became a target for Protestants and St. Mary's was captured and sacked by Richard Ingle in what was called Ingle's Rebellion. Claiborne, in the meantime, reestablished his claim over Kent Island. In 1646, the young Calvert managed to recapture his colony with the help of Governor William Berkeley of Virginia.

Down the coast from Virginia, the Albemarle colony was established by Virginians in the early 1650s in an effort to expand the colony's southern frontier. This territory later became North Carolina. An adventurous group of New Englanders founded a colony at Cape Fear in the early 1660s, but the venture ended in failure. Port Royal Sound was established in South Carolina, but its citizens, fearing the Spanish to the south, withdrew to the north, establishing themselves at Charles Town. In 1671, the colonists were at war with the local Indians as they expanded inland. A group of Scots formed the Port Royal colony in the early 1680s. The city of Charleston was established in 1680. By the early 1700s, the colony began to expand up the Santee and Savannah Rivers. Along the entire coast of the area that was soon to become the colony of North Carolina, the settlers continued to move inland, causing a new war with the local Indians.

Little data is available on what type of fortifications the colonists built in the Carolinas in the latter part of the seventeenth century. According to one history of the region, there were no defensive positions in North Carolina before 1710. In the hot sweltering climate of these coastal regions, wood and even earthen fortifications did not have a long lifespan. But the swamps, waterways, and alligator-infested areas provided natural impassable defenses in some cases, while the abundant forests supplied the materials needed to construct fortifications.

The local tribes and the Tuscarora, relatives of the Iroquois, who had been mistreated and even enslaved by the colonists, launched a last desperate effort to retake the coastal areas of North Carolina. Thus, the Tuscarora War broke out in September 1711. Those colonists who did not flee entrenched themselves in New Berne and Bath (founded in 1703) where they began working on defensive positions. A number of other settlers clustered together on farms where they built their own fortified refuges. Thus early in 1712, FORT READING was built on the Pamlico River. Since Great Britain was already involved in the War of Spanish Succession, the colonists could not count on the crown to defend them.

The Tuscarora War soon turned into a war of position as the Tuscarora built their own forts of timber and earth probably similar to those of their other Iroquois relatives. Colonel John Barnwell, with his thirty or so militiamen and several hundred Indian allies struck against the Tuscarora at the defended village of NARHANTES. The Indians had erected nine small palisaded forts to protect the village. Barnwell attacked the strongest fort and overcame the defenders. This allowed him to destroy the other forts and several villages. He then proceeded to a place known as HANCOCK'S FORT (named for the Indian leader King Hancock), a larger, well-protected palisaded fort of the

Tuscarora. He stopped to build FORT BARNWELL on the Neuse River to serve as his base of operations. But with victory in his grasp, he allowed the Tuscarora generous terms and restored the peace for a short time.

As more trouble flared up, the call for help went out once more. Early in 1713, Colonel James Moore responded with a new expedition of militia and Indians from South Carolina. He attacked the Tuscarora fort of NOHOROCA (NEOHEROKA), located about forty miles to the northwest of New Berne near Hancock's Fort. This irregular shaped fort, probably the largest Tuscarora fort in Carolina, included blockhouses, a covered passageway that led to the Contentea Creek, and a number of homes within its walls. Moore laid down a formal siege, establishing battery positions and an approach trench. He built his own blockhouse of sufficient height so his men could dominate the interior of the Indian fort. In addition, he had a mine dug toward the walls, but launched the assault on March 20, before he could complete it. After three days, Moore's men inflicted a major defeat on the Tuscarora. Soon after their surrender, the Tuscarora trekked north to join their brethren and become the sixth nation of the Iroquois Confederation.

Following the Tuscarora War, fear of other native tribes or retaliation from the Five Iroquois Nations spurred the colonists to build new forts in Virginia. One of the new forts was located in western Virginia. Another, FORT CHRISTANNA, was built in 1714 on high ground on a bend of the Meherrin River near Lawrenceville. It covered the route into North Carolina near the border. However, tribal resistance in the region was largely broken. By 1720, the frontier had moved far from this fort, which was no longer garrisoned.

Peace did not reign in the southern colonies for very long, however. The region extending from the Atlantic coast to the foothills of the Appalachian Mountains in Alabama, Georgia, and Carolina was home to the large Cherokee, Creek, and Choctaw nations as well as several smaller tribes like the Yamassee. The French, Spanish and English had all moved into this region, staking out their claims with trading posts and forts and trying to control the various tribes. Although the British blamed the French and Spanish for inciting the Yamassee against them, the real cause of the Native American's resentment was their mistreatment at the hands of the English merchants and settlers. When the Yamassee War broke out in April 1715, most of the tribes in the area, except the Cherokee, joined in. The conflict dragged on until the end of the 1720s, even though the threat presented by the Yamassee had been broken by 1716. During the first year of the conflict, the militia built PORT ROYAL FORT (BEAUFORT FORT) on Port Royal Island near Beaufort. Although it was little more than a typical earth and wood construction, the colonials maintained it during the next decade to protect the port until they replaced it with Fort Frederick.

FORT FREDERICK built on Cat Island in the early 1730s, consisted of four walls made of tabby. Additional defenses, including WILLTOWN FORT on the Edisto River twenty-eight miles southwest of Charleston, were built further inland in 1715. The militia garrison of

Willtown Fort beat off an Indian attack in July 1715. In the same year, deeper inland, the government built FORT MOORE on a high bluff on the Savannah River, opposite present-day Augusta. This fort had the typical square design with sides 150 feet long and artillery bastions on each corner. It housed a small garrison until 1746.

The colonists, too, began to erect their own defensive positions. Thus, Thomas Elliot fortified his home, known as ELLIOTT'S FORT, on his plantation about twelve miles west of Charleston. Soon other such "forts" appeared on the plantations, farms, and ranches in the area. Among these was SCHENCKINGH'S FORT on the Santee River, twenty miles from Moncks Corner, which was overrun and destroyed by the Catawaba Indians. More than one of these modest fortifications were taken by the Indians during the war and their garrisons were killed or captured. After the war in the 1730s, traders established FORT NINETY SIX, a trading post about ninety-six miles from Charleston. The English turned it into a major defensive position later in the century.

The colonists in South Carolina, like the settlers in North Carolina, despite the threat from Indians, the French, and the Spanish, expanded little effort in protecting their colony with defenses before the Yamassee War. Colonial CHARLESTON was fortified in the 1670s with earthenworks that included ditches and a palisade. When the town was moved to its present location in the 1680s, it was surrounded by even stronger defenses that included a number of bastions, demi-lunes and ravelins. Brickwork strengthened these defenses. Each of the bastions and outworks was endowed with artillery and a militia garrison during the early eighteenth century. In 1704, work began on FORT JOHNSON, the first actual fort at Charleston. The fort was sited on the east end of James Island to the south of the town. It was triangular and included corner bastions, a surrounding moat, and palisade walls. A ravelin covered the entrance and a battery position defended Charleston harbor. In 1735, a battery known as FORT BROUGHTON was also constructed at Charleston. The city received a new wall with five bastions in 1746. However, in 1752 a hurricane struck with such force that most of the city's fortifications had to be replaced or heavily repaired. By the end of the French and Indian War, the colonials neglected the city defenses, allowing them to fall into disrepair.

In 1721, Colonel John Barnwell built FORT KING GEORGE on the coast atop a bluff overlooking the Altamaha River. The fort served as a buffer against Spanish expansion. It consisted of a three-story high blockhouse, barracks, and a triangular earthen wall and moat roughly forming a triangle with palisades on one side. In 1726, a fire destroyed the blockhouse and barracks.

According to Douglas Leach, author of *Arms for Empire*, an expedition from Charleston led by Colonel John Palmer sailed along the coast to the St. Johns River to deal with the renewed threat from the Yamassee. His hundred or so militiamen disembarked and moved toward the fortified village of NOMBRE DE DIOS, within sight of St. Augustine. In February 1728, Palmer smashed the Yamassee, burned their village, and departed, largely bringing to an end the conflict with the Yamassee.

In 1732, James Oglethorpe, a former professional soldier, arrived in America with a charter to create a colony, which he named Georgia in honor of King George II. He arrived in Charleston in January 1733 with a group of about 115 colonists. Picking up an escort of militia and a local engineer, Colonel William Bull, he set out in search of a suitable site for his settlement. The group journeyed south to the site of present-day SAVANNAH and selected a location on the Yamacraw Bluff, on the south side of the Savannah River where the surrounding swamps would offer some degree of protection to the fledgling settlement. The settlers set to building their town, already laid out by Bull, inside a stockade enclosure. A sketch from 1734 shows a well laid out town on the bluff, surrounded by wooded and swampy terrain with masts of sailing ships on the river towering above the walls of the stockade.

Oglethorpe then directed his attention to the construction of inland forts to protect against hostile Indians and to sound the alarm if the Spanish appeared to threaten the colony. In the fall of 1733, he completed FORT ARGYLE on a bluff on the west bank of the Ogeechee River (at the present-day site of Fort Stewart) to block a key route. The fort's trace was an irregular square with sides of about 110 feet in length. The first fort included corner bastions and a two-story central blockhouse. It was a relatively small and weak stockade surrounded by a moat, which according to Oglethorpe was about 5 feet deep and 15 feet wide. Archaeological evidence and documents indicate Fort Argyle held four cannons. Fort Argyle was probably rebuilt twice. In 1740, it was rebuilt into a rectangular form. Its corner bastions were removed and the central blockhouse was replaced by a parade ground. The only brick used was in the chimneys of the barracks located on the eastern wall on the river side. The remainder of the fort was made of timber. The fort was built and garrisoned by twenty rangers and its first commander, James McPherson, a Scottish ranger from South Carolina. Fort Argyle, which served as a base for rangers throughout its existence, was abandoned in the 1750s. During the French and Indian War, the British rebuilt it, increasing its size and its garrison. In 1767, the fort was again abandoned when General Thomas Gage, commanding British forces in America, de-commissioned the Georgia Rangers.

In 1735, Scottish Highlanders established the settlement of New Inverness across the bay from Darien, Georgia. In 1736, Oglethorpe directed the construction of FORT DARIEN on a high bluff of the Altamaha River to protect the Scottish settlers. The fort consisted of a large stockade with two bastions and two half-bastions mounting artillery. South of Fort Darien, CARR'S FORT was built at modern-day Brunswick, on an inlet known as Turtle River that led to St. Simon Sound. It was a small fort of tabby construction located on a plantation. Before the Spanish landing at St. Simon Island, it withstood raids from Spain's Indian allies.

In 1736, Oglethorpe also fortified Cumberland Island, one of the barrier islands located south of St. Simon Island. FORT WILLIAM was situated so that it could command the entrance to the St. Marys River. FORT ST. ANDREW was built on the north end of the island.

Savannah 1734

(from University of Texas Collection)

Oglethorpe established FORT ST. GEORGE on an island near the mouth of the St. Johns River in Florida. He thought this would be an adequate southern boundary for Georgia and a good launching point for an invasion of Spanish Florida. Evidence indicates that the fort was a small earthwork with a palisade. Unlike most of Oglethorpe's fortifications, this one was not able to fend off the Spanish.

Ogelthorpe commissioned the construction of FORT AUGUSTA IN 1736, near the settlement of the same name. From there, he secured peace with the Cherokee and Creek. This expansion inland also formed an effective buffer between the Carolinas and the French and Spanish colonies, particularly as Oglethorpe won over four of the so-called Five Civilized Tribes (Choctaw, Cherokee, Creek, and Chickasaw, but not the Seminole who were not a factor yet).

In January 1734, Oglethorpe had explored the coast to the south and selected St. Simon Island as the site for a new settlement and two new forts to protect his colony from Spanish incursions. It was not until February 1736 that he began work on the first of these forts after finally establishing the planned settlement. Named FORT FREDERICA, it was placed to control a river passage on the west side of the island. It had a square shape with corner bastions, one of which was a large battery position situated to cover the river. The fort's walls were built of tabby. In March, Fort Frederica mounted its first artillery battery. Oglethorpe extended a line of defenses around the nearby town of Frederica and created an outer wall to enclose the forty-acre area. This polygonal enceinte included a dry moat, an earthen rampart, and a pair of 10-feet-high, mile-long palisades. Governor Oglethorpe took command of the 42nd Foot Regiment (a regular army unit) in 1739, which was to be based on the island. He had already formed militia units and the Georgia Rangers. A second smaller fort, FORT ST. SIMON, was constructed at the south end of the island.

In 1742, Spanish forces took to the offensive and moved against Georgia. Unable to reduce the forts on Cumberland Island, in July they landed on St. Simon Island forcing Oglethorpe to abandon Fort St. Simon in the face of superior numbers. He retreated to his command post at Fort Frederica from where he set out to ambush the approaching Spanish forces and defeated them at the battle of Bloody Marsh. While his offensive strategy had failed, his defensive strategy turned Georgia into a strong British bastion, anchoring their southern border in the continent.

English and Dutch Colonization North of the Chesapeake

Further up the coast, the Pilgrims landed in the *Mayflower* in December 1620 at PLYMOUTH. This was the second attempt of the Plymouth Company to establish a colony in America. The Pilgrims, aware of their lack of military skills, employed Miles Standish, a professional soldier, to take care of their security. Soon after they landed and established their settlement, Standish set them to work on a protective stockade. The first defensive work went up at one end of the settlement, on top of a hill from where they could dominate their surroundings. It consisted of a platform for mounting cannons. The heavy cannons for the gun platform on the hill were hauled up in February. The work on the fortifications was not completed until March 1621. The enclosure was designed for the convenience of the colonists rather than for resisting an attack, since the log walls were only 8 feet high and there were no bastions. They also placed three gates in the walls because the trace covered a relatively large area.

In 1622, the Pilgrims modified their fortifications, reported John Pory, whose ship stopped in Plymouth on the return voyage from Virginia to England. Pory also noted that the enclosing palisade was stronger than any he had seen in Virginia and that a completed blockhouse on top of the hill had replaced the earlier gun platform that commanded the site. According to Edward Winslow, it was the Indian uprising and massacre in Virginia that prompted the Pilgrims to strengthen their position and build the blockhouse. Captain John Smith visited the settlement in 1623. He reported that the settlement numbered about 180 people with their livestock. He figured that the palisade was 2,640 feet long, confirming John Pory's estimate of about 2,700 feet in the previous year. Smith also noticed the "well built fort of wood, loam and stone, where is planted their ordnance" on top of the height.

According to Isaac de Raiseres, an agent of the Dutch West Indies Company who visited the colony in 1627, the "fort" on top of the hill was a large square building that

Plymouth

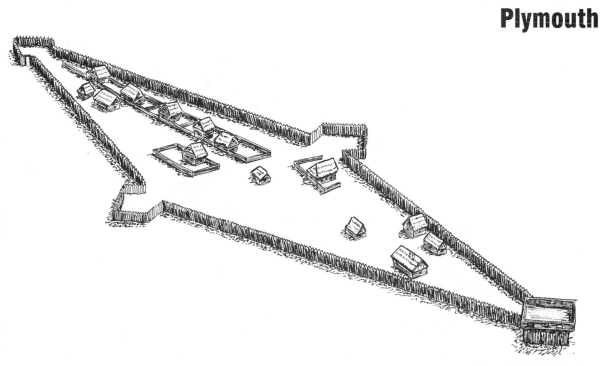

© TOMASZ IDZIKOWSKI

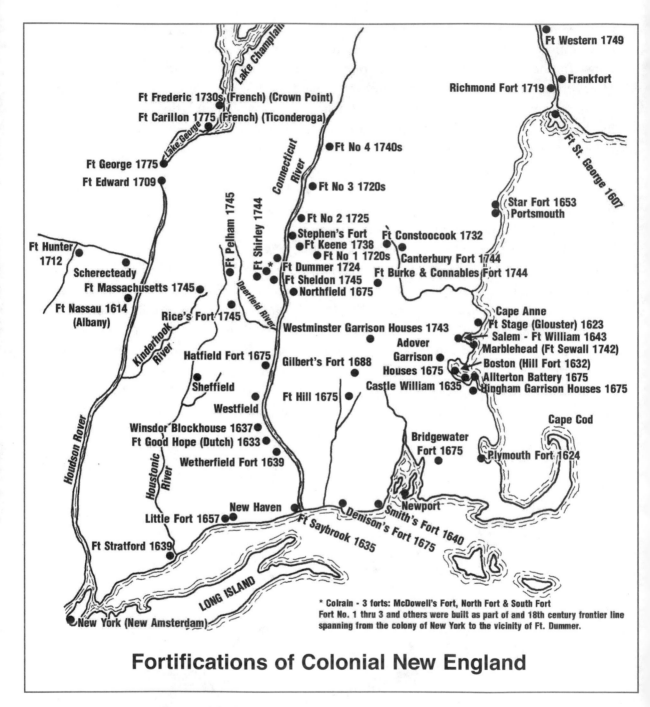

* Colrain - 3 forts: McDowell's Fort, North Fort & South Fort
Fort No. 1 thru 3 and others were built as part of and 18th century frontier line
spanning from the colony of New York to the vicinity of Ft. Dummer.

Fortifications of Colonial New England

housed six 4- or 5-pdr cannons and dominated the countryside. The lower part of the building was used as a meetinghouse. The second floor of this blockhouse projected over the first floor and was supposedly equipped machicoulis-like with openings that allowed the defenders to protect the foot of the walls. Raiseres also mentioned that Governor Bradford's house was a square stockade on which were mounted four small cannons that could enfilade the streets.

Sometime during the seventeenth century, the New England colonists developed a type of fortification known as a GARRISON HOUSE. This term applied to a variety of structures that could vary from a simple stoutly built home to a more elaborate blockhouse where members of a community could gather in case of attack. Instead of normal windows they had loopholes or windows of reduced proportions, no more than one foot by one foot and closed by heavy shutters. These houses were often surrounded by their own palisade. According to John Dow, author the *History of Hampton*, the garrison house torn down in 1855 was "heavily timbered, the eastern half of the second story projecting over the first, with openings here and there in the projection, through which shot may be fired downward, or waste poured if the savages pursued their favorite plan of setting fire to the house." Dow also claims that ordinary residences were also used as garrison houses in time of war, in which case a stockade was hastily put up around them.

The Pequot War of 1636 was the first major conflict to rock New England. The coastal Indians were virtually surrounded by New Englanders when hostilities broke out. FORT SAYBROOK (Connecticut), located on the west bank of the Connecticut River at its mouth, came under siege by the Pequot. This fort had only been built in 1635 in response to the Dutch setting up a fortified trading post with two cannons near today's Hartford. It was erected by a party of twenty men sent by ship by Governor Winthrop from the Massachusetts Bay Colony. Before it was even finished, its guns had driven off a Dutch ship on the eve of the Pequot War. Lion Gardiner, a master fortifications engineer, was sent from England to turn Fort Saybrook into a modern fortification. Gardiner began work in the spring of 1636, but when the war broke out, the fort was still unfinished. In the spring of 1637, an expedition of English and Indian allies struck at the fortified Pequot towns, virtually wiping out the tribe. One of the Pequot forts at PEQUOT HILL on the Mystic River was destroyed by a force of almost five hundred Englishmen and Indians (about four hundred Mohegans). Almost the entire population inside the palisade was massacred. Fort Saybrook, which was only a palisade work, burned down in 1647. It was replaced by a fort of earth and stone, but lost much of its strategic importance after the next war.

The next conflict, King Philip's War, took place when King Philip (the chief named Metacom) of the Wampanoag allied himself with the Narragansett and other tribes located between the Connecticut River and the coast. These Native Americans, virtually encircled by English settlements and suffering from European diseases, were being forcibly dispossessed of their lands. In 1675, a thousand-man colonial force under General Josiah Winslow, governor of Plymouth Colony, set out in a snowstorm to attack the Narragansett. On December 19, they launched an assault on the Narragansett fortified position known as FORT SWAMP or GREAT SWAMP FORT (today the site of South Kingston) on an island well inside of the Pocasset Swamp of Rhode Island. In *Soldiers in King Philip's War*, George Bodge claims that the Englishmen crossed the frozen swamp to attack the "rude fortifications" of a very strong position: "Without waiting for an organized attack, the Massachusetts troops ... rushed forward across the ice in an impetuous charge, and into the entrance, where the Indians had constructed rude flankers, and placed a strong blockhouse in front and flanks, and were forced back for a time; but others coming on pressed into the breach, and, though suffering terrible losses, at last stormed all the fortifications, drove the enemy from every line of entrenchments within the fort, and out into the swamps and woods beyond. The fort was burned and many slain, but many more Narragansetts escaped to join the Wampanoag who had already been attacking many towns in the Plymouth Colony." According to Joseph Dudley, who accompanied the expedition, the position was located in a cedar swamp and contained hundreds of wigwams inside the fortifications. The defensive works, he claimed, were breastworks with flanking positions that included many small blockhouses.

In 1675, some towns resisted the Indians better than others did. Northfield's residents had built a stockade about 10 feet high a year or so earlier, but all the homes and the defenses were destroyed in the first raid. The people of Hatfield were saved from several hundred Indians by their recently built stockade, which was about 10 feet high and surrounded most of the settlement. On February 10, 1676, the town of Lancaster was almost destroyed before a relief force arrived to save the defenders of a single garrison house. As the attacks continued, a new expedition set out against the Indians who, had two large fortified camps, one near WACHUSETT HILL and the other at MENAMESET near Brookfield (about twenty miles west of Worcester). The colonial force found Menameset abandoned early in March. In mid-March, the Indians attacked Groton, forcing its inhabitants into five garrison houses, one of which was destroyed. The colonists escaped while the others held out as their town burned. A number of other towns were heavily raided and both sides took heavy casualties. In the end, however, the Indians, fewer in numbers, were nearly exterminated by the war. The local fortifications, mostly garrison houses, generally stymied their attempts to drive the English out.

John Winthrop arrived with the Puritans at Salem in 1630 and later moved down the coast to a better site where he established BOSTON. The Boston settlement was on a protected position, on a neck of land almost surrounded by water, and it was not until 1632 that its first fort was built. This earthen fortification, called FORT HILL because it was built on a location known as Corn Hill at the time, was not completed until 1634 and quickly eroded away. In 1687, it was replaced by FORT ANDROS, named after the governor who ordered its construction, with a four-bastioned earthen fort with barracks enclosed by a palisade. It had limited strategic value because its location soon prevented it from protecting the rapidly expanding town. When a fire broke out in 1760, its magazine exploded, virtually destroying the fort.

In the 1660s, the SOUTH BATTERY was built a short distance to the east of Fort Andros. According to Gerald Butler, author of *The Guns of Boston Harbor*, it became the strongest battery in the colonies by the 1740s, when it housed thirty-five cannons in a bastioned stone fort with a large blockhouse in the center. On the other side of the old harbor, at Merry's Point, was the NORTH BATTERY, a masonry position that held several cannons. However, by the time of the American Revolution both of these batteries were in ruins.

Castle Island and Governor's Island were the keys to Boston Harbor. Governor's Island was only defended by a blockhouse throughout most of the seventeenth century. It was not until the end of the century that it was endowed with a fort that could form a crossfire with the fort on Castle Island. This fort too deteriorated within a few years. The fortifications of Castle Island were built in 1635. These works decayed as fast as the others in the Boston area did, but they were rebuilt and reworked until late in the century, when they were replaced by a rectangular stone fort with four corner bastions. The walls consisted of the standard tabby construction, except that the space between the masonry walls was filled with oyster shells. Unfortunately, the mixture did not work out very well and the fort began crumbling within ten years. Later known as CASTLE WILLIAM, it remained the main fort in the Boston area for many years. It was rebuilt more than once during the seventeenth century.

The Dutch built FORT AMSTERDAM on the south end of Manhattan Island in 1625 and the settlement of NEW AMSTERDAM grew around it. A year later, Governor Peter Minuit purchased the island from the Indians. According to Father Isaac Jogues, who described the settlement in 1643, the walls and four corner-artillery bastions of Fort Amsterdam had been reduced to crumbling mounds. Furthermore, the poor state of the walls made the gate irrelevant. Not long after Father Jogues's visit, the governor decided to restore the fort and to face the bastions and gates with stone. In 1646, the Dutch colonists erected a palisade a short distance away from the fort to protect the settlement from the native tribes. This palisade, which cut across the island, formed the northern boundary

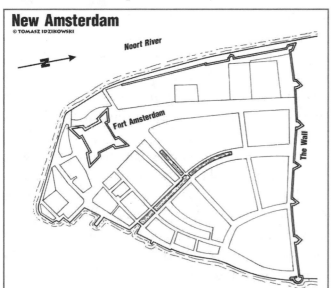

of the settlement. In 1660, the older palisade was replaced by a new, 12-foot-high wall that included seven stone bastions and two stone gates. Known as "The Wall," it was maintained and improved by the English and remained in use until the 1690s. Its location and name would be immortalized as Wall Street.

The Dutch built few defenses in NEW NETHERLANDS, even though their traders spread from the site of modern-day Hartford in the east to the Delaware River in the west. In

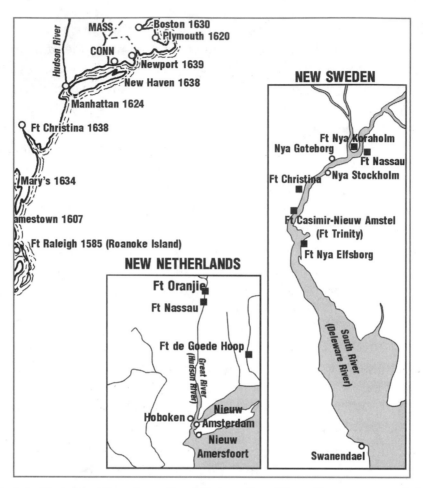

1652, about sixty Dutch settlers from the Albany site of Fort Orange moved down river to a point where the depth of the Hudson changed, almost midway from the mouth of the river to Albany. There they established a settlement and FORT ESPOUS, a stockade with a moat, at the site of modern-day Kingston. Dutch immigration was modest and the town's population numbered only about seven hundred souls when Peter Stuyvesant was appointed governor in 1647. Fort Espous was besieged by the Espous Indians for about twenty days in 1659. After that, it served as a base of operations to Peter Stuyvesant, who went after the attackers. Its stockade was expanded several times. Twenty years after Stuyvesant's arrival, the population more than doubled with the influx of immigrants from the homeland and a failed colony in Brazil.

In 1638, a group of Swedes, led by Peter Minuit, the former Dutch leader of New Amsterdam, settled in Delaware, naming the colony NEW SWEDEN. Near their first settlement, located at the site of present-day Wilmington, they built FORT CHRISTINA, which included four corner bastions and held a garrison of twenty-four men. During the first few years mostly Dutchmen came to settle and they were followed later by several ship loads of Swedes, who expanded into the region, building more forts as they went. In 1643, Johan Printz took over the governorship of the Swedish colony, determined to expand it. In 1643, Printz began work on FORT NEW ELFSBORG, near the mouth of the river. It mounted eight 12-pdrs and a mortar and had a garrison of only thirteen men. He also built FORT NEW GOTTENBURG up river from Fort Christina on Tinicum Island, where he moved the capital and built his home. Fort New Gottenburg was apparently little more than a log blockhouse mounting four cannons. It burned down in November 1645 when the sentry fell asleep with a candle burning. The fort was then rebuilt.

Governor Printz soon found himself engaged in a diplomatic game of chess with Governor Stuyvesant in which the Delaware region became their chessboard and the forts their pieces. Toward the end of the decade, there were only about two hundred colonists in New Sweden while the Dutch did not even have a dozen soldiers in the contested area. Neither the Swedish nor the Dutch governor had a large enough army to engage in open conflict.

In 1647, the Swedes built a log fort, FORT NEW KORSHOLM, on Province Island near the mouth of the Schuylkill River, the future site of Philadelphia. The new fort, which was not far from Fort Nassau, cut off the Dutch from the lucrative fur trade with the Indians. The Dutch soon retaliated by building FORT BEEVERSREEDE on the Schuylkill River to challenge the Swedes for the fur trade and to stop their expansion. The Dutch fort was little more than a house surrounded by a palisade. Next, Printz built a stockade in front of Fort Beeversreede to shut off its business with the Indians, forcing the Dutch out a few years later.

After that, in 1651 the Dutch built FORT CASIMIR not far from Fort Christina. In the same year, Printz had to abandon Fort New Elfsborg, whose insalubrious, swampy environment was decimating his garrison. Fort Korsholm was also abandoned. The new Dutch fort was succeeding in choking off the modest Swedish colonization effort. The Swedish colony had dwindled to a mere seventy souls when a new expedition from Sweden brought 350 new settlers. The new arrivals landed at Fort Casimir in 1654, forced the few Dutch soldiers to surrender, and renamed it FORT TRINITY. Finally running out of patience, the Dutch West Indies Company ordered Stuyvesant to forcibly remove the Swedes. Stuyvesant sailed up the Delaware with a few ships carrying several hundred soldiers in August 1655. He recaptured Fort Casimir and took Fort Christina (renamed Fort Altena). By September, New Sweden had disappeared from the map. The Dutch now occupied a wide and strong position between the English colonies of New England and Virginia.

In 1664, the small Dutch garrisons in New Netherlands surrendered to the British after a short war. The English changed the name of Fort Amsterdam to FORT JAMES and the name of the colony to New York, after the king's brother. The Third Anglo-Dutch War broke out in 1672, and as usual spilled over onto the American continent. Most of New Netherlands was recaptured by the Dutch, but was given back to England after the war ended in 1674. At this point, the English colonies stretched from New England to the Carolinas.

In the early 1680s, William Penn was given Delaware and the right to settle the lands later named Pennsylvania. Peace reigned for a relatively short period in the colony until the Indians realized they had been cheated out of their lands. During this time, the colonists, lulled by a false sense of security, built no fortifications. However, as the colonists spread inland, they built many log cabins with loopholes. Blockhouses also remained the main type of defensive positions for families fearing the hostility of their Native American neighbors.

Eighteenth-Century New England Frontier and King George's War

Before King Philip's War, the New Englanders had established a line of settlements along the Connecticut River valley. NORTHFIELD, and the area around it, was fortified before and after the war, and by 1722 it had received two new forts. But as the frontier became more secure on the eve of the French and Indian War, its citizens decided to dismantle the forts. Starting in the mid-1740s, a series of forts were built west of the Connecticut River, on the western frontier of Massachusetts, in order to secure it in case of war.

The General Court, or colonial legislature, also ordered the construction of forts. Two types of forts came into use at the time: those built by settlers, usually small, and those built by orders of the General Court, generally larger and manned by a garrison of colonial militia. Most of the forts built by the settlers were little more than palisaded works with walls 10 to 12 feet high encircling a varying number of homes in a settlement. The larger forts were more elaborate and served a military purpose.

Early in 1744, the Massachusetts General Court ordered the construction of FORT SHIRLEY at Heath on a tributary of the Connecticut River and FORT PELHAM at Rowe. Fort Pelham near the source of the Housatonic River was built as a four-sided stockade with four large watchtowers on each corner and held a twenty-man garrison. The General Court also commissioned the preparation of several other positions to cover the Mohawk Trail, an east-west route between New York and Massachusetts consisting mostly of Indian footpaths. Along the Housatonic River, several small positions were readied at the towns of Pittsfield, Stockridge, and Sheffield. Some of the better-known forts included FORT BURKE, a blockhouse mounting two small swivel guns enclosed by a square stockade with corner watchtowers and garrisoned by twenty men. These swivel guns, which filled the gap between cannons and muskets, were used in many colonial forts, especially when cannons were not needed or not available.

FORT DUMMER (Brattleboro, Vermont) was built in 1724 as part of the first settlement in Vermont, and might be considered, together with a few blockhouses in the area, the northern anchor of this line of forts. It was larger than the average fort on this frontier, each of its sides being 180 feet long. It was also not built like a typical stockade, but instead it was made of cut white pine timbers placed horizontally to form rather solid walls with loopholes cut into them. Buildings were placed at each corner and a single watchtower with loopholes stood at a corner near one of the two entrances. Fort Dummer was first garrisoned by about forty Massachusetts militiamen and a dozen Mohawks.

Another much looser line of forts was built along several of the rivers in Maine, including the Kennebec River. FORT FREDERICK at Pemaquid and FORT RICHMOND are probably fairly representative of the forts in the area. Fort Frederick dated from the 1630s and began its existence as an early stockaded trading post. It was later replaced by FORT CHARLES, a two-level wooden blockhouse surrounded by a stockade which was overrun by Penobscot Indians in 1689.

Fort Charles was replaced in 1692 by FORT WILLIAM HENRY, which had a large two-level stone corner-tower 29 feet high with twenty-eight gun ports. It is considered the first English stone fort in New England. The fort's walls ranged from 10 feet to 22 feet in height. The fort, armed with eighteen cannons, controlled the harbor entrance. One of its main weaknesses was its lack of an internal water supply since its well was located outside its walls. Fort William Henry was captured and destroyed by a small expedition led by Pierre d'Iberville in 1696.

FORT FREDERIC was built on the ruins of Fort Charles in 1729. The new fort included two corner bastions, but was not as strong as the fort it replaced. Its stone and brick walls were only 8 to 10 feet high. Even so, Fort Frederic was able to repel attackers twice in 1747. FORT RICHMOND was built in 1719 on the west bank of the river and was later enlarged and refurbished in 1740.

A number of blockhouses and forts had been built in the Massachusetts-owned territory of Maine before King George's War because of a boundary dispute involving Acadia and New England. The forts on the Massachusetts frontier, including coastal Maine, served as the main line of defense against the French and their Indian allies during King George's War. FORT MASSACHUSETTS, located in a meadow thirty miles west of Deerfield and four miles east of Williamstown on the western side of the Hoosac Mountains, was built in 1745. It was rectangular in shape and measured 120 feet by 80 feet. Its walls were made of horizontal pine logs rising to a height of 16 feet. It included two gun-platforms and watchtowers at opposite corners. Inside were a barracks and "Great House." The latter was a multifloored building that housed the officers's quarters and a storehouse. In August 1746, its garrison of only twenty-two men expended all its ammunition before it surrendered to a French and Indian force of over nine hundred men led by Rigaud de Vaudreuil. The prisoners were taken to Quebec and the fort was burned. In August of 1748, this fort, rebuilt after it was burned, was attacked again by a force estimated at up to three hundred Indians. However, its forty defenders under the leadership of Captain Ephraim Williams Jr. managed to hold out.

Other raids by French Indian allies took place throughout the frontier regions of New England in 1746, but had limited success. One of these raids penetrated as far as the New York colony. The attackers planned to attack FORT FREDERICK at Albany in 1745. Fort

Frederick had been rebuilt early in the century in masonry, replacing the old wooden fort built after a Dutch defeat. The new fort was quite formidable with its four corner-bastions that mounted over twenty cannons. Not surprisingly, it held off the French assault.

In 1748, the Indians managed to strike at detachments from Fort Dummer and FORT NUMBER 4, located at Charlestown and known also as PLANTATION NUMBER 4 (New Hampshire). It was built in 1743 near the Connecticut River and formed a large, rectangular log fort measuring 180 feet by 156 feet. It included a 30-foot watchtower in one corner. Its entrance consisted of a large, two-story building. The walls of the fort enclosed most of the village. When it was attacked in 1746, its defenders were forced to abandon it due to a shortage of food. In the spring of 1747, Captain Phineas Stevens returned with thirty militiamen to reoccupy the fort. A few days later, early in April, a large French and Indian force put the fort under siege. All attempts to set fire to the fort failed and the invaders withdrew.

In New England, CASTLE WILLIAM on Castle Island in Boston harbor remained the strongest position. When Colonel Wolfgang William Romer, the chief military engineer for North America, came to Boston in 1701 to fortify the harbor, he renovated and improved Castle William, giving it brick walls and adding a twenty cannon position in 1705. By the time he was finished, the distance between each of the bastions was 180 feet. Further improvements included a first line of defense on the waterfront, a secondary position behind it, and finally the four-bastioned fort itself now made of brick and wood. By that time, the defenses mounted fifty cannons. However, according to Gerald Butler, the mortar Romer used was of such poor quality that the fort began to come apart in the 1730s. In 1740, further repairs and additions were made. Bastion Shirley was added at this time and its twenty new 42-pdrs brought the total number of cannons to over eighty. Some of these cannons were taken by the colonial troops on the expedition to capture Louisbourg. Thanks to Castle William and its other fortifications, Boston remained one of the best-defended seaports in the British colonies in America until 1770. Even so, these fortifications were far from formidable.

One major addition to the British position in America came after the end of King George's War. Until then, the large peninsula of Nova Scotia had been defended by the ANNAPOLIS ROYAL, located on the Bay of Fundy. To the northeast of Nova Scotia, on the island of Cape Breton, stood the French fortress of Louisbourg. After the war ended in 1748, the British government decided that it needed a new and stronger position to replace Annapolis Royal. A site was selected on a peninsula formed by a river on one side and a natural harbor on the other. The harbor led northwest into Bedford Basin. Settlers quickly laid out the new town of HALIFAX and worked on the construction of FORT GEORGE, a square stockade 200 feet wide on each side with two-story bastions or blockhouses. The new fort was placed on top of Citadel Hill. Governor Edward Cornwallis reported that the town's fortifications consisted of a line of palisades with stockade forts that he called "squares," which consisted of double pickets, a second row

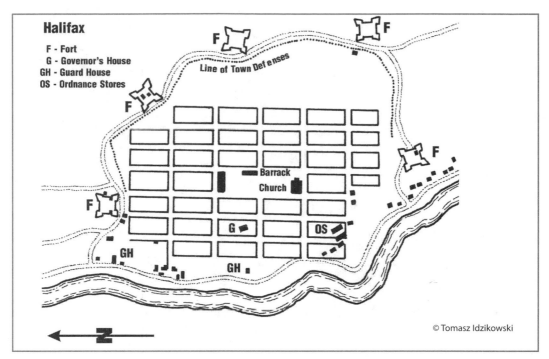

of timbers that covered the gaps in the first row and strengthened the entire wall. In addition to Fort George, there were four similar forts in the town palisade: FORT CORNWALLIS, FORT HORSEMAN, FORT GRENADIER, and FORT LUTTRELL. The walls included loopholes for firearms. During the next few years, a line of three blockhouses with triangular stockades was built in front of the city walls to form an advance position that also allowed for the city's growth. More blockhouses appeared as the settlement grew and the Indian problem diminished.

Halifax was on a peninsula that was part of larger peninsula partially formed by the Bedford Basin. As the community expanded, FORT SACKVILLE was built at the base of this large peninsula, not far from the north end of the Bedford Basin. In addition, FORT CHAROLETTE was built on Georges Island to protect the entrance to the harbor on the site of a seven-gun battery. FORT CLARENCE was built at Dartmouth, across the river from Georges Island in order to protect the harbor area further. During the French and Indian War, Halifax served as a depot for the English army and navy and became the assembly point for the assault on Louisbourg. After the war, Halifax replaced Louisbourg as the dominant coastal fortress on the American North Atlantic coast.

The French and Indian War: War of the Forts

The French and Indian War was sparked by the French ambition to control the Ohio Valley. The governor of Virginia disputed their control of the region, particularly after French forts appeared at Presqu'Isle and Le Boeuf and the French advanced to Venango on the Allegheny River. Lieutenant Colonel George Washington arrived at Fort Le

The Campaign against Ft. Duquesne 1754 to 1760

© TOMASZ IDZIKOWSKI

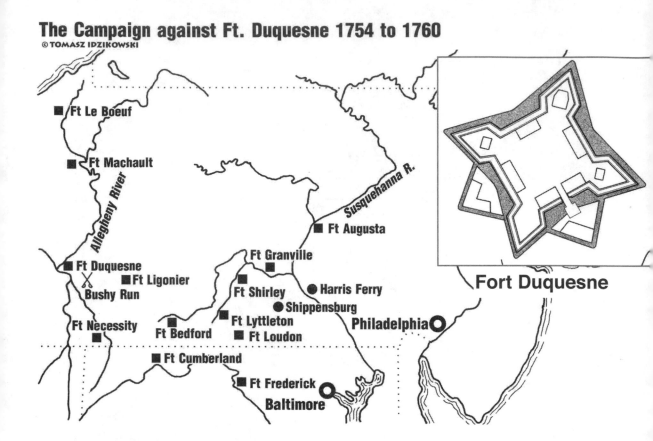

Fort Duquesne

Boeuf in late 1753 to demand the French withdrawal from the area. After their refusal, Virginia's Governor Dinwiddie sent a small company of militia to the confluence of the Allegheny and Monongahela Rivers to build a fort on a site deemed ideal by Washington in his journal entry of November 22, 1753. The French drove them off and then proceeded to construct FORT DUQUESNE on the same site. In the summer of 1754, Washington departed Virginia with militia from a newly formed regiment, marching toward the Monongahela River to attack Fort Duquesne. In order to undertake the campaign, he had to cut a road through the Allegheny Mountains as he advanced. Since the rivers in this region did not form good pathways, a man-made road was needed as much as the forts to effectively maintain territorial claims.

Washington built a small, palisaded fort, later named FORT NECESSITY, at the Great Meadows, a marshy valley surrounded by hills. After ambushing a small French contingent, he learned that the French forces coming from Fort Duquesne numbered over five hundred men, including Indian allies. Deciding that prudence was the better part of valor, Washington fell back to his small fort. There the remainder of the Virginia Regiment and an Independent Company of South Carolinians joined him. His men prepared entrenchments in front of the fort on June 9 and June 12. The question of the actual size and shape of Fort Necessity was disputed for many years, until archaeological evidence resolved the conundrum. Amazingly, Washington himself left no written description of the fort. On June 3 he merely wrote that "We have just finished a small palisado'd fort, in which, with my small numbers, I shall not fear the attack of 500

Fort Necessity

© Tomasz Idzikowski

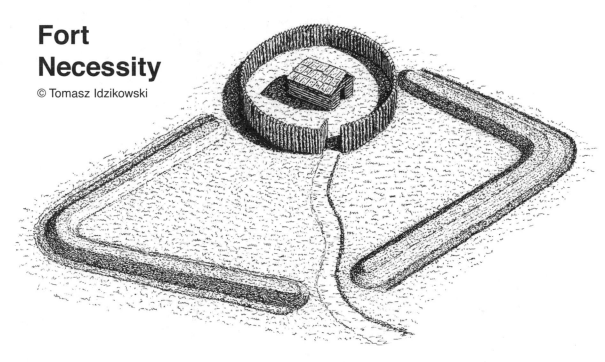

men." It is now known that the fort was circular with a diameter of 53 feet and enclosed a small, square log building 14 feet in length. Washington mounted several small swivel cannons in the fort.

The French arrived on July 3, after a pounding rain had flooded the entrenchments in the swampy area. Musket fire was exchanged, the swivel guns boomed across the fields, but Washington was not able to entice the French to attack through the open fields where he could take advantage of his defensive position. During the evening, the French isolated the fort and the next day they negotiated terms. Washington and his men marched out of the fort and returned to Virginia as the French proceeded to demolish the little fort.

Washington's defeat at Fort Necessity initiated the war, according to the English colonists. The French, on the other hand, reasonably contended that the event that actually sparked the war was Washington's ambush of their contingent. Be that as it may, British General Braddock arrived in Virginia with two regiments of regulars. At the same time, the colonials began putting up new forts and improving old ones along the frontier of Pennsylvania and Virginia. The same thing happened in New England and New York along the major invasion routes, which usually followed the river valleys.

General Braddock laid out the strategy for the war, ordering a four-prong offensive. He would personally lead his two regiments of regulars and colonial troops and an artillery train to take Fort Duquesne. Governor Shirley, Braddock's second in command, was to send a force of colonial regiments to reinforce Fort Oswego and then move against Fort Niagara to cut the French lifeline. Sir William Johnson, who had kept the Iroquois loyal to the British, was to lead a force against Fort Frédéric at Crown Point, on

French & Indian War

Virginian & Pennsylvanian Frontier Forts in the 1750s

Present day towns for reference

© TOMASZ IDZIKOWSKI

the main invasion route north. A fourth force consisting of colonials under Lieutenant-Colonel Robert Monckton was to move up the coast from Massachusetts and attack the French forts in Acadia. The French plan was to hold their forts and use non-conventional tactics learned from fighting on the American frontier.

In July 1755, Governor Dinwiddie ordered that the post at Willis Creek, a tributary of the Potomac, be turned into a major fort. Almost a year earlier Colonel James Innis, at his own discretion, had built a small stockade on a high point that was not well sited. Governor Dinwiddie wanted it enlarged so it could provision 1,200 to 1,400 men for half a year. The new fort was built during the winter and, after bearing the name of FORT MOUNT PLEASANT at first, it was renamed FORT CUMBERLAND in honor of the new British commander-in-chief. The new fort's outer works were about 400 feet long and 160 feet wide including the square fort with four bastions built according to what might be considered Vauban-type standards. Fort Cumberland was located on a hill above the bluffs overlooking Willis Creek. It consisted of four corner-bastions, each mounting four cannons, including eleven 4-pdrs. Its curtain walls were each about 50 feet in length. On one side of the fort, a long palisade enclosed three rows of barracks and a large parade ground. Trenches were excavated to provide a covered path to Willis Creek, but after Braddock's defeat, a well was dug within the fort. The barracks within the stockade held two hundred soldiers in addition to quarters for officers. Tunnels under the fort allowed the occupants of the fort to get water from the creek. It is at Fort Cumberland that General Braddock assembled his expedition of over two thousand men in June 1755 before he set off to drive the French from the Forks of the Ohio. After Braddock's defeat and death at the battle of Monongahela in July, Washington led the retreat back to Fort Cumberland. Even though Washington did not think it was worth maintaining, this fort was one of the few relatively strong fortifications on the Upper Potomac.

The forts along the Potomac and its tributaries were scattered. However, there were also many privately owned stockaded cabins or heavily fortified homes in the region before the summer of 1755. This practice was not uncommon on the frontier throughout the Thirteen Colonies, especially in the Southern and Middle Colonies. Most forts built by colonial governments were intended to either protect ports or cover river passages. Washington tried to set up a line of forts to protect the frontier, but the region, consisting of woodlands, valleys, hills, and mountains, restricted the construction of trails and roads. And the Indians could easily bypass the widely scattered forts since they did not have to rely on the few protected roads or river routes.

Some of the forts formed a loose line that stretched back into Virginia, Maryland, or Pennsylvania; however, they did not form a defensive line. They were used instead as points along the rivers or the few roads from which patrols could go out on escort missions or keep the area clear of hostile Indians. Supplying the forts was a serious problem, since civilian wagoners did not like to move through hostile territory without an escort. A military transportation corps was created in 1756 to solve this problem. Before

1756, many fort garrisons had run out of supplies during periods of hostilities. Most of the forts in the Thirteen Colonies were little more than stockades. Many of them were small, with garrisons of only ten to fifty men. If they did not defend lines of communication, they served as refuges for the settlers and depended on the local population for some support, existing in a symbiotic relationship with the civilian population.

Few regular troops were available for garrison duty on the frontier forts, which meant that the provincials provided the bulk of the troops in their respective colonies. This may have been an advantage, since a colonial soldier was usually a volunteer who worked well with the settlers in his region. He also may have been more skilled at building and maintaining a frontier fort than a regular army soldier from England. However, it was not unusual to find regulars in some of the more important forts. They were generally recruited from the working classes in the British Isles, and often developed a rocky relationship with the colonists. Loudoun The problem was further aggravated by some British requiring colonials to quarter the regulars when military barracks were not available. On the other hand, the provincials performed with mixed results on the battlefield, whereas the regulars were usually more efficient and dependable.

George Washington was responsible for establishing a number of forts on the Virginia frontier as protection against the Indians. FORT ASHBY was built in 1754 under a line of nearby low hills that allowed the Indians to send flaming arrows into the stockade. As a result, it was set on fire several times. It was from Fort Ashby that Washington would lead a relief force to breakup the Indian siege of Fort Cumberland in 1756. In July 1756, during a council of war, Washington and his officers decided to establish a loose chain of twenty-three forts to protect the frontier. Washington decided to maintain a garrison of 170 men at Fort Cumberland, which represented the strongest westernmost position on this line. The most advanced position was FORT NICHOLAS further up the river from Fort Cumberland. Built during the summer of 1755 by Captain Charles Lewis of the Virginia Regiment, it included four corner blockhouses.

The new frontier line also included pre-existing positions such as Fort Ashby. It was located beyond the line, but Washington considered it worthy of being maintained because it could provide escorts between Fort Cumberland and Romney. Late in 1755, on Washington's orders, Captain William Cocke and his ranger company built a stockade known as FORT COCKE further up Pattersons's Creek from Fort Ashby. He also placed about sixty men in garrison at FORT PEARSALL (present-day site of Romney, West Virginia). This fort, built in 1753, was actually a stockaded cabin on the south branch of the Potomac, and was typical of many privately created positions. Washington eventually ordered it enlarged and turned into a supply depot.

Before and after July 1756, Captain Thomas Waggoner built several forts, including FORT WAGGONER (or FORT BUTTERMILK). This small stockade on the south branch of the Potomac near Moorefield (West Virginia) held a garrison of seventy men, slightly larger than average. In February 1756, Captain Waggoner, under orders from Washington, built

FORT UPPER TRACT (West Virginia), further up the valley. Like many of the forts in the region, it was square with sides of about 90 feet in length and four corner blockhouses and held a garrison of about fifty men. FORT SEYBERT (West Virginia) was a privately built stockade on the south fork of the Potomac with two blockhouses dating from 1755. The conditions in which the troops in these forts had to live were far short of ideal, which led to mutinies, especially in 1757, which were all suppressed. In April 1758, forty Shawnee attacked Fort Upper Tract, then proceeded to place Fort Seybert under siege for two days. Their leader, Chief Killbuck, convinced the defenders to surrender, promising them that he would allow them to leave. However, after they opened the gate they were slaughtered and the few survivors were taken captive. The fort was rebuilt that summer.

FORT PLEASANT, also built by Captain Waggoner on Washington's orders of 1756, was located between Moorfield and Romney near the main road from Winchester. Washington's instructions for the building of the fort called for a basic quadrangle with 90-foot sides and bastions. Due to the loose terminology of the period, many historians had concluded that the bastions were in actuality mere blockhouses. However, West Virginia historian Terry Gruber has argued that Fort Pleasant was endowed with actual bastions.* Fort Pleasant was intended to serve as a key position on the frontier even though its garrison only averaged about sixty men. [*Note: Generally speaking, the bastion on a palisaded fort required double walls filled with earth and a platform inside. This type of structure took only a few days to build whereas a blockhouse required more work and time. A blockhouse would also serve the function of a bastion and even be found on a bastion. Given the speed with which this fort was put up, it is more likely that it had bastions. Furthermore, it is more likely that Washington, given his background and military experience, would have been more familiar with the task of building bastions rather that blockhouses. Nonetheless, because the term of bastion was rather indiscriminately applied to bastions and blockhouses alike, throughout this chapter the term of bastions will be applied to both.]

Other forts were positioned behind these first-line forts to the east covering road and river crossings. FORT COX was located on the Little Cacapon River. FORT DAWSON, FORT ENUCH, and FORT EDWARDS occupied sites along the Great Cacapon River, further down the Potomac. French-led Indians actually penetrated this far to attack Fort Edwards in 1756. In September of 1756 the Indians reached as far east as Martinsburg and massacred the garrison at FORT NEALLY.

The Virginia assembly authorized the construction of FORT LOUDOUN in Winchester in the spring of 1756. Construction began that summer and continued for two years, but the fort was never completed because the funds were cut off. Fort Loudoun was square shaped, 150 feet in length, and had corner bastions. Its walls consisted of two parallel rows of logs set upright with the space between them filled with earth. Inside the walls was an additional palisade. The barracks could accommodate as many as five hundred men. The bastions and walls mounted eighteen 4-pdr and 6-pdr cannons, a pair of howitzers, and four swivel guns. The normal garrison numbered seventy-five men whose duties included construction work. The war never reached Fort Loudoun, which served as a base for George Washington from which to coordinate the defense of the region.

North of the Potomac, Governor Sharpe of Maryland and Governor Morris of Pennsylvania ordered the construction of several small forts similar to those Washington built in Virginia. One of these was FORT CRESAP near the Little Cacapon River on the north side of the Potomac. It was a simple stockade built by Colonel Thomas Cresap around his home at the site of Oldtown, Maryland, to protect himself against roving bands of French-led Indians, who often moved through the region during the summer of 1756 on their way to attack other forts further east. After fending off many attacks in 1756, the colonel took his family and local settlers to FORT CONCOCHEAGUE, on the tributary of the same name.

The most impressive fort built in the region was FORT FREDERICK on the north bank of the Potomac in Maryland. Construction on this masonry fort began in the fall of 1756. Inspired by the Vauban school of military architecture, Fort Frederick was square and had corner bastions and standard defensive features. A two-floor barracks accommodated two hundred men. The fort was located a little more than forty miles from Fort Cumberland. The area in-between the two forts was covered by other smaller fortifications and a road linking them was finally built in 1759.

Benjamin Chambers built his own fort in 1756 a good distance from Fort Concocheague, up the river of the same name. FORT CHAMBERS was one of the strongest in the area besides Fort Frederick and Fort Loudoun (Pennsylvania). Armed with two 4-pdr cannons and some swivel guns, Chambers beat off two major Indian attacks from his fort.

The largest fort in the region inside of Pennsylvania was another work named FORT LOUDOUN. It was built in 1756 by Colonel John Armstrong and his Pennsylvania militia on the orders of Governor Morrison. It stood on the west branch of the Concocheague River, to the west of Fort Chambers. It served as headquarters to General John Forbes in the summer of 1758 when he assembled several thousand troops to move against Fort Duquesne. One of the more interesting fortifications in the region was FORT STEEL, built further down the creek from Fort Loudoun. It was actually a church enclosed with a stockade in the summer of 1755.

In Pennsylvania, a line of over a dozen forts and blockhouses ran along the Blue Mountains by 1756. There was chaos in the region in November 1755 when Delaware Indians attacked a Moravian mission at modern-day Lehighton in the Lehigh Gap of the Blue Mountains, where the Lehigh River cuts through. Benjamin Franklin, appointed as commissioner by Governor Morris late in 1755, was directed to restore order to the area and establish a line of forts in the northwest frontier, northwest of Bethlehem, between the Susquehanna River and east branch of the Delaware River. These forts were also intended to protect the approaches to Philadelphia.

Although Franklin did not feel qualified, he carried out his mission, creating innova-

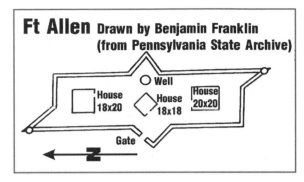

Ft Allen Drawn by Benjamin Franklin (from Pennsylvania State Archive)

tive fortifications like FORT ALLEN. Construction on this fort began in January 1756. The fort consisted of an elongated stockade 125 feet by 50 feet and two corner demi-bastions. In addition, Franklin placed two bastions in the center of the longer walls. (The bastions Franklin placed in the middle of the walls were two-faced projections sometimes called redans by the British. They had been in common use since at least the sixteenth century.) According to Franklin, "Each pine made three palisades of 18 feet long pointed at one end. When they were setup, our carpenters built a platform all round within, 6 feet high, for the men to stand on when to fire through the loopholes. We had one swivel gun, which we mounted on one of the angles...." He called the fort a "miserable stockade" and noted that it took a week to complete. The palisades projected 12 feet above the ground and were sunk 3 feet into the ground. The fort mounted two swivel guns.

Franklin sent detachments to build two other stockades, FORT NORRIS and FORT FRANKLIN, each about fifteen miles from Fort Allen. Fort Norris, he wrote, was square and had four half bastions. Its sides were 80 feet in length. Fort Franklin, on the other hand, was much smaller with sides of only forty feet. Both forts were held by small garrisons. At Fort Norris, there were only fifty men. As in Washington's forts in western Virginia, the garrisons of Franklin's forts suffered from boredom, isolation, and poor discipline, which eventually led to mutinies. After negotiating a treaty with the Indians in August 1757, only Fort Allen was garrisoned.

To the west of this line, on the east bank of the Susquehanna River at its forks near Sunbury, stood FORT AUGUSTA, which served as an advance post. Colonel William Clapham of Boston, recommended for the task by Franklin, directed its construction in 1756 using provincial labor. The fort was garrisoned until 1765 and was renovated during the intervening years. Although swivel guns were used in the other provincial forts of the colony, Fort Augusta mounted cannons and was the only fort with a glacis in the region. The fort was square, with

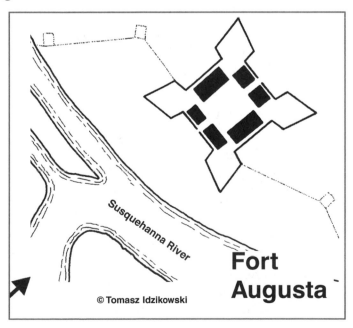

© Tomasz Idzikowski

Fort Augusta

204-foot sides and had four large bastions, each mounting two cannons. It had enough room to quarter four hundred men. A moat surrounded the fort and three of the walls above the scarp were built of horizontal logs while the side facing the river was a palisade of vertical logs. Another palisade was placed on the counterscarp of the moat. Plans show a palisade with two blockhouses apiece extending from two sides of the fort across from two of the corner bastions to the river. Fort Augusta saw little action. In the autumn of 1756, a French raiding party with three small cannons observed the fort under construction from Blue Hill. However, despite the partially completed condition of the fort, they decided that the number of troops present was too strong for them to take on, so they withdrew.

Colonel William Clapham also built FORT HALIFAX during the summer of 1756 at a location between Fort Augusta and FORT HUNTER, a gristmill turned into a stockaded blockhouse. Fort Halifax was placed near modern-day Harrisburg on the Susquehanna River. It was square, had earthen curtains and four corner bastions, one of which was circular. It also included a surrounding ditch, whose spoil formed the curtains. Troops from Fort Augusta were sent to garrison Fort Halifax, which remained occupied until the end of 1757 to protect the line of communications to Fort Augusta.

In 1758, General John Forbes arrived in Philadelphia to complete Braddock's task and lead the British offensive against Fort Duquesne. General Amherst was to attack Louisbourg and General Abercromby was to advance up the Champlain Valley. In June, Colonel Henry Bouquet and his advance party had built FORT BEDFORD at Raystown, on a bluff overlooking the river. This fort had five corner bastions, a moat on two sides, the bluffs on the other two, and a stockade built of 18-foot logs. The longest curtain wall was about 150 feet and the shortest of the five was about 70 feet. Fort Bedford became a major supply point for this operation.

By September, the major obstacle of the Alleghenies was crossed and the force was about halfway to Fort Duquesne. Forbes constructed FORT LIGONIER on the site of an Indian town known as Loyalhanna. This fort was built on a plateau running parallel to the creek. As far as regional historian Charles Stotz can determine, the fort's outer works included a breastwork that encircled most of the top of the plateau. The fort was square and had four corner bastions. Its east wall and its two flanking bastions were only 7 feet high, consisting of a pair of horizontally laid logs, several feet apart. Dirt was placed between the logs to form a solid wall; a fraise of angled stakes was added on the outer side. The other walls consisted of vertical posts, as in most stockades. The two bastions between the horizontal log curtain wall mounted the artillery. Another artillery position, a battery made of fascines, was situated just beyond the west wall. Major James Grant rushed westward into the wilderness ahead of the main column with a brigade of eight hundred troops hoping to take Fort Duquesne by surprise in September. He was captured after being engaged and defeated by a force of over two

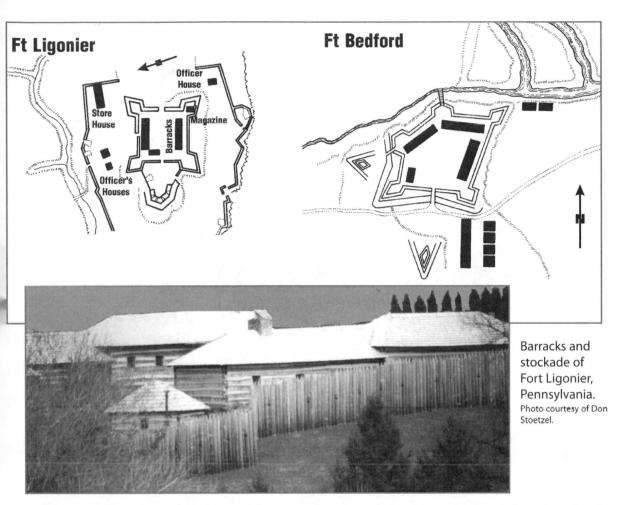

Barracks and stockade of Fort Ligonier, Pennsylvania.
Photo courtesy of Don Stoetzel.

thousand French and Indians. The French advanced with a force of four hundred French troops and one hundred Indians and attacked Fort Ligonier on October 12, 1758. Colonel James Burd, commander of the fort, drove them off. Shortly after this, late in October, most of the tribes of the area held a council with the British redcoats and declared a state of peace.

The French commander of Fort Duquesne, concerned about the loss of needed supplies, opted to abandon his fort. Forbes set off from Fort Ligonier in November only to find his quarry had been turned to ashes. The British began building FORT PITT near the ruins of Fort Duquesne. Work on a small, temporary square stockade with bastions was begun, and by January 1759, Colonel Hugh Mercer reported that the construction had advanced far enough to make the fort defensible. Two hundred Virginia militiamen remained behind to garrison the new fort and continue the work on it. By March 1759, the garrison had risen to 428 men, most of which were Virginia and Pennsylvania militia. Fort Pitt was laid out on a pentagonal trace with sides of unequal lengths and had five corner bastions, two overlooking the Monongahela. It was designed to be the most impressive fortress in the west. The entrance to Fort Pitt was approached through a rav-

Fort Pitt
© TOMASZ IDZIKOWSKI

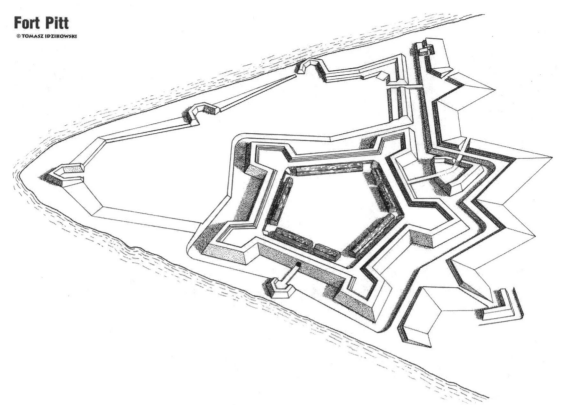

elin. The side facing the Allegheny River had outworks with three bastions or crown works, which extended from the fort to the river. The five curtain walls were about 200 feet in length and included casemates. The earthen ramparts on the two landward facing sides had brick revetments. A moat that could be filled with water surrounded the fort. In addition to a powder magazine, the fort included a barracks for officers and a barracks for four hundred men. The work was not completed until the summer of 1761, at which time Colonel Henry Bouquet was in charge and the garrison had increased to seven hundred men.

Lieutenant Colonel Robert Monckton moved up the coast with about two thousand colonial and 280 regular troops and naval support on the second prong of the British campaign of 1755. French resistance in Acadia was neither strong nor well organized, allowing Monckton to move into the Bay of Fundy and to bring his troops up to FORT BEAUSÉJOUR. Since it was critical for the French to maintain their position in Acadia, the fort was well defended by a garrison of over 450 men. In June, Monckton's troops joined the garrison of FORT LAWRENCE, forming a force of 280 regulars and 2,000 colonial troops. The British threw a bridge across the Mesaguash at Point Buot, where the French had destroyed the bridge, and managed to eject an entrenched force of French and Indians. The British destroyed the small French redoubt, which mounted four swivel guns. From there, they proceeded toward Fort Beauséjour, bringing up their artillery to engage the fort and its twenty-six cannons. The troops moved to within a mile and a half of the fort as the French set fire to the nearby village. Preparations were made for the siege. By June 12, all the artillery had been unloaded and work began on a parallel two hundred yards in length. The next morning the French began an artillery bombardment from their fort. The British, undeterred, continued to work on the siege trenches. A 13-inch mortar and three 8-inch mortars were placed behind the parallel and opened fire. On June 16, the French commander agreed to surrender. The next day, following the fall of Fort Beauséjour, the commander of FORT GASPEREAU decided that his situation was untenable and agreed to capitulate. Lieutenant Colonel Winslow led a detachment to occupy that fort on June 18.

Sir William Johnson led 3,500 colonial troops and 400 Indian allies in a third prong of the British campaign. He built FORT EDWARD at the portage between the Hudson River and Lake George, then advanced to the south shore of Lake George where he erected FORT WILLIAM HENRY. Meanwhile, French General Dieskau was on the move. The French had learned of the British plans from documents they had captured after Braddock's defeat. Seven hundred men were sent to Fort Frédéric in preparation for the British attack, while Dieskau moved south to Lake George. Dieskau at the head of 1,400 French regulars, militia, and Indians set up an ambush. Johnson's men retreated behind hastily erected field fortifications and Dieskau's regulars, with bayonets fixed, unsuccessfully tried to charge their position. Dieskau was wounded and captured. Johnson's men broke up the French force, but did not continue their advance as they continued to work on the construction of Fort William Henry.

Governor Vaudreuil dispatched Michel Chartier de Lotbinière to build FORT CARILLON at Ticonderoga on the south end of Lake Champlain. Work on Fort Carillon, which was then renamed FORT VAUDREUIL, began in October 1755. The fort was sited on a ridge overlooking the lake. Troops from Fort Frédéric were sent to work on the fort and, at one point, up to two thousand men were involved. The original layout was a square bastioned fort. In October 1756, Lotbinière wrote that he had reinforced the landward sides of the curtains with ravelins. The workers used cut oak logs, which they laid out horizontally in two rows 7 feet high and approximately 10 feet apart, linked with cross timbers placed between them and then filled in with earth to form the fort's curtain walls. Lotbinière observed that no stone was available to build a permanent work at that time. A large blockhouse in the southeast corner included embrasures for cannons. A parapet was placed on the two fronts exposed to artillery but not on the two fronts facing the water. Each of the bastions included a bombproof shelter. His men labored to create a moat that reached the bedrock as well as two demi-lunes. A covered way and glacis were prepared and a counter gard was planned to protect the single bastion exposed to attack on the landward side. Two stone barracks were built inside the fort and a storehouse and hospital were erected outside the walls. When the fort was

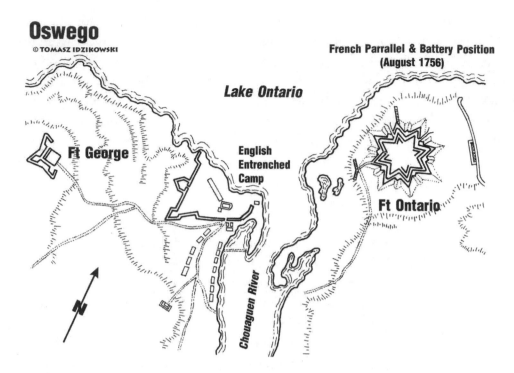

completed, it was armed with cannons hauled from Montreal and Fort Frédéric. In addition, when Fort William Henry was captured, some of its artillery was brought up the lake to the fort, which neared completion in 1758.

Governor Shirley, the interim British commander in America after Braddock's death, was unable to launch his assault on Fort Niagara because his progress across western New York was as slow as Johnson's to the north—he too stopped to build fortifications and secure his line of communications. On the French side, Vaudreuil's plans for taking Oswego were postponed because of the defeat of Dieskau's forces on Lake George.

In 1756, General Louis-Joseph Montcalm arrived in America. A skilled soldier in the European theater, he was relatively unfamiliar with the type of warfare in America. In 1756, the governor had already laid out the plans for breaking up the British presence on Lake Ontario at Oswego and ending the threat to Fort Niagara, which was the lifeline into the Ohio Valley. Montcalm departed from Fort Frontenac to strike at OSWEGO. He moved across Lake Ontario at the head of an expedition of three thousand men, which included 1,300 regulars of three regiments, 1,500 marines and militia, and about 200 Indians. His troops placed the town and fort under siege. Oswego's garrison consisted of over 1,100 colonials and regulars under Colonel James Mercer. The construction of a small fleet designed to dominate the lake was still underway. FORT GEORGE stood on the west side of the river and FORT ONTARIO on the heights on the opposite side of the river. To the south of Fort George lay the partially built FORT OSWEGO.

The Canadians and the Indians moved against Fort Ontario on the northern heights overlooking Oswego. However, soon after the siege began, Mercer allowed the garrison to withdraw across the river to join him. The French prepared new artillery positions for twenty cannons on the captured fort and began the bombardment of Oswego on August 14. The British commander, after holding a council of war, quickly concluded that his position was untenable and asked for terms.

Oswego offered the French a fortified base in the heart of the Iroquois Confederation from which to break that nation's loyalty to the British. It also presented a position from which to follow the newly improved British line of supply to subjugate western New York and remove a future threat to the Great Lakes and the French line of communications. However, instead of making the most of this opportunity, Montcalm destroyed the site and withdrew.

In 1757, the French returned to the offensive. Governor Vaudreuil sent Montcalm with a force of four thousand French and Canadian troops and one thousand Indians south, along Lake George, to attack Fort William Henry. Montcalm's forces assembled at Fort Carillon that summer. Their objective, FORT WILLIAM HENRY, had a square trace and included four log bastions and earthen curtain walls faced with logs. In mid-March, an advance force of 1,200 men led by the governor's brother surrounded the fort. The French force withdrew after several days, but not without destroying the shipyard and

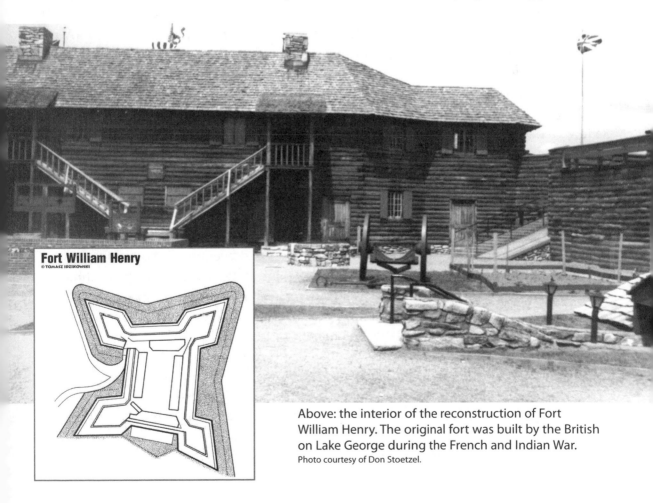

Fort William Henry
© TOMASZ IDZIKOWSKI

Above: the interior of the reconstruction of Fort William Henry. The original fort was built by the British on Lake George during the French and Indian War.
Photo courtesy of Don Stoetzel.

other facilities outside the fort first. At the end of July, Montcalm's force marched south on the western shore of Lake George with flatbottom boats, which carried the artillery, moving along the lake. When he reached Fort William Henry, the defenders numbered about 850 regulars, 95 rangers, and 1,400 colonial militiamen commanded by Lieutenant Colonel George Monro. At the beginning of August, the French troops began digging the siege trenches and preparing emplacements for the artillery. The bombardment began on August 6. As the French trenches moved closer to the western wall of the fort, Monro, who had lost some of his artillery during the fighting, decided to seek terms. As the British troops marched out in accordance to the terms of surrender, some of Montcalm's Indians got out of control and set upon the Englishmen, an event that inspired a famous scene in James Fenimore Cooper's *Last of the Mohicans*. Despite a major victory and with only Fort Edward blocking the path ahead, Montcalm once again failed to press on his advantage, destroying the fort instead and withdrawing to Fort Carillon.

While making preparations for the campaign against Louisbourg, General James Abercromby took charge of a force of sixteen thousand (including six thousand regulars) and attempted to drive the French from FORT CARILLON and open the invasion in June 1758. He moved his troops up the lake by boat. Montcalm placed most of his 3,000 to 3,500 men in field fortifications in front of the fort since it was poorly situated for landward defense. His men prepared entrenchments and felled nearby trees for log breastworks and abatis. Most of the work was done by July 7, although more time was needed to add traverses. The tree trunks were lying upon each other in front of the entrenchments, their branches cut and sharpened to create a chevaux-de-frise. The defenders stored stones and a few grenades to launch at the attackers if they crossed the abatis. Montcalm was not able to place artillery batteries on each side of his line, but his camouflaged defenses succeeded in tricking the British commanders who misjudged the strength of the position. On July 8, Abercromby attacked without his artillery and took heavy casualties, suffering a bloody defeat in the French abatis. The British withdrew to Albany.

British knowledge of LOUISBOURG was gleaned from their occupation in the previous decade and information gained by spying. A report had been prepared for an eventual siege of Louisbourg in 1757. It stated that the Island Battery mounted thirty-three 27- and 36-pdrs. They estimated that two ships of the line mounting seventy-four and sixty guns would be needed to eliminate this position. They also concluded that two 74-gun ships would be necessary to take out the thirty-two 42-pdrs of the Grand Battery (Batterie Royale). In addition, they estimated the fortress mounted over sixty guns requiring at least eight ships of the line to neutralize them. The accuracy of the information and the evaluation of the situation were subject to question, but there was no practical way of verifying it, a problem that all siege commanders have faced since ancient times.

At Halifax, General Jeffrey Amherst conducted landing exercises with the fleet to prepare his soldiers for a landing on a defended shore in the spring of 1758. At the end of May, he sailed from Halifax, escorted by Admiral Edward Boscawen's fleet that included twenty-three men-of-war, a number of other smaller vessels, and 127 transports carrying the 13,000-man invasion force. The defenders of Louisbourg numbered between 3,500 and 3,900 men augmented by a number of Indians and civilians. A company of marines was assigned to Port Dauphin and two to Port Toulouse. The French navy was heavily involved in the European theater of the war and could not support the fortress as efficiently as in the previous year. Ten warships were present, including three 64-gun and two 74-gun men-of-war.

The British expedition departed Halifax on May 28, 1758, and appeared off Isle Royale by May 30. However, foul weather delayed a landing until the seas became less choppy. The skies cleared on June 8. Meanwhile, a battalion of the Cambis Regiment landed at Port Dauphin to reinforce the garrison of Louisbourg. Governor Drucour ordered the preparation of trenches and gun emplacements along Gabraus Bay to the southwest of Louisbourg. He manned the positions with about two thousand men from the Artois and Bourgogne regiments and some marines. These forces were stationed in the place where Amherst had intended to land where the rocky beach offered the best foothold.

On June 8, the British troops set off in whaleboats toward the shore through the choppy surf, under the protection of the fleet's guns. On the left flank, Brigadier General James Wolfe, commander of one of the expedition's three divisions (organized from thirteen regiments) of the invasion force, led his troops, which included the elite units, to a more sheltered area than the designated site. He and his Grenadiers and Highlanders splashed ashore through the icy water. However, the landing was not without loss since a number of boats collided or were wrecked on the rocks. Wolfe and his men emerged on the rocky beach, quickly routed the few defenders in the area and drove the remainder back, clearing the way for the other two landing groups. As the beachhead was established, Drucour withdrew his men into Louisbourg. However, before the landing, he ordered the destruction of the Batterie Royale in order to prevent the enemy from using it against Louisbourg, as they had done in the last war.

As the British battalions advanced toward Louisbourg they began their siege lines. By June 10, Wolfe led about 1,400 men across the island to take Lighthouse Point only to find it abandoned. Before retiring, the defenders had pushed their cannons over the cliff. This key position now gave the British a height with commanding advantages once they brought their artillery up.

Even after the beachhead was secure, the weather did not cooperate. On June 11 a few 6-pdrs were brought ashore, and on June 16 supplies were landed. It was not until June 18 that the heavy artillery could be landed. It took a month to unload all the transports. A good portion of the expeditionary force, including the laundresses, had to drag the artillery over the island to its positions in the siege lines.

At Lighthouse Point the first pieces of Wolfe's artillery finally arrived on June 19 so he could counter the French guns firing from Battery Island. These guns immediately joined the batteries in the inner harbor in the bombardment of the French naval squadron. The next day, Wolfe began to pound Battery Island, and a heavy exchange of fire ensued for days as Wolfe's position received reinforcements. On June 25, Wolfe aimed his mortars and eight siege guns to smash the French positions on Battery Island whose garrison had received support from the battery at Rochefort Point just outside of Louisbourg. However, neither the guns at Rochefort Point nor those of the naval squadron had any significant effect on Lighthouse Point because of its height. The French naval commander scuttled some of his smaller ships in the channel to keep the British warships from entering the harbor.

On June 26, Amherst's troops secured Green Hill, to the west of the land defenses of Louisbourg. The next day, the French guns of the Dauphin Bastion, with the support of some of the warships in the harbor, attempted to drive the British troops from the hill. The British sappers, however, relentlessly continued to fortify the hill. Next, they began to dig the first parallel, as part of the formal siege, protected by gabions (wicker-like baskets) and fascines (bundles of sticks). The gabions were used to revet the trenches outer wall and were filled with excavated dirt from the trenches. The fascines were placed above the gabions and the remaining spoil was thrown over that side of the trench. Similar reveting was done on trenches for artillery battery positions and redoubts on the siege lines. Thus, in this battle, the British as well as the French resorted to formal European siege and counter-siege techniques and elements.

The French garrison launched several unsuccessful raids against the British positions. The French had several heavily gunned men-of-war, which could be maneuvered into position to bombard the siege lines. The British fleet stood beyond the harbor to prevent or interfere with relief forces. By the beginning of July, the siege lines had moved closer and even the heavy 24- and 32-pdrs on Lighthouse Point were able to drop rounds into the city. On July 3, British batteries of cannon and mortars bombarded the French ships from close range from a site west of Louisbourg. The French warships returned fire, giving as good as they got.

The French created a battery position at Black Rock Point, to the south of the fortress, to engage the British as the saps and trenches continued to advance. Wolfe moved his cannons and mortars forward, placing the town under almost constant bombardment. Only bouts of bad weather brought the French some respite. The town had been taking a significant amount of damage from British guns since July 6. The French garrison launched a major raid in the darkness of the early hours of July 9. Over seven hundred men attacked the British positions in front of the second parallel. The British counterattacked, driving the French back into the fortress. Soon the artillery on both sides, and the French squadron, were back in action. By July 13, the British installed a new battery that began pounding the Dauphin Bastion.

The bombardment made the situation for the vessels in the harbor precarious. On July 20, the Dauphin Bastion began taking serious damage as the siege lines advanced. Several hundred French sailors came ashore to work on the trenches. Early in the afternoon of July 21, a mortar shell exploded a small ammunition store on the French warship *L'Entreprenant*, which erupted into flames. In a short time, the fire leaped to two nearby ships which could not be moved away. After the conflagration and explosions of the night, only three burned-out hulks remained.

Without these ships to support it, the Dauphin Bastion literally crumbled under the intense bombardment. The next day, artillery on the British right flank began smashing the Queen's Bastion. At the same time, Wolfe, commanding the forces on the left, opened fire with six batteries, including mortars. Wolfe's guns set on fire the Citadel's buildings inside the King's Bastion. Flames erupted from many of the wooden structures in the fortress. The fire began devouring Louisbourg itself and there were few places for the residents to hide. The King's and Queen's Bastions came under heavy fire, which knocked out many of their guns. The British parallels and saps had advanced to a point where the assault could be launched once the breach was made. Finally, the Dauphin Bastion was breached on July 25 and British troops equipped with scaling ladders prepared for an assault.

On July 26, shortly after midnight, a few hundred sailors in whaleboats entered the harbor. One group of sailors clambered aboard the 74-gun *Le Prudent*, and, overcoming all resistance, set it ablaze while the other group captured the 64-gun *Bienfaisant*. As the rising sun bathed the city in light, the British batteries renewed their bombardment.

That morning, with only three cannons left at his disposal and having done more than honor required, Governor Drucour negotiated the surrender of the citadel. An honorable surrender assured the safety of the troops and the civilians under his command. On the other hand, if he waited for the assault to take place, he could expect to see his men massacred and the town within the fortress plundered. The terms the British imposed on Drucour were harsh. Isle Saint Jean was included in the surrender of Drucour's forces on Isle Royale. [Note: In 1760, the occupying British troops received orders from London to level the fortifications, just in case they might be returned to France.] Now that the Royal Navy controled the mouth of the St. Lawrence, British forces landed at Miramichi and Gaspe in September, encountering negligible resistance. Late in September, in Acadia, Colonel Monckton advanced up the St. John River further to undermine the French position. The lifeline to the fortress of Quebec was effectively closed.

As Louisbourg was under seige, another British force under Lieutenant Colonel John Bradstreet, on orders from Abercromby, moved west along the Mohawk River to the newly built Fort Stanwix with the mission of continuing on to Lake Ontario to strike at FORT FRONTENAC with his force of over two thousand colonials. On August 14, he moved through the abandoned ruins of Oswego where his men boarded bateaux for their journey to the northern corner of the lake. On the evening of August 25, they pulled their

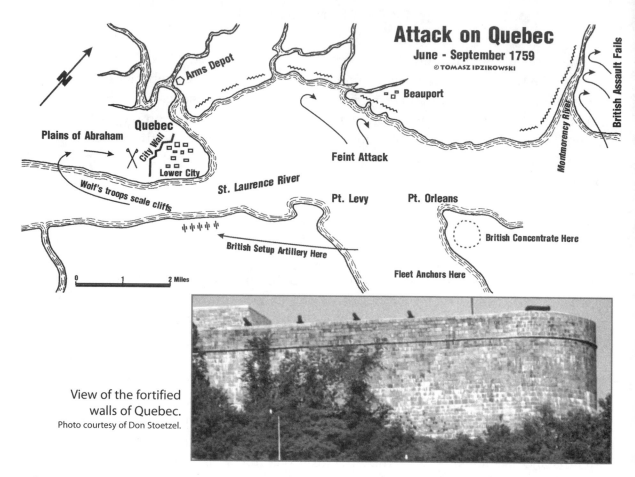

Attack on Quebec
June - September 1759
© TOMASZ IDZIKOWSKI

Arms Depot

Beauport

Quebec

Plains of Abraham

City Wall

Lower City

Wolf's troops scale cliffs

St. Laurence River

Feint Attack

Montmorency River

British Assault Fails

Pt. Levy

Pt. Orleans

British Concentrate Here

British Setup Artillery Here

Fleet Anchors Here

0   1   2 Miles

View of the fortified
walls of Quebec.
Photo courtesy of Don Stoetzel.

boats ashore and moved toward Fort Frontenac, whose garrison may have numbered as few as seventy men. The French, who had only a few of their cannons mounted, were taken by surprise. The French commandant surrendered on the condition that his men could depart for Montreal. Bradstreet now had the intact fort in his hand and could easily have tried to hold the position and choked the western line of communications for the French. The possession of Louisbourg and Fort Frontenac would have allowed him to place a death grip on New France. However, this was not to be because Bradstreet simply demolished Fort Frontenac after sending off its contents. He then withdrew, leaving the French with an open line of communications to the west.

By the end of July 1759, Montcalm had lost control of Lake Champlain to General Amherst's advancing force of twelve thousand men. French Colonel François de Bourlamaque with only three thousand men (half regulars) had abandoned Fort Carillon and Fort Frédéric. The death knell for New France was sounding on the St. Lawrence at Quebec. General Wolfe's 9,000-man force sailed up the St. Lawrence River to the island of Orléans at the end of June 1759. Montcalm awaited him with 16,000 men along the north shore from Quebec eastward. The French defenders held the area between the St. Charles River and the Montmorency River, which, though protected by tidal flats, was considered the most likely place for a landing. The cliffs that dominated the shoreline west of Quebec made it an unlikely place for a landing.

When Point Lévy was captured, the British ships found a safe anchorage between the point and the island of Orléans. Artillery batteries set up west of Point Lévy soon destroyed the Lower Town of Quebec. The French sent fire ships and then fire rafts against the British ships, but met with no success. Late in July, Wolfe tried to establish a position on the north shore of the river, by the mouth of the Montmorency River and the Montmorency Falls, but the operation failed. During the month of August, Wolfe attacked on the north bank, east of the city, but once again the results were unsatisfactory. On September 3, he evacuated all positions on the north shore moving most of his troops to Point Lévy and marched west. On September 12, they were ferried across the river and the first troops landed at the foot of the cliffs on the north shore under the cover of darkness and made their way up the heights before dawn. By morning, Wolfe led about 4,500 men to the Plains of Abraham, at the rear of Quebec. Montcalm faced him with a force of similar size. During the battle that ensued, both generals were killed; however, the French forces were defeated. This was one of the few European style battles fought in America up to this time involving major forces. It took place in front of the fortifications so that, when it was over, the remnants of the French army fled to the safety of the walls. Leaving a garrison behind at Quebec, Governor Vaudreuil retreated to Montreal with the army. On September 17, after increased bombardment of the city, the French commander asked for terms and capitulated the next day. The British made repairs to the city and left a garrison there before sailing off at the end of October.

While the campaign against Quebec was just beginning, another British force moved westward to FORT NIAGARA. Late in 1758, Sir William Johnson had won over the Iroquois Nations to the British cause. Thanks to this alliance, General John Prideaux was able to lead an expedition of several thousand men from Albany to the ruins of Oswego, where he worked on rebuilding the fort. On July 6, Prideaux at the head of two thousand troops (about half of them regulars) and fifteen hundred Iroquois proceeded by boat along Lake Ontario to a point several miles east of Fort Niagara. They carried their whaleboats and three disassembled cannons for five miles to the Niagara river where they launched them for the last leg of their journey.

Although Fort Niagara's artillery greeted Prideaux's force on the morning of July 7, the guns safely reached their destination and the men prepared fascines to set up and protect a battery position from which they would bombard the walls facing the river. Prideaux then began a formal siege involving parallels and saps, the first of which were dug on June 9. His main gun batteries of two 12-pdrs and four 6-pdrs were set up facing the landward walls of the fort. On July 17, the battery across the river fired hot shot into the wooden palisades and the roof of the main building, setting them on fire. On July 21, three 18-pdrs joined in the bombardment of the walls. On July 20, during the bombardment, Prideaux was killed by an accidental explosion and Johnson took command.

Captain Pouchot, the French commandant who had prepared and strengthened the fort since late in 1755, soon realized that his situation was becoming untenable without support. Since he had fewer than 450 Canadians and French troops under his command, he sent for reinforcements from Detroit and the Ohio Valley. A relief force of about six hundred French troops and possibly one thousand Indians almost reached his position on July 23. By this time, the situation at Fort Niagara was indeed desperate. On the previous day, three of the five guns on one of the bastion were blown off their carriages. Pouchot, whose force had already been reduced by over one hundred dead or wounded, was using every available hand to plug the breaches in the walls with bags of dirt. Pouchot's only hope centered on the relief column. Unfortunately, Johnson ambushed that force on July 24. At the same time, his artillery relentlessly bombarded the fort and his siege trenches inched to within one hundred yards of the walls. Realizing the hopelessness of his situation, Pouchot surrendered the heavily damaged fort. After British troops took possession on July 25, several hundred of their Indian allies swarmed over the walls and plundered it.

FORT ROUILLÉ at Toronto had already been burned down by its fifteen man garrison in June, who then retreated to Montreal. FORT PRESQUE'ISLE and FORT LE BOEUF were left without a supply line after the fall of Fort Niagara, and were put to the torch and abandoned in August of 1759. One by one, the French positions in the Ohio Valley began to collapse.

By January 1760, the main French forces at MONTREAL were virtually isolated. The French forces in Louisiana were cut off from New France, but maintained their line of communications with France. In Montreal, Governor Vaudreuil dispatched General François de Lévis, who replaced Montcalm, at the head of a force of about 8,500 men to recapture Quebec. In April, General James Murray, commander of the heavily outnumbered British forces at Quebec, tried to drive the French back from their positions on the Plains of Abraham. The British were defeated and withdrew into Quebec, using its fortifications to withstand a French siege in May. Only a little more than two thousand troops were probably available to defend Quebec. On the other hand, the size of the French force continued to grow. Murray's men successfully manned the landward defenses that the French had thought to be too weak. Finally, in mid-May, a few British warships arrived to drive off the six French frigates and break the siege. The French army withdrew to Montreal as most of its Indian and Canadian troops deserted.

During its withdrawal from the Champlain Valley forts in 1759, the French army worked on building fortifications on the FORT DE L'ILE AUX NOIRS, a small island in the Richelieu River. The strategy was to shorten the French lines in the face of superior British forces. This island was located at about half the distance from the St. Lawrence than Crown Point. From there, the French could block the Richelieu River and stop a British advance. However, the main problem was that both sides of the island were within range of heavy artillery placed on either shore. Instead of building a traditional fort, the French completed a series of poorly linked positions by 1760. François Fournier, an engineer newly arrived from France, had begun the work on the entrenchments in

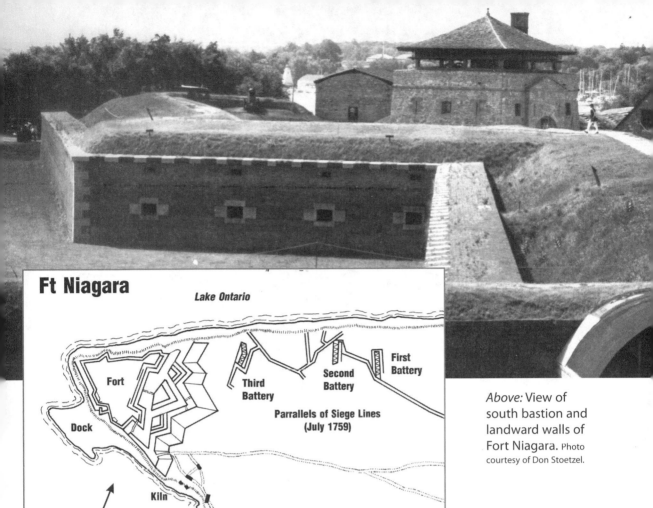

Ft Niagara

Lake Ontario

Fort

Third
Battery

Second
Battery

First
Battery

Parrallels of Siege Lines
(July 1759)

Dock

Kiln

N

Above: View of
south bastion and
landward walls of
Fort Niagara. Photo
courtesy of Don Stoetzel.

1759. When de Lotbinière took over in 1760, he added to the work and created two redoubts and a blockhouse that are not clearly defined. An 18-foot-wide ditch was excavated and a palisade was erected. Supposedly, the positions on the island required a garrison of over three thousand men while they had less than half that number. The island had at least seventy-seven pieces of artillery of various sizes, including three 16-pdr guns. The defenders put chains across the river on both sides of the island and guns on barges to act as floating batteries. In August 1760, British forces under General William Haviland with 3,400 men put the small garrison under siege. Bombarded by several batteries on the western shore and by guns from the ships already demoralized by the events taking place to the north, the French garrison soon surrendered.

The main British force under General Amherst, at the head of a force of over ten thousand soldiers and seven hundred of Johnson's Indians, moved from Oswego to the St. Lawrence on August 5. A week later, this invasion force moved down the St. Lawrence to Montreal and isolated Fort Lévi on Isle Royale. The French abandoned the older FORT LA PRÉSENTATION (also known as FORT LA GALETTE and renamed by the British as FORT OSWEGATCHIE), which had been rebuilt as a square earthwork fort with palisades on the 70-foot-long walls and four corner bastions on the south shore.

Forts of the French & Indian War
© TOMASZ IDZIKOWSKI

French forts:

Ft. Michilimackinac
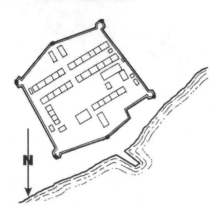

Ft. Venango
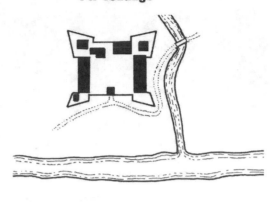

French forts in Canada:

Ft. Levi
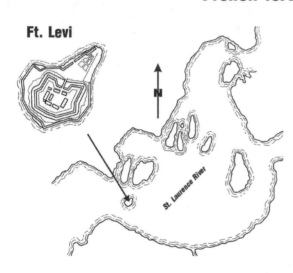

St. Laurence River

Ft. Frontenac

Battery

Gardens

Store House

Harbour

Battery

Artillery Park

Short Yard

Kitchens

Head of St. Laurence River

Montreal
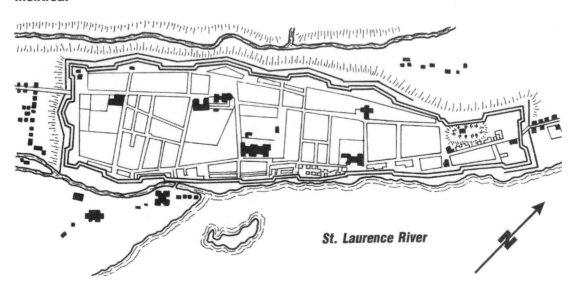

St. Laurence River

Captain Pouchot, who had surrendered the previous year at Niagara, defended the newly completed FORT LÉVI three miles down the river, halfway between Lake Ontario and Montreal. This too was a square fort, mounted five guns and held a garrison of over four hundred men. However, the British ships mounted fifty guns and the British army consisted of thousands of troops. On August 22, the British emplaced three batteries, and began bombarding the fort in tandem with their ships. Pouchot bitterly fought for three days, even sinking three British ships, but finally ran out of ammunition and was forced to surrender on August 25.

Located on an island as it was, MONTREAL should have been easily defended, except for the fact that it had been isolated since September 1760. The principal obstacle along most of the south side was a dry moat about 8 feet deep which, together with the St. Lawrence, surrounded most of the town. However, Governor Vaudreuil, who still had 3,600 men, chose not to endure a bloody siege. Therefore, on July 6 he surrendered to General Amherst, who was preparing to attack the city.

The Treaty of Paris of 1763, which formally concluded the war, also ended French control of New France and Louisiana, but gave France back its Caribbean Islands. The British returned Cuba, which they had captured from Spain during the war, in exchange for Florida (from the Atlantic to the Mississippi) which they divided into East and West Florida. The Spanish took over New Orleans. Once France was removed from the mainland, a new strategic contest emerged between England and Spain.

Other Forts of the Thirteen Colonies

To the south the provincials built other, less well-known, frontier forts strung out from the Maryland frontier to Georgia, where the main campaigns of the French and Indian War did not take place. South Carolina's Independent Companies garrisoned all these forts, which were needed to protect against the Frenchmen and Indians who crossed this wilderness with impunity. Some of the better-known frontier forts built by the British included FORT LOUDOUN. It was built by Governor William Henry Lyttleton of South Carolina far in the mountains, now Eastern Tennessee, on the Little Tennessee River in late 1756. It was designed by William Gerald DeBrahm, a German civilian engineer who immigrated to the colonies and was created to aid the Cherokee allied with the British. When it was completed, early in 1757, Fort Loudoun was garrisoned by ninety regulars and 120 militiamen of an Independent South Carolina Company. Its enceinte was an elongated diamond shape with very short curtain walls, each less than 100 feet long, and two large and two small corner bastions. The moat was about 50 feet wide and a ravelin masked the entrance. The fort was made of a 15-foot-high palisade placed on an earthen wall. Records from the South Carolina archives also indicate that these palisades, sharpened according to custom, were angled ten degrees outward from the vertical, apparently to obviate the need for fraise. This building method may have been used on many frontier forts, but details are lacking. Each bastion housed three swivel guns that had been hauled to the fort across the Smoky Mountains. The main problem was the fort's location, deep in Cherokee territory in the Tennessee Valley, four hundred miles from Charlestown and too far from any other forts for support.

FORT PRINCE GEORGE, named for the Prince of Wales, was the nearest post to Fort Loudoun, about 150 miles away on the other side of the mountains. It too had been commissioned by the governor of South Carolina in 1753 to establish a British presence in Cherokee country. It was located near the Cherokee village of Keowee, near the banks of the Keowee River. Its enceinte formed a simple square made of earthen walls crowned by palisades. The earthen walls were about 100 feet long and were crowned by a palisade of yellow pine logs. The four corner bastions were built the same way as the earthen and timber curtains. Each bastion's small interior was occupied by a platform positioned in the center, high enough for its small swivel gun to fire over the palisade. To do this they must have been at least 10 feet above ground. A 5-foot-deep ditch surrounded the enceinte. The walls enclosed a barracks, a guardhouse, a powder magazine, and a few other structures.

FORT NINETY-SIX was built on the Saluda River, between Fort Prince George and the place where the river meets the Broad River to form the Santee River. First established as a trading post in the 1730s, it was converted into a small stockade in 1759. In 1761, its stockade was strengthened in response to the problems with the Cherokees. Hostilities with the Cherokee erupted in 1759, and Captain John Stuart arrived with seventy men to reinforce Fort Loudoun. When an agreement made with the Cherokees failed, raids along the frontier intensified and the warriors blocked the line of communications to Fort Loudoun. Finally, in February 1760, they put the fort under siege. Fort Ninety-Six was attacked in February 1760. Fort Prince George had been under siege since January 1760 and its commander was killed in an ambush. Several Cherokee hostages at the fort were executed in retaliation, which triggered the Cherokee War. In a letter to Governor Lyttleton dated February 28, 1760, the second in command at Fort Prince George, pleaded for reinforcements. He also mentioned that all the loose boards had been gathered to use as "blinds to shelter the sentries and men as they walk the curtain lines." He complained that his men were easy targets for the Indians, who had a commanding position in the surrounding hills. Furthermore, he wrote, only two of the four guns were functioning. It is not clear if these were the swivel guns, because he also noted that he had a port hole cut in a bastion and had one of the cannons moved up to fire on the Indian town of Keowee. Finally, he informed the governor that he would forward all his messages to Fort Loudoun. However, the place had been cut off and not even the traders were brave enough to venture across the mountains.

The siege at Fort Prince George was lifted in June, when Montgomery finally arrived from Charlestown, spreading death and destruction on the Indian lands in his path. After a delay of several weeks, Montgomery's column moved on toward Fort Loudoun, but a costly engagement with the Indians forced it to abandon the rescue effort. By this time, the garrison of Fort Loudoun was surviving on minimal rations and succumbing to disease. Another relief column from Virginia moved too slowly to rescue the defenders of Fort Loudoun. The commander of the fort negotiated with the Cherokee chief. The garrison, 180 men and 60 women and children, were allowed to leave for Fort Prince George with everything they needed, including weapons. They departed on August 9, but the next day, after their Cherokee escort disappeared during the night, they were ambushed. The few survivors became hostages for exchange later. The next year, the British dispatched another expedition that laid waste to a number of Indian villages in retribution and finally forced the Cherokee to their knees in the summer of 1761.

In the hot and humid climate of the southern colonies, the earth and timber palisade forts decayed quickly and had to be rebuilt every few years. Fort Prince George and Fort Ninety-Six were both rebuilt after the war, but Fort Loudoun was destroyed by the Cherokees and not replaced.

In the north during the French and Indian War, the British also built other fortifications. Some of the more important ones were those protecting the routes to Oswego and Lake George in New York. Plans to enclose the key supply point of ALBANY with a stockade, a ditch, blockhouses, and two bastions were drawn up. In 1702, a new masonry fort had replaced the old Dutch fort that had been in ruins only two years after it was built. This new fort mounted over twenty heavy cannons. It had rectangular enceinte with corner bastions and was located within the palisades that formed the city walls.

FORT SARATOGA was located in a bend of the Hudson River. Rebuilt several times after the 1720s, it consisted of a square stockade with corner blockhouses. It was renamed more than once after renovations. The 1757 reconstruction was called FORT HARDY and remained in service until the end of the war.

Further up the Hudson, FORT EDWARD occupied a key portage site at the southern end of the Great Carrying Place on the eleven mile route to FORT ANN, a square bastioned fort rebuilt early in 1702 on Wood Creek which emptied into Lake Champlain. Fort Edward was rebuilt several times during the eighteenth century. When it was known as FORT LYDIUS during King George's War in 1745, it was destroyed by a French and Indian

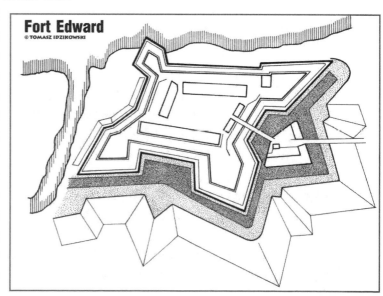

Fort Edward
© TOMASZ IDZIKOWSKI

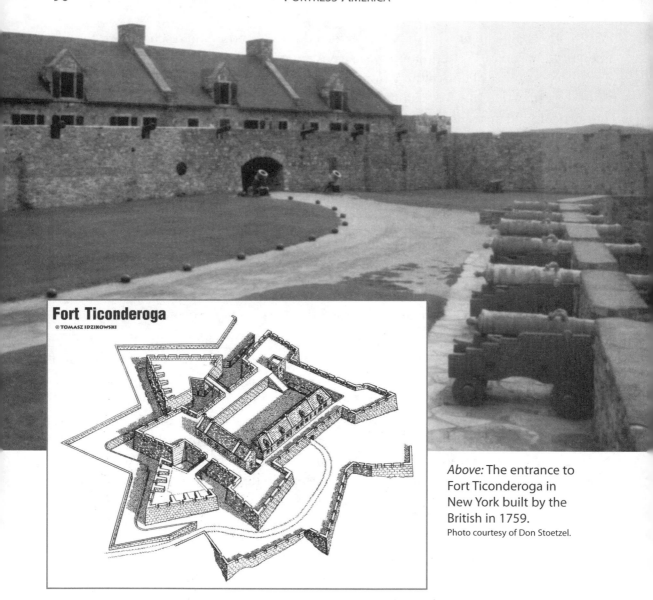

Fort Ticonderoga
© TOMASZ IDZIKOWSKI

Above: The entrance to
Fort Ticonderoga in
New York built by the
British in 1759.
Photo courtesy of Don Stoetzel.

raiding party. It was rebuilt once more as an earth-and-log structure. During the French
and Indian War, it was renamed as Fort Edward. Soon after that, a fire left it in ruins and
it had to be rebuilt again. Fort Edward was on the east bank of the river and had a diamond shape with three large bastions facing the landward sides and a small bastion facing the river. A large barracks erected in 1756 or 1757 on the nearby island could accommodate about five hundred men. It served as a base to Roger's Rangers. On the west
bank of the river stood the ROYAL BLOCKHOUSE, built in 1758. It had a square shape with
two corner bastions and was surrounded by earthworks. The blockhouse was abandoned in 1764.

On the Lake Champlain route, the British rebuilt FORT CARILLON between 1759 and
1760, renaming it FORT TICONDEROGA. British troops garrisoned Fort Ticonderoga and

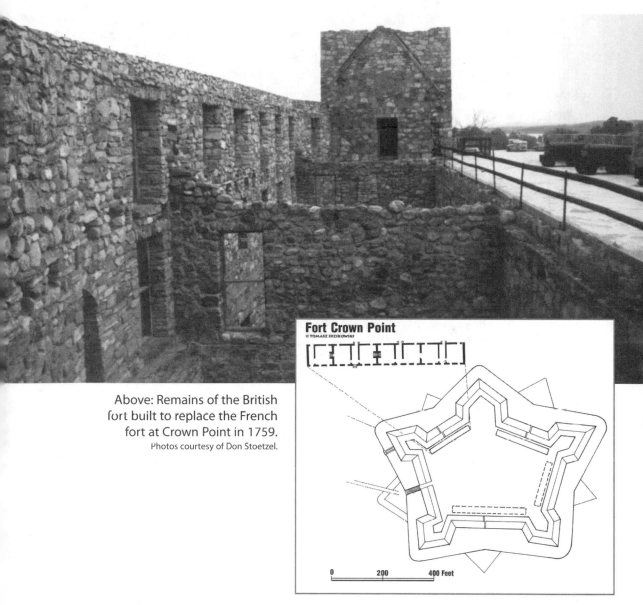

Above: Remains of the British
fort built to replace the French
fort at Crown Point in 1759.
Photos courtesy of Don Stoetzel.

Fort Crown Point
© TOMASZ IDZIKOWSKI

0   200   400 Feet

until the American Revolution, using it as a depot. To the north of Fort Ticonderoga, General Amherst replaced the French Fort Frédéric with FORT CROWN POINT in 1759. The British fort, which stood near the ruins of the French fort, was the largest fort the British built in the American colonies. It was pentagon shaped and had five corner bastions and consisted of earthen ramparts faced with logs and mounted 105 cannons. Inside, several large stone barracks were built for the garrison. Three small redoubts, each mounting ten cannons, defended the approaches to the fort. With the conclusion of the French and Indian War in 1763, work stopped on the fort. Later, in 1773, a fire badly damaged the log walls.

In addition to Fort Ticonderoga, a series of fortifications protected the route between Albany and Oswego. They included several fortified positions along the Mohawk River and Oneida Lake. FORT SCHENECTADY, at the east end, was a village surrounded by a stockade since the previous century. A new stockade, the Queen's Fort, was built in 1735 in the northeast corner and renamed FORT COSBY in 1755. The square fort, about 100 feet in length, consisted of a stone wall crowned with heavy timbers, resulting in a height of about 12 feet. It had four corner blockhouses and six cannons.

Further up the Mohawk was old FORT HUNTER dating from 1711. Strengthened in 1755, it had a square enceinte, with 150-feet-long sides and 12-foot-high walls with four corner blockhouses mounting cannons. At the headwaters of the Mohawk River, the British built FORT STANWIX in 1758, at the site of modern-day Rome. The fort, which secured the Oneida Carrying Place, was improved during the American Revolution. At the other end of this portage was FORT BULL, built in the fall of 1755 as a star-shaped stockade. It was destroyed by de Léry in March of 1756, after the fall of Oswego. It was replaced with an earthwork called FORT BREWERTON in 1759, built on the west end of Lake Oneida. During the American Revolution, the lifeline to Oswego, consisting of the Mohawk and Oneida Rivers, remained a major defended route, of almost as much importance as the Champlain route.

Indian Uprising of 1763

Much of the frontier was affected by the massive uprising known as Pontiac's Revolt of 1763. In the west, nine of twelve forts fell. In the autumn of 1759, the French had abandoned FORT MACHAULT, FORT LE BOEUF, and FORT PRESQU'ISLE, putting them to the torch as they departed. The British rebuilt the last two and built FORT VENANGO further up the river from the charred ruins of Fort Machault. Fort Venango fell to the Seneca in the spring of 1763 and its garrison was massacred. Fort Le Boeuf and Fort Presqu'Isle also fell in 1763.

After FORT PONTCHARTRAIN surrendered to Roger's Rangers in 1760, it was renamed as FORT DETROIT. In 1763, it became Pontiac's primary target. Major Gladwin, who defended the fort with a hundred men, learned in May that Pontiac intended to take the place by surprise by rushing the gates. He closed the gates before the Indians arrived, foiling their plan. Soon the fort was placed under siege. A relief force coming to its rescue was defeated at the end of the month. The Indians succeeded in taking other forts in surprise attacks, including FORT SANDUSKY (a blockhouse), FORT ST. JOSEPH, and FORT MICHILIMACKINAC, where the garrisons were massacred. At the end of July, a relief force of two hundred men finally reached Fort Detroit, but the siege continued. Further east, FORT LIGONIER was again put to the test, fending off a massive attack in June 1763. The 330-men garrison of FORT PITT, besieged in 1763, placed a palisade on the ramparts as an additional obstacle. However, some of the earthen ramparts on the sides that lacked brick revetments were washed out by a heavy rain before the siege and had to be restored. Early in August 1763, after the battle of Bushy Run, Colonel Bouquet dispersed the Indians and relieved Fort Pitt. Bouquet then continued toward Fort Detroit, lifting the siege in mid-October, after a relief attempt out of Fort Niagara had failed.

In 1764, Colonel Bouquet added a redoubt to FORT PITT. It was a brick blockhouse 16 feet by 15 feet and 22 feet high with a double layer of logs that included thirty-six portholes. Gradually, many of the frontier forts were abandoned or allowed to deteriorate. Only key positions like Fort Pitt were maintained until the next major war. British troops reoccupied FORT MICHILIMACKINAC's ruins in September 1764 and proceeded to restore it to service, making it the only garrisoned fort north of Detroit on the Great Lakes.

Group of 18th-century mortars at Fort Ticonderoga, New York. Photo courtesy of Don Stoetzel.

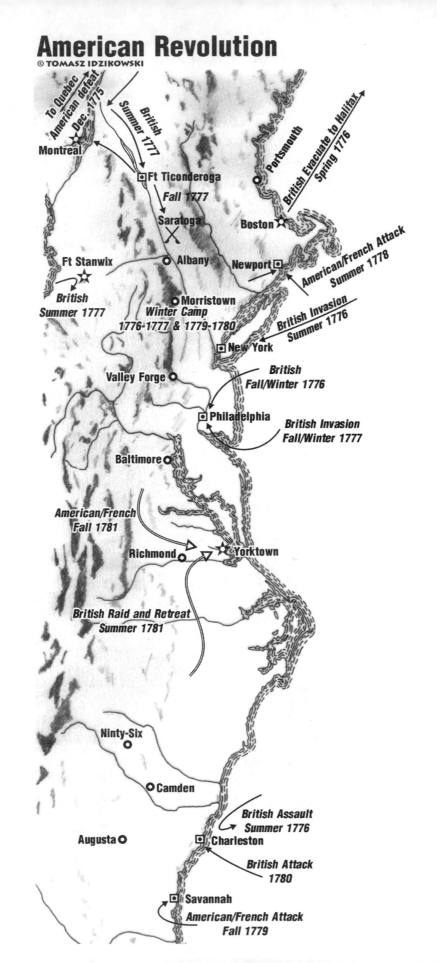

American Revolution
© TOMASZ IDZIKOWSKI

To Quebec
American defeat
Dec. 1775

British
Summer 1777

Montreal

Ft Ticonderoga

Fall 1777

Saratoga

Portsmouth

British Evacuate to Halifax
Spring 1776

Boston

Ft Stanwix

British
Summer 1777

Albany

Newport

American/French Attack
Summer 1778

Morristown
Winter Camp
1776-1777 & 1779-1780

British Invasion
Summer 1776

New York

Valley Forge

British
Fall/Winter 1776

Philadelphia

British Invasion
Fall/Winter 1777

Baltimore

American/French
Fall 1781

Richmond

Yorktown

British Raid and Retreat
Summer 1781

Ninty-Six

Camden

British Assault
Summer 1776

Augusta

Charleston

British Attack
1780

Savannah

American/French Attack
Fall 1779

Chapter 3

THE AMERICAN REVOLUTION

THE FRENCH AND INDIAN WAR IN AMERICA left Great Britain as the world's foremost naval and colonial power. Although the Industrial Revolution took place in Great Britain and even reached its American colonies during the eighteenth century, the great technological advances did not much affect the British fortifications in America. In fact, the forts in the Thirteen Colonies barely equaled many of the Spanish and French fortifications. The great debts incurred during the French and Indian War caused the Parliament to impose heavy taxes on the American colonists. Tensions between the colonists culminated in April 1775 when the opening salvos of the American Revolution took place at Lexington and Concord. After this, British troops with General Thomas Gage at their head were confined to the Boston area, turning it into a fortress. The defenses of Boston were too strong for the American forces, who lacked siege weapons at the time.

Early in May, Benedict Arnold and Ethan Allen at the head of the Green Mountain Boys struck at FORT TICONDEROGA. The fort's commander, Captain William Delapace, with a garrison of only fifty men at his disposal, was unable to withstand the attack and surrendered without much resistance. A small American force also moved up to FORT CROWN POINT, taking it easily. The two forts yielded over one hundred cannons to the Americans, sixty to seventy of which were put back into service. During the winter of 1775–1776 Henry Knox and his men hauled about sixty artillery pieces (fourteen mortars, two howitzers, and forty-three cannons) to the southeast, over a distance of three hundred miles, to join in the siege of Boston.

The British army of General Gage spent most of the remainder of 1775 and early 1776 trapped in Boston. Gage commanded fourteen regiments, in addition to marines and artillery, a total of about 6,500 men. Generals Howe, Clinton, and Burgoyne arrived in Boston in May. They convinced Gage that they must take both the Dorchester Heights and the peninsula occupied by Charlestown, which included Bunker Hill, to prevent

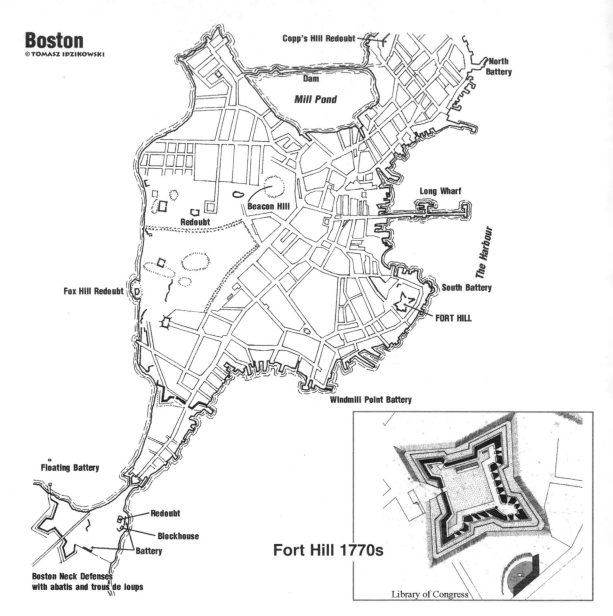

Boston
©TOMASZ IPZIKOWSKI

Copp's Hill Redoubt

North Battery

Dam

Mill Pond

Long Wharf

Beacon Hill

Redoubt

The Harbour

Fox Hill Redoubt

South Battery

FORT HILL

Windmill Point Battery

Floating Battery

Redoubt

Blockhouse

Fort Hill 1770s

Battery

Boston Neck Defenses
with abatis and trous de loups

Library of Congress

their besiegers from making the British position in Boston untenable, especially if the enemy should obtain heavier additional artillery.

At this point, the British defenses in BOSTON consisted of: Castle William on Castle Island just east of the unoccupied Dorchester Heights; Boston Neck, fortified earlier by Gage with field fortifications in the form of ditches and earthen positions; Copp's Hill, on the north end of Boston with a battery of eight 24-pdrs, which could fire on Charlestown across the river to the north; North Battery to the east of Copp's Hill which covered the wharfs, but was in ruins in 1775; the South Battery, located on the other side of the wharfs, backed by old Fort Hill on Corn Hill, which mounted a few field pieces; a few more batteries on the shore on the west side of Boston, between Beacon Hill and the Neck; the adjacent small island with a redoubt with four 12-pdrs; a redoubt on the east end of Beacon Hill with two 12-pdrs; two oar-propelled barges forming a couple of floating batteries mounting a 12-pdr or 18-pdr and lighter artillery weapons; and several warships. None of these positions could be considered formidable. Only the water barrier and the large number of Redcoat regiments prevented the American rebels from assaulting Boston.

The American commander in New England, Artemus Ward, a veteran of Abercromby's defeat at Ticonderoga in 1758, having been informed by spies of the intended British move on Dorchester, decided to move three regiments under Colonel William Prescott and a regiment of veterans of colonial wars into the peninsula with orders to fortify Bunker Hill. Prescott chose instead to build a redoubt on Breed's Hill, despite the fact that Bunker Hill had almost twice the height of his own chosen position. American troops worked through the night, quickly digging and setting up a redoubt on BREED'S HILL and took up positions along a fence line. Several other smaller positions were created. Stark, a captain in Rogers Rangers during the French and Indian War and quite experienced in colonial warfare, took up the left flank, ordering his men to set up their own breastworks by piling up rocks. A force of over two thousand men on barges prepared to land as artillery on Copp's Hill, floating batteries, and a warship bombarded the colonists. American militiamen prepared defenses on Bunker Hill and built breastworks to support their redoubt on Breed's Hill and some flanking positions. The building materials used by the Americans came from rail fences and walls. That afternoon they successfully repelled two assaults until they ran out of ammunition and had to retreat before the British bayonets. However, the retreating Americans inflicted heavy losses on their opponents, who were too exhausted to advance beyond Bunker Hill, which they took and fortified.

Both sides now settled in for a long siege. When George Washington arrived in July, he took over as commander-in-chief of the colonial forces. On the other side, Howe replaced Gage as commander of the British forces in America in October. British strength at Boston rose from 6,500 men in June to 11,000 in March of 1776. During the same period, the American forces, mostly militia, rose to a high of about 17,000, but also dropped because of the short enlistment periods. Throughout the fall and winter, both the Americans and British worked on their positions. The British built fieldworks and redoubts at key points around Boston and at Bunker Hill. The fort they built at BUNKER HILL, larger than any position defending Boston, effectively blocked any breakthrough at Charlestown Neck. It covered much of the top of the hill, running from northwest to southeast. The southeastern tip ended in a triangular position formed three bastions for cannons. The northwestern curtain included a battery of six cannons placed between two smaller bastions. From these two bastions, the walls continued toward a polygonal position with more artillery emplacements.

The Americans, on the other hand, set up three battery positions named Forts No. 1, 2, and 3. FORT NO. 1 and FORT NO. 2 were located just south of Cambridge on the Charles River. FORT NO. 3 was also known as PATTERSON'S FORT or PROSPECT HILL FORT since it was located on Prospect Hill, just north of Cambridge. Fort No. 3 overlooked both

Charleston and Cambridge and was the most formidable American position built during the siege. More fortifications were built in the vicinity of Prospect Hill, on Ploughed Hill, and near Bunker Hill, on Cobble Hill. The American position known as ROXBURY FORT covered Boston Neck and was instrumental in keeping the British confined to the peninsula. The Americans built several other "forts" and redoubts around the British fortress. Despite all this activity, Boston remained a fortress with few permanent fortifications.

In February 1776, Washington and his officers decided that they must prevent British reinforcements from arriving. To achieve this, they planned to take DORCHESTER HEIGHTS, which would allow them to dominate Boston. However, at that time of the year, the soil was still frozen and too hard to dig mines and make earthworks. Rufus Putnam, an engineer and veteran of the French and Indian War, came up with an ingenious solution: they would use portable fortifications. On the night of March 3, hundreds of American troops scrambled up the Dorchester Heights, pulling carts loaded with construction materials for field fortifications: barrels filled with earth to form an earthwork, fascines, gabions, and 'chandeliers' or wooden frames that could be filled with fascines. As the troops worked on the heights, Henry Knox's artillery bombarded Boston from Cobble Hill and Ploughed Hill to mask the sounds of construction. By the light of dawn, the British were astonished to see a new American fortified position. General Howe thought that at least twelve thousand men had been involved in the construction of the American position, but in fact only a thousand or so had been assigned to the task. Howe's artillery could not be elevated sufficiently to fire on the heights and the navy was not in a position to help. Accepting the fact that his position in Boston was no longer tenable, he began to evacuate on the morning of March 17. The garrison of Castle William blew up the fort before departing, but Boston suffered little damage. Fortunately for the rebels, many supplies and almost seventy cannons, including some 42-pdrs, were left behind. After the retreat, Washington ordered the creation of new fortifications on Fort Hill and the South Battery. Lieutenant Colonel Paul Revere was put in charge of the renovation of Castle William. The new fort was given the name of FORT INDEPENDENCE.

To the north in September 1775, General Philip Schulyer and his force of more than 1,200 men quickly eliminated the British positions along the Lake Champlain route. Montreal surrendered on November 13. Meanwhile, Colonel Benedict Arnold proceeded overland on a direct route through the wilderness to Quebec. He arrived at Point Lévi across from Quebec in November of 1775 with only six hundred men. Governor Guy Carleton defended Quebec with about seventy regulars and one thousand militia. Arnold took the same route Wolfe had used joined by three hundred of Montgomery's men as Carleton prepared for a siege. Arnold was wounded storming the Lower Town on New Year's Eve in a snowstorm. Daniel Morgan took over and used ladders to scale a 12-foot barricade and was then wounded and trapped by obstacles and forced to surrender. Montgomery's troops withdrew when he was killed moving below Point Diamond. The siege ended as the winter ice melted and the navy arrived with four thousand reinforcements under Burgoyne. The retreat to Montreal began.

After leaving Boston, Howe took his army to HALIFAX where he made continual improvements on the harbors fortifications. A dockyard established there in 1759 became an important repair facility. During the first year of the revolution, Colonel Richard Spry improved the positions on Citadel Hill. As the war continued, the fortifications were strengthened until Georges Island mounted almost fifty cannons. The harbor area was protected by up to fourteen forts during the period of the revolution.

In the south, most of the southern governors had been forced to evacuate their colonies as the American militias seized key locations. Early in 1776, Howe dispatched his rival, Henry Clinton, with an expedition to recapture the southern colonies and stir up Loyalist support. After sailing along the coast and meeting with the governors in exile, Clinton learned that the American fortifications at Charleston were incomplete, especially the fort on Sullivan's Island. In the meantime, the Americans worked frantically to build defenses in Charleston and several of the islands in the bay.

FORT JOHNSON, on James Island, the oldest fort in Charleston Harbor, had originally been built with palmetto logs as a triangular structure with bastions and mounted twenty cannons. A ravelin in its surrounding ditch protected its gateway. The fort became Colonel William Moultrie's command post in September 1775, when his forces took it over.

In February 1776, John Rutledge, the leader of the South Carolina government, ordered Colonel Moultrie to build a fort on Sullivan's Island, an ideal location to control the shipping along the few channels through the shallows near the island. Moultrie built FORT SULLIVAN using solely materials immediately available in the region: palmetto trees and sand. His men and a black labor force cut the trees and hauled the logs to the site where they laid out parallel rows of palmetto walls, about 16 feet apart, which they filled with sand. The soft mushy palmetto logs backed by sand may have seemed rather flimsy, but served as an effective shock absorber in stopping cannon balls. Work on Fort Sullivan was still in progress when a British expedition led by Clinton sailed into view. By then, only the southern and eastern walls and two corner bastions were completed. The remaining corner bastions and walls were only about 7 feet high and breastworks had been added to give them additional protection. The fort had gun emplacements for twenty-five 9-pdrs and 25-pdrs. When General Charles Lee took command of the forces at Charleston on June 4, he visited Fort Sullivan and concluded that it had to be abandoned because it was too isolated and too weak to be of any use. However, the governor refused to have the fort evacuated, ordering Moultrie to hold the fort. While Lee set up his headquarters in Charleston, Fort Sullivan's garrison of about 420 men, mostly from Colonel Moultrie's 2nd South Carolina Regiment, prepared for action.

A British naval squadron sailed into the harbor on June 7. The British force numbered eleven ships of various sizes and 262 cannons, the largest warships mounting as many as fifty guns. On June 28 the British ships bombarded Fort Sullivan for most of the day, not stopping the firing until after sundown. The Americans, who had limited ammunition and powder supplies because Lee had not wanted to risk too much on a doomed fort, stood their ground. Their fort held up surprisingly well as the British cannon balls were absorbed in the spongy palmetto and sand walls. Their success convinced Lee to send over more powder in the afternoon. The defenders directed their fire against two of the larger ships and inflicted a great deal of damage and casualties. The British naval units ceased fire and retreated the next morning, leaving behind one burning 28-gun warship. The Tories of the southern colonies would remain without the support of the British army for the next three years.

THE WAR FOR INDEPENDENCE BEGINS

On July 4, 1776, the only British force remaining in the Thirteen Colonies was Clinton's contingent waiting to be evacuated in South Carolina. The Second Continental Congress declared the colonies independent states and the revolution, which had begun with the colonists fighting for their rights as Englishmen, became a war for independence. At this point, time became a critical factor for the government in London because the rebellion had to be suppressed as quickly as possible, before other nations recognized the colonies's independence. The fact that the British had never heavily fortified the coasts of their thirteen colonies played in their favor now, since the Royal Navy controlled the sea.

The New England colonies were relatively isolated from the others by topographical features. Boston and the coastal region around it represented a major, weakly fortified enclave when the revolution began. There were smaller enclaves further north, however this was not a region on which to waste precious resources in order to subdue the remaining colonies. Once Boston was lost, only the coastal areas of Connecticut and Rhode Island retained strategic value in the British campaign.

Of the Middle Colonies, New York was the most important. New York City was as important as Boston as a commercial center and had a larger population. Its strategic location gave control of the Hudson Valley and offered direct access to New Jersey and Pennsylvania. There were few British fortifications in the port area and New York was not protected much better than Boston when the war began. Since Long Island was wide open to invasion, the Patriots were forced to hurriedly prepare forts in the vicinity of New York and on the Hudson River. In the Hudson Valley, there were already a good number of positions built to protect the Lake Champlain invasion route. In the Mohawk River Valley, there were also older fortifications that covered the route to Oswego. Beyond the river valleys, in the Catskill and Adirondack mountains the pristine wilderness was a haven for hostile Indians, many of whom preferred the British to the colonists who, in their eyes, were bent on dispossessing them of their land. Thus, the Iroquois alliance from the last war still held steadfast during most of the Revolution.

New Jersey was mostly too open, and except in the New York area, was not easily fortified. Philadelphia's strategic importance lay not only in the fact that it was a port, but also in that it was the political center for the Patriots. Since the main access to the city was, as in the past, along the Delaware River, a number of forts along its shore became increasingly important in the fight against the British. Most of Pennsylvania beyond the Philadelphia area was too mountainous and too wild for major operations to take place and held few positions worth fortifying.

The Southern Colonies south of Virginia had fewer cities and were more sparsely populated. The coastal plain up to the Appalachian Mountains was largely occupied and easy to negotiate. Large pine forests dominated the southern colonies and provided a good and plentiful source of timber for fortifications. In addition, except along the border areas, most of the Indian groups no longer presented a major threat. The long southern coast south of the Chesapeake consisted of largely open, low-lying areas dominated by swampy terrain like the Dismal Swamp in Virginia. The swampy South Carolina coast was devoid of pine forests, offering few building materials for fortifications. Rock quarries were few and far between, thus precluding the construction of masonry forts. The only construction material available in reasonable quantities was the palmetto, which had been used successfully in the building of Fort Sullivan. In addition, on the southern coastline there were a limited number of locations where deep river mouths offered sheltered harbors that could serve as main points of entry. One of the most important ports in the area was the city of Charleston.

Thus, the British as well as the Americans based their strategy on the Middle Colonies as the key to victory. The first site of primary importance was NEW YORK CITY. Its excellent harbor could accommodate the largest British fleet and the surrounding area provided enough suitable sites to deploy a larger army to strike eastward along the coast, westward in the direction of New Jersey, or northward up the Hudson Valley. Long Island was too large and isolated for the American Patriots to defend safely. Manhattan, on the other hand, would be too vulnerable once Long Island fell. In addition, its west side was exposed to the British who controlled the sea. In order to hold New York City at the south end of Manhattan, the Patriots needed to control Brooklyn Heights, on the tip of Long Island, which dominated the city.

In the summer of 1776, one of the largest and most critical campaigns of the war was fought for control of Long Island and Manhattan. General Howe reached New York late in June with 130 ships carrying 9,000 troops. In addition, Admiral Richard Howe arrived with 150 ships carrying 13,000 troops. To this army were added Clinton's 3,000 men returning from the ill-fated mission at Charleston. An additional 8,000 German mercenaries raised Howe's army to 32,000 men, the largest force assembled in the entire war.

Facing Howe was General George Washington, who had about 29,000 men in the New York area, at least on paper. In reality, however, they numbered no more than 19,000, still making this the largest force Washington would ever command in a single campaign. Neither side could afford a decisive defeat.

Washington had sent Charles Lee, a former officer of the British army who had served in Europe, to New York in February 1776 to evaluate the situation. After surveying the area, Lee prepared defensive plans. However, he informed his superiors it was impossible to defend Manhattan Island properly and make it impregnable as long as the British controlled the sea. The best that could be done, he pointed out, was to fortify the city in order to make it too costly for the enemy to attack. Following Lee's plan, a fort was placed at Horn's Hook to control Hell's Gate and close Long Island Sound with its link to the East River. Lee also recommended placing batteries at key points on Long Island, including Brooklyn Heights, to control the East River. However, he pointed out, the Hudson River was too wide and deep to control. He considered old Fort George at New York too risky to maintain and suggested that its northern curtain and two bastions be razed, thus leaving its landward side open so the British could not take and defend it. He also advised the construction of fortifications all the way to King's Bridge, which needed to be heavily fortified to protect the line of communications with Connecticut. It was Lee who first pointed out that Long Island was key to the defense of New York and proposed a chain of redoubts for a camp on the East River that required five thousand men to hold without counting the additional troops necessary to defend the remainder of the island. However, before he could take charge of any construction the Congress gave him command of the Southern Department in March. He was replaced by Brigadier General William Alexander, Lord Stirling.

Captain Jeduthan Baldwin, who served under Alexander, reported that battery positions were built on Governor's Island and Red Hook, and a fort at Hell's Gate. He wrote that a parapet was raised at the "old fort," apparently referring to Fort George. Lee's plans were modified by his successor, who advanced the proposed line of redoubts on Long Island further to the east so that they ran from Wallabout Bay to Gowanus Marsh.

Although Washington had come to similar conclusions as Lee about the vulnerability of New York, he still cautioned Alexander that New York "is the Place that we must use every endeavor to keep." Washington was concerned that if the harbor area were taken, the British fleet would be able to move up the Hudson, effectively separating the northern and southern colonies. He sent his engineer, Rufus Putnam to take charge of work on Long Island and Manhattan. On May 1, Washington informed Lee that a great deal of work had been completed and that "in a fortnight more, I think the city will be in a very respectable posture of defence." He also assured him that a large and strong work had been built on Governor's Island and was occupied by a regiment. At Red Hook a small but "strong barbet battery" [a battery whose guns fired over parapets instead of

Defenses of New York City Area during American Revolution

© TOMASZ IDZIKOWSKI

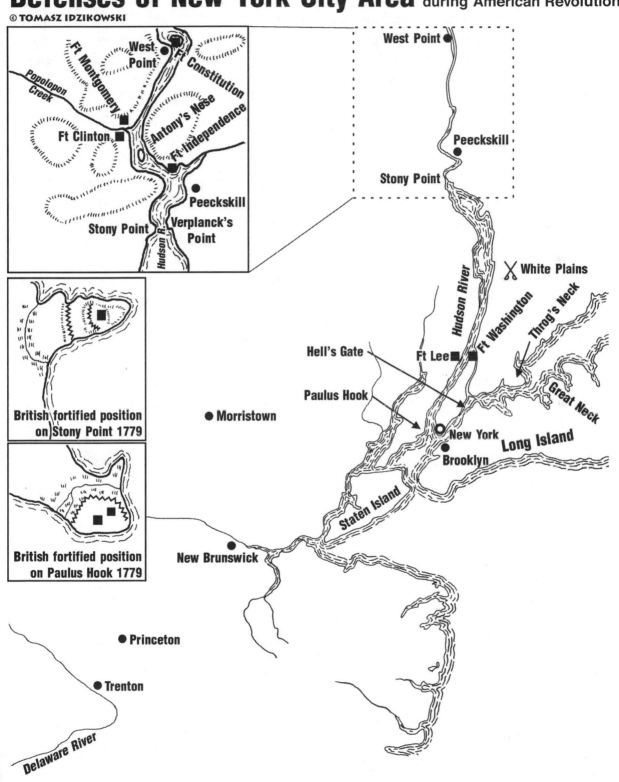

West Point

Ft Montgomery

Ft Constitution

Popolopon Creek

Antony's Nose

Ft Clinton

Ft Independence

Peeckskill

Stony Point

Verplanck's Point

Hudson R.

West Point

Peeckskill

Stony Point

Hudson River

White Plains

Ft Washington

Throg's Neck

Hell's Gate

Ft Lee

Great Neck

Paulus Hook

Morristown

New York

Long Island

Brooklyn

Staten Island

New Brunswick

British fortified position on Stony Point 1779

British fortified position on Paulus Hook 1779

Princeton

Trenton

Delaware River

through embrasures] was completed. Other works were also nearing completion, including the redoubts on Brooklyn Heights, which would be further strengthened during the summer. On July 3, Washington informed the president of the Congress that 110 British ships had appeared off Sandy Hook and that he was apprehensive about his position. On July 12, two British warships sailed forty miles up the Hudson, unhindered by the Patriot artillery batteries, confirming Washington's worst fears.

Earlier in June, George Washington had expressed concern about fortifications being built further up the Hudson River. In late June, he informed the New York legislature that the situation had not improved, but that he was unable to investigate it personally. He did not think the situation at Fort Constitution and Fort Montgomery on the west bank of the river was satisfactory. FORT MONTGOMERY, planned in 1775, was not begun until 1776. While it was still under construction, the engineer in charge realized that the heights across Popolopen Creek dominated the position. The problem was solved by building the smaller FORT CLINTON on the rocky outcrop. However, neither fort was finished in the next two years. Work was also begun on nearby FORT INDEPENDENCE (called FORT CONSTITUTION by Washington) at Peeksill, on a hill on the east bank of the river. Unfortunately, none of these forts would stand up to the British troops in 1777.

The excursion of the two British warships up the Hudson caused a great deal of consternation among the Americans. Robert Erskine—later appointed geographer of the Army in 1778 to relieve the engineers of mapping duties—suggested setting special chevaux-de-frise on the riverbed to stop ships from advancing up the river. On July 18, 1776, he sent a description and model of his invention to Brigadier General John M. Scott of the New York militia. They consisted of a tetrahedron with "four horned corners and three horns to each corner," requiring six wooden beams. He proposed a line of these contraptions be extended across the Hudson from the new FORT LEE to FORT WASHINGTON. These obstacles, used in Europe only on land, were soon set up in the American river. On August 5, Washington reported to the president of the Congress, "The Hulks and Chevaux de Frize that have been preparing to obstruct the channel, have got up to the place they are intended for, and will be sunk as soon as possible."

On August 11, Washington implored Rufus Putnam, who he had promoted to colonel of engineers, to sink vessels and other

It was during the New York campaign that David Bushnell designed and built the first operational submarine to be used as part of New York's coast defense. The odd-shaped vessel looked somewhat like a grenade and was pedal operated. It included a drill with which the operator could bore into the hull of a ship to attach an explosive. On the night of September 6, Sergeant Ezra Lee took the little vessel, called the *Turtle*, on its first mission. However, the operation failed because he was unable to penetrate the metallic bottom of Howe's flagship, the *Eagle*. A second attempt a week later also ended in failure.

obstructions in the Hudson near Fort Washington as quickly as possible. He also informed Putnam that Congress had sent two French engineers to help strengthen the defenses of Fort Washington and King's Bridge. In the General Orders of August 24, Washington mentioned that the East River had also been obstructed with chevaux de frises, which would prevent enemy ships from passing. By that time, however, Howe had already landed on Long Island.

In *The Battle of Brooklyn 1776*, John Gallagher writes that the Americans had not returned Fort George, the only British-built fort in New York City, to service but added more defenses. On Long Island, on the high ground where Fort Hamilton was later built across from Staten Island, they installed a battery of 9-pdrs to cover the Narrows. In addition, more artillery was placed on Governor's Island.

When the British landed virtually unopposed on Staten Island on July 2, 1776, they gained a base from which to launch an invasion of New York, rendering the American position in the New York area virtually untenable. The British had the entire western side of Manhattan at the mercy of their fleet. In addition, their army could land anywhere on Long Island and bring fresh reinforcements from Staten Island. Furthermore, the nearby British fleet was in a position to interdict the line of communications between Brooklyn Heights and Manhattan, effectively trapping the American defenders.

By August after months of preparation, Washington's fortified camp on the BROOKLYN HEIGHTS was enclosed by FORT BOX, FORT GREENE, FORT PUTNAM, and two redoubts. Fort Greene, the largest fort on Long Island, was a star-shaped earthwork that mounted six cannons. FORT STIRLING and FORT DEFIANCE (at Red Hook) were located to the rear and stood watch on the East River. Only a small part of Long Island was defended by elements of Washington's army. After trying to hold off the British as they landed on Long Island at Gravesend, Washington withdrew to the line of forts on Brooklyn Heights. At this point, over half of his army was at risk defending the Brooklyn area to secure New York. The British forces dominated Long Island and their fleet was ready to strike almost anywhere along the Hudson thus isolating the American army. The hoped-for suicidal British assault against the fortifications of Brooklyn Heights did not take place because the British chief engineer in America, Captain John Montresor, had concluded that the American position was too strong to be taken by direct assault and decided that a siege was in order. Within two days, the British erected a redoubt from which to bombard the American lines.

The Americans decided to evacuate Long Island rather than allow the army to suffer a major defeat and capture. By August 30, the entire American force had been evacuated, leaving behind only a few cannons. At this point, the wisdom of defending Manhattan Island was in question, because the American army was still at risk of being trapped. While the main body of the army prepared to abandon New York City, Rufus Putnam feverishly continued to create entrenchments on Harlem Heights and Mount Washington, on the northern end of Manhattan Island.

On September 1, 1776, Washington organized his army into three Grand Divisions, one of which numbered nine thousand men and was assigned to protect Harlem. Another division with five thousand men defended New York City. On September 8, General Nathaniel Greene and New Yorker John Jay urged Congress to abandon New York and put it to the torch. Congress steadfastly objected.

"I have never spared the Spade or Pick Axe," wrote Washington. The dilemma he faced was that "We are now in a strong Post, but not an impregnable one, nay acknowledged by every man of Judgement to be untenable, unless the Enemy will make the Attack upon Lines, when they can avoid it and their Movements indicate that they mean to do so." He also added that drawing the whole army into the New York City area would leave the country wide open. On the other hand, abandoning the city where so much labor had already been invested would hurt morale and weaken the American cause. American troops still held Fort Washington, Fort Lee, and King's Bridge.

Much like in the French and Indian War, this campaign and much of the war up to this point had depended on either taking or holding fortified positions and all the battles centered on them. The British troops had taken Montresor's Island at Hell's Gate across from the American fort at Horn's Hook. Washington realized that his position on Manhattan had become more precarious and that there now was the possibility of a landing to the north, which would outflank his defenses. On September 12, it was decided to evacuate New York as soon as possible while Putnam set up three lines of entrenchments at Harlem Heights. Washington, who waited with the main body of his army at Harlem Heights, repelled a British assault on his defenses on September 16. On October 12, Howe's troops moved up the East River and through Hell's Gate by ship to land on the mainland at Throgg's Neck and Pell's Point on Long Island Sound, forcing Washington to abandon all of Manhattan. After the battle of White Plains on October 22, Washington, evading Howe's army, moved his forces up the Hudson Valley and crossed to Haverstraw.

The only sizable forces left on the Hudson were Colonel Robert Magaw's 2,800 men at Fort Washington and the 2,000 men at Fort Lee. FORT WASHINGTON, located on a rock formation rising 200 feet above the Hudson, had some grave defects. Rufus Putnam, who had begun its construction in July, found that the bedrock was too hard to excavate. The fort, a weak, five-sided earthwork, did not even have a surrounding ditch because of the bedrock. It served as a last-stand position since its main line of defense was formed by a number of outworks. The total ensemble mounted thirty-four cannons. At noon on November 16, the British launched an assault, overwhelming the outerworks and forcing the garrison to retire into the fort with no possibility of escape. Magaw was forced to surrender.

Howe ferried his troops across the Hudson on November 18 and was about seven miles from FORT LEE. On November 19, Washington concluded that Fort Lee was no longer valuable without Fort Washington to support it in blocking the Hudson River.

He withdrew the two thousand men of the garrison rather then let them stand and see them sacrificed. Thus concluded the "War of Posts." If the Americans wanted to win the war, they could not do it by trying to hold fortified positions, especially on the coast, within range of the British fleet. With the exception of Sullivan's Island, most American attempts to hold fortified positions had failed. It took the British only a month to force the Patriots from New York and a little more than another month to clear the mouth of the Hudson.

During the next year and a half, the complexion of the war changed when Washington decided it was no longer wise to cling to fortified areas. Instead, he met the British in open battle, using the remaining American fortifications as shields. In December 1776, Washington's army took to the field to engage and defeat a British force of Hessians garrisoned at Trenton. Within a week, he scored another field victory at Princeton.

Howe decided to move against Washington's army and take the lightly fortified Patriot capital of Philadelphia. In July 1777, Howe sailed from New York with 18,000 of his men to the Chesapeake, landing at the head of the Elk River early in September and advancing on Philadelphia. The only fortifications of significance for Philadelphia were on the Delaware River and were powerless to stop an advance from the south. Washington, with about ten thousand men, attempted to defend a position along the Brandywine Creek. This time the Continentals were pushed back. By the end of September, the Congress and the Continental Army evacuated their capital. Howe occupied the city and during the next month, with the help of his brother's fleet, he cleared the American fortifications on the Delaware River. In October, Washington suffered a second reverse at Howe's hands at Germantown. His army spent most of the 1777 campaign fighting the British in the field and was not involved in laying sieges or defending major fortified sites.

At the close of the 1777 campaign season, Washington's army set up a fortified winter camp at VALLEY FORGE, next to the Schuylkill River outside Philadelphia, to accommodate over ten thousand men. General Louis Duportail was responsible for creating the defenses for this site, which included earthen redoubts and entrenchments around the thousand huts, each intended to be 14 feet by 16 feet, occupying the high ground. The site was well chosen, despite the difficulties caused by a severe winter. Redoubts #2 and #3 anchored the outer line of defenses along the high ridge on the south side of the position. Between Redoubt #3 and Redoubt #4 to the north, ran the inner line of defenses along Mount Joy, almost parallel to Valley Creek. Redoubt #1 stood about 350 yards northwest of Redoubt #4, on the high ground overlooking the Schuylkill River and Sullivan's Bridge. The bridge was built to secure a supply route to the north. From this strong and secure position, Washington, with the help of Baron von Steuben, forged the American army that would emerge in the spring of 1778.

Meanwhile in July 1777, British General Burgoyne, advancing through the restricted

Creation of the Corps of Engineers

The U.S. Army Corps of Engineers (CE) had its beginnings in the American Revolution. The need for such an organization became apparent when the Continental Army desperately needed skilled military engineers and trained troops to erect fortifications quickly to resist the advances of the British army.

Colonel Richard Gridley, George Washington's chief engineer in Boston, is considered the first chief of the Corps of Engineers. But Washington preferred Rufus Putnam, who replaced Gridley in April 1776 when Washington went to New York. As he worked on the fortifications of New York, Putnam put forth a plan for recruiting a corps of engineers. Putnam explained that the men for the new branch must learn to use their weapons first and then their "business" so they could work and fight as needed. Thus, they may be considered the first combat engineers. Putnam added that carpenters would be the largest group of artisans required for building anything the army needed, from obstacles to barracks. Washington endorsed the suggestions, but the Continental Congress failed to act upon them and the frustrated Putnam resigned to take command of a regiment.

In May 1777, Philippe Coudray, a Frenchman, arrived with a number of French officers to assume the position of chief engineer. However, many American officers resented the fact that he was given such a high rank and problems soon developed. Before Coudray even departed France, Louis Duportail, a French military engineer, had volunteered to serve the Americans in January 1777, on condition he be put in command of all engineers. He joined Washington in July 1777, but problems soon developed between him and Coudray. But the problem was solved when Coudray drowned crossing a creek in September. Colonel Duportail officially became the third chief of engineers.

In November 1777, General Duportail apprised Washington that more officers and troops were needed for the Corps of Engineers. His suggestions echoed Putnam's, except that he suggested that the sappers and miners should be recruited from regular army units so that they would already have the necessary military training. The main purpose of these troops would be the construction of fortifications. Once again Washington urged the Congress to act. In May 1778, Congress finally authorized three companies of engineers for the construction and repair of fortifications. It took until 1780 to find enough qualified officers and enlisted men to form the companies, all of which were under-strength when they were formed in the summer of 1778. Duportail remained chief of engineers until the end of the war. The army corps of engineers would be deactivated for a number of years after the war.

terrain of the Champlain route, defeated an American force at Fort Ticonderoga. A smaller force led by Barry St. Leger landed at Oswego late in July and was defeated by the end of August in an attempt to take Fort Stanwix. Burgoyne was soon engaged in one of the most important battles of the war. In October, Burgoyne went back on the offensive, attacking the Americans who were entrenched on Bemis Heights, just to the south of him. After a fierce battle, Burgoyne was defeated again. This battle, better known as the battle of Saratoga, yielded the victory necessary to gain foreign support. Although the fortifications of the Mohawk and Hudson Valley were used with great effect as shields, they no longer played a pivotal role for either side, as in past campaigns.

THE DELAWARE RIVER FORTS OF 1777

In 1776, the government of Pennsylvania took steps to protect the port of Philadelphia by constructing their own defenses. They employed the Polish military engineer Tadeusz Kosciuszko in the fall of 1776. Three forts formed the defensive system on the Delaware River below the city. Kosciuszko designed the Red Bank fort, known as Fort Mercer, on the New Jersey shore. On Mud Island across from Fort Mercer, was Fort Mifflin. By December 1776 a series of chevaux de frise, like those used at New York, blocked the channel between the two forts. Further down the river there was another group of obstacles, between Billing's Island and Billingsport where a fort was built on the New Jersey shore. These defenses looked good on paper, but the designs of the forts left much to be desired. And the river fort on the south side of Philadelphia appears to have been of little value at this time.

The fort at Billingsport was begun in the summer of 1776. The state government approved a plan for an earthen fort with four bastions and a maximum length of 700 feet with a 9-foot-deep and 18-foot-wide ditch. However, when the engineer in charge ran out of time to complete the fort, he turned a finished corner on the riverside into a redoubt only capable of covering the water obstacle. Two floating batteries with nineteen 18-pdrs held a position at Billings Island, protecting the other end of the line of obstacles.

FORT MIFFLIN (under another name) on the south end of Mud Island was started by British military engineer John Montresor in 1771. The Patriots completed it in 1776 and 1777. Originally designed to cover the main channel in the Delaware River, it had little protection on the west side, facing the Pennsylvania shore. Two sides of the fort included a stone wall with loopholes built by Montresor and faced the river front and the main ship channel. The fort included four wooden blockhouses, each mounting two guns on the lower platform and four on the upper. Three of these positions controlled the main channel and one faced the Pennsylvania shore. The main part of the fort was no longer than about 600 feet and much of it was enclosed by obstacles. The fourteen cannons of Fort Mifflin protected the main lines of chevaux de frise closing the shipping channel of the river and linked to the twenty cannons of Fort Mercer on other side of

Philadelphia Campaign of 1777
© TOMASZ IDZIROWSKI

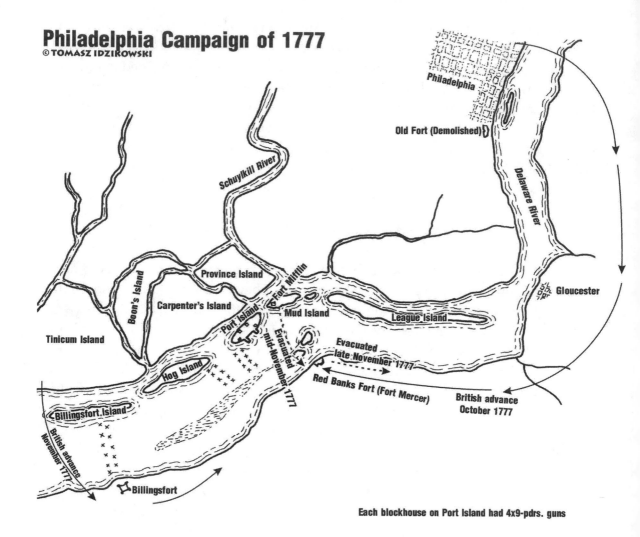

Each blockhouse on Port Island had 4x9-pdrs. guns

the river. FORT MERCER, also known as FORT RED BANK, the largest fort in the group, was also an earthwork with an effective design that included a large ditch and abatis on the landward side.

Tronson de Coudray, who inspected these forts in July 1777, commented that the fort at Billingsport would need two thousand men and that the planks and piles that supported the sand of the earthen fort were not high enough. He found Fort Mifflin so badly situated that half its guns stood in useless locations. He also commented that the slope of its walls was too straight, which explained why they were already collapsing. He did not believe that these forts could effectively prevent the passage of enemy warships.

When the British arrived in July 1777, they concluded that the river defenses were too strong to be taken on by the fleet alone. Consequently, General Howe decided to land his army at Elkton. After driving back Washington's Continental Army at Brandywine in mid-September and sending Cornwallis to take Philadelphia late in the month, Howe resolved that the time had come to clear the Delaware so he could use the port facilities of the city. Although Washington's army remained in the vicinity, the river forts could expect little help after its defeat at Germantown. The forts were actually under the command of Commodore Hazelwood who had a small fleet of galleys and a few larger ships.

Since the British naval squadron could not pass the obstacles blocking the channel by Billingsport, Howe's army had to help by eliminating the river forts. Cornwallis set up twelve cannons along Philadelphia's riverside. On September 27, Hazelwood sent his three larger ships and five galleys carrying a single gun each to take on Cornwallis's batteries. During the engagement, the *Delaware* ran aground when the tide went out and was captured. The British soon put it back into service against its former owners.

The redoubt at Billingsport mounted six cannons, mostly 9-pdrs, and held a hundred-man garrison. Its landward side, however, was virtually undefended. When a British force crossed the river and approached the fort from its weak side on October 2, the garrison had no recourse but to spike the guns, set fire to the barracks, and escape by ship. On October 5, a gap was opened in the obstacles, but the timely arrival of three hundred Americans forced the British to evacuate Billingsport. Although the Patriots attempted to close the gap in the chevaux de frise, the British reopened it within several days.

The British moved to tackle the next barrier. Fortunately for them, their chief engineer, Captain Montresor, was familiar with Fort Mifflin since he had initiated its construction. Montresor oversaw the installation of batteries on Carpenter's and Province islands during the month of October. As the British prepared to launch an attack on Fort Mercer and Fort Mifflin, the fleet moved up the river. The 400-man garrison of Fort Mercer, which had been reinforced with two regiments, braced for the onslaught under the command of Colonel Christopher Greene.

A Hessian brigade of 1,200 men with ten cannons was transported across the Delaware at Cooper's Ferry (modern-day Camden) to attack Fort Mercer. Since Greene did not have enough men to hold the fort, he ordered a new wall to be built as a retrenchment to shorten his defenses. The Hessian commander demanded his surrender or there would be no quarter when the fort was taken. Undaunted, Greene replied that he expected no quarter. On October 22, 1777, the Hessians attacked. Late in the afternoon, just as the light was beginning to fade, one of the Hessian regiments attacked the southeast side of the fort where the abatis had not been completed, using fascines to fill the ditches. Meanwhile, another unit launched an assault from the north, taking the section the defenders had abandoned. Next, they stormed forward, only to be met by cannon fire and musket volleys at the defended retrenchment. The unrelenting Hessians continued their attempts to breach the sharpened tree trunks and branches of the abatis in front of this new 10-foot-high wall. Some of the small American galleys fired into the flank of the attackers, forcing them to break off the attack. After smashing through the abatis and ditches, the Hessians realized that they could not negotiate the parapet without scaling ladders and retreated under a barrage of fire. The Americans

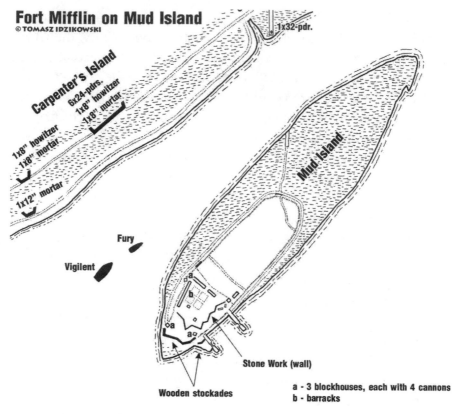

Fort Mifflin on Mud Island
©TOMASZ IDZIKOWSKI

Carpenter's Island

1x32-pdr.

6x24-pdrs.
1x8" howitzer
1x8" mortar

1x8" howitzer
1x8" mortar

1x12" mortar

Mud Island

Fury

Vigilent

Stone Work (wall)

Wooden stockades

a - 3 blockhouses, each with 4 cannons
b - barracks

inflicted over four hundred casualties on the Hessians while losing only thirty-four of their own men.

FORT MIFFLIN came under fire next. The British batteries on the nearby island were aimed at its incomplete ramparts. The naval squadron, delayed by bad winds, had not crossed the barrier before the attack began. The *Augusta*, a 64-gun ship of the line, was trapped in the mud while the *Merlin*, an 18-gun sloop, ran aground. On October 23, Hazelwood's mosquito fleet of twelve galleys and two floating batteries moved against the two ships. The *Augusta* went up in a huge explosion followed by the *Merlin*. The remaining British ships were forced to retreat down river by a fleet of fire rafts. Thus, a small naval victory was won by the Patriots on the Delaware. Meanwhile, Fort Mifflin was put under a heavy bombardment. However, heavy downpours inundated much of the fort and the British positions for almost a week.

At the beginning of November, Howe sent his troops back to Billingsport to cover the ships as they moved through the chevaux de frise. The Americans tried to block the naval advance by setting up another battery further up the river. On November 8, Howe's ships moved past the barrier. The British batteries opposite Fort Mifflin resumed their bombardment on November 10. Fourteen heavy pieces of artillery soon neutralized the four American cannons facing them, reducing to rubble the walls of the fort during the next three days. The pounding of British 24- and 32-pdrs left only one of the four blockhouses standing. On the night of November 12, a hundred reinforcements arrived at the fort. The 300-man garrison was relieved between the evening of November 14 and the early hours of November 15, as over four hundred replacements arrived from across the river. On November 14, the British moved forward with two floating batteries, but the fort's guns drove them back. [Note: According to contemporary accounts, one of the floating batteries mounted ten 18-pdrs on an enclosed barge about 59 feet in length and 22 feet across, with places for oars on each side between the gun embrasures. Some of these batteries may have included an upper deck for swivel guns and muskets]. The next day, a large 16-gun floating battery came within forty yards of the fort and laid down a devastating barrage while several British warships, including the 64-gun *Somerset*, dropped anchor near the underwater obstacles and laid down supporting fire. The little American mosquito fleet emerged again, but was powerless against such overwhelming odds. Fort Mifflin was down to only two cannons as darkness fell and 250 of its men had fallen. Major Simeon Thayer, almost out of ammunition, conceded that there was nothing left to defend. Early on the morning of November 16, he evacuated his remaining two hundred men to Fort Mercer. The tattered remains of the flag continued to fly over the smoldering ruins as the British landed near dawn.

But Fort Mercer still stood in the way of the British who strove to open the Delaware in order to use the port of Philadelphia. As Howe prepared to send a large force against the fort, Washington sent several thousand reinforcements to support it. However, the reinforcements did not arrive before Colonel Greene was forced to abandon the fort on November 2, blowing it up as he departed. [In 1778 the Americans would return and rebuild both Fort Mercer and Fort Mifflin.] After spending over a month besieging a few forts, the British finally took control of the river that November of 1777 and broke the chain blocking the passage of their ships to Philadelphia.

Americans returned in December 1777, to challenge the British for control of the river by employing floating mines. David Bushnell's plan was to use pairs of submerged mines moored to kegs with a floating device that detonate them on making contact with a ship. The Patriots launched twenty of these kegs late in the month, and one detonated and managed to kill a few innocent civilians.

DEFENDING THE HIGHLANDS OF THE HUDSON

The Highlands along the Hudson River between New York City and Albany served as the main line of defense in the struggle to prevent the British from splitting the colonies. The loss of New York City weakened the line of communications, but a route remained open as long as the Americans held the Highlands. To this end, in 1775 the Congress asked New York to set up a commission to defend the section of the Highlands that dominated the Hudson and to keep the British from taking control of the river route.

The site first picked for the main line of defenses was at the entrance to the

Highlands. Although West Point was more accessible for construction, Anthony's Nose was selected months after work had already begun on Constitution Island opposite West Point. The site was located several miles down the Hudson. The cliff face of Anthony's Nose rose up to 900 feet and provided little space on the east bank of the Hudson for a defensive position to dominate the river. Opposite it, on the west bank, was lower ground cut by the Popolopen Creek. Governor George Clinton and his brother, General James Clinton, preferred this site, especially after the work on Constitution Island was deemed insufficient.

In August 1775, a commission was appointed to oversee the works on the Highland fortifications. Bernard Romans took charge of fortifying the 'S' bend in the Hudson at WEST POINT. His plan called for fortifying Constitution Island, which formed much of the 'S' turn and was only separated from the eastern shore by a marsh. The northwest side of the island's shoreline was steep, with what were considered inaccessible precipices. Romans planned to build several blockhouses, batteries, and a large impressive position, which he called the GRAND BASTION, that was to have walls 30 feet thick and 18 feet high. ROMANS BATTERY, finished in March 1776, mounted thirteen 6-pdrs and one 9-pdr. Its walls consisted of an outer section of dry stone masonry and an interior one of stone with mortar. The gap between the two walls was filled with rubble, giving the wall a total thickness of 11 feet. This battery position included a brick magazine. ROMANS BLOCKHOUSE was finished in November 1775 and mounted eight 4-pdr cannons on its upper level. Next to the Grand Bastion, on the southeast side, was the MARINE BATTERY. Late in 1775, Romans's work was so heavily criticized that work on the Grand Bastion was interrupted. Plans were drawn for the addition of a couple of batteries at Gravel Hill and Hill Cliff. The first was to hold eleven 12- or 18-pdr cannons and the second, four 4-pdrs. Both batteries were built in May 1775. According to a report filed by Lord William Alexander Stirling in 1776, Romans's work was built at "very great expense," but offered little advantage since it was scattered and essentially defenseless. Lord Stirling claimed that Fort Constitution could only be maintained if it was supported by a position on West Point.

Work shifted from Constitution Island to the position at Anthony's Nose in the spring of 1776. FORT MONTGOMERY was built on a plateau on the east bank of the Hudson, across from the place where Popolopen Creek empties into the river. The fort was made of earth and stone, had an irregular, almost triangular trace, and included three bastions on its west side, barracks, and a magazine. The main barracks was large, measuring 80 feet by 20 feet, and consisted of two levels. In November 1776, the fort housed a garrison of 750 men and mounted twenty-nine cannons. When Lord Stirling inspected the site, he found that its south flank, the main direction of an enemy advance, was dominated by the high ground on the other side of the creek. In August 1776, the Americans built FORT CLINTON on top of that commanding hill to correct the situation. A pontoon bridge spanning the creek linked the two forts. To complete the defenses and deny the river to the British, it was planned to add a chain and boom across the Hudson between the two forts and Anthony's Nose.

Thomas Machin, one of the engineer officers who worked on the forts, was charged with the mission of procuring a chain strong enough to stop the British ships and getting it across the river. Machin obtained the chain by October and floated it across the river, anchoring its other end near Anthony's Nose. However, soon after it was in place the chain broke under the strain of the river's tide. Winter then blocked the Hudson with ice floes after Washington began his southward retreat late in November. In March 1777, as spring returned, Machin was able to put the chain back in place. No British ships could move north without neutralizing the pair of forts and breaking the chain. However, the two forts's Achilles heel was that they were not well prepared for landward defense. It was thought the paths on the western side of the river were narrow and arduous, making an overland assault impractical. Thus it appeared the river route was effectively blocked. The garrison dropped to as few as 150 militiamen in 1777 and Washington believed his defenses on the Hudson River were secure.

In the summer of 1777, General Burgoyne marched south along the Champlain route, taking Fort Ticonderoga early in July. The American commander had refused to follow the advice of his engineer, Tadeusz Kosciuszko, who had told him that he must defend the height overlooking the fort or face defeat. After this first victory, Burgoyne advanced on Albany in August. Meanwhile, Colonel Barry St. Leger, with a smaller force of eight hundred soldiers and one thousand Indians, landed at Oswego and advanced toward the Mohawk River. He was stopped and forced to withdraw after placing Fort Stanwix under siege in August.

FORT STANWIX was located on the mile-long portage between the Mohawk River and Wood Creek, the Oneida Carrying Place. Although built in 1758 during the last war, it had seen no action until now. It was rebuilt by General Philip Schuyler just before St. Leger's arrival. Fort Stanwix was a square log fort with four arrow-shaped corner bastions with walls up to 17 feet high. It was surrounded by a moat 40 feet wide and 14 feet deep, and its entrance was covered by a ravelin. At the time of St. Leger's attack, it was commanded by Colonel Peter Gansevoort and defended by a garrison of over seven hundred men. Fort Stanwix withstood the siege until Benedict Arnold came to the rescue in late August. Ironically, after successfully fending off the British attack, the fort succumbed to fire in 1781.

As Burgoyne met defeat at the battle of Saratoga in front of Kosciuszko's fortifications on Bemis Heights, Sir Henry Clinton was finally moving north up the Hudson with a contingent of two thousand men to link up with him. Clinton advanced to Verplanck's Point where he drew off Israel Putnam's troops to the east side of the valley. Meanwhile, Clinton's main force landed at Stony Point and did the unexpected by moving through the narrow defiles toward Bear Mountain where he split his force. One column of twelve hundred men led by Clinton himself moved near the shore, toward

Fort Clinton; the other, numbering nine hundred men, came around the mountain to take Fort Montgomery from the rear.

"The Battle of the Clintons," so called because it involved Sir Henry Clinton, Governor George Clinton, and his brother, General James Clinton, took place on October 6, 1777. Governor George Clinton, who held the rank of general, had stationed about six hundred men at Fort Montgomery and Fort Clinton. He sent out about one hundred men to stop the smaller British force heading toward Fort Montgomery. General James Clinton held Fort Clinton. Sir Henry Clinton's British troops stormed Fort Clinton after its commander refused to surrender. Fort Montgomery was also taken. However, Governor Clinton and his brother and many of their men evaded capture by melting into the darkness escaping through the rough terrain, leaving behind three hundred dead and wounded and about one hundred cannons. The British broke the chain the next day. Sir Henry Clinton's force continued up the river to FORT CONSTITUTION whose shaken defenders, having seen the stragglers from Fort Montgomery, evacuated on October 7. British troops landed unopposed on the island the next day. The British squadron continued up the river, burning the town of Kingston on October 16 and finally stopping about thirty-five miles south of Albany where they learned that Burgoyne had already surrendered. On October 22, Sir Henry Clinton

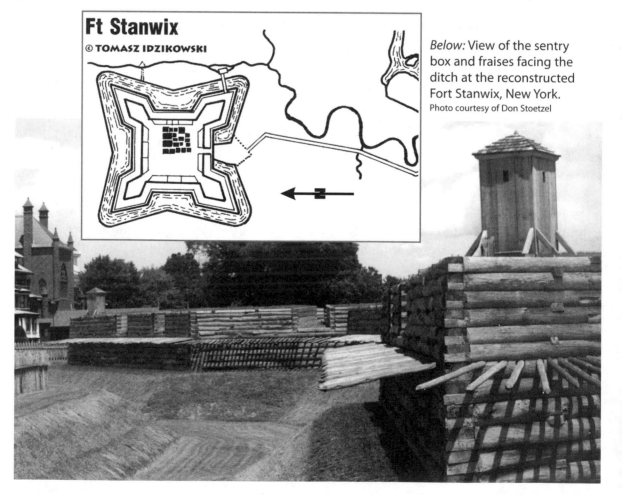

Ft Stanwix
© TOMASZ IDZIKOWSKI

Below: View of the sentry box and fraises facing the ditch at the reconstructed Fort Stanwix, New York.
Photo courtesy of Don Stoetzel

retreated to New York, having destroyed and leveled the fortifications of Fort Constitution, Fort Montgomery and Fort Clinton. Although the Americans built Putnam's Battery near the remains of Fort Montgomery, the next year, the main effort to defend the highland passage shifted to West Point.

Washington, who wanted the defenses of the Highlands restored, dispatched General Duportail, the chief of engineers, to investigate. The construction of the WEST POINT fortifications was beset from the very beginning with controversy over design and location. Lack of funds and materials and the threat of the return of the British up the Hudson in 1778 resolved the discord to a great extent. General Israel Putnam, who was in charge in the Highlands, and a special commission wanted to fortify West Point. Captain Louis de la Radière, a French officers who had accompanied Duportail, was assigned as Putnam's chief engineer. He contended that the old site above the Popolopen Creek was better suited for defense and less vulnerable to land attack. Overruled, de la Radière started drawing up plans to defend West Point. His original intention was to create a traditional Vauban-type fortress of solid masonry, a type of fort the Americans had not built during the Revolution. However, financial constraints ruled out his more ambitious plans. Putnam modified de la Radière's plan, so that the majority of the works were of earth and stone.

The main objective was to block the Hudson River and command it with artillery. To this end Thomas Machin was put to work on preparing a new chain while de la Radière selected the sites for two battery positions. The four-gun CHAIN BATTERY was originally intended to lay close to water level to deliver grazing fire against passing ships for maximum effect. However, the battery had to be placed a little higher than planned in order to cover the river more effectively, and many of the benefits of being at river level were lost. The two-gun WATER BATTERY could only be placed at a height where no grazing fire was possible. The poor performance of artillery in controlling the coast or waterways in the past inspired the idea of installing a chain to prevent enemy ships from passing. Since the two batteries were exposed on the landward side, de la Radière planned to build his Vauban-type fort not only to cover them but the river as well.

This fort of earth, stone, and wood that was built did feature many of the items de la Radière had included in his plans. In April, de la Radière was replaced by Colonel Kosciuszko, who had arrived a month earlier. Construction of all these positions began in March 1778. Since labor was provided by James Clinton's regiment, the fort became known as FORT CLINTON, but was shortly renamed FORT ARNOLD. Washington and his lieutenants wanted Fort Clinton to be able to resist for fourteen days rather than to withstand a long siege. Its mission was to protect the two water batteries, until a relief force arrived.

The first artillery pieces arrived late in March. In April 1778, Colonel Kosciuszko added two new water batteries: the three-gun LANTHORN BATTERY and the SOUTH BATTERY. In April, Thomas Machin floated the pieces of the great chain down river from the manufacturing site and began the assembly. Machin prepared the equipment to extend and secure it so that it would not break under the pressure of the tidal river. The chain and the boom created a formidable obstacle and were more likely to stop British ships from moving up river than the few cannons in the scattered batteries. In the winter, the chain was hauled in to prevent it from being broken by the ice floes that blocked the river. In the spring, the great chain was strung across the river again. The log boom was another problem because the wood rotted and had to be replaced more than once during the war.

Also in April, further additions were made to protect Fort Arnold. Among them were several redoubts known as FORT WEBB, FORT WYLLYS, and FORT MEIGS, which covered the landward approach from the south, and FORT SHERBOURNE, situated just northwest of Fort Arnold to protect against an enemy landing. Fort Webb had six guns and offered the final line of protection for Fort Arnold. To the south of Fort Webb, stood Fort Wyllys with a two-gun battery that covered Fort Meigs. Fort Meigs included a battery that was open in the rear. Still later in April, work began on FORT PUTNAM to the west of Fort Arnold. It was situated on the high ground to protect the western approach and the plateau on which Fort Arnold was located. As summer began, Kosciuszko proceeded with work on Constitution Island to secure the other end of the Great Chain with GREATON'S BATTERY. Fort Arnold, the water batteries, and some of the other positions were largely completed by November 1778. Work continued on most of the positions throughout the next few years. In 1779, a third set of fortifications was built further to secure the position at West Point. It consisted of redoubts, either hexagonal like Fort Wyllys, or pentagonal. They were identified as REDOUBTS #1 THRU #7 and REDOUBTS NORTH AND SOUTH. Redoubts #1, #2, #3, and #4 were on the high ground to the west of Fort Putnam, while #5, #6, and #7 were on Constitution Island. North and South Redoubt covered the landward approaches to the island from the south on the high ground. Redoubt #7 was actually begun in the fall of 1778. All these new positions formed an outer line of defenses. Another French engineer, Major Jean Louis Ambroise de Géneton Villefranche, who replaced Kosciuszko in August 1780, completed the water batteries and Fort Clinton, but abandoned the Sherburne Redoubt, which he deemed of little value.

Fort Arnold (Clinton) and Fort Putnam were the main positions at West Point. FORT ARNOLD's north and east sides with walls about 2.5 feet high overlooked the cliff face. The fort's other walls, made from the earth dug out to create the large ditch, were about 9 feet high. The gate, located in the western wall, was accessed by a bridge over the moat and was covered by two guns on both flanks in the bastion on the southwest corner and the demi-bastion on the northwest corner. The south wall was covered by two more cannons in the bastion and two cannons in the southeast demi-bastion. A glacis was added to the landward side for additional protection. The fort included a two-level barracks for six hundred men, a magazine, and other structures. The fort's garrison provided the crews for the water batteries below.

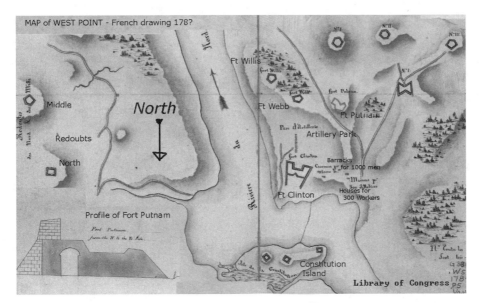

FORT PUTNAM, located on a 50-foot cliff overlooking the plateau, was built with the same type of construction materials as Fort Arnold and most of the other positions. According to 1780 reports, its walls were lined with stone that had to be replaced and repaired. Before 1784, lime mortar was added to the walls, but there are no detailed records on the subject. The fort mounted ten cannons and four mortars. A barracks accommodated part of the 420-man garrison.

Most of the batteries and redoubts of West Point were built in the style of field fortifications with earth, wood, and, in a few cases, stone. Most present-day reconstructions of these fortifications include fraises, a defensive device consisting of a line of stakes placed on the ramparts, which served as an additional obstacle to infantry assaults.

The fortifications of West Point were not heavily garrisoned, but the British never attempted to breach them. After taking command of the fortifications in August 1780, Benedict Arnold betrayed his compatriots. The intelligence he gave the British was recovered when British Major Andre was captured during Arnold's escape in late September. The documents prepared for the British by Arnold provide much of the data available today regarding the fortress of West Point in 1780. Arnold's report reveals that: FORT ARNOLD was in very poor condition at the time and the dry fascines and wood rendered it highly flammable; FORT PUTNAM, although made of stone, was in need of major repairs, especially on its eastern side, which was down; FORT WEBB was made of wood and fascines that were also very dry and its approaches were only covered by light abatis; FORT WYLLYS was a stone work 5 feet high, but the upper parts of its walls were made of planks filled with earth; REDOUBT #1 was made of wood and 9 feet thick on the south side and 4 feet thick on the east and north sides with no ditch; REDOUBT #2 was similar to #1; REDOUBT #3 was made of very dry wood and its walls were only 3 feet thick; REDOUBT #4 was of wood and about 10 feet high, but its west side was faced with a stone wall 8 feet high; The NORTH AND SOUTH REDOUBTS had stone walls 4 feet high topped by dry wood filled with earth. They had no ditch, but unlike, the other redoubts, had bombproofs. Arnold also gave Andre a report from the artillery commander, Major Bauman. This showed a total of one hundred artillery pieces mounted in all the works at West Point.

As a result of Arnold's betrayal, Fort Arnold was again renamed Fort Clinton and renovations and improvements, such as barracks and magazines, were set in motion. By 1782, only Fort Putnam, Fort Wyllys, North Redoubt, and South Redoubt had powder magazines. The large powder magazine near Fort Clinton served all the other positions at West Point. Fort Webb was abandoned altogether. Bombproofs and magazines were planned for most of the redoubts, but were not completed before the end of the war. Alexander Hamilton referred to the fortress of West Point as the "Key to America," but this key was rather fragile since its works were incomplete and its garrison consisted largely of militia. Although the Continental Army never built up enough strength to force the British from New York City, American forces did venture down the Hudson before Arnold's betrayal. For a short time, Washington even moved his headquarters to West Point.

The British struck the entrance to the Highlands on June 1, 1779, at the King's Ferry crossing, with Stony Point on one end and Verplanck's Point on the other located on heights about 150 feet above the river. The Americans had built a blockhouse and begun work on some fortifications at STONY POINT, where they posted only forty men. Across the Hudson at Verplanck's Point stood the small FORT LAFAYETTE held by about seventy men. The Americans burned their defenses and fled before the British troops landed at Stony Point while the garrison at Fort Lafayette was quickly isolated and forced to surrender. The British immediately began to improve both positions.

In July, Washington dispatched a small American force of a little over one thousand men under General Anthony Wayne to Stony Point. By that time, the British had created two lines of abatis, the first at the bottom of the hill at the base of the peninsula, facing the marshes. The British built three fleches as advanced positions, which included embrasures to cover the few access paths. The flèche to the north mounted a 12-pdr and two mortars serviced by nine men. The flèche in the middle mounted two Coehorn mortars with fifteen gunners. The southern work had a 12-pdr and twenty men. About two hundred yards up the hill lay the second line of abatis and behind it a partially enclosed fort on the top of the hill. In this second line were two flanking batteries, each with a 12-pdr and an 18-pdr for long-range fire. Between them stood a battery with a single 12-pdr and another with an 8-inch howitzer. There was another 12-pdr to the rear. Offshore, the sloop *Vulture* lay at anchor. Lt. Colonel Henry Johnson stationed over six hundred men at Stony Point.

To overcome these defenses, Wayne divided his force into two main columns on each flank and a holding force in the center. The attack took place in the dark, when the long-range naval 12-pdr and 18-pdrs, as well as the mortars, would be of little use. Moving through the swamp, the lead teams were able to hack down the abatis, penetrate the

British line, and storm the enemy position, capturing most of Johnson's men. After this, Wayne's men turned the guns against Fort Lafayette across the river. However, the British reinforced that position and soon Wayne's men abandoned Stony Point on Washington's orders. The British returned and refortified the position.

This feat was repeated further down the Hudson, across from New York on August 19. This time four hundred men of Major "Light Horse Henry" Lee moved against PAULUS HOOK, located across the Hudson River from New York City. This small peninsular position was isolated from the mainland by a marsh and a creek through which the British had dug a moat whose depth varied with the tides. The defended position was on the higher ground behind the moat and included a large magazine, a redoubt mounting five guns, and three barracks. Most of the position was encircled by earthworks. British Major William Sutherland commanded about two hundred men, including a number of Hessians and Tories. Lee's men, who had dwindled to three hundred at this point, attacked after midnight in order to cross the moat at low tide. They stormed the British positions, capturing about 150 men. However, the commander eluded them. Lee had to abandon the position at dawn because his force was not strong enough to resist the British forces stationed in nearby New York.

OTHER FORTIFIED POSTS AND CITIES OF THE AMERICAN REVOLUTION

The American Revolution did not end without involving other fortifications. In August 1778, a battle for the city of NEWPORT took place in Rhode Island. General John Sullivan, leading a force of ten thousand men against the 3,000-man British contingent dug in at Newport. Despite the support of four thousand French troops and a dozen French ships of the line, Sullivan was not able to overcome the British fortifications and, after the French troops and fleet departed almost half of his troops went home as well. At the end of August, Sullivan attempted to hold the fortifications at the other end of Rhode Island, but realized he could not hold out for long. On the night of August 30, the Americans pulled off an evacuation as successful as the one at Brooklyn two years earlier.

The British also moved into Penobscot Bay to establish a base from which to raid New England. In June 1779, General Francis McLean and over 750 men established an earthen fort, named FORT GEORGE, on the Bagaduce Peninsula, which dominated the bay. A thousand militiamen from Massachusetts tried to dislodge them late in July. However, instead of attacking the largely incomplete fort, whose walls were only a few feet high and not yet fully enclosed, the Americans built their own defenses opposite the British position. When the British fleet showed up in mid-August, the poorly coordinated American effort fell apart in front of the British fortifications.

In the West, the campaign unfolded much in the same way as the French and Indian War. Each side occupied key sites defended by forts and the battles revolved around the capture of the strongholds. American pioneers like James Harrod and Daniel Boone had already established their own forts in Kentucky before the revolution began. FORT HARROD was built in 1774 and FORT BOONESBOROUGH at the time the revolution began. Both were stockaded towns in which the walls of buildings formed an integral part of the curtain walls. LOGAN'S FORT, built in 1775 by Colonel Benjamin Logan, stood about ten miles from Fort Boonesborough. The garrison of Fort Boonesborough expanded in 1776 and with it the fort itself. Corner blockhouses were added and the fort grew to approximately 250 feet by 150 feet. It withstood a number of British and Indian attacks, the most significant of which was a thirteen-day siege in August 1778. Over four hundred Indians and a few Canadians participated in the siege, which was part of an attempt by the British to wrest control of the frontier from the Americans. Among the defenders was Daniel Boone. The Americans successfully beat off the attackers flaming projectiles intended to set the fort ablaze, and even a tunneling effort.

Colonel George Rogers Clark with a contingent of 175 men trekked from western Pennsylvania to the Mississippi in the summer of 1778. On this journey, he stopped at the site of the future city of Louisville on the Ohio River where he built a fort on Corn Island to protect his supplies. The next year his settlers built another fort on the shore. In 1781, they constructed a more permanent structure named FORT NELSON, a large fort with logs laid out horizontally to form the walls and four corner bastions. It also included a moat and a palisade on the counterscarp. On July 4, 1778, Clark took the British garrison of Kaskaskia (Fort Gage) by surprise. FORT GAGE, renamed as FORT CLARK, was an old Jesuit compound where the British had thrown up a stockade. Shortly after taking Fort Gage, Clark forced the surrender of FORT CAHOKIA, an old stone building used as a barracks. In February 1779, Fort Gage was renamed one more time, becoming FORT PATRICK HENRY.

On December 1, 1778, a British force out of Fort Detroit attacked Vincennes (Indiana), after an arduous seventy-day journey though the wilderness. The expedition, led by the lieutenant governor of Canada, Henry Hamilton, numbered 175 soldiers and a few hundred Indians. The town of Vincennes did not resist since its fort was weak and lacked facilities. With the help of his remaining thirty-five men and the local militia, Hamilton rebuilt the fort and added a barracks and a pair of large blockhouses that mounted five cannons each. The walls of the stockade rose to 11 feet and formed a quadrangle whose longest side measured 275 feet. Hamilton named the place FORT SACKVILLE. Clark arrived from Kaskaskia with two hundred men, half of whom were volunteers, soon after the fort's completion, after trekking through the winter wilderness over a hundred miles for about two weeks. He used a ruse to trick the British into believing that his force was much larger than it actually was. As a result, many of Hamilton's allies changed sides. Clark's riflemen kept Fort Sackville under accurate fire for a whole day, forcing Hamilton to surrender on the next day, February 25, 1779.

Although he wanted to undertake an expedition against Fort Detroit, Clark was unable to do so as trouble with the Indians flared up again when Joseph Brant's tribe went on the warpath. FORT JEFFERSON, built by Clark in 1780 near the mouth of the Ohio River, was abandoned a year later in the face of British and Indian opposition.

FORT DETROIT, originally known as FORT LERNOULT, was erected by the British in 1778, up-river from the older Fort Pontchartrain, and was designed to resist artillery fire. It had demi-bastions and earthen walls 11 feet high and 26 feet wide. Its shape is unusual because each of the half-bastions was designed to cover one of the fort's four sides, which could not be done unless the half-bastion protruded from one end of each curtain wall. Fort Detroit remained in British hands until July 1796.

In December 1778, Sir Henry Clinton sent a British expedition of 3,500 men under Lieutenant Colonel Archibald Campbell into the south. Campbell landed unopposed on the Georgia coast near SAVANNAH, engaged the one thousand militia under American General Robert Howe, and took the city. This sparked a Tory uprising in the south. In September 1779, the fleet of French Admiral Charles d'Estaing, numbering over thirty warships, disembarked four thousand French troops near Savannah. This force, joined by General Benjamin Lincoln with thirteen hundred Americans (half militia), put Savannah under siege. General Augustin Prevost, who defended the city with a contingent of 3,500 men, asked his chief engineer, Captain James Moncrieff to prepare a line of fortifications. The defenses consisted of several redoubts and a ditch backed by abatis from the river on the east side to the redoubt on the southwest corner, known as SPRING HILL REDOUBT. The western side was largely covered by swamp.

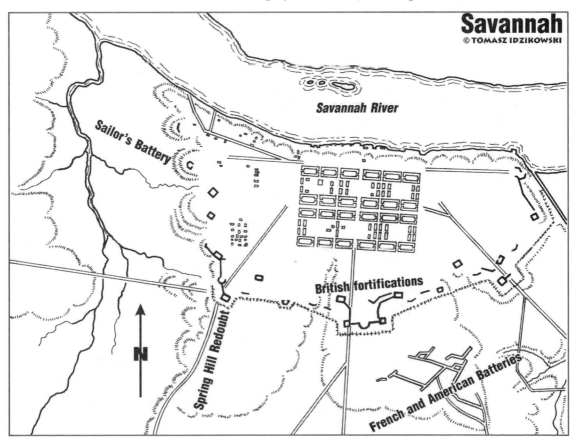

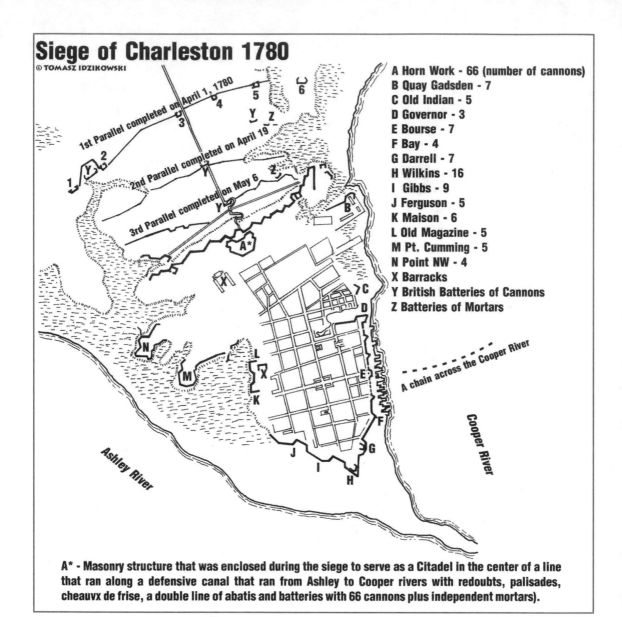

Siege of Charleston 1780

© TOMASZ IDZIKOWSKI

1st Parallel completed on April 1, 1780

2nd Parallel completed on April 19

3rd Parallel completed on May 6

A Horn Work - 66 (number of cannons)
B Quay Gadsden - 7
C Old Indian - 5
D Governor - 3
E Bourse - 7
F Bay - 4
G Darrell - 7
H Wilkins - 16
I Gibbs - 9
J Ferguson - 5
K Maison - 6
L Old Magazine - 5
M Pt. Cumming - 5
N Point NW - 4
X Barracks
Y British Batteries of Cannons
Z Batteries of Mortars

A chain across the Cooper River

Cooper River

Ashley River

A* - Masonry structure that was enclosed during the siege to serve as a Citadel in the center of a line
that ran along a defensive canal that ran from Ashley to Cooper rivers with redoubts, palisades,
cheauvx de frise, a double line of abatis and batteries with 66 cannons plus independent mortars).

The parallels of the French siege lines advanced toward the main bastion on the southern side of the defenses. Meanwhile, the French navy bombarded the British on October 8. The attack on the city was launched on October 9, when the French, together with an American contingent under Francis "Swamp Fox" Marion, moved against the Spring Hill Redoubt on the southwest corner. A diversion against the SAILORS' BATTERY failed when the group sent to attack through the swamp got lost. In the meantime, Marion's men and the French worked their way through the ditch, broke through the abatis, and stormed the redoubt, only to be forced back out. The French and American forces suffered heavy losses. The French admiral, also wounded in the battle, took his men and ships and departed at the end of the month.

After his victory at Savannah, Clinton voluntarily gave up Newport in December 1779, taking eight thousand men by sea for an assault on CHARLESTON to expand his position in the south. In February, Clinton gathered additional troops in the south, almost doubling his army as it advanced on Charleston from the landward side. The man in charge of the defense of the city was General Benjamin Lincoln, who had about 5,500 troops under his command. New fortifications consisting of a line of redoubts and abatis were erected across Charleston Neck, along a canal between the Cooper and Ashley Rivers. Charleston itself was surrounded by a number of batteries, including the Grand Battery on the eastern end of the waterfront. A chain barrier was placed across the entrance to the Cooper River. The British naval squadron appeared in the harbor early in April, after Clinton's troops had taken Fort Johnson on March 6 as they moved across James Island. The siege of Charleston began on April 11 and the bombardment on April 13. According to Mark Boatner, author of the *Encyclopedia of the American Revolution*, the British, like the Americans at Boston, used prefabricated mantelets to advance their positions. [Note: These mantelets, prepared in New York, were 6 feet tall and 14 feet long and had three legs. They were moved into position by eighteen men and covered with dirt in front, creating an impromptu wall for a battery or redoubt.] The British siege lines continued to advance during the next few days. The third parallel was ready by April 25 and the first line of abatis taken on April 26. This placed British troops on the wet ditch, which they drained on May 6. On the same day, Fort Moultrie fell, leaving Charleston at the mercy of the British fleet on one side, and Clinton's troops on the other. The American lines could not hold much longer and provisions were low. On May 12, Lincoln was forced to surrender to avoid further destruction. The American force of over five thousand men was the largest Patriot contingent to surrender during the Revolutionary War.

Rebels and Tories continued the war in the South that led to the American defeat at Camden in August 1780 and then the defeat of the Tories at King's Mountain in October. Fortified posts proved vulnerable for the British, especially after their decisive defeat at Cowpens in January 1781, followed in March by a pyrrhic victory at Guilford Court House. In May 1781, American forces moved against FORT NINETY-SIX. The British garrison had not received their orders to evacuate the fort. They had strengthened their position by having slaves dig trenches and adding abatis. The Star Redoubt with 14-foot-high walls was added and linked to the town's stockade by a covered way. To the west, FORT HOLMES was built to protect access to the water supply. On May 22, the 28-day siege began with General Kosciuszko directing the work on the parallels. He built a Maham Tower 30 feet high and 30 yards from the Star Redoubt. (The Maham Tower was Hezekiah Maham's version of a modern siege tower like those used against castles. It consisted of a tower of prefabricated log cribs with a platform to give riflemen an elevated protected position so they could fire into the enemy defenses. It was first used in the American attack on FORT WATSON located between Charleston and Fort Ninety-Six in April 1781 where it kept the defenders from manning their positions and forced them to surrender.) Kosciuszko also opened a mine at the third parallel which was 6 feet below the surface, but did not reach the Star Redoubt in time for the premature assault

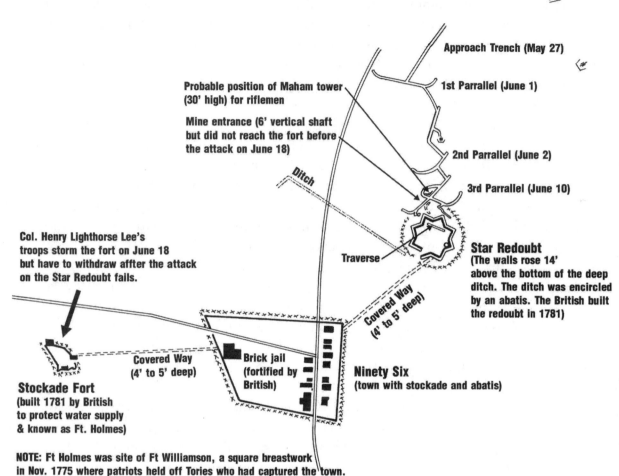

Siege of Ninety-Six
May-June 1781

© TOMASZ IDZIKOWSKI

Rebel Battery Positions (late May)

Kościuszko's Siege Works

Approach Trench (May 27)

Probable position of Maham tower (30' high) for riflemen

1st Parrallel (June 1)

Mine entrance (6' vertical shaft but did not reach the fort before the attack on June 18)

2nd Parrallel (June 2)

3rd Parrallel (June 10)

Ditch

Col. Henry Lighthorse Lee's troops storm the fort on June 18 but have to withdraw affter the attack on the Star Redoubt fails.

Traverse

Star Redoubt (The walls rose 14' above the bottom of the deep ditch. The ditch was encircled by an abatis. The British built the redoubt in 1781)

Covered Way (4' to 5' deep)

Covered Way (4' to 5' deep)

Brick jail (fortified by British)

Ninety Six (town with stockade and abatis)

Stockade Fort (built 1781 by British to protect water supply & known as Ft. Holmes)

NOTE: Ft Holmes was site of Ft Williamson, a square breastwork in Nov. 1775 where patriots held off Tories who had captured the town.

on June 17, launched because a British relief force was on the way. The Americans suffered numerous casualties and withdrew after failing to take the Star Redoubt and Fort Holmes. The relief force arrived on June 21 and the British evacuated the site.

While Sir Henry Clinton was campaigning in the South, the Patriots and their French allies planned to retake New York City, which had been left with a garrison of fifteen thousand redcoats. General Jean Baptiste de Rochambeau landed his army of five thousand at Newport in July 1780, preparing to join Washington in the campaign to recapture the city. Clinton returned with some of his troops in August to reinforce New York. But the British fleet kept the French in check at Newport, preventing the operation from going forward.

In the meantime, Lord Cornwallis was left in command in the south where he engaged in several actions against the Americans during the year that followed, as he moved north toward Virginia. Young General Lafayette was sent to keep an eye on

Cornwallis's army, which outnumbered his. Finally, Cornwallis moved into the Peninsula where Clinton ordered him to secure a base. He selected Yorktown, around which his 7,000-man contingent began building defenses. On August 30, 1781, Admiral François de Grasse's force of twenty-eight warships and 2,500 troops joined Lafayette. Cornwallis now found himself trapped as Washington and Rochambeau advanced from New York with thousands more troops.

As Washington's army moved from New York to Virginia to engage Cornwallis at Yorktown, one more important raid took place on September 6, 1781. Benedict Arnold, now serving the British, led a force estimated at eight hundred men against New London (CT) on the Thames River. On the west side of the river stood FORT TURNBULL, which had been started before the revolution but was not completed. It was occupied by only about twenty-five men so the defenders fired one volley, abandoned the fort, and moved over to Fort Griswold as Arnold's men plundered and burned New London.

FORT GRISWOLD, located on the east side of the river on Groton Heights, was a more formidable position and was manned by about 150 soldiers under Colonel Ledyard. A four-sided fort made of earth and faced with stone, its longest side was about eighty yards that included a salient (or redan) in the center. The other curtain walls, all about 12 feet high, were thirty to forty yards long and connected to two bastions. There were cannons in embrasures in all the walls, except the west wall between the two bastions and one of the southwest bastions where the battery was mounted en barbette. Except for the side with the guns en barbette, the remainder of the fort was surrounded by a deep ditch. Fraises on top of the walls further secured the position. The main gate on the north side was covered by a ravelin. A sally port in the form of a tunnel was located on the south side and led to a covered way that went down the hill to the Water Battery. The British demanded the Americans surrender Fort Griswold or receive no quarter. The British troops fixed their bayonets and stormed the fort taking considerable casualties, but they managed to fight their way inside forcing Colonel Ledyard to surrender. Although both sides agreed that the fighting was intense, they disagreed about what happened next. Over half the garrison was killed and most of the remainder was severely wounded. The Americans claimed there had been a massacre, while the British denied any such allegations

At YORKTOWN, Cornwallis now held an awkward position since there were few features amenable to defense. He set up an inner line of defenses, forming a semicircle around the city, but only about three hundred yards from the river at most points. Ten redoubts reinforced the entrenchments. A strong redoubt, called the FUSILIER'S REDOUBT, stood on the western flank. On the eastern flank were REDOUBTS #9 and #10, which played a key role in breaking his position. On the Hampton Road to the south, was a large crown work. Beyond it were several redoubts serving as outworks. Across the York River, at Gloucester, Cornwallis built entrenchments and reinforced them with four more redoubts. Unfortunately for Cornwallis, the British Royal Navy was no longer able to control the American coast in the autumn of 1781. After its defeat at the battle of the Virginia Capes on September 5, Cornwallis's position became quite precarious.

At the end of September, Washington's forces moved into position to begin the siege of Yorktown and Cornwallis decided to abandon the redoubts of his outworks. French and American troops began digging the first parallel on October 7 and the artillery moved into place on the 9th. The second parallel was begun on October 11, but could not be extended to the river until Redoubts #9 and #10 were taken. On the night of October 14, the French attacked Redoubt #9 and the Americans assaulted Redoubt #10. The assaults were preceded by a massive bombardment of the two positions. The besiegers worked their way through the abatis, quickly covering the last twenty to twenty-five yards toward the redoubts. Before working their way through the fraises protruding from the redoubts, they had to get over the ditch. Mark Boatner, author of the *Encyclopedia of the American Revolution*, believes that the Americans reached their objective sooner than the French because they did not wait for pioneers to clear a path for them and not that Redoubt #10 was defended by 45 men instead of 120 like at Redoubt #9. Besides a small sortie from the crown work to raid the American positions early in the morning of October 16, the British did not defend themselves vigorously. An attempt by Cornwallis to evacuate that night to Gloucester failed. Early on October 17, 1781, the sixty-five artillery pieces at Yorktown were overwhelmed by a French and American cannonade of up to one hundred guns set in the siege lines. Cornwallis surrendered his army on the same day. The main British force under Clinton remained holed up in the defenses around New York. However, after Yorktown, no further major battles followed and the Treaty of Paris brought the war to an end in 1783.

From the very beginning to the end, the American War of Independence heavily involved fortifications. From Ticonderoga to Yorktown, many battles were fought around earthen, masonry, earth-and-stone or timber-and-log works built either prior to or during the Revolutionary War. More often than not, these works resembled field fortifications rather than the durable defenses strewn across Europe. Nonetheless, they represented a great expenditure of capital and labor and became an integral part of the early history of the United States of America.

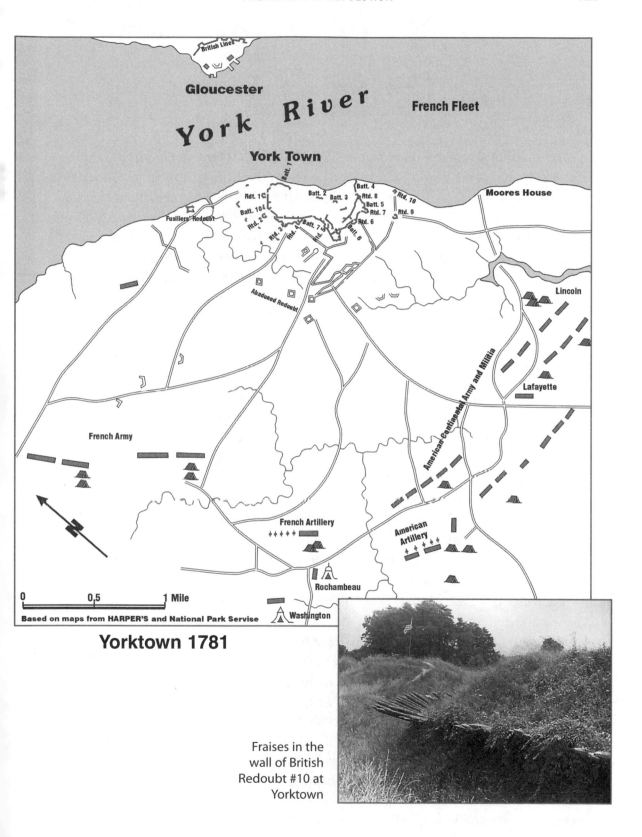

British Lines

Gloucester

York River

French Fleet

York Town

Batt. 1

Rdt. 1
Batt. 10
Batt. 2
Batt. 3
Batt. 4
Rtd. 8
Batt. 5
Rtd. 7
Rtd. 10
Rtd. 9

Moores House

Fusiliers' Redoubt
Rtd. 2
Rtd. 3
Rtd. 4
Batt. 7
Batt. 6

Abadoned Redoubt

Lincoln

American Continental Army and Militia

Lafayette

French Army

French Artillery
+ + + + +

American Artillery
+ + + +

Rochambeau

0   0.5   1 Mile

Based on maps from HARPER'S and National Park Servise

Washington

Yorktown 1781

Fraises in the wall of British Redoubt #10 at Yorktown

The Spanish Conquest of the Floridas: Five Forts that Failed

At the end of the Seven Years War in 1763, the French were expelled from Louisiana and the Spanish exchanged Florida for Cuba with the British. The Spanish took over Louisiana and its capital at New Orleans as the British occupied the French and Spanish fortifications in Pensacola, Mobile, and Natchez on the Mississippi. Although the British controlled a large part of the Lower Mississippi, they could not use the main shipping exit at New Orleans. While developing a water route to bypass New Orleans, they built FORT BUTE (also known as FORT MANCHAC) in 1766 at the point where the Iberville River branches off from the Mississippi and leads to Lake Pontchartrain. This stockade that held a garrison of fifty men was rectangular in shape and had demi-bastions.

Further up the Mississippi in 1764, the British rebuilt old Fort Rosalie, first constructed by Bienville in 1716, at the site of modern-day Natchez and renamed it FORT PANMURE. But the main British stronghold on the Mississippi was FORT NEW RICHMOND at Baton Rouge, also known as the Spanish FORT SAN CARLOS. This earthen fort was built by Lieutenant Colonel Alexander Dickson in 1779 when it was feared that the Spanish would enter the war. Fort New Richmond mounted thirteen cannons capable of dealing with any threat from the river or landward side. Its walls were 18 feet thick and were surrounded by a 9-foot-deep moat.

The British also held Biloxi, Mobile, and Pensacola as part of West Florida (Florida was divided into East and West at the Appalachicola River). At the time about two-thirds of the population of West Florida lived near the Mississippi. Pensacola, the capital of West Florida, was home to a third of the population of West Florida.

When the British took over West Florida, they found it already fortified by the French and the Spanish. In Mobile, they renamed Fort Condé, built of brick by the French, as FORT CHAROLETTE. When they first landed in 1763, they also found a Spanish blockhouse, known as FORT SAN MIGUEL, near the bay shore of Pensacola. There they built FORT PENSACOLA, a stockade that rotted within a few years. The fort was designed by the engineer Captain Elias Durnford and General Haldimand. In 1767, it was expanded in all directions from the bay to span about 1,400 feet at a distance of about 850 feet from the shore. Norman Simons, author of "The Pensacola Fortifications," informs us that the fort was a five-sided stockade shaped like a house, with a peaked roof pointing north. It was reinforced with four two-story blockhouses. Simons also mentions an advanced redoubt 150 feet by 75 feet with a wet moat and cannon located north of the fort.

In 1778, shortly before the Spanish declared war, General John Campbell was dispatched from New York with a contingent of British troops and German mercenaries to take command in West Florida. Shortly after his arrival, he began improving the defenses of Pensacola. According to Simons, Parker began upgrading the Pensacola defenses by closing off the entrance to the bay and building the ROYAL NAVY REDOUBT (or RED CLIFFS REDOUBT) in 1780, at a point near present-day Fort Barrancas. Located on the highest ground, the redoubt built of fascines held eleven cannons (five 32-pdrs taken from Fort George and six 6-pdrs).

In 1780, at a point over one thousand yards north of Pensacola and the fort on top of Gage Hill, Campbell rebuilt the blockhouse and stockade known as FORT GEORGE, a square earthwork with palisades, about 240 feet on each side and demi-bastions in each corner. It also had a dry moat and a glacis and had room for twenty cannons. It included a hornwork on the southwest slope that protected the water supply. Only three hundred yards to the north stood the PRINCE OF WALES REDOUBT, the last position built by the British in the area. Built between 1780 and 1781, the redoubt was another earthwork built to mount five cannons. The QUEEN'S REDOUBT or ADVANCED REDOUBT was built shortly before the Prince of Wales Redoubt, about three hundred yards to the northwest to control the high ground. This earthwork was designed for fifty men and four cannons. Campbell concentrated his men and cannons at Fort George and the two earthen redoubts to the north, assigning more cannons to these positions then they were originally designed to hold.

In 1779, FORT BUTE fell before a quick assault by Spanish forces and many of its defenders retreated to Baton Rouge. Weeks later, FORT NEW RICHMOND failed to hold out longer than a day after the Spanish began the bombardment. Its commander surrendered and ordered FORT PANMURE at Natchez to surrender as well. Mobile's FORT CHAROLETTE fell after a day of bombardment in 1780. It took the Spanish several weeks in 1781 to maneuver into position at Pensacola after landing on Santa Rosa Island. When they finally got close enough to begin the bombardment of the British positions, they targeted the Queen's Redoubt. Shortly after the cannonade began, the redoubt's magazine exploded, inflicting a great deal of destruction and thus allowing the Spanish to seize the position. Before the day was over, Campbell surrendered Fort George before the Spanish could move their cannons into position. None of the West Florida forts resisted more than several hours of bombardment and assault during the entire campaign.

Source: *SIEGE: Spain and Britain: Battle of Pensacola*, edited by Virginia Parks, and *Guardians of the Gulf* by James and Irene Coleman

War of 1812
© TOMASZ IDZIKOWSKI

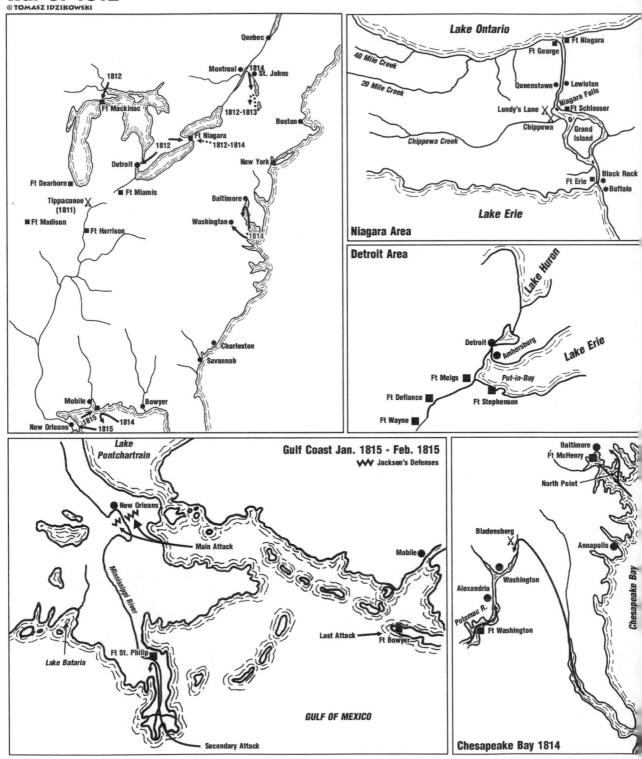

Niagara Area

Lake Ontario
40 Mile Creek
20 Mile Creek
Ft Niagara
Ft George
Queenstown • Lewiston
Lundy's Lane ✕ Niagara Falls
Ft Schlosser
Chippewa
Chippewa Creek
Grand Island
Ft Erie
Black Rock
Buffalo
Lake Erie

Quebec
Montreal • 1814 • St. Johns
1812-1813
Boston
1812
Ft Mackinac
1812
Ft Niagara
1812-1814
Detroit
New York
Ft Dearborn
Ft Miamis
Tippacanoe ✕
(1811)
Baltimore
Ft Madison
Washington
Ft Harrison
1814
Charleston
Savannah
Mobile • Bowyer
New Orleans 1815 1814
1815

Detroit Area

Lake Huron
Detroit
Amhersburg
Lake Erie
Ft Meigs
Put-in-Bay
Ft Defiance
Ft Stephenson
Ft Wayne

Gulf Coast Jan. 1815 - Feb. 1815
〰〰 Jackson's Defenses

Lake Pontchartrain
New Orleans
Main Attack
Mobile
Mississippi River
Last Attack
Ft Bowyer
Lake Bataria
Ft St. Philip
GULF OF MEXICO
Secondary Attack

Chesapeake Bay 1814

Baltimore
Ft McHenry
North Point
Bladensberg ✕
Annapolis
Washington
Alexandria
Potomac R.
Ft Washington
Chesapeake Bay

Chapter 4

FORTIFYING AMERICA:
1783–1815

THE NEW NATION THAT EMERGED FROM the American Revolution had a government based on the Articles of Confederation, which organized the Thirteen States into the United States of America bound together by a weak central government. The individual states retained a great deal of sovereignty, being actually like true nations. The Confederation had no power to tax or raise an army. The states had the burden of financing the central government and providing troops for the army, but their obligation was limited. Each state was required to maintain a militia force, and by the end of June 1784, there was virtually no regular army, as Congress had disbanded it. The only force that remained was a contingent of eighty artillerymen under Major John Doughty, the highest-ranking officer in the U.S. Army. Later, Congress ordered the formation of a force of about seven hundred militiamen, which became the 1st Regiment of a new army in September 1784. Congress sold off the navy's last ship in 1785. As far as fortifications were concerned, West Point and Fort Pitt were the only forts with garrisons. Thus, besides the state militia and one lonely regiment, there was no U.S. army to oppose the British troops still occupying part of the Northwest Territory including Detroit. With the adoption of the 1787 Constitution, Congress authorized the creation of a regular army, which numbered about eight hundred men in the spring of 1789 at the time the War Department was created.

Occupation and Defense of the Northwest Territory

During the late 1780s, a few forts were built in the Ohio country. FORT HARMAR, built in 1785 by Major John Doughty, was one of the earliest of these frontier forts. It was situated near the Virginia border at Marietta where the Muskingum River flows into the

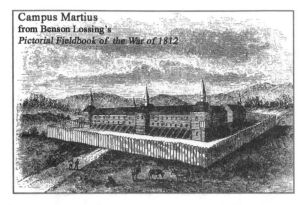

Campus Martius
from Benson Lossing's
Pictorial Fieldbook of the War of 1812

Ohio. From this five-sided stockade with five corner bastions General Josiah Harmar led one of his first unsuccessful expeditions against the Maumee Indians in 1789. FORT FINNEY was also built in 1785 in the southwest corner of Ohio, on the Miami River.

Harmar established a chain of forts stretching all the way to Vincennes, Indiana. One of these forts, known as CAMPUS MARTIUS (Field of Mars), was actually a fortified settlement, built in 1788 a short distance from Fort Harmar, up the Muskingum River. Established by a group of settlers from New England led by veteran general Rufus Putnam, it was an impressive site with four corner blockhouses and walls 180 feet long built completely of logs. Initially the fort consisted of houses or cabins forming a square with four corner blockhouses whose roofs later sprouted guardposts in the form of cupolas. The walls of the houses, which formed the exterior of the fort, were built of four-inch thick planks placed horizontally. A later drawing of Campus Martius shows an angled palisade sited between blockhouses and a stockade around the original site. After suppressing the Indians, the army abandoned the fort and its settlers hauled off the logs for their own use.

The method of construction employed at Campus Martius, called "TENON-AND-MORTISE," used in many log fortifications in the west, was extremely practical because it permitted rapid replacement or expansion of a structure. It consisted of placing planks with tenons into specially prepared vertical framing posts. The frame, like the wall of a house or a barn, was assembled first and placed upright on a foundation, usually of stone. Once the frame was in position, the planks were added. These planks were usually up to 4 inches thick—enough to stop a bullet. (See Glossary: tenon and mortise.)

In 1790, Major John Doughty oversaw the construction of FORT WASHINGTON on the site of modern-day Cincinnati. David Simmons, author of *The Forts of Anthony Wayne*, notes that it was built on a major ford of the Ohio River used by the Indians. This fort, built with the same tenon-and-mortise method as Campus Martius, measured 200 feet by 200 feet and had four five-sided, two-storied, corner blockhouses projecting out like bastions. Each blockhouse had a distinctive cupola for a sentry box on the roof and mounted cannons on the upper level. These blockhouses resembled the ones built by Doughty years earlier at Fort Harmar. Their walls were lined by two-story buildings, mostly troop quarters. On two sides, additional walls projected out to form a triangular ravelin-like structure,

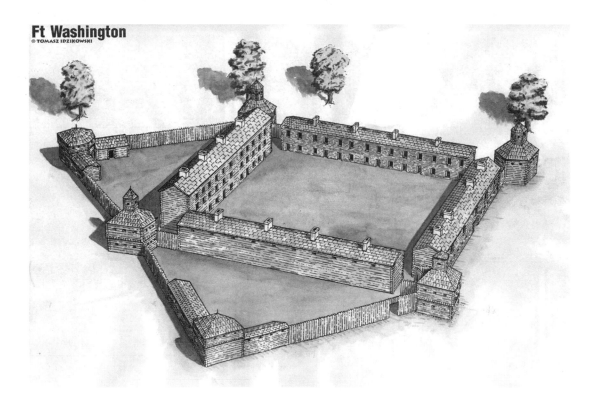

Ft Washington
© TOMASZ IDZIKOWSKI

more like a salient (see Glossary) because it was not separate from the fort, with a simple blockhouse at each corner. The fort also housed an underground magazine measuring 10 feet by 12 feet. In 1790, General Harmar moved his troops from Fort Harmar to Fort Washington, making it his main base of operations.

Following devastating Indian raids, the army, heavily reinforced with militia, engaged the Maumee tribe in the northwest between 1790 and 1792, suffering several defeats and the loss of most of its soldiers. After Harmar's 1790 expedition failed, Governor Arthur St. Clair received command of the army in 1791 and Congress authorized the creation of a second regiment. St. Clair tried to establish a line of forts to secure his lines of communications, but did not have the resources to achieve his aim, according to Simmons. In addition, his regulars were poorly trained and equipped and the militia, which made up the bulk of his force, were unreliable. In fact, these troops proved to be better at building than fighting.

In 1791, St. Clair set his men to work on FORT HAMILTON, to the north of Fort Washington, on the Great Miami River. This rectangular palisade with four corner bastions was later reinforced with blockhouses placed on top of the northern and southern bastions. Further to the north, FORT JEFFERSON was built in a period of ten days by two hundred of St. Clair's men in October 1791. Its 114-feet-long walls were connected with corner-bastions, two of which had two-story blockhouses. The larger upper-level of the blockhouses formed an overhang to protect the base of the walls and served as machicoulis, a relatively standard feature in American forts of this period. According to

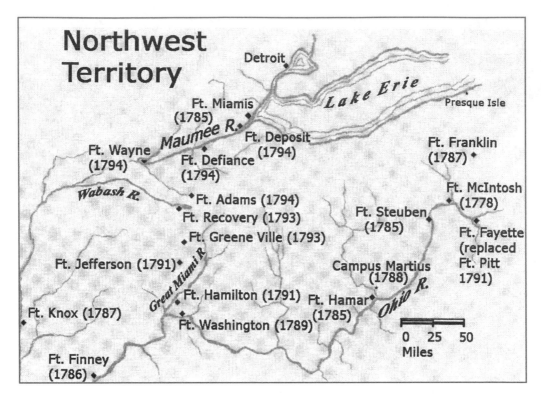

Simmons, Fort Jefferson and Fort Hamilton were built by William Fergueson and their design was similar to Fort Ligonier which St. Clair had commanded during the Revolution. Like Campus Martius, Fort Jefferson began as a square enclosure formed by log buildings with four corner blockhouses. Later loopholes were cut into the barrack walls that formed the fort's exterior. The idea of incorporating the barracks into the curtains was first implemented at Fort Washington, also built by Fergueson. These common features, according to Simmons, seem to indicate that St. Clair and Fergueson were both involved in the design and construction of these forts and that they continued to use styles they were familiar with since they had no other guidelines. Since there were no regulation designs for frontier forts at the time, the only rule that applied was that the walls be thick enough to stop musketballs.

After building these forts, St. Clair's army moved on, leaving about ninety men incapable of continuing the march to garrison Fort Jefferson. St. Clair's army was ambushed and almost wiped out near the Wabash in November 1791. This unnamed battle on the Wabash, sometimes referred to as St. Clair's defeat, was the army's worst defeat at the hands of Native Americans. Appalled by this debacle and finally made aware of the inadequacy of the militia, Congress authorized a larger regular army in 1792. The army was reorganized into a mixed-arms force of infantry, cavalry, and artillery, and was given the name of Legion. General Anthony Wayne was appointed as its leader. After training his new troops, Wayne moved to Fort Washington on the Ohio River, determined to reduce the Indian population.

While the new army was forming, FORT JEFFERSON remained exposed deep in Indian Territory. In spite of poor morale and desertions, it gamely held out until 1793. After Wayne moved into western Ohio, he restored several of the old forts and built new ones as he advanced northward. In 1792, General James Wilkinson took command of the forts in the territory and expanded Fort Jefferson in preparation for the coming offensive. He extended it with a new section of wall by adding stables and granaries with the loopholed walls. The fort was to serve as a supply depot for the Legion's advance. At FORT HAMILTON, Wilkinson added a redan on the south side and a rectangular enclosure on the north side that included a granary and barracks for dragoons. Further to the north, in 1792, Wilkinson set to work on FORT ST. CLAIR, a square fort with short curtains and four large bastions.

Early in 1794, at a short distance to the north of Fort Jefferson, Wayne completed FORT GREENE VILLE, the largest of the frontier forts. As was his custom, notes David Simmons, he built redoubts around his encampment before beginning work on the main fortifications in order to protect the workers, mostly soldiers. Fort Greene Ville was a stockade forming a rectangle about 900 feet by 1,800 feet. Its 10-foot-high walls connected the four corner bastions.

At the end of July 1794, on his way north, Wayne advanced past FORT RECOVERY, which had been built only a few months earlier near the site of St. Clair's defeat, to support his 1794 campaign. Fort Recovery included four corner blockhouses that were later given a second story by the fort commander, Captain Alexander Gibson. It saw action as soon as June 1794, when it was put under siege by an Indian contingent that destroyed a supply column of about one hundred soldiers. However, this siege lasted only a day or so. At Wayne's approach, the Indians, still recovering from the losses they had incurred in their successful ambush, broke off the siege despite the taunts of the fort's garrison.

Having bypassed Fort Recovery, Anthony Wayne stopped to build FORT ADAMS further north on the St. Marys River. This fort was designed as a small square with two large blockhouses at opposite corners measuring 18 feet by 18 feet, that were almost as large as the fort with its 24-foot-long curtains.

Proceeding north in early August, Wayne set up another fort on a commanding site at the place where the Auglaize River empties into the Maumee River and named it FORT DEFIANCE. The fort's palisade was sixty feet long. A palisaded ravelin pointed toward the angle formed by the two rivers. At each corner of the fort was a square blockhouse with 22-feet-long sides and one embrasure on each side for artillery.

In mid-August 1794, Anthony Wayne moved east along the Maumee River with 3,500 men. On August 18, he stopped briefly to build FORT DEPOSIT, a fortified encampment with three large enclosures made of breastworks and corner bastions. Wayne left about two hundred men behind to complete this position and guard the baggage as he proceeded to engage the Indians in battle. He defeated the Indians at the end of the month at Fallen Timbers, near the site of modern-day Toledo, within sight of the British at Fort Miamis.

The British FORT MIAMIS was quickly built in 1794 about fifty-five miles from Detroit, on the site of an older army post near the mouth of the Maumee River and its rapids. It was intended as an advance position to protect the British forces in the Northwest Territory, which, according to the terms of the Treaty of Paris of 1783, should have been withdrawn. The impressive earthen fort included two large diamond-shaped corner bastions on either side of the gate and a formidable deep ditch with a wide belt of abatis beyond the counterscarp and ramparts bristling with fraises. A large triangular ravelin in front of the gate covered the curtain between the two large bastions. At least one of the large bastions had an artillery platform. The side of the fort facing the river included two smaller bastions and a large river battery. This fort was designed not only to resist musket fire but also artillery rounds. According to some sources, it mounted as many as fourteen cannons. The defeated Indians pleaded for protection from the British, but the fort's commander, Major William Campbell, turned them away to prevent an incident. Wayne demanded the fort's surrender, but Campbell refused. Wayne chose not to put the fort under siege because a few militiamen captured with some Indians revealed that the garrison was 400-men-strong and had a number of artillery pieces. He was also informed that over a thousand militiamen had assembled at Detroit and were on their way to relieve the fort. It appeared that John Graves Simcoe, lieutenant governor of Upper Canada, had ordered the Canadian militia to move to Fort Miamis. Nonetheless, Wayne tried to provoke Campbell into action by burning crops and Indian villages in the area, but the British officer did not rise to the challenge. Finally, Wayne withdrew to FORT DEFIANCE, opting to improve its defenses by making it artillery proof in the event the British became aggressive. He encircled the fort with a 14- to 16-foot-wide and 8-foot-deep ditch. The dirt excavated from the ditch was used to create the earthen walls around the timber fort to resist artillery. Fraises and a drawbridge were also added.

After securing his position at Fort Defiance, Wayne moved up the Maumee River to the junction of the St. Marys and St. Joseph Rivers in the heart of Miami territory. There,

Fort Wayne before the War of 1812.

in October 1794, he built FORT WAYNE, near the site of an earlier French fort known as Fort Miami. Wayne's chief engineer and artillery officer was Major Henry Burbeck, a veteran of the Revolutionary War who had served under Colonel Richard Gridley, the army's first chief engineer. According to Walter Font, author of an article titled "A Garrison at

Miami Town: Fort Wayne," the first step in building Fort Wayne was selecting the site. The second step was clearing the site, which took about 250 soldiers to accomplish between September 18 and September 20. In the meantime, the design and layout of the fort were completed and workers staked out the site. On September 22, the soldiers began cutting timber and hauling it back to camp to build the barracks and block-houses. Wooden forms were set out to indicate where the earthen walls would be erected. On October 6, about a hundred men began digging up the soil necessary for the fort's walls. In another six days, the wooden elements of the walls were completed and the troops continued hauling or shoveling the earth into them. By October 22, the men had finished most of the fort's perimeter, including a 16-foot ditch. The rest of the work was left for those who remained behind as a garrison. They finished the earthen defenses, roofed the barracks, and worked on some additional wooden structures that required much more time to complete. However, the new fort was ready to go into operation just over a month after the initial construction had begun. Fort Wayne turned out to be a square fort of 250 feet (272 feet according to an old plan drawn by Burbeck) with a bastion at the two southern angles and only a small space between them. The bastions had earthen platforms for artillery. The earthen curtains were lined with the walls of the barracks and other structures. A guardhouse was placed over the entrance on the northern curtain facing the mouth of the Maumee River. Like Fort Defiance, the fort was given an earthen wall as protection against artillery.

Fort Wayne was the only fort Anthony Wayne initially built in the west to resist artillery with earthen walls instead of wooden walls, like the other forts he built during the campaign. In the years that followed, however, the trend in frontier fort building returned to the use of wooden walls since the main opponents were Native Americans who did not have artillery. Bastions, so important in the age of artillery, were largely replaced with wooden blockhouses for the same reason.

The old FORT MASSAC, built by the French in 1757, stood near the mouth of the Ohio River on its north bank. After the French left, it fell into disrepair and was rebuilt by Anthony Wayne in 1794 to protect the frontier against the Spanish.

The army broke the resistance of the Indians in the region during the next year and the Treaty of Greenville was signed in August 1795. The Ohio territory was open and secure thanks to the forts. Wayne's forts remained for only a few years, until the British evacuated the Northwest Territory, including Fort Miamis and Fort Detroit in July 1796. The Americans occupied Fort Miamis for a short time, but soon abandoned it along with most of Wayne's forts, except for Fort Wayne, Fort Defiance, and Fort Washington, which were not maintained and deteriorated.

After the treaty at Fort Greenville in 1795 ended the resistance of the Indians and Jay's Treaty forced the withdrawal of the British from the northwest, the American military did additional work to secure the frontier. The British evacuated FORT LERNOULT in Detroit in 1796, leaving it to the Americans. This fort consisted of an earthen rampart with four half bastions, a ditch, and a palisade in its center. One of the last forts to be built at the present site of Chicago was FORT DEARBORN, named for the secretary of war in August 1803. Encircled by a 12-foot-high stockade, the fort had two tall blockhouses and stood at the mouth of the Chicago River. FORT ADAMS was built to protect the frontier against the Spanish by General Wilkinson between October 1798 and 1799 on Loftus Height, Mississippi, overlooking the Mississippi River. This earthwork included a barracks and was so heavily garrisoned that an additional cantonment had to be built. It was abandoned in 1810.

Supplying the Forts:
The Quartermaster General's Department

Early in the nineteenth century, the U.S. Army still consisted of only combat branches with no supply or support services beyond a handful of officers appointed to handle those functions by contracting civilians. The common method of employing civilian contractors to supply the forts and military posts was through newspapers. Thus, the March 19, 1807, issue of the *American Mercury* published in Hartford (CT) carried a notice dated February 23, 1807, posted by the War Office:

Notice is Hereby Given,

That separate proposals will be received at the Office of the secretary of the department of war, until 12 O'clock at noon of the first day Wednesday in June next, for the supply of all rations that may be required for the use of the United States, from the first day of October 1807, until the 30th day of September 1808 ... at the following places ...

The places listed in the notice included Detroit, Michilimackinac, Fort Wayne, Chicago, Cherokee Nation, Nashville, Fort Massac, Vincennes, Chickasaw Bluffs, Aransas, Fort Adams, St. Louis, St. Charles, Chokia, New Orleans, Natchitoches, Charleston, Fort McHenry, Fort Mifflin, Pittsburgh, Fort Jay, West Point, Fort Trumbull, Fort Wolcott, Fort Independence, Portsmouth, Portland, and a number of other posts. This gives an idea of how the military garrisoned its forts and relied almost entirely on civilian services from the coast to the frontier. It was not until March 1812 that the Quartermaster General's Department was formed. The Quartermaster Corps was formed in May and a year later, a commissary general of purchases was appointed to put these supply activities under military control. However, it was not until 1842 that the Quartermaster General's Department finally took over all supply functions. But the garrisons in the far-flung outposts of the United States had to rely for the most part on a civilian supply system for many years after.

The Construction of America's First Frontier Fortifications

By David A. Simmons

The Northwest Territory, established in the 1780s was the United States's first real frontier. To establish control, the American army began building a series of frontier forts. The construction of these forts followed certain patterns and was based on three important considerations: first was the public's concern about keeping costs low; next they had to be large enough to house and provide for the movement of stores and supplies; finally, they needed to be small enough for a minimal garrison. Those who designed the frontier forts initially made them strong enough to resist nothing more than bullets, since the Indians had no artillery. Anthony Wayne changed the design of his forts to make them resistant to artillery should the British became hostile. Many frontier fort walls were timber stockade, but some also included "modern" features such as bastions or half-bastions. Blockhouses were frequently added to bastions, especially when the enemy was not believed capable of deploying heavy artillery. Some fort plans included a star shape, supposedly a French creation that eliminated the need for bastions by including a redan-type position, salients, on each wall. It lowered both the cost and construction time. The triangular-shaped fort was useful when only a small garrison was available. It provided the least number of walls to defend but left too much exterior ground exposed.

The blockhouse was a common form of independent defensive position and was often erected by civilian forces. They were usually two-story structures whose upper floor extended out over the sides of the lower. Openings in the projections allowed defenders to cover the base of the blockhouse. These were usually all-wood structures, but the first level was occasionally masonry.

The most common type of frontier fort wall was the stockade. A single line of logs was stood on end in a trench and reinforced with bracing to keep them stable. Spaces were often left between logs but officers preferred either to close the gaps between the logs with boards or to add a second row of smaller logs to seal these openings. In some cases, fort walls were made of horizontal logs as was done in most blockhouses. At other times, a pair of such walls was laid parallel to each other and the space filled with earth. This made them capable of resisting artillery but was not as effective against cannon fire as earthen walls.

An earthen fort was erected by first laying out a wooden framework to mark the limits of the parapet. Workers excavated the outer ditch and used the spoil to fill the framework and create the earthen wall. Slabs of sod could be used to protect the fill from weathering and maintain its shape, but if that was not possible, fascines, hurdles, or gabions were used. The engineers could also create a revetmented scarp by using stone or timber to maintain the shape of the wall.

Blockhouse at Fort Dayton in New York.
Photo courtesy of Don Stoetzel.

Creation of the Army Engineers
and the First System of Coastal Defenses

Before 1796, tensions had continued to mount between Great Britain and the United States as American ships were stopped by the Royal Navy on the high seas. This problem was compounded by the fact that the British military refused to abandon its forts in the Northwest Territory. In addition, American shipping was constantly threatened by the Barbary pirates of North Africa, a problem that was temporarily solved when the Americans agreed to pay them tribute in the early 1790s. In January 1794, America's virtual helplessness on the high seas in the face of British aggression finally spurred Congress to authorize the creation of a navy. Six frigates were built, however this fledgling navy was not adequate to protect the American coastline in the event of foreign invasion. As a result, the army examined the problem of coastal defense in 1794 with the specific object to deter a British invasion. In February 1794, Congress authorized the appointment of temporary engineers to direct the construction of fortifications for key American ports, to protect them from invasion and defend the new navy's bases of operation. Secretary of War Henry Knox selected seven Frenchmen for the job, one of whom was Pierre Charles L'Enfant, the man who had designed the new capital of Washington, D.C., in 1791. Knox first called upon Major Stephen Rochfontaine, who had arrived during the Revolutionary War and made a significant contribution at the siege of Yorktown. In 1795, Congress created the Corps of Artillerists and Engineers, a single regiment that remained under the command of Lieutenant Colonel Rochfontaine until May 1798. His second and third in command were Major Lewis Tousard and Major John Jacob Ulrich Rivardi. For the first time since the end of the revolution, military engineers were organized for the army and again a Frenchman was in charge.

On March 20, 1794, Congress authorized funds for the construction of coastal fortifications at sixteen designated sites to which it later added four more. During that year, a number of Frenchmen escaping the French Revolution, including the two already mentioned, served as temporary engineers to repair some of the older fortifications. Rochfontaine directed the construction of fortifications on the coast of New England at New London, Newport, Boston, Marblehead, Salem, Cape Ann, Portsmouth, and Portland. Most of these fortifications, except those at Boston where the state government blocked his efforts, were completed by the end of the year. Charles Vincent handled the defenses of New York. Charles L'Enfant handled the work at Philadelphia and Wilmington (DE), J. J. Ulrich Rivardi was appointed as the engineer for Baltimore and Norfolk, while John Vermonnet took charge of the work at Annapolis and Alexandria. Nicholas F. Martinon was the engineer for Wilmington (NC) and Ocracoke Inlet. Paul Hyacinte Perrault was assigned to the Deep South at Charleston, Georgetown (South Carolina), and Savannah. All these engineers had their projects well underway before the end of the year except Martinon and Vermonnet, who achieved very little.

Following instructions, these engineers built earthen batteries with timber reinforcement in areas where the soil was not adhesive enough to hold together. According to the custom of the day, the earthen walls were sloped and covered with sod or short creeping grass, known as knot grass, in order to prevent erosion of the ramparts. The most important and the largest batteries that defended the key harbors were usually protected by an enclosed fortification or redoubt. The secondary batteries had the protection of a wooden blockhouse. Congress preferred earthen forts not only because they afforded the best protection against cannon fire, but also because they were more economical in the short run.

These coastal forts of the 1790s are considered part of the 1ST SYSTEM OF COASTAL FORTIFICATIONS and were identified as such by General Totten in the mid-1850s. At the end of 1794, FORT JAY (New York), FORT MIFFLIN (Philadelphia), FORT WHETSTONE (renamed FORT MCHENRY in 1798), and FORT JOHNSON (Charleston) represented the major works of this new system. Each was assigned a garrison of one company from the Corps of Artillerists and Engineers. As the years passed, these American fortifications eroded, turning mostly into piles of dirt. Meanwhile, the British and Spanish continued to maintain and build masonry fortifications to secure their New World possessions.

According to a 1928 article titled "Early Coast Fortification" in the *Coast Artillery Journal*, the batteries of these early American forts mounted either 12-, 18- or 24-pdr cannons or 8- or 5.5-inch howitzers or mortars ranging from 5.5-inch to 16-inch most of which dated from the Revolution. In 1794, Congress authorized 24-pdr and 32-pdr cannons for these forts. It was estimated that 450 cannons of these calibers were needed, however, only 150 were available. The individual states were expected to provide the same number and private industry was to manufacture the remaining 150. In addition, Congress authorized the purchase of one hundred cannons of each caliber to have sufficient stocks on hand. Congress allotted about 60 percent of the appropriations for the construction of the fortifications to the procurement of two hundred cannons. In 1801, the 42-pdr cannons were installed in some of the batteries.

In 1798, as these new fortifications were deteriorating from exposure to wind and rain, and the country became involved in an undeclared war with France, Congress authorized a second project to improve the works of the 1st System. Although no new sites were created, several were abandoned, including Cape Ann, Wilmington (DE), Annapolis, Alexandria, and Georgetown (SC). The project was intended to repair and restore the works at the most important positions and bolster the defenses of Newport, New York, Philadelphia, Baltimore, and Charleston. The project of 1798 also gave the funds needed to make some improvements on a few batteries and forts. In addition, five major ports that had not been adequately defended received new positions. However, most of the work was finished or stopped in 1800.

The 1st System positions could hardly be considered formidable, but Rochfontaine, as commandant of engineers, could do little to change the situation considering the limitations imposed by Congress. Until that time, Major Tousard had worked on improving the defenses of West Point and designing a more modern Fort Mifflin. In May 1798, Lt. Colonel Henry Burbeck succeeded Rochfontaine as commandant and held the position until April 1802. Major Tousard was appointed as the inspector of fortifications in March 1799, a function he had performed since 1797. He had also been the inspector of artillery since 1798. Tousard held these positions until the end of 1801.

The fact that the four battalion Corps of Artillerists & Engineers in 1798 included few men trained as artillerymen or engineers was a serious problem. French involvement remained strong under Burbeck simply because of this lack of trained American engineers. Included in the improvements of the 1798 project, were the defenses of Narragansett Bay designed by Tousard and the construction of the masonry fort of Fort McHenry at Baltimore. Jean Foncin worked on Boston's Fort Independence in 1799. Tousard finished L'Enfant's work at Fort McHenry, which was based on Foncin's design. Another Frenchman, Bureaux de Pusy, directed work on the defenses of New York City. However, the situation of these French engineers became awkward under the presidency of the Anglophile John Adams. When Thomas Jefferson replaced John Adams in 1801, their circumstances changed again.

In the South, in Charleston harbor, Governor William Moultrie resumed work on FORT MOULTRIE in 1794, employing slaves and white workers alike. But construction stopped at the end of 1795 and did not resume until the next war scare in 1798 when the original plan was modified and reduced in size. The people of Charleston had to contribute to the financing to supplement federal funds. When it was finished, the fort was a pentagonal structure with an 8-foot-deep moat and 50-foot-wide glacis. It mounted several 12-pdrs and ten old French 26-pdrs. It also had a brick magazine and a hot-shot furnace.

Little attention was given to the western frontier after the British withdrawal from the Northwest Territory in 1796. As war with France loomed on the horizon in 1798, a second regiment was added to the Corps placed under the command of Lt. Colonel John Doughty, the builder of the forts in the Ohio country during the Indian wars, who came out of retirement. Since this arrangement was not producing engineers capable of handling the construction of America's forts, Lt. Colonel Burbeck recommended the reformation of the Corps of Engineers in 1800. However, the Corps did not materialize until 1802. Although Burbeck had built forts during Wayne's campaign in the Northwest, he was trained as an artilleryman and became commander of the new artillery corps. He went on to develop the first American produced cast-iron cannons that were needed in the new forts.

Major Jonathan Williams, more scientist than soldier, was promoted to commander of the new Corps of Engineers in April 1802, after Secretary of War Henry Dearborn began removing the French officers who had helped establish the army engineers. Williams held this position until he resigned in June 1803. President Jefferson convinced him in April 1805 to return to active service, as commandant of the Corps of Engineers and promoted him to colonel. Williams remained in this position until July 1812. During his tenure, he had to face a new problem. After the purchase of the Louisiana Territory from France, he had to take into consideration the defenses of the new western frontier beyond the Mississippi.

In addition to the creation of the new Corps of Engineers, a school for training officers was established at West Point to produce the skilled military engineers the country lacked. In 1802, besides serving as chief engineer, Williams became the first commandant of the military engineer school at West Point where the headquarters of the Corps of Engineers were located. *The Elements of Fortification* by French General de Belairs, a book Williams had translated in 1799, became the basic engineer manual through the War of 1812. The academy at West Point was left in the hands of the most senior instructor in 1807 as the engineers were stretched thin with Williams working on the harbor defenses of New York and other officers of the Corps of Engineers fortifying other cities.

Some significant changes took place during the last phase of work on the 1st System. Willard Robinson, author of *American Forts*, points out that during the project of 1798 an Englishman named Benjamin H. Latrobe instituted an important design change during his work at FORT NELSON at Norfolk, Virginia, that would characterize American fortifications in the early 19th century. Instead of using the embrasures for cannons that Rivardi had designed for the 1794 project, Latrobe devised a continuous parapet for the guns. In addition, he added bastions to the parapet and made other improvements. The continuous parapet allowed the artillery to be mounted en barbette, or on high carriages that could fire over the walls, eliminating the possibility of enemy cannonballs funneling through the embrasures, wiping out the gun and crew. Although this method had been adopted in France in the late eighteenth century, it had not been implemented by the French engineers working in America.

At the end of 1802, the American coastal defenses were vulnerable once again since most of them were still earthen constructions subject to rapid deterioration. The only forts of the 1st System that did not succumb to the ravages of time and the elements were Baltimore's Fort McHenry and Philadelphia's Fort Mifflin. The garrisons of the coastal forts consisted of relatively small artillery detachments that rarely numbered more than seventy-five soldiers. Out of twenty-six sites, sixteen had garrisons of fifty or fewer men who were responsible for maintenance as well as defense. Some posts were not even occupied. The only exception was the fort at New Orleans, which held 118 soldiers in 1803.

Jefferson's secretary of war, Henry Dearborn, who had little faith in permanent coast batteries, favored building fewer fortifications and more mobile batteries and small gunboats. Jefferson enthusiastically supported Dearborn's ideas since they were more economical. However, in 1807 he was faced with the necessity of building larger and more permanent fortifications as gunboats were no longer considered an effective means of defense.

Congress had only authorized the most economical types of fortifications in every harbor along the Atlantic coast. When the 1st System was created, the secretary of war had provided guidelines as to the type of positions required, but had given no design specifications, which led to a hodgepodge of positions on the American coast. The Undeclared Naval War or Quasi War with France in 1798 spurred Congress into considering coastal defenses and increasing the size of the navy. The War with the Barbary pirates between 1801 and 1805, which resulted in the capture of an American warship, stretched the U.S. Navy to its limits and emphasized the need for coastal fortifications since the navy was not large enough to protect all the major ports of the nation. In addition, British impressment of Americans on the high seas reached a critical point with the Chesapeake Incident in June 1807. In November, Congress authorized a new fortifications project, later known as the 2nd System. In 1808, the last year of Jefferson's presidency, Congress made its largest appropriations for fortifications since 1794. The 1st System was replaced by the 2nd System of coastal fortifications as fear of war intensified. But once again, the government failed to provide detailed design guidelines as construction and renovations were set in motion.

The Second System of Coastal Defenses

The Undeclared Naval War with France was followed by a few years of relative calm that did not last. As Napoleon rose to power in France sparking off conflicts in Europe, and the British navy continued to stop American ships and impress American seamen into the service of the king, the United States became increasingly concerned about coastal defenses. According to General Joseph Totten, the coastal forts built up to that time were too small and weak. They had been built with economy as the main consideration. The "cheap materials" and poor workmanship, Totten claimed, resulted in "very perishable" positions.

The 2ND SYSTEM was formally created in November 1807 under Colonel Williams. In December of that year, Congress designated primary and secondary coastal sites to be protected. Under the 2nd System, additional open batteries and masonry-faced earthen forts were repaired or added. When war was declared in 1812, the government had to call out large numbers of militiamen to create vast fieldworks to protect these positions. However, this effort did not increase the effectiveness and security of the weak battery positions of most of the coastal towns. Virtually every sizable coastal town was defended by one or more batteries before 1812. However, by the end of the War of 1812 more changes were required. Under the 2nd System a limited number of all-masonry coastal forts were built. However, many forts, like Fort McHenry, still consisted of a combination of earth and masonry. Fort McHenry was completed in 1806, before the beginning of the 2nd System, but like similar 2nd System forts it would stand up well in combat.

In 1805, Colonel Williams was sent by Secretary of War Henry Dearborn to evaluate

1st and 2nd System Forts 1790-1812

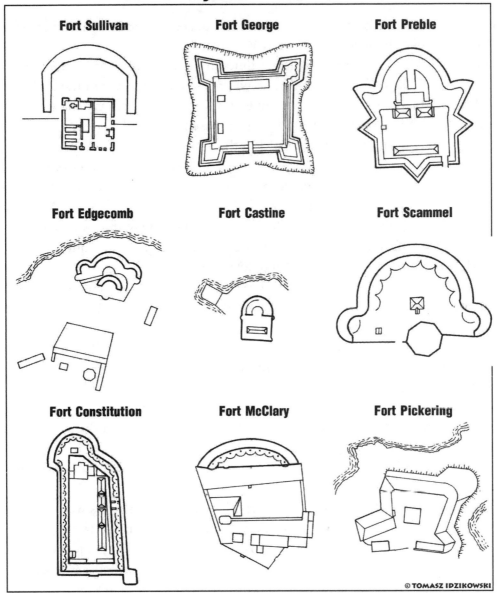

Fort Sullivan

Fort George

Fort Preble

Fort Edgecomb

Fort Castine

Fort Scammel

Fort Constitution

Fort McClary

Fort Pickering

© TOMASZ IDZIKOWSKI

the possibility of building a circular battery for twelve guns on Digges Point, a bluff on the Potomac. The site had been recommended in 1794 by George Washington, who was familiar with it because it was just across the river from Mount Vernon. Captain George Bomford, a recent graduate of West Point (Class of 1805), was given the task of designing FORT WARBURTON based on the plans for Fort Madison at Annapolis. He had to modify the plan and reduce the size to fit the fort into a site that he considered unsuitable. The result, he wrote, was "An enclosed work of masonry comprehending a semi-elliptical face with a circular flank on the side next to the Potomac." Construction was begun in April 1808 and was completed in December 1809. A masonry tower for one company and six cannons, also of brick and stone, was built to the rear of the position. Fort

Warburton was intended to hold 120 men, but housed fewer than half that number in 1814. Its name was changed later to FORT WASHINGTON.

Colonel Williams introduced a major innovation into the 2nd System. Instead of mounting the artillery solely on the walls where they fired through the embrasures or over the parapets (en barbette), he employed the casemated battery. The technique was not new in the Old World since the first gun casemates had appeared in a series of masonry coastal forts built by Henry VIII in the 16th century. Williams came upon this concept when he translated the work of René de Montalembert, the dominant French military engineer in the late eighteenth century, for use as a text at the new academy at West Point. According to Ian Hogg, author of *The History of Fortification,* Montalembert considered the siege to be an artillery duel in which the side with the most effective and best-protected artillery came out the winner. Thus, instead of mounting guns in the open, behind the parapets, he preferred to use casemates and tower-like structures where the artillery could be concentrated in several tiers of guns creating a "perpendicular fortification." Montalembert advocated this type of fortification for harbor defense, believing that the towers crammed with artillery casemates would present a smaller and more difficult target for ships firing back as they rolled with the waves. Montalembert's ideal fortification was too elaborate and expensive for the French to build, and certainly beyond the means of the Americans. The British Martello towers, first built in 1805, were undoubtedly a more modest version of Montalambert's grandiose scheme and were modeled after a tower on Corsica that British warships had exchanged fire with in 1794.

CASTLE WILLIAMS, built on the waterfront of Governor's Island, New York, is a good example of the Montalembert design. The circular, multilevel fort had three tiers of casemated guns built of red sandstone shipped from New Jersey. Its walls were about 8 feet thick at the base and rose 40 feet from ground level, tapering off to a thickness of 7 feet at the top. The casemated walls enclosed a courtyard. Emanuel Lewis, author of *Seacoast Fortifications,* writes that each tier had twenty-six vaulted casemate positions for guns and that the lower level mounted the American-manufactured 42-pdr built on a French pattern. However, most sources cannot agree on the armament. About the same number of the newly designed and constructed American 50-pdr Columbiads were placed en barbette on the terrace. The fort's second level held medium-caliber guns and the third housed about three hundred troops. Cannons were added later. The fort was named for Colonel Williams, who in 1812 became its first commander. However, Williams's rapport with the garrison, which consisted mostly of artillerymen, was rather poor because the men resented being commanded by an engineer, especially one better known as a scientist than a soldier. As a result, Williams eventually resigned from his post.

When Colonel Williams directed the work in New York harbor in 1807, many citizens, fearing that the British might return to occupy the city, volunteered to work on the fortifications. Thus, Williams was able to focus on the construction of Fort Jay and Castle Williams on Governor's Island. [The New Yorkers participation in the construction of fortifications was not unique. At Norfolk, the citizenry came out to help complete the 40-gun FORT NELSON and repair old FORT NORFOLK, which was converted from an earthwork to a brick fort for thirty cannons between 1808 and 1812.]

While he worked on Governor's Island, Williams also erected CASTLE CLINTON on the rocks on the southwest end of Manhattan Island. Castle Clinton was to provide crossfire with Castle Williams to close the channel between them. Castle Clinton was simply known as the Western or Southwestern Battery until it was renamed for the governor. When it was finished in 1811, it was not built beyond its first tier of twenty-eight casemated guns positions. Its magazines were located along the rear wall. Its entrance included a drawbridge and a wooden causeway leading to the mainland, turning the fort into an island. In the 1820s, the fort was

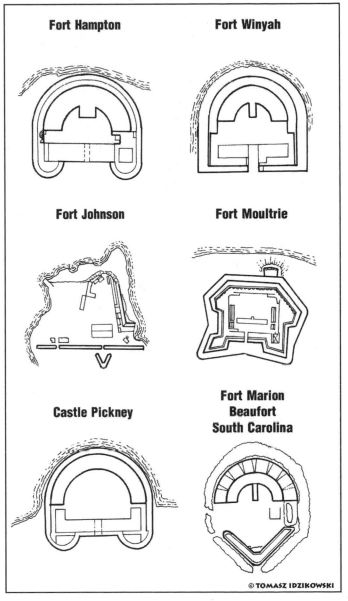

1st and 2nd System Forts 1790-1812

Fort Hampton

Fort Winyah

Fort Johnson

Fort Moultrie

Castle Pickney

Fort Marion
Beaufort
South Carolina

© TOMASZ IDZIKOWSKI

decommissioned and turned into a restaurant. In 1812, volunteers and troops built the South Battery, shaped like a redan to which a second floor was added in 1834. This battery covered Buttermilk Channel.

FORT JAY, on Governor's Island, had been built as a traditional square, four-bastioned fort at the end of the previous century. It was torn down in 1806, except for the counterscarp wall, and rebuilt with stronger materials. In 1808, Williams added a ravelin and a few other features. The fort was renamed as FORT COLUMBUS in 1807. A zigzag tunnel later linked it with Castle Williams. During this era, the military did not consider the construction and design of forts to be a major secret. Descriptions were made available to the public in newspapers and magazines. For instance, the *Aurora and General Advertiser,* a newspaper printed in Philadelphia, carried an article on October 21, 1808, describing Fort Columbus when it published a letter from a Doctor Mitchell to a Judge Spencer: "Fort Columbus is now finished excepting one barrack just ready to be covered, and the opening in the covert way opposite the gate, purposely left for the conveyance of materials. It consists of four bastions, three curtains, and an attached casemated ravelin with two retired flanks, the whole capable of mounting 97 guns, and might without inconvenience bring half its force at one instant against any passing ship, while it completely commands the East River...." Doctor Mitchell covered other details of the New York fortifications, including Bedloe Island's mortar battery, which was part of a position with an irregular trace that became Fort Wood. He wrote that it "commands all the channel and anchoring ground to the full distance that a shell can be sent," mentioning that the front wall of this battery had almost reached its intended height. He also described the works at Ellis Island and in New York City.

Before the outbreak of war in 1812, Colonel Burbeck ordered a hulk towed into New York harbor for target practice. His artillerymen at several batteries and forts pounded the derelict with over three hundred rounds before setting it afire. Although Castle Clinton and Castle Williams fired only a small number of rounds, they had a high percentage of hits. [These "castles," along with Castle Pinckney in Charleston, became symbols of strength for the army engineers and eventually became incorporated in the insignia for the army's Corps of Engineers.].

During the War of 1812, additional masonry forts were built or completed in New York harbor. The newly built FORT GIBSON on Ellis Island was ready to be garrisoned when the war began. FORT GANSEVOORT on Manhattan's Hudson shore, which covered the river with its casemated guns, was also ready to be occupied. FORT WOOD (today the pedestal for the Statue of Liberty) on Bedloe's Island, was begun in 1808, completed in

Castle Clinton, New York City 1812
from Benson Lossing's *Pictorial of the War of 1812*
(1869)

1ˢᵗ and 2ⁿᵈ System Forts 1790-1812

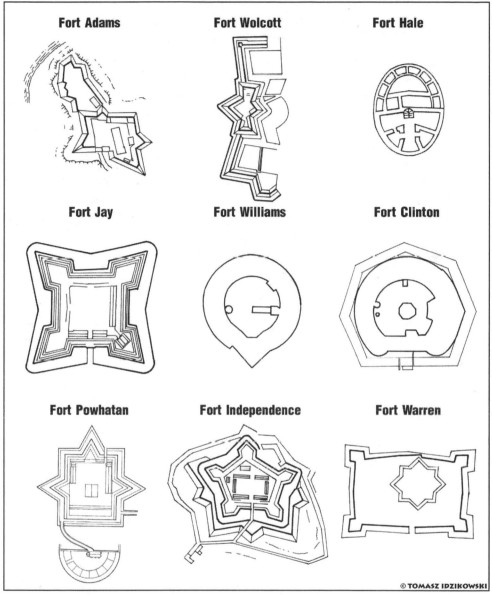

Fort Adams   Fort Wolcott   Fort Hale

Fort Jay   Fort Williams   Fort Clinton

Fort Powhatan   Fort Independence   Fort Warren

© TOMASZ IDZIKOWSKI

1811, and named in 1814. It was a twelve-point star-shaped fort with thirty 24-pdr cannons en barbette. On Staten Island, additional casemated forts were completed in 1814: FORT RICHMOND, a semicircular masonry fort, and FORT TOMPKINS, a pentagonal-shaped fort with five round bastions. FORT STEVENS at Hallett's Point included a casemated tower overlooking Hell's Gate. Across from this fort, a small garrison occupied a wooden blockhouse on Mill Rock in the middle of the river. Also in 1812, construction began on FORT DIAMOND (renamed FORT LAFAYETTE in 1823) on Hendrick's Reef near Brooklyn in the Narrows. It was a stone fort for seventy-two cannons placed in casemates and the uppers walls. However, this fort was not completed until 1822. At the outbreak of the war, a temporary battery was set up on the foundation of Fort Diamond. Thus, New York became the most heavily defended harbor area of the 2nd System.

Charleston, South Carolina, received much attention during the construction of the 2nd System. In 1804, a storm destroyed the earth and timber Fort Moultrie built in the harbor area in 1798. In 1808, one of Williams's engineers, Major (later general) Alexander Macomb, erected a new FORT MOULTRIE on Sullivan's Island. The new Fort Moultrie was completed in 1809. Like many forts of the 2nd System, it had an irregular trace and was made of masonry. It included two bastions to cover the landward approaches and demi-bastions to protect the landward flank of the walls facing the sea. It had 15-foot-high brick walls and a large brick magazine. Its forty cannons were either mounted en barbette on the seaward sides, or stood behind embrasures on the landward side. and another brick fort, CASTLE PINCKNEY, which was completed in late 1809. This castle-like fort consisted of a single level of casemated artillery with additional artillery on the roof mounted en barbette. The magazine was at the rear on the straight base of this semi-circular fort. Macomb also was responsible for work done on the coastal defenses of Georgia and the Carolinas until just before the War of 1812.

On December 7, 1807, Secretary of War Henry Dearborn submitted a report on the status of the fortifications of the major harbors and ports that had to be defended by the works of the 1st and the 2nd System (see sidebar opposite page). The report described the twenty sites designated for fortifications in 1794 and additional sites from the Louisiana Purchase of 1803. Henry Dearborn's report revealed the state of the coastal defenses of the nation when war was imminent and Congress finally appropriated the funds needed to undertake proper work on the 2nd System. By 1812, the army had completed a good deal of this work.

Canada Before the War of 1812

In 1782, Sir Guy Carleton replaced Henry Clinton as commander-in-chief of the British forces in America and took on the responsibility of evacuating British forces and Tories (Loyalists) from New York and other territories in the Thirteen States. He settled many of the Loyalists in Nova Scotia and later encouraged settlement of lands to the west to help create a buffer and defend the heart of the province, which ran along the St. Lawrence from Quebec to Montreal. As governor of Quebec in 1786, Carleton pushed through a plan to divide Quebec into Upper and Lower Canada, each under a lieutenant governor. This was done in 1791. Carleton remained as governor until 1796. In 1794, he attempted to prepare his provinces for an invasion, expecting an attack from an American army coming through Vermont and along the old Lake Champlain route.

The fortified front along all the traditional invasion routes from the United States was

1. Portland (ME), including Fort Sumner—"A small inclosed work with a block-house, magazine and barracks, and a detached battery, near the water for heavy cannon, with a store house and furnace for heating cannon ball; authorized by an act of congress, of March, 1794. The sites of the works were injudiciously selected; new ones will be necessary."

2. Portsmouth (NH), including Fort Constitution—"The remains of an ancient fortification, which have been repaired at different periods. Considerable progress has been made within the last three months in the improvement of the works."

3. Cape Ann (MA)—"Fortifications authorized by act of congress ... March 1794. A block-house and battery were erected, but are now out of repair."

4. Salem (MA)—"A block-house, magazine, and battery; authorized by act of congress ... 1794: out of repair.

5. Marblehead (MA)—"A block-house, magazine, and battery; authorized by act of congress ...1794: wanting repairs."

6. Boston Harbor (MA), including Fort Independence—"A regular, strong, inclosed work of masonry, with magazine, quarters ... commenced in the year 1800, and completed in 1803: in good repair.

7. Newport (RI), Fort Adams and Fort Wolcott—"Two enclosed works, with batteries, magazines and barracks; and in addition to a stone tower at the entrance of the harbor, and a block-house and battery on Rhode Island, near ... Newport, an extensive regular fort was commenced on a small island, but no part completed, except a range of stone barracks. These works were principally erected in the years 1798, 1799, and 1800. To complete the whole would require very large expenditures; and when completed, would not, in the smallest degree, annoy ships of war; but in one of three open and convenient passages, by which Rhode Island may be approached. The two first mentioned works have recently been put into a tolerable state of defence."

8. New London (CT), including Fort Trumbull—"Fortified in the ... revolutionary war. Several repairs have been made, at different periods since, with considerable improvements: further repairs are necessary."

9. New York Harbor, including Fort Columbus—"An enclosed work of earth and wood, on Governor's Island [Fort Columbus], and faced with permanent mason work, and is nearly completed, and may be considered as a strong, well constructed, regular fort. A strong marine, casemated battery has been commenced on the extreme western point of the same Island [Castle Williams]; and some progress has been made in forming foundations for batteries at other points in the vicinity of the city: a train of heavy cannon, mounted on traveling carriages, has been placed in the city."

10. Mud Island below Philadelphia (PA), including Fort Mifflin—"A regular, enclosed work, with batteries, magazines and barracks, principally erected in the years 1798, 1799, and 1800: and now in a good state of defence."

11. Wilmington (DE)—"A selection and survey of a site for a fortification; and authorized ... March 1794: but no works erected."

12. Baltimore Harbor (MD), including Fort McHenry—"A regular fortification of mason work, with batteries, and barracks, erected principally in the years 1798, 1799, and 1800: no considerable repair necessary." *(continued on next page)*

13. Annapolis (MD)—"An examination and survey of a site for fortifications, but the works not completed."

14. Alexandria (D.C.)—"Temporary works erected in the year 1795, now in ruins."

15. Norfolk (VA), including Fort Nelson—"Commenced in ... 1794, repaired and improved in the years 1802, 1803 and 1804, with extensive batteries, a magazine and barracks. Considerable improvements and repairs are now progressing."

16. Ocracock Harbor (NC)—"On ... Beacon Island, a work was commenced in ... 1795, but not completed; and in ... 1799, measures were directed for the erection of an enclosed work on the ruins of the former one: but form a belief that no work could be erected and supported at that place, which would afford any considerable protection to the harbor, none has been erected. It is presumed that gun-boats would more securely protect the harbor, than any fixed batteries which could be erected."

17. Cape Fear River (NC), including Fort Johnson—"The site of an ancient fortification. In ...1799 and 1800, some progress was made in erecting new works on the old site, which from unfortunate arrangements and delays, on the part of the ... [contractor] to complete them, are yet unfinished. When completed they will be insufficient for the protection of the river, or ... Wilmington, without the aid of gun-boats, or other floating force."

18. Georgetown (SC)—"Some cannon were mounted in the year 1794, but no works erected."

19. Charleston (SC), including Fort Moultrie, Fort Pinckney and Fort Johnson—"The old forts are in a state of ruins; and, as no sites have been ceded and designated by the state of fortifications, until the month of August last, no effectual measures could, with propriety, be adopted, for the defence of the town and harbor until within a few months past, in which time all necessary reassures of preparation have been pursued for commencing and completing the contemplated works, on the most permanent and durable principles."

20. Savannah, including Fort Green, and (21.) St. Marys (GA)—"On ... Cockspur [Island], near the mouth of the river, irregular fortifications were erected, in ... 1794, with a battery, magazine and barracks. In ... 1804 the works and barracks were totally destroyed, and a part of the garrison drowned, by a storm which occasioned such a rise of the water as overflowed the island to a considerable depth; but as no cession has been made to the United States, by ... Georgia, of any suitable site or sites for permanent fortifications, and it not having been in the power of the executive of the United States to procure any, on reasonable terms, either on the Savannah river or the St. Mary's, no considerable expense has been incurred on the sea coast of Georgia, for the last five years, and the garrison has been removed form St. Mary's as well as from fort Green."

22. New Orleans, including Fort St. Louis, Fort St. Charles and Fort St. Philip—"... New Orleans is surrounded, except the front, by a mud wall, with three redoubts in the rear and two in front; the two latter called forts. About fifty miles below the town there is an ancient fortification called St. Philip, with a battery, magazine and barracks, which require considerable repairs and improvements. At the junction of Bayau St. John with Lake Pontchartrain, a small ancient work remains, intended to guard the communication with New Orleans, against the approach of an enemy, by way of the lake. This work is out of repair and will probably require considerable improvement. Within the last twelve months a considerable sum of money had been expended in repairing the ancient works about the town, and for materials and workmen for repairing the other works, and erecting new ones."

rather thinly held. According to Donald Graves, author of *The Incredible War of 1812*, the British army maintained six regiments of about 2,500 men in Upper and Lower Canada and another four regiments in Nova Scotia. Like a rope that can be reinforced with knots, Canada could be strengthened with fortified sites from Louisbourg to the Great Lakes, but if cut in any single place an entire section could be quickly lost, since there was little depth possible. The waterways from the Great Lakes to the Atlantic were vital to Canada's defense. The first and main line of defense did not consist of the few forts and fortresses, but rather the British navy operating out of Halifax and West Indies ports like Jamaica. The British navy was further supported by a militia fleet, later taken over by the Royal Navy, that the lieutenant governor of Upper Canada assembled on Lake Erie and Lake Ontario.

On May 18, 1812, Sir George Prevost, commander of British forces in America, sent a dispatch to the prime minister listing Canada's defenses. FORT ST. JOSEPH, about 1,500 miles from Quebec, consisted of a blockhouse with a small garrison protecting the fur trade in the region. FORT AMHERSTBURG [Malden] included a dockyard and arsenal for the Upper Lakes. The fort was a temporary fieldwork in poor condition and was being repaired by its garrison of 120 troops and 500 militiamen from the area. FORT GEORGE, also a temporary work, was being repaired. Its garrison consisted of four hundred men and two thousand militiamen from the area. Prevost gave no details about Fort Erie and Fort George, which formed the line of communications between Lake Erie and Ontario. York had a good harbor, a dockyard, and an arsenal, but a small garrison and it needed to be fortified. Prevost gave few details about KINGSTON, a critical point between Upper and Lower Canada on the St. Lawrence, which also had a small garrison. The island that had been incorporated into the city of Montreal remained undefended, depending on a flotilla and defenses to the south for its protection. ST. JOHNS, a frontier post at the end of Lake Champlain's navigable waters, consisted of fieldworks. FORT CHAMBLY no longer held an important position and served only as a staging area. FORT WILLIAM HENRY, at the junction of the Richelieu and St. Lawrence Rivers, was the most important depot on the southern shore. QUEBEC, the only permanent fortress in the Canadas, was the key to controling them. According to Prevost, it needed bombproof casemates and its garrison numbered 2,500 men. The provinces of New Brunswick and Nova Scotia were considered vulnerable at many points. Only HALIFAX, wrote Prevost, was well protected with a garrison of 1,500 men. Newfoundland, Cape Breton, and Prince Edward Island had no significant defenses. Prevost's report clearly indicates that Canada was extremely vulnerable to attack from its southern neighbor, who, on paper at least, possessed a much larger army.

The War of 1812

The United States entered the War of 1812 with ambitions of taking Canada away from the British empire. The American army reinforced with militia forces heavily outnumbered the imperial and militia forces in Canada. Meanwhile, the British army and navy were heavily committed to the defense of the empire elsewhere and fighting Napoleon in Europe, leaving mainly smaller ships of fifty or fewer guns for the defense of the Americas.

Over a year before the outbreak of war, a preliminary campaign took place under General William Henry Harrison, governor of the Indiana territory. The Americans believed that the British were supporting the Shawnee leader Tecumseh and his brother, the Prophet, who were organizing the various Native American tribes into a new con-

Navy Yards

When Congress decided to establish a navy in the 1790s in response to French privateers and North African pirates, private contractors were given the task of building the ships. At the beginning of the next century, the Navy Department found that the private sector was not able to meet the needs of a rapidly expanding navy. Thus Benjamin Stoddert, the first secretary of the new Navy Department, ordered the creation of six federal navy yards, which would build, repair, and maintain the navy ships. The first federal navy yard was a private shipbuilding yard at Portsmouth, New Hampshire, purchased in June 1800. It was followed by the Charlestown (Boston) Brooklyn yards. In 1801, three more naval yards went into operation at Philadelphia, Norfolk, and Washington, D.C. At the beginning of the War of 1812, the navy opened yards at Presqu' Isle and Sackets Harbor on the Great Lakes. However, only Sackets Harbor stayed in operation until the 1870s. As the country expanded, other naval yards followed at Pensacola (1825), Mare Island (1853), the Mound City yard on the Mississippi (1862), and the New London naval yard (1868).

In the 1880s, with the development of steel ships, many of these yards closed down. Private shipyards took over most of the construction of steel ships, but new federal navy yards also appeared to take up the slack at Charleston (SC) in 1901 on the east coast and at Puget Sound in 1891 on the west coast. A yard was also created at Pearl Harbor in 1900. After World War I, new yards appeared on the west coast at Long Beach in 1935 and Hunter's Point in 1939.

These naval yards were major naval port facilities where many warships were built, maintained, and repaired. They required, therefore, coastal defenses such as forts and naval support. The 2nd and 3rd Systems of fortifications for coastal defense were developed to provide protection for these facilities.

federation that threatened American interests in the region. Harrison led a military campaign to remove the threat. In September 1811, Harrison marched up the Wabash with a force totaling about nine hundred men to the Indian encampment. En route, Harrison halted near the site of modern-day Terre Haute where he erected a rectangular stockade with three corner blockhouses on a bluff rising over thirty feet above the river. His troops completed the work by the end of October, naming it FORT HARRISON. Harrison warned the assembling tribes to disperse as he secured his position, and then continued his advance toward the Indian encampment. He stopped once again to build a blockhouse on the Wabash River near its juncture with the Vermilion River. The eight-man garrison of this small blockhouse was intended to protect supply boats moving up the river to support Harrison's army. Harrison, like Wayne a decade before him, was securing his line of communications with fortifications.

On November 7, the Prophet, despite instructions to the contrary from Tecumseh, attacked the American camp near Tippacanoe and was defeated, but not without inflicting 180 casualties. Harrison then destroyed the Indian village. American garrisons were installed at FORT LERNOULT (Detroit), FORT MICHILIMACKINAC, and FORT DEARBORN (Chicago) to keep the British from interfering. Fort Dearborn, a new addition, was built in 1803. It consisted of a 12-foot-high stockade and two blockhouses. These three forts were sufficient to prevent British encroachment into the Michigan, Indiana, and Illinois Territories.

The impressment of American seamen was a continued irritant that led the United States to declare war on Great Britain on June 18, 1812. Unable to challenge the Royal Navy on the high seas, the Americans decided to confront the British on land. There were only three major invasion routes, each blocked by fortifications. An invasion of Upper Canada from Detroit was considered an excellent option because only the British Fort Malden at Amherstburg stood in the way of an advance on the provincial capital of York, up the peninsula. York (present-day Toronto) had no significant defensive positions and eventually proved vulnerable to amphibious attacks across Lake Ontario. The second route into Canada was across the Niagara River where both sides had erected a fort on their respective bank. If the Americans managed to advance across the Niagara River, it would secure a more direct route to York. The third invasion route was the Lake Champlain path into Lower Canada, used frequently in the previous two major wars. It was still defended by several forts that were no longer in prime condition. But before advancing on the capital located at Quebec, the Americans would have to take Montreal.

General Sir George Prevost, who had arrived late in 1811, took command of all military forces in Canada, ordering General Isaac Brock, commander of Upper Canada, to abandon his province. However, Brock convinced Prevost to countermand his orders, insisting that if he managed to take the American outposts in the west, he would be able to win over the various native tribes with the help of Tecumseh.

A month after the declaration of war, General William Hull set in motion the American invasion of Canada from Detroit. Bypassing Fort Malden at Amherstburg, he

Fort Mackinac
from Benson Lossing's
*Pictorial Fieldbook of
the War of 1812*

moved cautiously up the peninsula. FORT MALDEN, built on the Detroit River after the British evacuated the Northwest Territory in 1796, stood about five miles south of Detroit. It was a square fort with four corner bastions and a ravelin in front of the curtain facing the river. It was manned by about 250 soldiers when the war began.

However, when FORT MACKINAC (FORT MICHILIMACKINAC) fell to the British, Hull was forced to retreat to DETROIT within a month and go on the defensive. Detroit's population of about two thousand represented almost half of the settlers of the Michigan Territory. Palisade walls extended from both sides of the city to Fort Lernoult, located behind it. The two walls included two bastions each. FORT LERNOULT had a rather unusual shape with four half-bastions forming much of the fort and four to five embrasures for cannons on each side of the fort. Hull concentrated his troops in the fort, on the town's defenses and at points from which he hoped to stop the British from crossing the Detroit River.

While Brock was striving to stop Hull's advance from Detroit, his small westerly garrison at Fort St. Joseph went into action. FORT ST. JOSEPH was little more than a blockhouse surrounded by a stockade on an island at the mouth of the waterway linking Lake Huron with Lake Superior. It was garrisoned by a company under Captain Charles Roberts. According to Donald Graves, author of *The Incredible War of 1812*, Roberts received orders from Brock to attack Fort Mackinac (Michilimackinac) and began the operation as soon as he got word that the war had begun. Taking several hundred Indians, some volunteers, and most of his garrison, he headed along Lake Huron by canoe and boat to a point near Mackinac and set siege to Fort Mackinac. The fort, which sat on a bluff on Mackinac Island, held a garrison of about sixty regulars, mostly physically unfit, and some light artillery. The original fort had stood on the mainland, but was abandoned by the British during the Revolutionary War. In 1780, it had been rebuilt by the Americans on Mackinac Island. After bringing a pair of 6-pdrs into position, Roberts rounded up the locals outside the fort. He then convinced Lieutenant Porter Hanks, commander of the fort, to surrender without a fight on July 17. After that, Roberts decided to leave Fort St. Joseph in the care of a couple of men and transfer his garrison to Fort Mackinac, from which he could more easily pursue the frontier war and help the Indians further to the south.

When Hull got wind of Robert's action, he decided to withdraw to the border because he feared that an Indian uprising against the settlers he had to protect was now more likely. He even sent orders for the evacuation of Fort Dearborn to consolidate his forces. Thus, the fall of a single fort brought an end to his campaign and American attempts to retake Fort Mackinac during the two years of war that followed failed.

In August, Captain Nathan Heald, the commander of Fort Dearborn received the order to withdraw. His contingent of about fifty-five regulars, a few militia, and some civilians totaling about 150 accompanied by an escort from Fort Wayne was attacked by the Potawatomi Indians a few miles from the fort and massacred. The Indians burned Fort Dearborn so that both the garrison and fort were lost to General Hull. The area was now wide open to the British while Hull remained under siege in Detroit.

The last of Hull's troops returned to American territory on August 11. General Brock advanced on FORT DETROIT on August 15, 1812, and entrenched a battery of two 18-pdrs and an 8-inch howitzer at a commanding point over the town and fort. Some of the twenty-four heavy cannons at Fort Detroit were moved to stop the British from crossing the Detroit River. Since the town was located between the fort and the river, many civilians took refuge in the fort. Brock demanded Hull's surrender, explaining that he would not be able to exert control over the Indians once they entered the fray. Hull refused and soon the British artillery opened fire on the town. Hull ordered many of his troops to withdraw into the fort which aggravated the situation as the place was already overcrowded with civilians. He also did not leave enough troops to hold the town's defenses and prevent a British crossing. Several hundred of Tecumseh's Indians did cross two miles down river under the cover of darkness, outflanking and isolating the defenders. At dawn, Hull withdrew the remainder of his troops into the fort. When the first artillery rounds fell within the walls of the overcrowded fort, killing a number of troops and civilians, he was convinced that he and his men could not hold out for long, and fearing many more casualties surrendered Detroit on August 16, 1812.

Soon after, Brock traveled to the threatened sector on the Niagara River, leaving Colonel Henry Procter to secure the situation and threaten the exposed American territories. Colonel Procter sent Tecumseh and his Indians south. On August 28, the Indians reached Fort Wayne and Fort Harrison. At the beginning of September, Major Muir followed with a British detachment with the objective of advancing up the Maumee River and joining the Indians in a siege of FORT WAYNE, a well built-stockade with two blockhouses. Apparently, the old earthen protection along its walls was gone, so that the fort could no longer resist cannons. Fort Wayne was held by seventy regulars armed with four small cannons. According to Benson Lossing, author of *Pictorial Field-Book of the War of 1812* published in 1868, Tecumseh, who had fomented an uprising among the tribes, led them against Fort Wayne and Fort Harrison, isolating the two forts and plundering the countryside between them. Since Muir's troops advanced too slowly for the impatient Indians, they decided not to wait for him. On September 4, they engaged FORT HARRISON, held by Captain Zachary Taylor. Fort Harrison was also a stockade with three corner blockhouses and held about fifty regulars, most of whom were ill. They succeeded in setting the lower blockhouse on fire, destroying it along with most of the fort's supplies stored in it. As the flames spread to the rest of the fort, Taylor's men fought from the walls while Taylor directed a bucket line to put out the fires. Taylor, rallying his faltering men, was able to contain the fire by tearing off the roofs of nearby structures and watering them down. However, the burned-down blockhouse left a gaping breach almost 20 feet wide. To close the gap, the garrison raised a 5-foot-high breastwork before dawn. Despite all the shooting that night in the eight-hour engagement, Taylor sustained only one casualty and lost a couple more who panicked and deserted. The Indians, unable to make an assault on the breastworks in the breach, withdrew in the morning, destroying everything in their path. On September 5, Taylor made repairs to the breach by removing logs from the guardhouse and using them to create a new stockade wall. He still had to wait for Harrison's troops to relieve Fort Wayne before they could come to his aid.

From Fort Harrison, Tecumseh and his warriors proceeded to FORT WAYNE, placing it under rifle fire on the night of September 5. The next night about six hundred Indians assaulted the fort, but failed to scale its walls. In the morning, they set up two log "cannons" to trick the garrison into surrendering. The defenders, who were not fooled, rejected the offer. On September 9, the Indians launched a twelve-hour attack that ended the next day. The Indians then launched another unsuccessful assault, which they broke off on September 12, when they learned that General Harrison's relief column was approaching the fort.

In 1812, the American army was plagued with poor leadership, especially in the territories where General James Winchester was in command. It was not until Harrison took effective command of operations in the area that the situation finally turned around. However, by that time the United States had lost all the forts along the Great Lakes. The British even reoccupied the remains of old Fort Miamis, near the mouth of the Maumee River. Harrison spent the fall and winter of 1812 preparing for a new campaign in January 1813 when he advanced on Detroit only to be beaten back. He reoccupied old Fort Defiance on the Maumee and built a log stockade nearby.

As Harrison's forces came to a halt just short of Detroit, the remainder of the frontier along the Mississippi River remained open and vulnerable to hostile Indians and raiding parties since the large American forces were concentrated in the north. FORT MADISON was built in 1808 at a site north of present-day St. Louis. It was meant to protect a government trading post and to secure that area on the Mississippi. The fort had two corner blockhouses overlooking the river on the squared side of the fort (instead of a fourth wall, two walls forming an angle were joined by a blockhouse). From the central blockhouse the palisades extended for a short distance, forming a passage called the "tail" which ended at another blockhouse on a ridge behind the fort. It was garrisoned by a detachment of the 1st Infantry Regiment. Fort Madison was attacked by Black

Hawk, a Sauk chief, and a party of Sauk, Winnebago, and Fox Indians on September 5, 1812. For three days, the Indians tried to set the blockhouses and barracks on fire and put to the torch other structures outside the fort. The Indians withdrew on September 8 when they got wind that a relief force was on its way. But the twenty-man contingent did not reach the fort until two weeks after the onset of the battle. Skirmishing continued in 1813 until the garrison, tired of being harassed and shot at with fire arrows, torched the fort themselves and escaped down river in September 1813.

After Brock's early victories, the British had to juggle their troops around the northern front and shift units, mostly wracked by disease, from the West Indies to Quebec and other places. Both sides built small fleets on Lake Ontario and Lake Erie. The key front ran along the Niagara River and included Fort Niagara and Fort Schlosser on the American side and Fort George and Fort Erie on the British side.

FORT NIAGARA, located at the north end of the Niagara River, had not changed much since the last war. FORT SCHLOSSER, named after the German officer who built it in 1760 to replace the older Little Fort Niagara, was a large earthen fort with four corner bastions located near the falls. FORT GEORGE, which faced Fort Niagara across the river, served as the British army headquarters. It was a large six-sided fort with six corner bastions and a surrounding moat. In 1812, it consisted of earthen walls and cedar palisades walls 12 feet high. It included five blockhouses, garrison quarters, a stone magazine, and other structures. Its artillery included two 24-pdrs. FORT ERIE stood on a knoll at the south end of the river to avoid the fate of its predecessors, which were built nearer the river and were destroyed by severe winter storms. This new fort, begun in 1804, was a square masonry work with four corner bastions, and remained incomplete in 1812 because the construction was done intermittently over the years. It had 3-foot-thick walls and was designed for three hundred men but only held a garrison of fifty men and a pair of light artillery pieces in 1812. In addition, the British had a small stockade known as FORT CHIPPEWA just above Niagara Falls.

During the month October 1812, Fort Niagara and Fort George engaged in an artillery duel. The Americans crossed the river and moved against Queenstown, finally taking the redan, an earthwork on the heights that dominated the battlefield. General Brock died trying to retake the half-moon redan that mounted a pair of 18-pdrs. General Roger Scheaffe, who took over command, defeated and captured most of the Americans in a counterattack with bayonets. The victory boosted the morale of the outnumbered British and Canadian militia. On November 28, American troops tried again to drive the British back. This time they crossed the river a couple miles below Fort Erie and the falls, but were driven back once again. The region around the Niagara River became the scene of many of the major clashes between the two armies in 1813 and 1814.

In November 1812, General Dearborn led the main American thrust against Canada at the head of a force of 4,500 to 5,000 men. He chose the Lake Champlain route to

Montreal. However, he never had a chance to test the British defenses because his militia troops refused to cross into Canada, forcing him to turn back. Also in 1812, both sides strove to build fleets for the Great Lakes. The ship building sites at SACKET'S HARBOR in New York and KINGSTON in Canada became major bases to be defended. As the main American warship, the 20-gun brig *Oneida* built in 1809, lay at anchor at Sacket's Harbor, it was attacked by a squadron of British ships in June 1812. It was saved by a barrage of fire from the shore batteries.

In the 1780s, Guy Carleton had created new shipyards and naval installations at Haldimand Bay (Navy Bay), on the other side of the river from Kingston. In November 1812, a fleet led by the *Oneida* even bombarded the defenses of Kingston. The Americans also had a navy yard at Black Rock, across from Fort Erie on Lake Erie. The British built a few warships at the yards they controlled on the Detroit River, arming one with cannons from Fort Malden, which allowed them to maintain naval dominance on Lake Erie.

In the early weeks of 1813, Harrison began a campaign with the objectives of retaking the lost forts at Mackinac and Detroit and invading Canada by first taking Fort Malden. Stopped not far from Fort Malden, Harrison was hit hard by Procter's troops, who crossed the ice to counterattack. As he withdrew, Harrison decided to secure his position by building FORT MEIGS a few miles upstream from old Fort Miamis on the Maumee River. Captain Charles Gratiot, an 1806 graduate of West Point, designed this large timber stockaded fort that could hold 2,500 men. The fort included seven blockhouses and several bastions with gun batteries. Located on a high bluff overlooking the river rapids, Fort Meigs formed an elongated trace in a good defensive position. As

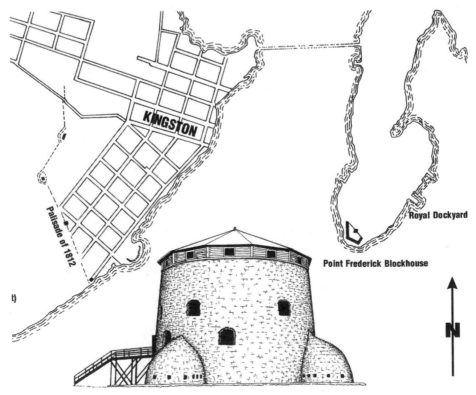

General Procters's troops and Tecumseh's Indians approached the fort in the spring, Harrison reinforced his new fort. A row of tents was left in front of the fort's walls as the British built their camp near Fort Miamis and installed their batteries to bombard the fort. At the beginning of May 1813, the tents were taken down to reveal earthworks in front of the fort's wooden walls. The garrison had only a limited amount of shot to return fire and had to use British balls recovered inside the fort as the British continued a heavy but unsuccessful bombardment that failed to damage the new earthen walls— the wet weather turned the walls into a muddy mix that absorbed the cannon balls like a sponge.

When General Green Clay came to the rescue with his Kentucky brigade, over half of his men were sent across the river to capture and spike the British artillery. Although they fulfilled their mission successfully, many were led into an ambush and killed by the Indians. A party sallied from the fort to storm the British battery across the river. Although Procter managed to inflict many casualties on the Americans and take hundreds of prisoners in minor skirmishes, he was forced to break off the siege and withdraw toward Detroit when his artillery was put out of action. At the end of July, Procter returned to the attack with a smaller force. After crossing Lake Erie, he put Fort Meigs under siege once more. However, after he failed to draw out the garrison, he returned to Lake Erie where he embarked for the Sandusky River hoping to attack Fort Stephenson, a main supply position for the Americans.

FORT STEPHENSON was built by Ohio militia on the west bank of the river in 1812. It was a square stockade, with a 7-foot-deep and 12-foot-wide ditch, with a pair of blockhouses and a bastion, but it was armed with only one 6-pdr cannon. The small fort was designed for about 200 men but it held only 160 regulars when a force of 500 British regulars and some Indians advanced upon it. General Harrison and his officers determined that Fort Stephenson could not resist heavy artillery, so a few days before the British arrived they sent orders to the fort's commander, Major George Croghan, to destroy the fort and withdraw. However, since the Indians were already at the gates and with the memory of the disastrous evacuation of Fort Dearborn still fresh in his mind, Croghan opted to fight. On August 1, Croghan informed Procter: "We give up the fort when there's not a man left to defend it." Procter did not have heavy artillery. He used his cannons to open a breach in one corner of the fort, but the damaged section was easily closed with sandbags. After a relatively ineffective bombardment, Procter's troops launched an assault, but without ladders they were not able to get past the ditch and scale the 12-foot-high stockade. Thus Procter's force, having suffered significant losses without taking either of Harrison's forts, withdrew empty-handed.

A 1,700 man expedition led by Zebulon Pike departed Sacket's Harbor in April 1813 to raid York with its large stock of supplies. Only a pair of batteries behind earthworks, a blockhouse and an unfinished fort defended the capital. Pike was killed when the main magazine was detonated and the Americans withdrew.

Sackets Harbor

© TOMASZ IDZIKOWSKI

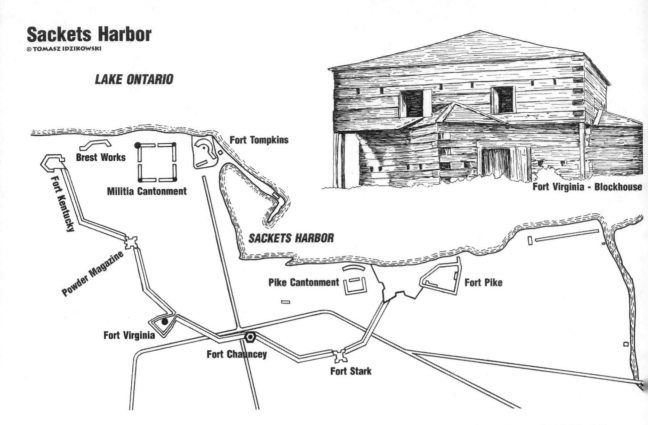

LAKE ONTARIO

Fort Tompkins

Brest Works

Militia Cantonment

Fort Kentucky

Powder Magazine

SACKETS HARBOR

Pike Cantonment

Fort Pike

Fort Virginia

Fort Chauncey

Fort Stark

Fort Virginia - Blockhouse

The fortifications on Lake Ontario also played a role in the War of 1812. The Americans fortified SACKETS HARBOR between 1812 and 1813. These defenses included FORT TOMPKINS, a blockhouse on the lakeshore with a battery of twenty cannons behind earthworks that covered the harbor. A large palisaded cantonment with four corner blockhouses stood nearby. FORT VIRGINIA, a square stockade with corner bastion and a central blockhouse mounting fifteen cannons, was built to cover the landward side and encircle the town with fortifications. FORT VOLUNTEER (later renamed FORT PIKE), a rather weak position on the shore, completed these defenses. The British launched a naval expedition against Sackets Harbor on May 29, 1813. General Jacob Brown was in charge of the defense at the head of five hundred militia and a few regulars. The British troops landed west of the town, forcing many of the Americans to retreat to Fort Volunteer. However, some American detachments held the entrenchments and managed to repel the invaders. After that minor victory, additional defenses were erected at Sackets Harbor, including a palisaded earthwork called FORT KENTUCKY, located to the west of the cantonment. A new stone tower named FORT CHAUNCEY and an earthwork called FORT STARK occupied the position between Fort Virginia and Fort Volunteer, which was renamed Fort Pike after it was renovated, and the Pike Cantonment not far away. Entrenchments linked the fortifications, creating a perimeter around Sackets Harbor, but the British never returned to test the fortress.

The American naval force joined Fort Niagara in bombarding FORT GEORGE for two days and then landed troops on May 27, 1813. The landing force occupied the ruins of Fort George and about four thousand Americans cleared the west bank of the Niagara including Fort Erie. With victory at hand, the American forces advanced inland for several miles only to be defeated at Stony Creek on June 6. Many American troops retreated to the ruins of Fort George where they were trapped while the British cleared most of the west bank of the Niagara River. Fort George was finally evacuated late in 1813 and a few days later the British silently crossed to the American side in freezing weather and stormed into Fort Niagara, taking the garrison of about four hundred by surprise and capturing most on December 19.

In October 1813, General Wade Hampton led about four thousand men into Lower Canada along the Lake Champlain route. Once again, this invasion force soon withdrew to New York. Later that month, a large expedition under Wilkinson departed Sackets Harbor, sailed into the St. Lawrence bypassing Kingston, and disembarked above Fort Wellington which controlled the river near Prescott. FORT WELLINGTON, begun in December 1812, was a large single-level blockhouse surrounded by earthen defenses that controlled the river with a pair of 9-pdr cannons. Sir George Prevost had ordered its construction to keep the Americans from closing the St. Lawrence River at Prescott. The presence of this fort delayed Wilkinson's expedition long enough to bog it down in the battle of Chrysler's Farm in mid-November, halting its advance on Montreal. Finally, the Americans withdrew the way they had come.

The only positive event for the Americans was Perry's defeat of the British naval force on Lake Erie in September 1813, which gave him control of the lake. Thanks to this victory, General Harrison was able to move against Detroit and Fort Malden, forcing Procter's troops to retreat into the peninsula where they were defeated. The outposts to the west of Detroit remained in British hands, despite American efforts to take them back. Croghan, who had distinguished himself at Fort Stephenson a year earlier, tried to take back Fort [Michili]mackinac in August. Unfortunately, since the ships that came with him were not able to elevate their guns high enough to fire on the fort, his landing force could not reach it. At this time, many of Harrison's regulars were shifted east and one brigade was sent to defend Sackets Harbor.

In 1814, the American and British troops on the northern front were on the move again, but the most important actions took place along the eastern seaboard of the United States. Wilkinson led his army up the Lake Champlain route one last time only to be turned back in April. In May, a British expedition crossed Lake Erie to attack FORT OSWEGO, which had just received a garrison of 290 regulars. Their naval squadron landed over six hundred men who advanced on the fort, forced the Americans to abandon it, and captured a large stock of supplies in the harbor. Meanwhile, the Americans were preparing to arm a 62-gun ship built at Sackets Harbor and the British were rushing to complete a 102-gun warship at Kingston.

Fighting resumed along the Niagara front under the direction of General Jacob Brown, who replaced Wilkinson. On July 3, General Winfield Scott led an assault on FORT ERIE with 3,500 men. The British, who were stretched thin, were trying to hold Fort

Niagara with 1,500 regulars, where they hoped to engage the Americans. The commander of Fort Erie, with only 150 men at his disposal, surrendered, realizing that his situation was hopeless with no relief in sight. As Scott moved northward and the fighting became centered on Chippewa, the troops he left behind strengthened and altered Fort Erie. After the battles of Chippewa and Lundy's Lane, General Brown withdrew his army across the Niagara River, leaving a bridgehead at Fort Erie, which was endowed with new earthworks and bastions quickly completed. The new earthworks connected the fort to the shoreline on the north side. On the other side, they stretched almost five hundred yards to create a fortified camp between the fort and the shore of Lake Erie. On August 15, three thousand British troops advanced on Fort Erie carrying ladders to scale the walls and grenades to clear out the defenders. The attackers moved through woods in the early morning darkness and the rain and soon engaged in bloody combat, capturing one of the bastions. That bastion's magazine exploded, killing almost two hundred British troops. Other columns of the British assault force ran into problems in the woods and the darkness and were unable to participate in the attack or even attack the entrenched camp. Thus the defenders, fewer than two thousand, won a striking victory. The British next established siege positions, moving three batteries into place by mid-September and building their own field defenses, including blockhouses. On September 16, Fort Erie's American garrison, reinforced with another thousand men, sortied and destroyed two of the three British siege battery positions before retiring behind their walls. In November 1814, the Americans evacuated Fort Erie, blowing up the fort as they departed. Thus, the year of 1814 was characterized once more by blunted American incursions into Canada and British offensives against the key facilities in the United States that put the defenses of the 2nd System to the test.

In 1813, the British had attempted to maintain a blockade of the American eastern coast and extended it to the southern coast from Maryland to North Carolina with raids. One major raid was launched on Hampton Roads in 1813. General Robert B. Taylor, in command at NORFOLK, did not believe that Fort Norfolk and Fort Nelson would present an adequate defense, even though he had prepared them himself. FORT NORFOLK, converted from an earthwork to a masonry fort in 1808, had an unusual curved battery facing the Elizabeth River and mounted thirty guns. FORT NELSON was across from it on the west side of the river with its continuous parapet for mounting cannons en barbette. It had also been turned into a masonry fort of the 2nd System at the same time as Fort Norfolk. Taylor had Lieutenant Colonel W. K. Armistead from the Corps of Engineers assigned to him to work on the defenses of Norfolk. Armistead fortified Craney Island with a blockhouse on the north end and some redoubts with a battery extending most of the length of the island after a feared British invasion failed to materialize in March 1813. The American defenders on the island, barely more than five hundred in number, repelled a British landing force of over two thousand men in June 1813 [some sources indicated both sides had larger forces]. It was a minor victory for the Americans, since the British went on to strike at Hampton, which had little in the way of defenses. As a result, the partially completed FORT POWHATAN with a curved masonry water battery detached from the fort on the James River about thirty miles from Jamestown, was armed in 1814. However, no work was done at Point Comfort at the site of old Fort George.

Things changed drastically in 1814. The citizenry of New York was concerned about the inability of the American forces to stop these raids and began to fear another British occupation of New York City. Records at the Corps of Engineers Office show that Joseph Swift, chief engineer of the army, had already taken on the task of completing and strengthening the harbor defenses in 1812. However, when British warships appeared off the coast in mid-1814 the New York Committee of Defense called upon him to take emergency action. He proposed two lines of field fortifications: one, similar to the line of 1776, placed along the hills of Brooklyn would defend against a new British invasion of Long Island; the other was to be drawn across the northern end of Manhattan Island from the Hudson to the mouth of the Harlem River. He called upon New Yorkers to help build these defense lines that required ditches, breastworks, and redoubts. During the fall of 1814, about 38,000 civilians from all age groups and social strata answered his call, laboring to protect their city. Those unable to do the manual labor contributed money or helped to make more than five thousand fascines. Their efforts may well have forced the British to look for easier targets when they decided to move against the Chesapeake.

In April 1814, with Napoleon on his way to exile, the Royal Navy became free to concentrate its forces off the American coast, and the veteran regiments in the European theater were now able to take part in the American campaign. By this time, the British naval command in North America was split into the North American Command under Admiral Sir John B. Warren and the West Indies Command under Vice-Admiral Sir Alexander Cochrane. In April 1814, the latter extended the blockade to cover the entire eastern coastline of the United States. Late in July, General Robert Ross assembled four thousand Royal Marines and regulars of his own regiment at Bermuda and sent them to the Chesapeake. There was little in the region to stop this raiding force except for about one thousand regulars and many unreliable militiamen. Ross marched on the almost defenseless capital of WASHINGTON, D.C., brushing aside an American force at Bladensburg. He took the new capital at the end of the month and burned the navy yard and other structures including the White House. At FORT WASHINGTON, Captain Samuel T. Dyson and his garrison of fifty men who manned twenty-six guns watched the British fleet take up positions on the evening of August 29. Only nine of his cannons were able to fire down river. As the British opened fire the next morning, "The garrison, to our great surprise, retreated from the fort; and a short time afterward Fort Washington was blown up," reported British Captain Gordon. After they finished the destruction of the fort, the British moved on to take Alexandria. Dyson, on the other hand, was court-martialed for his action.

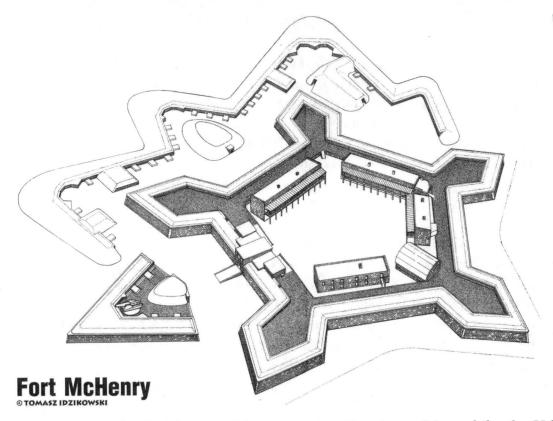

Fort McHenry
© TOMASZ IDZIKOWSKI

On August 30, the British moved by sea against BALTIMORE. Meanwhile, the U.S. Navy blocked the harbor with sunken ships and the citizens built earthworks around the defenseless city. On Hampstead Hill, just east of the city, they built ROGER'S REDOUBT, which included artillery positions and a mile of earthworks. At dawn on September 12, Ross landed at North Point at the head of three to five thousand British troops and moved north, pushing the defenders back toward the city. The British fleet of over forty ships began its bombardment of Baltimore and Fort McHenry on September 13, but it failed to inflict significant damages on Baltimore's defenses. As a result, the heavily outnumbered British force, unable to take on the formidable defenses of Baltimore, cancelled the planned siege and withdrew on September 14.

FORT MCHENRY, designed by J. J. Ulrich Rivardi in the late 1790s, has often been labeled as a star-shaped fort. Actually, although it included five curtains and five bastions, it had no salients usually associated with true star forts. The citizenry of Baltimore had helped finance this expensive project before the actual 2nd System was funded by the federal government. Most of the work was completed by 1806. In 1814, there were several brick structures in the fort, including two single-level barracks, officer's quarters, a magazine, and a guardhouse. Fort McHenry was not entirely built with masonry; its parapets were sod-covered earth walls but its 12-foot-high scarp was bricklined. The fort had no revetment walls and its terreplein was tree-lined, as can be seen in drawings of Fort McHenry at the time. Oak planks in the bastions provided a stable floor for the artillery. A bastion in the northwest corner included a small sentry post. The bridge from the ravelin included a removable span in front of the fort's entrance. The ravelin, located in the surrounding moat, faced an 8-foot-high brick-faced scarp at the time, but was mainly an earthwork with no room for artillery. Just beyond the ravelin were the high and low water batteries consisting of earthworks and plank decking for the guns. In 1814, each curtain was about 115 feet long, creating enough space inside to hold one thousand men. In 1814, the fort mounted twenty-three 18-pdr and 24-pdr cannons, including the four guns in each bastion. The Upper and Lower Batteries outside the fort mounted thirty-six 18-pdr and 36-pdr guns taken from a French warship damaged in 1808. Early in 1813, Colonel Swift sent Captain Samuel Babcock to supervise improvements at Fort McHenry. Babcock was responsible for the addition of the three hot-shot furnaces for the water batteries, and a 32-pdr or 36-pdr gun battery near the shoreline. He also added defenses to other areas near Baltimore to deter a landing.

Other positions built in the area in 1813 included FORT COVINGTON, a wedge-shaped brick fort mounting ten 18-pdrs located about two miles west of Fort McHenry on the site of modern-day Port Covington; FORT LOOK-OUT (FORT WOOD in 1814), an earthen redoubt covering the landward approaches to Fort Covington; FORT BABCOCK (Battery Babcock), an earthwork mounting six guns located between Fort Covington and Fort McHenry; and LAZARETTO BATTERY with three guns located across from Fort McHenry that closed the entrance to the harbor. During the battle, the defenders of Fort McHenry included the regular garrison of artillerymen and Maryland militia under Major George Armistead. In addition, there were sailors from Joshua Barney's flotilla that had been trapped and scuttled when the British fleet moved up the Chesapeake.

The bombardment of Fort McHenry on September 12–13 lasted for twenty-five hours. Despite the British long-range bombardment from two miles out, the fort's artillery was able to drive back Cochrane's ships. During the engagement, an estimated 1,500 rounds were fired, including bombs and Congreve rockets. Five British bomb ships lobbed 10-inch and 13-inch mortar bombs at the fort. [Bomb ships were small two-masted vessels that usually carried two mortars of 10-inch and/or 13-inch mounted on platforms in the center of the ship.] The British bombardment had little effect and only served to turn Fort McHenry, with its large flag waving in the night sky, into a symbol of defiance and national pride. Colonel Arthur Brooke's troops waited in vain in front of the eastern defenses of Baltimore for the reduction of Fort McHenry and for their naval support. The amphibious landing that was to support their attack failed to materialize when the frigate carrying the troops was driven off by the guns of Fort McHenry and Fort Covington.

As the British departed the area, Pierre L'Enfant was sent to redesign FORT WASHINGTON on the Potomac to protect the capital. When the war was over, a year later, additional land was purchased to build the fort properly this time based on L'Enfant's new plans.

To the Americans, the situation seemed to deteriorate as the British struck at will. On July 11, 1814, British forces advanced from New Brunswick into Maine, taking Eastport in the disputed border region. British warships not only blockaded, but also threatened several ports. The ports of Maine had been somewhat fortified before the war, but there remained many problems. In 1808, army engineer Major Moses Porter had been sent to select sites for fortifications. FORT EDGECOMB, near the town by the same name, was built to defend the busy port of Wiscasset at the mouth of the Kennebec River. The batteries and large hexagonal blockhouse of the fort were completed in 1809. In the summer of 1814, British warships landed raiding parties and engaged the position.

Further up the coast, at the mouth of the Penobscott River, Porter had selected a site at Castine for a small work called FORT MADISON. Before the war, troops had been too scarce to man the battery. When the war began, it was manned by only a skeleton garrison because of a dispute over the legality of the war. Since the Federalists, including the governor, were against the conflict, the local militia refused to cooperate. The locals, in the meantime, started rebuilding nearby FORT GEORGE from which they had stripped bricks for years. In September 1814, a British invasion force approached the virtually undefended Fort Madison, fired a salvo, spiked the guns, and retreated. After Castine fell, the expedition sailed up the river to Bangor. At the same time, another British landing force took Machias, located further up the coast, closer to Eastport. The garrison of nearby FORT O'BRIEN, an old, lightly armed earthwork built during the Revolutionary War, fled instead of putting up a resistance.

Fort Washington, Virginia, on the Potomac. Designed by Pierre L'Enfant, this hybrid 2nd/3rd System fort was built after the War of 1812 to replace the one that was blown-up during the war. Below is a view of the entrance looking at the Potomac.

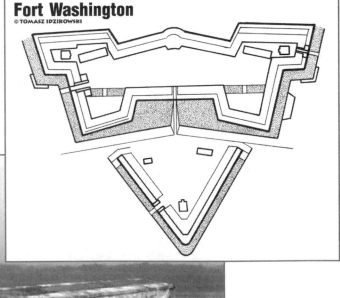

Fort Washington
© TOMASZ IDZIKOWSKI

These raids were minor nuisances compared with the threat represented by Prevost, who was advancing down the Lake Champlain route with ten thousand men. No permanent fortifications barred his path. However, the American army at PLATTSBURGH had erected field fortifications during the summer. In addition, General Alexander Macomb, an army engineer, was left in command of about three thousand troops to block Prevost's advance. The troops stationed in advanced positions near the border quickly withdrew in the face of the advancing enemy. According to J. M. Hitsman, author of *The Incredible War of 1812*, Macomb withdrew behind the Sarnac River, which divided Plattsburgh, and took up positions in the three redoubts and two blockhouses previously built. This was not a very formidable position, except for the advantage offered by the river obstacle. On September 11, while Prevost's troops advanced on Plattsburgh, the British and American fleets on Lake Champlain clashed nearby. After several hours, the Americans defeated the British naval squadron. As a result, Prevost called off his assault on the American defenses and retreated because he believed that he must control the lake to secure his advance.

Also in September, a small naval force off the Florida coast attempted to capture the American fort at the entrance to Mobile Bay at Mobile Point. Thus, with the bombardment of Baltimore, the British invasion of Maine, Prevost's thwarted advance at Plattsburgh, and the attack on Mobile Point, September 1814 turned out to be a critical month for the United States. Ironically, all these events took place while peace negotiations, begun in August, continued at Ghent.

In 1814, Andrew Jackson, a former militia general, commanded the Southern Department. He had risen to prominence fighting the Red Sticks, a coalition of Creek tribes incited against the Americans by Tecumseh and supported by the British. The first significant event of the Creek War was an attack on a hastily built stockade around the home of Samuel Mims, near a ferry crossing on the Alabama River about thirty-five miles north of Mobile. Major Daniel Beasley took command of FORT MIMS and its garrison of over two hundred troops in July of 1813. Although instructed to build blockhouses for the fort, he failed to do so. Neither did he post sentries around the fort. Thus on August 30, the Creeks launched a surprise attack, rushing into the fort through an open gate. Of an estimated 550 soldiers and civilians in the fort, only thirty-six survived. Jackson led the militia against the Creeks that year, inflicting major defeats on them. On March 27, 1814, he attacked the heavily defended Tohopeka village of the Creek Indians at Horseshoe Bend on the Tallapoosa River. The village, located inside a peninsula formed by a bend in the river, was sealed from the mainland by an impressive log stockade. General John Coffee's troops and some Cherokee allies took up positions on the opposite side of the river to prevent the Creeks from escaping as Jackson's main force began an artillery bombardment of the stockade with 6-pdr guns, which inflicted no significant damage. Coffee's Cherokees set the village ablaze with fire-arrows, while Jackson's men attacked the stockade, driving the warriors back. By the time the battle was over, over nine hundred Creeks were killed. After that, Jackson was commissioned into the regular army, taking command of the Southern Department.

Mobile had just been occupied by Americans when an expedition of six hundred men from New Orleans came to reinforce it in mid-April 1813. The American troops began to build a position on the west end of a spit of land called Mobile Point, site of the future Fort Morgan. From this point, artillery was able to control the entrance into the bay. Colonel John Bowyer, who took charge of the construction in June, named the fort after himself. The redoubt for FORT BOWYER was completed in November. In January 1814, General Thomas Flourney, commander of the region, was informed that the landward defenses of Fort Bowyer were weak and exposed to attack from the sand dunes only two hundred yards away where cannons could easily be mounted. In July, the general ordered Colonel Bowyer to destroy the fort and withdraw to Fort Charolette (the Spanish garrison of the latter had surrendered to Bowyer in April). However, Andrew Jackson ordered the reoccupation of Fort Bowyer in August and Major James Lawrence and 130 men of the 2nd Infantry Regiment took up position at Fort Bowyer at the end of the month and restored the structure, a semicircular battery 400 feet wide flanked by two 60-foot-long curtains joined by a single bastion. The sand ramparts lined with pine stakes on the inside were 15 feet thick. The rear of the fort on the landward side was covered by the bastion. Its two flanks accommodated one cannon apiece. The distance between the bastion and the parapet of the battery was 180 feet. A dry 20-foot-wide moat with a small glacis and without a covered way encircled the entire position. By September 20 cannons, including two 24-pdrs, six 12-pdrs, eight 9-pdrs, and four 4-pdrs, were mounted in the fort but there were no bombproofs to protect them. Of these guns, only a 9-pdr and three 4-pdrs were located on wooden platforms on the bastion for the landward defenses. However, the fort remained vulnerable from that quarter because the gun crews were exposed. On September 12, four small British warships under Captain William H. Percy landed a force of sixty Royal Marines and some artillery to the east of the fort. Over one hundred Indians joined in the assault. Foul weather delayed naval attack until September 15. The fort's artillery grounded the 28-gun *Hermes*, which burned and later exploded. The defenders silenced the enemy battery in the dunes. Only two of the fort's cannons were dismounted and the infantry garrison, which had no experience in firing artillery, did quite well.

The attack on Fort Bowyer, which was undertaken in preparation for the British campaign against NEW ORLEANS, failed to open Mobile Bay for them. Jackson hurried to New Orleans, which was threatened by 7,500 British troops. After the British troops landed on December 13, 1814, and began their approach, Jackson's engineer, Major A. L. Latour, created a rampart along the Rodriguez Canal. The canal was 4 feet with a 12-foot width and Latour used its spoil to create a 4-foot-high rampart (20 feet thick in some places) reinforced with wood from nearby fences to keep it from washing away in the rain. A redoubt for an artillery battery was created to anchor the line on the river. After an initial attack on December 28, Jackson's 6,700 troops expanded his defenses on the left into the cypress swamp creating a log and earth rampart and strengthened the original position by adding a firing step (banquette) to the ramparts. On January 8, 1815, the British force was smashed against Jackson's mile-long entrenchments in the climatic battle of New Orleans, although on the other side of the river a smaller British force cleared the American defenses. (The war had actually ended on December 24, but the news did not arrive until February 1815.)

Meanwhile, British warships blockaded and bombarded FORT ST. PHILIP on the Mississippi for over a week. This fort, originally built by the Spanish, was taken over by American troops in 1808 and rebuilt with bricks in 1810. It had two bastions that faced the river and mounted most of the fort's artillery, which consisted of twenty pieces. On January 18, the British squadron withdrew having caused little damage to Fort St. Philip while taking a number of damaging hits.

Admiral Cochrane re-embarked the troops. However, before accepting defeat, he landed five thousand troops on Dauphine Island opposite FORT BOWYER. The fort's garrison, totaling four hundred men after reinforcements, faced over thirty British ships. Three British regiments landed on Fort Bowyer's side of the channel, driving the defenders back into the fort. The fort riposted, inflicting some casualties and neutralizing several siege guns. The British troops cleared the dunes, coming close enough to clear the American gunners from the ramparts with musket fire. On February 10, another regiment landed and the British sappers advanced their trenches to within forty yards of the fort's moat. Artillery was moved to the top of the dunes from where it could fire into the fort. On February 11, a heavy artillery bombardment finally persuaded Major Lawrence to surrender on the next day. This small victory hardly benefited the British because the war had been over since December and they had to return the fort.

The War of 1812 showed that Canada's borders were relatively secure even with a limited number of fortifications. For the United States, the war exposed the weakness of the fortifications of the 2nd System and the inability of the U.S. Navy to protect the long coastline from raids and invasions.

View of Chalmette Battlefield outside of New Orleans where Andrew Jackson created earthworks which defeated the British assault in January 1815. The naval 32-pdr gun on the left was Jackson's heaviest gun.

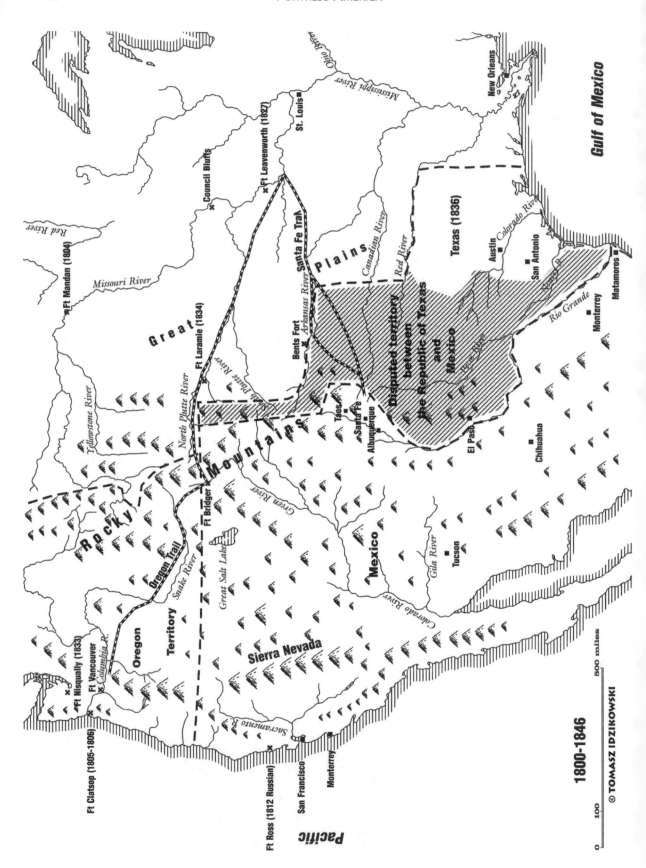

Gulf of Mexico

New Orleans

Mississippi River

Ohio River

St. Louis

Ft Leavenworth (1827)

Council Bluffs

Red River

Ft Mandan (1804)

Missouri River

Yellowstone River

Great

Santa Fe Trail

Arkansas River

Plains

Canadian River

Red River

Texas (1836)

Austin

Colorado River

San Antonio

Matamoros

Nueces R.

Rio Grande

Monterrey

Ft Laramie (1834)

North Platte River

South Platte River

Bents Fort

Disputed territory between the Republic of Texas and Mexico

Taos

Santa Fe

Albuquerque

Pecos River

El Paso

Chihuahua

Rocky

Mountains

Ft Bridger

Green River

Mexico

Gila River

Tucson

Oregon Trail

Snake River

Great Salt Lake

Colorado River

Ft Nisqually (1833)

Ft Vancouver

Columbia R.

Oregon

Territory

Sierra Nevada

Ft Clatsop (1805-1806)

Sacramento R.

Ft Ross (1812 Russian)

San Francisco

Monterrey

Pacific

1800-1846

© TOMASZ IDZIKOWSKI

0   100   500 miles

Chapter 5

FORTIFICATIONS OF
THE EXPANDING FRONTIERS

THE WAR OF 1812 NOT ONLY REVEALED the inability of the United States to defend its borders, but also witnessed drastic changes in the Americas. Spain had proven to be a power in decline even before the war began, as the United States gradually wrested West Florida from its control by securing the area around New Orleans first and the entire coast of Louisiana and Mississippi next. During the war, American forces had marched into Mobile, and in November 1814, Andrew Jackson had sent his troops into Pensacola. Spain was convinced to cede the territory, giving the United States a continuous coastline from Maine to Louisiana and increasing the number of sites that needed defenses. Earlier, the frontiers of the United States and New Spain along the newly acquired Louisiana Purchase had also been contested. However, after the War of 1812, Mexico became independent presenting a weaker neighbor on the American border who could only rely upon the old Spanish presidios to protect its borders. Early in the century, Lewis and Clark had traveled beyond the boundaries of the new acquisition and reached the Pacific where one of the first outposts of the United States was set up near present-day Astoria. This entire region soon became an area of contention between U.S. and British trading interests and almost precipitated another war with the British in the 1840s.

The Frontier and Foreign Encroachment

In the first half of the nineteenth century, the overriding reason for Americans to build fortifications had been the necessity to protect the country from European invasion. Thus, the emphasis had been on coastal fortifications and the protection of the border with Canada and the Lake Champlain route. However, priorities shifted after the War of 1812.

On the Canadian border, few new forts were built. In 1840, the U.S. army concluded that the increase in population and trade on the Great Lakes reduced the need for fortifications in the area. The need to establish national boundaries with potentially hostile nations [Spain and Great Britain], however, still provided a reason to build fortifications. As the Americans moved west of the Mississippi, forts also became a necessary protection against the Native Americans to control the displaced tribes, enforce treaties, and keep the Indians on their reservations. The westward movement across the Great Plains and Rockies also necessitated forts to protect travelers on the trails from hostile Indians.

President Monroe intended to begin a more aggressive frontier policy with the establishment of a fort in Arkansas. Andrew Jackson received orders to establish an American bastion, which eventually became FORT SMITH, on the Arkansas River in 1817. Major Stephen Long and a five-man party of engineers selected the site for the fort on a bluff overlooking the river. Late in the year, a company of the army's Rifle Regiment began the construction. Long had laid out plans for a square stockade with sides 132 feet long. Blockhouses at opposite corners measured 28 feet in length and extended 10 feet beyond the fort walls, creating an overhang to defend the walls. Following the typical fort design, Long included a dry moat. Initially, the fort's mission was to maintain peace between the Osage and Cherokee tribes. As was the case for other frontier forts, supply lines were tenuous at best. [The re-supply of forts like Fort Smith became even more problematic in 1819 when Congress passed a new budget-saving plan. Instead of contracting civilians to supply the army and its forts on the frontier, an officer of the garrison was appointed to handle commissary needs, which included disparate duties like purchasing necessities and sending out hunting parties.] In 1822, Colonel Matthew Arbuckle and five companies of the 7th Infantry Regiment occupied Fort Smith, then the main fort in the west. Since the fort only had accommodations for one company, Arbuckle built additional barracks. A small town grew around Fort Smith during the next few years, a not uncommon event in the nineteenth century. In 1824, Arbuckle received orders to abandon the fort. He moved further up the Arkansas River, to the junction of the Grand and Verdigris Rivers, where he established CANTONMENT GIBSON (later FORT GIBSON). At Fort Smith, the locals stripped the abandoned stockaded fort that was falling into ruins.

In the early 1830s, President Andrew Jackson forced many southeastern tribes on the "Trail of Tears," resettling them in the west, beyond Fort Smith, mainly in modern-day Oklahoma. Most of the frontier forts in this area were built at that time, including FORT ARBUCKLE on the Arkansas River at the mouth of the Cimarron River, whose only defenses consisted of a palisaded blockhouse. [Note: This Fort Arbuckle was abandoned in 1834, and should not be confused with another fort without any defenses of the same name built further to the south near the Washita River in 1851.] The army's objective was to establish and control the resettlement of the tribes from east of the Mississippi.

The Lewis and Clark expedition, the first to move up the Missouri River, had built a string of temporary forts all the way to the Pacific in the future Oregon Territory. It had spent its first winter at FORT MANDAN, a stockaded position they built on the Missouri River in the territory of the Mandan Indians in present-day North Dakota. After reaching the Pacific in November 1805, Lewis and Clark had moved south of the Columbia River and early in December built a stockaded outpost for the winter. Named FORT CLATSOP after a local tribe, it consisted of two buildings with seven contiguous rooms facing each other and forming two sides of the enclosure. They were linked to each other by two walls where two gates allowed access. The thirty men of the expedition occupied the site and foraged the area for food for 106 days, 94 of which were drenched with rain. They abandoned the site in late March 1806 leaving behind the first U.S. army post on the Pacific. In 1808 to control the fur trade and reduce Indian resistance Lewis assigned Clark to go up the Missouri where he established FORT OSAGE (first named FORT CLARK), a five-sided fort with five blockhouses serving as bastions. The army did not garrison Fort Osage during the War of 1812.

It was not until after the war that the government finally took interest in the region of the Upper Missouri. British and American fur companies had already begun competing in the Oregon Territory and the British were pushing their claims south, to the banks of the upper Missouri River. A military expedition under Colonel Henry Atkinson reached Council Bluffs (near modern-day Omaha) in 1819 where they set up Camp Missouri to sit out the winter. However, the site was too close to the river and suffered from flooding, so it was moved a mile away to a more elevated position in 1820. The dimensions of this fort were 455 feet by 468 feet. Later renamed FORT ATKINSON, this outpost represented the first military stockade west of the Missouri and was, for several years, the military post furthest west in the U.S. territory. It served as a jumping off point for westbound expeditions.

To stop encroachment from British Canada, the army sent Lieutenant Colonel Henry Leavenworth with troops of the 5th Infantry further east in Minnesota where he established FORT SNELLING in 1819. In 1820, the army moved the fort from its initial site to a more prominent position not subject to flooding. Fort Snelling, situated on the heights above the point where the Minnesota and Mississippi Rivers meet, was turned into a large stone fort. It had four straight sides and a curved side, and included a bastion at each corner and one in the middle of the curved side. The fort played a major role in controlling traffic on the rivers and maintaining relations with the various tribes in the region for many years.

In 1824, funds became available for Colonel Atkinson to continue on his exploratory mission and he set out the following year. However, this expedition had limited success. Since no viable route to the Oregon Territory had been opened along the Missouri, the army abandoned Fort Atkinson at Council Bluffs in the summer of 1827, leaving only the newly created FORT LEAVENWORTH as the main outpost in the west. Fort Leavenworth had been built by Colonel Henry Leavenworth after he departed from Jefferson Barracks in April 1827, taking with him four companies of the 3rd Infantry.

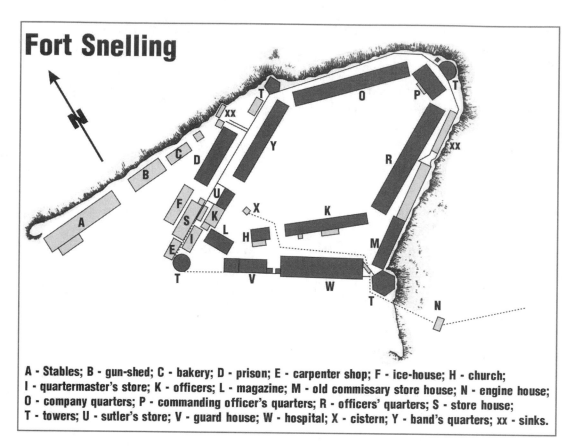

Fort Snelling

A - Stables; B - gun-shed; C - bakery; D - prison; E - carpenter shop; F - ice-house; H - church;
I - quartermaster's store; K - officers; L - magazine; M - old commissary store house; N - engine house;
O - company quarters; P - commanding officer's quarters; R - officers' quarters; S - store house;
T - towers; U - sutler's store; V - guard house; W - hospital; X - cistern; Y - band's quarters; xx - sinks.

Traveling by keelboats, they moved up the river to establish the new post. Leavenworth reported that the site he selected was 150 feet above the river on dry rolling country near the mouth of the Little Platte River. Major General Brown, commander of the Western Department ordered the 6th Infantry to evacuate Fort Atkinson and deliver any useful property and stores to Leavenworth's new fort. Fort Osage was soon abandoned as well. Leavenworth began by building a number of log huts, and then surrounded the camp with a crude stone wall. However, the fort soon outgrew its wall and by the 1840s, its only defenses consisted of two blockhouses. The new fort served two missions: to protect the Santa Fe Trail running just to the south, and to inspect boats moving up the Missouri, in an effort to control the illegal alcohol traffic with the Indians. The Santa Fe Trail linked the first series of forts needed to establish control over the Comanche, Arapahoe, and Pawnee, who found the trade caravans tempting targets for raiding.

American and British fur-trading companies took up the initiative started by Lewis and Clark and began staking out new claims. Some of the better-known posts of the next thirty years were Fort McLoughlin, Fort Langley, and Fort Victoria in present-day Canada, and Fort Nisqually, Fort Vancouver, and Fort Astoria in present-day Washington and Oregon. In 1811, John Jacob Astor, an American entrepreneur, had sent two expeditions, one overland and one by sea, to establish a fur-trading center on the Pacific Coast. Astor's ship expedition sailed into the mouth of the Columbia River and built a large stockade

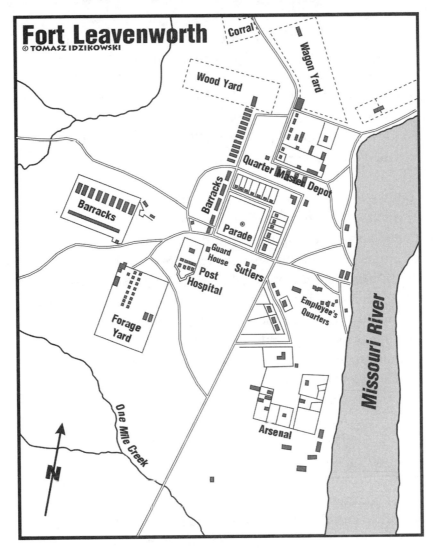

with blockhouses called FORT ASTORIA, on the south side of the river, at the site of present-day Astoria. The region, rich in timberland and devoid of termites, favored the construction of timber forts. The main problem was wood-rot fostered by the humidity of the region. In 1813, Fort Astoria and its assets were sold to the British North West Company after the War of 1812 put it in a precarious position. A British warship took possession of the fort, renaming it FORT GEORGE. It appeared that the British were in control of the Columbia/Oregon territory by dominating the mouths of both the Fraser and Columbia Rivers. Despite the Treaty of Ghent, which directed a return to the status quo, the situation did not change on the Pacific Coast. The problem was resolved in 1818 when the United States and Great Britain agreed on a joint occupation. In 1825, the British North West Company moved their base of operations further up the Columbia River and built the first FORT VANCOUVER. But in 1829, the company ordered the fort to be rebuilt closer to the river. The fort's 15-foot-high stockade encircled several large buildings. The garrison farmed the area around the fort and raised livestock to be self-sufficient.

The American Fur Company built FORT UNION (North Dakota) on the upper Missouri among the Mandan in 1829. According to Robert Athearn, author of *Forts of the Upper Missouri*, it was built of strong cottonwood log walls 25 feet high and its enceinte enclosed 52,800 square feet. At two opposite corners it had 30-foot-high stone bastions with a typical double entrance. Fort Union was occupied during the Civil War, but it was in poor condition and later abandoned. Other fur traders built a rival post, named FORT PIERRE, further down the river in South Dakota. This small fort later played an important role with the army.

To the west of the Rockies and beyond, the trails suitable for a "modern" supply column were few and the terrain was difficult. The prize at the other end was the Oregon Territory on the Pacific. It was claimed by four contenders: Great Britain, Spain, Russia, and the United States. Russian ships had visited the coast of the Pacific Northwest since the eighteenth century. The Russians established their presence as far south as northern California with the construction of FORT ROSS. However, by the beginning of the 1820s, the Spaniards and the Russians had withdrawn their claims to the area, but the Americans and the British still contested it. British dominance only lasted until the 1830s, when American settlers began moving in along the Oregon Trail. By the mid-1840s, American settlers poured into the region coming to farm and displacing the fur industry. Until that time, the flags of trading companies had flown over a large array of forts. After 1845, the British and Americans agreed on a boundary line that is now the present-day U.S./Canadian border. National flags largely replaced company flags and many of the old trading forts became military posts.

FORT VANCOUVER became an American army post in 1846. By 1845, a year before the Pacific Northwest became U.S. territory, the fort's stockade had already been expanded several times. At the time, the fort measured 734 feet by 318 feet and had a three-story-high corner blockhouse mounting eight 3-pdr cannons on the upper floor. In many ways, Fort Vancouver was representative of both the large and the small trading posts of the northwest and the Rocky Mountains. It had high stockades without wall-walks because there were usually not enough company personnel to defend them. Many of the other trading posts also included one or more blockhouses, often incorrectly identified as bastions. In some cases, however, these blockhouses did serve as bastions by providing flanking fire along the walls, but more frequently, they were used for storage rooms and quarters. Nonetheless, they were one of the few places in the forts from which the occupants could defend themselves. In many ways, these "forts" were similar to the older frontier blockhouses surrounded by palisades, but they were probably stronger.

Further north, the British had gotten a firm hold on the Fraser River Valley. Their presence had been established in the region when Simon Fraser founded the first settlement west of the Rockies at FORT McLEOD in 1805 and traveled down the Fraser River

The Russian Foothold in America

Russian fur-trading companies established several forts in the Kenai region of Alaska, including FORT ST. GEORGE (1791), FORT ST. NICOLAS (1791), FORT ALEXANDROVSK (1785). Fort Alexandrovsk is recognized as the first European settlement in Alaska. Fort Alexandrovsk was one of the largest Russian military posts and included a 12-foot palisade and two bastions with a square enceinte of about 120 yards on each side enclosing over twenty buildings. In 1793, the Russians built FORT VOSKRENSENSKII, a large rectangular stockade with two tall watchtowers, at the head of Resurrection Bay. Outside this fort was a shipyard encircled by chevaux-de-frise. New Archangel (Sitka) was established and became the capital of Russian America in 1804. Alexander Baranof built the REDOUBT ST. GABRIEL in Sitka in 1799 near a fortified town of the Tlingit Indians. This large stockaded blockhouse held two hundred troops. In 1802, the Tlingit destroyed this redoubt. Other Russian sites along the coast included the YAKUTAT BAY FORT built in 1796 in the eastern Gulf of Alaska and FORT NAKNEK on the mouth of the river of the same name. Both were stockaded blockhouses from the 1830s. On Wrangell Island, there was REDOUBT ST. DIONYSIUS, a fortified trading post.

In 1812, a Russian expedition moved down the North American coastline seeking greener pastures. Passing the Columbian/Oregon region, the ship anchored north of San Francisco, beyond the range of the Spanish settlements.

The Russians quickly built a fort, completing it by mid August 1812. They named it FORT ROSS, short for Rossyia, their homeland. The fort's stockade and buildings were made of stout California redwood. The fort included two blockhouses: a seven-sided blockhouse on the north (northwest) side and an eight-sided blockhouse on the south (southeast) side. Fort Ross stood on a terrace overlooking the Pacific above the shoreline with a forest on its east side. Inside the fort were barracks, storehouses, offices, an Orthodox-style church built in 1825, a well, and other facilities. The settler's homes were located outside the walls.

In a report dating from 1833, Lieutenant Vallejo put the length of the walls of Fort Ross at about 300 feet forming a square with sentry positions on the two corners without blockhouses. By this time, the walls of the fort had badly deteriorated due to the ravages of the elements and had not seen any significant repairs. They were unable, the lieutenant observed, to stop any cannon balls. The fort and settlement numbered about three hundred people. A shipyard was built near the beach, but its production was limited in the 1830s. The colony was unsuccessful in supplying Alaska for a variety of reasons. Finally, in 1839, the Hudson Bay Company negotiated an agreement with the Russian-American Fur Company, agreeing to supply Alaska with foodstuffs. Thus, the Russians abandoned Fort Ross and the California colony in 1841.

in 1808. This river was much more treacherous than the Columbia and not as inviting for exploitation of the region. Still, the British created a chain of trading posts along its course, including FORT ST. JAMES (1806) on Lake Stuart, FORT KAMLOOPS (1812), FORT ALEXANDRIA (1828), FORT YALE (1847 or 1848), and FORT HOPE (1847). More forts were established further north and west of the Fraser River Valley. They included FORT SIMPSON (1831) on the Nass River and FORT MCLOUGHLIN (1833) further down the coast that was replaced by FORT RUPERT (1849). However, the last two were located in hostile territory and failed. After the 1846 boundary settlement with the United States, the British were no longer able to use the Columbia River route into the interior of their Canadian territories. In preparation for this event, they began developing the Fraser River route in the 1840s. At this time, the company built FORT YALE between Fort Kamloops and Fort Langley and FORT HOPE as trans-shipment points for floating goods down the Fraser to Fort Langley. The main purpose of Fort Hope was to provide a site where the trappers could pasture the herds of horses used for carrying the furs and supplies. As the fur and salmon trade waned in the 1850s, gold was discovered near Fort Kamloops and the Fraser route and its forts took on new importance. The British government soon took over, founding the colony of British Columbia. Fort Yale served as the final provisioning post for miners during the 1858–1860 gold rush, and as a result, a town grew up around it.

FORT LANGLEY, which went into operation in 1827, was one of the largest and better-known forts of the Hudson Bay Company and it occupied a key position in the region. It was garrisoned with fewer than twenty men in 1828 and only eight men in 1833. In the 1830s, the company even decided to replace Fort Langley with Fort Nisqually on Puget Sound (near the site of modern-day Tacoma), which offered easier access than the Fraser, but the advent of steam-powered vessels on the Pacific made the move unnecessary. In 1837, Fort Langley's 25-man garrison was attacked by a party of six hundred Yuculta Indians coming down the river in canoes. Even though the attack was repelled, James Douglas claimed that the fort was in poor condition. Fort Langley was probably larger than most of the other trading posts in British Columbia. The first fort was about 120 feet by 135 feet with two blockhouses. In 1839, it was replaced by a larger fort, which included four blockhouses and was located more than a mile away from the original. After this fort succumbed to fire, a final fort was built with a stockade roughly 669 feet by 242 feet. The stockade of this fort was made of timbers squared only on two faces to provide a closer fit. Each log, about 8 to 10 inches in diameter, stood about 20 feet above the ground. The stockade was assembled with the tenon-and-mortise method known in this region as the Red River frame construction technique. The logs were sawed in a pit by a two-man crew who shaped the flat sides of each log. Tenons projecting from the ends of the logs and planks fit into a mortise or groove cut into vertical posts, holding the wall tightly in place. Once placed upright in the ditch, a squared brace was fitted into the lower slots of the logs forming the wall and a similar brace in the upper slot. A series of wooden dowels held the braces in place. When it was necessary to remove or expand a building, the old logs could be easily disassembled and reused. Since the wet climate caused the logs to rot within ten to fifteen years, this method made it easier to replace deteriorating sections of walls without rebuilding the entire structure.

Fort Langley included two corner blockhouses facing the river, each mounting two 9-pdr cannons. The blockhouses projected outward from walls serving as bastions to cover the face of the fort's walls. A wall-walk linked these two blockhouses since the riverfront was considered the most vulnerable. Archaeological evidence suggests that there were two other bastions, probably blockhouses serving as bastions, but documentary evidence confirms the existence of only one in the southeast corner. An 1858 drawing shows it facing the lowlands to the east. In addition to storehouses, the fort included the "Big House," which served as the main office and residence of the company's representative, and a blacksmith's shop. Since these trading posts had to store and ship produce or fish, they also had a cooperage for making barrels.

Besides Fort Langley, one of the most important forts in British Columbia was FORT VICTORIA, built in 1843 on Vancouver Island, near the present city of Victoria. This fort's mission was to serve as a control center when it became evident that American settlers would soon dominate the Oregon Territory. Five years later, the island became a British colony, and in 1858, British Columbia joined the empire, virtually ending the independence of the Hudson Bay Company when the government took over the larger trading forts.

Earlier, when the British had planted their flag in British Columbia and the Oregon Territory, Americans began moving overland along routes opened through Indian Territory only made somewhat secure by the presence of frontier forts. FORT SMITH was reoccupied in 1831, and in 1838 work began on a new and larger fort intended to be a fortress, but it was never completed. The fort became the center of expansion from the Arkansas River while St. Louis and the Missouri River served as the main gateway to the west for settlers moving along the Oregon Trail. In April 1836, Secretary of War Cass wrote in a report to the president that to protect the western frontier and roads in the region of the Great Plains "stockaded forts, with log block-houses, have been found fully sufficient for all the purposes of defence against Indians." Since they were inexpensive and easily built, he suggested that they were all the army needed on the frontier. More permanent fortifications, he claimed, were superfluous in the west because the frontier was constantly receding. In many cases, the frontier "forts" did not even have a stockade or blockhouse.

In 1842, the 2,000-mile-long Oregon Trail rather than the undeveloped Missouri/Columbia River route became the main westward route. Leaving from St. Joseph, Missouri, the wagon trains passed by Fort Kearney and Fort Laramie and wound their way through the Rockies before they reached their final destination. The arduous journey from Missouri to Oregon took four to six months, depending on the weather and other conditions.

Competing fur traders had established posts in the vicinity of the Laramie River since the 1830s. One of these, called FORT JOHN, was built in 1841 with adobe walls and would eventually be FORT LARAMIE (See pages 186-188). Contemporary drawings show a typical enclosed trading post/fort that looked quite formidable on the outside. Travelers on the Oregon Trail reached this fort at a time when its fur trading business was dying out. In 1849, it was acquired by the army and improved over the years with additional buildings and even a moat. However, the old walls decayed since they played no role in a largely open post built around a large parade ground. Its first military garrison consisted of an infantry company and two companies of mounted riflemen.

FORT KEARNEY (Nebraska) was built in 1846 to protect the Oregon Trail on the Great Plains, but it was abandoned when it proved to be too far from the trail to be useful. On June 1848, a new Fort Kearney, better-suited to carry out its mission, was built on the Platte River.

Beyond Fort Laramie the Oregon Trail ran to South Pass through the Rocky Mountains and on to FORT BRIDGER, a trading post established in 1842 by traders Jim Bridger and Louis Vasquez. This fort became a major stop for the pioneers. However, the fort's owners soon found themselves at odds with Brigham Young's Mormons in the 1850s. The Mormons eventually took over the fort. During the Mormon War in 1857, when Colonel Albert Sidney Johnston advanced on the fort, the Mormons put it to the torch and fled. The U.S. Army then occupied the fort, replacing the burned-down stockade with additional buildings.

After Fort Bridger, the last major stop on the Oregon Trail was at FORT HALL, a small walled trading post built by a fur trader from New England named Nathaniel Wyeth in

Fort Hall, Idaho, was established as a trading fort on the Oregon Trail. The log buildings were surrounded by whitewashed adobe walls.

1834. His fort had 15-foot-high walls of cottonwood and formed a square with 80-foot sides and two corner bastions. The Hudson Bay Company bought it in 1836 and expanded it with whitewashed walls of adobe bricks. The company abandoned the fort in 1856, and in 1859 the U.S. Army moved in to protect the wagon trains.

After it left Fort Hall, the trail cut across modern-day Idaho, passing by FORT BOISE, a fort built by traders in 1834 to compete with Fort Hall. The Hudson Bay Company owned it until the mid-1850s. Finally, the trail led into Oregon and FORT WALLA WALLA in Washington. This post too belonged to the Hudson Bay Company from 1821 to 1860, when it was abandoned. It had a 20-foot-high stockade and measured 200 feet in length. The 9th Infantry moved into the vicinity and built a stockaded blockhouse in 1856.

The army left the Upper Missouri in the hands of the trading companies until the 1850s, when the government finally decided to create a route. The U.S. Army's presence in the region was re-established with the acquisition of FORT PIERRE and with Colonel William Harney's retaliatory expedition against the Sioux in 1855. Fort Pierre was to serve as a supply base, but it proved to be too small, as Harney discovered when he tried to quarter his troops there for the winter. In 1856, FORT RANDALL, located further down the river, was turned into the supply fort and Fort Pierre was dismantled. Fort Randall was able to accommodate two companies of the 2nd Infantry and four companies of the 2nd Dragoons, but its isolated position was not good for morale.

In 1858, according to Athearn, Captain A. A. Humphreys of Topographic Engineers, who was sent to evaluate the situation, reported that there was no satisfactory route westward along the Missouri above Fort Pierre. Despite his report, the army under the direction of Secretary of War John Floyd, planned to link the Missouri River route to Fort Walla Walla with a road later named the Mullan Road after the army engineer lieutenant who built it. Floyd's goal was to link Fort Benton by road to Fort Walla Walla. FORT BENTON, built in 1845, was the property of the American Fur Company and was located far up the Missouri in western Montana, where steamships could only reach it for half of the year. Lieutenant John Mullan of the 2nd Artillery and his work party completed most of the road and its bridges covering over 630 miles. In Montana, Mullan setup winter camps for his work crews: Cantonment Jordan (1859–1860) at De Borgia and Cantonment Wright (1861–1862) at Milltown. The road was inaugurated after the first steamboat reached Fort Benton in 1860. Although this new route improved communications with the west, it led to deterioration in Indian relations so that the army had to establish more posts in the region during and after the Civil War.

Although the Santa Fe Trail was older than the Oregon Trail, it was not an emigrant route and saw less traffic than the Oregon Trail. For this reason, only one important trading fort operated along the Santa Fe Trail in the late 1840s: BENT'S FORT, or BENT'S OLD FORT. Located on the Arkansas River in southeastern Colorado, it was built by the brothers Charles and William Bent in partnership with Ceran St. Vrain in 1833, although

Fort Laramie

FORT LARAMIE is typical of many of the early army installations in the West. It began as a trading post named Fort John established by the American Fur Company in the 1830s. Unlike many other trading posts, it became important when the Oregon Trail passed by it as the fur trade was drying up in the area. Contemporary drawings show that, like most trading posts or forts of the period, it had 15-foot-high adobe walls and two corner block-houses. The company hired Taos Indians to build the adobe walls since there were no timber resources in the area. Two brass cannons projected over the gate that opened on the Laramie River. In the days of the Oregon Trail, it was a busy trade center. For the pioneers moving west, it was a secure place where they could outfit themselves for their journey into the mountains.

When the army found it necessary to protect the Oregon Trail, the government purchased the site. However, the army had no use for the adobe structure, preferring to lay out the buildings of a larger fort around a huge parade ground. The fort presented some defensive advantages because it occupied a bend in the Laramie River. However, the river was not a formidable obstacle and most of the fort was open. In 1865, the garrison excavated a defensive ditch, using wooden stakes to create revetments to protect the fort when the Indians in the area resumed hostilities. The ditch did not last long because timber was at a premium in an area virtually devoid of trees and it was needed for buildings. Thus, Fort Laramie, like many other forts in the west and southwest, continued to be a fort without defenses. Apparently the army believed that maintaining a large garrison was sufficient to deter Indian raids.

The structures found at Fort Laramie were typical of most forts of the nineteenth century. It included barracks that were renovated or replaced over time. The main buildings stood around the parade ground of the fort. The oldest remaining structure on the site is Old Bedlam, the BOQ, a two-story structure built in 1849. The commanding officer and his wife lived on the upper floor, which also included a conference room/officers mess. There was an infantry barracks for two infantry companies built of adobe that included mess halls and kitchens for each company. A larger, one-floor, wooden infantry barracks from 1867 housed three companies and included mess halls and kitchens for each company. The troops lived in tents until these barracks were built. A guardhouse, known as the Old Guardhouse built in 1866, replaced the first guardhouse. It had room for forty prisoners on the lower level, but often accommodated more. The upper level held the guards and two small cells. After the post surgeon complained about the unhealthy conditions in the old guardhouse, the New Guardhouse was built in 1876. The cavalry barracks, built in 1874 of lime-concrete, was the largest structure on the fort. The troopers slept on the second floor. It was not located next

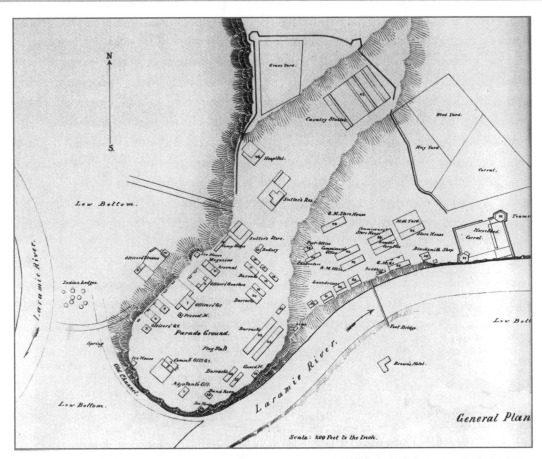

Fort Laramie had no walls and the large parade was surrounded by buildings including these. This two story structure was the BOQ, nicknamed "old Bedlam." To the left are the ruins of the married officers's housing. At top is one of the original plans for the fort.

to the parade ground. Officer's quarters in three individual buildings made of lime-concrete appeared in 1881, next to the parade ground. The post surgeon's quarters, built in 1875, included his residence and office. Bakeries with large brick ovens were built beyond the parade ground in 1876 and 1883. Sewage was a problem and the post surgeon recommended the construction of a latrine for four companies near the river in 1866. However, the problem was not resolved because the river was turned into a sewage ditch, particularly in the summer months when the river was low. Other buildings on the post included a commissary, post trader, and administration buildings built at various times in Fort Laramie's history. The stables were near the cavalry barracks, and a hospital, built in the 1870s, was situated on a rise just outside the fort near a cemetery dating from the 1860s. A number of laundresses were allowed to live in tents near the bakery buildings. The number of these women generally depended on the size of the garrison.

Initially this open fort, like many others in the west, was built around a parade ground giving it a square or rectangular shape so that the buildings might offer some defensive advantages if need be. At the end of the nineteenth century, structures were added without great concern for defense since the Indian problem had waned.

there is some question as to the exact date of its construction. Sitting astride the Santa Fe Trail, Fort Bent looked more like a fort than a trading post. It included two round corner bastions at opposite corners, one of which mounted a cannon. The storerooms and quarters were placed in such a way that their back walls formed three of the fort's four walls, including the side with the entrance. The roofs on the entrance side served as a fighting platform and gave access to the bastion. The adjacent wall was made of two-level rooms and did not have positions on the roof, but a second corner bastion flanked that wall. The back wall was similar to the wall with the entrance but consisted of single-level buildings. The fourth side also consisted of single-level structures, but it formed an inner wall because beyond it was a wall running from the corner bastion to a point near the back wall on the east side of the fort. The enclosed area formed an inner corral that included a wall-walk. Behind the back wall was a larger outer corral. This adobe brick structure measured 142 feet by 122 feet. The walls were about 4 feet thick and 15 feet high, and at the time the fort was occupied cactus grew on top forming an obstacle like barbed wire to keep out intruders. The entrance to Bent's Fort consisted of double gates. The inner gate was closed during trading, and bartering took place through the trade-room that opened into the entrance corridor formed by the two gates, denying the Indians access to the fort. This type of double-gate entrance was not uncommon in trading forts of the period.

The Bents got along well with the Indians, including the Southern Cheyenne, espe-

Bent's Fort, Colorado. Established as a trading fort, it was located along the Santa Fe Trail and used by the army during the War with Mexico. This is a view of the wall walk and corner bastion of outer wall which formed a corral with the inner wall.

cially since one of them took an Indian woman for his wife. Although the forty to sixty men that usually occupied the fort could probably have easily defended it against a small war party, the need never arose. After the War with Mexico, Bent tried to sell his fort to the army, which had used it as a supply point during the Mexican War and later. Bent finally abandoned the fort in 1853 because the U.S. Army's presence had ruined trade. In 1853, Bent built BENT'S NEW FORT, a similar but smaller and bastion-less version of the old fort. This sandstone structure included the other fort's only cannon and stood on a bluff accessed from only one side. The army leased this fort in 1860.

Although the frontier policy regarding the territories west of the Mississippi appeared to be rather confused between 1820 and 1860, it was not. The first forts established west of the Mississippi during the period beginning after the War of 1812 and

Jackson Barracks 1834-1835

© TOMASZ IDZIKOWSKI

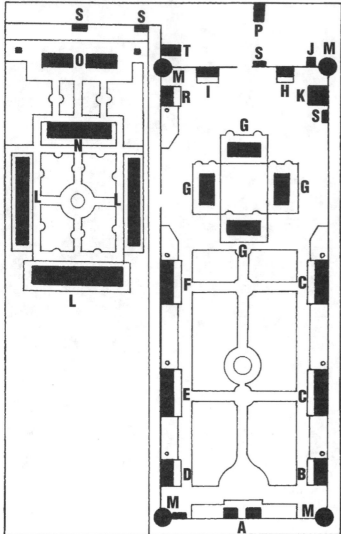

A Headquarters
B Chaplain's Quarters
C Officer's Quarters
D Quartermaster's Quarters
E Surgeon's Quarters
F Asst.'s Surgeon's Quarters
G Barracks
H Prison
I Commissary Storehouse
J Barracks Bakery
K Engine House
L Hospital
M Tower
N Dining Room
O Kitchen
P Hospital Bakery
R Ordinance Sgt. & Hosp. Stewards Qts.
S Privies
T Laundry

Jackson Barracks, outside of New Orleans, was built early in the nineteenth century and included four towers like this (two remain) at the corners of the bricks walls that enclosed it. The towers included musket embrasures and places for small cannons on the roof.

ending in the 1820s were mainly meant to stop British encroachment from the north and to maintain control over the local tribal groups. When Stephen Long mislabeled most of the Great Plains as the Great American Desert, the War Department saw little need to venture further west. After President Jackson implemented the policy of Indian removal from the southeast, Secretary of War Lewis Cass proposed the establishment of a line of forts built along a military road running along the frontier from Minnesota to Louisiana. Although the road did not reach Fort Snelling, as intended, in the 1840s it did link Fort Leavenworth to Fort Scott, Fort Gibson, Fort Smith on the Arkansas, and Fort Townsown on the Red River. FORT SCOTT was typical of many of these Plains forts. According to Leo Oliva, the author of *Ft. Scott,* it was built in 1842 and consisted of a settlement built around a parade ground that served as a supply base for the army. It had no actual stockades or blockhouses. Further to the south in Louisiana, FORT JESUP had been built to guard the U.S.-Mexican border and was abandoned after the beginning of the War with Mexico.

The army also built JACKSON BARRACKS a few miles down the river from New Orleans in 1834. It consisted of high brick walls enclosing an area of about 560 feet by 1,500 feet with four three-story crenelated round towers at the corners. These towers served as bastions flanking the walls with embrasures for muskets and cannons. Four large two-story wooden barracks and a large brick magazine, used as a powder depot, were the main features. A hospital complex was added outside the north wall in 1848. Jackson Barracks served as a depot and staging site for the Seminole Wars, the Mexican War, and then the movement westward. (The site is still used today by the Louisiana National Guard.)

Until the War with Mexico in 1846, the army built few forts beyond the old frontier line that ran between Fort Jesup and Fort Snelling and along the Santa Fe and the Oregon Trails. When the army started buying forts from traders or building new forts in the late 1840s and early 1850s, there were still only a few forts at key points along the trails. Most of the forts on the Great Plains, such as Fort Larned on the Santa Fe Trail, were hardly impressive. Because of a lack of wood, many forts were made of sod or sod and adobe. They were open positions where most of the structures served as shelter for the troops.

In the mid-1850s, Secretary of War Jefferson Davis still thought of the Great Plains as the Great American Desert and considered it of little economic value. He thought it preferable to invest in a few large forts for large garrisons than in numerous small outposts that would tie up large numbers of troops. Little change occurred in the west under Secretary of War Floyd, except for the opening of the Missouri route. However, in the northern states, railroads developed between the 1820s and the 1850s creating an effective network of communications in most of the eastern and northern states. As a result of the General Survey Act of 1824, the Corps of Engineers assumed the task of surveying routes for private railroads in 1826. In the 1850s, the U.S. government proposed the construction of a transcontinental railroad and early in the decade, army engineers were surveying possible routes. Many of these lieutenants and captains worked on military roads that linked key forts, such as those in Oregon, to areas with expanding populations. When the Civil War began, Secretary of the Army Simon Cameron found that the funds appropriated in the 1850s to complete a road from Fort Union (New Mexico) to Santa Fe and Taos were insufficient. In addition, other roads, such as the one from Fort Snelling (Minnesota) to the Red River, were still unfinished. The Civil War brought a halt to much of this work and the few main routes west continued to be vulnerable.

Seminole Wars and the Forts of Florida

In the spring of 1816, the 4th Infantry built FORT SCOTT (Georgia) on the Flint River at a point before it flows into the Apalachicola. Its mission was to control hostile Creek Indians. Secretary of War Calhoun sent Andrew Jackson to Fort Scott in 1817 to deal with the continuing problem of Indian raids coming out of Florida. Runaway slaves and Seminoles had operated almost with impunity for months. The British, who had built a fort near the mouth of the Apalachicola River on Prospect Bluff in 1814, had encouraged the Indians and Blacks and when they departed in 1816, Florida went back to Spain and the British turned the fort over to the Indians and Blacks. The fort became known as NEGRO FORT because it was occupied by escaped slaves who shared their crops with the Seminoles. The white settlers in Georgia asked the government to destroy the fort and close the area as a refuge. Negro Fort mounted British artillery and included a central magazine surrounded by an octagonal earthwork. The timber walls of the fort's enceinte formed a rectangle reaching the river and included two bastions on the eastern landward side. The former slaves had learned from the British how to use the artillery. American gunboats supporting the advancing infantry engaged Negro Fort in battle in the summer of 1816. A round hit the magazine, causing a massive explosion that killed about three hundred men, women, and children. Only about sixty people survived the blast. Jackson destroyed the fort and ordered Lieutenant James Gadsden to build a new, smaller fort on the riverbank. FORT GADSDEN was to protect supplies arriving by sea from New Orleans. Jackson proceeded east to force the surrender of the fort at Spanish St. Mark and then moved west to take Pensacola, despite the fact that Spain was at peace with the United States. In 1818, Spain, anxious to avoid further conflicts, ceded Florida to the United States. Despite the American takeover, the number of hostile Seminoles and runaway slaves remained high in Florida.

The Second Seminole War began when the Seminoles under Osceola refused to move to the western reservations. Small skirmishes and an ambush near FORT KING triggered all-out war in 1835. The fort, built in March 1827 as a trading post at the site of Ocala, was a stockade 152 feet by 162 feet with a single blockhouse and large barracks when the army took over. General Winfield Scott, in charge of the campaign, attempted to assemble a large military force from his headquarters near St. Augustine. He was seriously hampered by problems in supply and transportation. His attempt to smash the Seminoles failed when they scattered and began a long drawn-out guerrilla war. Scott was replaced by General Thomas Jesup, who established new posts on the east coast, including FORT PIERCE and FORT JUPITER, in the winter of 1837–38. However, both positions were abandoned in 1842. In November 1837, General Zachary Taylor, coming out of Fort Brooke, present-day site of Tampa, moved to the Kissimmee River and Lake Okeechobee, building FORT GARDINER and FORT BASINGER to cover his line of communications. He engaged in battle in December at Lake Okeechobee, driving the Seminoles east. However, he had to withdraw because he suffered over one hundred casualties while inflicting only about twenty-five on his enemy.

FORT BROOKE, built in 1824, served as the main base on the west coast of Florida. This large fort held 680 men during the campaign. It was one of several forts built to secure coastal and interior positions. Other Florida forts included FORT OGDEN near the Peace River; FORT NEW SMYRNA, the militia post of FORT MICANOPY (1835), taken over in 1836; FORT MYERS, destroyed in a hurricane in 1841; FORT LLOYD; FORT MCRAE, built on the east side of Lake Okeechobee; the stockaded blockhouse of FORT LAUDERDALE; and FORT DALLAS at the mouth of the Miami River. FORT HARNEY, built in 1839 as a trading post near the Everglades, was transferred to the army for trapping the Indians, who soon burned it.

Finally, in 1839, General Zachary Taylor took charge, launching a systematic campaign. According to Robert Roberts, author of the *Encyclopedia of Historic Forts*, Taylor divided northern Florida into 18-mile squares, placing small posts for twenty men in the center of each. Taylor numbered each fort for the square where it was located, except for the pre-existing named forts. He then organized searches to eliminate resistance. However, in spite of his success, his superiors questioned his tactics and replaced him with Colonel William J. Worth in 1841. The first operations began in the summer. In the past, the army had avoided summer campaigns because of the prevalence of insect-borne diseases and because the Florida fauna was most active in that season. Since Worth was able to use Taylor's many forts as bases for his operations, he destroyed the Seminoles's sources of food and hunted them down in the swamps.

In 1849, the War Department ordered the construction of a line of forts from Fort Brooke to the Indian River on the east coast to secure a line of communications. In 1855, more problems developed with the remaining Seminoles who had not been deported to the west. A few new forts were added in Florida and the Seminoles were largely contained and defeated. It is estimated that the army built over three hundred forts ranging from small camps and blockhouses to large walled forts during the seven-year war. Many were used, abandoned, and rebuilt, but after the war, most were left vacant.

Wars of Expansion and New Forts on the Frontier

After the Mexican War of 1846–1848, the United States would expand west establishing numerous forts to protect the route to California and defend the newly acquired territories from hostile Indians. The Republic of Texas was created in 1836 after it revolted against Mexico. During the Texas War of Independence, there were few fortifications in the territory beyond the Spanish presidios belonging to the Rubio Line or built even earlier. When Santa Anna's army marched on San Antonio, the possible positions that the Texians could use for defense consisted of only a few missions. They selected the abandoned mission furthest north, now popularly known as the ALAMO. Adobe walls and buildings and the now famous chapel formed the bulk of the defenses. The Texians added a wooden stockade to link the chapel to the main gate complex since the unfinished sanctuary had never been located within the adobe walls of the original mission compound. The old convent, part of which is known as the Long Barracks, had occupied a central position in the compound. The Texians built a ramp leading to the roof of the sacristy of the chapel where they installed artillery platforms. An earthwork with timber revetments and cannon positions was placed in front of the gate. The Mexican forces set up a siege battery in front of the north wall, one of the Alamo's weak points. From there, the Mexican army of over four thousand overwhelmed the defenders in March of 1836. The Alamo fell after thirteen days and most of the survivors were put to death.

Colonel James Fannin occupied a much better position at Goliad in East Texas since he held the presidio of LA BAHIA, an enclosed position with adobe walls and corner bastions. However, he opted to move out of the fort rather than defend it. The decision cost him dearly since he was defeated on March 20 by the Mexican army and his 440-man contingent was executed by Santa Anna.

Alamo
© TOMASZ IDZIKOWSKI

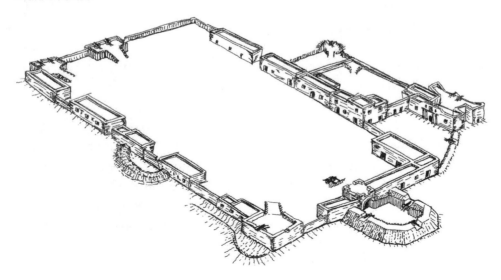

Ten years later, the United States annexed Texas and disputed the border with Mexico, claiming the Rio Grande. Mexico, on the other hand, claimed the Nueces River further to the north. After absorbing Texas, the American army had no time to build fortifications. General Zachary Taylor led his army into Texas in June 1845, and in March 1846, he moved down to the Rio Grande. The Mexican army began fortifying the city of Matamoros at the end of March and the U.S. army built a fort on the opposite side of the Rio Grande from Matamoros. Designed by Captain Joseph K. F. Mansfield, the new six-sided earthen fort was named FORT TEXAS. It included walls 9 feet high and 15 feet thick, six bastions, and a surrounding dry moat. Taylor was able to bombard Matamoros from this position. The Mexican army crossed the Rio Grande at the beginning of May and Taylor moved out, leaving Major Jacob Brown in charge of Fort Texas, which was renamed FORT BROWN shortly after the major died during the siege. On May 3, the fort's 550-man garrison faced a force of about 1,200 Mexicans with two artillery batteries totaling six cannons. The Mexican artillery bombarded Fort Texas for several days, while the troops isolated it. However, when Taylor returned with his main force from the coast, the Mexicans called off the siege, engaging the Americans in the battle of Palo Alto on May 8, 1846. The Mexicans were defeated during this first battle of the war and Fort Texas was relieved. The next day, Taylor's forces inflicted a major defeat on the Mexican army at Resaca de la Palma, but the American advance was slowed. The U.S. government did not formally declare war until May 13. Taylor slowly advanced into Mexico. After American forces overcame the fortifications of Monterey, Vera Cruz, and Mexico City the war came to an end. The Treaty of Guadalupe Hidalgo, signed in 1848, stripped Mexico not only of the lands disputed with Texas, but also of the territories of New Mexico, Arizona, and California.

The annexation of Texas and the acquisition of territory from Mexico through military action reconfigured the southern border of the United States. Now the frontier ran from the Gulf of Mexico, along the Rio Grande, to the Pacific. The former border between Fort Jesup and Fort Snelling that had been guarded by a dozen forts was greatly expanded. The new border with Mexico and the Santa Fe and Oregon Trails had to be protected all the way to the Pacific coast. In some cases volunteer militia units on the West Coast, where the population was growing rapidly in the 1850s, built their own forts. The army set up several forts along the main routes west. In most cases, especially in the southwest and on the Great Plains, these forts lacked much in the way of defenses and, in many cases, they were open positions consisting of buildings around a parade ground. In line with Jefferson Davis's policy of maintaining large garrisons at a small number of forts, most of these forts simply served as posts where the army could make a show of strength.

On the Rio Grande border with Mexico, the hastily built earthworks of FORT BROWN (Fort Texas) were replaced with a series of buildings in nearby Brownsville with no classical fortifications. When the bandit Juan N. Cortina attacked the town in 1859, there

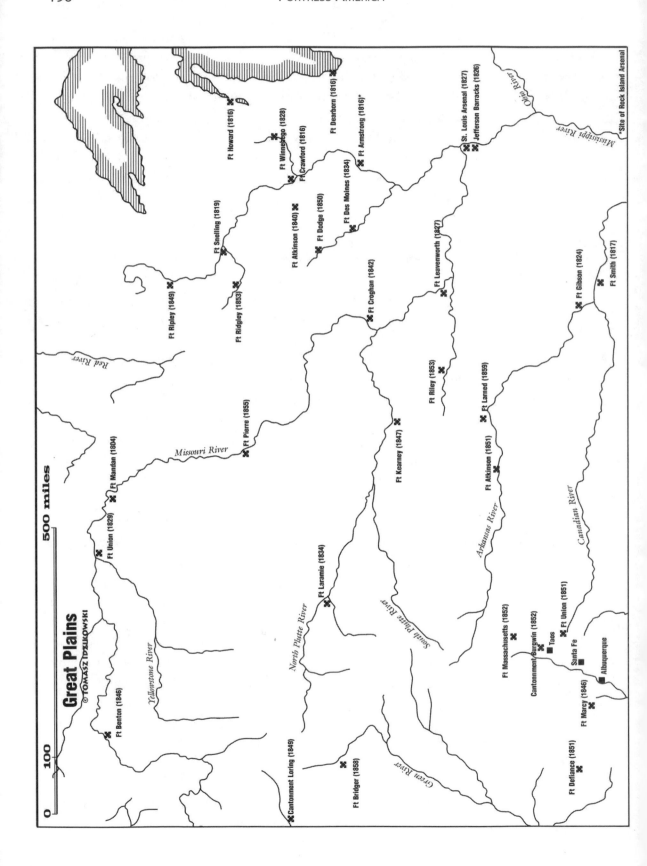

Great Plains
© TOMASZ IDZIKOWSKI

0   100   500 miles

*Site of Rock Island Arsenal

St. Louis Arsenal (1827) ✖
Jefferson Barracks (1826) ✖

Ft Dearborn (1816) ✖

Ft Howard (1816) ✖
Ft Winnebago (1828) ✖
Ft Crawford (1816) ✖
Ft Armstrong (1816)* ✖

Ft Des Moines (1834) ✖

Ft Snelling (1819) ✖
Ft Atkinson (1840) ✖
Ft Dodge (1850) ✖

Ft Ripley (1849) ✖
Ft Ridgley (1853) ✖

Ft Croghan (1842) ✖
Ft Leavenworth (1827) ✖

Ft Gibson (1824) ✖
Ft Smith (1817) ✖

Red River

Ft Riley (1853) ✖

Ft Larned (1859) ✖

Ft Pierre (1855) ✖

Missouri River

Ft Mandan (1804) ✖

Ft Kearney (1847) ✖

Ft Atkinson (1851) ✖

Ft Union (1829) ✖

Yellowstone River

Ft Laramie (1834) ✖

North Platte River

South Platte River

Arkansas River

Canadian River

Ft Massachusetts (1852) ✖
Cantonment Burgwin (1852) ✖
Taos ■
Ft Union (1851) ✖
Santa Fe ■
Albuquerque ■

Ft Benton (1846) ✖

Cantonment Loring (1849) ✖

Ft Bridger (1858) ✖

Green River

Ft Marcy (1846) ✖

Ft Defiance (1851) ✖

Ohio River

Mississippi River

was no garrison at Fort Brown to offer protection and the city had to rely on the Mexican militia from across the border to drive him out. FORT MCINTOSCH was estab-

lished at Laredo in 1849, but it was almost as defenseless as Fort Brown in the early 1850s with its garrison still living in tents.

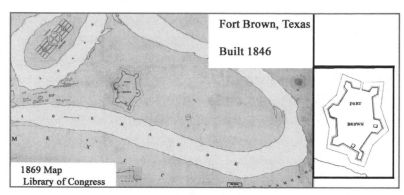

Fort Brown, Texas

Built 1846

1869 Map
Library of Congress

In New Mexico (including Arizona), Colonel Edwin V. Sumner was put in charge of the newly created Military Department 9 in 1851. He established seven forts—UNION, FILLMORE, DEFIANCE, CONRAD, WEBSTER, and MASSACHUSETTS—in his jurisdiction by 1852. These forts were necessary not only to protect the border, but also to maintain control over a population that, unlike that of Texas, included a majority of Mexicans who had no interest in separating from Mexico.

FORT RILEY (Kansas) was one of the largest frontier posts built on the Great Plains in 1853. It was another open post, but larger than most. Unlike many of the other forts, it was built by a group of several hundred civilians. It was garrisoned by the 1st Dragoons (redesignated the 1st Cavalry in 1855). Fort Riley and other forts during the 1850s secured safe-passage for emigrants and convinced various Indian tribes to sign treaties with the United States by a show of force.

The Yakima War spread throughout the Oregon Territory in 1855 and eventually sparked the Rogue River Indian War. The Indians were eventually defeated and placed on the Grande Ronde Reservation which was then encircled with three forts. Also in 1855, Colonel William Harney operating out of Fort Kearney, Nebraska, defeated the Brulés. From there he advanced to Fort Laramie to cow the Sioux and then to Fort Pierre for the winter. In 1857, Colonel Edwin V. Sumner replaced his rival Harney and launched a campaign against the Cheyenne from Fort Kearney. Operating from a small number of posts, the army eventually stabilized the situation in the West just before the Civil War.

CAMP VERDE was set up in Texas in 1856 as part of an experiment with camel caravans, an innovative idea endorsed by Secretary of War Jefferson Davis. In 1857, a caravan of camels traveled from this camp to Fort Defiance, Arizona, in the New Mexico Territory. After 1857, Camp Verde became their permanent station, but the army made little use of the camels, despite their ability to cross rough terrain where wagons could not go.

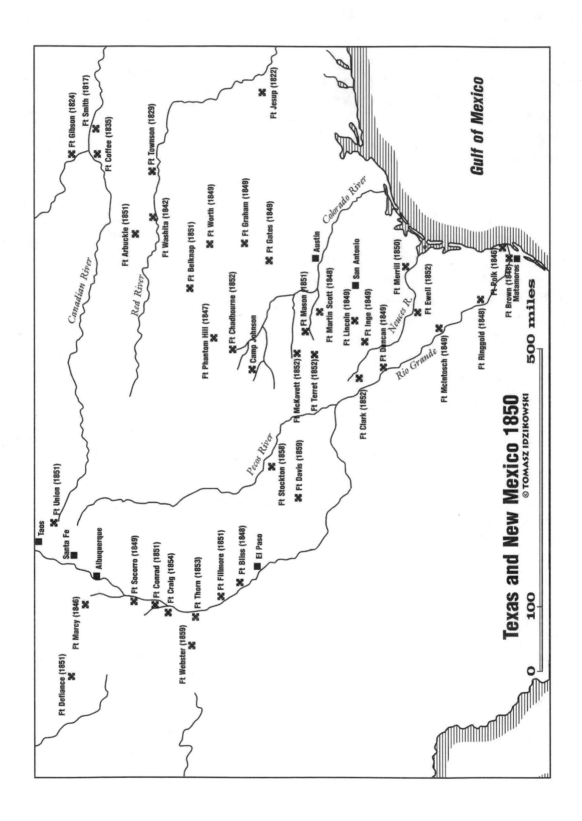

Texas and New Mexico 1850
© TOMASZ IDZIKOWSKI

Ft Gibson (1824)
Ft Smith (1817)
Ft Coffee (1835)
Ft Townson (1829)
Ft Jesup (1822)
Ft Arbuckle (1851)
Ft Washita (1842)
Ft Worth (1849)
Ft Graham (1849)
Ft Gates (1849)
Ft Belknap (1851)
Ft Phantom Hill (1847)
Ft Chadbourne (1852)
Austin
Ft Mason (1851)
San Antonio
Ft Martin Scott (1848)
Ft Merrill (1850)
Camp Johnson
Ft Lincoln (1849)
Ft Inge (1849)
Ft Ewell (1852)
Ft McKavett (1852)
Ft Terret (1852)
Ft Duncan (1849)
Ft Polk (1846)
Ft Brown (1846)
Matamoros
Ft Clark (1852)
Ft McIntosh (1849)
Ft Ringgold (1848)
Ft Stockton (1858)
Ft Davis (1859)
Ft Union (1851)
Taos
Santa Fe
Albuquerque
Ft Socorro (1849)
Ft Conrad (1851)
Ft Craig (1854)
Ft Thorn (1853)
Ft Fillmore (1851)
Ft Bliss (1848)
El Paso
Ft Marcy (1846)
Ft Webster (1859)
Ft Defiance (1851)

Gulf of Mexico
Canadian River
Red River
Colorado River
Pecos River
Neuces R.
Rio Grande

0   100   500 miles

The Mansfield Report on Frontier Forts in New Mexico and Texas after 1848

In 1853, Secretary of War Jefferson Davis sent Colonel Joseph K. F. Mansfield of the Corps of Engineers on an inspection tour of army outposts. Mansfield reported that there was no settlement on the Santa Fe Trail between Fort Leavenworth and Fort Union. Between the new Fort Atkinson (a sod and timber fort located at present-day Dodge City) and Fort Union he reported "the mail and traveler are exposed to the exactions, depredations, and attacks of the Arapahoe Indians...the Cheyenne and Kiowa...and Comanche Indians...." According to Mansfield, the forts of the New Mexico Territory he inspected were open forts with buildings around a parade ground and few defenses. What follows is his brief description in the order he visited the forts:

1. FORT UNION, general supply depot for the department: Built 1851, no defenses, garrison of 160 men. Located on shortest route to Santa Fe, the fort was exposed to the enemy from the mesa above. Recommendations: add a blockhouse on mesa.

2. FORT MASSACHUSETTS: Built in 1852, no defenses, garrison of 125 men. Located in the Valley of San Louis it was at an elevation of 8,000 feet. The garrison had not been paid in five months [This fort was abandoned in 1858 for a new one named FORT GARLAND.]

3. FORT MARCY in Santa Fe: Built in 1846 (by Kearney), garrison of 80 men. Located on a mountain spur and laid out in an irregular pattern it was the "only real fort in the Territory." Defenses included a surrounding ditch and a two level blockhouse outside the fort covering the entrance. It had no water source.

4. FORT DEFIANCE: Built in 1851, no defenses, garrison of 167 men. Recommendations: build two small blockhouses on the nearby ridge to protect the fort [one was built in 1858].

5. FORT CONRAD: Built 1850, no defenses, garrison about 100 men, located on Rio Grande, and had buildings all in poor condition. Recommendations: abandon the fort [abandoned in 1854 and replaced by FORT CRAIG built several miles away].

6. FORT WEBSTER: Built in 1852, no defenses, garrison of 200 men, located on the Mimbres River near the Santa Rita Copper mines. An older presidio existed at the mines, which had operated for only a short time. Neither position was adequate.

7. FORT FILLMORE: Built in 1851, no defenses, garrison of 280 men, located on the Rio Grande. Most fort garrisons maintained their own gardens to supply some of their agricultural needs. Mansfield noticed that Fort Fillmore was one of the few where conditions were actually good and the troops could grow most of the food they needed.

(continued on next page)

The morale and training of the troops at most of the forts Mansfield visited was good to excellent. The paymaster came to pay troops at remote locations like Fort Massachusetts about once every five months, but there were not too many places for the troops to spend their money. The majority of troops were poorly clothed and some rations like coffee, sugar, and salt were inadequate. According to Mansfield, the garrisons of the forts of this department were too isolated and were deep in Indian Territory. In addition, he pointed out, these open forts required large garrisons if they were not to be easily overrun. Thus, he concluded, a number of improvements were necessary if troop morale was to be preserved.

Mansfield trekked all the way to El Paso, which he noted was defenseless and in need of a fort. He also pointed out that there were no forts between El Paso and FORT CLARK (another typical open fort built in 1852), leaving too large a gap. The border further down the Rio Grande in the Department of Texas was inspected by Lieutenant Colonel W. G. Freeman in 1853 and Mansfield in 1856. Both found it to be poorly defended. FORT MCINTOSCH, established in 1849, was no more impressive than Fort Brown, Freeman noted. In 1853, it lacked defenses and its garrison still lived in tents. FORT RINGGOLD set up by the 1st Infantry in 1848, was located between Fort McIntosch and Fort Brown at Rio Grande City. At the time, it was known as Davis Landing and was accessible by steamboat. These forts were abandoned and reactivated in 1859 to subdue the bandit Cortina. In the early 1850s, other frontier forts in Texas included FORT DUNCAN (1849), FORT INGE (1849), and FORT LANCASTER (1855).

Probably as a result of Mansfield's report and problems with the Apaches between El Paso and Fort Clark, the army filled the gap, adding FORT BLISS, FORT STOCKTON (1859), and FORT DAVIS (1854). Fort Bliss was built at the beginning of 1854 at the site of an earlier post from 1848 that had been abandoned in 1851. Additional forts were also built in West Texas between Fort Clark and Fort Worth (1849), to secure the frontier and handle the Indian problem during the 1850s: FORT MCKAVETTE (1852), FORT CHADBOURNE (1852) FORT PHANTOM HILL (1851), and FORT BELKAMP (1851). According to the inspectors, Fort Phantom Hill was one of the most desolate posts in the West and was abandoned in 1854. All these forts were open posts, typical of the Southwest.

Sources: *Mansfield on the Condition of the Western Forts* edited by Robert Frazer (1963), *Tour Guide to Old Western Forts* by Herbert Hart (1980), and *Frontier Forts of Texas* by Charles Robinson (1986).

The Mansfield Report on Frontier Forts in the Pacific Division after 1848

Colonel Joseph K. F. Mansfield also inspected the forts in the Pacific Department in 1854. In California, he visited Monterey and found it without a garrison. The place was of no military value, he noted. In San Diego he found the Mission of San Diego, six miles from the town, occupied by an 85-man company of the 1st Artillery and a company of about the same size from the 3rd Artillery. When American troops had taken control of the town in 1846, they had taken over the ruins of an old presidio, turning it into the post of FORT STOCKTON. Then in 1847, the army took over the mission. The troops lived in shabby adobe buildings and the church was being converted into a barracks. The mission, which occupied a commanding position overlooking the valley, was enclosed with walls 4 feet thick and maintained as an army post until the end of the 1850s.

From San Diego, Mansfield made the hazardous journey to Fort Yuma, at the junction of the Gila and Colorado Rivers. FORT YUMA, established in 1850, was briefly abandoned and then reoccupied in 1851 by the 2nd Infantry, who moved the post to the heights on the west side of the river. The fort protected the southern emigrant route into California. The garrison of about one hundred men was well-disciplined and in good spirits despite the location and terrible heat, observed Mansfield. A small steamer traveled up and down the river bringing in supplies. According to historian Herbert Hart, author of *Tour Guide to Western Forts*, only nine men remained at the post during a short period in 1851 while the rest of the garrison went to get supplies. The Indians took advantage of the situation to put the post under siege. After a month, the defenders were forced to leave the fort. They returned with reinforcements a couple of months later to reoccupy the post after driving away several hundred Indians.

Back into California, Mansfield inspected the site of FORT TEJÓN where he found only a few soldiers and an Indian agent. The fort, located in the Grapevine Canyon, was intended to replace Fort Miller, over 150 miles to the north, to protect the Indians, and to guard the pass through the Tehachpi Mountains. Fort Tejón happened to be on the fault line and was near the epicenter of the earthquake of 1857. The curtain-less fort had a typical garrison of over two hundred men.

Mansfield next visited FORT MILLER on the San Joaquin River, which was built by the 2nd Infantry in 1851. Its garrison of about seventy-five men consisted of troops of the 1st Dragoons. Mansfield was not impressed with the training, discipline, or equipment of the troopers. Even though the fort had a blockhouse, its surrounding adobe wall was only 5 feet high. *(continued on page 203)*

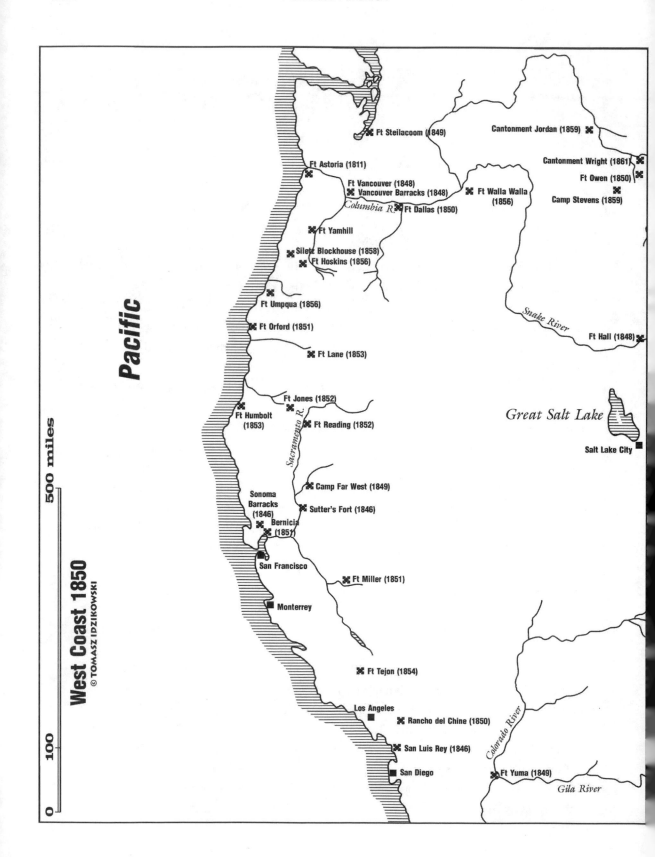

Pacific

West Coast 1850
© TOMASZ IDZIKOWSKI

500 miles

100

0

✖ Ft Steilacoom (1849)
✖ Cantonment Jordan (1859)

✖ Cantonment Wright (1861)

✖ Ft Astoria (1811)
✖ Ft Owen (1850)

✖ Ft Vancouver (1848)
✖ Vancouver Barracks (1848)
✖ Ft Walla Walla (1856)
✖ Camp Stevens (1859)
Columbia R. ✖ Ft Dallas (1850)

✖ Ft Yamhill

✖ Siletz Blockhouse (1858)
✖ Ft Hoskins (1856)

✖ Ft Umpqua (1856)

✖ Ft Orford (1851)

✖ Ft Lane (1853)

Snake River

✖ Ft Hall (1848)

✖ Ft Jones (1852)
✖ Ft Humbolt (1853)
✖ Ft Reading (1852)

Sacramento R.

Great Salt Lake

■ Salt Lake City

✖ Camp Far West (1849)
✖ Sutter's Fort (1846)

Sonoma Barracks (1846)
✖ Bernicia (1851)

■ San Francisco

✖ Ft Miller (1851)

■ Monterrey

✖ Ft Tejon (1854)

■ Los Angeles
✖ Rancho del Chine (1850)

✖ San Luis Rey (1846)

Colorado River

■ San Diego
✖ Ft Yuma (1849)

Gila River

Near San Francisco, Mansfield inspected the BENECIA BARRACKS and the harbor area whose coastal defense forts were still under construction. About sixty troops manned these defenses. The Benecia Arsenal, established in 1851, stood nearby. It had forty-five men to protect it. The magazine was located in an inadequate wooden building where much of the powder deteriorated and had to be condemned. At the time of Mansfield's visit, it was to be replaced with a stone magazine 105 feet long and 36 feet wide. This new magazine was to store all the powder needed in the department. This site also included a quartermaster's depot and a subsistence depot.

In northern California, Mansfield visited two forts built to protect the gold miners and a supply depot. Established in 1852 by the 2nd Infantry, FORT READING held a garrison of about ninety troops from the 3rd Artillery and 4th Infantry. Mansfield was impressed with the discipline and morale of these troops. At FORT HUMBOLT, on the coast, he found sixty-six soldiers from the 4th Infantry. This fort, built in 1853, could only accommodate one company but served as a supply depot for northern California. Mansfield went on to FORT JONES, built in 1852 by the 4th Infantry, which held only thirty men when he arrived.

Of the other army posts in California, one of the most important was SUTTER'S FORT established with permission of the Mexican government in 1841 by John Sutter as a trading post at the site of Sacramento. It was enclosed by adobe brick walls 18 feet high and included two corner bastions. The fort measured 330 feet in length and 183 feet at its widest point. The U.S. Army took over the fort in 1846, but abandoned it in 1850, after which time it fell into ruins. In California, there were also positions in the coastal towns built during the War with Mexico by the U.S. Marines and the U.S. Army.

After inspecting California, Mansfield traveled into the Oregon Territory to inspect forts there:

1. FORT LANE: built in 1852 and garrisoned by 50 men. Twenty men deserted to join the gold rush. The mission of the fort was to protect the Indians. [The fort was abandoned in 1856.]

2. FORT VANCOUVER: Former trading post taken over in 1848 and had a garrison of 140 men. It included walls and a blockhouse.

3. FORT DALLAS: built in 1850 on site of a trading post, it had a garrison of 47 men. (Used as a headquarters for the army east of the Cascades).

4. FORT STEILACOOM (in Washington Territory): built in 1849 and had a garrison of about 55 men. (Located near Tacoma.)

On his return trip to California by sea, Mansfield stopped at FORT ORFORD, Oregon, a small post established in 1851 that failed to impress him. Despite his recommendation to the contrary, the post was improved and lasted a few more years.

Sources: *Mansfield on the Condition of the Western Forts* edited by Robert Frazer (1963), *Tour Guide to Old Western Forts* by Herbert Hart (1980), and *Frontier Forts of Texas* by Charles Robinson (1986)

Nineteenth-Century Inventions Affecting Defenses

In the 19th century, several new inventions besides weapons improved the defenses of the United States. The development of STEAM-POWERED SHIPS pioneered by Robert Fulton in America not only affected coastal defenses, but made it possible to supply and support forts located along navigable rivers.

The STEAM LOCOMOTIVE and the RAILROADS revolutionized land transportation, allowing the quick and efficient distribution of large quantities of goods and merchandise. Railroads supplied and supported inland forts as well as coastal forts. However, the network of railroads was well developed only in the northern states east of the Mississippi where it was possible for troops to move quickly to any threatened port on the east coast or critical points on the northern frontier with British Canada. The rail system in the south was not as extensive, but it linked all the major fortified coastal sites. The major flaw of the American rail system of that period was that it included six different gauges of rail lines. The two main gauges used in the north were narrower than those used in the south.

One of the most important inventions of the era was Samuel Morse's TELEGRAPH, perfected in 1844. Although telegraph lines were not strung very far west of the Mississippi, to the east of the river they followed virtually every major rail line, linking most cities, towns, and military posts during the 1850s. However, telegraph wire was not used solely for communications. Both sides in the Civil War began to use telegraph wire to create entanglements for defense.

Other technological developments included METHODS FOR PRODUCING IRON AND STEEL that dramatically changed the quality of the metal produced. The BESSEMER PROCESS, developed in 1856, relied on the Bessemer Converter or blast furnace to convert a large amount of iron into steel, mass-producing the metal. This technology led to the development not only of more effective types of artillery, but also of armor for defenses and armored turrets for forts.

Two important inventions of the first half of the nineteenth century that eventually revolutionized the art of warfare were the SUBMARINE and the SUBMARINE MINE. Despite its rocky beginnings during the Revolutionary War, the submarine did not lose its fascination. After the Civil War began, the U.S. government contracted to build a submarine. The Confederates also worked on their own versions. This new weapon presented a new challenge for harbor defense and blockading ships. The submarine mine or sea mine was first used in the American Revolution. Robert Fulton took a hand in designing a more effective type of mine (torpedo) at the turn of the century. The Civil War caused the Americans to reconsider this previously rejected device and they played a key role in coastal defense.

The Third System of Coastal Defenses

President Madison took the problem of coastal forts in hand after the War of 1812. The seaborne invasions in the Chesapeake, at New Orleans, and at Mobile demonstrated the inadequacy of the nation's defenses. Chief of Engineers Joseph G. Swift intended to make improvements, but lacked enough qualified officers for the task because the Corps of Engineers was authorized fewer than two dozen officers and West Point was only turning out a small number of skilled engineers a year. Madison thought to have recourse to French engineers, long known for their work in fortifications, but Swift was not as enthusiastic about bringing back foreigners. In April 1816, Congress created the Board of Engineers for Fortifications (shortened to Fortifications Board). The board included five members: Brevet General Simon Bernard (one of Napoleon's former military engineers), Brevet General Joseph Swift, Colonel William McRee, Lieutenant Colonel Joseph Totten, and naval Captain J. D. Elliot. Swift, as chief engineer of the U.S. Army, served as president of the Fortifications Board. Both Swift and McRee disliked the idea of a French officer, Bernard, receiving equal rank and serving on such an important board. Finally in 1818, both Swift and McRee resigned from the army in protest and Bernard took the presidency of the board, imposing his ideas without opposition. Totten continued working with Bernard, who forced him to alter some of his plans. Nevertheless, they worked relatively well together and laid out the forts of the 3rd System. When Bernard returned to France in 1830, Totten became the senior engineer for fortifications projects. For the next thirty years, he carried out the construction of the 3rd System with designs and methods of his own choosing. He turned out to be even less tolerant of the ideas of others than Bernard had been, according to John Weaver, author of *A Legacy in Brick and Stone*. The Fortifications Board was suspended in 1826 when only Bernard and Totten remained as sole members, but was reconstituted later to include the superintending engineers for each area. However, these men were not considered regular members.

From 1818 until 1821, the board produced a yearly report that identified priorities, explained where and what fortifications were needed, and gave an account of those under construction. In 1821, the board concluded that national defense was dependent on five elements: a strong navy, adequate coastal defense, a regular army, an organized militia, and improved internal transportation. It gave cursory attention to the northern land front with Canada.

In 1821, Secretary of War Calhoun concurred with the board's recommendations and ordered the army engineers to investigate the status of inland river navigation as part of the internal transportation development. The engineer studies, which revealed an urgent need for military and commercial waterway improvements, led to the creation of a separate Board of Engineers for Internal Improvements in 1824. Its members included Bernard, Totten, and John L. Sullivan, a civilian engineer. Thus, Bernard and

Totten were forced to divide their attention between the 3rd System of fortifications and projects involving canals and waterways.

In their February 1821 board report, the Fortifications Board issued recommendations for the development of a system of defenses that eventually was named as the 3rd System in Totten's 1851 report (Totten also identified the earlier systems as the 1st and 2nd in that report). Although Bernard and Totten made the major decisions, the Frenchman tried to impose European standards on the projects at Fort Monroe (VA) and Fort Adams (RI), which, in Totten's and the other members of the board's opinion, were too grand. But the depression of 1819 caused Congress to curb many of Bernard's plans.

Bernard and Totten, realizing the importance of the navy in coast defense, gave priority to the defense of naval bases and facilities. The 1821 report proposed sites for fortifications. John Calhoun explained that "the projected fortifications have been distributed into three classes, according to their relative importance" and that the first class would be built first "previous to the commencement of the second and third classes." However, he wrote, the repairs at Fort St. Philip and the construction on a proposed fort at Bayou Bienvenue, two first-class projects, would be postponed in favor of new constructions at Mobile Point and Dauphin Island [Fort Gaines and Fort Morgan]. The latter required much more work than the two forts in Louisiana.

The report also identified the three most important coastal sections, which had already been surveyed: the Gulf coast, the coast between Cape Hatteras and Cape Cod, and the coast between Cape Cod and the St. Croix River. Areas of lesser importance included the coast between Cape Hatteras and Cape Fear, and the South Carolina and Georgia coasts. The report also pointed out that, except for Charlestown (near Boston), all the navy yards were improperly placed in regard to defense. It stated that: "A defensive system for the frontiers of the United States is therefore yet to be created; its bases are first, a navy; second, fortifications; third, interior communication by land and water; and, fourth, a regular army and well-organized militia," which must be combined to form a complete system of defense.

For the navy, the 1821 report proposed "great naval arsenals" at Burwell's Bay in the James River and at Charlestown near Boston. It identified HAMPTON ROADS, BOSTON, and NARRAGANSETT BAY as the main rendezvous for the fleet. The proposed forts were to serve one or more of the following purposes: 1. Close important harbors to the enemy and secure them for the navy; 2. Deprive the enemy of "strong positions" where he may establish bases from which to operate; 3. Protect the major cities from attack; 4. Prevent the blockading of major interior waterways at their entrance to the ocean; 5. Protect coastal and interior navigation; 6. Protect the great naval establishments. These main themes appeared repeatedly in the reports to Congress for the next thirty years. Except for some modifications, the 1826 report included a similar assessment as the 1821 report.

The Corps of Engineers was assigned not only the task of building fortifications, but also that of improving ports and building seawalls, which, in cases such as Boston

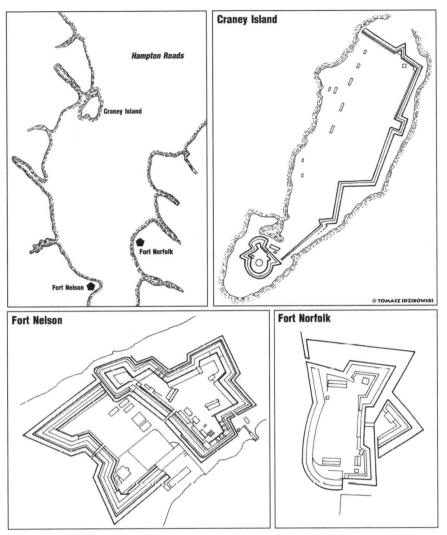

Fort Nelson and Fort Norfolk, built to protect Norfolk and the Hampton Roads at the turn of the nineteenth century would virtually disappear by mid-century. Fort Nelson would be replaced by a naval hospital and Fort Norfolk would fall into ruin due to neglect. New 3rd-System forts would be built to protect Hampton Roads—Fort Monroe and Fort Calhoun.

Harbor and St. Augustine, protected the fortifications from being eroded by the sea. With so many responsibilities, the Corps of Engineers stretched its manpower to the limits. Its officers, fewer than two dozen, had to serve on special commissions formed to investigate fortification sites and supervise work on internal navigation. The Corps of Engineers had to contract out to civilian firms for the construction of forts. Usually, after a site was evaluated by a commission that included members of the Fortification Board, it was necessary to appoint an engineer officer to supervise the work and make sure it was built as required. Most of the young engineer officers from West Point began their careers on such duties, including Robert E. Lee. The army imposed no restrictions on the type of labor employed. Thus, many of the civilian contractors used slave labor in the South and imported Irish immigrants wherever they were available. On occasion, military prisoners were put to work on the forts. Even so, lack of labor rather than funds often brought construction to a halt.

The type of materials used in construction depended on the region. For the 3rd System all the forts were made of masonry, many of brick, but also some of granite. Indeed, the foundations, entrances, and other features requiring more durable material than brick in many southern forts were made of New England granite (and in some cases granite from New York). Forts built on marshy areas or shoals required firm foundations usually made of a timber grillage, which sometimes created problems when the weight of the newly constructed walls was added causing it to settle unevenly. The size of the walls and the number of casemate tiers had to be reduced in some cases, such as at Fort Calhoun and Fort Pulaski. Earth was used on many fortifications to protect the landward walls, but on sandy beaches in the south, sand was used instead.

Expenses were always a major consideration. Thus, granite from Cape Ann was hauled all the way to Fort Independence because it turned out to be cheaper than granite from the nearby quarry. It was more common, however, to use local material. Thus, local manufacturers usually produced most of the brick, except in a few southern forts, where brick was shipped from Baltimore and other far-off locations. One issue that usually caused significant delays and jacked up the price of construction was the acquisition of property rights. This problem delayed construction at Fort Gaines for months.

Another serious problem was control of funds. Initially, the Corps of Engineers was able to allot the funds to the forts at will, but in the 1820s, Congress began appropriating money for specific projects, which resulted in work stoppage on many projects in the 1830s. By 1834, much of the construction came to a halt because of little or no government funding. An additional expense once the forts neared completion was the purchase of the artillery and ammunition needed to arm them.

Andrew Jackson's Secretary of War, General Lewis Cass (1831–1833), who did not believe that European-style fortifications were needed for the defense of the nation, decided that a number of the projects were too extravagant. Furthermore, he thought that forts in general were a waste of manpower, pushing instead to replace forts with floating batteries, an idea that had come up in the late 1820s with the advent of steam-powered vessels. Ignoring Totten's report, which contradicted Cass, Congress began cutting funding, despite the protests of a number of congressmen who wanted more fortifications in their districts.

Between 1835 and 1838, the Jackson and Van Buren administrations ended most appropriations, virtually halting work on the fortifications. In 1838, Congress resumed making appropriations, albeit small ones, allowing construction to proceed at a snail's pace on a few selected sites until 1844. Construction resumed in 1846 when Congress allotted a record $1.3 million. However, the War with Mexico brought another drastic cut, slowing down construction once again in 1847. Totten and other engineers were called up to take part in war operations since the number of engineer officers in the Corps of Engineers was still small. In 1846, when the army created the first regular company of engineer troops, the need grew for more engineer officers for all the corps duties. The siege operations at Vera Cruz, which resulted in the conquest of the fortified city, also brought into question the value of the 3rd System fortifications.

For three decades, the Corps of Engineers stayed with its original plan to concentrate on the major port areas and to create several major fortified regions. It also gave some attention to secondary ports. However, the emergence of steampowered ships and larger vessels requiring deep harbors changed the landscape of the coast, affecting the defense requirements, and affecting the importance of some ports. The major fortified areas were Boston Harbor, Newport, Narragansett Bay, the New York Harbor, Hampton Roads, Charleston, Pensacola Bay, Mobile Bay, and New Orleans. In the 1840s, the "Keys" on the Florida Straits and San Francisco on the Pacific coast were added to the list. These areas were already defended by one or more very large forts and/or several small forts of the 3rd System.

BOSTON, which was centrally located along the New England 500-mile-long coast, included the important naval facilities of Charlestown and a number of islands controlling the passage toward the harbor area. The main ship channel passed by George's Island into the outer harbor and then between Castle Island and Governor's Island into the inner harbor. These last two islands had been fortified in the past, but Bernard had given priority to a massive fortification on George's Island to keep the enemy well out of range of the harbor area. The War Department had rejected Swift's plan before the War of 1812 to defend George's Island, accepting instead Bernard's proposal for a huge granite fort later named Fort Warren. Between 1834 and 1851, Colonel Thayer supervised the construction of Fort Warren, Fort Independence, the other large granite fort, and Fort Winthrop. FORT WARREN, which occupied much of the island, had large granite block walls and brick vaulted casemate roofs. In the 3rd System forts, vaults like these supported the terrepleins above, making them strong enough for a tier of guns en barbette. One of Fort Warren's most important features was a large ravelin with gun positions that covered the channel. Most of its artillery was located en barbette. According to the 1851 report, Fort Warren was designed to hold over two hundred 42-pdr, 32-pdr, and 24-pdr cannons, a number of flanking howitzers to defend the fort, and more than a dozen heavy 10-inch mortars. FORT INDEPENDENCE, on Castle Island, was also a large granite structure with a pentagonal shape and five corner bastions. Two of its fronts included artillery casemates, but the majority of cannons were mounted en barbette. Fort Independence was slated for about eighty of the same type of cannons as Fort Warren, flanking howitzers, and a smaller number of mortars. FORT WINTHROP was a defensive tower surrounded by several artillery battery positions that were supposed to include forty-one 24-pdr cannons and twenty-five heavy 8-inch mortars. Fort Independence was near completion in 1854, but Fort Warren was not ready for armament until after 1854. The two larger forts effectively covered the approached to Boston Harbor.

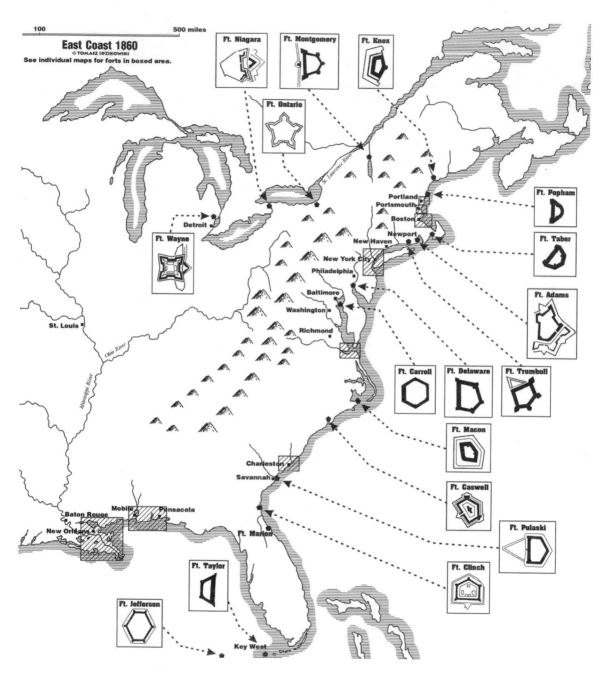

The area north of Cape Cod was described in Totten's 1840 report as a jagged, rocky, island-studded coastline with many deep harbors that, in some seasons, are shrouded with fog. West of Cape Cod, the coast was less rugged, but included a number of excellent harbors. Fourteen sites in this area were declared as needing some type of defenses by early nineteenth-century standards. However, only the ports of Portland and Portsmouth, the latter with a navy yard, were fortified, but received no new installations until the 1840s and 1860s respectively, except for Fort Knox in 1843, which closed the Penobscot Bay. FORT KNOX was a large pentagonal-shaped fort with a single bastion covering the entrance and two front walls. This fort, intended for a garrison of five hundred men, included two casemated batteries on the two seacoast-walls barbette above, and external batteries for a total of 135 cannon positions. In 1851, plans were made to purchase ninety-five 32-pdr and 24-pdr cannons, but as was often the case, the number and types of artillery changed by 1860. By 1854, work was still in progress on the casemates, the walls of the scarp and counterscarp, and the glacis.

Repairs and additions were made to the older fortifications in this region, especially from the early 1830s on. The most notable renovations took place at Eastport, Wiscasset, Portland (where the old forts were improved before they were rebuilt in the 1840s), Portsmouth (where an improvement phase preceded a period of rebuilding and additions in the 1860s), Salem, and Marblehead. Similar work was carried out at New Bedford, Newport, New London, and New Haven, on the southern New England coast.

PORTSMOUTH, one of the New England ports that received low priority, was an unusual case. Its priority level was lowered after the 1820s, most likely due to limited funding. In the 1830s, only repairs were done on its two 2nd System forts. No additional repairs were made on the two old forts in the 1850s. It was not until the Civil War that new forts were added on the sites of the two older ones. A pentagonal fort was started around old FORT CONSTITUTION in 1863, but it was never finished. The original plans had called for three tiers of artillery casemates crowned with cannons en barbette on the terreplein above, holding a total of 149 guns. Out of the three projected artillery tiers, only part of the first was completed. It included the newly designed Totten embrasures. Plans were also drawn up for a second brand-new fort at Portsmouth to be built next to the old FORT MCCLARY. Begun in 1863, this fort was left unfinished as well, with the shape of a truncated pentagon. The points of interest in the plans of the new Fort McClary are the new features adopted for the 3rd System forts. Fort McClary was to have included a caponier on the south side, between its two seacoast fronts. In addition, the rear of the fort was to have two bastions with casemate positions for four flanking howitzers each. The plans for the new Fort Constitution and Fort McClary were some of the most avantgarde for the 3rd System. Unfortunately, they were not completed because new developments during the Civil War rendered them obsolete before they were even finished.

NEWPORT at Narragansett Bay was put on the priority list because Totten classified it as the best harbor on the entire coast of the United States and Bernard feared that if it was not defended a potential enemy would seize it to gain control of this roadstead. Thus, the construction of one of the largest of the 3rd System forts, Fort Adams, began at the entrance to the Newport harbor.

FORT ADAMS was built at Brenton's Point on the east side of the bay. The original plans for Fort Adams called for a fort for 2,400 men and 468 cannons. Work at Fort Adams began under the direction of Lieutenant Andrew Talcott, assisted by Lieutenant

Fort Adams
© TOMASZ IDZIKOWSKI

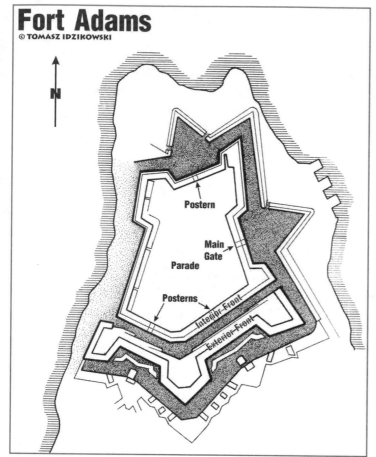

N

Postern

Main
Gate

Parade

Posterns

Interior Front

Exterior Front

Mansfield. The actual construction began in 1825 and three hundred Irish immigrants, including about fifty masons, were recruited as the labor force. Work at Fort Adams was not much different from at other sites from the initial period of excavations and preparation of the foundations to the raising of the masonry walls. Even when promoted to chief of engineers, Totten kept a keen eye on the progress at Fort Adams and a firm hand on the details of construction. He tested a number of his own designs on this fort. By 1838, the scarp on the northern front was complete and the glacis was almost finished. The work on galleries and countermines that linked with the outworks continued, despite threats to end it. In 1841, the fort received a garrison, but by the early 1840s it became quite apparent that the casemates were too damp, a problem that plagued a number of the new forts. The humidity made it difficult to keep the powder dry and created unhealthy conditions in livingquarters, which were decried by the surgeon-general. Various measures were undertaken to correct the problem, including increasing the size of the openings in the walls.

Fort Adams included a large crown work with three bastions and two tenailles. The fort itself included a large northwest bastion facing the bay and a half or demi-bastion just to the east, forming the northern side of the fort. Another demi-bastion on the south corner covered the main sally port. A redoubt was built a few hundred yards to the south of the fort toward the end of the construction. This redoubt was designed for landward defense of the approaches to the fort. It was a rather complex structure with two surrounding ditches, caponiers, and counterscarp galleries linked to the main fort by a covered way. The outworks of Fort Adams included an underground gallery system that linked the crownwork to other positions and included countermines. Nothing on this scale was found in other 3rd System forts. Fort Adams included artillery positions for guns to be mounted en barbette and casemates along the seacoast wall facing the bay. Its casemates were unusually large and divided into two levels, allowing for two tiers of casemated guns. The floor of the upper tier was made of wood and was at the same level as the parade ground, while the lower tier was accessed by a trench. Each casemate included positions for two guns per level. By 1851, the fort already mounted fifty-seven 24-pdrs and one hundred 32-pdrs and forty-three howitzers for flanking fire against troops. Although second in size to Fort Monroe and Fort Jefferson, Fort Adams was far more complex, yet between 1853 and 1857, its garrison only consisted of a caretaker. Captain John Magruder's artillery company moved into the fort in 1858, but departed in October 1859 leaving the caretaker in charge once again.

The complex of forts designed for the defense of the NEW YORK HARBOR area was the largest of all the projects. The British invasion of 1776, which exposed the vulnerable areas, helped in the planning of the 1st and 2nd System forts. During the development and construction of the 3rd System, the Fortifications Board tried to seal the remaining gaps and push the defenses out far enough to cope with technological changes. The inner harbor formed by Manhattan, Staten, and Long Islands had received all the previous fortifications. The 2nd System had added defenses to the Narrows, between Staten and Long Island, which included Fort Diamond/Lafayette, built on a shoal and works on the Staten Island side. FORT DIAMOND/LAFAYETTE, renamed for Lafayette after his New York visit in the early 1820s, was only started during the War of 1812, and remained incomplete for several years. Unlike Castle Clinton, this fort was not circular, but square with three tiers of artillery casemates. In most forts, the landward sides were reinforced to protect the masonry, but since this fort was on an island, it was not strengthened. However, since it was close to the shoreline, its walls were quite vulnerable to heavy land-based artillery. Fort Lafayette was a transitional fort presaging the 3rd System. In the new generation of forts, the exposed landward walls were usually covered with earth. Island forts without landward walls were also reinforced, unless they were well beyond the effective range of shore batteries. Robert E. Lee, assigned to repair the forts at the Narrows in 1841, undertook major repairs at Fort Lafayette, which was re-occupied later that year. The artillery of the fort was mounted en barbette and the fort ready for action by 1845, in anticipation of a war over Oregon or Texas.

On Staten Island, across the Narrows, two small batteries were repaired. Totten wanted to replace the old Fort Tompkins and Fort Richmond with new forts. Lee devised a scheme that encouraged the state to exchange the property so that in the late 1840s the sites were ready for the new forts. With Fort Lafayette, these forts effectively sealed the Narrows. FORT RICHMOND presented an impressive sight with its three tiers of casemated artillery and guns en barbette totaling 116 cannons on its three-seacoast ramparts. Its fourth side, the gorge, was less impressive, but included howitzers to cover it from infantry assault. FORT TOMPKINS just above it offered additional protection. Fort Tompkins, like a number of other such forts, included non-artillery casemates, and mounted all its

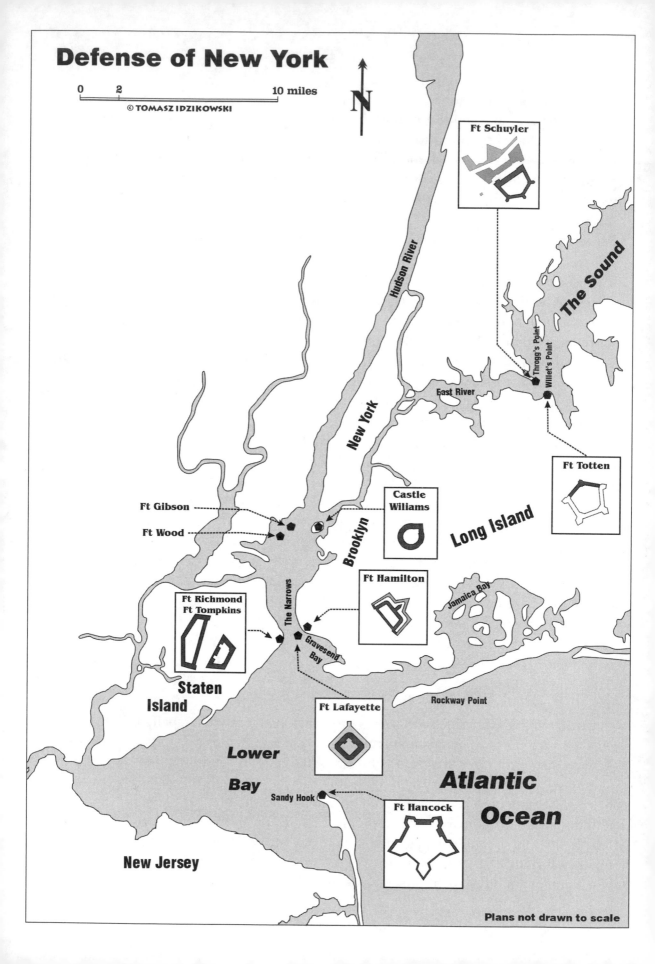

artillery en barbette. Any ships managing to slip through this barrier of forts would still have to deal with the older 2nd System forts protecting the inner harbor.

FORT HAMILTON, which protected Fort Lafayette on its landward side, was home to Lee at the beginning of his assignment to New York, until it was garrisoned later in 1841. The mission of this fort was to prevent a potential landing at Gravensend, but it was not possible until Lee extended its terreplein so it could mount twenty-three guns en barbette. In 1842, its casemates leaked badly and a storm caused heavy damage to its seaward slope, causing Lee to recommend the reduction of the slopes. This fort, which included a casemated tier of artillery as well as a tier en barbette, covered the seacoast on one front and Fort Lafayette on another.

Thanks to the development of the steamship, shipping no longer had to wait favorable winds and tides to enter harbors like New York. Thus all ports became more vulnerable since an attack could come at any time. The approach to New York's inner harbor along the East River through Long Island Sound and by Hell's Gate was no longer an obstacle. Therefore, the board planned to close that entrance with a large fort at Throgg's Neck. Work on FORT SCHUYLER, which did not start until the 1830s, was not completed. The fort's large divided artillery casemates were similar to those at Fort Adams. Four sides of the pentagonal fort faced the channel. The fort mounted 316 guns in two casemated tiers and a tier en barbette. Three caponiers instead of bastions protected the seacoast walls. Like Fort Adams, it included impressive outworks that included a hornwork and a ravelin covering the gorge.

Across from Fort Schuyler, FORT TOTTEN was built as a late addition and was not started until 1863. It was not named "Fort Totten" until the end of the century, before that it was simply referred to as the fort at Willet's Point. Only the first level of this pentagonal fort was actually built even though the original plans called for four tiers of casemated artillery with sixty-eight guns in its two-seacoast walls. Had it been completed, it would have been the most advanced of the 3rd System forts.

Another late addition to the New York defenses was FORT HANCOCK, whose construction began on the eve of the Civil War, but was never completed. It was located on Sandy Hook, New Jersey, so that its 170 or more gun positions could cover the outer harbor and threaten enemy warships trying to stay out of range of the guns of the main defenses at the Narrows.

Philadelphia's obsolete FORT MIFFLIN was repaired in 1835, after the port's main defensive position, Fort Delaware, located downriver on Pea Patch Island, burned down in February 1831. Work on FORT DELAWARE had begun in 1815. When construction flaws surfaced in the 1820s, a dispute erupted between the engineer officers, which culminated with the courtmartial of Captain Samuel Babcock, the engineer in charge. The star-shaped fort was completed in 1825 and troops from the 4th Artillery moved in, staying until the fire of 1831 when the fort had to be rebuilt. Captain Richard Delafield, who took over the project in late 1832, drew up a new design. A property dispute delayed construction until 1847 when Major John Sanders was put in charge of the project. In 1852, Lieutenant James St. Clair Morton was appointed as his assistant. Both men later challenged the value of Totten's 3rd System. Most of the work at the fort was completed in 1856 when the installation of three new Totten embrasures began. In 1859, two casemate tiers were ready and work was about to begin on the barbette level. The fort was intended for about 283 cannons in casemates and en barbette on the curtains and bastions. However, only a small number of cannons were mounted by the time the fort was completed in 1860.

On the other side of the Delaware peninsula, FORT MCHENRY and other forts were repaired, restored, and/or modified to protect BALTIMORE, but the Naval Academy took over FORT MADISON at Annapolis. The only 3rd System fort was FORT CARROLL, built on an artificial island downriver from Baltimore. Colonel Robert E. Lee, in 1848, after serving in the Mexican War, replaced the engineer in charge of construction of this fort. During the first few years, after assuring himself that the foundation was secure, he created a seawall. When it was finished in the 1850s, this casemated fort formed a hexagon, but it was not able to mount 225 cannons in four tiers of casemates because the number of tiers had been reduced to a single level. According to John Weaver, author of *Legacy of Brick and Stone*, work stopped not long after the first tier of casemated artillery positions was built because the army realized that the fort was too close to Baltimore to protect it from the newer long-range artillery. But the fort was armed and put into service.

The old and oddly shaped FORT WASHINGTON was modified and rebuilt after the War of 1812. It was situated to block access to Washington, DC, up the Potomac. The fort had an unusual trace with large bastions and demi-bastions. A rather unique transitional fort, it included large casemated demi-bastions and a tier of cannons in barbette to dominate the river.

Closer to the entrance to the Chesapeake Bay, stood the fortress complex built to protect Hampton Roads. It included two older forts on both sides of the Elizabeth River, of little value by 1860, which defended the naval facilities at Norfolk. Fort Monroe, built at Point Comfort, became the largest of all the 3rd System forts. Across from it, in the channel on the Rip Raps, stood Fort Calhoun (later renamed Fort Wool), which required a major alteration in plans.

FORT MONROE was a seven-sided fort with bastions on each side. Its trace, rather irregular, was wide (ranging from 60 feet to 150 feet). Its 8-foot-deep wet moat sets it apart from most of 3rd System forts. It included a tier of casemated artillery and a tier en barbette. A casemated Water Battery was added on the other side of the moat. The fort with its moat was virtually an island within an island. Although largely incomplete, the fort was occupied and in 1824, becoming home to the Artillery School of Practice and ten companies from the 1st, 2nd, 3rd, and 4th Artillery Regiments. In 1828 half of the artillery companies departed Fort Monroe to garrison other forts that were nearing completion. In 1835, the fort mounted a single 42-pdr and twenty-two 32-pdrs in casemates and about a dozen 24-pdrs en barbette. It still needed more work and more artillery since, in 1851, the army estimated it would mount 371 cannons. Fort Monroe was largely completed in the 1850s.

FORT CALHOUN helped Fort Monroe close the passage into the James River and Hampton Roads, which lay between them. Construction on this granite fort ceased in the early 1830s because the fort was sinking under its own weight with only one tier of casemates for artillery. Construction did not resume until 1858, after Totten reported in 1853 that the subsidence appeared to have ended. The renovations only involved the addition of Totten embrasures, but no major construction took place. Thus, by 1860, the defense of Hampton Roads and the approaches to Norfolk fell to Fort Monroe and Fort Calhoun. On the other hand, FORT NELSON and FORT NORFOLK, which had protected Norfolk at the turn of the century, had virtually disappeared by mid-century. Fort Nelson had been replaced by a navy hospital and Fort Norfolk had fallen into ruin by 1849 due to neglect.

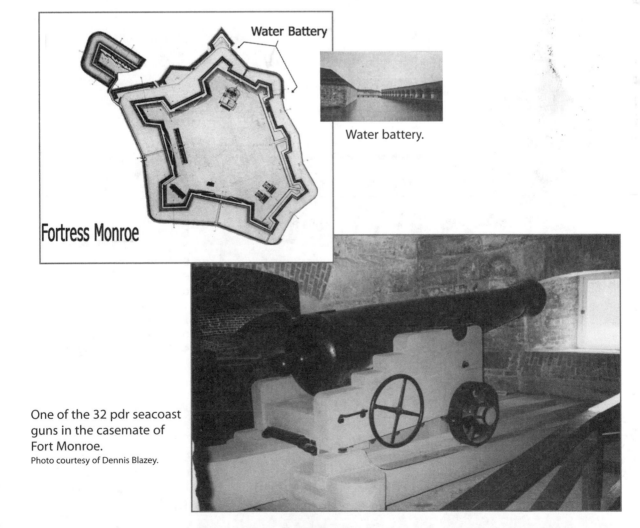

Water Battery

Fortress Monroe

Water battery.

One of the 32 pdr seacoast guns in the casemate of Fort Monroe.
Photo courtesy of Dennis Blazey.

Identified as an area of secondary importance by the Fortifications Board, the southern Atlantic coastline was not surveyed until 1821. Construction of the few forts recommended for this area began in the mid-1820s. In North Carolina, FORT MACON, an unusual five-sided brick fort was completed in 1834, but encroaching waves damaged it within a year. It defended the inlet leading to Beaufort. In 1840, Totten sent Robert E. Lee to study the situation and draw up plans to extend the jetties.

FORT CASWELL near Cape Fear was built further down the coast to guard the approaches to Wilmington, up the Cape Fear River. This five-sided fort had a regular pentagonal shape. A feature that set it apart was its three sets of two caponiers that covered three bridges over a wet moat. In the center of the fort was a cross-shaped citadel that did not rise above the ramparts. The fort was completed in 1838, and, like Fort Macon, it suffered sea damage soon after its completion, necessitating repairs.

CASTLE PINCKNEY, one of three "castle" or tower forts built under the 2nd System, was begun in 1809, completed in 1810, and renovated in the 1820s. This semicircular brick tower on Shutes Folly, a marshy island near Charleston, included a tier of casemated artillery and one en barbette. Although it received a sea wall between 1829 and 1832, Totten still considered it unsatisfactory in 1853 because storms continued to damage it. In 1832, Castle Pinckney was garrisoned and readied for the "nullification" crisis of 1832–1833 caused by Jackson's tariff. It was repaired in 1858 and used as a powder storehouse.

Fort Macon
© TOMASZ IDZIKOWSKI

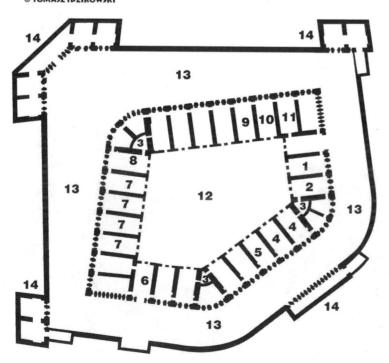

1. Guardhouse
2. Officers quarters
3. Magazines
4. Officers quarters
5. Mess
6. Main gate
7. Troop quarters
8. Ordnance store room
9. Kitchen
10. Commisary
11. Storage room
12. Parade
13. Ditch
14. Couunterscarp gallery

32-pdrs cannons at Fort Moultrie.

FORT MOULTRIE in Charleston was a product of the 1st and 2nd Systems which was later renovated. It was a five-sided fort with earth and timber walls rising 17 feet above the ground. After it was destroyed by a hurricane in 1804, Congress authorized its reconstruction as a brick fort in 1807. It was finished in 1809, but it now had a new, irregular shape with three fronts mounting most of the artillery. It included one large bastion and one large half-bastion on the gorge side. During the 3rd System, work was done on the parapet.

FORT SUMTER though was the key fortification at Charleston. In 1826, the Fortification Board had suggested the possibility of building a fort on the shoal opposite Fort Moultrie to defend Charleston more efficiently. Its location was carefully chosen so that it could create a crossfire with Fort Moultrie to close the main channel to Charleston harbor. In addition, in combination with Fort Johnson and Castle Pinckney, the forts covered the harbor area with artillery. In 1827, plans were prepared and Lieutenant Henry Brewerton took charge of construction late in 1828. Construction progressed slowly because of the lack of funding in the 1830s and disputes over ownership of the property. A Charlestonian who had purchased 870 acres of unidentified land in the harbor claimed that the proposed site for Fort Sumter belonged to him. It took several years for the state to resolve the problem. Work resumed in 1841 under the direction of Captain A. H. Bowman, who decided to use a different method of stabilizing the foundation than at Pea Patch Island and the Rip Raps. Instead of using a "grillage of continuous square timbers" on the rock, Bowman laid several courses of granite blocks to prevent worms from eating the wood and reducing its supporting strength. The granite was shipped from New England whereas the brick for the walls was purchased locally. Building on a shoal turned out to be an arduous affair. After the foundation was laid, work slowed down because access to the site was limited and there was too little

Fort Sumter
© TOMASZ IDZIKOWSKI

(Labeled illustration: Granite Wharf, Gorge Wall, Officer's Quarters, Left Flank, Enlisted Men's Barracks, Sally Port, Enlisted Men's Barracks, Stair Tower, Stair Tower, Right Flank, Right Face, Left Face)

space to store the construction materials. Even before it was completed, Fort Sumter was an impressive sight. It was pentagonal with walls that rose 50 feet high. Four walls included two tiers of artillery casemates surmounted by a tier for guns mounted en barbette. The gorge wall, which mounted weapons only on the parapet, was three-stories-high and accommodated the officers's quarters, storerooms, magazines, and the guard-house. The enlisted barracks consisted of two large three-story buildings running along the right and left flank walls. The fort was the strongest position in Charleston harbor, but at the end of 1860, it was still accepting delivery of its artillery. Many of these cannons were laying on the parade when Major Robert Anderson moved his men into the fort in 1861. The embrasures in the second tier of casemates had not yet been installed, leaving numerous gaping openings.

Interior of gun casemate at Fort Sumter

The Carolina and Georgia coast was low and largely swampy, like much of South Carolina, making it less inviting for an invasion and limiting the number of points that needed to be heavily defended like Charleston. The unhealthy working conditions slowed down the work force. In addition, the construction of foundations in the soft ground and marshes was more expensive and arduous than in the north.

SAVANNAH was one of the most important ports in the area with a river access that needed defenses. The construction of old FORT JACKSON on Salter's Island had been directed by Captain William McRee in 1808. The brick fort was enlarged between 1845 and 1860 with the addition of a 9-foot-deep moat, brick barracks, a magazine, and the rear wall. Its 20-foot-high walls mounted cannons en barbette.

FORT PULASKI was built further downriver on Cockspur Island. Even though its location was selected in 1821, work did not begin until 1829 under the direction of Major Samuel Babcock with the assistance of Robert E. Lee. Lee was responsible for the creation of a drainage system on the island to alleviate the problems faced by previous forts on the site. Joseph K. F. Mansfield took over the project in 1831. Plans for caponiers and a second tier of casemated guns were abandoned because the ground was too soft to support them. This large fort required over 25 million bricks purchased near Savannah. However, the hardened bricks needed for the embrasures and arches came from manufacturers in Alexandria (VA) and Baltimore (MD), and the granite was quarried in New York. The pentagonal fort included artillery casemate positions in four walls and positions for guns en barbette on the terreplein. The walls consisted of seven and a half feet of brick with huge masonry piers. The gorge wall, like Fort Sumter's, accommodated officers's quarters, offices, and other facilities. After the Civil War, a larger ravelin with magazines was added to cover the gorge. Before this, the area contained buildings and a less fancy ravelin. A water-filled moat 7 feet deep and 32 to 48 feet wide surrounded the fort. In the early 1850s, mud was silting the ditches and the canal that fed the moat. The entrance to the fort consisted of a drawbridge, a portcullis mounted in granite, and embrasures for rifles opening into the interior of the entrance passage in true medieval style. The fort included two half-bastions covering the gorge. While P. T. Beauregard claimed that Fort Sumter was Charleston's Gibraltar, J. G. Totten thought that Fort Pulaski was as strong as the Rocky Mountains. (See pages 255–256.)

A new fort, FORT CLINCH, was also built on Amelia Island on the Georgia-Florida border, to cover the St. Marys River. The plan was for a pentagonal fort, similar to Fort Gaines on Dauphin Island. Both forts had a Carnot Wall, theoretically a wall in the moat masking the scarp. At first sight it appears the masonry wall is the scarp until the sloping scarp behind it is revealed. The artillery mountings were for guns en barbette behind the parapets firing over the Carnot Wall in front of the scarp. Fort Clinch included five corner bastions. Its construction started in 1847 and was still incomplete before the Civil War began.

On the western end of the Florida panhandle, four forts protected the naval yard at Pensacola: Fort Barrancas, Advanced Redoubt, Fort Pickens, and Fort McRee. FORT BARRANCAS occupied the site of the old Spanish fort on a bluff at the entrance to Pensacola Bay. The ADVANCED REDOUBT to its rear covered the landward approach. Work began on Fort Barrancas in 1839 and on the redoubt in 1845 and ended in 1859. The four-sided Fort Barrancas was kite shaped and included the old Spanish Water Battery. The long counterscarp gallery, laid out in the form of a "V", protected the two rear walls. The gallery included rifle embrasures and casemated howitzers that could fire down the ditch. A glacis sloped away from the counterscarp. Across the moat from the counterscarp, the 4-foot-thick scarp rose to a height of twenty feet. The entrance was approached from above the counterscarp and over a drawbridge. Near the entrance, stairs led down to a tunnel leading under the moat and into the counterscarp gallery. On the other side of the fort, an underground passageway led beneath the front walls to the Spanish Water Battery. This battery was at a lower level than the fort, giving its cannons the ability to ricochet their shot off the water. The fort mounted nineteen guns en barbette and thirteen on the Water Battery.

FORT PICKENS was built at the west end of Santa Rosa Island, to improve the protection of Pensacola Bay. Together with Fort McRee on the east end of Perdido Key, it closed the entrance to the bay. The plans for Fort Pickens were drawn by Totten in the 1820s, but they were revised by Bernard, who deemed them too expensive. Totten's design had included two large bastions flanking the gorge and one of two curtains.

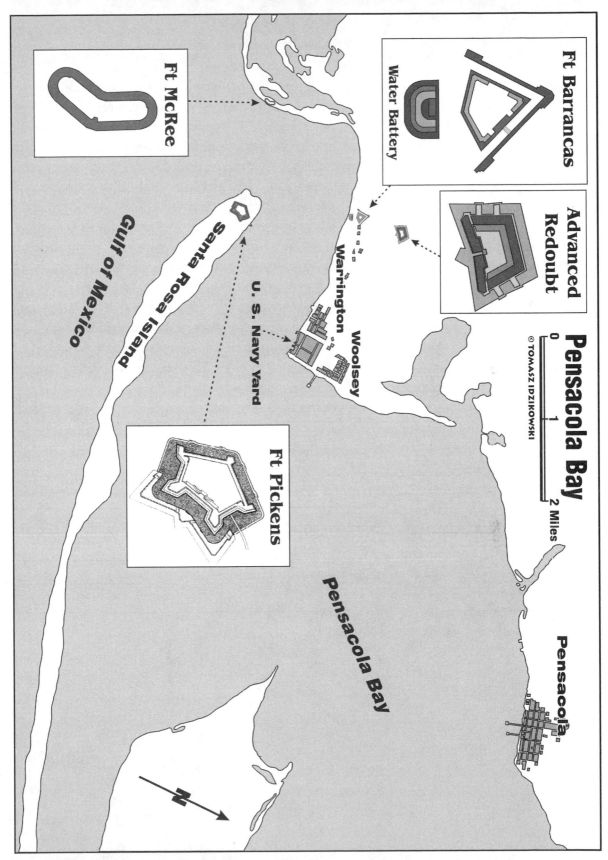

Ft McRee

Ft Barrancas

Water Battery

Advanced
Redoubt

Pensacola Bay

© TOMASZ IDZIKOWSKI

0   1   2 Miles

Warrington

Woolsey

U. S. Navy Yard

Santa Rosa Island

Gulf of Mexico

Ft Pickens

Pensacola Bay

Pensacola

N

Left: This corner section of Fort Pickens was destroyed in an explosion late
in the nineteenth century. It exposes the gallery created by the casemates
and gives a cross-sectional view of the arches and upper level.

Bernard reduced the size of the fort and eliminated the two large bastions, creating a five-sided fort. The new plan followed the trace of the two originally planned seacoast fronts linked by a small bastion. The final design of the fort included artillery casemates on the seacoast walls, none for the gorge, two large bastions, and outworks to defend against a landward attack. The large artillery casemates mounted two guns each. A 10-foot-deep ditch surrounded the fort. Underground works included mine chambers in the two landward bastions. Fort Pickens was completed in 1834. The next year, construction began on FORT MCREE, a casemate tower, similar to Fort Calhoun, shaped somewhat like a bent sausage. It was meant to hold sixty-eight cannons, two-thirds of them in casemates. The terrain added to the defensive advantages of the entire area.

Two forts were built at the entrance to Mobile Bay. The largest was FORT MORGAN, which was one of the few forts shaped like a true pentagon. (Most of the other five-sided forts were irregular or shaped like a truncated hexagon, although we refer to them as pentagonal in shape.) Work had begun in 1819. The fort included five corner bastions, a wide moat, and outworks. The walls of Fort Morgan had one tier of case-mated artillery and another above en barbette. A large ten-sided brick citadel occupied most of the parade.

Fort Morgan
©TOMASZ IDZIKOWSKI

Right: The remains of Fort Morgan's citadel after being bombarded in 1864 during the Civil War.

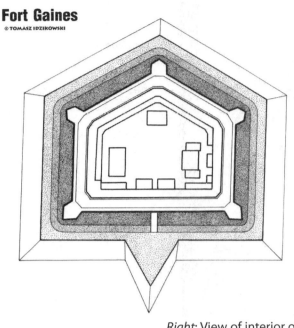

Fort Gaines
© TOMASZ IDZIKOWSKI

Right: View of interior of
casemate barracks of Fort Gaines
Photo courtesy of Dennis Blazey

Across from this huge fort was FORT GAINES on Dauphin Island. It was a five-sided fort similar to Fort Clinch in shape and with a carnot wall. The engineers dropped the plans for a grander fort to match Fort Morgan during the 1820s and this change resulted in a delay in work until the 1850s.

The city of NEW ORLEANS received a number of forts scattered at key locations to protect the seaward approaches. FORT PIKE and FORT MACOMB covered the two channels leading into Lake Borgne. These small brick forts were among the first built and easily recognized by their shape. Other positions included the TOWER DUPRE and PROCTOR LANDING TOWER on the lake. FORT LIVINGSTON, similar in shape (but little else) to Fort Barrancas except it had no water battery, was on Grand Terre Island covering the main pass into Barataria Bay. In 1840, Captain J. G. Barnard directed the construction on this remote site. By 1853 Totten reported it could be quickly armed and garrisoned, but that work soon needed improvements to prevent the encroachment of the sea. On the main channel of the Mississippi at Placquemine Bend, in the river's bird foot delta, were FORT ST. PHILIP and FORT JACKSON. The former was restored and improved, but considered not enough, so Fort Jackson was built across from it on the right bank of the

Fort Pike, Louisiana. View across the interior of the fort showing the slice-of-pie shape and citadel in the center.

Fort Livingston
© TOMASZ IDZIKOWSKI

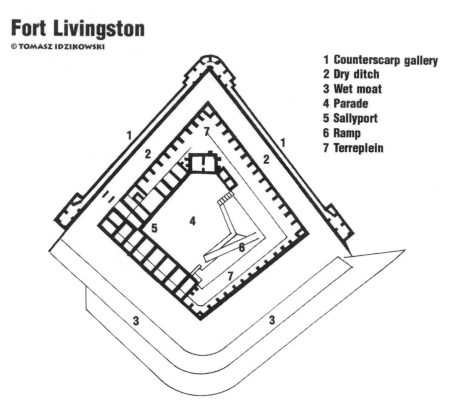

1 Counterscarp gallery
2 Dry ditch
3 Wet moat
4 Parade
5 Sallyport
6 Ramp
7 Terreplein

river. It had a pentagonal trace and, like Fort Morgan, included five corner bastions and a ten-sided citadel. The two seacoast fronts included casemated artillery. This brick fort had walls 25 feet high, and 20-foot-thick earthen ramparts protected the landward walls. The army built Fort Jackson between 1824 and 1832.

The other brick forts of the gulf coast were Fort Taylor at Key West and Fort Jefferson on Dry Tortugas. FORT TAYLOR was a four-sided fort with two tiers of gun casemates and positions for guns en barbette allowing it to mount 130 cannons on its seacoast fronts. Construction of this fort began in 1845, but it was not complete until after the Civil War. FORT JEFFERSON, located to block a passage in the keys, was even larger, and formed a hexagon with two tiers of gun casemates and positions for guns en barbette totaling 450 gun positions.

In 1850 the Board of Fortifications was divided into an Atlantic Board and a Pacific Board. The Pacific Board of Fortifications recommended major work on the Pacific coast at San Francisco Bay, such as batteries for San Francisco. Before long, new forts were under construction at the Golden Gate and on Alcatraz. The surveys for ALCATRAZ were completed by 1853, but before construction could begin, the island of Alcatraz had to be reshaped: a 90-foot cliff had to be blasted and two peaks were cut down. When it was finished, Alcatraz consisted of a citadel that overlooked all the island's batteries. The death of the chief engineer for Fort Point at the Golden Gate caused a slight delay, but his replacement resumed work in 1853. FORT POINT was an irregular five-sided fort with two bastions. Its walls were 45 feet high and 7 feet thick and held three tiers of casemated artillery and one tier of guns en barbette. The fort had enough room for 141 cannons. However, when it was completed in 1861, only 69 guns were installed in its gun positions. Its sea wall was not finished until 1869.

The only other water frontier the United States had in the 1850s was on the Great Lakes, where some fortifications were also developed. At FORT WAYNE in Detroit work began in 1845. This fort was shaped like a five-pointed star, but when it was ready for occupation a treaty agreement with Great Britain demilitarizing the Great Lakes prevented the army from arming it. FORT PORTER at Buffalo was not armed for the same reason. In 1839, FORT NIAGARA and FORT ONTARIO were in need of repairs even though Fort Ontario had previously undergone extensive renovations. On Lake Champlain at Rouses Point, FORT MONTGOMERY, which included a tier of casemates and barbette positions for artillery, was only half finished by 1854. A survey delayed the work when it was determined that the site was on the Canadian side of the border and work did not resume until an 1842 treaty realigned the border. Construction continued during the Civil War, but the army never garrisoned it and the fort was not finished until 1865.

Although Totten reported in the early 1850s that the system still required a lot of work before it could be declared completed, he pointed out that the American defenses were stronger thanks to the railroad and telegraph, which made it possible for the military to identify quickly any area threatened and rush troops to the scene. Unfortunately, other inventions, including new developments in artillery, would threaten the integrity of his 3rd System.

View of right seacoast wall of Fort Taylor at Key West from cannon embrasure in bastion showing the stone foundation and the brick walls above.

Some Features of Third System Forts

Although the forts of the 3rd System were by no means standardized since they were designed to suit the surrounding topography, they had several features in common. These common traits included casemates with vaulted brick arches that could support the weight of another casemate level above and the terreplein designed to mount guns en barbette. Their architectural designs often draw praise for their beauty and form, even though they were built for practical purposes. The piers that supported the brick arches were of either brick or stone. The relieving arches were built in a row, creating a gallery in the Romanesque style. The casemate gallery was divided into chambers that served as artillery positions, embrasures for musketry, rooms for storage, and even quarters. However, the main drawback was that often the living quarters had no embrasures of any type. Casemates not used for artillery were usually sealed with a brick or wooden wall, and often given doors and windows. According to Dennis Mahan, author of *Summary of the Course on Permanent Fortification*, when casemates served as quarters they were separated into two stories. The upper one had a bombproof arch while the lower had a timber ceiling. A ventilation flue was supposed to dry the air and circulated it, but often it did not work very well. Walls and their casemates facing the landward front had an earthen mask for protection, but the sea fronts designed for engaging ships had no such protection.

Casemates with embrasures might include only a cannon embrasure or musket embrasure, and sometimes both types. Musket or rifle embrasures to deflect bullets came in several designs. Hardened bricks or stone blocks formed the cannon embrasures. In the late 1850s, Totten designed an efficient iron embrasure and shutter system that was installed in some 3rd System forts. The Totten shutter consisted of a two-piece 2-inch thick iron shutter that sealed the embrasure. When the gun was pushed out, the shutters sprang up, after the gun fired and recoiled, it sprang closed. It served to protect the gun crew from grape shot and small arms. A vent over the embrasure siphoned off the smoke when the artillery fired. In some forts, ventilation flues ran from the top of the carriage recesses through the masonry of the scarp wall, carrying off the smoke. Other flues passed through the casemate arch to vent on the parapet. In addition, the back of the casemate was open to the parade to allow smoke to escape. According to Mahan, the early two-gun casemates, like those at Fort Adams, were weaker and more vulnerable to damage than the single-gun casemates.

Special mounting positions were prepared for the guns on the terreplein mounted en barbette and those in casemates. Heavy artillery en barbette required a solid foundation of heavy stone set in concrete and a semicircular set of rails on which the gun could traverse without impediment. Artillery in the casemate required a tongue hole, a recess below the embrasure that received the tongue of the chassis. The gun traversed on a pintle placed in a pintle hole at the center of the throat of the embrasure as deep as the

Left: Model of a Totten embrasure. *Right*: Most forts before the end of the Civil War included a hot-shot furnace where the rounds were heated up and then fired at wooden ships. This furnace was built at Castillo San Marcos at St. Augustine in the 19th century when the army installed a seacoast battery outside the fort's walls.

tongue hole. Curved rails, like those for the barbette guns, allowed the carriage traverse wheels to move.

Due to their design, casemates were usually identified as "bomb proofs." Totten had originally expected the garrison to live in casemates, but his superiors convinced him that they were generally poorly ventilated, damp, and inadequate and that proper barracks were needed in forts. By the 1850s, his reports show that he had taken the necessary steps to design adequate living quarters for the troops. When casemates were actually used for quarters, their walls were lined with plaster and fireplaces were installed. The doors, floors, and window frames in the forts were made of wood. At the end of 1853, Totten requested additional funds to repair and complete barracks at a number of forts.

Water was a critical concern in many forts. Fort Calhoun, located on the Rip Raps, lacked a fresh water supply. On the opposite shore at Fort Monroe, attempts to sink a well for potable water failed in the 1850s, so, as in many other forts, the garrison had to rely on large water cisterns. All the forts had some type of latrines for their garrisons, usually located along one of the curtain walls.

Brick magazines and hot-shot furnaces were located on or near the parade. In some forts, a central citadel served as a last line of defense inside the fort. Usually two-levels high, the citadel included firing positions and served as barracks. In most forts, ramps gave access to the terreplein for lighter cannons and ammunition. Strangely, at Fort Morgan only a set of rather steep stairways allowed access to the parapets. Several forts included either lighthouses or navigation lights inside or nearby to help mariners navigate the channels safely.

The Challenge of the 1850s

Conflicts in Europe soon demonstrated that masonry forts were so vulnerable to the new developments in artillery that major changes in fortification designs were essential. However, General Totten disagreed, drawing more criticism during the 1850s. In 1853 Jefferson Davis, then secretary of war, also proclaimed that steam navies and new, larger cannons had made the forts more important than ever, supporting Totten.

After conducting tests with embrasures and cannon fire at West Point in 1852, 1853, 1854, and 1855, Totten presented the results in the 1857 report. Brick and stone embrasures were tested by re-creating fort walls on the testing ground and by firing various calibers of artillery at them to determine how they withstood the punishment. This test demonstrated that a brick embrasure laid in cement mortar could withstand hundreds of discharges, while other types of brick embrasures quickly fell apart. Similarly, shutters of various thicknesses were tested with musketballs, canister, and grape shot. Only solid shot of sixty-eight pounds inflicted any significant damage. Cannon fire tested the iron throats characteristic of the Totten embrasures. A 24-pdr firing solid shot at ninety-five yards caused no damage on the iron throat on the first hit, but successive hits wreaked considerable damage. A few hits with solid shot of sixty-eight pounds cracked and blew away the cast-iron throat. When grape hit a side cheek of an embrasure, the shot fragments were funneled through the throat with enough force to wound the gunners (screens were placed behind the embrasures for this test). Further experimentation demonstrated that reducing the exterior and the throat openings gave the best results.

Totten also tested areas around the embrasures on scarp walls of various types. Solid shot hitting granite blocks caused vibrations and threw off stones on the interior facings. Both large and small shot, 128 pounds to 24 pounds, penetrated the granite blocks slightly but even the smaller shot created cracks on the first hit. The larger sized blocks suffered just as badly as the smaller ones, but sandstone proved more resistant than granite since it was less brittle. All these tests led Totten to conclude that a 5-foot thickness was sufficient for scarps. The embrasures required a wall of brick, cement concrete, or granite of 5-foot thickness, which Totten concluded should resist several hits, even from the 10-inch Columbiad. If the wrought iron throat plates were 8 inches thick and had a backing of 3 feet of solid masonry, they would be the equivalent of 5 feet of masonry. Totten noted that "were it not for the vastly greater cost, the whole scarp might be faced in iron—indeed might be made of iron only..." He wrote that until there was more proof that a naval broadside could breach a wall, the construction of masonry batteries with "the cheaper construction may be safely followed—especially as, should such a necessity ever arise, they may be externally plated with iron." Thus, he concluded, the best solution was to install iron facing on his masonry forts to withstand heavier artillery.

Nevertheless, Totten was working with a type of permanent fortification whose days were numbered because artillery too was making giant strides forward. During the Civil War, the most effective type of fortifications proved to be earthworks, which were merely temporary positions. By the end of the Civil War, a new type of permanent fortification that did not rely on traditional rules was needed and it appeared late in the century.

Newly-elect president James Buchanan appointed John Floyd as the new secretary of war. Floyd, who did not see eye-to-eye with Totten on the value of the 3rd System forts, sent Lieutenant James St. Clair Morton to examine the New York defenses. The young engineer, who also disagreed with General Totten, prepared three reports for Floyd in 1858 and 1859 in which he examined the existing fortifications of New York Harbor and proposed his own plan.

In his study of New York Harbor, Morton opined that Totten's explanations and system of defenses were unrealistic. In his report entitled "New Plan for Fortification ..." Morton challenged the effectiveness of the 3rd System forts and proposed terminating all construction. It was best, he thought, to create a system of defended fronts that ranged from 550 to 750 yards and whose main part consisted of detached bastions. These bastions should be casemated batteries with an interior redoubt, scarp walls backed by earth. A ditch and counterscarp used with a glacis would conceal the scarp from the enemy. He thought that there should be no outworks beyond the counterscarp because the besiegers could turn them to their advantage during a siege. Morton recommended these largely earthen fortifications for Key West, Pensacola, and other Gulf Coast sites.

Morton also pointed out that the lower casemates of the 3rd System forts were vulnerable to assault and that not even the new Totten shutters could prevent this. The advantage of a lower tier was the ability to ricochet rounds across the water, but, he pointed out, during tests at Fort Sumter he saw large waves deflect the rounds or even stop them. However, he failed to note that such waves would have a similar effect on ships firing at the forts. One serious problem, Morton found, was the inability of the forts to respond to a sustained bombardment. He believed that the magazines of these new forts, especially the smaller ones and the larger forts in isolated positions, were not capable of holding sufficient amounts of powder and stores for a long siege.

After this barrage of criticism, Totten's 3rd System appeared to be quite obsolete. The Civil War would prove the criticism was largely well founded since the forts were able to endure only limited periods of heavy bombardment by modern artillery. On the other hand, during the Civil War when these forts were damaged and were repaired and modified in battle, they became formidable positions, but the repairs reduced them to the category of fieldworks.

First U.S. Arsenals

During the first years of the Republic, the U.S. military depended on civilian and even foreign sources for their armament. The army's only arsenal was the SPRINGFIELD ARSENAL in Massachusetts, created by George Washington during the Revolutionary War to produce powder. Another powder magazine at Carlisle (PA) began producing in 1776, shortly before the Springfield Arsenal.

In 1794, an act of Congress designated Springfield and Harper's Ferry as national armories for manufacturing some of the weapons for the armed forces. Harper's Ferry did not begin producing weapons until 1801. In the years that followed, additional arsenals were created, including WATERVLIET ARSENAL in New York which became the site of production of much of the military's artillery in 1813. It was located across the Hudson River from Troy. The Erie Canal was later built through the arsenal. By the time of the Civil War, it had considerably expanded, employing two thousand workers, five hundred of which were children.

In 1862, the U.S. Congress authorized the ROCK ISLAND ARSENAL in Illinois. This arsenal, situated on an island three miles long and a one-and-a-half miles wide in the middle of the Mississippi River, would also serve as a prison camp for Confederates. Work on this arsenal, which was to replace Harper's Ferry, began in 1863. In 1865, the decision was made to make it into the main arsenal in the West. Between 1866 and 1893, ten huge stone buildings were built. In 1880, it supplied all the militia units in states and territories of the Mississippi Basin and half of the regular army stationed on the frontier. Rock Island Arsenal supplied the U.S. armed forces with a variety of field equipment, rifles, machine guns, artillery carriages and equipment, and even ammunition. In 1915, it produced the army's first armored vehicles, but became better known for carriages and recoil systems for artillery pieces. It remains the largest military operated arsenals in America and perhaps in the world.

The ALLEGHENY ARSENAL in Pittsburgh, one of the most important arsenals until the end of the Civil War, went into operation in 1814. The WATERTOWN ARSENAL near Boston, completed in 1816, began producing cannons for the army and navy. Much later, it became the main site for advanced technology devel-

15-inch Rodman at Fort Moultrie.

opment. The WASHINGTON ARSENAL, known at the time as the U.S. Arsenal at Greenleaf's Point, renamed in the 1880s as the WASHINGTON BARRACKS, and as FORT LESLEY MCNAIR after World War II, was opened in 1816 along with the FRANKFORD ARSENAL near Philadelphia and the BATON ROUGE ARSENAL. The AUGUSTA ARSENAL in Georgia was completed in 1817, the FORTRESS MONROE ARSENAL in 1824, KENNEBEC ARSENAL in Maine in 1827, the MOUNT VERNON ARSENAL in Alabama in 1829, the NEW YORK ARSENAL on Governor's Island in 1835, and the SAN ANTONIO ARSENAL in 1855. The BENICIA ARSENAL in California was opened in 1851 to serve the Pacific region. After 1827, the ST. LOUIS ARSENAL became one of the more important sites. However, rather than manufacturing the weapons, it was used for assembling them.

On the eve of the U.S. Civil War, there were twenty-two arsenals in the United States, eleven of which were in the south and two in the West (BENICIA ARSENAL in California and VANCOUVER ARSENAL in the Washington Territory). Some, like the St. Louis Arsenal did not actually manufacture weapons. Springfield Arsenal held the greatest number of small arms—a total of 240,000. Washington Arsenal contained approximately 76,000 weapons, Watervielt Arsenal (NY), 56,000; the St. Louis Arsenal (MA), 33,000; the Watertown Arsenal, 31,000; the Kennebec Arsenal (ME), 24,000; the Harper's Ferry Arsenal (VA), 18,000; the Frankford Arsenal (PA), 16,000; the Allegheny Arsenal (PA), 13,000; and the Baton Rouge Arsenal, 13,000. The others had less weapons on hand, ranging from only a few dozen to 11,000. Thus, when the Civil War began, the major arsenals held enough weapons to arm over 600,000 men even before wartime production cranked up. At the time, the United States was becoming a major power capable of arming and defending itself.

Battery of Union mortars outside of Yorktown during the Civil War.

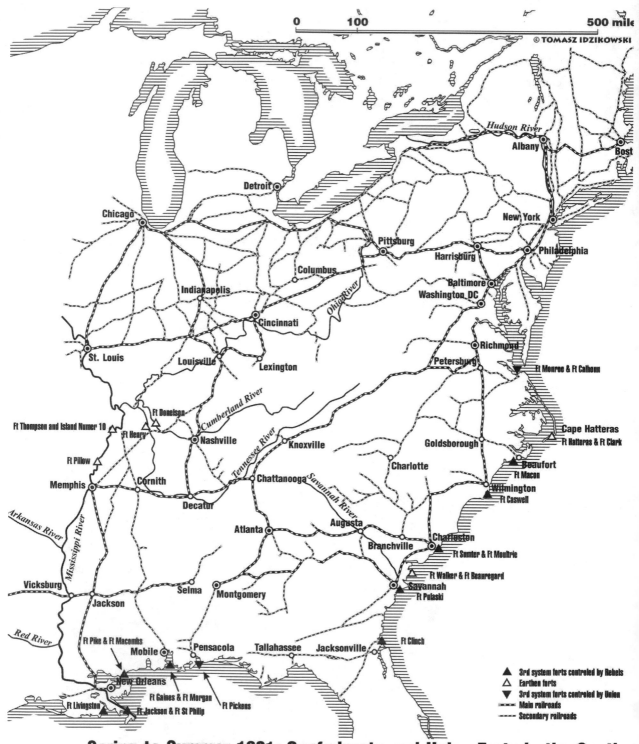

0   100   500 miles

© TOMASZ IDZIKOWSKI

Hudson River

Albany

Bost

Detroit

Chicago

New York

Pittsburg

Philadelphia

Harrisburg

Columbus

Baltimore

Indianapolis

Washington DC

Ohio River

Cincinnati

Richmond

St. Louis

Louisville

Petersburg

Lexington

Ft Monroe & Ft Calhoun

Cumberland River

Ft Donelson

Ft Thompson and Island Numer 10

Nashville

Cape Hatteras

Ft Henry

Knoxville

Ft Hatteras & Ft Clark

Goldsborough

Tennessee River

Ft Pillow

Charlotte

Beaufort

Memphis

Cornith

Chattanooga

Ft Macon

Savannah River

Wilmington

Decatur

Ft Caswell

Arkansas River

Atlanta

Augusta

Mississippi River

Branchville

Charleston

Vicksburg

Ft Sumter & Ft Moultrie

Selma

Montgomery

Ft Walker & Ft Beauregard

Jackson

Savannah

Ft Pulaski

Red River

Ft Pike & Ft Macombs

Ft Clinch

Pensacola

Tallahassee

Jacksonville

Mobile

▲ 3rd system forts controled by Rebels

New Orleans

△ Earthen forts

Ft Gaines & Ft Morgan

▼ 3rd system forts controled by Union

Ft Livingston

Ft Pickens

Main railroads

Ft Jackson & Ft St Philip

Secondary railroads

Spring to Summer 1861: Confederate and Union Forts in the South

Chapter 6

THE AMERICAN CIVIL WAR

THE ELECTION OF 1860 GAVE ABRAHAM LINCOLN the presidency and pushed South Carolina into seceding from the Union in December. As other Southern states followed suit in the months that followed, their militias attempted to seize Federal property and forts. At the time, many of the forts from Maine to Louisiana were manned by a lone caretaker rather than complete garrisons. In other forts, such as at Fort Delaware, only a small fraction of the artillery was on hand, or even mounted in position. This left most of the forts in the states in rebellion vulnerable to a quick takeover. Some arsenals fell quickly and naval facilities were soon in jeopardy as well. The only positions the Union retained in the South were those where the local commander had sufficient men and had acted promptly. In those few cases, the Union forces had to move swiftly and take up positions near the forts. At Pensacola, Federal troops held off a takeover of Fort Barrancas. When Virginia finally seceded, the garrison at Fort Monroe repelled the Virginian troops that stormed the place. The naval base at Norfolk capitulated, but not before the base commander set fire to what he could, including the warship *Merrimack*, and evacuated the port. At Charleston, Major Robert Anderson, though a Southerner, remained loyal to the Union. He evacuated Castle Pinckney, since he had only a small force, and temporarily took up the defense of Fort Moultrie, which was not combat-ready. According to Captain Abner Doubleday, a contemporary eyewitness, Fort Moultrie was little more than a sea battery with sand drifts so high against the walls that cows could graze onto the ramparts. In November, Anderson worked on clearing the sand and strengthening the entrance. He gave Doubleday permission to purchase over 5,000 feet of telegraph wire to entwine between the stakes of the fraises they had hastily erected. This would have been the first use of wire obstacles in the war, but the next day Anderson evacuated the fort before the wire was strung. Realizing his position was too vulnerable to landward attack on the Sullivan's Island side, Anderson withdrew to the still incomplete Fort Sumter. At the time, the fort's cannons were just in the process of being mounted. The Rebel forces took up positions at the abandoned forts, set up additional batteries, and closed the harbor area, preventing Federal ships from resupplying Major Anderson's garrison, thus igniting the Civil War.

First Actions: Battles of the Forts

Events evolved quickly in the states that seceded. Rebel forces took Fort Johnson near Charleston on January 2, the next day Georgia's volunteer forces occupied Fort Pulaski, and on January 4, Alabama's troops seized the U.S. Arsenal at Mount Vernon. Florida's militiamen seized the Federal arsenal at Chattahoochee on January 6, and the next day troops on the east coast seized Fort Marion (Castillo San Marcos at St. Augustine) and Fort Clinch even though Florida did not secede until January 10, 1861. In North Carolina, the citizens of Smithsville took Fort Johnston on January 9, and the next day, with men from Wilmington they seized Fort Caswell. The governor of North Carolina, whose state was still in the Union, ordered the leader of the small militia force occupying Fort Caswell to return it to its caretaker. On January 10, Louisiana's militia took over the Federal arsenal and barracks at Baton Rouge. On January 11, the Louisianans seized Fort Jackson and Fort St. Philip at the entrance to the Mississippi River. They also took over Jackson Barracks at New Orleans and Fort Livingston on Grand Terre Island. As Florida seceded, Federal troops secured Fort Taylor at Key West on January 14. In Louisiana, the militia took Fort Pike on January 14 while troops from Mississippi crossed over to Ship Island to seize Fort Massachusetts on January 20. The Georgians took the U.S. Arsenal at Augusta on January 24, and two days later occupied Oglethorpe Barracks and Fort Jackson. On February 8, the Federal Arsenal at Little Rock, Arkansas, was in Rebel hands. In Texas, the U.S. Arsenal and Barracks at San Antonio were taken on February 16, and two days later most military posts in the state surrendered. During the next six months, Union troops abandoned military posts in the remainder of Texas and New Mexico.

Since many of the coastal and inland forts had telegraph communications, the Rebels's actions did not come as a complete surprise. Most of the forts taken by the Rebels were in poor condition. When Georgian troops took FORT PULASKI from the two caretakers they discovered that it had only twenty unserviceable cannons, and that the moat was silted up and overgrown. The situation was not much different in other forts left in the charge of caretakers for years. However, this was not too much of a drawback since the Confederates had many months to prepare the forts to resist a Union invasion.

By spring only one Union position remained in northern Florida. It was at Pensacola where 1st Lieutenant Adam J. Slemmer, a Pennsylvanian, commander of Company G, 1st U.S. Artillery, moved his fifty-one soldiers and thirty sailors by boat from FORT McRee and FORT BARRANCAS to FORT PICKENS, located on the west end of Santa Rosa

Island, which had been deserted since 1850. Before departing, Slemmer destroyed the powder stored at Fort McRee and spiked all of its 24-pdr and 32-pdr that faced the channel as well as those at Fort Barrancas. Slemmer mounted some of the artillery pieces at Fort Pickens, from whose ramparts his cannons controlled the harbor. Slemmer had given first priority to the flanking positions, supplying the casemate guns with grape and canister to repel a ground assault. Colonel William Chase, who had criticized Totten's 3rd System fortifications, had also worked on the forts at Pensacola and now led the Confederate troops. After he took over the abandoned Fort McRee, Fort Barrancas, and the Advanced Redoubt, Chase tried to convince Slemmer to surrender. On January 28, after Slemmer turned down all entreaties to surrender, the future Confederate secretary of the navy, Stephen Mallory, who resided in Pensacola, negotiated a truce guaranteeing that the Rebels would not fire on Fort Pickens as long as no reinforcements were landed. During the following weeks, Slemmer prepared the fort which had forty cannons mounted. He installed wooden shutters to seal the fifty-seven casemates that had no artillery and placed fourteen more cannons on the walls and in casemates. The ships with supplies and reinforcements stayed offshore for weeks while Lincoln and his cabinet tried to decide whether to support Fort Sumter or Fort Pickens first. After the firing began on Fort Sumter on April 13, 1861, the situation changed quickly. Colonel Harvey Brown at the head of one thousand troops landed at Fort Pickens and took command with a naval squadron in place to support him. Thus, one of the 3rd System forts that Colonel Chase had disparaged in the 1850s now held the key to victory for both sides at Pensacola.

Meanwhile, the action that finally ignited the war took place on the Carolinian coast around Fort Sumter. On December 27, 1860, Rebel militia crossed over to CASTLE PINCKNEY held by Lieutenant R. K. Meade and a couple dozen laborers. Using scaling ladders, the Rebels climbed over the walls into the fort. Recognizing that resistance was futile, Meade refused to allow his men to fight and the Rebels transferred them to Fort Sumter as they ran up their flag. The militia at Castle Pinckney took possession of four 42-pdrs, fourteen 24-pdrs, four 8-inch seacoast howitzers, a 10-inch mortar, and an 8-inch mortar.

In the meantime, Anderson had withdrawn from FORT MOULTRIE to Fort Sumter on the night of December 26, 1860, but not before spiking the guns and torching their wooden carriages. Rebel forces moved into Fort Moultrie on December 27, while the gun carriages were still smouldering. Despite Anderson's efforts, the Rebels were able to salvage sixteen 24-pdr, nineteen 32-pdr, ten 8-inch Columbiads, a 10-inch seacoast mortar, four 24-pdr howitzers, and several smaller pieces of artillery with their ammunition. The burnt carriages were rebuilt and the guns damaged by the spiking were easily repaired in most cases. On December 30, the Rebels took over the U.S. Arsenal in Charleston, forcing the storekeeper and about a dozen of his subordinates, trapped there for days, to yield.

When Major Anderson arrived with his two companies numbering eighty-five men from the 1st U.S. Artillery, he found that FORT SUMTER was far from complete, especially in regard to the final trimmings and amenities needed for garrison duty. The quarters were not ready, the embrasures of the second tier of casemates had not been installed, leaving 8-foot gaping holes in their place, and only a few cannons had been installed. He put his men to working immediately to put the fort in order. They began bricking up some of the unfinished embrasures, creating bombproofs and traverses on the parade, and mounting some of the artillery laying on the parade. According to Captain James Chester, his artillerymen were busy for weeks with these repairs. There was no shortage of construction materials, since they had been already delivered in preparation for construction. There were also enough provisions to keep the garrison going for several months.

Fort Sumter had been intended for 135 guns, but only 15 guns were already mounted and another 66 were on their carriages on the parade when Anderson arrived. By early April 1861, 38 guns were placed in the first tier of casemates or en barbette on the parapets. The lower tier was armed first because it was less arduous to place the cannons there than on the top tier, 50 feet up to the terreplein. According to Captain Chester, they had wanted to mount the 10-inch Columbiads on the parapet because they were the only weapons capable of taking on the ironclad batteries, but they did not have the equipment to move those heavy pieces. However, Chester wrote, they did manage to mount at least one, but as they hoisted the second, it broke loose and fell to the ground. A few of the guns remained on the parade to serve as defensive weapons. In the end, the fort numbered about sixty serviceable cannons, but no gun larger than a 32-pdr was mounted on the walls. Of the fort's three 10-inch Columbiads, one was set on the parade, fixed at a high angle so it could serve as a mortar. Several 8-inch Columbiads were similarly installed. A small arsenal of 42-pdr, 32-pdr, 24-pdr guns, and a few 8-inch seacoast howitzers remained on the parade because there were not enough gun crews to man them. Anderson's eighty-five men, including the band, simply were too few to

Fort Sumter. Gun in casemate position.
Photo courtesy of Dennis Blazey

operate a fort built for over six hundred men. Although Anderson had more cannons than gun crews, he was able to distribute the artillery so that there were enough pieces for his crews to man on any given wall. To prevent the assailants from storming the fort, Anderson's men prepared fougasse along the esplanade, built wooden machicoulis on the flanks and faces of the fort, and converted 12-pdr and 10-inch shells into giant grenades to be dropped through the machicoulis. Chevaux-de-frise were installed outside the gorge.

While Anderson prepared Fort Sumter for battle, the Confederates were busy preparing positions around the harbor to prevent Union ships from entering and for the bombardment of Fort Sumter if Anderson continued to defy them. The Rebels prepared a floating battery covered with iron rails at Steven's Point. Other batteries were set up on Morris, James, and Sullivan's Islands. At Fort Moultrie, the garrison closed the embrasures with bales of cotton, which proved effective in stopping shot. The Rebels mounted their only English 12-pdr Blakely on Morris Island. Early on the morning of April 12, a mortar shell from Fort Johnson was fired, signaling the opening of the bombardment of Fort Sumter and the beginning of the first battle of the Civil War. Major Anderson held his fire for over two hours, and when he did fire it was with his casemate guns. Abner Doubleday directed fire against the floating battery, but it proved to be too far to suffer any damage. After that, Doubleday decided it best to direct his effort against Fort Moultrie, but the shot was easily absorbed in the cotton bales stuffed in the embrasures. When the Rebel's Blakely breached the walls of Fort Sumter, the Union ships waiting outside the harbor were unable to breakthrough and come to the rescue. Shot and shell landed in and around the fort, and the next morning the barracks were set on fire by hot shot. Within several hours the flames began to threaten the garrison. Having satisfied the demands of honor, Anderson surrendered the fort on April 13. His men evacuated the next day after firing a salute. The gun exploded, causing the only death of the battle. Confederate troops took over Fort Sumter and continued to strengthen the defenses of the harbor. Charleston faced years of fighting and witnessed the deployment of almost every major and new type of weapon from mines to ironclads during the war.

After Fort Sumter surrendered, the situation continued to worsen for the Union. On April 15, the governor of North Carolina sent the militia to take Fort Macon and Fort Caswell. In Virginia, Federal troops abandoned Harper's Ferry after putting it to the torch on April 18. The Rebels took a Federal Arsenal at Liberty, Missouri on April 20, and the one at Fayetteville, North Carolina, on April 22. General Winfield Scott devised the Anaconda Plan. The goal was to employ the Union navy to put a stranglehold on the South by blockading its ports and seizing positions on the coast while the main forces of the army moved south. Fort Taylor and Fort Jefferson provided valuable stations for enforcing the blockade. In addition, the failure of the Confederates to capture Fort Pickens allowed the Union a firm foothold on the

Confederate Gulf Coast. While both sides recruited and prepared to build up large armies, which would engage in battle by 1862, the Union Navy actively engaged in implementing the Anaconda Plan.

General Braxton Bragg was in command of several thousand Confederates preparing to attack FORT PICKENS during the summer of 1861. Five additional earth and timber batteries had been built outside Fort Pickens during the summer to supplement its main defenses, which pointed toward the coast and the channel. On October 9 Bragg landed a large force on the east side of Santa Rosa Island to assault Fort Pickens. The garrison sallied out and defeated the Rebel force. In November, a massive bombardment lasted two days. Neither side suffered any significant damage nor casualties. Fort Pickens's walls held up well. On November 22, two ships joined Fort Pickens in a bombardment of FORT MCREE. The Confederates had easily repaired the guns spiked by Slemmer's men when they had abandoned the fort and mounted additional guns. The bombardment quickly silenced the fort's guns and those of the Water Battery six hundred yards away. The Water Battery, also a brick structure, was heavily damaged. On New Years day, 1862, a second bombardment targeted the navy yard. Fort McRee was also involved and was badly damaged when a magazine exploded, putting the fort out of action.

Up to ten thousand Confederate were tied up by the smaller Union garrison and the navy. Union success in Tennessee forced Bragg to evacuate the Pensacola area on March 10, 1862, and head north to stop the advance of Union forces. Some troops stayed behind because Colonel Thomas Jones refused to evacuate the area. But when David Porter's squadron showed up off Mobile Bay on May 7, Jones had to send his troops to protect Fort Morgan. Before leaving, Jones put the remaining wooden parts of Fort McRee and the navy yard to the torch. By May 10, 1862, the Rebels were gone, leaving much of the area in flames. The mayor of Pensacola surrendered to the Union. The Yankees took Pensacola and the naval yard, which served as a major base of operations for the remainder of the war. Fort Pickens vindicated the value of 3rd System forts. In fact, Fort Pickens held up better than the more compact casemate tower of Fort McRee. Even though it was designed for coastal defense, Fort Pickens prevented Pensacola from becoming a major Confederate base of operations.

Western Theater of War 1862

The main actions on the Western Theater took place along the Mississippi River and its tributaries. The Corps of Engineers had never contemplated building fortifications through the center of the country prior to the Civil War because there was no need for them. When the Confederate States realized that they would have to be on the defensive due to their limited resources in manpower and equipment, they quickly began fortifying key points in the Western Theater. Thus they erected Fort Donelson and Fort Henry on the Cumberland and Tennessee Rivers to close this avenue of advance into

Tennessee. They also built fortifications along the Mississippi River from New Madrid to Memphis, including positions on ISLAND NO. 10 and later FORT PILLOW, FORT RANDOLPH, and FORT HARRIS. Since there was no time to build large masonry works, these positions did not resemble the 3rd System forts in any way. Instead, the Confederate fortifications were largely earthen works with revetments, trenches, bombproofs, rifle pits, and many of the standard obstacles like abatis, ditches, and so on. In the end, this did not turn out to be a drawback, but rather an advantage because earthen defenses stood up to the new artillery of the period better than permanent fortifications.

In September 1861, Rebel forces advanced into Kentucky, ending its position of neutrality in the conflict. Moving up the Mississippi, the invaders fortified Columbus and placed artillery batteries on the high bluffs to dominate the river. Across the river, an outpost was setup at Belmont. In 1861, after occupying Paducah, Kentucky, General Grant ordered the construction of defenses, including the earthen FORT ANDERSON that covered the mouth of the Tennessee River. This fort saw no action until March 25, 1864, when Nathan Forrest attacked it and was repulsed.

In late 1861, Major Gilmer, a former army engineer officer who had worked on the 3rd System forts, inspected the Confederate fortifications in the West. He was also present at the battle for Fort Henry and Fort Donelson, which played a key role in General Albert Johnston's campaign of 1862.

FORT HENRY, located near the Kentucky border on the east bank of the Tennessee River, had been poorly sited with higher ground behind it. It was a good site for ricochet fire against enemy ships coming up the river, but that was small compensation for being on the river's flood plain. FORT HEIMAN was built on the heights across the river from Fort Henry to protect it from the higher ground in the back, but it was not finished when Union forces turned up. Gilmer noticed watermarks on the trees around the fort that indicated the river had flooded in the vicinity of the fort in the past. Fort Henry's garrison numbered 1,885 men and there were another 1,100 across the river at the incomplete Fort Heiman. The fort mounted ten 32-pdrs, two 42-pdrs, a rifled 24-pdr, a 10-inch Columbiad, as well as some smaller artillery pieces. Only the rifled cannon and the Columbiads formed the long-range heavy artillery. Of the seventeen pieces, eleven were mounted en barbette and the heavy guns were behind sandbagged embrasures.

When the battle started on February 6, 1862, the river began to rise following heavy rains and the Confederate soldiers had to build up earthworks to hold the river back. The Rebels abandoned Fort Heiman to move across the river. General Lloyd Tilghman, the Confederate commander, ordered everyone from the fort, except for the gun crews, to keep casualties down. Fort Henry's heavy battery poured devastating fire upon advancing Union ships. Soon, the river fleet came within range of all the Rebel guns, which scored a large number of hits and tore through the armor of the ironclads. Nonetheless, the Rebel situation began to deteriorate because their two long-range rifled guns were knocked out. In less than an hour and a half, Tilghman was ready to

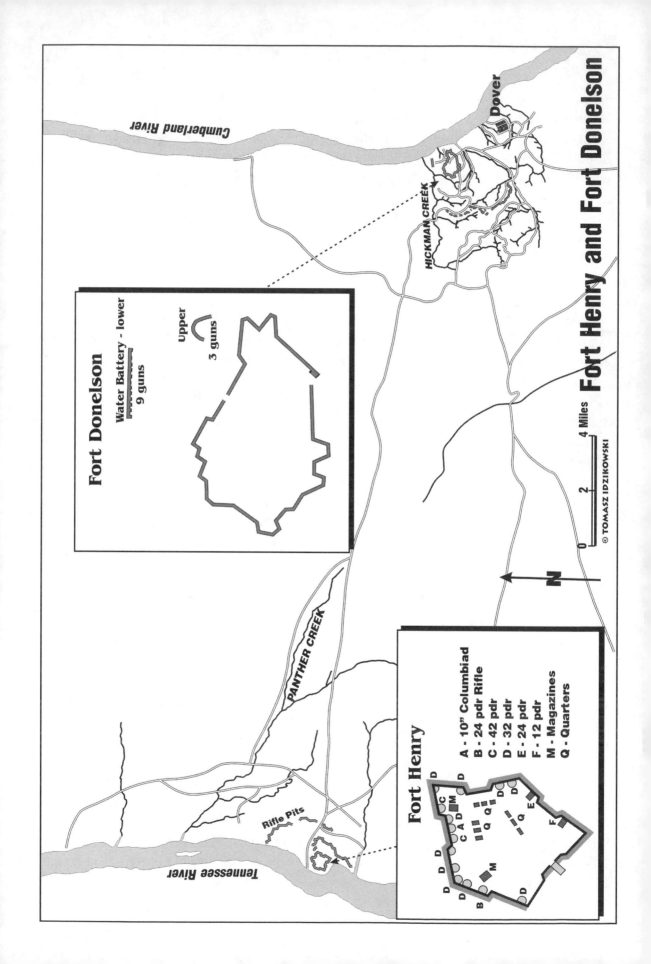

Fort Henry and Fort Donelson

Cumberland River

Dover

HICKMAN CREEK

Fort Donelson

Water Battery - lower
9 guns

Upper
3 guns

PANTHER CREEK

Tennessee River

Rifle Pits

N

0   2   4 Miles

© TOMASZ IDZIKOWSKI

Fort Henry

A - 10" Columbiad
B - 24 pdr Rifle
C - 42 pdr
D - 32 pdr
E - 24 pdr
F - 12 pdr
M - Magazines
Q - Quarters

surrender, but not before sending most of his command to Fort Donelson. The earthen fort was badly battered and near flooding from the rising river. Tilghman surrendered with seventy-eight of his men, having lost fewer than twenty. The Tennessee River now lay open to Federal gunboats. The dozen or so torpedoes in the river inflicted no damage whatsoever on the Union ships.

FORT DONELSON was built a short distance to the east about a thousand yards north of the town of Dover on the Cumberland River. It was an irregular-shaped earthwork about 1,200 feet long and 1,040 feet wide, filled with about four hundred small log huts where the troops spent the winter. The water batteries were placed on the bluffs on the west bank of the river, northwest of the fort. They consisted of embrasured works made with coffee sacks. The Lower Battery had nine 32-pdrs and a 10-inch Columbiad and the Upper Battery mounted two 32-pdr carronades and a rifled 32-pdr. The fort sat on a ridge above them. To protect its landward side, outworks consisting of a line of logs and rifle pits were added. Seven two-gun batteries occupied a hill to the west of the fort and three more batteries stood on another fortified hill to the southwest. An additional five batteries stood on a hill to the west of Dover. Johnston sent sixteen thousand men to occupy these extensive field fortifications. Gilmer inspected Fort Donelson in January 1862, but these defenses were not finished until February 1862.

General Gideon Pillow, who assumed command of the defenses on February 10, wrote that on his arrival he found the troops demoralized by news of the loss of Fort Henry, and by the cold, wet weather. He immediately began improving the positions and mounted the 10-inch Columbiad and a 32-pdr rifled cannon of the water batteries (most of the important artillery pieces had already been delivered). Pillow wrote that he ordered Gilmer to build defenses on the chain of hills west of Fort Donelson that dominated the site. General John B. Floyd, former secretary of war, took over command from Pillow when he arrived before the work was completed.

On the morning of February 13, Grant practically surrounded the Rebel positions with a force of twenty thousand men, while Admiral Foote proceeded up the Cumberland River with his little fleet. Fort Donelson was the last earthen fort to stand between Grant and victory over the Confederate front from the Tennessee to the Cumberland Rivers. On February 14, Foote's small fleet escorted the transports that landed the Union troops and proceeded to bombard Fort Donelson. In the afternoon, Foote's four ironclads advanced under the Rebel fire to within five hundred yards of the water batteries. At 350 yards a cannon shot tore through the pilothouse of the flagship and after an hour-and-a-half-long engagement the navy withdrew. The Union navy took fifty-four casualties.

On February 15, the Confederates appeared to be pushing back the Union right wing, but a counterattack soon sent them reeling back to their defenses. Union forces attacked all along the Rebel lines, breached the line of abatis, and took part of the line of rifle pits under a barrage of artillery from Fort Donelson. Since neither Floyd nor Pillow wanted to surrender, they turned the command over to General Simon Buckner (all three were brigadier generals) and fled the battlefield with Nathan Forrest's help. Grant savored his first major victory. The routes to Nashville up the Cumberland River and to the states of Mississippi and Alabama up the Tennessee River now lay open. Albert Johnston's army had lost almost half of its troops in the battles of Fort Henry and Fort Donelson. The encounter also revealed that Foote's armored gunboat flotilla was inadequate in neutralizing earthen fortifications since shore batteries easily penetrated the ships's armor.

As Fort Donelson fell, General Beauregard withdrew from Columbus on the Mississippi and took up positions on the newly raised defenses of Island No. 10 and Fort Pillow. ISLAND NO. 10 had been neglected during the advance to Columbus in 1861, but the Rebels soon fortified it and set up about fifty 32-pdr guns or larger on the island and across from it on the east bank of the river. They built an earthen fort on the next bend of the river at New Madrid, which was put under siege during the first two weeks of March 1862. Foote's gunboats moved past Island No. 10 and almost daily, mortar boats armed with 13-inch mortars lobbed their bombs at the Rebel batteries, driving the gun-crews from their positions. After a three-week siege, Union troops took Island No. 10, considered one of the strongest positions blocking the Mississippi. General Pope's army took over seven thousand prisoners as the Rebels retreated further south to the earthwork known as Fort Pillow.

Between April 14 and May 10, Federal mortar boats towed by gunboats, bombarded FORT PILLOW. May 10 saw the first naval battle of the war, when Confederate gunboats engaged the Federal ships under the guns of Fort Pillow. The Union ships beat off the attack and the Rebels abandoned Fort Pillow on June 4. Dense clouds of smoke over the fort signaled that it had been put to the torch; explosions continued throughout the night. The Union troops landing the next morning found the fort in ruins, but proudly raised the Stars and Stripes over the stronghold all the same.

The Confederate earthen forts proved to be surprisingly strong and resisted with some degree of success against Union ironclads in Tennessee, but they continued to fall under heavy bombardment. Union forces slowly tore open the Western Theater as they overran the Rebel forts.

More Southern forts in the Western Theater fell in the spring of 1862. This time it was the 3rd System forts protecting New Orleans, including the older but renovated Fort St. Philip, whose original mission had been to defend against a hostile fleet and invasion force. When they became integrated into the 3rd System, the New Orleans forts had no longer been expected to stand alone, but to fight with the support of the navy. However, the Confederates did not have an effective sea-going navy that could support the forts.

Early in 1861, a small work crew had begun construction of casemates for the 3rd

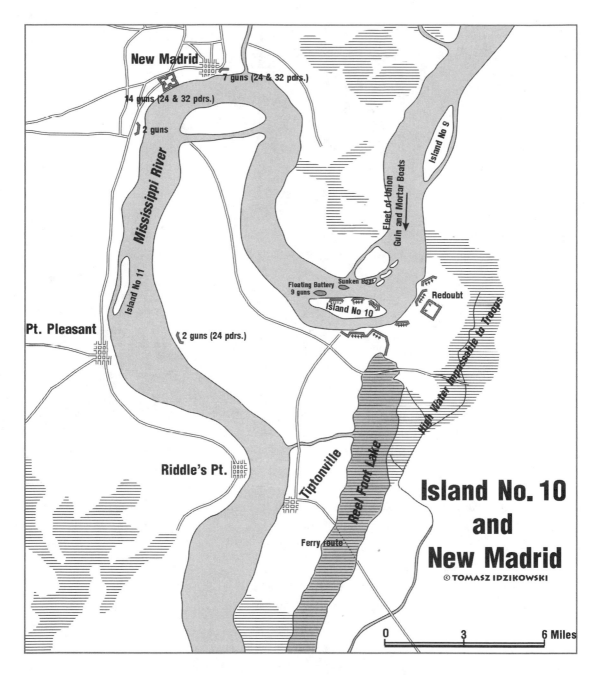

New Madrid

7 guns (24 & 32 pdrs.)

14 guns (24 & 32 pdrs.)

2 guns

Mississippi River

Island No 9

Island No 11

Fleet of Union
Guin and Mortar Boats

Pt. Pleasant

Floating Battery
9 guns

Sunken Boat

Island No 10

Redoubt

2 guns (24 pdrs.)

High Water Impassable to Troops

Reel Foot Lake

Riddle's Pt.

Tiptonville

Island No. 10
and
New Madrid
© TOMASZ IDZIKOWSKI

Ferry route

0   3   6 Miles

System fort on Ship Island. Rebel militia landed on the island and work came to a stop. Confederate marines occupied the island that summer, followed by troops from Louisiana. The Rebels took over the strengthening of the fort under Colonel Johnson Duncan who named the place FORT TWIGGS. However, during the first half of September 1861, after sighting the Union warship *Massachusetts*, the Rebel commander decided it prudent to abandon the partially built fort. Two thousand Union troops subsequently established themselves on the island. In December, they began working on the fort,

Right: View of the side of Fort Massachusetts on Ship Island near New Orleans showing the casemates and gorge.
Above: Interior of Fort Massachusetts. The enclosed stairway is in the tower-like position and in the left corner is the hot-shot oven.
Photos courtesy of Dennis Blazey

renaming it FORT MASSACHUSETTS after the warship that had helped drive the Confederates off the island. Chances of the Confederates returning against such strong opposition were nil, so the island, a base of operations for two centuries, became Admiral David Farragut's headquarter during the campaign against New Orleans. Farragut's small fleet was reinforced with David Porter's mortar flotilla in May 1862.

The Confederates had had a year to prepare their forts on the Mississippi Delta. They had brought reinforcements since 1861 and made improvements on the forts. In addition, their navy moved a small number of ships to support Fort Jackson and Fort St. Philip. The new ironclad ram *Manassas* and the ironclad *Louisiana* took up positions by the forts. The Rebels sank eight old hulks in the channel and used rafts to stretch a chain across the river and through the hulks. They also readied fire rafts to launch against any Union ships attempting to break the barrier.

FORT JACKSON included forty-two guns en barbette, twenty-four in casemates, and a 6-gun Water Battery. The fort's artillery included three 10-inch Columbiads, three 8-inch Columbiads, a rifled 42-pdr, and five 10-inch seacoast mortars brought from Pensacola after its evacuation. The Water Battery, which had not been finished before the war, was now completed to cover the river approach. It included two bombproof magazines for its two 32-pdr rifles, one 10-inch Columbiad, a 9-inch Columbiad, three 32-pdrs, and a 10-inch seacoast mortar. Fort Jackson's brick citadel was well stocked in case of a siege. The bombproofs were covered with sandbags creating a 5- to 6-foot barrier against the heavy mortars they knew the Federals had. Unfortunately the foundation of the fort had settled somewhat and the rising river had left the parade of Fort Jackson and its casemates under a few inches of water, an additional irritation for the garrison.

Half a mile up the river stood FORT ST. PHILIP with its fifty-two guns en barbette and brick walls covered with earth. The small Confederate fleet lay at anchor along the shore, just above Fort St. Philip. To provide a clear view and field of fire for Fort Jackson and the Water Battery through the bend in the river, the surrounding trees had been cleared on a radius of about one thousand yards to the east of the fort. Fort St. Philip, on the other hand, had an unobstructed view straight down the river. The woods remained intact along the shore behind Fort St. Philip and Fort Jackson.

Farragut planned to bypass and neutralize this formidable complex. On March 18, the Union fleet moved into the Delta with four steamers towing the mortar schooners past the bar at Passe à l'Outre. As Porter's flotilla cleared the bar, Farragut's larger ships struggled to move past the bar at the Southwest Pass, taking twelve days to accomplish the passage. On April 16, after preliminary operations before the forts, Farragut's fleet anchored three miles away. The mortar-schooners took up position along the wooded bank. Porter camouflaged his vessels with brush to confuse the Rebel gunners and placed one of his three divisions on the opposite bank.

The bombardment began on April 18 at 9:00 A.M., setting off one of the largest battles between ships and forts of the Civil War. The ships fired about three thousand rounds, and by the end of the day Fort Jackson was in flames and its gunners were observed leaving their positions to fight the fire. The garrison, who had already lost most of its bedding in the partially flooded fort, lost the remainder as the living quarters in the bastions and throughout the fort burned down. The citadel was ablaze throughout the day. Even worse, several of the fort's best artillery pieces had taken serious hits. The mortar schooners had also taken some hits. The mortars boomed again early in the morning of April 19, wreaking more havoc upon Fort Jackson. The defenders lost a 10-inch Columbiad, an 8-inch Columbiad, a 32-pdr, a 24-pdr, and a 10-inch siege mortar in the fort. Two 32-pdr rifles on the Water Battery were knocked out. The defenders repaired what guns they could during the days that followed. The Union artillery had been extremely effective. In five days, its mortars fired 16,800 shells on the Rebel positions, losing only one vessel.

During the early morning hours of April 24, 1862, under cover of the pre-dawn darkness, Farragut's fleet moved to pass the forts. The ships, painted a mud color to hide their profile, advanced with lowered chains over the sides as extra protection. The

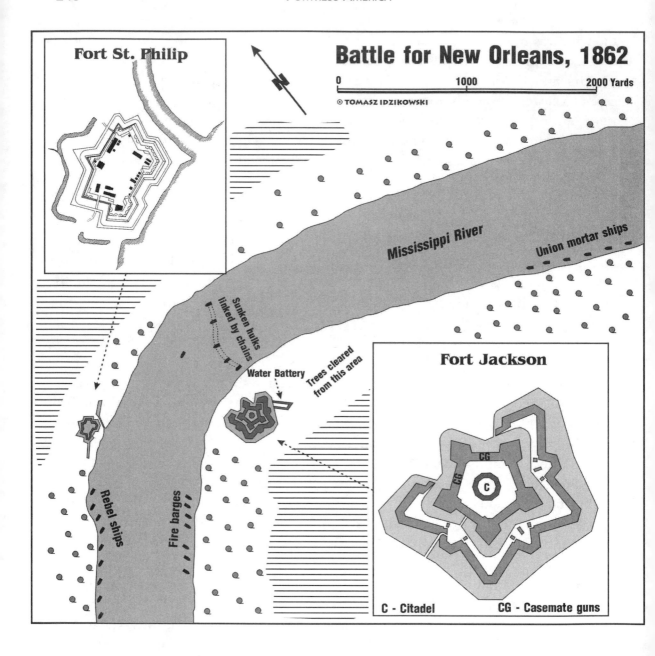

Battle for New Orleans, 1862

Fort St. Philip

© TOMASZ IDZIKOWSKI

0   1000   2000 Yards

N

Mississippi River

Union mortar ships

Sunken hulks linked by chains

Water Battery

Trees cleared from this area

Rebel ships

Fire barges

Fort Jackson

CG

CG

C

C - Citadel   CG - Casemate guns

movement began at 2:00 A.M. as the first ship passed through a break in the chain. Ninety minutes later, as the fleet moved upriver, both forts opened fire. The mortar flotilla directed its fire against the Water Battery. The small Confederate fleet moved to engage the enemy, inflicting some damage with its two rams. Nonetheless, the Union fleet dominated the scene and its large warships poured a withering fire onto Fort St. Philip, driving the gunners from the walls. The grape and canister shot proved devastating. After silencing the Water Battery, Porter's mortar vessels directed their fire on the fort. Farragut took 184 casualties (thirty-seven dead) but succeeded in isolating the two Confederate forts.

Farragut proceeded past the last batteries to New Orleans, which was quickly evacuated by the few Rebel troops, who set the docks, warehouses, cotton bales, and the unfinished ironclad *Mississippi* on fire. In 1861, in addition to the outer line of 3rd System forts, the city had been fortified with the strengthening of the old CHALMETTE LINE (remains of earthen rampart built along the Rodriguez Canal east of the city) where Jackson defeated the British in 1815, and a new position on the west side of the city later known as CAMP PARAPET. The latter, just west of the city on the east bank of the river, consisted of one and a half miles of zigzag parapet that was 9 feet high and 30 feet wide at the base with a 6-foot-deep moat in front and a large redoubt known as FORT JOHN MORGAN with about two dozen 24- and 42-pdr guns. Farragut's approach up river made all these positions useless. The Rebels also abandoned Jackson Barracks and out on Lake Borgne they evacuated Dupre Tower, the two level hexagonal Martello Tower, with five 24-pdrs. On April 27, a steamer escorted by the mortar-schooners landed troops near Fort Jackson. General Johnson Duncan signed the surrender of Fort Jackson and Fort St. Philip on April 28 aboard a Union ship. The day before, the 300-man garrison of Fort Livingston had abandoned their isolated positions on Grand Terre Island at the entrance to Barataria Bay. On April 29, Farragut landed an armed party with a battalion of marines to take control of the city. One of the largest and most important Confederate cities with more fortifications than any other Southern port had fallen. The Union forces used the Camp Parapet position for their own defenses and constructed FORT BANKS across the river from it in December 1862.

The battle between ships and forts had dragged on for six days. In May, Union General Weitzel, an engineer officer, inspected the forts and reported that Fort St. Philip "with one or two slight exceptions, is to-day without a scratch." As for Fort Jackson, he wrote, it had been "subjected to a torrent of 13-inch and 11-inch shells during 140 hours" and to an "inexperienced eye it seems as if this work were badly cut up." Nevertheless, he concluded, "it is as strong to-day as when the first shell was fired at it." After the surrender, Captain Harris reported that of the seventy-five guns at Fort Jackson, only four had been dismounted and eleven carriages damaged. However, 116 guns had remained intact at Fort Jackson as well as at Fort St. Philip. On April 22, the combined garrisons of the two forts had suffered fourteen casualties and four deaths and by April 28, their losses amounted to fewer than forty men. It seemed, therefore, that the 3rd System forts had again passed the test of fire. Though the outcome might have been different if torpedoes (mines) had been deployed.

After April 24, the Confederates abandoned all the forts around New Orleans. When two Union gunboats arrived at FORT PIKE on May 4, they found that the Rebels had spiked the guns and burned the gun carriages, the buildings, and the citadel before leaving a week earlier. The Federals garrisoned the fort and rearmed it with forty guns.

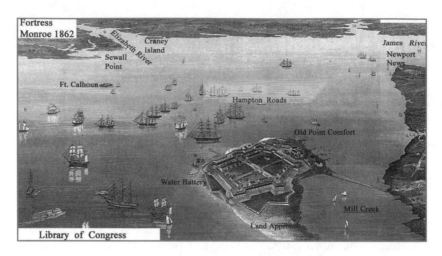

Fortress Monroe 1862 · Elizabeth River · Craney Island · Sewall Point · Ft. Calhoun · Hampton Roads · James River · Newport News · Old Point Comfort · Water Battery · Mill Creek · Land Approach

Library of Congress

The Eastern Theater of War

At the end of April 1861, the Confederates controlled the coast from Norfolk, Virginia, to Jacksonville, Florida. The one key site they did not hold was FORT MONROE, at the end of the Peninsula, where the Union held on. Fort Monroe proved worthy of every dollar spent on it. The Federals later launched a number of expeditions from this great fortress at Point Comfort.

Early in the war, Secretary of the Navy Gideon Welles formed a Blockade Board placing Captain Samuel Du Pont in charge. The board came up with a few recommendations, including an amphibious operation to take Fernandina, defended by Fort Clinch, and a couple of other weakly held positions on the Carolina coast to serve as bases for the fleet. Late in the summer, the navy opted for a proposal to strike at a weak Rebel position on the Carolina coast in order to score a quick victory, thus compensating for a dismal summer of campaigning. The site selected was the Hatteras Inlet where the Rebels had begun to build two small forts: FORT CLARK and FORT HATTERAS. The latter mounted twelve 32-pdrs and formed a crossfire with Fort Clark's five 32-pdrs. A single 10-inch gun was available, but had no ammunition. Fort Hatteras was a simple square with sides of 250-feet and earthen (mainly sand) ramparts 25 feet thick and 6 feet high. About six hundred men defended the two forts. Union warships bombarded the forts while Butler's men struggled ashore through the heavy surf. Cowed by the bombardment, not the landing force, the 85-man garrison of Fort Clark spiked the guns and retreated to Fort Hatteras, which surrendered the next day. The poorly armed earthen forts were too puny to stand up to the fleet. Had they been better armed, the outcome might have been different. Further north from Hatteras Island, the Rebels were fixing Roanoke Island as a base of operations to drive the Federal forces from the area. To the west of Hatteras, the Rebels strengthened Fort Macon and placed obstructions in the Neuse and Pamlico Rivers. In October 1861, General J. K. F. Mansfield, in command of the Union forces, reported that the position at Hatteras was secure, but that it was not

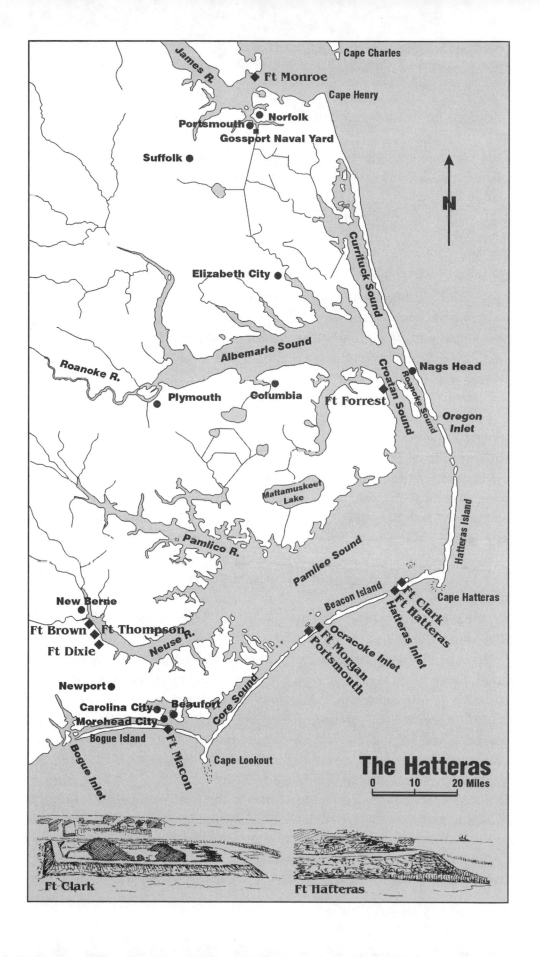

Cape Charles

Ft Monroe

James R.

Cape Henry

Norfolk

Portsmouth

Gossport Naval Yard

Suffolk

Currituck Sound

N

Elizabeth City

Albemarle Sound

Nags Head

Roanoke R.

Croatan Sound

Roanoke Sound

Plymouth

Columbia

Ft Forrest

Oregon Inlet

Mattamuskeet Lake

Hatteras Island

Pamlico R.

Pamlico Sound

Beacon Island

Ft Clark

New Berne

Ft Hatteras

Cape Hatteras

Ft Brown

Ft Thompson

Ocracoke Inlet

Hatteras Inlet

Ft Dixie

Neuse R.

Ft Morgan

Portsmouth

Newport

Carolina City

Beaufort

Core Sound

Morehead City

Bogue Island

Ft Macon

Cape Lookout

Bogue Inlet

The Hatteras

0   10   20 Miles

Ft Clark

Ft Hatteras

a good base for operations against the interior. A look at the terrain and existing lines of communications made that clear, but the site continued to serve as a base for supporting naval operations.

After the Federals strengthened their position at Hatteras, gunboats were sent there in early February 1862, against the Rebel gunboats and three forts on the northwestern end of Roanoke Island in Croatian Sound: FORT HUGER with twelve guns, FORT BLANCHARD with four guns, and FORT BARLOW with nine guns. Three brigades landed on the island, forcing the Confederates to surrender after a two days battle. This victory allowed the navy to push north to the mainland and take Elizabeth City.

In March 1862, the Federals attacked NEW BERNE. A number of field fortifications, including entrenchments, ditches, and earthen forts covered the river and the city. A double row of piles and sunken ships blocked the channel. FORT THOMPSON, an earthen fort, stood at the end of the line of defenses. On March 15, the Union forces under General Ambrose Burnside took New Berne and its nine forts, which mounted forty-one heavy guns.

To complete the campaign, Burnside moved against FORT MACON, the 3rd System fort protecting Beaufort where Colonel Moses J. White, commander of the Confederate forces at New Berne, was in charge. During the first year of the war, the Rebels had re-armed the fort with over fifty weapons including two 10-inch Columbiads, five 8-inch Columbiads, a 5.82-inch rifled Columbiad, and four 32-pdr (rifled). Many troops defending this coastal area had moved north to defend New Berne, so when Burnside arrived in March 1862, there were only five companies of artillery in the fort, less than 450 inexperience soldiers, with little support from the outside. The unhealthy marshes and winter weather not only affected the attackers, but many of the Confederates as well. The fort held several months of supplies, but only enough gunpowder for a few days. According to Paul Branch, park historian and author of *Ft. Macon a History*, on March 23, 1862, Fort Macon was already isolated and its commander was asked to surrender. On March 26, Federal troops occupied Beaufort as the fort's garrison prepared for the impending siege. As the actual siege began on March 29, a number of the defenders deserted. Fort Macon was located on the eastern end of the barrier island known as Bogue Banks and occupied a rather dry sandy area. The narrow island is shaped like a hook, at the bottom of which stood the fort, facing the Beaufort Inlet. The area inside this hook shape and behind the beach is largely marshy. Thus, the Union troops, confined to the sandy beach, used the dunes for protection. The Rebels had eliminated most of the few buildings that obscured their fields of fire.

The Union troops advanced their siege lines in the sand dunes and set up a battery of four 10-inch mortars and, in advance of it, a battery of four 8-inch mortars. The defenders had no mortars with which to bombard the entrenched Union positions. Federal artillerymen moved a powerful battery of three 30-pdr Parrott rifles into position between the two mortar batteries. The fort's guns were ineffective since they could not see the Union batteries concealed by the dunes. To make matters worse, the garrison's defective powder rendered most of their shells ineffective. Colonel White used his 32-pdr carronades and, like Anderson at Fort Sumter, turned 10-inch Columbiads into mortars, but with little effect. Approximately one fourth of the garrison was on sick call every day.

Finally, at dawn on April 25, 1862, the Union batteries supported by gunboats began the bombardment of Fort Macon. The defenders drove off the gunboats. The siege batteries were ineffective at hitting the fort, masked in the smoke from its own gunpowder. Following directions sent by signals from the top of a hotel in Beaufort where observers could see where the shells were landing, the Union gunners corrected their fire by noon. Round after round smashed into the fort and mortar shells exploded inside. The Union artillery began knocking the fort's guns out of action and damaging the casemates with the Parrott rounds. By 4:00 P.M., the last of the fort's guns went silent. However, the walls had protected the garrison adequately from the landward side, despite the accuracy of the Parrotts. The Union fire now concentrated on one of the magazines and the penetrating rounds were close to detonating it when Colonel White realized that he must surrender. Fort Macon suffered devastating damage despite attempts to reinforce exposed walls with iron rails from the nearby railroad. Rifled cannons seemed to have rendered the 3rd System forts obsolete.

In mid-October 1861, while the sounds at Hatteras were still being secured and before the campaign against Fort Macon and New Berne, General Thomas Sherman and Flag Officer Dupont set out on an expedition against Port Royal and Fernandina. Departing from Fort Monroe, the invasion fleet sailed past Cape Hatteras where it encountered bad weather and suffered significant losses. On November 7, the fleet moved up the channel between the two earthen works of FORT WALKER and FORT BEAUREGARD and began their bombardment. According to Rowena Reed, author of *Combined Operation in the Civil War*, General Beauregard, while in command of Charleston, refused to build gun batteries because he was convinced that they could not defend the mouth of the Broad River leading to Port Royal. The state governor overruled his decision, ordering him to build two forts. The forts were not armed with 10-inch Columbiads, as Beauregard desired, because none were available. The design of his forts was altered by removing the protective traverses in order to accommodate additional smaller artillery pieces. Fort Walker included two 6-inch rifles, seven 32-pdrs, a 10-inch Columbiad, three 7-inch seacoast howitzers, and an outwork with five 32-pdrs and an 8-inch howitzer. Fort Beauregard had a 6-inch rifle, a 10-inch Columbiad, an 8-inch Columbiad, and several 32-pdrs.

"The beautifully constructed work on Hilton Head [Fort Walker] was severely crippled and many of the guns dismounted," wrote Sherman after the battle, adding that "much slaughter had evidently been made there, many bodies having been buried in the fort, and some twenty or thirty were found some half-mile distant...." Three of the 32-pdrs were dismounted and their carriages destroyed. Several naval personnel landed in the early afternoon to find Fort Walker abandoned. The victory at Port Royal gave the Union a second foothold on the hostile southern coastline. The exploding shells fired by naval guns dominated the campaigns at Hatteras as well as Port Royal, devastating the earthen forts, which had resisted solid shot so well. What the Union commanders did not realize at the time was that the defenders were plagued with faulty material, including defective ammunition for their best pieces.

In January 1862, General Sherman prepared to move against Fort Pulaski at the mouth of the Savannah River. Robert E. Lee had ordered the evacuation of Tybee Island and the removal of the artillery, leaving the Union troops a good landing site. Sherman sent his chief engineer, Quincy Gillmore, to prepare for an assault since he preferred not to starve out the garrison. On February 21, the navy landed the equipment and ordnance needed for the siege. The Union engineers set about preparing the ground between Tybee Island and the Fort Pulaski, laying out makeshift roads over the marshes to move in their siege artillery. Since the whole operation was carried out as stealthily as possible, the preparations for the siege lasted until April 9. According to Gillmore, it took 250 men and extraordinary effort to haul just one 13-inch mortar into place. The troops also built gun platforms from local pine and created revetted sand ramparts for the batteries, most with embrasures in the parapet. The Lincoln Battery mounted its three 8-inch Columbiads in timber casemates covered with earth and with sod walls one-inch thick. Each battery was given magazines and splinter-proof shelters. By the time all preparations were finished, the Federals had eleven batteries in place, including six with 13-inch mortars, one with 10-inch mortars, two with 10-inch Columbiads, one with 8-inch Columbiads, rifled cannons in two batteries including five 30-pdr Parrotts, one 48-pdr James, and two 64-pdr James. [The James referred to smoothbores that had been rifled by a technique developed by General Charles T. James in 1841.] Finally everything was ready for the siege, but there was no response from the garrison of the fort.

FORT PULASKI had a garrison of 385 men under Colonel Charles Olmstead. The fort mounted on its ramparts five 8-inch and four 10-inch Columbiads, 24-pdr Blakely rifle, along with two 12-inch, and a 10-inch seacoast mortar facing Tybee Island. In casemates were four 32-pdr guns and an 8-inch Columbiad. Other artillery brought the fort's total to forty-eight pieces though it was designed for 140 guns. When Robert E. Lee briefly visited the fort, he asked Olmstead to prepare traverses in the fort and place sandbags between the guns. He had also ordered the garrison to dig pits on the terreplein where the artillerymen could take cover, cut trenches across the parade to trap rolling shot and to protect the garrison, and lay heavy square timbers against the rear of the casemates to create blindages to protect the gun crews from splinter fragments. He also informed

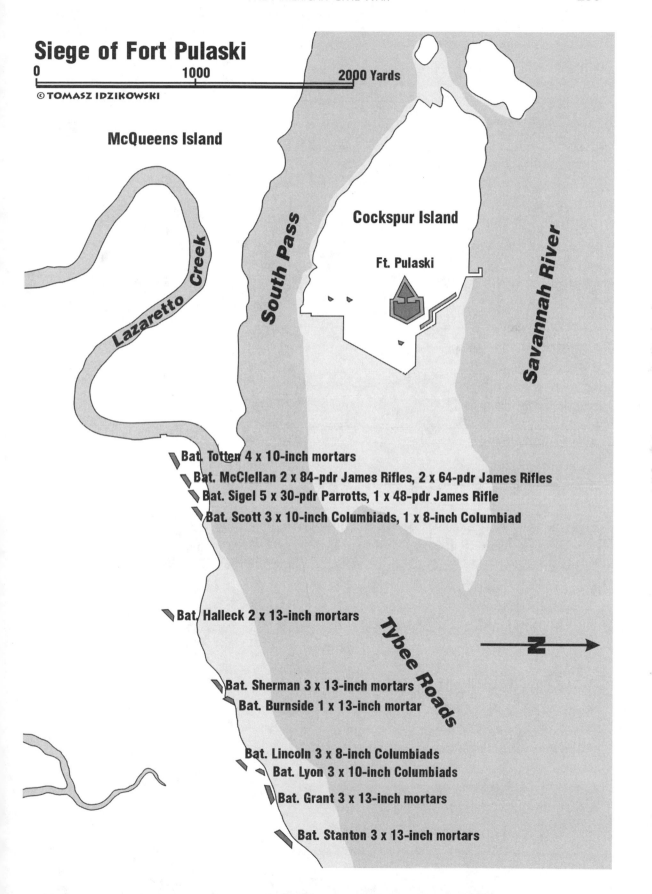

Siege of Fort Pulaski

0   1000   2000 Yards

© TOMASZ IDZIKOWSKI

McQueens Island

Lazaretto Creek

South Pass

Cockspur Island

Ft. Pulaski

Savannah River

Bat. Totten 4 x 10-inch mortars

Bat. McClellan 2 x 84-pdr James Rifles, 2 x 64-pdr James Rifles

Bat. Sigel 5 x 30-pdr Parrotts, 1 x 48-pdr James Rifle

Bat. Scott 3 x 10-inch Columbiads, 1 x 8-inch Columbiad

Bat. Halleck 2 x 13-inch mortars

Tybee Roads

N

Bat. Sherman 3 x 13-inch mortars

Bat. Burnside 1 x 13-inch mortar

Bat. Lincoln 3 x 8-inch Columbiads

Bat. Lyon 3 x 10-inch Columbiads

Bat. Grant 3 x 13-inch mortars

Bat. Stanton 3 x 13-inch mortars

Fort Pulaski

© Tomasz Idzikowski

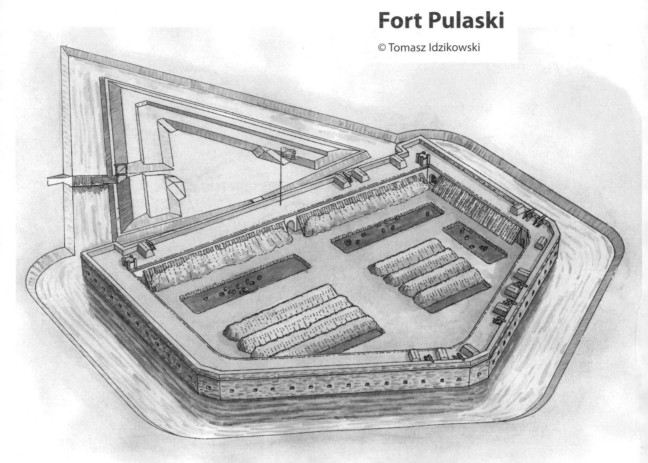

Fort Pulaski. Damage is from the Union artillery bombardment of the fort in 1862. The walls were repaired by Union troops and some of the cannon balls left in them.

the commander that from Tybee Island "they [the Federals] cannot breach our walls at that distance" (about 1,500 yards). Evidently, Lee, like most officers at this point in the war, did not realize that heavy artillery could penetrate masonry fortifications at ranges beyond eight hundred yards. Even Totten insisted that "the work could not be reduced in a month's firing with any number of guns of manageable calibers."

On April 10, 1862, Gillmore's batteries opened fire at 8:15 A.M. While the heavy mortars did little damage, much of their blast effect was absorbed in the dug-up parade. The rifles began opening a breach in the wall just after noon. The next morning saw more rounds penetrate the walls, and the fort's magazine, with thousands of pounds of powder, was in peril. The long-range rifles opened breaches up to 30 feet wide in two casemates. The debris from the scarp created a ramp the attackers could use to storm the fort. At 2:00 P.M., Olmstead hauled down the colors and surrendered with his 360 men. The Federals had fired 5,275 rounds, or about one-fifth of their ammunition supply.

Effects of Artillery Against Brick Walls

Captain Q. Gillmore was able to evaluate the effectiveness of the artillery used to subdue Fort Pulaski in April 1862. He found that the old rifled cannons of 42-pdrs (James 84-pdr after rifling) could penetrate 26 inches of brick wall at 1,650 yards and a 32-pdr (James 64-pdr after rifling) 20 inches. The 30-pdr Parrott rifles penetrated 18 inches of brick at 1,670 yards. The 10-inch and 8-inch Columbiad smoothbores at 1,740 yards penetrated 13 inches and 11 inches respectively.

Gillmore also observed that "against brick walls the breaching effect of percussion shells is certainly as great as that of solid shot of the same caliber," and although they did not penetrate as far, by bursting they formed a broader crater. He believed that these shells would also break granite walls. General David Hunter, who replaced Sherman, commented in a report that "no works of stone or brick can resist the impact of rifled artillery of heavy calibre," adding that a radical change in the construction of fortifications was necessary. Despite this, his engineer officer set about repairing the brick walls of Fort Pulaski during the remainder of April and May in order to put the fort back in service.

Hunter also found that the 13-inch mortars were too inaccurate and when they did strike the fort, the damage appeared minimal. He wrote that mortars were unreliable for use against casemated forts like those of the 3rd System. Gillmore, like Hunter, believed the heavy rifled cannon meant the end of the brick and stone fort.

Source: *Siege and Reduction of Ft. Pulaski* by Brig. Gen. Q. A. Gillmore

Fort Delaware - Prison Camp   Pea Patch Island

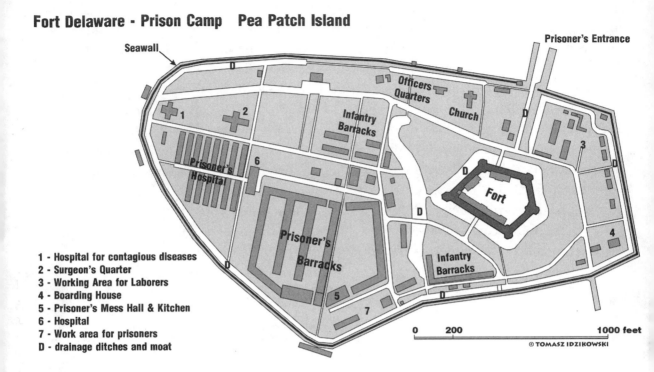

1 - Hospital for contagious diseases
2 - Surgeon's Quarter
3 - Working Area for Laborers
4 - Boarding House
5 - Prisoner's Mess Hall & Kitchen
6 - Hospital
7 - Work area for prisoners
D - drainage ditches and moat

The North had little use for most of its coastal forts during the war from Fort Delaware on the Delaware River to Fort Warren in Boston Harbor. Many of the larger forts became prisons for POWs and their commanders had to install additional facilities to handle the large volume of prisoners. Initially, FORT DELAWARE housed high-profile military and political prisoners, but in 1861, when over two thousand POWs arrived, its commander had to build barracks outside the fort, turning the entire island into a large prison camp. He also had to build dikes to keep the island from flooding at high tide. Conditions were difficult at best. By 1863, when General Albin Schoeph assumed command of the fort, the overcrowded island held about eight thousand POWs. During the winter, the POWs suffered from the cold and competed for space around the stoves in the chilly barracks. FORT LAFAYETTE, because of its location on an island, served as a prison in New York Harbor. CASTLE WILLIAMS on Governor's Island, and FORT SCHUYLER on Throgg's Neck, also became prisons.

Not all Northern forts became prisons. FORT CONSTITUTION at Portsmouth mounted twenty-five pieces of artillery in 1861, including 32-pdr guns and 100-pdr Parrott rifles. A militia company of only two dozen men garrisoned the fort. More local troops arrived later, and in 1862, work began on new walls outside the fort as part of a new 3rd System fort despite the lessons gleaned at Fort Pulaski and Fort Macon that spring.

FORT HAMILTON in New York was rearmed with heavy artillery. FORT ADAMS in Newport was rearmed with heavier weapons, including 10-inch Rodmans in the casemates and 15-inch Rodmans en barbette on the ramparts in 1863. Similar heavy artillery pieces were also shipped to captured coastal forts in the South, apparently in the belief that they would compensate for the weaknesses of the forts in the face of rifled artillery.

In the meantime, General Lee ordered the evacuation of as much heavy artillery as possible from FORT CLINCH and the defenses of Fernandina after the fall of Port Royal in the fall of 1861. When Du Pont's ships arrived at the beginning of March 1862, the last of 1,500 Confederate soldiers were embarking on the last train out. Most of the artillery had already been hauled out and Fort Clinch was deserted.

A few days later, FORT MARION (CASTILLO DE SAN MARCOS) and the town of St. Augustine were also evacuated and Union troops took possession. The occupation of Jacksonville involved some problems, but nothing major. Thus, by the spring of 1862, most of the Atlantic coast forts, except for Fort Caswell at the entrance to the Cape Fear River and the forts at Charleston had returned to Union hands.

The Union navy was able to

> Fort Monroe also witnessed the first SUBMARINE operations. On October 9, 1961, under the cover of darkness, a two-man Confederate submarine tried to sink the warship *Minnesota* anchored off Fort Monroe in Hampton Roads. The attempt failed and the little submarine moved back to the nearest shore from where it was hauled back to Norfolk. On June 23, 1862, Brutus Villeroi's submarine, the *Alligator*, arrived off Fort Monroe, too late to take action against the Rebel ironclad *Virginia*, which had been scuttled the previous month. This unusual submarine, powered by sixteen men working sixteen oars, went up the James River to assist in the campaign against Richmond. However, it returned within a few days because the Union naval commanders did not know what to do with it.

control the Chesapeake and support the expeditions launched against the Atlantic coast from FORT MONROE. Although most of the forts of the period had direct communication by telegraph, Fort Monroe was isolated. Early in 1862, a submarine cable had to be laid across the Chesapeake to link Fort Monroe to the telegraph system. In March 1862, General McClellan, encouraged by the president, used Fort Monroe to assemble and build up an army of 100,000 and began his advance up the Peninsula. Confederate General John Magruder had put up a line of defenses from Yorktown to the Warwick River and across the peninsula, but withdrew before the Union attack in May.

At Drewry's Bluff (FORT DREWRY, called FORT DARLING by the Yankees), about seven miles south of Richmond, Robert E. Lee ordered the construction of fortifications and the installation of artillery on the bluff over 80 feet above the James River. Fort Darling gained in strength during the war, and repelled attacking Union troops in 1864. This bastion on the James remained in Rebel hands until the very end of the war.

Failure of the Forts in the Western Theater in 1863

In 1862 and 1863, Union troops advancing up the Mississippi from New Orleans and down the Mississippi from Cairo moved against the last strongholds on the river to split the Confederacy. The Federals drove Rebel forces from Kentucky and much of Tennessee. Transportation lines were limited, so the Southern commanders could not rely on quick reinforcements, especially when most attention was riveted on the battles in the Peninsula and in northern Virginia.

After the battle of Shiloh in April 1862, Grant's army advanced on Corinth, effectively severing the only rail connection between Richmond and Vicksburg. South of Nashville, General Buell's army was poised to attack Chattanooga, a key rail hub for the South. The loss of this city would greatly hinder Rebel attempts to reinforce the Western Theater. Therefore both sides struggled to control these lines of communications. The Union Army built blockhouses at key points like bridges to keep the railways operating and safe from raids and irregular forces. In May 1862, Farragut sent his gunboats upriver from New Orleans to demand the surrender of Vicksburg. In the meantime, Foote's river flotilla was still busy subduing Fort Pillow above Memphis. After the Confederates evacuated Fort Pillow and Fort Randolph in June 1862, Union forces marched into Memphis. At the end of June, Captain Charles Davis moved south to join Farragut in the bombardment of Vicksburg. Without sufficient troops to force a landing, the Federal ships withdrew to their bases. The Confederates occupied Port Hudson and Baton Rouge and started preparing defenses for Vicksburg and Port Hudson.

Work on the VICKSBURG defenses had begun in the spring of 1862. Captain D. B. Harris, a Confederate engineer officer, who was in charge of preparing the defenses of Vicksburg after the fall of New Orleans, hired free blacks to build battery positions below the city to cover the river. General Martin Luther Smith took command of Vicksburg in May 1862, and in June, S. H. Lockett arrived from Bragg's army to serve as his chief engineer. The garrison was set to work on new batteries and bombproofs. Lockett set up several new batteries on commanding heights. At the time, the Rebels had twenty-nine guns, including two 10-inch Columbiads. He later recalled how difficult it was to defend against the bombardment by mortar boats, even with bombproofs, because their heavy rounds penetrated 17 inches into the compacted clay. Lockett laid out the positions for a line of defense to the rear of the town to cover the landward approaches after a month-long survey and study of the site. Next, he created a system of redoubts, redans, lunettes, and small fieldworks on prominent points, linking them with rifle pits to form a continuous line. The construction began in September 1862, with free blacks and slaves doing the bulk of the work.

At the outset of the Vicksburg campaign, the Union scored a minor victory when General McClernand launched an assault against FORT HINDMAN at Arkansas Post up the Arkansas River. There 5,500 Confederates held a position from which they could interdict traffic on the Mississippi. Grant did not think that the position presented a threat or that its elimination was worth the effort. The earthen fort, located on a bend in the Arkansas River, was surrounded by a ditch. It formed a square with four corner bastions and curtains about 200 feet in length. On the side facing the river, two gun casemates mounted 8-inch guns: one in a bastion and the other in the curtain. The casemate's embrasures were 3 feet wide and made of squared timbers; the ceilings of oak timber were six and a half feet above the floor. Above the ceiling, a timber gabled roof was covered with flat iron plates, each seven-eighths of an inch thick and 3 inches wide. The rear of the casemate was open. The bastion facing the river included a 3-inch Parrott with an embrasure in the parapet and a 9-inch gun en barbette.

On January 3, 1863, McClernand moved up the river at the head of 32,000 troops on transports escorted by three ironclads and six gunboats of Porter's fleet. On January 10, the ironclads opened fire on Fort Hindman and the next day the Federal troops established positions nearby, joining in the fray. The Federals advanced on the narrow line of rifle pits flanked by the river on one side and woods and swamp on the other. The bombardment lasted thirty hours and knocked out the casemate guns and the 9-inch gun. Generals George Morgan's and William Sherman's Corps took the first line of rifle pits, and moved on to the last line of rifle pits, isolating the Rebel position. When the gunboats next directed their fire against the line of rifle pits extending from the fort, the

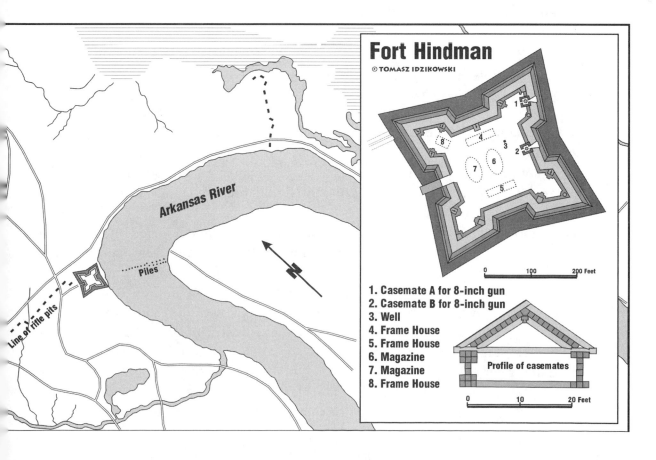

Fort Hindman
© TOMASZ IDZIKOWSKI

Arkansas River

Piles

Line of rifle pits

0   100   200 Feet

1. Casemate A for 8-inch gun
2. Casemate B for 8-inch gun
3. Well
4. Frame House
5. Frame House
6. Magazine
7. Magazine
8. Frame House

Profile of casemates

0   10   20 Feet

Rebel commander surrendered. Much of the battle was fought against Confederate troops in defensive positions beyond the fort, which took a toll on the Union troops, causing over one thousand casualties. The defenders counted only sixty men dead and about eighty wounded, but almost 4,800 surrendered on January 11, 1863. The loss of so many men greatly weakened the Confederate army in Arkansas. [Today the river has changed course and the remains of Fort Hindman are under water.]

Grant continued his advance on VICKSBURG. On May 17, 1863, after failing to stop Grant from crossing the Big Black River, Pemberton sent Lockett ahead to prepare the defenses of Vicksburg as his troops pulled back toward their earthen fortress. Lockett again put the garrison to work on the defenses. The main works, he wrote, included exterior ditches 6 to 10 feet deep and ramparts with a parapet and banquette for the infantry and embrasures and platforms for the artillery. To his dismay, the winter rains had already washed away and weakened the previously prepared earthworks. While work parties went up to prepare the positions, all the field artillery, the Parrott guns, and siege artillery were moved into position. When the army showed up on May 18, 102 guns were in position, not including the river batteries. The defenses of Vicksburg included nine earthen forts: FORT HILL overlooking the river north of the city, the STOCKADE REDAN, THIRD LOUISIANA REDAN, the GREAT REDOUBT, the SECOND TEXAS LUNETTE, the RAILROAD REDOUBT, FORT GARROTT, the SALIENT WORKS, and SOUTH FORT overlooking the river south of the city. Various obstacles, which included abatis and wire entanglements made of telegraph wire, were also set up.

By May 19, Grant's forces launched probing attacks against the Confederate fortress. On May 22, hoping to avoid a siege, Grant launched a major assault on a three-mile front between Fort Garrott and the Stockade Redan which included six of the fortress's nine forts. The Federal troops struggled to the top of several forts to plant their flags. However, unable to hold their precarious positions, they were ruthlessly driven back. When Grant finally broke off the assault, he had suffered three thousand casualties and realized that he must lay a formal siege. The siege began in a traditional manner as the Union troops dug parallels, advanced saps, and finally prepared mines while the Rebels tunneled out countermines.

On June 25, a large mine filled with 2,200 pounds of powder detonated under the 3rd Louisiana Redan, one of the most formidable forts of the entire line. The explosion tore apart a section of the redan, leaving a crater 12 feet deep and 40 feet in diameter. The 45th Illinois Infantry stormed into the crater and the defenders withdrew to a retrenchment. During the next twenty-four hours, the Rebels pinned the Union troops in the crater, hurling explosives at them. Most of the redan was still intact. The Union soldiers held a section of the crater where they put up a parapet to protect themselves. The miners used the crater to begin a new mine leading to the left side of the fort. On July 1, they detonated this second mine under the redan, blasting a crater about 20 feet deep and 50 feet in diameter and destroying most of the Confederate fort. The Rebels stubbornly held

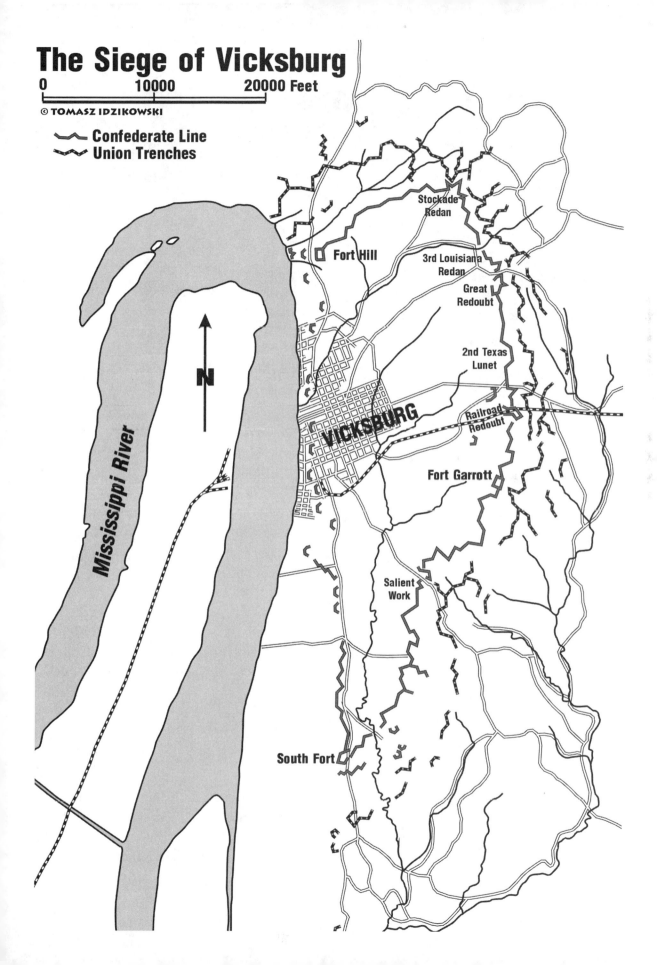

Vicksburg, Mississippi. Reconstruction of a Confederate battery position.

on to their retrenchments despite the heavy bombardment, finally driving back the attackers. On July 2, they prepared a dozen countermines loaded with 100 to 125 pounds of powder about 20 feet beyond their works to use against enemy sappers whose mines were advancing toward their lines. However, the countermines were not used.

Pemberton was totally isolated with the Union Army on three sides and Porter's gunboats holding the river line. Starvation and disease took its toll on troops and civilians. There did not seem to be any hope of relief. To avoid the bombardment that was devasting the town, many civilians took refuge in caves. Pemberton, finding his situation untenable, surrendered on July 4, 1863. Despite everything, his fortifications had held and he had inflicted over nine thousand casualties on the Union forces, a ratio of about nine to one. The fortress on the Mississippi and its garrison were lost, a fatal blow to the Confederacy.

Only PORT HUDSON remained in Confederate hands on the Mississippi, but it did not have the importance of the position at Vicksburg. In October 1862, the largest piece of artillery at Port Hudson was a 10-inch Columbiad. In addition, there were a few dozen other pieces of artillery. The garrison numbered less than a thousand men. By December 1862, however, 5,500 men gathered there under the command of General Franklin Gardner, an engineer. Gardner immediately set out to improve the river defenses to stop advancing ships. His men, mostly slaves, prepared a series of lunettes about four hundred yards apart to defend the land front for a distance of about eight miles. As in Vicksburg, the Confederates mounted their artillery on the bluffs facing the river. On March 14, 1863, General Gardner's twenty heavy guns on the river batteries engaged Farragut's fleet in a three-hour battle, sinking one warship. By then, Gardner's garrison

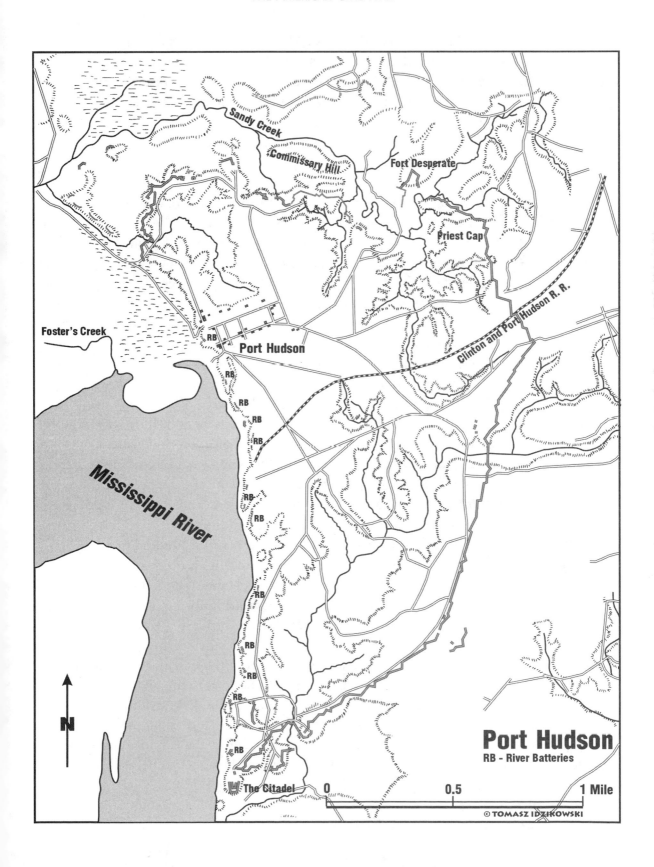

Sandy Creek

Commissary Hill

Fort Desperate

Priest Cap

Clinton and Port Hudson R. R.

Foster's Creek

RB

Port Hudson

RB

RB

RB

RB

Mississippi River

RB

RB

RB

RB

RB

RB

N

RB

The Citadel

Port Hudson
RB - River Batteries

0   0.5   1 Mile

© TOMASZ IDZIKOWSKI

had grown to over eleven thousand troops. On May 22, General Banks placed the fortress under siege and launched several assaults. Despite ferocious combat, the siege lines advanced relentlessly as both sides resorted to mining and countermining. When the news of Vicksburg's capitulation finally reached Gardner, he decided to raise the white flag on July 9. The garrison lost about 670 men between May 21 and July 9, whereas the Federals suffered over 4,000 casualties. Despite these heavy losses, the Union navy and army were in control of the Mississippi.

As the Union troops took over the Confederate fortifications they restored in many cases the masonry and earthen forts to protect their own lines. In the summer of 1863, General Orlando Poe was assigned the task of fortifying KNOXVILLE, which sat on the rail line between Richmond and Chattanooga. After inspecting some Rebel earthworks on a bluff overlooking the railway station, Poe decided that they were not adequate and built Fort Sanders on the site. He also erected another fort (FORT HILL) on the east side of town at Temperance Hill. The work was done by an engineer battalion and a group of freed slaves, but it was not finished until after the next siege.

FORT SANDERS was an irregular quadrangle with a maximum length of 125 yards and a minimum length of 85 yards. It included two completed bastions on its western front, but its eastern side was left open. A 12-foot-wide ditch, 6 to 8 inches deep covered the bastions and the fort had almost vertical scarps. The counterscarps included a banquette from which the defenders could lay down grazing fire. The Union troops made creative use of telegraph wire during this siege: they strung the wire around tree stumps, letting it hang a few inches off the ground to trip up the advancing enemy soldiers. Fort Sanders's northwestern bastion housed a lone 12-pdr gun. Three more 12-pdr were located on the northern front. The fort also had four 20-pdr Parrotts, two 3-inch rifles, and two 12-pdr in addition to those used by the garrison of five hundred men.

The defenses around Knoxville formed a semicircle whose ends rested on the Holston River. The Confederate attack on Fort Sanders began with a bombardment at dawn on November 29. Twenty minutes later the assaulting force passed through the wire entanglements and abatis. The defenders laid down heavy fire from the ramparts as the Rebels jumped into the ditch and swarmed toward the scarp walls where they were blasted with canister, grenades, and musketry from the bastions on their flanks. During the siege, General McLaws ordered his sharpshooters to fire on the embrasures of the unfinished Fort Sanders to pin down the gunners. The Rebels climbed over the shoulders of their own comrades to reach the parapet where they planted their flags and rallied, only to be killed or captured. The remainder of the Confederate force retreated, breaking off the siege on the night of December 4.

In central Tennessee, the Union forces had strengthened their position at NASHVILLE back in 1862. Captain James St. Clair Morton supervised the construction of FORT

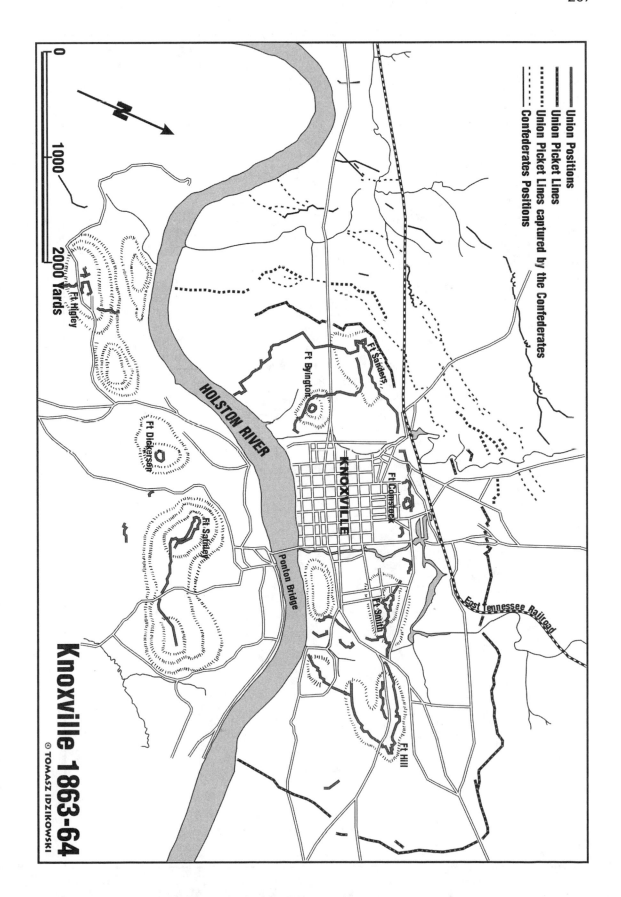

Knoxville 1863-64
© TOMASZ IDZIKOWSKI

Union Positions
Union Picket Lines
Union Picket Lines captured by the Confederates
Confederates Positions

HOLSTON RIVER

Ft Higley
Ft Dickerson
Ft Stanley
Ft Byington
Ft Sanders
KNOXVILLE
Ft Comstock
Ft Smith
Ft Hill
Ponton Bridge
East Tennessee Railroad

N

0
1000
2000 Yards

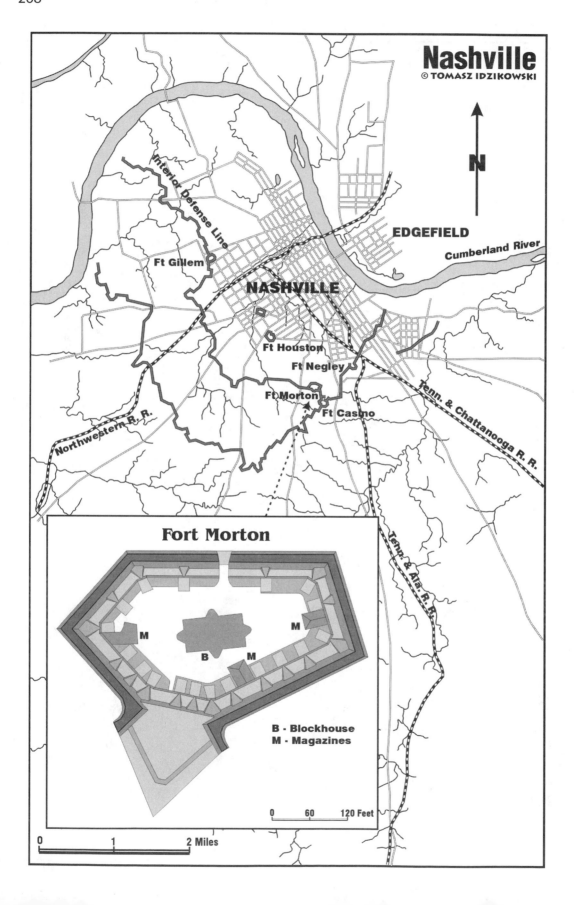

Nashville
© TOMASZ IDZIKOWSKI

N

EDGEFIELD

Cumberland River

Interior Defense Line

Ft Gillem

NASHVILLE

Ft Houston

Ft Negley

Ft Morton

Ft Casno

Tenn. & Chattanooga R. R.

Northwestern R. R.

Tenn. & Ala. R. R.

Fort Morton

M

M

B

M

B - Blockhouse
M - Magazines

0   60   120 Feet

0   1   2 Miles

NEGLEY, FORT MORTON, FORT HOUSTON, and FORT GILLEM on the hills on the outskirts of the city. He also built defenses around the capitol building on a hill in the city. Morton drew new plans up for Fort Houston and Fort Morton, which were to serve as independent strongholds if the city fell. However, his designs, which included stone scarps for the two forts, were considered too grand for the number of men and amount of materials available.

Before he departed for his next assignment, Morton completed the large FORT NEGLEY, one of the most interesting forts built during the war. It consisted of a central 12-foot-high wooden square stockade, with four wooden corner turrets and ravelins on the east and west sides, within a larger rectangular enclosure that measured 600 feet by 300 feet. The east and west faces of the fort consisted of several redans that ran from the bastions to the northern scarp. The fort, which occupied most of the hill, included two large half-bastions with bombproofs on its south side. In most places, earth covered the fort's stone scarps and the parapets were 9 feet thick. On the West Ravelin, above the south scarp, two artillery casemates held a 30-pdr Parrott rifle and included defenses made of iron. About two thousand free blacks and slaves worked on the fort to complete it in December 1862.

A minor Rebel raid against Nashville took place early in November 1862. In December 1864, the city braced itself for a major attack from a Confederate contingent led by General John B. Hood, which never materialized.

Fort Negley
© TOMASZ IDZIKOWSKI

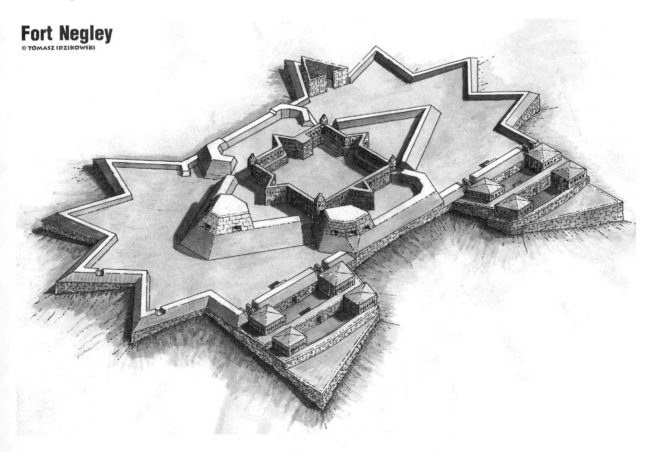

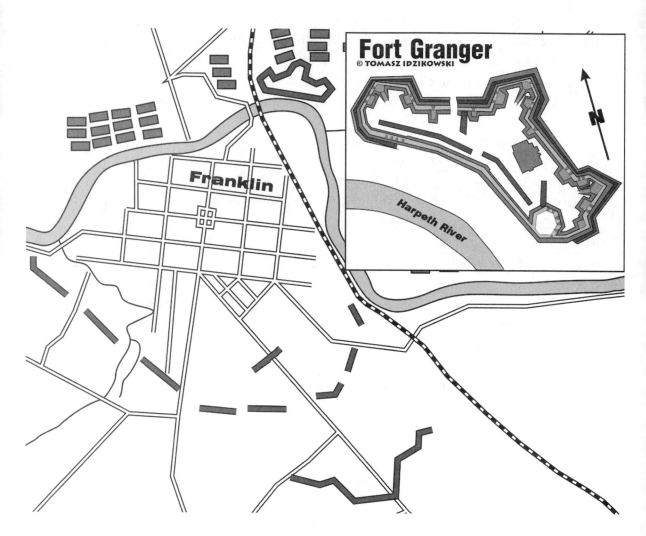

Several days earlier Hood's army had attacked the Federal fortifications at Franklin, Tennessee, which included the large earthwork of FORT GRANGER. Built in the spring of 1863 by Union troops, this fort was used to repel Confederate cavalry raids that year. Hood's troops first attacked the defenses of Franklin located on the south side of the Harpeth River. Fort Granger, which was on the north side of the river, covered the main railroad crossing. When the Confederates came within three hundred yards of the breastworks, a cannon in Fort Granger roared into action. The Rebels gave their famous yell and charged forward. The clash lasted for six hours as Hood's troops stormed the first line of breastworks and then broke into the main line of defenses only to be counterattacked and ejected. By the time the fighting died down in the evening, the Rebels had lost over six thousand men. The Federals withdrew across the river under the guns of Fort Granger, and evacuated the fort a little later. Hood advanced on Nashville where winter and a much larger force of Union troops, outnumbering his by more than two to one, brought his momentum to an end.

Clearing the Coast—1863 to 1865

In 1863, the Rebels still held the ports of Wilmington, Charleston, and Mobile, which all became the sites of major battles. Charleston represented a strategic and psychological target, since that was where the rebellion had begun. Admiral Samuel Du Pont waited for the completion of more ironclad monitors before he launched a naval assault on Charleston. The Union also embarked on other naval operations further down the coast, south of the Savannah River.

FORT MCALLISTER was situated on a bluff on the south bank of the Ogeechee River several miles south of Savannah. This Confederate fort, made largely of marsh mud and sand, was built by a company of Georgian infantry under the supervision of Confederate engineer Captain John McCrady. It was built in the summer of 1861, at the southern end of a line of coastal defenses in Georgia that began at the Savannah River. Robert E. Lee suggested improvements needed such as a water obstacle made of pilings in the river, which were implemented in 1861. Initially, the armaments consisted of four 32-pdrs forming a simple battery, but by the fall of 1862, the garrison had added more positions, including a detached position for a 10-inch mortar, and created earthen walls to encircle the fort. By the end of 1862, the fort mounted an 8-inch and a 10-inch Columbiad, which was transferred elsewhere in March 1863 and replaced with a 24-pdr rifle (32-pdr rifle?). The fort's other armament included a 42-pdr, three 32-pdrs, small guns for the landward defenses, and a couple of howitzers to cover the sally ports. The gun positions facing the river included large earthen traverses, some with magazines. The mortar position was detached to prevent the vibration from its discharge from damaging the soft earthen walls. The fort included a large central bombproof, built with the original 1861 position, which served as the fort's hospital and supply depot. The hot-shot furnace served the nearby 32-pd gun. During 1864, the fort's landward defenses were expanded to include a dry moat in which a line of sharpened stakes was embedded. Two drawbridges spanned this moat. The garrison also cleared a glacis and created a line of abatis with a primitive minefield made of shells in front of the moat. A covered way (an earthen embankment) gave access to the mortar position.

Fort McAllister exchanged fire with Union ships in July 1861 and again in July 1862 when a blockade runner sought shelter under its guns. Since the mouth of the Savannah was controlled by the Federals in 1862, the Ogeechee River was the only waterway open to blockade runners. In January and February 1863, Admiral Samuel Du Pont sent the monitor *Montauk* against the fort. The fort scored forty-eight hits on the *Montauk*. In February, several Rains Torpedoes were delivered at the fort. The next naval attack achieved little beyond damaging a gun carriage. An ironclad's 15-inch shell pierced a 17-foot-thick parapet made of marsh mud, but the sand parapets held up better. The garrison only suffered a few casualties. The men's worst inconvenience was getting covered with sand when the ramparts were hit. On March 3, 1863, three monitors began

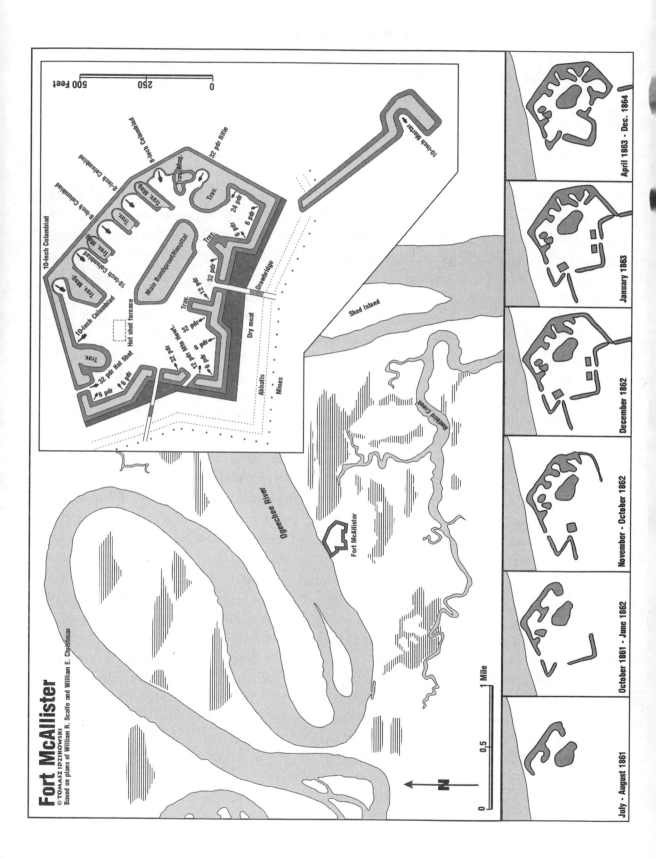

Fort McAllister
© TOMASZ IDZIKOWSKI
Based on plans of William R. Scaife and William E. Christman

Fort McAllister, Georgia, in December 1864 with Union ships anchored nearby. National Archives

blasting the fort for the last time. After a fruitless eight-hour bombardment, the navy ceased its operations against Fort McAllister. For months the fort's garrison suffered from boredom as the war raged to the north and south. Finally in December 1864, a division of Sherman's army on its "March to the Sea" was detached to remove this last Rebel bastion south of Charleston. In a quarter of an hour, the fort was taken. Forty-eight men of the garrison died in the engagement and the remaining 230 were taken prisoners. The Union troops lost 134 men storming the position.

By the end of March 1863, there were eight ironclads at Port Royal: the *Montauk*, the the *Passaic*, the *Patapsco*, the *Nahant*, the *Weekawken*, the *Catskill*, and the *Nantucket*, and the *Keokuk*, an experimental vessel. The monitors had turrets with 11 inches of armor, a hull with 5 inches of armor, and the pilothouse with 8 inches of armor. Their main weakness was against plunging fire because their decks had only an inch of armor. The turrets mounted a 15-inch and an 11-inch SB Dahlgren. The 11-inch guns were used because there was a shortage of the larger weapons. The *Keokuk* was protected by 4 inches of armor and had two gun towers with three embrasures each and an 11-inch SB Dahlgren. Thus, each of these ships was a virtual floating fort.

Admiral Du Pont sent the ironclads against FORT SUMTER on April 7, 1863, in the first major contest between a 3rd System fort and the best the navy could offer. Fort Sumter controlled the entrance to Charleston Harbor with the help of a number of earthen forts, built after the beginning of the war, and some batteries. The ironclad squadron, including the *New Ironsides* (an ironclad warship with eighteen heavy guns, including 11-inch Dahlgrens), sailed past Battery Wagner in good weather conditions before they approached Fort Sumter and Fort Moultrie and fired the first salvos at 3:00 P.M. The sea between Fort Sumter and Sullivan's Island was littered with obstacles and torpedoes. As the *Keokuk* and the *Nahant* closed to within 1,100 yards of Fort Sumter, the *Nahant* took three dozen hits. The *Keokuk* came within nine hundred yards before Rebel guns riddled it with holes and its two turrets were damaged. By the time the ironclad withdrew, it had taken ninety hits, including nineteen below the waterline, and was on the verge of sinking—it sank the next day. Of the 139 rounds the ironclads fired at Fort Sumter, only thirty-four hit its walls, but they caused little significant damage. It is believed that the gunners had aimed too high in an attempt to take out the barbette guns of the fort. The Confederate gun crews at Fort Sumter and neighboring fortifications hurled two thousand rounds at the squadron, scoring 520 hits. The *New Ironsides* was unable to reach a position from which to fire at the fort, but was hit ninety-five times. The monitor *Weehawken* took fifty-three hits, some of which penetrated its deck and shattered its armor plate. The *Passaic*, after taking thirty-five hits, limped off, its 11-inch gun knocked out and its turret jammed. The *Nantucket* was struck fifty-one times and its 15-inch gun disabled; the *Nahant*, *Passaic*, and *Keokuk* were all disabled and the *Nahant* was forced to withdraw. The battle ended when the remaining monitors retired. Thus it turned out that the navy was not able to overcome well-defended 3rd System forts. Admiral Du Pont was relieved at his own request because his superiors would not accept the fact that a squadron of ironclads was not adequate to reduce forts of the 3rd System. Admiral Dahlgren took over his command.

The task of taking CHARLESTON fell to the army, which resorted to its heavy guns to smash the forts. By July 10, 1863, General Gillmore crossed from Folly to Morris Island to clear the southern shore at the entrance to Charleston Harbor. On July 12, the Federal troops attacked FORT WAGNER, on the north side of the island, with naval support. The earthen fort on Morris Island held off the initial attack. After several days of bombardment, another and even larger assault was led by the 54th Massachusetts. The black troops of the regiment reached the ramparts, but were driven back, taking heavy losses along with the white regiments that followed. The battle for Fort Wagner, one of the bloodiest of the war, cost the Union over fifteen hundred casualties and the Confederacy fewer than two hundred. As Union forces bombarded the fort for seven more weeks, their sappers advanced the siege lines with five parallels. On September 6, the head of the sap reached the ditch in front of the fort from the fifth parallel. That same night the Confederates quickly evacuated the fort and Battery Gregg behind it. They had intended to destroy the fort, but the fuses left behind in the magazines of both positions failed to detonate.

According to General Beauregard, Fort Wagner had never been more than a battery and not the fort that Gillmore claimed it was. Nonetheless, its earthen ramparts seem to

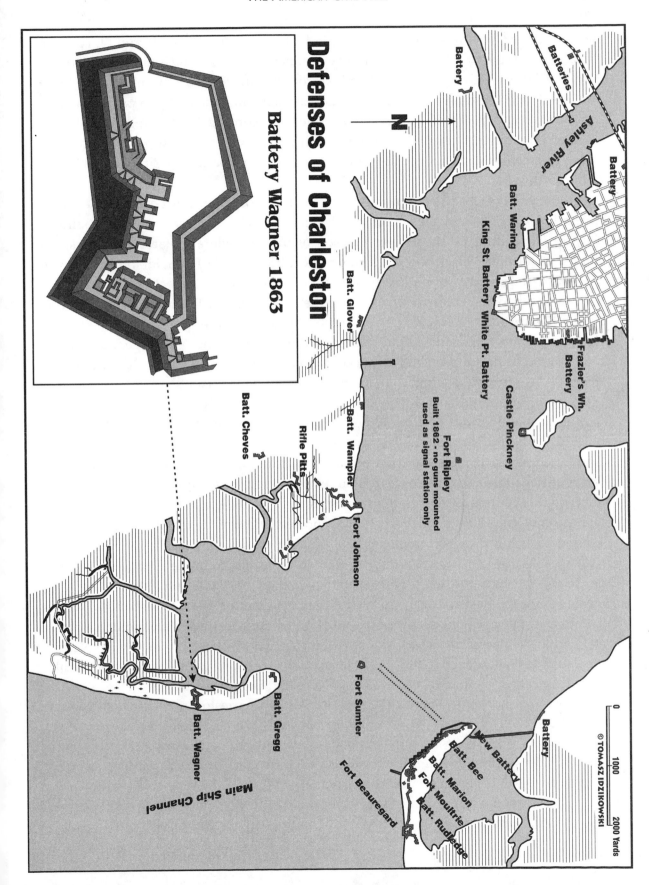

Defenses of Charleston

Battery Wagner 1863

N

Ashley River

Battery

Batteries

Battery

Batt. Waring

King St. Battery

Battery White Pt. Battery

Frazier's Wh. Battery

Castle Pinckney

Fort Ripley
Built 1862 - no guns mounted
used as signal station only

Batt. Glover

Batt. Wampler

Fort Johnson

Rifle Pits

Batt. Cheves

Batt. Gregg

Batt. Wagner

Main Ship Channel

Fort Sumter

Battery

New Battery

Batt. Bee

Batt. Marion

Fort Moultrie

Fort Beauregard

Batt. Rutledge

© TOMASZ IDZIKOWSKI

0   1000   2000 Yards

indicate that it was more than any simple battery position. It had only eleven gun embrasures, three of which were for heavy calibers (two 10-inch Columbiads and one 32-pdr rifle). The other guns were 32-pdr carronades and 12-pdr mortars, but the bombardment disabled most of them. Beauregard strengthened the position to include traverses and bombproofs that sheltered 750 men. (According to Beauregard, Gillmore claimed that they sheltered sixteen hundred men). He also placed a parapet along the gorge to enclose the position, thus transforming it from a battery position into a formidable earthwork.

But the prize of this campaign was FORT SUMTER. Thus, after they occupied the northern end of Morris Island, the Union troops moved their batteries into position to fire on the fort. According to Major John Johnson of the Confederate States Engineers, Du Pont's failed naval attack had left a crater 6 feet high and 18 feet wide on the exterior eastern wall. A section of the parapet had been loosened on 25 feet of its length and some bricks had been blown out, exposing the gun carriages. The four magazines were placed in pairs (an upper and a lower) at the ends of the gorge. The Confederates abandoned the upper magazines before the fall of Morris Island since the gorge faced Morris and James Islands. Johnson had to inspect the magazines hourly and "by the aid of a little bull's-eye lantern hanging from my finer, and casting fantastic shadows on the piled-up kegs of cannon powder, I would enter the chamber, apply my ear close to the surface of the massive wall, and await the coming of the next rifle-shell, to hear how much more it shook the fort than the last, and to estimate its gain of penetration." When the firing died down at night, he went out to inspect the damage and finally ordered the lower eastern magazine to be cleared out even though it was not breached. Dahlgren attempted a landing at Fort Sumter on September 8, 1863, but the Rebels laid down heavy small-arms fire from the parapets and hurled grenades at the assailants. The Confederates killed or captured over a hundred of the 400-man landing force.

For weeks after, the Union artillery pounded the walls to rubble forcing the defenders to fill the huge breaches with sandbags and place fraises on exposed sections. Rubble from the battered walls formed ramps into the fort. By December, the Rebels had created interior defenses since the walls no longer constituted a formidable obstacle. Eighteen months of bombardment had turned Fort Sumter into a pile rubble, but the defenders had turned it into a large formidable earthwork. The Confederates finally abandoned the fort until February 17, 1865, as Charleston was evacuated.

Blockading ships effectively closed the harbor of Charleston and occasionally even bombarded the city during 1864, but the harbor fortifications managed to keep them at bay most of the time. At the same time, the Confederates made a desperate attempt to turn the tide, sending the *Hunley*, a hand-powered submarine, to break the blockade. The *Hunley* engaged in the first successful submarine attack in history, sinking the Union warship *Housatonic*, but it was lost on its return to port. The incident proved, nevertheless, that the submarine could be an effective and deadly weapon in harbor defense.

In 1864, the Confederates enlisted a brigade of Cherokees to fight the Union troops holding FORT GIBSON and FORT SMITH. The Rebels moved between Fort Gibson, the strongest position in the region, and Fort Smith, isolating it. They drove back the Union outposts in the area. A year earlier, in April 27, 1863, Colonel William Phillips had built earthworks according to "scientific principles," declaring them almost impregnable in a letter to his commanding officer. When they were completed, they covered over a mile, making it the strongest fort in the west. In the summer of 1863, Confederate forces had come close to the fort and tried to take it, but in 1864, they only isolated it. In September 1864, over ten thousand troops and civilians were trapped at Fort Gibson with limited supplies. Luckily for them, the Indian troops left for the winter, ending an operation that might be considered a distant blockade rather than a siege.

Admiral Farragut was not able to begin the long awaited operations against MOBILE, the last Confederate port on the Gulf Coast to the east of the Mississippi, until August 1864. He had wanted to eliminate it earlier that year, but had not been allowed the necessary ships and troops. While Farragut awaited troops and ships, the Confederates had been busy erecting defenses and building three ironclad rams, including the *Tennessee*, the largest and best built of the Confederate navy, which was anchored near Fort Morgan.

FORT GAINES and FORT MORGAN covered the main entrance leading to Mobile. Most of the deep-water channel was mined, although a gap was left free for blockade-runners. At Grant's Pass, the other entrance to Mobile Bay, the earthen work known as FORT POWELL, built after the war had begun, was far from complete in 1864. By the summer of 1864, a telegraph linked the three coastal forts to Mobile. The guns in the three forts were provided with three hundred rounds apiece and all the forts were well provisioned. The battle of Mobile Bay began on August 5 when Farragut's ships entered the bay, passing Fort Morgan where they first ran into the mines. A line of monitors to the starboard of a line of wooden vessels shielded them from the batteries of Fort Morgan. The gunners of Fort Morgan and its Water Battery blasted away at the ships in line. During the passage of the channel, the fort managed to fire 491 rounds. The return fire from the ships, on the other hand, did little damage to the fort. General Page, commander of Fort Morgan, claimed most of the torpedoes (mines) had been ineffective because of the depth of the water and strong tides, although they did sink one monitor.

After bombardment by the monitor *Chickasaw*, Fort Powell's garrison evacuated the site and blew up the fort. On August 6, the monitor *Chickasaw* bombarded Fort Gaines as Union troops prepared the siege. The attack knocked out the fort's three 10-inch guns, leaving twenty artillery pieces still in operation. Fort Gaines's commander surrendered the next morning. On August 9, Union troops landed near Fort Morgan and proceeded to set up siege lines. General Page prepared to defend the fort by constructing traverses between the guns and removing wooden structures that were obstructions

Inside the Confederate Redoubt #4 at Fort Blakeley, Alabama.

in the fort. He had his four hundred men work night and day adding earthen protection. The monitors, gunboats, and frigates bombarded the fort daily until it became evident to Page that the brick walls would not hold up much longer. On August 21, the Union sappers came within two hundred yards of the glacis. A day-long naval bombardment took place the next day while sharpshooters picked off the fort's gunners, silencing their guns. Only two guns remained after Fort Morgan's walls were breached. The Union mortars devastated the fort setting the citadel on fire. As the fire raged, Page tried to flood his magazines, which were now exposed. With his artillery gone, his quartermaster stores destroyed, and the fort turning into rubble, Page raised the white flag on the morning of August 23. Farragut's battle of Mobile Bay had effectively closed the port, but Mobile still had a triple line of fortifications with three hundred guns, plus several forts to the east on the northern shore. The city held out until the spring of 1865 when the last battle of the war involving fortifications was fought at FORT BLAKELEY, one of the forts east of the city. The earthen fort, with its nine redoubts, fell to a Union assault on April 9, 1865.

After the fall of Fort Gaines and Fort Morgan, the Gulf Coast east of the Mississippi was in Union hands. On the East Coast, only Charleston remained and the North Carolinian ports were closed down from 1863 until 1865. In 1863, Louis Trager, who served as a spy for Grant, observed the conditions in the Confederacy, including troop strengths and fortifications. In a report forwarded to General Halleck he warned that the Rebels were building earthworks at Atlanta and that Richmond was already strongly fortified. The good news, he reported, was that the port of Wilmington (NC)

Part of Fort Fisher on the Cape Fear River after it fell to Union troops early in

could fall at any time. General W. H. C. Whiting, commander of the Wilmington defenses in January 1863, warned the commanders of Fort Fisher and Fort Caswell to ready for a major Union offensive later that month.

FORT FISHER waslocated at the south end of the peninsula on the eastern side of the Cape Fear River. Although it was begun in mid-1861, Fort Fisher was little more than a collection of sand batteries until July 1862 when Colonel William Lamb took command. Lamb, relying heavily on slave labor, turned it into the strongest earthwork coastal fortification in the South. The fort became known as Wilmington's "Malakoff," a reference to the Russian fortress at Sebastopol in the Crimean War. It also had telegraph connection to Wilmington. Fort Fisher formed an 'L' shape and had casemated and barbette guns, but was designed only to defend against naval attack and amphibious assault. It had large traverses used for magazines and bombproofs. It also served to protect the gun positions from enfilading fire. Battery Buchanan, at the end of the peninsula on its own high mound, consisted of four guns (including two 11-inch) that covered the land approach to the open rear of the fort and the inlet. It also served as the fort's citadel. Fort Fisher's armaments included several 8-inch and 10-inch Columbiads and 6-inch and 7-inch Brooke rifles. The shorter arm of the 'L' shape closed off the peninsula on the north side of the fort with a 20-foot-high parapet in front of which stood a 9-foot-high wooden palisade. In addition, there was a crude minefield whose "torpedoes" were wired into a bombproof with the electrical batteries as a detonating device. Three mortars stood in position behind the northern wall. The two arms of the 'L' were linked by the large 45-foot-high northeast bastion. The long arm of the 'L', which faced the coast and extended for three-quarters of a mile, had a 12-foot-high parapet mounting twenty-one cannons. Most of these guns were emplaced so they could use ricochet fire against ships. The Mound Battery, anchoring the end of this arm, was a 60-foot-high sand mound with a ramp that allowed access to the two guns. These cannons could place plunging fire on the decks of attacking ships.

FORT CASWELL was strengthened with "iron-clad casemates." However, Fort Caswell was the weak link in Wilmington's defenses. Whiting had not been able to block the channel effectively, but hoped that the mines designed by General Rains would be more successful. FORT ANDERSON stood on the west bank of the Cape Fear River about fifteen miles south of the city in 1862. Other smaller fortifications such as FORT PENDER (former Fort Johnson) were strengthened as much as possible. Heavy sand traverses protected most of the forts. There was only one 10-inch Columbiad and one 42-pdr rifle for all the outer defenses. As no assault materialized during 1863, heavier weapons were delivered and Lamb continued to strengthen Fort Fisher. Robert E. Lee sent Hoke's division to reinforce the defenders, explaining to Colonel William Lamb that Fort Fisher was the key to Wilmington and crucial to his own army's survival at Richmond.

In December 1864 the defenders of Fort Fisher were able to hold off an attack by Union land and naval forces. In January 1865 over forty ships of Porter's fleet commenced the bombardment of Fort Fisher. After two days, they managed to dismount several of its guns and cut the wires to the minefield thus neutralizing it before the Union troops stormed the fort. The landing force attacked on January 15, and took the fort after taking heavy losses. The Confederates, who fought to the bitter end did not spike their guns. A magazine near the northeast bastion blew up, killing hundreds. When the fort fell approximately two thousand men in the fort including their commanders were taken prisoner.

The loss of Fort Fisher led to the evacuation of FORT HOLMES on Smith's Island (Bald Head Island) on January 16, of Fort Caswell on January 17, and of Fort Pender and other positions on Oak Island shortly afterward. Fort Anderson fell in mid-February.

In Defense of Washington D.C.

Major John G. Barnard, the department engineer, ordered his engineer officers, including Captain Horatio Wright, to build field fortifications around Washington D.C. in May 1861. As a result, several earthen forts, including FORT CORCORAN, FORT HAGGERTY, FORT BENNETT, FORT RUNYON, FORT ALBANY, and FORT ELLSWORTH, were built, mainly to defend bridges. When the rebellion was not crushed early, a strong fortress ring had to be developed to defend Washington, D.C. The new Union commander, George McClellan, undertook the massive effort. The entire project would last four years. The forts built in the summer of 1861 were only temporary and had to be rebuilt because they were unsatisfactory. By the end of 1862, the fortress ring included fifty-

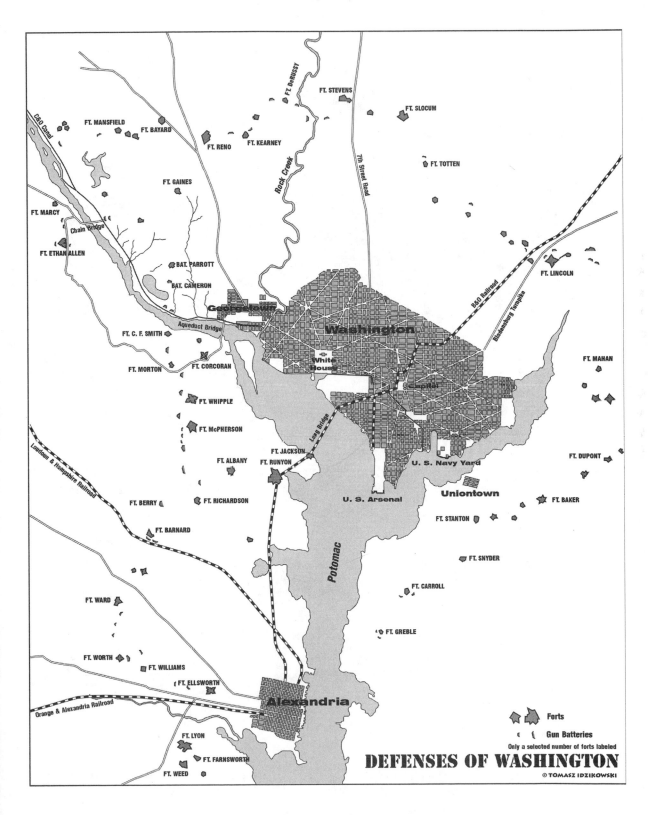

DEFENSES OF WASHINGTON
© TOMASZ IDZIKOWSKI

Fort Slocum

0   100   200 Feet

Nine gun platforms for a Field or Siege Gun
Five gun platforms for a 4.5-inch Rifle
One position for a 24-pdr on a barbette carriage
One position for a 10-pdr Parrott
One position for a 24-pdr Siege Gun

A-B   C-D

E-F   G-H

Fort Slocum and Fort Ethan Allen were two of the more than sixty forts that were built for the protection of Washington D.C. during the Civil War.

Fort Ethan Allen

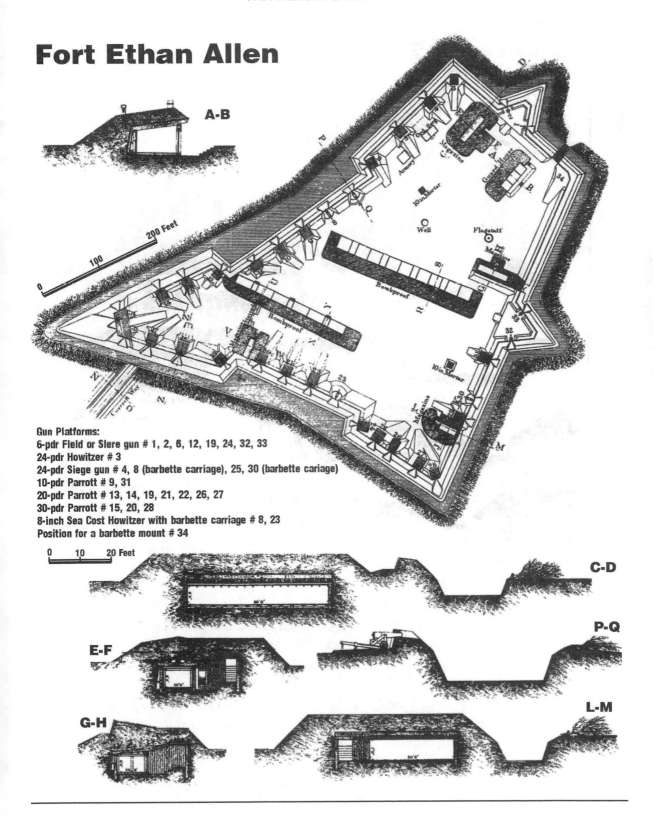

A-B

200 Feet
100
0

Gun Platforms:
6-pdr Field or Siere gun # 1, 2, 6, 12, 19, 24, 32, 33
24-pdr Howitzer # 3
24-pdr Siege gun # 4, 8 (barbette carriage), 25, 30 (barbette cariage)
10-pdr Parrott # 9, 31
20-pdr Parrott # 13, 14, 19, 21, 22, 26, 27
30-pdr Parrott # 15, 20, 28
8-inch Sea Cost Howitzer with barbette carriage # 8, 23
Position for a barbette mount # 34

0   10   20 Feet

C-D

P-Q

E-F

L-M

G-H

Blockhouse

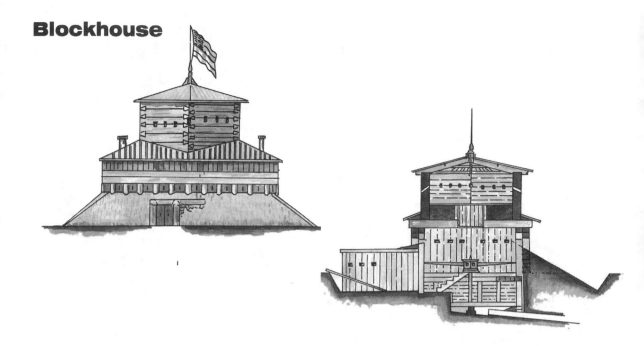

three forts and twenty-two batteries with 643 guns and seventy-five mortars and, it is believed, required a 34,000-man garrison. In October 1862, the secretary of war formed a commission for the defense of the capital that included Totten, Barnard, and several other officers and provided the guidelines for the fortifications. In 1863, Barnard ordered the addition of more forts to the ring so that by the end of that year, there were sixty forts and ninety-three batteries with 837 guns—but only 23,000 men to man them. J. G. Barnard wrote in a postwar report that by April 1865, sixty-eight enclosed forts and batteries had been completed, forming an aggregate perimeter of 22,800 yards or thirteen miles with emplacements for 1,210 guns. However, he pointed out, only 807 cannons and 98 mortars had been actually placed in these positions. In addition, ninety-three batteries for field guns had been prepared, but had not been armed; this gave a total of 401 emplacements. In addition, he had erected three blockhouses, excavated 35,711 yards or about twenty miles of rifle trenches, and built thirty-two miles of military roads. The entire circuit of the fortifications extended for thirty-seven miles.

According to Benjamin Cooling, author of *Mr. Lincoln's Forts*, many of these forts were not fully enclosed earthworks. Even though Barnard ordered the addition of wooden stockades to cover their gorges, they should be classified as lunettes. Their main armament consisted of 24-pdr and 32-pdr cannons on seacoast carriages because those were the only ones available. The large earthen forts stood about a half a mile apart and their front parapets ranged from 12 feet to 18 feet in thickness. In a postwar report, Barnard mentioned the forts were built according to the specifications of D. H. Mahan's *Treatise on Field Fortifications* with parapets 7 to 9 feet high and 8 to 12 feet thick. The thickness was increased to 18 feet on exposed fronts. The exterior slopes were built at a 45 degree angle and plank, or sod if timber was unavailable, revetments lined the interior to prevent erosion. The cheeks (the sides) of the embrasures were made of turf-filled gabions. The slopes were covered with sod and the ditches were about 6 feet deep. A glacis studded with abatis was prepared around each fort. The bombproofs were covered with at least 8 feet of earth, usually occupied positions along the gorge, and had loopholes cut in their back walls. The more important forts had a well, the deepest of which at Fort Stanton was 212 feet deep. The forts's magazines and supplies allowed them to be self-sufficient.

BLOCKHOUSES were placed in wide gaps between forts to prevent raids. According to Barnard, the ground plan of these blockhouses was in the shape of a Greek cross. The blockhouses were made of logs 16 to 18 inches in diameter with two sides squared, and placed vertically. There were loopholes for musketry and an embrasure on each side for the two 12-pdr howitzers they housed. The magazine was on the lower level. The blockhouses were partially covered with earth and surrounded by a deep ditch. Their garrisons usually numbered sixty men.

Barnard also built military roads to facilitate communication and reinforcement. Work on this system of roads first began in 1861 and was finished in 1864.

In 1864, as Grant's troops engaged in more costly battles in the south, he took troops from the Washington defenses. General Jubal Early led a raid into Maryland and stood before the capital's defenses in July 1864. However, he found the Washington defenses too strong to attack even though many of the defenders belonged to the militia. General Early launched a brief, but unsuccessful attack on FORT STEVENS before retreating on July 12. Lincoln arrived at Fort Stevens during this action and became the only American president who ever came under enemy fire while in office. The Washington defenses successfully served as a shield that the Rebels simply could not break or dent after 1861.

In Defense of Richmond

McClellan's Peninsula campaign in 1862 motivated the South to build strong defenses for RICHMOND, where Robert E. Lee took command. The work was already underway in the summer of 1861 when a committee of the city council asked Lee for advice. In March of 1862, the acting chief engineer, Major Alfred L. Rives, reported to Secretary of War Judah Benjamin on the state of the Richmond defenses. His report concerned the positions along the James River, a route that had to be readied to stop Union vessels and troop landings. It included FORT BOYKIN, which stood on the bluff at Days Neck, with ten 42- and 32-pdrs and a hot-shot furnace. The fort was a seven-pointed earthen structure from the War of 1812. The Confederates refurbished it in 1862 and added a bombproof. FORT HUGER at Harden's Bluff had thirteen guns, including a rifled 10-inch Columbiad, four 9-inch Dahlgrens, two 8-inch Columbiads, and six 32-pdrs for hot shot. Fifteen casemates at the Mulberry Island Point Battery, known as FORT

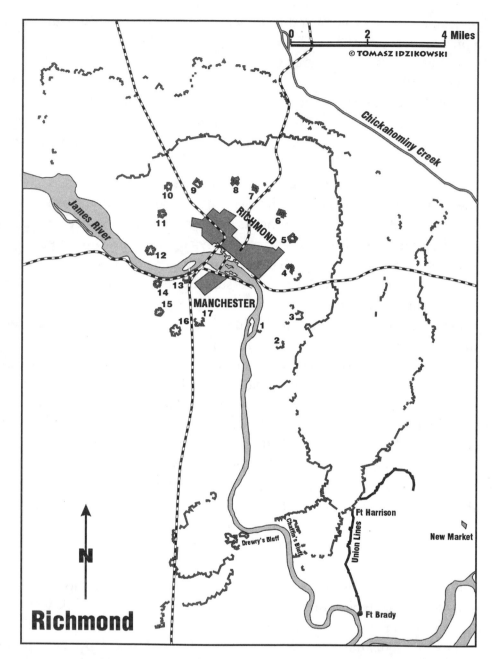

0   2   4 Miles

© TOMASZ IDZIKOWSKI

Richmond

CRAWFORD, begun in 1861, were about to be completed. The battery mounted five 32-pdrs. However, Fort Crawford was abandoned in May 1862. The Jamestown Island batteries had four 9-inch Dahlgrens, four 8-inch Columbiads, and five 32-pdrs for hot shot. The DREWRY'S BLUFF BATTERY was still under construction as well as the river obstacles it protected. This battery was one of the few key positions the Federals were never able to take. Of the projects mentioned in the report, only Fort Boykin was finished (it was the furthest down river), but the others were rapidly nearing completion as bombproofs were added. After a careful evaluation, FORT POWHATAN was reoccupied in March 1862.

According to General Leadbetter, the fortifications around Richmond were situated too close to the city, but since many were almost complete, Leadbetter ordered Rives to finish them. Nevertheless, some contemporary plans show that the inner line was moved further out the next year. Similar comments appear in a report to the Confederate Congress by Colonel Charles DImmock in February 1862. He too claimed that the seventeen existing batteries, and the two still to be built, which covered seven and a half miles, were too close to the city and could only be used as a last resort. Since they were near completion, he also recommended they be finished. These batteries were a half to three-quarters of a mile apart and mounted guns en barbette. Dommick recommended embrasures for the most important ones and pointed out that, although they required over 140 guns, only eleven guns were actually mounted and twelve were still lying on the ground. The four battery positions, and two not yet built, on the south side of the James River at Manchester had similar problems. Rives also complained about the paucity of guns for these positions and about the fact that the finished works remained unoccupied. Despite instructions to keep the magazines drained, Dommick noticed that many magazines were wet and some were even filled with a couple feet of water. To avoid water problems, Dommick suggested building the magazines above ground and adding bombproofs and breastworks. He also recommended pushing the defenses forward to the banks of the Chickahominy River. Later in 1862, as Lee assumed command of the army, he did some additional work.

One year later, in August 1863, Colonel T. S. Rhett, commander of the Richmond defenses, reported that the batteries of the inner line were not in optimal condition. Even though they were ready for combat, the wooden revetments had rotted and needed replacing. Colonel W. H. Stevens of the engineers suggested enclosing all the battery gorges with rifle pits, which required additional, mainly slave, labor. These batteries were known as No.1 through No.10; the largest were No.6 and No.7; Battery No.2 was the most prominent. A year later, in 1864, the Richmond defenses were readied and entrenchments were prepared in the face of Grant's advance. By then, batteries No.11 through No.17 had been added, several on the south side of the river, and the entrenchments were placed in advance of all these defenses. The Richmond defenses also included five forts with letter designations A through E, most of them star-shaped.

The defenses of Richmond consisted of three permanent lines, the inner line, the intermediate line, and the outer line. The outer line reached to the banks of the Chickahominy River in the north and the intermediate line was a short distance behind it. These two lines were up to ten miles from the city and spanned over sixty-five miles, covering the city north of the James River. The intermediate line was probably begun in the spring of 1862, after the inner line, which was probably started in 1861 and consisted of many earthen strongpoints like batteries and forts linked by trenches. South of Richmond, this line was anchored on the Randolph Farms, about three miles from the outskirts of Richmond, just west of the Osborne Turnpike. The outer line was similar, but not as complete and was anchored on the south by an entrenched camp at Chaffin's farm, about eight miles from the edge of Richmond, across from the defenses of Drewry's Bluff. A few forts with earthworks and trenches between them were situated in advance of this line. From 1861 to 1863, the government built an inner line within two to three miles of the city and included the first seventeen works located close to the city. The strongpoints consisted of a number of earthen forts and batteries. The Confederate field fortifications and earthen forts were similar to those built by the Federals since many Southern engineer, infantry, and artillery officers were graduates of West Point and had also learned their craft from D. H. Mahan.

According to Lieutenant Colonel P. S. Michie of the Union Army, who wrote in 1861, "General Wise erected some works at Chapin's Farm ... known as 'Wise's line of 1862.' Across the river was Drewry's Bluff and like Chapin's Farm both had large camps, and were entrenched in 1862." Michie wrote that "the lines of intrenchments were of a very simple character; in plan tenaille, in profile very slight {with} the strongest positions in the line at Chapin's Farm were Forts Harrison and Gilmer, the latter being a bastioned field work with a stockaded gorge." After 1862, the Rebels linked this fortified site to Richmond with a "line of earthworks and rifle-trenches, east of, and parallel to, the Osborn Turnpike," wrote Michie. Their purpose was to defend against an advance from the east.

FORT DARLING at Drewry's Bluff, a bastioned fieldwork with deep and wide ditches, sat on top of the bluff from which it dominated the James River. A line of entrenchments, including open batteries, redans, and lunette fieldworks tied together by rifle trenches surrounded Fort Darling. According to Michie, a system of fieldworks encircled Richmond and Petersburg, creating two entrenched camps. The Confederates did not extend the line beyond the south side of the James River linking these two entrenched camps until after General Butler's failed attack on Fort Darling in May 1864. The extension of the line had no enclosed works, but consisted of a series of epaulements for field artillery linked by rifle trenches. The protective ditch, which had no abatis or other obstacles, was not much of an obstacle being shallow and narrow. However, it was never attacked by Federal troops.

According to Michie, a third line "extended from ... Chapin's Farm, which it connected with at Fort Harrison, and crossed the country, at the average distance of about six miles from Richmond, to the bluffs overlooking the valley of the Chickahominy, the crests of which it followed till it came to Brook Run," from there it ran west to the James. This line was better developed than the one south of the James, its infantry parapets were thicker, its ditches deeper. It had up to three lines of abatis dotted with "torpedoes" and placed within musket range. According to Michie, the other sections near the Chickahominy remained in primitive conditions until the end of the war. Michie downgraded the importance of works like Fort Harrison because they were open at the rear. The Confederates used bombproof shelters and even excavated listening galleries to warn of mining operations. They also built dams on small watercourses to flood areas on this front.

In May 1864, General Butler assembled 39,000 men to strike at the Confederate defenses between Richmond and Petersburg. General Beauregard, in command at Petersburg, used George Pickett's troops to try to drive Butler back. Butler advanced on FORT CLIFTON, a new earthen structure built between 1863 and 1864 on an elevated site at the junction of Swift Creek and the Appomattox River. The fort had bombproofs and mounted about fourteen heavy and light guns. On May 9, it engaged Union gunboats, sinking one of them with its heavy artillery. The gunboats were supporting Butler's attack, which failed. Butler retreated, establishing a line of defenses in front of the Bermuda Hundred. Butler next attempted to strike at Fort Drewry (named Fort Darling by the Yankees) on Drewry's Bluff on May 11, 1864, but this also failed.

Meanwhile, Grant's forces advanced toward Richmond. On June 3, 1864, Grant tried to break Lee's army and its advanced position at Cold Harbor and breakthrough the outer line of defenses on the other side of the Chickahominy River. Since Lee had entrenched his troops in the area for several days, Grant had to dig trenches of his own before he began a major bombardment and launched an assault. When he launched the final charge, Grant was severely repulsed, suffering seven thousand casualties.

FORT POWHATAN, a major obstacle to Union control of the James River, had fallen to Union naval forces the year before on July 14, 1863. This 2nd System fort, which held twenty-two pieces of artillery in 1863, was put back into operation by the Federals. On May 21, 1864, a force of Rebel cavalry tried to recapture the fort but the defenders and two Union warships drove them off.

June of 1864 was a busy month for the Union engineers as Butler's Army of the James was ordered to move forward from the Bermuda Hundred to lay Petersburg siege and Grant sent Meade's army, fresh from its repulse at Cold Harbor, across the James River to join him. A major achievement was the construction of a 2,100-foot-long pontoon bridge across the James River south of Windmill Point during the evening of June 14, done while advance elements of Meade's Army of the Potomac were ferried across the river. General Lee's army had maintained positions covering both Richmond and Petersburg while the numerically superior Union forces maneuvered and effectively began the siege of the fortified complex.

A 90-foot signal tower was built above the Appomattox River at Cobb's Hill. When it was completed on June 14, it was 125 feet high, and from it an observer could see Petersburg, Fort Clifton, Port Walthall Junction, and other Confederate-held positions. On June 15, the Federal engineers sank four schooners in the James River about eight hundred yards above Aiken's Landing, and linked them with chains to keep the Confederate gunboats confined. General G. Weitzel, chief engineer for the department, ordered Michie to build redoubts and a corduroy road through the marsh. The needed timbers were cut in the heavily wooded area, but shortage of labor delayed the work.

In addition to the road, the engineers had to place more pontoon bridges across the James. Despite the fact that Weitzel was heavily involved in the siege of Petersburg, the job was largely accomplished by July.

With Grant's main forces south of the James, the siege of PETERSBURG began. An inner and outer line of entrenchments and forts formed a semicircle around the city, resting on the Appomattox River on the right flank. Since the work on these defenses, begun in 1862, had been carried out under engineer Colonel Charles Dimmock, this line of defenses is sometimes referred to as the Dimmock Line. It consisted of battery positions numbered from one to fifty-five. As the siege began, coal miners from a Pennsylvania regiment excavated a tunnel over 500 feet in length that ended beneath a position in the Confederate outer line. They filled it with 8,000 pounds of gunpowder (in 320 kegs) and detonated it on July 30, 1864, creating a huge crater. The Union troops advanced into the crater where 280 Rebels lay hurt or dying from the explosion—but they stayed in the crater too long, allowing the Confederates to reorganize and counterattack. The Union troops took heavy losses in this battle of the Crater and finally the Rebels drove them back.

Early in the siege, Grant's troops built their own line of entrenchments and forts to keep the enemy trapped. Lieutenant Peter S. Michie, acting chief engineer for the Department of Virginia and North Carolina, reported in early October 1864 that the army had made much progress on its entrenchments. The Union troops had the luxury

Above: Entrance to the mine dug beneath the Confederate lines at Petersburg which led to the battle of the Crater.

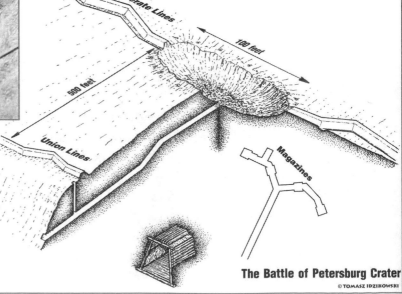

The Battle of Petersburg Crater

©TOMASZ IDZIKOWSKI

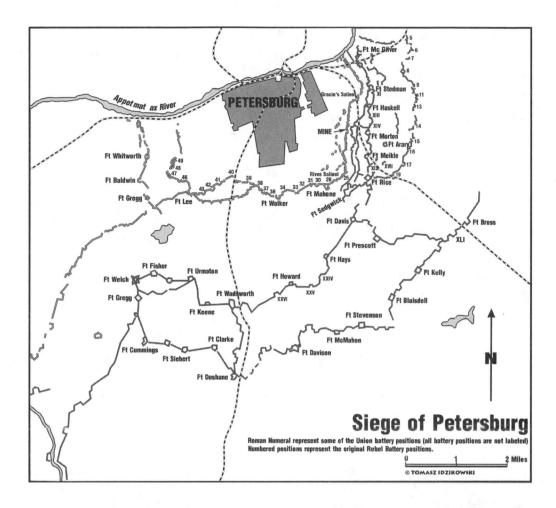

Siege of Petersburg

Roman Numeral represent some of the Union battery positions (all battery positions are not labeled)
Numbered positions represent the original Rebel Battery positions.

0   1   2 Miles

© TOMASZ IDZIKOWSKI

of using rails for the revetments of their trenches. Michie reported that a number of large bombproofs and battery positions were completed or nearing completion. Three faces of the redoubt on Signal Hill were finished, seven embrasures cut, and four guns already mounted. Other redoubts were under construction.

Late in September 1864, Grant tried once again to break the Confederate line at RICHMOND with General Butler's army while Meade's army remained in front of Petersburg. On September 28, his men took FORT HARRISON, an earthen fort held by two hundred men with artillery and one of the strongest points on the line, after hand-to-hand fighting. The Union troops also attacked FORT GILMER to the north, but failed to take it, suffering heavy losses. The Federals strengthened Fort Harrison and extended their lines toward FORT BRADY on Chaffin's Bluff. The Confederates had to give up over 1,200 yards of entrenchments that led to Fort Harrison because the fort's guns looked right down the length of them. On September 30, Lee launched a major assault to retake Fort Harrison but was repelled. The loss of this key fort forced the Rebels to move their artillery from the outer to the intermediate line and FORT JOHNSON became the anchor of their new line. The Confederates also created new entrenchments to link the line to FORT

HOKE after the loss of Fort Harrison. In mid-October, work began on extending the new outer line northward across the Darby Road and Charles City roads, a distance of about four miles, strengthening the outer line which held until April 1865.

As the situation deteriorated during the winter of 1864–1865, Lee had to prepare to evacuate his positions at Richmond and Petersburg or undertake a decisive action to break the Union siege. He decided to move on the Petersburg front to break the Union Line. General John Gordon's troops launched the surprise attack on the Union FORT STEDMAN and on the adjacent sections of trench line and battery positions garrisoned by eight companies of heavy artillery. FORT HASKELL stood to the south of Fort Stedman on lower ground and exposed to the enemy's artillery but fronted by wooded and marshy terrain. and FORT MORTON was beyond that. A bastioned work, Fort Morton stood on an elevated site. On Fort Stedman's right, to the north, FORT

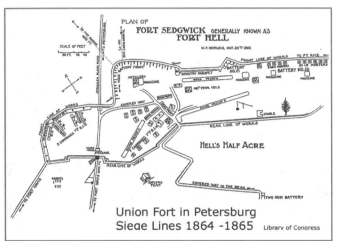

Union Fort in Petersburg
Siege Lines 1864 -1865   Library of Congress

Fort Sedgwick, a Union seige fort outside of Petersburg known as "Fort Hell." The walls are supported by gabions and given added height with sandbags. National Archives

McGilvery stood beyond the range of the Confederate heavy artillery. Lee hoped that the fall of Fort Stedman would throw Grant off balance since it was on a direct route to his supply base. The Confederate attack began before dawn on March 25, but was repelled along the line of entrenchments on the left flank of the fort. It was followed by a second assault by a larger force. The attack, which involved over ten thousand men according to Union estimates, was contained. The Union forces counterattacked, driving the Rebels from the trenches and Fort Stedman.

The siege of Petersburg and Richmond was coming to an end as the Confederates forces suffered significant losses due to desertion, hunger, and disease. At the same time, Grant's army increased, Sheridan's Union troops operated in the rear of Lee's position, and Sherman advanced north through the Carolinas. Lee was forced to withdraw and the defenders of Petersburg were pushed back to the inner line resting on the Appomattox River. Two small earthen forts, FORT GREGG and FORT WHITWORTH, were to check a Union advance on the west side of this line. The garrisons of the two forts, estimated at 200 and 60 respectively, were ordered to hold out for several hours to protect Lee's retreat. The garrison of Fort Gregg accomplished its mission as it repelled several attacks until it was overrun after ferocious hand-to-hand fighting.

On April 3, 1865, Union forces from FORT SEDGWICK (Fort Sedgwick had earned the nickname of "Fort Hell" because it was the closest Union position to the Petersburg lines and suffered from constant bombardment for months) moved on FORT MAHONE, the Rebel fort opposite them, nicknamed "Fort Damnation." The Union troops overran the abandoned Rebel lines ending the sieges and taking Petersburg and Richmond.

Four Fortresses and the Keys to Victory

In the final analysis, during the American Civil War four fortresses determined the outcome of the conflict: Washington D.C., the Richmond-Petersburg complex, Vicksburg, a fortress town as well, and Fort Monroe, the only one of these fortresses that centered around a 3rd System masonry fort.

It is a fact that FORTRESS MONROE was more than a thorn in the side of the Confederacy. It provided a base from which Union forces could strike at Richmond and from which the navy launched expeditions to recapture a number of positions on the southern coast. It also prevented the Rebels from taking maximum advantage of the naval yard at Norfolk. If Fortress Monroe had fallen, the Confederate forces could have threatened or even blocked traffic on the Chesapeake.

Pemberton's decision to defend VICKSBURG is a controversial event as it cost him his army and caused the collapse of most of the western theater. If he had abandoned his fortified position and joined Joseph Johnston's army, Grant might well have been defeated. By holding Vicksburg, Pemberton put Grant in an exposed position and with a tenuous line of communications. On the other hand, if Johnston had been able to move against Grant in time, he would have been able to relieve Vicksburg, which would have been a major setback for the Union. Thus, the choice was either to give up the Mississippi and put the large garrison to better use or to try to hold the fortress and hope to inflict a defeat upon the besiegers, tilting the entire situation in the Western theater in favor of the Confederacy.

Although many critics of the 3rd System seem to think that the loss of major cities was not as important in the United States as it was in Europe, they are mistaken. The loss of WASHINGTON D.C. would have been a terrible psychological, political, diplomatic, and military defeat for the Union because by this time in American history the capital held more significance than Philadelphia had during the Revolution. Fortunately for the Union, the Army of Northern Virginia never achieved the strength to strike at the capital's ring of earthen forts.

The loss of RICHMOND would have had a similar effect on the Confederacy and also resulted in the loss of one of the South's few industrial areas. In addition, establishing an effective defensive line further south would have been more difficult. Thus, the line of earthen forts and entrenchments that extended from around Richmond to Petersburg was critical. Its loss meant the loss of the war.

The Civil War showed that the brick-and-stone fortifications of the 3rd System were not able to defend themselves in most situations from land and naval attacks and that earthen forts withstood the new rifled artillery far better. But the attack on Fort Fisher showed that, given the right circumstances, even the strongest earthen forts could be neutralized almost as quickly as the 3rd System forts. However, the 3rd System forts originally had been intended to resist for only thirty to fifty days, until reinforcements arrived. Thus, Fort Pickens was able to fulfill its mission successfully because it was relieved in time by the Union forces. Fort Sumter, on the other hand, fell into Confederate hands because the reinforcements came too late to save it. However, Fort Sumter lasted much longer than fifty days for the Confederates. Even Fort Macon lasted over thirty days. However, in the case of most Confederate-held forts, there was no relief force to come to the rescue.

Despite claims to the contrary, fortress warfare was as important in the United States as it was in Europe at the time. Indeed, some of the most important battles of the Civil War were fought around permanent or field fortifications. The American Civil War, with its new developments in artillery, ushered in a new era of fortress warfare and profoundly influenced military architecture, changing the character of fortifications not only in the United States, but in Europe as well.

Mines and Torpedoes of the Civil War

The Confederates developed mines and obstacles primarily to defend their waterways and harbors. Union forces also used them, but to a more limited extent. The obstacles of the Civil War period were similar to those of the American Revolution and included a variety of devices. Sunken hulks filled with rubble and linked by chains blocked water channels. Piles could include rock-filled cribs and vertical or angled timbers to block shallow areas. The torpedoes (sea mines) were employed in deeper channels where piles were not effective.

Land mines consisted of artillery shells with a friction primer (when someone stepped on it, the resulting pressure caused it to detonate). The Confederates used them at Yorktown, at Spanish Fort near Mobile, and on some of the roads leading to Richmond in 1864.

In 1862, Gabriel Rains improved the fuses of contact mines. He replaced the simple friction fuse with one using sulphuric acid in a glass tube. When the tube broke, it started a chemical reaction that ignited the fuse.

Hunter Davidson developed the electrically controlled mines used in the James River in 1863 and 1864. Fort Fisher had a minefield that relied on the same method to detonate the mines. During the war, twenty-seven ships, including three monitors, were either sunk or damaged by these torpedoes (mines). And a blockading Union ship at Charleston was sunk with a spar torpedo delivered by the submarine *Hunley*.

Not to be outdone, the Union resorted to these unconventional weapons as well. Thus, Lieutenant William Cushing sank the Confederate ironclad *Albermarle* with a spar torpedo. The Federals also developed methods to protect their ships from torpedoes, which included extending rigs of various types from the ships and even sweeping for mines with fishnets.

The keg torpedo was a sea mine consisting of a powder-filled barrel covered with tar with wooden cones on each end. It was detonated by a primer attached to the keg. These sea mines were commonly used in many Confederate harbors and waterways. The crews that deployed them in small craft called yawls had to anchor the mines to the seabed to keep them from floating away and to prevent them from riding high in the water where they could be detected.

The Rebels also buried keg torpedoes in the ground, turning them into land mines, especially at Fort Wagner in 1863. At Fort Esperanza, Texas, the Confederates buried the sea mines not used to block the channel around the fort. Supposedly, hundreds of mines were planted around Fort Gilmer and Fort Harrison in the defenses of Richmond.

In March 1865, a report to the U.S. secretary of the navy on Charleston revealed some facts about the minefields gleaned from the Rebels. The Confederates kept forty to fifty mines on hand to deploy as needed. Francis Wood, who had assembled the torpedoes for almost a year, explained that "they were constructed from lager beer barrels, tarred inside and outside with build pitch, tar, and resin." The barrel was then filled with sixty or sixty-five pounds of coarse cannon powder and attached to "sensitive fuze [*sic*] plugs." Finally, a cone was attached to each end of the barrel. In addition, Wood stated, to lay down torpedoes "dark nights were always selected, using a yawl-boat for the purpose, carrying three or four torpedoes, taking from half an hour to an hour to put down the four." Between Fort Sumter and Fort Moultrie, sixteen mines of the keg type were deployed outside the rope obstructions.

To prevent accidents, the Confederates developed a system of marking their minefields on land and sea. When attacks were expected, the markers were removed. The naval minefields formed an integral part of the defenses, but needed artillery batteries coverage to prevent the enemy from removing them. At the time, no distinction was made between a torpedo and a mine. With time, the term mine became associated with torpedoes that were not self-propelled.

In addition to mines or torpedoes, the Confederates employed small vessels known as "Davids" and rams to defend ports and harbors. Occasionally, when available, ironclads were also used. The rams, primarily designed to defend the harbors, had no other use. The "David" was a small, fast, steampowered vessel for a two-man crew that carried a spar torpedo. The 10-foot vessel rode only a few inches above the water, but was easily swamped by waves or the wake of a passing ship. The "David's" success was limited to one incident when one of its kind slightly damaged the ironclad *New Ironsides* at Charleston in mid-1863.

Confederate Torpedos (Mines)
© TOMASZ IDZIKOWSKI

A. A mine made of a tin casing less than 2' in length. The were to detonate it came out the bottom and was attached to a float or even a position on shore.

B. River mine held by anchors. About 5 1/2' long and had prongs pointing to surface which triggered its detonation when struck by a ship.

C. A type of bouyant mine held beneath the surface by an anchor. It was linked by wire to a shore position and detonated electrically by a spotter.

D. The keg mine was one of the most common mines in use. Thse are characterized by the cone shaped ends attached to the keg. A precussion or chemical fuse was at the top which detonated the mine whcih held from 50 or more pounds of powder.

E. Unusual mine which was only about 1 1/2' in length which was used to drift in channels and once stopped the propeller began to move triggering the detonation of the mine.

F. Brooke torpedo. It consisted of a copper csing and it was attached to an anchor.

G. Singer's Mine. A ship stricking the cap and forcing it off the mine triggered the detonation of the mine.

Chapter 7

POST-CIVIL WAR ERA
AND TRANSITION

THE END OF THE AMERICAN CIVIL WAR presented new challenges for the U.S. Army Corps of Engineers and the U.S. Army. Since the 3rd System had yielded mixed results as far as its ability to defend American shores was concerned, the coastal defenses had to be re-evaluated, particularly in light of the new developments in artillery. At the same time, the U.S. government faced enormous social, economic, and political problems with the reconstruction of the South and the westward expansion. Lines of communication to the West Coast had to be opened and new problems with Native American tribal groups on the frontier had to be dealt with.

Winning the West

The Civil War was followed by a period called the Reconstruction, during which the Federal government struggled to return the Southern states to the fold. Although military garrisons stationed in the South imposed martial law in many cases, they did not require forts for defensive purposes. Many Southerners, discontented with the situation after the Civil War, decided to emigrate west. Many Northerners, whose lives had been disrupted by the war, also moved west, encouraged by the Homestead Act of 1862 that offered them free acreage in exchange for developing the new territories. As a result, many settlers took up farming on the Great Plains, soon encroaching on Indian territory and hunting grounds. The pioneers headed for the West Coast also passed through Indian territory. In addition, miners searching for gold and other valuable minerals also began encroaching on Indian lands. At the same time, the government pursued its prewar plans to build a transcontinental railroad, completing the project in 1869, and creating an even greater problem for the Indians as people often stopped and settled along its route. Soon other railroads followed the first transcontinental railroad. The numbers of white settlers increased, and the Native Americans, whose very livelihoods were threatened, became increasingly hostile. The population movement into the Great Plains and Rocky Mountain region finally sparked off a new series of Indian wars.

Before the Civil War, white settlers such as Kit Carson had suppressed the Navajo in the New Mexico Territory, but the Apaches remained a problem in the Southwest. During the Civil War, most of the posts in the West were garrisoned with U.S. Army volunteer regiments. Later in the war, "Galvanized Yankees" (Rebels who changed allegiance to avoid staying in prison camps) appeared on the frontier. Then regular army troops replaced the volunteer units after the war.

The telegraph line that ran from Omaha to Sacramento also required army protection. Known as the Telegraph and Overland Emigration Route, it extended along the emigrant routes, mainly the Oregon Trail. Begun in 1860, the line was not completed until October 1861, after the war had started. It required frequent repairs since the Indians hacked down its poles and weather and other natural disasters damaged the lines.

FORT CASPAR, known as the Platte Bridge Station, one of the forts assigned to keep the telegraph line in operation, was reoccupied in May 1862 after having been abandoned years earlier. It consisted of several buildings, including a telegraph office, storerooms, barracks, a horse corral, and a stockade located a short distance from the privately owned Platte River Bridge. On July 26, 1865, a small detachment from the fort led by Lieutenant William O. Collins was ambushed and only a handful of his men made it back to the safety of the fort. The incident signaled the beginning of serious unrest in the region. The opening of the Bozeman Trail exacerbated the situation.

After the Civil War, hostilities with the Apache grew, and then the Sioux and Cheyenne, disappointed by the empty promises of the American government, went on the warpath as well. These mushrooming problems required an increased presence of the U.S. Army on the frontier. An increased number of forts was needed to protect emigrants, settlers, and miners from the Indians. The new forts were built along transportation routes and near major settlement areas. Little concern was shown at this point for the protection of the borders with Mexico and Canada.

One source of friction between Canada and the United States during the 1860s and 1870s were the "whiskey forts" established by American traders. When they were forbidden to sell whiskey to the Indians in their own country, these traders moved north from Fort Benton, creating several trading posts along the "Whoop-Up Trail" in Southern Alberta and Saskatchewan. There they sold whiskey to the Indians to cheat them out of their trade goods, causing many problems in the process. As a result, the North West Mounted Police (the Mounties) was formed in 1873 to drive the Americans out of places like Fort Whoop-Up. Cities eventually emerged around the wooden stockaded forts of the Mounted Police in Canada's Prairie Provinces.

Most of the important western forts had been largely built before the Civil War (see

Fort Caspar, Wyoming. One of the western forts built to protect the main line of communications to the Pacific.

Chapter 5). Additional forts appeared after the Civil War to extend control, but their layouts hardly changed at all. Most forts on the Great Plains consisted of a cluster of buildings around a parade without walls since there were no forestsfrom which to draw lumber. Since wood for the buildings had to come from distant sources, it was used sparingly and sod became the alternative building material. On the northern plains, where the tribes were larger and more hostile, many forts required stockades with blockhouses. In Texas and the Southwest, most forts were also a collection of buildings around a parade. In west Texas, many buildings were of limestone, but in many cases, as in the Southwest, adobe prevailed. The thick adobe walls of some forts also helped insulate against the summer heat.

Even though many battles and skirmishes took place between the Indians and the U.S. Army, few involved an actual assault on a fort. The forts, which mainly served as bases of operations, were usually avoided by the Indians who did not consider them easy targets, even when they lacked a surrounding stockade. Nonetheless, there were several actions that took place during and after the Civil War that directly involving some of the western frontier forts.

In the southwest in 1860, as hostilities increased, the Navajo actually tried to drive the army from FORT DEFIANCE, Arizona. The fort, which consisted of a cluster of buildings around a parade, some made of pinewood and some of adobe or stone, was situated at the entrance of Canyon Bonito, a lush oasis in the arid region, greatly prized by the Indians. It was built in the 1850s to control the Navajo. In January 1860, the Navajo tried to isolate it. In April, a thousand warriors attacked the three companies of the 3rd Infantry stationed at the fort. They reached the outer buildings in a pre-dawn assault but the soldiers drove them out. The fort was abandoned a year later at the outbreak of the Civil War when the garrison was recalled to Fort Lyon.

Life in the Frontier Forts

Most of the soldiers living on the frontier between the Mississippi River and West Coast states suffered hardships. Life in the forts in southern Texas and the Southwest was not too uncomfortable, except in summer. Those troops stationed further north, from Kansas to the Dakotas and Colorado to Montana had to put up with harsh winters, which brought freezing temperatures and, in some cases, isolated their posts. In the summer, on the other hand, temperatures often soared to 100 degrees Fahrenheit or higher. The climatic conditions caused various types of respiratory ailments, including bronchitis. Intestinal problems and rheumatism were high on the list of ailments and diarrhea, for obvious reasons, was a common problem. Isolation often increased problems with alcohol. In forts located near settlements, the rate of sexually transmitted diseases increased, but strangely, the rate of mortality was low.

Soldiers and officers maintained vegetable gardens, but in the northern posts it was more difficult to have an adequate supply of vegetables in the winter when scurvy reared its ugly head. To supplement the diet of their men, fort commanders would send out hunting parties who might travel as far as one hundred miles. Occasional shipments of luxuries such as lemons, sardines, and berries arrived from time to time. During the winter, the soldiers relied heavily on canned or salted products such as pork and fish.

The living quarters in many forts were less than satisfactory. The soldiers often slept in poorly built barracks with dirt floors. In most cases, forts garrisoned for long periods had permanent barracks. Sanitary facilities in many forts were lacking. In some frontier posts, where proper facilities were not established, the men washed in pits filled with water and relieved themselves against the walls of the fort.

The army provided the troops with standard uniforms that were not suited for extreme summer and winter temperatures, but few changes occurred until the area ceased to be a frontier. Laundresses were an important part of the frontier forts. Usually they were the wives of enlisted men. Civilians at the forts performed other functions including operating the sutler's store. They were usually contracted to deliver wood, coal, and animal feed. In some cases, they also maintained the livestock.

Source: *The Army Post on the Northern Plains 1865-1885* by Ray Mattison.

In 1861, a 25-year conflict began with the Apaches. The army had to abandon many of the southwestern forts in 1861 because of the Civil War. In 1862, General Carleton sent Kit Carson and his New Mexico volunteers to reoccupy Fort Stanton. In the fall of 1863, they also reoccupied Fort Defiance in the campaign against the Navajo. In January 1864, Carson was sent to remove the Navajo from their stronghold at CANYON DE CHELLY, a steep-walled canyon in which the ruins of the Anasazi civilization still formed a redoubtable fortress with limited access. Carson succeeded in removing the starving Navajo from their stronghold and escorted them back to a reservation. After this, Fort Defiance was abandoned for the final time.

In the Dakotas and Minnesota, the Sioux became a problem during the Civil War when the government failed to live up to its obligations. In August 1862, as the commander of Fort Ridgely went to investigate the problems on the reservation, the Sioux struck at the nearby German settlement of New Ulm and at the fort, held at the time by only thirty men. FORT RIDGELY was an old fort, built in 1853, that consisted of a cluster of buildings huddled around a parade. The fort received some reinforcements, bringing the number of defenders to 180 soldiers when, on August 20, over four hundred Sioux attacked. They reached the northern perimeter, which consisted of a row of loghouses. The soldiers rallied on the parade ground and as they began to waiver, six old howitzers blasted canister rounds into the attackers driving them back. On August 22, eight hundred Siouox warriors returned to the attack. This time, the defenders were ready. The Indians assaulted all sides and breached the southwest corner where they set fire to anything that would burn, but once again, the artillery drove them off. The total losses in both attacks numbered five soldiers and one hundred Indians killed.

Undaunted, the Sioux continued their campaign. On September 3, 1862, they attack FORT ABERCROMBIE, on the west bank of the Red River just north of Fargo. Established in 1858, it was the first fort in North Dakota and was located along the west bank of the river, which was subject to flooding. In 1860 it was moved to a higher position on the riverbank. At the time of the siege, it had no defenses. The volunteers from Minnesota (the regulars had been sent east) held off the Sioux for six hours with their few artillery pieces. Later they added a stockade and a blockhouse to the fort.

The army established several more forts in the Dakotas after the Civil War. FORT RICE, built in 1864 on the Missouri River in North Dakota, became a key control point for a number of years. The square trace was largely formed by the fort's buildings with wooden walls filling the gaps between them. In addition, the fort had two corner blockhouses. FORT ABRAHAM LINCOLN, a stockaded fort built on the west bank of the Missouri River in 1873, was relocated a few months later near the site of Bismarck to provide protection for workers on the Northern Pacific Railroad. This large fort accommodated nine companies of cavalry and infantry. On the bluffs 270 feet above stood FORT MCKEEN, built before Fort Abraham Lincoln. It consisted of three blockhouses with a stockade protecting its two western sides while the bluff dropped off at its open sides. It eventually became part of the Fort Abraham Lincoln complex.

In 1866 after the end of the Civil War, General Sherman met with Indian leaders at Fort Laramie in an attempt to negotiate for rights to open the Bozeman Trail and protect it with a series of forts in the Powder River country (Wyoming). Two mountain men had blazed the trail in 1863 to link the Oregon Trail to the gold mining region in Montana. Even though the negotiations with the Indians failed, Sherman sent Colonel Henry B. Carrington with seven hundred men of the 18th Infantry to establish a line of forts. Carrington proceeded to Fort Reno (Fort Connor) in July 1866.

An expeditionary force of 745 soldiers and civilians led by General P. E. Connor had departed Fort Laramie in July 1865, and established FORT CONNOR in August. Initially General Connor built a small square stockade of cottonwood 120 feet on each side, which only enclosed two storehouses. The fort was renamed FORT RENO in November. Colonel Carrington was ordered to relieve the 5th Volunteers stationed there and to abandon the fort. Because he had more supplies than was practical to move on with, he left the excess at Fort Reno, ordering Captain Joseph Proctor's company to garrison the fort. Proctor's men built a stockade around the post's wooden buildings adding corner bastions. In June 1867, Major James van Voast took command, continued improving the defenses and the buildings, and even expanded the stockade. He replaced Proctor's bastions with three hexagonal blockhouses built in wedding-cake style and added a square bastion. The fort mounted six artillery pieces, including a 12-pdr howitzer (all but one were mountain howitzers) when Carrington arrived, but he had taken four of those weapons with him.

While Proctor worked on the stockade of Fort Reno in 1866, Carrington sent Captain Nathaniel Kinney to establish FORT C. F. SMITH in Montana on a bluff overlooking the Big Horn River. This square fort had 300 feet long walls and corner blockhouses.

Carrington concentrated his efforts on the construction of FORT PHIL KEARNY, at an ideal site, according to him, on the trail at Piney Creek at the foot of the Big Horn Mountain on a plateau with a slope that created a natural glacis. The fort was only a few miles from all the timber, coal, and hay that he needed. Although not a West Pointer, Carrington had solid ideas about fort construction. The fort's walls and buildings were built using a method very similar to the Red River style. The walls of the timber stockade rose 8 feet above the ground and there was a wall walk, only about 3 feet above the ground, for the defense of the walls. The trace formed a rectangle 790 feet by 580 feet and included two corner bastions. A stockaded area forming a trapezoid attached to the south wall of the fort was known as the Quartermaster Corral. It included the teamster's quarters, offices for the wagon master and quartermaster, a mess hall, warehouses, a blacksmith shop, stables, and a storage area for hay. This stockaded area had two entrances from the outside and a blockhouse in the southwest corner. The stockade included a large parade, occupying the northern two-thirds of the fort, and surrounded by barracks (infantry barracks near the walls and cavalry barracks on the south side), warehouses, the bakery, sutler store, post headquarters, guardhouse, commander's quarters, surgeon's quarters, and the officers's quarters. The magazine was on the southwest section of the parade. Cavalry stables, laundry quarters, a quartermaster store, and a saddle shop occupied the other third of the fort on the south side of the cavalry barracks. Over four thousand logs were cut for the stockade and 130,000 bricks were produced for the buildings. The fort was completed by October, but the troops that came to reinforce the garrison were barely trained. Carrington installed the four 12-pdr howitzers he had brought from Fort Reno, including one field howitzer.

Large reconstructed corner bastion for artillery at Fort Phil Kearny on the Bozeman Trail in Wyoming.

The Sioux and Arapahos virtually isolated the three forts—Fort Reno, Fort C. F. Smith, and Fort Phil Kearny—but did not attack them directly. In December 1866, a relief column led by Captain William Fetterman was wiped out. The incident came to be known as the "Fetterman Massacre." Carrington's situation deteriorated, worsened by the winter snows. A volunteer, John "Portugee" Phillips, rode 265 miles through a blizzard in four days with warriors in hot pursuit to get help from Fort Laramie. A relief column was dispatched, but the Indians maintained the pressure throughout 1867. In August 1867, the Indians attacked a wood gathering party, but the woodcutters and their military escort turned the wagons into a makeshift fort and held off the assault at the "Wagon Box Fight." Due to Indian hostility and the fact that the Union Pacific Railroad was providing an alternate route, the government abandoned the Bozeman Trail in the spring of 1868 and destroyed the three forts. Thus, just this once, the Indians succeeded in pushing soldiers and forts out of their lands.

FORT STEEL, built in southwestern Wyoming in the summer of 1868, replaced the three forts on the Bozeman Trail. Its main mission was to protect the workers of the Union Pacific Railroad (the Transcontinental Railroad project). The fort stood across the tracks from the railroad town that later grew in the area and occupied a bend in the North Platte River. An open post, it had no defenses and included about a dozen buildings. In 1881, its commander built a masonry magazine a good distance from the fort on the other side of the tracks. Although it was recommended to place the magazine away from the other buildings of the fort in case of explosion, it was not a practical arrangement for a fort that was built to serve as a defensive position. Fort Steel was abandoned in the 1880s.

The 1880s witnessed the last actions of the Indian wars in the west, and soon the forts lost their defensive value and their role and would serve mainly as training camps. Of the numerous forts that remained in the western states, most had no stockades and few even had a defensive blockhouse. FORT RILEY, built in Kansas in 1852, known as Camp Center, had the distinction of being near the geographical center of the United States. It had no unusual features, occupied an area about 553 feet by 606 feet, and included six company-sized barracks (88 feet by 40 feet) of hammered magnesian limestone. The barracks, like many others found in western forts, had two levels. The first floor was subdivided into a kitchen, dining room, and orderly room. The upper floor housed a dormitory with a fireplace at each end. By the 1870s, stoves replaced the fireplaces. The latrines were 100 to 300 feet away from the barracks, depending on the fort. Fort Riley, an open fort like Fort Leavenworth, was retained by the army because of its location and large size. By the 1880s, many frontier forts disappeared from the landscape. But by the end of the century, the need for defensive fortifications resurfaced as a result of new territorial acquisitions.

Canadian Defense Against the United States

While the American Civil War raged on, the British and Canadians became concerned about the U.S. reaction to their neutrality, which stemmed from their need for Southern cotton. The British sent additional troops to Canada, fearing an American invasion. Their primary concern was for QUEBEC, whose lifeline could be cut off if American troops reached the shores of the St. Lawrence. Quebec's ramparts and Martello Tower were inadequate for its protection. A commission headed by Colonel John W. Gordon of the Royal Engineers arrived in 1862 to study the problem. It recommended the construction of a line of detached forts on the heights of Point Lévy, opposite Quebec. William D. Jervois, assistent inspector general of fortifications, drew up a more economical plan in 1863. He concluded that the British army should abandon Canada west of Montreal in time of war and proposed fortifications south of Montreal, at Sorel and Point Lévy. Eventually, the Canadian colonial government and parliament agreed to build four forts at POINT LÉVY. In 1864, when arrangements were still underway, it was decided that only three forts would be built. FORT NO.1 was built by the army, and FORT NO.2 and FORT NO.3 by civilian contractors. The first was pentagonal and the last two were rectangular. Their style did not differ much from European designs, which included troop casemates beneath the terreplein, a surrounding ditch, a masonry scarp with a massive earthen rampart covering the cement, and brick casemates. The gorge wall and counterscarps were made of masonry. The forts included impressive bricklined vaults and underground passages to the caponiers. The bridges over the moats retracted into the fort over the rails on which they were mounted. The work was begun in 1865 and was not completed until 1872, due to delays and disputes with contractors. The guns were to be mounted en barbette, but only one was ever mounted because the position had become obsolete after it was completed.

The British shifted their main line of defense to HALIFAX and coastal fortifications, which gained importance on the Canadian Atlantic and Pacific coasts alike. The third, largely wooden, citadel at Halifax had fallen into ruin after the War of 1812, and after an investigation in 1825, a new masonry citadel with two demi-bastions, two salients, a redan that was part of the enceinte, and three ravelins were built. The construction lasted from 1828 to 1856. Colonel Gustavus Nicolls of the Royal Engineers designed the CITADEL's numerous casemates for troops and artillery. He also added a musketry gallery that surrounded the fort. When completed, the Citadel was able to accommodate over a thousand soldiers. In 1856, it mounted twenty 24-pdrs in casemates that protected the moat and another forty-five 32-pdrs on the ramparts. The Citadel overlooked the Northwest and Point Pleasant batteries at the end of the peninsula, and behind them FORT OGILVIE. The Grand Battery on the east side of the peninsula faced Fort CHARLOTTE on an island and FORT CLEARENCE on the mainland, which closed the channel. With the addition of Fort Ives and several other forts and batteries by the end of the century, the entire harbor area was well covered. In 1861, there were only ten defensive positions mounting 167 weapons, including 68-pdr, 8-inch, and 32-pdr guns. By 1880, the armament included 7-inch, 9-inch, and 10-inch rifled guns, giving more effective protection than the guns at any American port of the time.

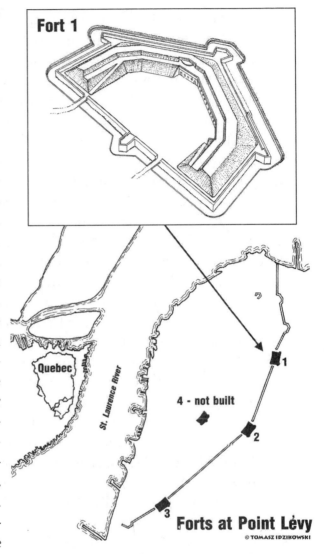

In the 1870s, the British established fixed coastal batteries on Canada's west coast where they faced only two potential adversaries: the United States and Russia. These batteries of rifled muzzleloaders, located at Esquimalt, protected the naval base at Esquimalt Harbor and Victoria Harbor. Meanwhile, the coast defenses of the United States lagged behind.

The Question of Fortifications and Coast Defense

The end of the Civil War presented the Corps of Engineers with the immense problem of determining the type of fortifications needed to defend the nation. Despite the realization that the masonry forts had seen their day, the U.S. government continued improving the existing structures, while the Corps of Engineers looked for alternatives.

FORT MCHENRY is an interesting case. This 2nd System fort was already obsolete because it was too close to Baltimore and was actually being replaced by the 3rd System Fort Carroll when the Civil War began. After the war, some improvements were made on Fort McHenry's outer works where new artillery pieces were placed. It is not clear why the War Department believed that Fort McHenry could be of use in 1870 when it had been considered obsolete at the beginning of the Civil War.

In addition to the renovation of existing forts, at a number of harbors some earthen positions were added and larger pieces of artillery were installed. Congress was reluctant to make any major investments in fortifications when new developments in artillery rendered them obsolete as soon as they were built, or even before they were finished. Congress's skepticism remained firm, despite attempts by the Corps of Engineers to find viable solutions. For the next twenty years, the army engineers worked on efficacious designs for the coastal fortifications and endorsed the use of mines as a vital element in coastal defense.

The defenses on the Northern Frontier were largely ignored, with the exception of some repairs to Fort Wayne near Detroit in 1870. Fort Porter, near Buffalo, was renovated at the behest of the city council. Fort Niagara and Fort Ontario received some repairs at the same time, while Fort Montgomery at Rouses Point continued to decay. On the East Coast, Fort Knox, Fort Popham, and Fort Georges either needed repairs or had to be completed. Some of this work was done until the funds ran out in 1876. Besides the renovation of the East Coast forts, the main project in the 1870s was the construction of the earthen batteries. In most cases, the money allotted by Congress ran out between 1873 and 1876 so that almost all the positions remained incomplete by the end of the decade. Such was the case of the new earthen batteries at Fort Preble, Fort Scammel, Portland Head, Gerrish's Island, Jerry's Point, Long Island Head (Boston Harbor), Fort Hamilton (New York), Staten Island, Fort Mifflin at Finn's Point (New Jersey side of the Delaware River), Fort McHenry, Fort Foote (on the Potomac), Fort Taylor (Key West), Fort Jackson, Fort St. Philip, the entrance to San Diego, Fort Point, and both sides of the Golden Gate Bridge in San Francisco. Fort Tompkins was ready to receive heavy artillery and equipment for a torpedo station by 1876, but remained unarmed in 1880. On Staten Island, the Glacis Gun Battery and Glacis Mortar Battery were completed by 1872 and 1873 but remained unarmed throughout the decade. The reconstruction of Fort Sumter began in 1870 and continued throughout the decade. In 1870, modifications were made at old Fort Jackson, outside of Savannah, to accommodate heavy guns, but the funds ran out in 1873. At Fort Pulaski the demi-lune was modified between 1872 and 1875, but the new wooden gun platforms rotted away by 1880. Extensive repairs and modifications were done at Fort Pickens and Fort Barrancas between 1869 and 1876 when funding ran out. At Fort Morgan, the gun platforms were modified in 1873 and 1874 and construction of two water batteries for heavy artillery began in 1875, but work was suspended the next year for lack of funds. Plans to renovate Fort Pike and Fort Macomb in 1870 never got off the ground because Congress failed to provide funds.

The Fortifications Board conducted tests at Fort Monroe and Fort Delaware on experimental constructions of iron and masonry in late November and early December 1868. Following the tests, the board reported that "the results thus far obtained do not enable the board to recommend any plan of construction for casemates or shields for seacoast or harbor defense batteries." The only recommendation the group made was that work should be restricted to earthworks while they conducted an investigation on the use of iron in seacoast batteries in Europe. Three engineer officers were sent to Europe in 1870 to study the subject.

In Europe, France, Germany, Austria, Italy, Russia, and Great Britain were searching for the most resistant structures to stand up to the rapidly evolving artillery. While the American engineers were investigating and testing new materials, Vicktor von Scheliha, a former Confederate army engineer, published his *Treatise on Coast Defense* based on his wartime experiences. Scheliha pointed out that exposed masonry could not withstand the fire of modern artillery and that earthen fortifications offered better protection. In addition, he wrote, the downfall of the Confederacy demonstrated that no forts of the era could deny access to an enemy fleet without relying on obstructions as well. Scheliha's treatise caught the attention of European and American military engineers, who took his theories to heart. The Fortifications Board also followed with interest the developments in Great Britain where iron had been extensively used for naval and land batteries since 1862. However, the high cost of iron was a primary consideration and the War Department wanted a thorough investigation before committing the military to its use in coastal batteries.

In his report submitted after his return from Europe, Colonel J. G. Barnard concluded that iron battery positions had proven superior to any masonry types. British experimental firings against test sections in the 1860s demonstrated an "... attack on a properly constructed iron-built battery would be hopeless, except with steel or hardened shot, at a range not much exceeding 600 yards." Tests revealed that a cast-iron shot easily destroyed granite casemates at one thousand yards. British Lieutenant Colonel Inglis wrote in a Royal Engineer report of 1868 that British casemates built of granite, similar to those used in America, with an English-made iron shield proved superior in strength to those of any other nation. Barnard agreed that the British armor plating was stronger than anything tested at Fort Monroe and Fort Delaware. Barnard also had witnessed Prussian test firings against a Gruson iron casemate in 1867 with 24-pdr, 72-pdr, and 95-pdr cannons with steel shot and different types of chilled iron shell. In ideal conditions, some hits dented the armor and a few even caused fracturing, while others damaged the masonry. The results of the experiments, reported Barnard, indicated that this type of casemate would stand up well in combat.

The idea of iron turrets was not new, and even preceded the creation of the turrets of the monitors. During the Civil War, engravings of circular sea forts similar to the British forts appeared in *Harper's* magazine. They included Theodore Timby's pre-war drawings of a huge revolving turret with a dozen or more cannons that were to serve as a fort. By the early 1880s, the British mounted breechloading rifles (BLR) on their warships. America's aging fleet, on the other hand, needed a major overhaul, as did its coastal fortifications.

Brigadier General Horatio G. Wright, then chief of engineers, summarized the state of American fortifications between the end of the war and the beginning of the 1880s in the Report of the Chief of Engineers of 1881. At that time, the Corps of Engineers had 106 officers, many more than before the Civil War, but their responsibilities had increased. Less than a quarter of these officers were assigned to fortifications, a number comparable to the prewar count. During the first fifteen years after the war, the engineers concentrated mainly on "protection, preservation, and repair" of existing American seacoast defenses, according to Wright. Despite constant rebuffs, Wright repeatedly urged Congress to make reasonable appropriations because "the necessity of a *commencement* [his emphasis], if nothing more, in the modification of, and additions to, our works of fortifications on which the safety of our maritime cities, our navy-yards, and depots of supply must sooner or later depend." The existing fortifications, he pointed out, built before "the introduction of modern ordnance and armored ships ... and although there were none better in their day, are now most of them utterly unfit to cope with modern ships of war." The more recently constructed earthen batteries needed reinforcement against modern ordnance and the casemated works were no longer

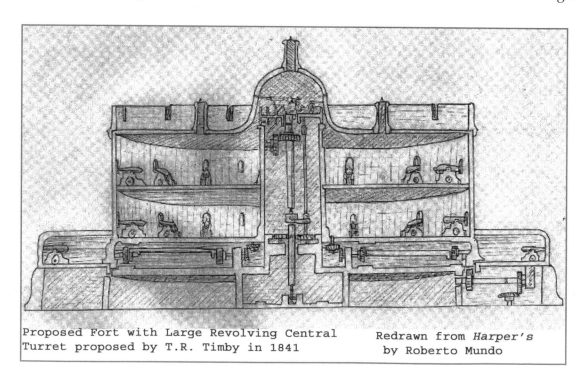

Proposed Fort with Large Revolving Central
Turret proposed by T.R. Timby in 1841

Redrawn from *Harper's*
by Roberto Mundo

adequate to stand up against warships. Wright warned that other great maritime nations had heavily armored ships of war carrying guns of up to one hundred tons (15-inch guns) and that they were also building armored coastal defenses. He reported that the British had installed over five hundred guns in armored defenses while the War Department had not even begun work on any such position for a single gun. Wright attempted to convince Congress that a single well-built fort cost less to build than it cost just to maintain a single major warship.

Lieutenant Colonel Gillmore, on the other hand, took a different tack. He cautioned instead that all the forts needed to protect the nation adequately would cost a tenth less than the damage caused from the loss of one of the country's great cities. In his 1881 report to the Board of Engineers, Lieutenant Colonel Gillmore emphasized that the British had reacted to the developments of the American Civil War by quickly appropriating funds for the defense of their key harbors. "It is upon our maritime frontier that we are most exposed," he wrote, and "our coast for three thousand miles is washed by the ocean which separates us from those nations who have made the highest advances in all the arts." America, because of its commercial and political relationships, was likely "to be drawn into collision," he warned. The U.S. coast offered too many exposed points and enemy warships only needed thirty-six hours to steam from Halifax, six hours from Havana, or ninety-six hours from Victoria to appear before a major American harbor. There would be little time to "to meet assaults of these fast-running, sea-going, armored ships, ships clad with from 6 to 24 inches of iron armor, carrying rifled guns from 9 inches to 17 inches bore, which are more powerful than any gun we have in our service." Even if the United States could muster 100,000 men in twenty-four hours to meet a single battleship bombarding a harbor, this force would be helpless against it. Troops rushed to meet such an attack, warned Gillmore, were impotent against such a threat, even if they had the standard 32-pdr, 42-pdr, and 100-pdr rifles. However, the timing of Gillmore's presentation was not favorable and it fell on deaf ears.

The modern weapons of the U.S. arsenal included one hundred and ten 8-inch rifles. The Ordnance Department, having had more success than the Corps of Engineers, received appropriations for the construction of four breechloading 12-inch rifles based on the Krupp model. These weapons, which fired an 800-lb shot, compared to the 180-lb shot of the 8-inch rifles, were considered the minimum size needed to match a modern armored warship. The Ordnance Department planned to convert all 325 of its 15-inch smoothbore into 11-inch breechloading rifles firing a 500-lb shot. Gillmore emphasized the fact that the major European powers were replacing their old guns with rifled weapons of large calibers, including 12-inch and 16-inch firing 800-lb and 1,700-lb shots respectively. They were even developing a 17-inch rifle that could fire a 2,000-lb shot. He insisted that this was what America needed to challenge modern armored warships.

These new weapons created new problems for coastal defenses. The earth and sand parapets and traverses would have to be three to four times thicker than during the Civil War, Gillmore estimated. The new artillery and its ammunition were so heavy that it had to be operated and moved with new "mechanical appliances." The Corps of Engineers required large appropriations if it was to make the necessary modifications to casemated works and build barbette and mortar batteries that could accommodate the appropriate weapons. According to Gillmore, the only areas that needed to be defended with permanent works were the "avenues to the great commercial cities and naval and military establishments," since the coast was too long and could be struck at almost any point. He felt that the selected sites must: 1. Close all-important harbors from an enemy; 2. Deprive the enemy of a site from which they may establish a bridgehead for further operations; 3. Cover the great cities from attack; 4. Prevent the major avenues of interior navigation from being blockaded at their outlets to the sea; 5. Must cover coastal and interior navigation; 6. Must protect the great naval establishments. In addition, Gillmore recommended using electrical torpedoes to obstruct harbor mouths and channels. The electrical connections had to be placed in subterranean galleries leading out to deep water and the electric machinery for controlling these mines had to be placed in the fortification and out of the line of enemy fire. At the time, only two hundred engineer soldiers were trained for working with mines.

Furthermore, the heavy mortars had to be located in large numbers where they could command any likely anchorage for enemy ships. It was the "torpedoes," Gillmore wrote, that would hold the enemy ships exposed in front of the fortifications where the artillery could engage them. The engineer department supported mounting much of the required artillery en barbette, but also believed that the existing casemated works needed modifications to accept the heaviest calibers and that armor plating must be added. In some cases, new works had to be built.

Members of Wright's Board of Engineers, Colonel Z. B. Tower, Colonel John Newton, and Lieutenant Colonel Henry Abbot, also reported on the state of coast defenses. At that time, they believed, nothing less than earth parapets and iron shields were suitable to protect coastal guns although the positions would remain vulnerable to plunging fire. Since the ships of the time only had direct fire weapons, this was not considered a problem. They also did not favor iron shields combined with masonry scarps because they were vulnerable to new heavier artillery with increasing velocities. They conceded that turrets would provide a good solution for harbor defense, recommending them for important harbors. Designs were being prepared for a turret to mount a 100-ton gun. Site location would restrict the use of costly iron scarps and turrets, while earthen fortifications were much more economical. Many of the earthen barbette batteries begun in the 1870s finally neared completion and theoretically would be able to mount 12-inch rifles.

All the plans of the 1870s finally began to bear fruit under a new presidential administration. When Grover Cleveland took office in March 1885, he showed interest in national defense and not only began work on a "steel navy," but also began an investigation into the construction of modern coastal defenses. A special board, known as the Endicott Board, was formed for that purpose.

The Endicott Board and a New System

By presidential order, in March 1885, Secretary of War William Endicott formed the Endicott Board to study fortifications. The members included Brigadier General Stephen V. Benét (chief of ordnance), Brigadier General John Newton (chief of engineers), Lieutenant Colonel Henry L. Abbot (corps of engineers), Captain Charles S. Smith (ordnance department), Commander William T. Sampson and Commander Caspar F. Goodrich of the navy, Mr. Joseph Morgan Jr. of Pennsylvania, and Mr. Erastus Corning of New York. The board completed its report one year later. It consisted of about twenty-five pages and included reports by five separate committees that total over three hundred additional pages.

The Endicott Board's report read much like those of the chief of engineers from the 1880s and shed no new light on the subject of fortifications, although it began a new era in American fortifications. The report stressed the fact that forts that had been able to withstand the 10-inch Rodman of 1860 could not stand up to the new heavy artillery. It also cited the Gun Foundry Board's estimate that it would take a minimum of three years to establish a plant for modern artillery and an additional two years to produce the first 16-inch guns. Once work began on the new guns, emplacements, magazines, shell rooms, engine rooms, and other facilities would be needed to maintain and service them, which meant that nothing would be ready before the 1890s.

The Endicott Board concluded that priority for construction of fortifications must be given to a select number of key locations exposed to naval attack. Concluding that the field army could handle any attack on a land front, the board prepared a list of twenty-seven ports by order of urgency. Eleven of these ports received top priority: New York, San Francisco, Boston, Great Lakes ports, Hampton Roads, New Orleans, Philadelphia, Washington, Baltimore, Portland, and Narragansett Bay. The board recommended both fixed and floating defenses for these sites. Floating defenses did not refer to armored sea-going warships, which were for offensive operations. They referred instead to floating batteries more heavily armed than sea-going warships and designed for operation in shallow water. Shore batteries were to consist of armored turrets (fixed or revolving and presumably of cast iron), armored casemates, and emplacements for barbette mounts. Steel was preferred, although iron was an option for the armor. Since all these options required a great expense, Congress looked more favorably at less costly barbette batteries, which, according to the report, were "earthen parapets and traverses, sometimes arranged with a core of concrete or rubble masonry to gain resistance to shot." Although these structures may have required a greater volume of materials, they were cheaper than iron or steel. The extra labor required was the least of the expenses involved.

Like earlier reports from the chiefs of engineers, the Endicott Report emphasized the fact that batteries alone would not stop an enemy fleet. It concluded that submarine mines and buoyant mines must be placed in deep channels, and ground mines in shallow water, all of them preferably electrically detonated. In addition, these minefields needed facilities for operating and maintaining the mines and gun batteries to protect them. Electric searchlights were a requisite for keeping the minefields under observation. Torpedo boats and older smoothbore guns, no longer suitable for fighting heavily armed ships, would serve as an additional means of defense for these minefields. The board also referred to the self-propelled Whitehead torpedo, and other models, and to the unknown factor of the possibility of using "submarine boats" to defend the harbors. A key section of the report contained recommendations for the type of weapons to be used and where.

The casemates, turrets, and barbette positions alone for the fortifications of all these port areas were estimated at $55,483,000, exclusive of the cost of the weapons. Five gun turrets were roughly estimated to cost the same as ninety disappearing and non-disappearing gun positions or ten gun positions in casemates. The casemates and turrets would not be built since their cost was about $30 million of the $55.48 million. Fifteen planned turrets were estimated at over $15 million while eight casemate positions were about $15 million. Two floating batteries were recommended for New Orleans and three for San Francisco with an estimated cost of almost $19 million not including their huge guns. Not only the price, but their practicality, were questioned later and they were not built. Congress looked more favorably at the submarine mines. The minefields required for all the harbors totaled over six thousand mines, fifty operating rooms and associated facilities, and two hundred electric searchlights at an estimated cost of $4,334,000. The board also recommended 150 torpedo boats for the first thirteen ports on the list at an estimated cost of $9,720,000. The total cost for all the items the Endicott Board recommended came to over $126 million.

The Endicott Board tackled the problem of carriages and mountings since all the new guns were to be breechloaders, which also alleviated some problems associated with loading the heaviest pieces. The barbette mount had been considered the most practical and effective option during the Civil War, but it left the crew and gun exposed. After considering several unusual alternatives, the board settled on the disappearing carriage. As it turned out, the Americans exercised their options at the right time because years of experimentation and bad choices had forced the Europeans to scrap many faulty artillery designs. The same was true about fortifications, in which the Americans had not invested. Great Britain had spent huge sums on iron fortifications, which had to be replaced with steel and concrete works by the late 1880s. Since Congress was not about to appropriate the huge funds required for steel turrets and casemates, the new American fortifications would rely heavily on DISAPPEARING CARRIAGES for the heaviest guns and barbette mounts for small calibers.

The Endicott Phase began a new era in American fortifications. It was followed by the Taft Phase, the World War I Phase (lasting until the 1930s), and the World War II Phase (beginning in the late 1930s) in the twentieth century. This era was characterized by the last heavy gun-bearing fortifications in the United States. Most of the work resulting from the Endicott investigation did not begin until 1890 and lasted over ten years. Items like turrets, casemates, and floating batteries, which were considered too extravagant by Congress, were the first to be removed for funding consideration. The projected cost of over $126 million for the entire package recommended by the board turned out to be an underestimate for much of the armament.

In fact, Congress refused outright to appropriate any funds for fortifications in 1886. A year after the Endicott report the condition of America's coast defense had changed little. In an article entitled "Our Unprotected Seacoast" published in the March 1887 issue of *Frank Leslie's Popular Monthly*, Joseph Nimmo Jr., chief of the Bureau of Statistics wrote, "During the last twenty years we have actually grown weaker ... while almost every other maritime nation, by adopting the modern instrumentalities of military science, has grown stronger." General Newton, quoted in the same article, opined that at that time the United States was "left in a condition to invite attack from any third-rate Power piratically inclined." Nimmo also wrote, "At the present time New York City is absolutely defenseless," while "Fort Hamilton ... and Fort Wadsworth ... which look so grand and formidable, would constitute no obstacle to the passage even of second or third rate armored ships of foreign nations right into our harbor." He added that "too much reliance has been placed upon torpedoes and submarines mines," which, he believed were devastating weapons but "are practically useless when unprotected by forts, or mortars or ships." Nimmo also questioned their effectiveness in rough and deep water. With the support of officers from the army and navy and their reports, he pleaded the case for coastal defense. Still, it was not until 1890 that Congress appropriated funds for fortifications at New York, San Francisco, and Boston.

The 16-inch guns of American design, not yet perfected, did not appear until the next century. The main heavy artillery that went into production were the 12-inch, 10-inch, and 8-inch guns as well as the 12-inch mortars. All the heavy guns had flat trajectory and maximum elevation of 15 degrees, like the guns of a warship, which limited their range. The preferred positions were disappearing mounts because naval guns of the era, with their flat trajectory, could not hit a gun in the depressed position. In addition, if the artillery were placed at an elevated position above sea level, it would be more difficult to target when the gun was in the firing position. By this time, the Europeans had developed a number of models. Inspired by the transatlantic designs, Colonel Adelbert Buffington and Captain William Crozier of the Ordnance Department perfected a carriage that used a heavy counterweight for raising the gun into firing position above the parapet. Once fired, the recoil pushed the gun back below the parapet into the loading position. The BUFFINTON-CROZIER CARRIAGE became the standard type for American disappearing guns.

The Endicott Board had recommended several GUN LIFTS, which were later developed. One consisted of an elevator (lift) capable of lifting a heavy piece of artillery on its mounting to a firing position and lowering it to a safe position for reloading. The Board of Ordnance and Fortifications had been developing its own gun lift, designed by Colonel Henry Abbot, since 1888. An experimental battery consisting of two lifts in a large two-floor concrete structure was built at FORT HANCOCK in New York between 1891 and 1893. At first, French manufacturers built many of the components since American industry was not ready to meet the needs of the military. The first American-produced 12-inch gun made with French steel was mounted on one of the lifts in 1892. Testing began that same spring. The main power source was a large boiler room in the center of the position that operated the pumps, which, in turn, fed the accumulators that could raise both gun lifts. When in operation, the guns were loaded below ground, on the upper floor. A hydraulic lift delivered ammunition from the lower level. It took a little under a minute to raise the guns into firing position and the same amount of time to lower them. The total time elapsed from loading to firing was about seven minutes, but the complex system worked well. Thus, the Corps of Engineers decided it needed over a hundred more in 1895. However, only one gun-lift battery, Battery Potter, was ever completed because the Buffington-Crozier Carriage for 8-inch and 10-inch guns was already going into production in 1894, and in 1896 they were experimenting with a carriage model for a 12-inch gun that was ready for production the next year. The disappearing carriage cost about a quarter of the price of the gun lift. In addition to being cheaper, it required no complex machinery or power source and its rate of fire was under a minute per round.

The gun-lift position was more fortification-like than the disappearing-gun position. It consisted of a large block position made of concrete and earth while the disappearing gun position was open with up to 20 feet or more of concrete in front of the gun and an additional earth covering. In many cases, the disappearing guns mounted upon supporting concrete positions had no protection to the rear or overhead. This was the wave of the future for the American coast defenses. Many of the platforms for the disappearing carriages were built in or adjacent to 3rd System forts, which were modified to accommodate the new seacoast battery positions. By the turn of the century, disappearing batteries appeared in FORT WARREN, FORT DELAWARE, FORT WOOL, FORT SUMTER, and FORT MORGAN, while similar batteries were erected near FORT RICHMOND, FORT WASHINGTON (a transitional fort), FORT MONROE, and FORT PICKENS. Some of the batteries were not placed in existing forts, but were clustered together to form new positions such as FORT CASEY in the state of Washington.

The battery positions usually included two to four, and sometimes more, seacoast guns that required an immense amount of concrete, not counting the material needed to build associated positions such as magazines, control rooms, and engine rooms. David Clary, author of *Fortress America*, quotes a supervisor's report stating what a 10-

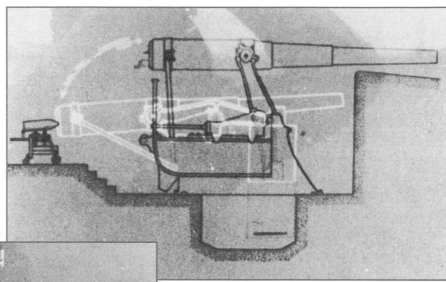

OPERATION OF THE GUN

Heavy counterweights lift the gun into firing position above the thick concrete parapet which gives protection to the gun and gunners. The gun is lowered into loading position by the recoil force which lifts the counterweights.

Above and Left: Operation of a disappearing gun. National Park Service
Below: As part of the Endicott Program new batteries, many with disappearing guns like this 6-inch-gun battery at Fort Pickens, were created on or near existing 3rd System forts.
Photo courtesy of Dennis Blazey.

inch-gun battery at Fort Monroe required: "The sand foundation for these platforms was thoroughly rammed and settled with water. The surface of the platforms was covered with 4,700 square feet of granolithic finish, 2 inches in thickness, in the composition of which 88 barrels of Portland cement, 20 cubic yards of fine broken stone, and 15 cubic yards of sand were used." This did not include, writes Clary, the massive parapet structures built previously. The Americans were not at the cutting edge of technological development at the time of the Endicott defenses construction period. In Europe, experiments finally led to the application of reinforced concrete (concrete poured into a form reinforced with steel rods or ribar) which was more resistant and required less concrete. It was not until early in the twentieth century that the U.S. army engineers began to work with reinforced concrete.

The supporting structures for the disappearing gun batteries generally occupied more physical space than the gun blocks of the battery and were the largest structures on the battery site. These structures, like the gun positions, were shielded from view from the sea, and were exposed in the rear. A few gun emplacements actually had all-around cover, but no overhead protection. Some of the supporting positions were protected by the terrain to their rear, but they were designed to serve for coast defense and not all-around defense. Batteries for guns under 8-inch caliber generally required fewer and smaller facilities and were often mounted en barbette, usually with a gun shield.

The Endicott Board favored the use of both. The War Department and Congress dropped many of the board's pet projects, saying they were either unreasonable and/or unperfected. Undaunted, General Henry L. Abbott of the Corps of Engineers pushed forward his ideas. During the 1890s, he not only designed the gun lift built at Fort Hancock, but also developed a submarine minefield policy and advocated the use of heavy mortars in seacoast defense. But the large seacoast mortar proved inadequate against warships, since by the time they were developed and mounted, warships had acquired armored decks. In addition, these weapons were not accurate enough, as scoring a hit on a ship with high angle plunging fire is more difficult than with direct fire, even with the type of barrage fire Abbott advocated.

The mortar batteries of the 1890s usually consisted of two concrete mortar pits well concealed in the front by a high parapet with the huge stubby breechloaded 12-inch mortars out of the direct line of fire from an enemy's ships. Each pit contained a cluster of four mortars whose proximity presented a potential danger in case of accident. The more efficient 1911-model 12-inch mortar came into service in the twentieth century, leading to the reduction of the number of mortars per pit from four to two.

One important feature of these batteries and the forts they served was range-finding equipment. The gunners no longer had to peer down the barrel to aim the large breechloading guns as they had done with the old smoothbores. These new guns were outfitted with equipment and sighting devices similar to those on ships and were usually placed in tower-like structures. At Fort Monroe, an impressive tower was built next

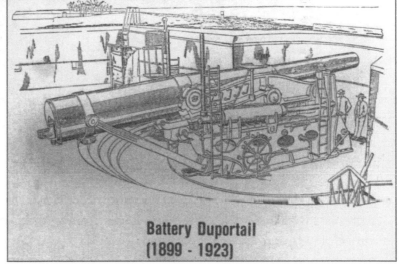

Above: As with many 3rd System forts an Endicott battery was built into Fort Morgan. This is Battery Duportail which mounted two 12-inch guns. *Right:* A sketch of one of the guns for Battery Duportail.

Battery Duportail
(1899 - 1923)

to the battery. However, when the guns fired, the vibrations they produced made it difficult to control their fire. Early in the twentieth century, horizontal base stations were built a little away from coastal batteries. Usually, two or four of these stations transmitted data to the command center to compute range and fire direction. The command center was located in one of the supporting structures of the battery. The base stations were generally small structures built of wood instead of concrete, whose dampness affected the sensitive instruments. Early in the twentieth century, a form of concrete stucco was used on these base stations to make them more permanent.

Special equipment for communications and operating electrical equipment had to be developed for these new fortifications and the old forts that continued in service. The telephone took on an increasingly important role in transmitting orders, but since the gun crews could not hear them during firing exercises, the Signal Corps had to develop other alternatives.

By 1898, only about 150 artillery pieces had been installed in the newly built fortifications. But the Spanish American War spurred Congress into increasing funding. The

3-inch gun with shield at Fort Casey in Washington.

chief of engineers reported the next year that 288 heavy guns, 154 rapid-fire guns, and 312 mortars were ready. The Endicott seacoast defenses became a reality at last, but the number of weapons and emplacements actually built remained far below the rather extravagant recommendations. The Endicott fortifications were found at the mouth of the Kennebec River, Portland (ME), Portsmouth, Boston, New Bedford, Narragansett Bay, Long Island Sound, New York Harbor, Delaware River, Baltimore, Potomac River, Hampton Roads, Cape Fear River, Charleston, Port Royal Sound, Savannah, Key West, Tampa, Pensacola, Mobile, Mississippi River, Galveston, San Diego, San Francisco, the Columbia River, and Puget Sound.

At the end of the 1890's, some forts mounted the new "dynamite guns" and a large number of rapid-fire or quick-fire weapons of 3-inch to 5-inch caliber. These smaller weapons were pedestal mounted and protected by an armored shield. A number of batteries for 8-inch and 10-inch guns became operational. Work on the Endicott fortifications ended at most sites by 1910, as a new phase was getting under way. During the first decade of the twentieth century, most of the sorely needed 12-inch guns replaced the 8-inch guns that were no longer effective against modern battleships. In addition, early in that same decade, the War Department scrapped the few batteries of "dynamite guns."

Experimentation on MINE CASEMATES took place at Willet's Point (site of FORT TOTTEN) before any were actually built. The first of these casemates were completed by 1893 at

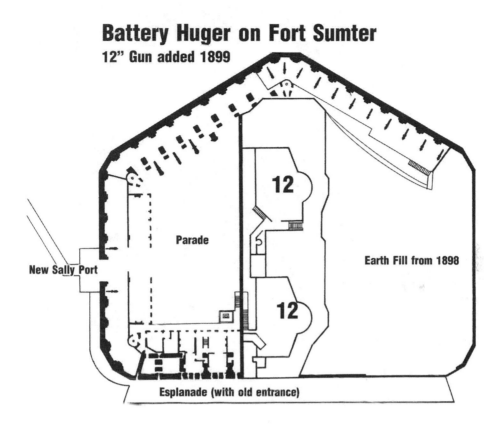

Battery Huger on Fort Sumter
12" Gun added 1899

Parade

New Sally Port

Earth Fill from 1898

Esplanade (with old entrance)

Fort Monroe, Hampton Roads, and San Francisco. These fortifications were built specifically to operate and handle mines (which were referred to as torpedoes until the early twentieth century). The unfinished 3rd System fort at Willet's Point (New York) had been converted into an engineer depot at the end of the Civil War. The site served as the only engineer depot for many years. In the early 1870s, a torpedo depot and a large concrete storage facility consisting of mine storage casemates for submarine mines was added to the complex. A large concrete mining casemate from which mining operations were directed was built by 1876. The fort also included the School of Submarine Defense until early in the twentieth century. At the turn of the century, the army acquired four minelayer (referred to as mine planter in the army) vessels to create the submarine minefields. In the early 1880s, Henry L. Abbott experimented with the Sim's Torpedo, an electrically propelled torpedo. In addition to developing mines, Abbott tested electric searchlights at Willet's Point.

With the new American coastal defenses under construction, in the early 1900s President Theodore Roosevelt's administration conducted another examination of these defenses and the needs of the newly acquired territories beyond the forty-seven states. Secretary of War William H. Taft organized the TAFT BOARD (National Coast Defense Board) at Roosevelt's request in January 1905. In a letter dated February 27, 1906, Taft

Dynamite Gun
© TOMASZ IDZIKOWSKI

Questionable Defensive Weapon

The last quarter of the nineteenth century witnessed the appearance of a number of defensive weapons and equipment of questionable value. The biggest boondoggle of them all was the Pneumatic Dynamite Gun. This weapon came in a 15-inch and 8-inch caliber and served to launch dynamite packages. Invented by Mr. Meddford of Ohio and perfected by Captain E. L. Zaliniski, an artillery officer, in 1888 it was adopted by both the army and the navy. This air gun reportedly could fire a full 1,000-lb. projectile (including weight of projectile and dynamite) 2,400 yards. According to official statistics, it fired a projectile with 500 lbs. of dynamite 2,000 yards and one with 50 lbs. of dynamite 5,000 yards. The gun, operated by one man, was manipulated with electrical power. Carriages and emplacements for this weapon were built at Fort Hancock, Fort Wright, and Fort Winfield Scott. The navy experimented with the dynamite guns also. The Holland submarine mounted one of the Zaliniski 8-inch dynamite guns in its bow. The U.S.S. *Vesuvius* mounted three of these guns and used them against Santiago de Cuba in the Spanish American War. The weapon proved to be a failure and was declared obsolete in 1902 by the Board of Ordnance and Fortification. All the guns of this type went to the scrap yards by 1904.

described the condition of the defenses: "The details of the system of defense have been modified and added to from time to time to keep pace with the advances in ordnance, electrical appliances, methods of construction, and with changes in design and armament of war vessels. The present system is, therefore, the result of a gradual development and, in addition to the heavy or high-power guns and submarine mines proposed by the Endicott Board, defended ports are now equipped with rapid-fire guns, and to some extent with power plants, searchlights and range finding and fire-control systems, necessary adjuncts of an adequate defense to-day, though not so considered in 1886."

Taft's board revised the sites to be fortified, including sites already on the list like the eastern entrance to Long Island Sound, Tampa, and Puget Sound, which needed to be completed. The board endorsed adding new defenses at Cape Henry and Cape Charles to block the entrances to the Chesapeake Bay, which were undefended. The board recommended that priority be given to the defenses on Long Island Sound which were considered important because they would obviate the need to defend New London and New Haven. In addition, the board determined that the defenses at Penobscot, Cumberland Sound, and Port Royal Sound, where the naval yard was closed, were no longer needed. It recommended leaving the care of these facilities to a caretaker. According to the Taft report, the four-mile wide entrance of the Puget Sound was too deep to be mined. The board recommended extending a second line of gun defenses about seventeen miles from the outer entrance, from Foulweather Bluff to Double Bluff, to keep out enemy warships. Tampa took on greater importance during the Spanish American War as a staging area that needed defenses. Since the United States had expanded its territory across the seas, the board also recommended that overseas naval bases and coaling stations receive fortifications if the United States was to maintain control of its insular possessions. The Taft Board urged that the "great" naval bases of Guantanamo, Subic Bay, and Pearl Harbor and the cities of Manila and Honolulu be fortified. [Note: It is curious that these sites were described as "great" naval bases since none of them had actually been developed enough at the time to qualify for the title.]. In addition, the board recommended defending the coaling stations at Guam and San Juan. In Central America, the construction of the Panama Canal was already under way and the Taft Board included Panama in their list of needed port defenses.

On March 6, 1906, President Roosevelt wrote in the Taft Board Report presented to Congress, "The necessity for a complete and adequate system of coast defense is greater to-day than twenty years ago" because "the vast wealth of the nation invites attack from fleets which can reach and strike American shores in a much shorter time than in the past." Furthermore, he stated, "The fact we now have a navy does not in any wise [sic] diminish the importance of coast defenses; on the contrary, that fact emphasizes their value and the necessity for their construction."

The Russo-Japanese War and the development of the British dreadnought played a major role in determining America's needs in regard to its coast defenses. The HMS

Dreadnought was only begun late in 1905 and was not completed before the Taft Board had finished its work. But the American navy had already drawn up plans for, and laid down the U.S.S. *South Carolina*, a dreadnought with superimposed turrets of even more modern design and thus, the members of the board knew what to expect from big-gun warships.

The Taft Board evaluated the work done since the Endicott Board report and examined the rapidly changing technology that had inspired some of the more fanciful requests of the previous board. They concluded that the defense of the American coast and its insular possessions required: 1. Guns of no less caliber than 12-inch and 12-inch mortars and rapid-fire guns to protect the minefields in important harbors; 2. 10-inch guns for channels only accessible to enemy cruisers; 3. 6-inch guns for places vulnerable to naval raids and minefields beyond the range of 3-inch guns. The board based these conclusions on the reach of the improved range-finding equipment, improved communications for firing data, searchlights at night, and increased effective range of coastal guns allowing for ranges up to twelve thousand yards as opposed to the past effective ranges under three thousand yards. The Russo-Japanese War demonstrated that only heavy-caliber weapons could damage armored warships. On the other hand, the board's naval officers concluded that first-class coastal defenses were vulnerable to nothing less than battleships.

The Taft Board's report pointed out the inadequacies of the U.S. defense system. For instance, four mine-planter vessels were not sufficient to serve all the important U.S. ports; and the coastal batteries needed reserve powerhouses because a hit on the single power generating equipment could cripple an entire position. The board also underscored the growing importance of searchlights, and the need to improve command and control equipment to make the batteries more effective. It recommended burying all communication and submarine cables to protect them from enemy fire. It recommended laying submarine cables from Key West to Panama and the insular possessions in the Caribbean. However, frequent cable breakdowns along the American coast alone required more ships than were available to service them. Fortunately, wireless telegraph (the radio) was coming into service, making coordination with naval and land defenses easier and more practical than ever before. The board was glad to point out that the recent addition of horizontal base stations resulted in more effective fire control, but requested additional funds to improve the system.

The Taft Board recommended additional mines and range finding and fire control equipment. It also urged the modernization of old emplacements. The new expense list included a supply of ammunition for the artillery, which had not been considered by earlier boards. Since the new battleships and the British dreadnoughts reduced the effectiveness of the 12-inch coastal gun, the board recommended the adoption of a 14-inch gun because the 16-inch gun relied too heavily on mechanical devices for its operation, significantly reducing its advantage in firepower. Additional work on the improvement and development of the disappearing carriages was also recommended. There was no need for floating batteries and torpedo boats permanently assigned to a harbor since the navy would need them elsewhere in time of war. A few old pre-dreadnaught ships and several monitors were assigned to some of the ports. However, the board considered the shallow draft monitors to be rather poor and unstable firing platforms.

Searchlights no longer just served to protect minefields from enemy sweeping operations at night but also helped the artillery sight targets. They illuminated enemy ships, allowing the base stations to gather range data that was sent to the plotting room whose calculations directed the heavy artillery. The best projectors were 36-inch and 60-inch ones because smaller ones lacked the needed power. According to the 1902 specifications supplied by the General Electric Company, the 60-inch searchlight had 194,000,000-candlepower and its beam could reach a distance of twelve miles on a dark night, allowing one to read ordinary print in its light. Other electrical equipment was necessary for the efficient operation of the gun battery from lighting to hoisting ammunition.

The administration and Congress were more receptive to the Taft Report than they had been to the Endicott Report, despite the huge costs. Thus, plans went forward and work was underway within a short time. By the time World War I began in 1914 (1917 for the United States), most of the work was well underway, but still incomplete.

Above: 10-inch gun in loading position at Fort Casey in Washington.
Right: 10-inch gun in firing position.

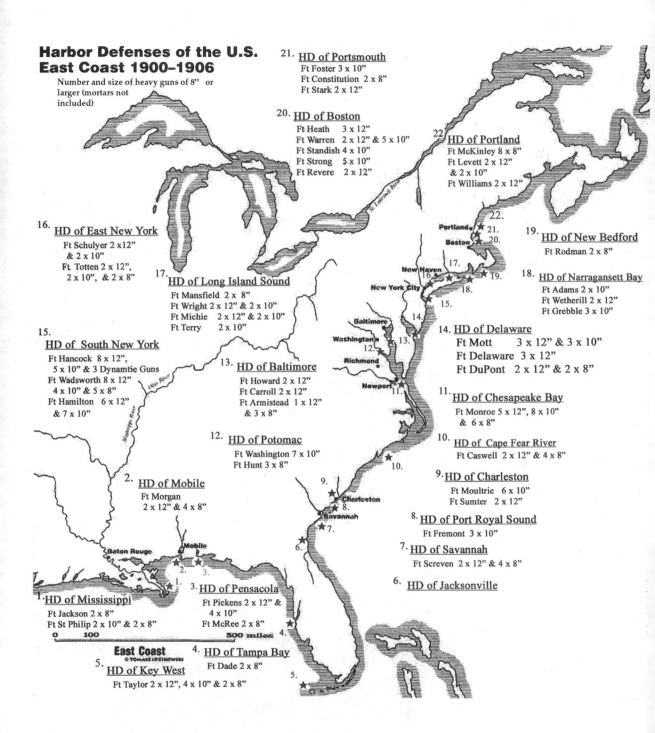

Harbor Defenses of the U.S. East Coast 1900–1906

Chapter 8

THE END OF ISOLATION AND THE BIG-GUN FORTIFICATIONS

EARLY IN THE TWENTIETH CENTURY, American coast defenses had progressed and most of the harbor areas were sufficiently protected by fortifications begun in 1890 under the Endicott plan and modified in 1907 on the recommendations of the Taft Board. In 1898, the United States had gone to war with Spain over the Cuban problem after the sinking of the U.S.S. *Maine*. Although the war was short, it lasted long enough for Congress to become concerned about the state of American coastal defenses. At the end of the war, the Philippines, Guam, and Puerto Rico became insular dependencies of the United States by treaty. In addition, the Cubans leased the base of Guantanamo in southeastern Cuba to the United States. The war inspired the American government to annex Hawaii. The military believed the Hawaiian Islands were an excellent base needed to maintain control over the new Pacific possessions. After the American-instigated Panamanian revolt against Columbia in November 1903, the United States received a 10-mile wide strip, later known as the Canal Zone, in perpetuity. In 1904, American engineers began work on the Panama Canal, completing it by 1914. All of these new possessions received some form of fortifications to protect them.

Change in Fortifications and Weapons

Construction of the new coastal defenses began in 1890 and by 1914 almost every major port area in the United States and most of its insular possessions included a number of heavy-gun batteries mounted en barbette or on disappearing carriages. These batteries were grouped together to form a new type of fort. Like most of the army posts found throughout the United States during the end of the nineteenth century, the new

Fort Drum
© TOMASZ IDZIKOWSKI

coastal defense forts had no walls, unless they were part of an older fort. Except for a peripheral fence, most army forts, including the coastal forts, were relatively open posts with permanent, fixed gun positions, and defenses generally facing seaward. Coast Artillery companies specially trained to use the complex weapons systems manned the coastal fortifications in the early twentieth century. Later, when enemy aircraft had to be dealt with, the first antiaircraft battalions came from the Coast Artillery Corps because the army believed that these troops had the best training for firing at moving targets.

The United States had ambitious projects underway overseas. HAWAII received immediate attention after the Taft Board's recommendations because it was a vital station on the lines of communication to America's Pacific empire. Preparations for the construction of the first fortifications began in 1906. In the Philippines in 1902, at the entrance to Manila Bay the engineers began converting the island of Corregidor into a fortress position named FORT MILLS. By 1910, it had nine heavy batteries. Forts (battery positions) built at Cavite and on three smaller islands at the entrance of Manila Bay formed the main line of defense for the harbor. One of these small island forts was located across from Corregidor on El Fraile Island where the engineers had begun leveling operations in 1909. Between 1909 and 1918, the Corps of Engineers reshaped the island, covering it with a reinforced concrete shell with a deck 18 feet thick and sides 25 to 60 feet thick. FORT DRUM had the appearance of a ship and its interior consisted of three decks with

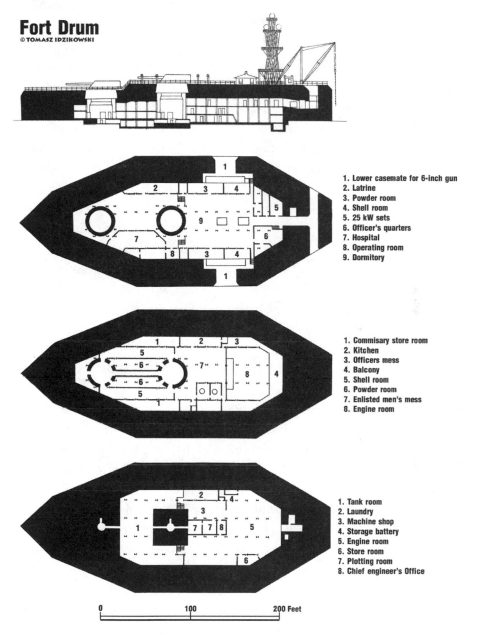

Fort Drum
© TOMASZ IDZIKOWSKI

1. Lower casemate for 6-inch gun
2. Latrine
3. Powder room
4. Shell room
5. 25 kW sets
6. Officer's quarters
7. Hospital
8. Operating room
9. Dormitory

1. Commisary store room
2. Kitchen
3. Officers mess
4. Balcony
5. Shell room
6. Powder room
7. Enlisted men's mess
8. Engine room

1. Tank room
2. Laundry
3. Machine shop
4. Storage battery
5. Engine room
6. Store room
7. Plotting room
8. Chief engineer's Office

0   100   200 Feet

engines and the plotting room on the lower deck, magazines and the mess on the next deck, and the barracks on the top deck. The fort had two turrets, each mounting a pair of 14-inch guns, much like the turrets of a battleship. On the port and starboard sides, batteries of 6-inch guns protruded in armored casemates. Behind the turrets was the cage mast, which also mounted the searchlights. This, combined with the other features, earned the fort the nickname of "The Concrete Battleship." It represented the most unusual fortification built by the United States. The Coast Artillery Corps took over the fort in 1918, but its turret guns were test-fired only once in the 1920s.

On American shores, work began to protect the PANAMA CANAL's sets of locks at both entrances. A Panama Fortifications Board met in 1909 to make its recommendations, under the direction of General Leonard Wood. The board recommended a pair of 14-inch disappearing guns and eight 12-inch mortars for FORT SHERMAN and FORT RANDOLPH on the Atlantic side of the canal. Both forts received a pair of 6-inch disappearing guns in addition to the other guns, even though the board had recommended all four of these guns for Fort Randolph. However, the board did not recommend any heavy artillery for FORT DELESSEPS. On the Pacific side, the board proposed four 14-inch and 6-inch disappearing guns for FORT GRANT. However, the weapons actually emplaced there included six 14-inch guns, the requested number of 6-inch guns, twelve 12-inch mortars, and a 16-inch gun. The board also recommended an inner line of defense consisting of 12-foot-high walls, bastions, infantry redoubts, and wire obstacles to protect the rear of these new positions. Major Eben Winslow was transferred from Hawaii to direct the work on the fortifications in Panama in the spring of 1911. Work on the land defenses began in December 1913 and lasted about a year, but the board's plan was only partially implemented. A concrete wall 12 feet high, 12 inches thick, and about one thousand yards long was built, but only to the rear of the batteries at Fort Sherman.

The Characteristics of Coastal Fortifications until 1920

Some characteristics of battery positions remained standard throughout their ten to thirty year lifetime in the twentieth century. According to Colonel Eben Winslow's *Notes on Seacoast Fortification Construction* published in 1920, DISAPPEARING CARRIAGES had a restricted traverse of about 170 degrees, while most barbette mounts usually had a greater traverse. On the other hand, the disappearing guns could be loaded faster since the recoil pushed them into the loading position. Adjustments made to these carriages in Panama allowed an increase of elevation of 15 to 20 degrees, giving the weapon a longer range. Special bolts that could withstand the great pressure exerted by the firing of the heavy guns held the mounts to the concrete platform.

To cut costs in these batteries, sand replaced CONCRETE as fill in certain areas such as between floors. A concrete blast apron in front of the parapet where the guns fired prevented the earth cover from being blown away during firing. According to the Board of Engineers report of 1903, either 45 feet of concrete or 90 feet of sand were required as protection against the heaviest naval guns based on tests of Rosendale cement. In 1899, the army switched from Rosendale cement to Portland cement, which had higher resistance. As a result of this switch, new standards were set for the 10-inch and 12-inch gun blocks in 1903. Fifteen feet of concrete and 45 feet of sand, which theoretically equaled 30 feet of Portland concrete, were sufficient in front of a magazine. In front of a gun, 15 feet of concrete and 40 feet of sand equaling 28.3 feet of concrete were recommended. The vertical cover for a magazine was 10 feet of concrete. For the Panama batteries, the standard protection was 20 feet of concrete or 45 feet of sand in front of a position, which was considered excessive. For overhead protection, 7 to 8 feet of concrete covered by a minimum of 10 feet of sand was required. As in the case of earthen forts of the last few centuries, sod was planted to prevent erosion. Because concrete tends to acquire a bright white coloring when it dries, tint or paint had to be added to the mixture to eliminate the glare. In some regions, certain rocks were added to the aggregate, in others, certain oils were used to yield a dark coloration. The interior was less problematic, especially after electric lighting replaced oil lamps. Gray oil-based paint was usually applied to the lower 3 to 4 feet and the upper part of the wall was left white (the unpainted concrete). A 3-inch band of black paint often marked the boundary between the gray and the white areas.

The ceilings in battery blocks were reinforced with I-beams and their foundations and walls included either steel bars or wire mesh (creating a position of reinforced concrete). SPEAKING TUBES insured communication within the block. Fire control communications were normally done by telephone because the speaking tubes were impractical. During firing operations, the tubes picked up every noise around them, from the rumbling of trucks or trolleys moving through the corridors to the activity on the loading platform above and all the attending noises of battle. One solution was to hang the tubes from the ceilings and keep them out of contact with the concrete. Powder and shells from the magazines were moved with hoists and trucks to an assembly point at the same level. After being assembled on ammunition preparation tables, the shells were transferred to shot carts and carried to the heavy guns. The process was less complex for rapid-fire guns. The MAGAZINES FOR SHELLS AND POWDER usually were located on the lower level of the battery block. Stairways led from one level to the other, but in some cases, ramps with gentle inclines were also included. The ceilings were at least 8 feet high in sections where ammunition trolleys circulated and 6 inches higher in batteries for 14-inch guns. The height requirement for battery blocks of 6-inch guns was slightly lower.

Another important component of a battery was a PLOTTING ROOM that sent firing data to the gunners. In early works, the plotting room was actually in the battery block. In later constructions, the plotting room was placed in an observation station often located in an outside frame structure, where the vibrations from the firing guns and the dampness of the concrete would not interfere with the accurate col-

Armored door to magazine of Battery 234 outside Fort Pickens. Photo courtesy of Lee Unterborn.

Observation and plotting rooms of Battery Worth at Fort Casey

lection of data. The newer towers built for vertical range finding were two-stories high and included sufficient space for a plotting room below the observation room that the earlier towers lacked. For the mortar battery, the plotting room was generally at the rear of the central traverse, between mortar pits. Small alcoves extended to the flanks that had shafts for "mechanical indicating apparatus which displayed the data through slots at the ends," according to Winslow. The men in the mortar pits could see this firing data information. A set of wooden slides with numbers and letters for displaying the firing data to the gunners was located in the mortar battery booth of reinforced concrete, at the rear of the mortar pit. After 1903, experiments with similar mortar battery booths led to the adoption of these slides. The practice of chalking the information on a blackboard and sliding it out to show the data was less effective because sometimes the recorder's data, hurriedly scribbled on the board, was barely legible or was washed away if it was raining. The plotting room transmitted the firing data to the mortar booth by telephone. In the plotting room, the range and elevation were determined from data sent from base and range-finding stations. The azimuth was also determined here, but if it was not, a gunner could resort to the telescope on the sighting platform of the gun. The guns could also be aimed without data from the plotting room, but the mortars relied totally on the information supplied by observers.

Underground Switchboard Room at Fort Casey's Battery Worth.

Other facilities associated with fire control included the BATTERY COMMANDER'S STATION, which usually was in or near the plotting room, in the battery, or at an observations station. SWITCHBOARD ROOMS linking the various sites were important and were placed either in older buildings or in a subterranean position. A small METEOROLOGICAL STATION located in a high position, sometimes an abandoned fire-control tower, provided important data such as temperature, wind direction, and barometric pressure, which allowed the plotting room and fire control to make adjustments.

In addition to the telephone, communications with other forts and ships were carried out with flags and even radios. Thus, SIGNAL STATIONS for flags and radio rooms were important features of the new forts. They normally included a telephone link to the battery command post. These stations usually were located in a three-level timber building with facilities for their small crews.

Like the modern European fortifications, American forts also included a POWER PLANT for powering the electrical equipment, the electric searchlights, which could not be manually operated, the range scales on the guns, the range-finding instruments, the hoists, the gun, and the order transmitting equipment. The battery power for the submarine mines could be replaced with a direct electrical link. The modern communications equipment also relied on wires. Therefore, ducts had to be installed to carry all these lines from the outside into the fort, and from the point of entry to various parts of the fort. Buried cables passed through concrete trenches lined with tiles or fiber ducts between blocks and other points that needed these links, and were accessed through manholes. A special room was reserved for a generator and transformers, but in some cases, the power plant was located outside the block.

LATRINES were either in the battery block or nearby. Officers had separate facilities. In some cases, the blocks included troop quarters. To reduce and eliminate condensation, the engineers finally resorted to using gratings on doors and windows so when the block was closed, air could continue to circulate through these openings. Heating became a necessary feature in many of these blocks, especially to control humidity. VENTILATION was required for many magazines and galleries though in many parts of the United States, air circulating through open doors and windows was sufficient. In Panama, where humidity is high, special ventilation equipment was necessary. Large fans forced air into the battery block, helping to maintain tolerable living conditions.

Many of the forts included MINING CASEMATES and MINE BUILDINGS. The mining casemates acted as operating rooms for the mine system. In the older forts, the rooms tended to be located in casemates. The cables controlling the mines ran into these rooms. The mining casemates included a room for the operating boxes and test instruments, a power plant with a generator, a storage battery room, and a room for the crew. Unlike other gun battery rooms, there were no steel beams until after 1903 because of the sensitive equipment. The walls were 20 feet thick on the side facing the enemy and 10 feet on the rear wall. The designs changed shortly before World War I, when an open casemate appeared. However after 1917, when the airplane entered the battlefield, designers returned to the enclosed mining casemate. If the distance from the casemate to the shore exceeded 200 feet, the cable conduits required manholes and a cable terminal in the form of a large manhole near the shoreline. Other requirements for mining were cable tanks for the submarine cables, which worked best if they were constantly submerged. The mines were kept in a special storehouse. In Panama, they were kept in a two-story concrete building, but there were several different designs for the store-

Fort Stevens. One of the few good remaining examples of a mine casemate. Photo courtesy of Dennis Blazey.

room. The mine planters were loaded with their deadly cargo at torpedo wharves, which included a derrick for lifting. Tramways led from the wharf to the cable tank, torpedo storehouses, and torpedo loading room, cables, and other items associated with mining. Observation stations connected to fire control and plotting rooms tracked vessels moving through the minefield.

After the batteries were completed, work usually began on the supporting facilities of a new fort. Coast Artillery companies often occupied the batteries of the fort while waiting for their permanent barracks and other facilities to be finished.

Modernization of the Coastal Defenses after 1920

World War I came and went without putting America's defenses to the test. Even though an American army went to Europe when the United States entered the war, the Germans presented no serious threat to the American coastline. The bold German war plans for an invasion of America formulated earlier in the century were too unrealistic, even under favorable conditions. Thus, the only big guns of the American arsenal to see action were the railway pieces sent to Europe.

As the military completed its new defenses in the first decade of the century, it seemed to ignore the ramifications of the Wright brother's successful flight on the dunes of North Carolina at Kitty Hawk in 1903. Ironically, even before that fateful date, a special board had planned to procure still non-existent airplanes for the army. By 1908, the Army Signal Corps purchased its first aircraft. It was not until early in the next decade that the airplane became a weapon of war. For the American coastal forts, this meant that the crews of disappearing guns or low profile guns en barbette operating behind the ramparts were now exposed to assault from the air. This did not present an immediate problem because no enemy aircraft or dirigibles had the range to reach the

German Invasion Plans for America

As early as 1897, the German admiralty had worked on war plans against the United States. Lieutenant (later Admiral) Eberhard von Mantey prepared these plans, which included attacks on Portland, Hampton Roads, and New York City. His plans also called for a decisive naval battle. The harbor fortifications, well known to the Germans, were taken into account. Vice Admiral August Thomsen proposed the occupation of Puerto Rico as an alternative to Norfolk, but others considered it too far away to serve as a base. One of the interesting aspects of the plan was that some ships were to be towed across the Atlantic to solve refueling problems.

Early in the twentieth century, the Germans again worked out war plans that included an attack on the United States and its possessions. The German admiralty concluded that a decisive naval encounter was necessary. They determined that an invasion of the islands of Culebra and Puerto Rico would allow the German navy to control the eastern approaches to the Panama Canal and thus draw the U.S. Navy into battle. Operations Plan III, prepared between 1903 and 1906, called for the German navy to escort an occupation force of 12,000 to 15,000 men to Ponce, Puerto Rico. The United States had not fortified Puerto Rico at that time, and the first installations in the Canal Zone, which would not be finished before 1910, could not have deterred a blockade of the canal. One of the prerequisites for the German plan was Great Britain's neutrality or even friendship. However, in 1906 the Germans determined that that was unlikely and scrapped their plans.

Source: *Politics of Frustration: The United States in German Naval Planning 1889-1941* by Holger Herwig.

American coast. However, by World War II, with the improvement of aircraft technology and the development of aircraft carriers, the situation became much more serious, especially the threat to some of the U.S. insular possessions. Antiaircraft protection generally consisted of machine guns and rapid-fire 3-inch guns mounted on a new type of carriage. However, the small number of weapons provided for the forts offered little protection. The antiaircraft battalions detached from Coast Artillery units proved more effective, but they were not designed specifically for the defense of forts.

In the early 1920s, the army continued perfecting its coastal forts. Improved mounts lengthened the range of old 12-inch guns and allowed the employment of new long-range 16-inch guns. A Board of Review headed by General Hugh L. Scott, the chief of staff, recommended these changes in November 1915. It also recommended the use of 16-inch mortars to penetrate the heavy deck armor then in use on warships. When this weapon, which could be considered a "super" mortar, was perfected, it was designated as a Model 1920 Howitzer. Fort Story and Cape Henry received the first of these weapons in 1922. Within a short time, production of the 16-inch howitzer and the 16-

inch guns stopped when the army received sixty naval 16-inch guns. Because of the Washington Naval Treaty of 1922 that had restrictions on battleships, the navy no longer needed these surplus weapons. When it was discovered that the 16-inch gun was capable of achieving the same high angle as the 16-inch howitzer, the "super" mortar was discontinued.

General Scott informed Congress "the supply of antiaircraft guns for the protection of existing defenses is an urgent necessity" and urged their procurement that year. The board also recommended one hundred and thirty-four 3-inch antiaircraft guns for the coastal defenses, seventeen for the Pacific islands, and eight for the Canal Zone.

Some work was done between 1916 and 1920, but in the 1920s, the coastal forts received limited improvements. One welcome addition were the diesel-powered mine planters, but there were still too few to serve more than a few harbors. Work done in the 1920s was modest but significant. Many of the naval 16-inch guns were installed. In 1924, a second battery of 12-inch guns on the new long-range barbette carriages, as recommended by the Review Board of 1915, was added to Portland's FORT LEVETTE on Cushing Island. Boston's harbor defenses received the same type of battery position at FORT RUCKMAN in Nahant. On Hog Island near Boston, a battery of two 16-inch guns on long-range barbette carriages was completed at FORT DUVALL in 1927. A second 12-inch gun battery recommended by the board was not built. New Bedford's FORT RODMAN was similarly reinforced with a 12-inch gun battery. In 1923, New York Harbor's eastern approach through Long Island Sound was strengthened with the addition of a battery with a single 16-inch gun on a disappearing carriage at FORT MICHIE on Great Gulf Island.

The board had recommended the installation of five more of these guns as well as "super" mortars. In 1924, the southern approaches to New York received a two-gun battery of 16-inch howitzers (the "super" mortar) mounted on a long-range barbette carriage at FORT TILDEN, though the board had wanted more at Rockaway Beach in the vicinity of Fort Tilden, considering the area of primary importance. The defenses of the Delaware River received all the items requested by the board: two 2-gun batteries of 12-inch guns mounted on long-range carriages. In 1922, at the entrance of the Chesapeake Bay positions were built for four 16-inch guns mounted on long-range howitzer carriages at the new post of FORT STORY. However, the wartime batteries of 6-inch and 5-inch guns had already been destroyed by the surf before 1920. The board had also requested four 6-inch guns and additional "super" mortars for Fort Story.

A battery of 12-inch guns was set up at FORT PICKENS, Pensacola. Other improvements recommended for the southern coast were also carried out. FORT TRAVIS at Galveston received two 12-inch guns on long-range barbette mounts in 1922 and a similar battery was added at FORT CROCKETT in 1924. On the Pacific coast, Los Angeles's FORT MACARTHUR, which had not been on the board's list, received a two-gun battery of 14-inch railway guns to reinforce its four single-gun batteries of 14-inch disappearing guns

14-inch gun on railway mount M1920
© TOMASZ IDZIKOWSKI

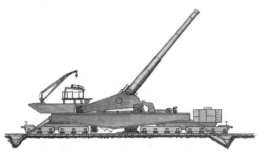

In World War I, the American Expeditionary Force in France used railway guns. After the war, these guns, first introduced in the American Civil War, became part of American defensive strategy. In the 1920s, 14-inch railway guns were sent to California and Panama. In Hawaii, an additional line of tracks was laid for the island's 8-inch railway guns.

The army's 14-inch guns consisted of the same railway gun tube used by the navy, but the railway mounting was distinctive. The weapon included a power rammer that did the work of a dozen men. Like the heavy coastal artillery, it was electrically operated. A steel boxcar carried the ammunition supply and a second boxcar contained the plotting board that served a two-gun battery. For best results, these pieces were deployed on curved sections of track so they could change their direction of fire. The weapon had a maximum range of 48,000 yards. Test firings had to be restricted in California because they damaged civilian property, shattering windowpanes and causing excessive vibrations.

built during the war. San Francisco's FORT BARRY received a two-gun battery of 12-inch guns on long-range barbette carriages in 1919. However, the additional batteries with two 16-inch guns, two 6-inch guns, and four "super" mortars recommended by the board did not materialize. A 12-inch mortar battery at FORT CANBY was built on the Columbia River instead of the 16-inch howitzers requested by the board. No other major additions took place between World War I and the 1930s. The board's request for 16-inch guns and other weapons for Puget Sound were ignored.

The situation was slightly better in the Hawaiian Islands. FORT KAMEHAMEHA received a battery of 12-inch guns on the long-range barbette carriages and FORT WEAVER had two-gun battery of 16-inch guns mounted on similar carriages. This was more firepower than the 1915 board had recommended. In the Panama Canal Zone, the army bolstered the defenses at the Atlantic entrance with the addition of two two-gun batteries of 12-inch guns on long-range barbette carriages at FORT SHERMAN and a two-gun railway battery of 14-inch guns at FORT RANDOLPH on Margarita Island. The growing threat presented by Japan led to major additions to the Pacific entrance: two two-gun batteries of 16-inch guns mounted on long-range barbette carriages were completed at FORT KOBBE in 1926 and a railway battery of two 14-inch guns were added to FORT GRANT in 1928. This was in line with the Review Board's requests, which had also included the expense of building railroad car mounts for 14-inch guns to convert those weapons into railway artillery. However, before many of the new batteries could be built on the American coast and the overseas territories, the U.S. government had to arrange for the purchase of the land needed, which sometimes caused considerable delays.

The Lean Years

After its reorganization of February 1924, the Coast Artillery Corps (CAC) numbered about twelve thousand men, far below its authorized strength. According to General F. W. Coe, chief of the Coast Artillery at the time, the situation was deplorable since the corps was at its lowest strength since its creation in 1901. In his annual report of September 1924, General Coe claimed that many of the nation's fortified harbors were almost without protection. After its creation in 1901, the CAC consisted only of companies that were occasionally grouped into larger formations on a temporary basis. The new orders redesignated the CAC companies as batteries, and created sixteen permanent regiments (numbered 1 thru 16) and a regiment of antiaircraft artillery (the 65th CA) for the defenses of Panama, and two Filipino CA regiments (91st and 92nd Philippine Scouts). In the United States, the regiments serving in harbor defenses included an HQ battery and seven to ten lettered batteries (three batteries to a battalion).

Early in the 1920s the U.S. government had returned to a policy of isolation. Congress and the president had no interest in maintaining national security through the strength of the armed forces or coastal fortifications, preferring to rely on geographic distances. Canada only needed to maintain the defenses of St. Johns, Halifax, and Vancouver Island, covering the only overseas gateways into the country. In exchange, it had the help of Great Britain, which used Esquimalt-Victoria as its main base for its Pacific fleet.

The American War Department developed a number of color-coded scenarios—the Rainbow Plans—for each potential enemy, including Canada and Great Britain, even though these two countries were not considered a serious threat. To the south, the military considered Latin America to be beyond the range of most great powers and no threat to the United States. Argentina, Brazil, and Chile (the ABC Powers) maintained one or two battleships each to retain their status as naval powers. Brazil also fortified Rio de Janeiro with modern coastal fortifications. Nonetheless, Americans foresaw no problem for the future and the professional politicians who became presidents, Warren Harding and C.alvin Coolidge, had little understanding of military affairs and national security, allowing America's strength to dwindle.

General F. W. Coe's pleas to maintain the coastal defenses that had already been completed fell on deaf ears. He was forced to put many of the forts under caretaker status. Whereas during the previous century inactive forts were left under the care of an ordnance sergeant, now they were assigned to a battery of coast artillery troops, as required by regulations dating from 1914 that strove to preserve military property for future use. The mechanical equipment, machinery, and complex weapons systems required routine inspection and maintenance. These detachments had to do everything from cleaning and oiling weapons and equipment, to painting buildings and cleaning out gutters, according to Mark Berhow, author of an article titled "Caretaker Status in the Coast Artillery."

In the 1920s, the Coast Artillery regiments were largely skeleton units assigned to the various Harbor Defenses (the HD acronym came into use after 1925). By the end of the decade, there were twenty-five HDs. Some of the old thirty-four coast defense areas, established in 1890, were maintained as Harbor Defense (HD) commands. Others were eliminated or combined with other areas to form a Harbor Defense command. Only ten HDs were active and the remaining fifteen were in caretaker status. In 1930, the active HDs included only Long Island Sound and the Chesapeake Bay on the East Coast. The defenses of New York, all of New England, and the South, except for Pensacola, including many of the newly armed forts of the 1920s, were placed on caretaker status. Even within the active commands, some of the forts went on caretaker status and others were only partially garrisoned. On the West Coast, only the HD of San Francisco and the HD of Puget Sound stayed active. The remaining six active commands were all overseas.

Reservists and National Guard units did their annual training at many of the forts under caretaker status. Only limited work took place on the fortifications west of Hawaii after 1922 because of the Washington Naval Treaty that restricted the United States from creating new defenses in that part of the Pacific. For most of the decade little happened to strengthen America's defenses as the public was reassured and blinded by its leadership and encouraged to believe that war was outlawed for good by the Kellogg-Briand Treaty of 1928. When the careless economic policies of the business oriented administrations led to the stock market crash of 1929, plunging the United States and other industrial nations into the depths of the Great Depression, the American armed forces were weaker than ever.

One of the improvements that took place between World Wars included the design of the PANAMA MOUNTS for the old 155mm GPF artillery bought from France and used late in the 1920s to supplement coast defenses. The mounts had a circular form for the gun's trails and a central pivot position for the gun. These prefabricated Panama Mounts were emplaced in the desired position. A similar version was used for even larger weapons, but was not prefabricated.

In 1931, Americans ignored the echoes of war from distant Manchuria. In 1933, Franklin Roosevelt's new administration could not bring immediate relief, and the armed forces and American defenses remained on the back burner. When Japan became an increasing threat and the rise of aggressive dictatorships began to jeopardize world peace, the American government finally turned its attention to its defenses. During the 1930s, improvements were made in the Philippines by skirting the Washington Naval

American Coastal Defenses in 1924

Note: Some Coast Artillery (CA) regiments were reassigned after this initial reorganization, but the following list gives a basic idea of where American defensive efforts were concentrated. Only eighteen harbor areas were retained and many of their forts were on caretaker status. Third System Forts italicized. HD or Harbor Defense Command was the title given after 1925 to the coastal regions. Active HD in bold type. AA=Antiaircraft. CA=Coast Artillery.

HD of Portland (Ft. Lyon on Cow Island, Ft. McKinley on Great Diamond Island, Ft. Levett on Cushing Island, *Ft. Prebble*, Ft. Williams): 8th CA (HQ at Ft. Prebble).

HD of Portsmouth (Ft. Foster on Gerrish Island, Ft. Constitution on Newcastle Island, Ft. Stark): one battery (caretaker duty) of 8th CA.

HD of Boston (Ft. Ruckman, Ft. Banks, Ft. Heath, Ft. Warren, Ft. Standish on Lovell's Island, Ft. Strong on Long Island, Ft. Andrews on Peddocks Island, Ft. Duvall on Hog Island, Ft. Revere): 9th CA (HQ at Ft. Banks).

HD of New Bedford (Ft. Rodman): one battery (caretaker duty)10th CA

HD of Narragansett Bay (*Ft. Adams*, Ft. Wetherill and Ft. Getty on Conanicut Island., Ft. Greble on Dutch Island, Ft. Kearny): 10th CA HQ at Ft. Adams).

HD of Long Island Sound (Ft. Mansfield, Ft. Wright on Fisher's Island, Ft. Michie on Great Gull Island, Ft. Terry on Plum Island, Ft. Tyler on Gardnier's Point Island): 11th CA.

HD of Eastern New York (Ft. Slocum on Davids Island, *Ft. Schuyler, Ft. Totten*): 62nd CA (AA).

HD of Southern New York (Ft. Tilden, *Ft. Hamilton, Ft. Wadsworth, Ft. Hancock*): 5th CA, HQ of 7th CA (at Ft. Hancock).

HD of Delaware (Ft. Mott, *Ft. Delaware* on Pea Patch Island, Ft. DuPont, Ft. Saulsbury): 3 batteries of the 7th CA.

HD of Baltimore (Ft. Howard, *Ft. Carroll*, Ft. Armistead, Ft. Smallwood).

HD of the Potomac (*Ft. Washington*, Ft. Hunt)

HD of Chesapeake Bay (*Ft. Monroe, Ft. Wool,* Ft. Story): 12th CA (HQ at Ft. Monroe), 42nd (Railway)CA, 61st (AA) CA–(12th CA de-activated in 1930).

HD of Cape Fear River (*Ft. Caswell*).

HD of Charleston (*Ft. Moultrie* on Sullivan's Island, Ft. Sumter): 2 batteries of 13th CA.

HD of Port Royal Sound (Ft. Fremont, Ft. Welles).

HD of Savannah (Ft. Screven).

HD of Jacksonville.

HD of Key West (*Ft. Taylor*): 2 batteries of 13th CA.

HD of Tampa Bay (Ft. Dade, Ft. DeSoto).

HD of Pensacola (*Ft. Pickens* on Santa Rosa Island, *Ft. McRee* on Perdido Key): HQ and 3 batteries of 13th CA.

HD of Mobile (*Ft. Morgan, Ft. Gaines*).

HD of the Mississippi (*Ft. Jackson, Ft. St. Philip*).

HD of Galveston (Ft. Travis, Ft. San Jacinto, Ft. Crockett): 3 batteries of 13th CA.

HD of San Diego (Ft. Emory, Ft. Rosecarns): 1 battery (caretaker duty) of 3rd CA.

HD of Los Angeles (Ft. MacArthur): HQ and 2 batteries of 3rd CA.

HD of San Francisco (Ft. Funston, Ft. Miley, Ft. Winfield Scott, Ft. Mason, Ft. McDowell on Angel Island, Ft. Baker, Ft. Barry): 2 batteries of 3rd CA, 6th CA, 63rd (AA)CA.

HD of the Columbia (Ft. Stevens, Ft. Columbia, Ft. Canby): 3 batteries of 3rd CA.

HD of Puget Sound (Ft. Ward, Ft. Whitman, Ft. Flagler, Ft. Casey, Ft. Worden): 14th CA (HQ at Ft. Worden).

<u>HD of U.S. Possessions:</u>

Hawaii: 55th CA, 64th (AA)CA.
    HD of Honolulu (Ft. Ruger, Ft. DeRussy, Ft. Armstrong): 16th CA.
    HD of Pearl Harbor (Ft. Kamehameha, Ft. Weaver): 15th CA, 41st (Railway) CA.
Panama: 65th (AA)CA.
    HD of Critobal (Ft. Randolph on Margarita Island, Ft. DeLesseps, Ft. Sherman): 1st CA, 2nd CA (2nd CA transferred to Ft. Monroe in 1932).
    HD of Balboa (Ft. Kobbe, Ft. Amador, Ft. Grant): 4th CA.
Philippines: 59th CA , 60th CA(AA), 91st (P.S) CA and 92nd (P.S.) CA.
    HD of Manila and Subic Bays (Ft. Mills on Corregidor Island, Ft. Frank on Carabao Island, Ft. Drum on El Fraile Island, Ft. Hughes on Caballo Island, Ft. Wint on Grande Island).

Treaty. Meanwhile, the army slowly began rebuilding and reorganizing. In 1937, the navy set in motion the construction of its first capital ships since the 1922 Washington Naval Treaty. During the 1930s, a major change to the War Plan Orange (war with Japan) left the Philippines isolated since the armed forces did not have sufficient ships or men to secure the islands. The new strategy drew the main line of American defense in the Pacific from Alaska to Panama through Hawaii. In the Philippines the commander of the harbor defense area used local funds to build the MALINTA TUNNEL maze on Corregidor for Fort Mills in the 1930s to avoid treaty restrictions. Otherwise, things went on as usual in the islands.

In Hawaii, the island of OAHU had an impressive array of defenses. Honolulu had FORT RUGER's two batteries with twelve 12-inch mortars, FORT DERUSSY with a battery of two 14-inch guns and another of two 6-inch guns, and FORT ARMSTRONG with a battery of two 3-inch guns. An additional battery of 8-inch rail guns was delivered in 1935 to Fort Ruger. At Pearl Harbor, FORT KAMEHAMEHA had two batteries of two 12-inch guns and FORT WEAVER had one battery of eight 12-inch guns. In 1924, a battery of two 16-inch howitzers was added at Fort Weaver. In the mid-1930s, a battery of two 16-inch guns on long-range carriages was built at FORT BARRETTE.

One of the more impressive features on Oahu was the LEAHI FIRE CONTROL SITE on the 761-feet-high Leahi Peak at Diamond Head. This four-level position, cut into the very peak, was completed in January 1911. Each level of this unique site consisted of four large concrete-lined chambers, with ceilings reinforced with I-beams. The observation openings were protected with steel shutters. Four separate plotting stations supplied fire directions to Fort DeRussy and Fort Ruger. The commander's post was on the top level with Station 1, which directed the 12-inch mortars of Fort Ruger. Level three housed Station 2, also assigned to Fort Ruger. Station 3 was located on level two and

Leahi fire control station
© TOMASZ IDZIKOWSKI

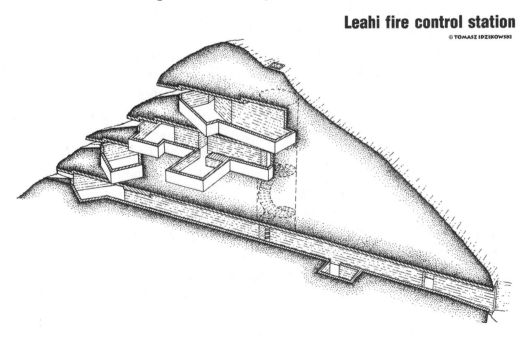

served the 14-inch guns and a 6-inch gun battery at Fort DeRussy. Station 4 was housed on level one and served Fort DeRussy as well. The control station at Leahi Peak took on additional functions in the late 1930s as these forts received additional armament. A trail in the crater led to a steep set of stairs that linked to a 225-foot-long tunnel that ran through one of the crater's interior ridges and led to the Leahi Peak site. A spiral staircase gave access to each level of the complex. Fort Ruger was on the north side of the crater with its batteries nearby. In 1916, BATTERY HULINGS was excavated into the northeast side of the crater lip for landward defense. It was an interesting position consisting of two 4.7-inch guns in casemates, but it did not remain long in service.

Preparing for War

The army and navy began to modernize after the mid-1930s, as the world situation worsened. However, the number of personnel in the armed forces was still insufficient and equipment was lacking. The Coast Artillery Corps (CAC), considered one of the more prestigious branches of the army, slowly received funds and began making improvements. Some of the skeleton commands of the HD areas began to fill out. Most recruits received on-the-job training in all the branches of the army. It was a common practice to take new enlistees, give them a uniform, a brief indoctrination, send them off to their duty assignment such as the Philippines, and let them learn the necessary skills on location.

The army included the Army Air Corps, which needed a number of airbases throughout the country and the territories to be effective. These airbases became part of the American defensive system. The Army Air Corps, with its new B-17 bombers at the end of the decade, shared the role of coastal defense with the Coast Artillery Corps. However, the bombers turned out not to be highly successful in coast defense during the war. The army was to defend the coast while the navy was to act as an offensive force. Both the army and navy shared the responsibility for mining. The CAC was to mine channels with electrically controlled buoyant mines directed from mine casemates and the navy minelayers were to place contact mines in the outer areas.

Strategy was another problem the military had to work out. A line from Alaska to Hawaii to Panama formed the primary defense boundary on the Pacific Coast, leaving Guam, the Philippines, and the island possessions beyond on their own. Shortly before World War II, Marine Defense Battalions arrived at several key islands to prepare defensive positions; the most notable, Wake Island, would eventually come under direct assault.

While the British and Germans confronted each other in 1940, the Americans took over certain British bases in the West Indies where they established positions to defend the Western Hemisphere from Axis aggression. Plans for airbases on these islands and later for coast artillery positions were drawn up. Additional bases were established in British Guiana and Newfoundland, all with the purpose of interdicting American waters to enemy warships and submarines. In 1940, Congress authorized a draft, allowing the American army to expand rapidly. In addition, a partial call-up of National Guard units permitted the military to prepare for an adequate defense. Before the United States even joined the war, German U-boats were occasionally spotted by Army Air Corps aircraft on patrol off the coast. During the previous war, a few U-boats had operated off the American coast but had inflicted little damage.

The American defenses rapidly improved with the addition of more efficient communications systems and radar. New radar units, both mobile and fixed, were installed in Panama and Oahu in the fall of 1941, but their reliability was not sufficiently tested. The United States turned to Canada for support in regard to radar because it had the already tested British system. In the United States, radar was still in its infancy in 1941, but soon proved decisive in detecting targets and directing gunfire, especially for anti-aircraft (AA) units, which played a critical role in defense. Radar was much more effective than the sound locators (giant listening horns) when used to calculate the range and distance of enemy aircraft.

During the 1930s, some forts were finally abandoned, in some cases resulting in the deactivation of the HD to which they belonged. These positions included Fort Baldwin in the HD of the Kennebec, Fort Schuyler in the HD of Eastern New York, all four forts in the HD of Baltimore, both forts in the HD of the Potomac, old Fort Caswell in the HD of Cape Fear River, Fort Screen in the HD of Savannah, both forts of the HD of Tampa Bay, Fort McRae in the HD of Pensacola, both of the old 3rd System forts in the HD of Mobile, the two old forts of the HD of the Mississippi, and Fort Ward in the HD of Puget Sound. Other forts, once relatively well-armed, were reduced in strength. They included Fort Mansfield in the HD of Long Island Sound that had no artillery, Fort Totten in the HD of Eastern New York reduced to only a 3-inch. At Fort Mott in the HD of the Delaware the remaining artillery (three 10-inch guns) was sent to Canada in 1942, and the three 12-inch guns of Fort Delaware were sent to Puerto Rico. Fort Dupont's remaining heavy artillery (12-inch mortars) went out of service in 1942.

World War II Comes to America

At the time of the attack on Pearl Harbor on December 7, 1941, the armed forces of the United States had been growing in strength for well over a year, but were still caught off balance. The Japanese attack on Hawaii crippled the Pacific Fleet. However, the Japanese forces did not have the capability to invade Oahu and had to reduce other American possessions in the Pacific first. Guam, which was virtually undefended, fell quickly. The Philippines were not able to hold out for more than a few months. American strategy there had been to withdraw to the Bataan Peninsula, but despite pre-war planning, this site was not prepared for defense. The forts at the entrance to Manila Bay, including Corregidor, were the key to the American strategy, but their usefulness was limited.

As a result of the attack on Pearl Harbor, America quickly mobilized from coast to coast and all coast defense positions went on full alert. To bolster the coastal defenses the army built a number of Panama Mounts for 155-mm guns. When Germany went to war with the United States right after the American declaration of war on Japan, the American forces on the East Coast, which had been engaged in neutrality patrols for over a year, were ready.

Although Japanese submarines ringed Oahu, they had little success and withdrew on December 17, 1941. In December nine Japanese submarines also lurked off the shores of the West Coast. At the time, California's air defenses consisted of searchlights, antiaircraft guns, and sixteen modern aircraft. The few military units available rushed to the West Coast to repel a possible Japanese invasion and local commanders hastily devised defensive plans. Troops strung barbed wire along the beaches and all units went on full alert. However, the threat of an invasion was greatly overblown because it was beyond the capabilities of the Japanese forces.

Nevertheless, the West Coast did witness some military action. On December 24, the first ship went down within sight of the California coast after a torpedo attack and shelling from a Japanese submarine. The next day a single 75mm gun from a field artillery battalion at Redondo Beach fired on a Japanese submarine in the first encounter between the American defenders in the continental United States and an enemy ship. On February 13, 1942, the Japanese submarine *I-17* dropped a few rounds on Goleta, California. Ten days later, early in the evening, the same submarine fired sixteen more rounds at an oil refinery at Ellwood (near Santa Barbara), California. The total damage inflicted consisted of minor damage to oil pumps and rigging and a pier.

Blackout restrictions became the norm, the windows of many factories and even office buildings were painted black, and shiny surfaces toned down. More than once air-raid sirens warned of an impending enemy air attack that never materialized. One of the most memorable false alerts was probably the one that happened February 24–25. On the night of February 24, the alert was sounded on the California coast, but when no threat materialized, the tension eased. Early the next morning, one of the radar units detected an incoming target at about 120 miles west of Los Angeles. Shortly after 2:00 A.M., the antiaircraft units were put on full alert and soon the blackout signal was given. The blip on the radar screens had disappeared, but ground observers imagined they saw enemy aircraft in the early morning darkness. Soon the Los Angeles area was lit up with antiaircraft fire. The "battle" against the invisible enemy raged for about three hours until the light of dawn revealed that there were no enemy aircraft. Although rumors persisted, this incident, sometimes called the Great Los Angeles Air Raid, revealed the inadequacy of the warning system and the means of detecting and firing at targets.

On the night of June 20, 1942, the Japanese submarine *I-26* surfaced and fired about thirty rounds against the lighthouse at Point Stefan on the west coast of Vancouver

Island, inflicting no damage. However, Canadian/British defenses did not respond because the main British base was at Victoria on Vancouver Island where the only modern fortification was the VICTORIA-ESQUIMALT FORTRESS, which included FORT RODD HILL, built in 1893. Between 1936 and 1939, the Canadians had moved two 9.2-inch guns, standard British heavy coast artillery, from Signal Hill to Albert Head, several miles from Fort Rodd Hill. The command post for the fortress was located a few miles behind Albert Head at Triangle Mountain. In 1939, observation and 6-inch gun positions were built at Mary's Hill, further to the northwest, to replace the old 6-inch batteries at Fort Rodd Hill. By the spring of 1941, a third 6-inch gun was installed at Mary's Hill. The plotting room for the fortress was located in an underground facility adjacent to the Lower Battery of Fort Rodd Hill. In the spring of 1941, two 8-inch railway guns, on loan from the U.S. Army, were mounted at Christopher Point. They had sufficient range to cover the entrance to the Juan de Fuca Strait. Before the attack on Pearl Harbor, American and Canadian commanders had established a radio link to coordinate the defense of the straits. Despite all these preparations, on the day of the lighthouse attack a British ship was torpedoed at the entrance to the straits while the Canadians stood impotently by.

A day after it shelled Point Estevan, *I-27* surfaced off the mouth of the Columbia River under cover of darkness and fired on FORT STEVENS, the only continental coast defense installation in the United States to actually engage enemy naval forces in the twentieth century. The Fort Stevens garrison was taken by surprise. Armed with two batteries of 10-inch guns and a battery of 6-inch guns on disappearing carriages, and a battery of 12-inch mortars, the fort should have easily matched the 5.5-inch gun of the submarine. According to Marshall Hanft, author of *The Cape Forts*, the officer on duty, Jack Wood, recalled racing to the command station and sighting the muzzle flashes after the first round landed about three hundred yards from the battery. However, he quickly concluded that the target was beyond the range of his guns. The maximum range of the submarine's 5.5-inch deck gun was about 17,500 yards or about 1,000 yards greater than the fort's old 10-inch guns. The submarine fired less than a dozen rounds, scoring no hits. The startled gun crews, who quickly moved to their positions, were unable to fire a single riposte since the submarine was beyond their range.

War also came close to the East Coast of the United States in early 1942, as Americans watched ships burning off the coast after U-boat attacks. Americans on the East Coast were seized by the same type of panic that reigned on the West Coast, even though they did not expect an invasion. Since blackout security had not been instituted when the German marauders showed up, the bright lights silhouetted buildings in the coastal areas in the darkness of night, offering easy targets. As on the Pacific coast, few aircraft were available for patroling, but the navy later began sending out blimps for longer patrols. After sinking twenty-five ships during the first two weeks of their campaign, the German submarines journeyed south with the remainder of their torpedoes. The oil

America's Icebox

Purchased from Russia in 1867, Alaska completed America's mission of "Manifest Destiny" of expansion on the continent. Besides a gold rush late in the century, not much happened in the territory until the twentieth century. Most activity centered on the coastal fringes where small forts were built and abandoned. The only major outpost remaining in Alaska after 1923 was FORT WILLIAM SEWARD (also known as CHILKOOT BARRACKS), located at Haines. This fort established in 1898, was named after Seward in 1904 and was renamed Chilkoot Barracks in 1922. It remained in service until June 1943.

During a hearing in 1935, Billy Mitchell told Congress "Alaska is the keystone to the Pacific arch" from which the United States could launch air raids on Japan or vice versa. He also warned that the Japanese would try to take Alaska to strike at the United States. However, it was not until 1939 that the navy made plans to build air stations in Alaska. The Alaska Defense Force, created in July 1940, numbering fewer than one thousand men of the 4th Infantry, moved into Chilkoot Barracks. During that first year, the army began building its first airfields in Alaska. At the same time, the navy began the construction of air and submarine bases at Sitka, Kodiak Island, and Dutch Harbor. However, work did not progress as planned because the army and navy squabbled over how to conduct operations in 1940. Since the army troops assigned to the defense of Dutch Harbor had no place to stay, the army began building FORT MEARS nearby in January 1941. Between 1940 and 1941, FORT RICHARDSON, located on the site of an old 1919 post at Anchorage, became the main army base. By December 7, 1941, over 22,000 soldiers were stationed in Alaska. They took the same precautions as on the West Coast for fear of a Japanese attack. Alaska soon became a base for ferrying aircraft to the U.S.S.R. as part of Lend-Lease after the German invasion of Russia in mid-1941.

seeping from the sunken tankers, their main targets, continued to wash up on American beaches for months. Another seventeen ships were sunk in the Caribbean from Trinidad to the American coastline during the month of February as the U.S. Navy stood impotently by. The new bases on Trinidad, St. Lucia, Jamaica, and Bermuda were still largely under construction. In late February, the U-boats moved back up the American coast, between Florida and the Carolinas, sinking more ships. They even intercepted a convoy out of Halifax further north.

By the end of February, Admiral King, who was responsible for the naval forces defending the Atlantic coast, was forced to call back more destroyers and smaller craft to patrol American waters. The United States finally decided to institute a convoy system for ships sailing in American coastal waters before the situation deteriorated any further. In April, the Germans sent eighteen more U-boats into American waters off the coast of Florida and nine large Type IX U-boats into the Caribbean. By May, the Milch Cow, a new type of German submarine, appeared off the coast of Bermuda. This vessel, designed as a tanker, could refuel over a dozen U-boats, extending their patrol time by several weeks. It also carried a few torpedoes on its deck to resupply at least one U-boat.

Before the end of August 1942, dozens of merchant vessels were lost in American waters off the coast of Panama, the Gulf of Mexico, the coast of Venezuela, in the Caribbean, the East Coast of the United States and Canada, and even in the mouth of the St. Lawrence River. American air, sea, and land defenses appeared woefully inadequate. The coast artillery was unable to deal with submerged submarines and the navy and air resources were stretched thin during the first few months of the war. Within a little over six months, the U-boat offensive in American waters was brought to an end, but not before 397 Allied ships had been sunk for the loss of seven U-boats.

During the summer of 1942, the American forces braced themselves for possible enemy retaliation for the Doolittle air assault on Japan in April 1942. Before the war, army and navy planners, had speculated that the Japanese, masked by a weather front in the North Pacific, could move their aircraft carriers off the West Coast for a surprise attack. When the long-awaited Japanese invasion force finally materialized, it did not appear off the West Coast, but in Alaskan waters. Sixteen aircraft from one of two aircraft carriers struck at Dutch Harbor, killing twenty-five soldiers at FORT MEARS on June 3, 1942. But when Admiral Yamamoto's main battle fleet was defeated at Midway, the Japanese called off the planned invasion of Dutch Harbor and Adak. The Japanese commander of the Aleutian invasion force decided instead to land his troops at Attu and Kiska, further to the west. The Japanese landed on June 7 and captured the 12-sailor garrison of a weather station. Except for the small native population, there were no American troops on Attu. The invasion of American territory did not pay big dividends for the enemy.

America's "Atlantic Wall"

Between 1940 and 1944, the United States erected the American equivalent of Hitler's Atlantic Wall along its eastern seaboard, although the American coastal defenses were never given an official name. The two systems of fortifications are roughly contemporary and built along similar principles. Until the end of 1942, the Germans strove to heavily fortify the ports in the occupied territories while the Americans also defended their most important harbors. The main difference was the Germans extended their coverage to intermediate areas and planted vast minefields after 1942, while the Americans never had to. The Americans also extended their defensive line along the Pacific coast. The unfounded fear of a Japanese invasion spurred Americans to build defenses, albeit weak ones, on every likely beach along the Pacific coast.

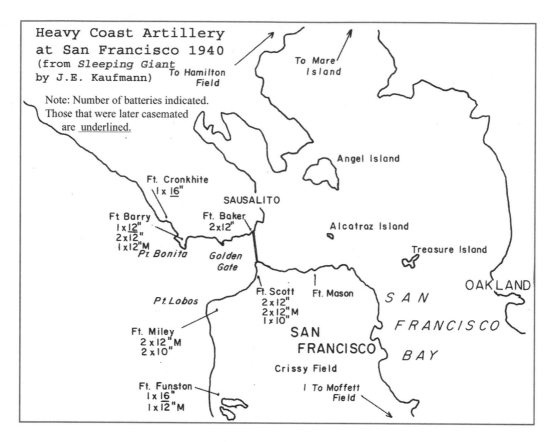

Heavy Coast Artillery
at San Francisco 1940
(from *Sleeping Giant*
by J.E. Kaufmann)   To Hamilton
                        Field

Note: Number of batteries indicated.
Those that were later casemated
    are <u>underlined</u>.

To Mare
Island

Angel Island

Ft. Cronkhite
1 x <u>16</u>"

SAUSALITO

Ft Barry   Ft. Baker
1 x <u>12</u>"   2 x 12"
2 x 12"M
1 x 12"M
Pt. Bonita   Golden
                Gate

Alcatraz Island

Treasure Island

OAKLAND

Ft. Scott   Ft. Mason   S A N
2 x 12"
2 x 12"M
1 x 10"   F R A N C I S C O

Pt. Lobos

SAN
FRANCISCO   B A Y

Ft. Miley
2 x 12"M
2 x 10"

Crissy Field

Ft. Funston   1 To Moffett
1 x <u>16</u>"   Field
1 x <u>12</u>"M

The centerpiece of the proposals of the Harbor Defense Board (established in 1931) was to casemate the naval 16-inch guns the army had been given. Plans also included preparing a number of batteries of 8-inch and 6-inch guns. In 1936, when appropriations had been made, the army engineers went to work on a prototype casemate for a 16-inch gun at FORT FUNSTON in the HD OF SAN FRANCISCO. According to Brian Chin, author of *Artillery of the Golden Gate*, the guns were test-fired after being mounted to help settle the foundations into the sandy terrain before the actual construction of the casemates began. The battery's two casemates stood about 600 feet apart and were linked by a gallery that housed centrally located magazines, a power plant, workshops, a plotting room, and other facilities. The entire complex was covered with earth, creating a man-made ridge. Just below this earthen cover, between the concrete structure and more earthen protection, was a 2-foot-thick concrete burster layer, a feature found on most subterranean concrete European forts since the turn of the century. In February 1939, with its camouflage in place, BATTERY DAVIS became the first modern American gun casemate of reinforced concrete to be completed.

A second prototype 16-inch-gun battery was also built in the HD of San Francisco. It was located on the other side of the Golden Gate at FORT CRONKHITE in the Marin headlands. According to Chin, this battery tunneled into the terrain so that the engineers had to build the casemates first and then bring in the guns. Thus, there was no test firing to

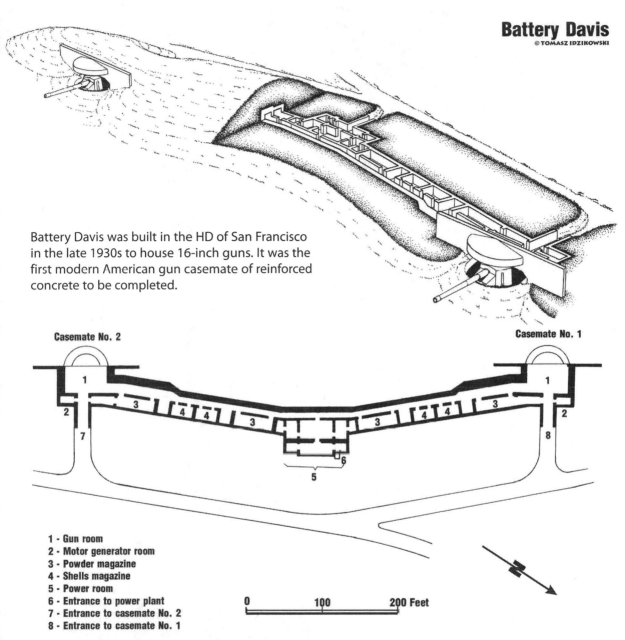

Battery Davis
© TOMASZ IDZIKOWSKI

Battery Davis was built in the HD of San Francisco in the late 1930s to house 16-inch guns. It was the first modern American gun casemate of reinforced concrete to be completed.

Casemate No. 2   Casemate No. 1

1 - Gun room
2 - Motor generator room
3 - Powder magazine
4 - Shells magazine
5 - Power room
6 - Entrance to power plant
7 - Entrance to casemate No. 2
8 - Entrance to casemate No. 1

0   100   200 Feet

settle the foundation of the gun, but the ground was much firmer than at the first battery site. Begun several months later than Battery Davis, the casemates of BATTERY TOWNSLEY were also finished a little later. In July 1939, the guns were hauled in through the rear of the casemates and mounted. So by September 1939, two modern long-range batteries protected the entrance to San Francisco Bay, yet these weapons were not test fired in their new position until a year later. Battery Townsley was the first to fire its guns on July 1, 1940. First Lieutenant Arthur Kramer, in charge of the firing, evacuated the battery because this was a first-time event. The test consisted of firing five rounds electrically, to verify their maximum range and observe the effects on the casemates.

16-inch gun battery

© TOMASZ IDZIKOWSKI

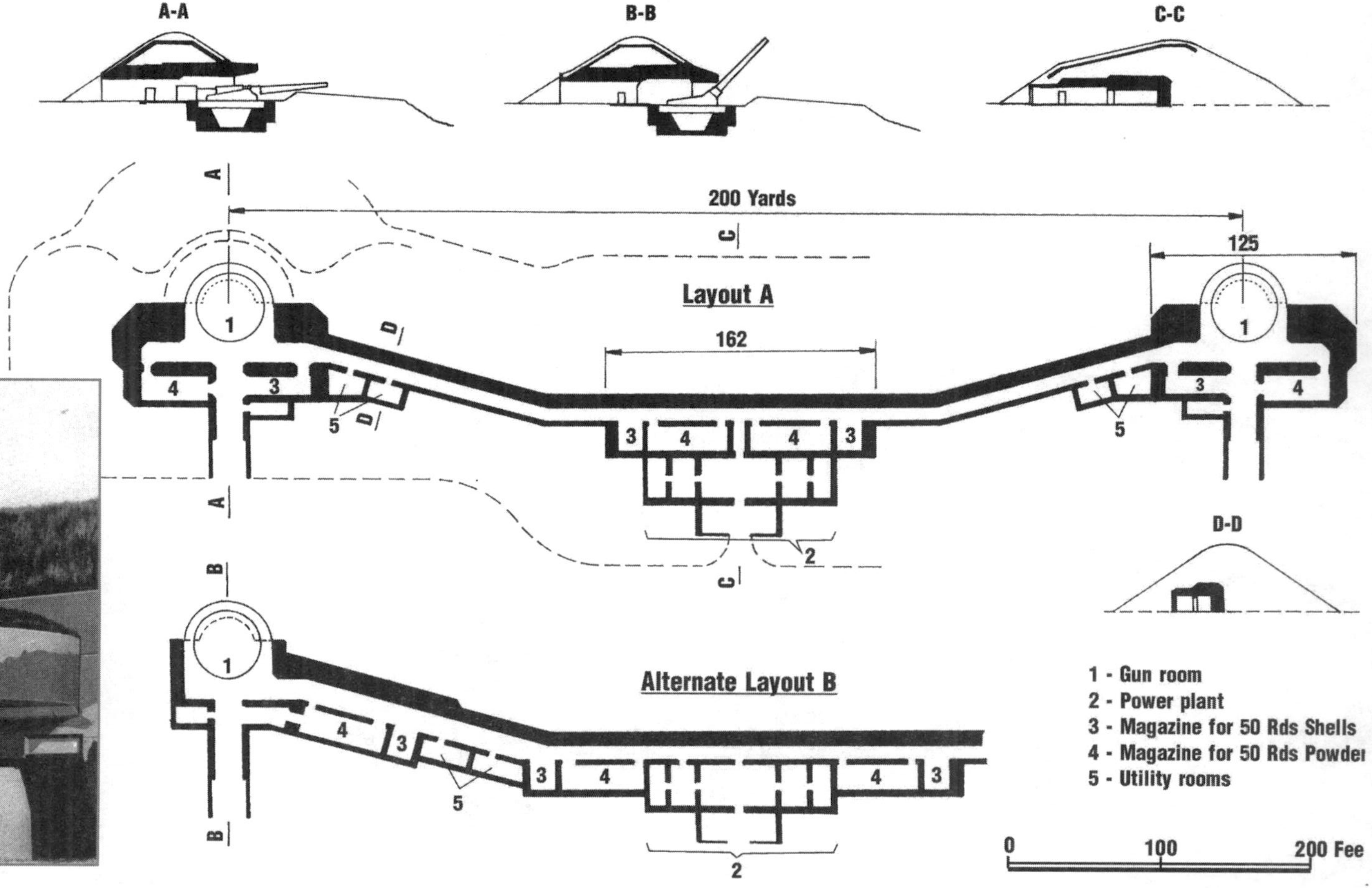

A-A

B-B

C-C

D-D

200 Yards

125

162

Layout A

Alternate Layout B

A

A

B

B

1 - Gun room
2 - Power plant
3 - Magazine for 50 Rds Shells
4 - Magazine for 50 Rds Powder
5 - Utility rooms

0   100   200 Feet

This drawing is based on: Study for Emplacement of Two 16-inch Guns on Barabette Carriage 1919M1 with Overhead Cover prepared March 15, 1937 by Corps of Engineer

16-inch gun in casemate.

Battery Townsley
© TOMASZ IDZIKOWSKI

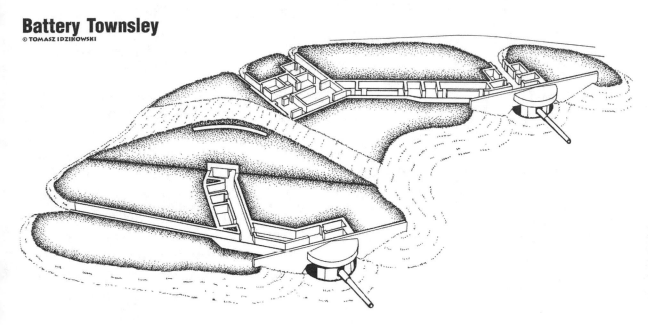

The exercise was an unqualified success. After Battery Davis tested its guns that autumn, preparations went ahead to build more.

The designs of the 16-inch-gun casemates were relatively standard but came in several variations. Battery Davis was built according to one of two plans drawn in 1937 by the Corps of Engineers. Its magazines and power plant were concentrated in the central area instead of being strung out along the central corridor. A second design, which was favored for 16-inch-gun batteries, placed the facilities next to the gun positions. Battery Townsley was probably one of the most unique of these casemates because it was tunneled into the terrain and its corridors and gun casemates did not conform at all to the standard plan. Naturally, the terrain did not allow all battery positions to fit those standard plans. In most cases, they served only as a guideline and the final layout of a casemate or battery was determined by topography. For instance, at BATTERY BUNKER in the HD OF LOS ANGELES, the No.1 Gun Position did not face in the same direction as the No.2 Gun Position. The No.2 Gun Position was at a standard 90-degree angle from the main gallery and faced almost southwest. The No.1 Gun Position, on the other hand, had any additional thirty-five degree (approx.) divergence from the alignment with the other casemate and pointed more to the west.

An important feature of the casemates was the M1-1919 BARBETTE CARRIAGE on an electrically rotating platform over a well-like position. Most of the gun barrels protruded beyond the overhead canopy in order to allow the weapon to elevate to 46 degrees to obtain its maximum range. The front concrete gallery wall linking casemates in older plans was 8 feet thick. According to the early plans, the frontal concrete casemate wall on either side of the gun positions was supposed to be about 25 feet thick. However, it is unlikely that they actually were that thick. After all, the thickest walls of

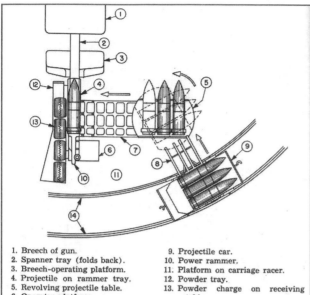

1. Breech of gun.
2. Spanner tray (folds back).
3. Breech-operating platform.
4. Projectile on rammer tray.
5. Revolving projectile table.
6. Operator platform.
7. Parking table, projectiles.
8. Lock bars (side rails of car).
9. Projectile car.
10. Power rammer.
11. Platform on carriage racer.
12. Powder tray.
13. Powder charge on receiving table.
14. Circular track about gun platform.

Figure 92. Loading mechanism, 16-inch gun barbette carriage M1919, open emplacement.

WWII fortifications in Europe seldom reached 12 feet thick.

Two 6-foot wing walls projected out on each side of the opening of the 16-inch gun casemates. According to the early plans, the gun room was protected by a concrete roof about 8 feet thick, a 10 to 18 foot layer of earth, and a 2-foot concrete burster layer. Some plans show about 15 feet of overhead concrete. In *Military Annals of Nahant*, Gerald Butler gives the following dimensions for the 16-inch-gun BATTERY GARDNER: exterior walls of 4 to 10 feet thick and a roof slab of 8 to 12 feet thick covered by sand and above that an irregularly configured 2 to 3 foot thick burster slab. He also mentions that the average ceiling height was 8.5 feet and 10.65 feet in the power plant. The sand or earth covering, which included a burster layer, formed a man-made hill covering the entire position. The batteries built during the war were initially classified by three-digit numbers in the 100s, but some were later given names.

In 1937, the army also received sufficient funds for the construction of an 8-inch-gun battery that was to include wrap-around gun shields. As a result, BATTERY STRONG was built in the HD OF SAN DIEGO, but its cannons were never equipped with gun shields. Although construction began in 1937, Battery Strong did not become operational until 1942. Built between 1939 and 1940, BATTERY REILLY at FORT CHURCH in the HD OF NARRAGANSETT BAY was turned over to the CAC in 1942. It was the only 8-inch gun battery in casemates. The few 8-inch-gun batteries, including some built in tunnels on Oahu, were classified as Series 400 casemates.

Plans were also drawn up for two-gun 6-inch-gun batteries to serve as secondary batteries. Most of these guns were old and some had been used with disappearing mounts. They received a wrap-around gun shield made of cast steel about 2-inches thick. A central traverse between the guns contained the magazines and other facilities in concrete structures under earth cover. The prototype for these batteries, BATTERY WORCESTER, originally designed as #224, was built at FORT STORY in 1941 and completed in 1942. More of these positions were built in the United States and the territories. Most were classified as Series 200, but some had a Series 300 classification.

In May 1940, General Joseph A. Greene, the chief of Coast Artillery, a prominent member of the Harbor Defense Board, complained that "With but few exceptions our seacoast batteries are outmoded and today are woefully inadequate. Nearly every battery is outranged by guns aboard ship of the same caliber. More alarming than this is the fact that every battery on the Atlantic Coast, and all but two of the batteries on the Pacific Coast, have no overhead cover so are open to attack from the air."

In 1940, the Harbor Defense Board included the chiefs of the Coast Artillery, Engineers, Ordnance, Artillery, Signal Corps, Chemical Warfare Service (CWS), and Air Corps. Each of these men had special areas of concern. The Coast Artillery, which needed batteries that could defend the HD, worked with the Artillery to select the proper weapons and equipment. The Engineers had to prepare acceptable designs and carry out the construction. Ordnance was responsible for much of the equipment and had taken over the responsibility of the operation of power plants from the engineers. The Signal Corps was responsible for communications and later radar equipment. The CWS had to insure that the positions were gas-proof. Finally, the Air Corps took part in the coordination of the defenses.

The Harbor Defense Board submitted its report on July 27, 1940, to the chief of Coast Artillery, recommending the creation of twenty-seven additional casemated batteries for 16-inch guns to modernize American coast defenses. It also requested fifty new 6-inch-gun batteries, even though the prototype was not built until the following year. Initially, the board favored 6-inch guns in turrets, but later settled for wrap-around shields. The 1940 Program was set in motion in September with the approval of the secretary of war, after Congress appropriated the necessary funds. Although the army built the casemated batteries, the chief of the Coast Artillery did not receive the antiaircraft guns he needed to protect his vulnerable batteries—the antiaircraft guns had higher priority assignments.

Local boards were formed in each of the eighteen Harbor Defense (HD) commands in the United States. These local boards selected the exact locations for the new batteries and made recommendations that, in many cases, favored an increase in the number of batteries. In some instances, the local board and the Harbor Defense Board did not reach an agreement until the attack on Pearl Harbor. But as the United States mobilized for war, a massive fortification construction effort was set in motion, especially on the East Coast.

In 1940, the Harbor Defense Board selected twelve HDs for batteries of long-range 16-inch guns. The board wanted some form of partial air cover for the twenty-three existing batteries mounting 8-inch and larger guns. At this time, there were also sixty-three secondary batteries of 6-inch and 3-inch guns still in service. The Harbor Defense Board believed that once the seventy-seven new batteries were completed, they could abandon the 128 coastal batteries that were obsolete. The ultimate goal was to reduce the number of coast artillery troops manning the defenses with the construction of new and more efficient batteries. Cost estimates continued to grow in 1940 until $60 million became $82 million, but the army's argument was simple, the entire coastal fortification system still would cost less than a single new battleship.

By June 1941, as work went ahead only on a few primary batteries and a prototype of the 6-inch battery, the War Department decided that work should be restricted to the primary and secondary batteries that could be completed by June 30, 1944. In November, the War Department officially deferred the construction on fourteen of the thirty-seven planned batteries and shifted the main effort overseas for the construction of twenty new 6-inch gun batteries.

In October 1941, the secretary of war ordered the creation of HARBOR ENTRANCE COMMAND POSTS (HECP) in seventeen harbors, which became the most important element in the command structure at each major harbor. A joint army and navy command was to coordinate operations. The president ordered HECP to initiate wartime operations in December 1941. Each HECP had an army and navy officer on duty at all times. This was necessary because the army operated the coast artillery positions and the navy operated the barrier nets and was responsible for controling all shipping going in and out. All vessels entering the defense zone of an HECP were restricted to doing so during daylight and good visibility.

The HECP usually occupied a concrete position at a key location. In some cases, like at FORT TAYLOR in Key West, the HECP was located with the army's Harbor Defense Command Post (HDCP). In the HD OF CHARLESTON, subterranean rooms were specially built in 1943 whereas at FORT MOULTRIE the HECP was housed in an older concrete structure in a corner of the old fort. In the HD OF SAN FRANCISCO, the HECP occupied the old underground facilities of a dynamite gun emplacement at FORT SCOTT with concrete observation positions on the fort's parapet. When older facilities were used, they often had to be renovated and gas-proofed. In the HD OF BOSTON HARBOR, the HECP was located in a concrete structure at FORT DAWES. In the HD OF NARRAGANSETT, the HECP was set up in a few frame structures at Jamestown, Rhode Island. In 1942, FORT BURNSIDE was established at this site and in July 1943, a two-level reinforced concrete bunker with twenty-four rooms replaced the old HECP's structures. At the HD OF SAN DIEGO, the HECP was at FORT ROSECRANS. It was located in a two-level concrete position. This HECP had a tunnel that formed an incline downward to the actual command post, which was largely underground with its own power supply, communications room, and operations room. Some other HECPs had these features on the main observation structure, which was usually larger than the one at San Diego. Usually this observation section was two levels, the smaller upper level with the signal equipment that naval personnel operated.

In New York Harbor, the situation was complex. The HECP located at FORT WADSWORTH did not have facilities large enough to control and monitor traffic. Therefore, two Advance HECPs (also identified as HARBOR ENTRANCE OUTPOST—HEOP) were set up at FORT HANCOCK (Advance HECP #1), and at FORT TILDEN (Advance HECP

An HECP atop the central magazine of the 12-inch mortar battery, Battery Worth at Fort Pickens, Florida.

#2). Advance HECP #2 was located in a gas-proof casemate with an air lock. It included two large rooms for operations, latrines, radio room, and a boiler room. These Advance HECP positions were smaller than the main HECP and included the same SCR-582 radar found at most HECPs.

Since most of these two-level structures tended to stand out, they were often camouflaged. For instance, the HECP at FORT BURNSIDE was disguised as a farmhouse. At FORT MOULTRIE it was painted in camouflage colors. In other places the HECPs were disguised as stores or other types of commercial buildings.

The army HD commander also had a HARBOR DEFENSE COMMAND POST (HDCP), a permanent structure sometimes located near the HECP. Sometimes this was next to or included the HARBOR DEFENSE OBSERVATION POST (HDOP). Both the army and navy deployed surveillance equipment to protect the harbors. The army's mines could be set so that instead of detonating they sent a warning signal when a ship passed. Early in the war, the new RADAR systems, usually a SCR-582 model that could operate under all weather conditions, supplemented the lookouts at observation positions. The coast artillery batteries used the SCR-296 radar for fire control. Most of the radar equipment for fire direction was not installed until 1943 when many of the new gun batteries were declared ready.

Army Radar

One of the most important additions to the coastal batteries was radar. Although the anti-aircraft units had already used it effectively, it was still a new device for the gun units. The army had studied the idea of using radar for fire control with seacoast artillery since 1937. The Signal Corps had worked on search and targeting radar systems. Some of the most important research took place at the Radiation Laboratory of the Massachusetts Institute of Technology early in the war. There the Signal Corps developed the fire control radar for the gun batteries identified as SCR-296 (SCR=Signal Corps Radar) and the SCR-582 search radar used in harbor defense.

The SCR-296 required a five-man crew: four operated the radar and one its power plant. Once the harbor radar made a contact or an observer had a visual sighting, this unit locked onto the target to determine the range and azimuth. Including all its components, the unit weighed over forty-eight tons. Its antenna was placed in a cylindrical shelter on top of a tower. These towers ranged from 25 feet to 100 feet in height to achieve the proper elevation above the terrain for effective operation and were usually located near the commander's battery command post rather than near the guns. All the old primary batteries and the new primary and secondary ones completed between 1942 and 1943 (the 100 and 200 Series) were equipped with SCR-296A radar units for controling fire against surface ships. The SCR-296A was to track shells and adjust fire, but had its limitations. Postwar tests gave a reliable range data for large ships 40,000 yards out and destroyers up to 20,000 yards. Thus, the CAC units still had to rely on their traditional ranging equipment and base stations to take advantage of the range of the 16-inch guns, which was greater than 40,000 yards. In 1944, the new 90mm AMTB batteries were to receive SCR-572.

An RC136 IFF system added to the SCR-296 position required its own antenna and a separate transmitter/receiver in the operating room. Friendly ships carried a Mark III transponder, which was activated by this system so the operator could identify friendly and unknown ships. However, they had to be beyond a minimum distance to appear on the radar screen.

The SCR-582, made for harbor surveillance, linked directly to the HDCP. Tested at Fort Dawes in 1941, it was found at most HDCPs by 1942. The antenna and equipment were usually placed in towers or in specially designed buildings with two or more stories as it was a line-of-sight radar, meaning the higher the elevation, the greater the range. Unlike the SCR-296, this radar was able to track multiple targets. Each Harbor Defense command was issued a long-range SCR-582/682 search radar set. The SCR-582 sets could detect surface vessels 90,000 yards away. The system was able to identify low-flying aircraft 40,000 yards out. Only fifty-five of these units were produced, and they were declared obsolete in 1945, not because they were not effective but due to a parts shortage. A mobile version, the SCR-682A, was used with mobile batteries. It had a maximum range of 240,000 yards and an effective range of 35,000 yards.

The SCR-270/271 was an early type of radar used at Pearl Harbor on December 7, 1941, which detected the incoming Japanese aircraft at 132 miles out. The first search radar produced by the army, it was developed in 1937 by the Army Signal Corps Laboratory and manufactured by private industry. This type of radar had the designation of SCR-270 (a mobile unit) and SCR-271 (a fixed station unit using a rotating 100-foot tower for antenna). The first unit served the Army Air Corps in Panama in the fall of 1940. Normally it was operated by a three man-crew, but on the morning of December 7, 1941, a two-man crew was using it for practice. The SCR 270/271 had a range of up to 150 miles and served as the main early warning radar throughout the war. By mid-1942, there were about 250 of these radar units in the United States, mostly on the West Coast.

Before the war, antiaircraft batteries, 3-inch and 90-mm, had relied on an M-1 optical height finder. During 1941, a radar unit with more effective fire control was developed. The SCR-268 was a 14-ton unit developed for directing the antiaircraft searchlights and had an effective range of 40,000 yards (twenty-four miles). It remained in service until 1944 for antiaircraft fire control and until the end of the war for directing searchlights.

The SCR-547 combined with the M-1 with an M-9 gun director could direct a battery of 90mm guns against surface and air targets, which the SCR-268 could not do. It could also track enemy aircraft at 20,000 yards. For 90mm batteries, the SCR-547 system was replaced with the SCR 584/598, which could handle fast moving targets and was not vulnerable to jamming by "window" (aluminum strips).

Source: "Seacoast Artillery Radar" by Danny R. Malone in American Seacoast Defenses; U.S. Army Signal Corps
Museum at Fort Gordon, GA (http://www.gordon.army.mil/ocos/Museum/ScrComponents/scrf.asp)

SCR 582 radar installation at Fort Dawes, Boston Harbor

© Tomasz Idzikowski

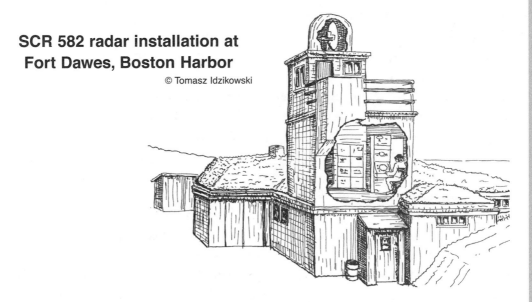

In 1939, the coast artillery contingent numbered only 4,200 men or an average of about 250 men for each of the seventeen harbors. By the fall of 1941, that number had risen to 45,000 troops for the entire coast defense system. This included six regiments of tractor-drawn 155mm guns needed to cover gaps in the defenses, including sites waiting for the construction of the new 6-inch gun batteries. Over thirty coast artillery regiments defended the HDs. After the war began, regular field artillery batteries with 105mm and 75mm guns were pressed into coastal defense service to fill in the gaps. By 1942, 70,000 troops were assigned to coastal defense, but this number dropped after mid-1943 as the threat of invasion evaporated and new positions went into service.

In the autumn of 1942, as American forces went on the offensive in the Pacific at Guadalcanal and launched the invasion of North Africa in the European/African theater, the army abandoned ten more of its 16-inch-gun battery projects from the earlier list of deferred positions since it was apparent the war would end before their completion. Since the army needed to produce more field guns, the number of planned 6-inch-gun batteries was also reduced during the next year. America's "Atlantic Wall" thinned out quickly as the tide of war turned.

Work on the new 6-inch gun batteries only started in 1942 after the prototype was completed. Since 1941, the Coast Artillery Corps (CAC) had determined that the most effective weapon for stopping fast attack vessels was the 90mm antiaircraft gun, which they intended to use as their AMTB (Anti-Motor Torpedo Boat) gun to replace the 3-inch guns by late 1942. These 90mm AMTB units included two fixed 90mm AMTB guns with gun shields and two mobile ones with two mobile 37mm or 40mm antiaircraft guns. Many of the 90mm AMTB units and even some of the 16-inch-gun batteries occupied positions beyond the old forts of the HDs and on military reservations where they effectively covered the harbor approaches. By the end of the war, these were the only positions still manned by the CAC in some harbors.

As the engineers completed a number of new batteries and turned them over to the CAC in 1943, they began removing from service the obsolete 12-inch-mortar batteries and guns mounted on disappearing carriages. When radar was introduced in the new batteries to improve fire control, the old fire-control systems remained in place as backup.

The price tag for the 1940 Program for modernization of the coast artillery rose from $80 million to $220 million by 1945. Eighteen 16-inch-gun casemated batteries were completed by 1945 and five were nearing completion or awaiting gun installation. Forty-one 6-inch-gun batteries were completed in the last year of the war and another twenty-nine were near completion or awaiting gun installation. Three older 16-inch-gun and eight 12-inch-gun batteries had received casemates and casemates were built for two new 12-inch-gun batteries. All eighteen new 16-inch batteries were in the United States as well as two of three of the old positions with casemates added. The third old position was in Panama (one of the 16-inch batteries in Panama was to be casemated and the third bat-

Right: 6-inch gun with wrap-around shield.
Photo courtesy of Dennis Blazey.

Harbor Defenses of 1944

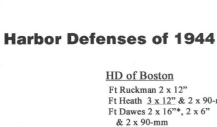

1. Newfoundland Defenses
Ft McAndrew (at Argentia) 4 x 6"
Ft Pepperell (at St. John's) 2 x 8"+
plus British batteries.

HD of Boston
Ft Ruckman 2 x 12"
Ft Heath 3 x 12" & 2 x 90-mm
Ft Dawes 2 x 16"*, 2 x 6"
  & 2 x 90-mm
Ft Warren 2 x 12"
Ft Standish 2 x 90-mm
Ft Duvall 2 x 16"
Ft Revere 2 x 90-mm
Brewster Islands 2 x 6" &
  2 x 90-mm
East Pt Mil.Res. 2 x 16" & 2 x 6"
Fourth Cliff Mil.Res. 2 x 6"

HD of Portland
Ft Levett 2 x 12" & 2 x 90-mm
Ft Williams 2 x 90-mm
Cape Elizabeth Mil.Res.
  2 x 6"*
Peak's Is. Mil.Res.
  2 x 16", 2 x 6" & 4 x 90-mm
Jewell Is. Mil.Res.
  4 x 90-mm
Long Is. Mil.Res. 4 x 90-mm
  4 x 90-mm at other points

HD of Portsmouth
Ft Foster 2 x 90-mm
Ft Stark 2 x 12"
Ft Dearborn 2 x16", 2 x 6" &
  2 x 90-mm

2. HD of Narragansett Bay
Ft Church 2 x 16", 2 x 8" & 2 x 6"
Ft Getty 2 x 90-mm
Ft Burnside 2 x 6"
Ft Varnum 2 x 90-mm
Ft Greene 2 x 16", 2 x 16"* & 2 x 6"

HD of New Bedford
Ft Rodman 2 x 12"
Mishaum Pt Mil.Res. 2 x 6"
8 x 90-mm at other points

3. HD of Long Island Sound
Ft Wright 2 x 16"*, 2 x 6", 2 x 6"*
  & 2 x 90-mm
Ft Michie 1 x 16"+, 2 x 12" & 2 x 90-mm
Ft Terry 2 x 90-mm
Camp Hero 4 x 16" & 2 x 6"

HD of the Delaware
Ft Saulsbury 2 x 12"+
Cape May Mil.Res. 2 x 6" & 2 x 90-mm
Ft Miles 2 x 16", 2 x 12", 4 x 6"
  & 4 x 90-mm

4. HD of Southern New York
Ft Tilden 2 x 16" & 2 x 6"
Ft Wadsworth 4 x 12"
Ft Hancock 4 x 12", 2 x 10" & 4 x 90-mm
Highlands Mil.Res. 2 x 16" & 2 x 6"

Harbor Defense of Chesapeake Bay
Ft Monroe 2 x 12" & 2 x 90-mm
Ft Wool 2 x 6"*
Ft Custis 2 x 16" & 2 x 6"*
Ft Story 4 x 16", 4 x 6", 4 x 90-mm
  & 4 x 16" howitzers+

Data from American Seacoast
Defenses by Mark Berhow

HD of Charleston
Ft Moultrie 2 x 10"
  2 x 6"* & 2 x 90-mm
Ft Sumter 2 x 90-mm

HD of Pensacola
Ft Pickens 2 x 12"
  & 2 x 6"* & 2 x 90-mm

Note: Guns of only 8" or larger noted
New 6" gun positions with shields
and 90-mm AA/Anti-Boat guns
(non-casemated) also indicated.
Underlined weapons indicate non-
casemated guns positions from before
1920.
+ non-casemated post 1920 positions
* Position completed by not armed.

0   100   500 miles

East Coast
© TOMASZ IDZIKOWSKI

HD of Key West
Ft Taylor 2 x 12", 2 x 6",
  2 x 6"* & 2 x 90-mm

Newfoundland Defenses

Sydney (British)

Saint John (British)

Halifax (British)

Portland

Boston

New York City

Washington

Charleston

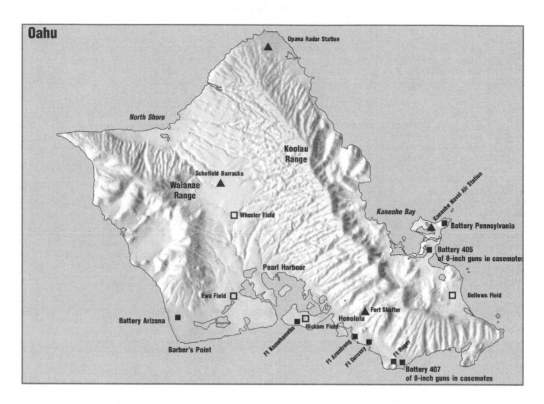

tery, a single gun on a disappearing carriage, was deactivated in 1943). Twenty-seven of the new 6-inch-gun batteries were also in the United States (the territories of Alaska and Hawaii not included) as were all ten of the 12-inch-gun batteries with casemates. The American totals do not include the number of mobile guns available or the 90mm AMTB or 3-inch-gun batteries. The 406mm was the equivalent of the American 16-inch gun of which the Americans mounted thirty to Germany's ten. Not included in the above totals are 8-inch (200mm) naval guns mounted on railway cars, which the Americans deployed between 1942 and 1945. The West Coast had two-gun batteries of these at Puget Sound and Los Angeles. The remaining twenty guns were on the East Coast (Fort Hancock, Fort Miles, and Fort Custis).

No enemy warship could approach any major American harbor without facing a volley from the heavy coastal guns, which were more than a match for most battleship weapons. And the old geographic distance factor still played a major role in the defense of America's Atlantic and Pacific Walls. None of the Axis Powers had a base within close enough range to sustain a landing. Any invasion of the United States would have required a direct assault on, or quick takeover of, one of America's harbors and none of the Axis powers had that capability after December 1942.

After the war began, the American army also expanded coastal defenses into the West Indies where work began on several batteries, mostly for 6-inch guns. In Puerto Rico and the Virgin Island, the engineers built a 12-inch-gun battery at FORT AMEZUITA in the HD OF SAN JUAN (Puerto Rico) along with several 6-inch-gun batteries at FORT MASCARO. An

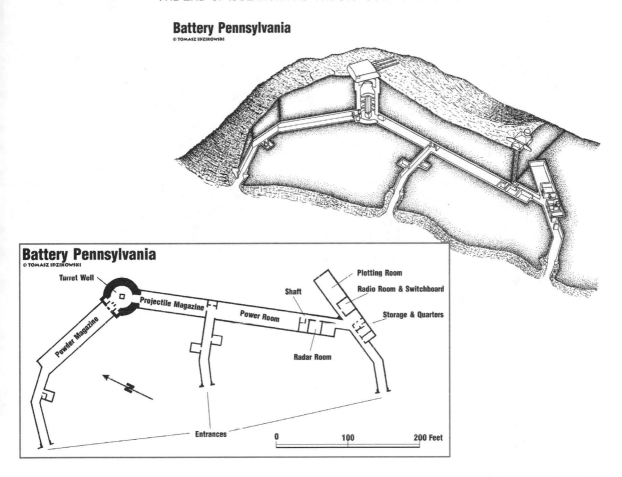

Battery Pennsylvania
© TOMASZ IDZIKOWSKI

8-inch-gun battery occupied a position in the HD OF VIEQUES SOUND with several 6-inch gun batteries. In 1940, after the destroyer exchange for bases with Great Britain, the army built and manned several modern batteries on bases loaned to the United States, including two 6-inch-gun batteries with wraparound shields built at Stone Hill and FORT VICTORIA in Bermuda.

In Alaska, the army set up several batteries of 6-inch guns at the forts of Sitka, Seward, Kodiak, and Dutch Harbor, but most were never completed. A battery of 8-inch guns was completed at FORT J. H. SMITH in the HD OF KODIAK and another at FORT SCHWATKA in the HD OF DUTCH HARBOR.

A number of new batteries were added on OAHU, HAWAII during the war. Two of the sunken battleship *Arizona*'s three-gun 14-inch turrets were used to make two new land batteries, BATTERY PENNSYLVANIA and BATTERY ARIZONA, which were also fitted with an army radar fire control system. Neither the Pennsylvania nor the Arizona battery was fully operational at the end of the war, but they were the most impressive battery positions built by the American army. Like all the other fixed batteries, the government dismantled them a few years after the war ended. Four batteries (KILPATRICK, BURGESS, RIGGS, and RICKER) each consisting of a twin 8-inch naval gun turret removed from the aircraft carriers *Lexington* and *Saratoga* were ready in 1942 and later also fitted with army radar.

One of two 4.7-inch Mark IVs at Fort Amherst at St. John's, Newfoundland. Photo courtesy of Paul Ozorak.

American defenses on the Atlantic coast extended to Canada's Newfoundland, where a major U.S. naval base was built in 1942. Two 6-inch-gun batteries for coast defenses were built at the American post of FORT MCANDREW at Argentia. These batteries belonged to the new 200-series battery positions. In addition, 90mm antimotor torpedo boat batteries and 3-inch gun batteries were setup. At Fort Pepperell, a battery of 8-inch guns on barbette mounts was setup on Redcliff Head. Newfoundland had never been a site of a major military base until right before World War II when the British RAF established the Gander Air Base. The American naval base was set up at Argentia in Placentia Bay in 1942. At the same time, Gander Air Base was expanded, becoming a major refueling stop for aircraft on the way to Europe. The two forts, naval base, and air base retained their importance during the Cold War while the U.S. Air Force and U.S. Navy operated from all four bases.

The British and Canadians also built up their defenses in Canada at Halifax, Nova Scotia, and Saint John, New Brunswick. The harbor at SAINT JOHN had boasted six 4.7-inch guns and a searchlight on Partridge Island since World War I. During World War II these defenses were improved with underground facilities and the addition of two 6-inch naval guns, two 18-pdrs, a more modern searchlight, and observation and communication equipment. Other positions were set up at FORT MISPEC, including concrete facilities and a battery. This battery of three 7.5-inch guns was emplaced in 1940, instead of the 9.2-inch-gun battery projected for the site in 1938. At the COURTNEY BAY BREAKWATER BATTERY in Saint John Harbor the 18-pdrs were replaced in 1944 with the modern rapid-firing twin 6-pdr in June. Concrete facilities and a battery of 4.7-inch field guns were added at the DUFFERIN BATTERY at Negro Point. Partridge Island had a battery of 6-inch guns and searchlights.

The HALIFAX DEFENSE COMPLEX included several batteries and forts that covered the harbor. Several positions included 4.7-inch, 12-pdr QF, and 6-inch-gun batteries. Below the Citadel (Fort George) at Point Pleasant, a number of concrete positions served a battery. Three 9.2-inch guns were located at DEVIL'S POINT BATTERY. The traffic control center was located at the York Redoubt, which stood on a commanding point. In 1942, a Fire Command Post was added to control the harbors defenses. The harbor was protected by two minefields and an antisubmarine net that stretched across the harbor from the York Redoubt to McNab's Island, and was controlled from the redoubt. FORT NCNAB was the inspection point for arriving ships. Across from it STRAWBERRY BATTERY, built in 1939, served the antisubmarine net and covered the entrance with searchlights. The harbor's

Devil's Point Battery at entrance to Halifax Harbor. Photo courtesy of Paul Ozorak.

shipyards made repairs on seven thousand ships damaged in the "Battle of the Atlantic."

On the Pacific Coast, the Canadians improved the defenses of the Victoria-Esquimalt Fortress. At FORT RODD HILL, the Belmont Battery acquired the new remote controlled

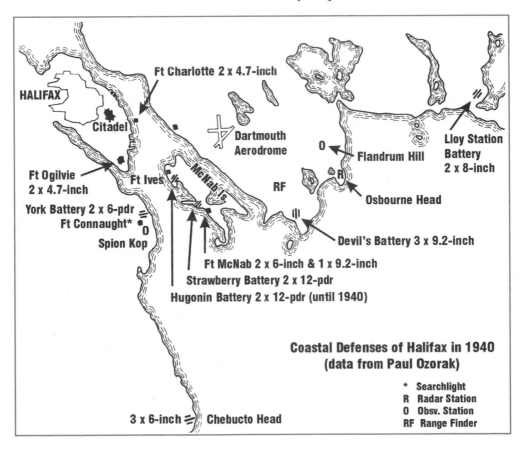

Coastal Defenses of Halifax in 1940
(data from Paul Ozorak)

Ft Charlotte 2 x 4.7-inch
HALIFAX
Citadel
Dartmouth Aerodrome
Lloy Station Battery 2 x 8-inch
Flandrum Hill
Ft Ogilvie 2 x 4.7-inch
Ft Ives
McNab's
Osbourne Head
York Battery 2 x 6-pdr
Ft Connaught*
RF
Spion Kop
Devil's Battery 3 x 9.2-inch
Ft McNab 2 x 6-inch & 1 x 9.2-inch
Strawberry Battery 2 x 12-pdr
Hugonin Battery 2 x 12-pdr (until 1940)
3 x 6-inch   Chebucto Head

*   Searchlight
R   Radar Station
O   Obsv. Station
RF Range Finder

The twin 6-pdr remote-controlled guns installed in 1944 at Fort Rodd Hill in British Colombia.

twin 6-pdr QF gun in 1944. The same type of weapon was installed at Duntze Head, on the other side of the entrance to Esquimalt from the Belmont Battery. These new weapons also replaced the 12-pdr batteries at Ogden Point, which covered the entrance to Victoria harbor. The batteries at Albert Head (9.2-inch guns) and Mary Hill (6-inch guns) received radar for fire control. All this took place late in the war as the Canadian defenses were being downgraded, like those in the United States.

Army Mines, Mine Planters, and Mining

Before the war began, the navy prepared booms and nets to guard the harbor entrances and laid CONTACT MINES in the outer region of some harbor areas. The army had a stock of five thousand mines. In February 1941, the coast artillery deployed minefields in Panama, at Cristobal and Balboa, on each side of the canal, in the Philippines in mid-summer, and along the East Coast in the fall. However, it did not get around to laying any minefields on the West Coast after the war began. By the end of 1941, the army had planted 1,200 mines. Early in 1942, minefields were completed in Portland (ME), Boston, Narragansett Bay, New York, Chesapeake Bay, Portsmouth (VA), and San Francisco. Navy minelayers laid the outer minefields at about the same time.

Eight new ships were ordered for the army in 1941 and eight more the next year, but the first was not ready before June 1942.

Army mine planter the *General Mills*.
Photo courtesy of Casemate Museum, Fort Monroe.

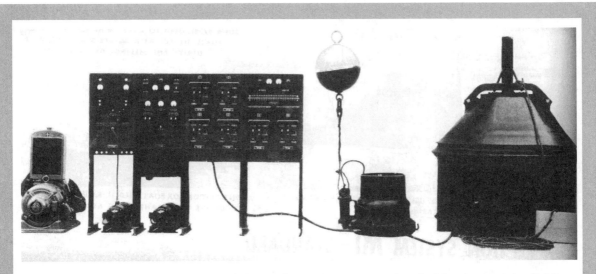

This photo from a technical manual shows the equipment associated with an army minefield. From Left to right: generators, the control panels found in the mine casemates for controlling the minefields, a buoy, distribution box, and ground mine.

As these ships entered service between June 1942 and May 1943, they were sent to Fort Monroe, Newport (RI), Portland (ME), Fort Miles, Boston, the Columbia River, New York, Little Creek Mine Base near Fort Story, each entrance to the Panama Canal, and San Francisco. Fort Miles, New York, Fort Monroe, and the Columbia River each received two mine planters.

The Coast Artillery troops used mine planters and other vessels to lay controlled minefields operated from the submarine mine casemates. However, these minefields did not necessarily represent the main line of defense against submarines, unless the mines were activated for detonation on contact, which was seldom the case. In most instances, the BUOYANT MINES served merely as a warning system, which was fortunate, since friendly ships often snared the lines of mines. According to K. L. Waters, author of an article entitled "The Army Mine Planter Service," the mines did not contain enough explosives to seriously damage most vessels, including submarines. Generally, the mines were laid in groups of nineteen, each connected to a distribution box, which in turn, was linked to a cable leading back to a terminal position on the shore and from there to the mine casemates. The casemate was in communications with the plotting room and a couple of observing stations that fed it the information to determine when to detonate a mine or mines.

In 1943, the new M-3 GROUND MINE replaced the buoyant mine. It contained almost 2,000 lbs. of TNT and could inflict serious damage on most vessels. According to Charles Bogart, author of *Controlled Mines*, one control board could handle 130 mines or ten groups of thirteen mines. The mines lay on the seabed

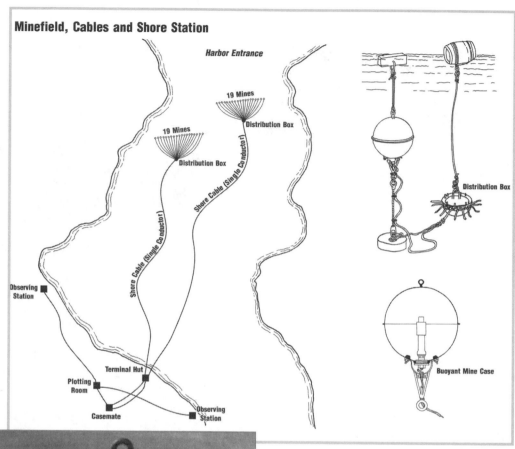

Minefield, Cables and Shore Station

Harbor Entrance

19 Mines

19 Mines

Distribution Box

Distribution Box

Shore Cable (Single Conductor)

Shore Cable (Single Conductor)

Distribution Box

Observing Station

Terminal Hut

Plotting Room

Casemate

Observing Station

Buoyant Mine Case

Buoyant mine

where a ship could not foul them. At the time they were deployed, these mines served mainly to stop submarines because it was unlikely that a warship would try to breach the harbor defenses. To be effective against submarines these mines had a magnetic firing pin that activated when a submarine passed within one hundred feet. If necessary, the mine battery commander could detonate the mines manually, either individually or as a group. Other options were to set mines armed for automatic detonation in response to a ship's magnetic field. If they were not armed, the mines could set off an alarm in the command post, warning of approaching ships.

In spite of these precautions, accidents happened occasionally. Thus, mines planted in the HD of New York Harbor and the HD of the Chesapeake Bay apparently sank three friendly ships in the summer of 1942. The minefields did not destroy any enemy vessels in American waters, but served as a deterrent. The army's submarine mine-fields remained in place until the summer of 1945 when their removal began. Some mines had to be destroyed in place.

U.S. Navy Mark 6 mine.

The navy used mines as offensive weapons as well as defensive weapons. Mines used for coast defense were mainly moored mines from World War I and included the MARK 5 with 500 lbs. of explosives and the MARK 6 with 300 lbs. of explosives. The Mark 6 could be moored at depths of up to five hundred fathoms, making it ideal for covering the outer approaches. This mine detonated if a ship struck its antenna. The Mark 6 was replaced with the MARK 16, which held 600 lbs. of explosive. One version of this mine had an antenna and the other an acoustic detonator. The navy also had ground mines that were primarily used for offensive operations in enemy waters.

In addition to mines, several other devices were developed to protect American harbors. In some places, BOOMS AND NETS were deployed. In other harbors, approaching ships were detected with HYDROPHONES, some of which had a range of up to two miles. MAGNETIC DETECTION LOOPS were set up at a number of ports with their operating stations in the HECP. Some of the harbors using this system included Argentia (Newfoundland), Saint John (New Brunswick), Portland (ME), Portsmouth (NH), Nahant (MA), and New York. The main purpose was detection of enemy submarines. When submarines or a vessel passed over the loop its magnetic field would send out a small electrical charge through the loop alerting the operator. The navy personnel manning the Loop Receiving Station (LRS) were referred to as watchstanders. In some cases the cable used for this loop system was run adjacent to or through minefields, so if a vessel was detected the appropriate mines could be activated. In other places, sonobuoys sounded the alarm. However, some of these systems were not effective or in use when German U-boats laid mines off of American harbors, including New York in 1942. In September 1942, the defenders of Charleston quickly identified the enemy mines laid by the *U-455* and navy minelayers neutralized them, which became a matter of routine at most ports.

Bunkers

Well before the war began, the army engineers drew up designs for bunkers which were classified as field fortifications, samples of which can be seen in the 1940 edition of FM 5-15 *Engineer Field Manual: Field Fortifications*. The designs of these field fortifications were heavily influenced by the trench warfare of the previous war. During the early 1930s, experimental work was carried out on the construction of machine-gun bunkers in the Hawaiian Islands. Twelve bunkers were built between 1933 and 1934, including five in the Honolulu Harbor. They were roughly 14 feet by 14 feet and included long narrow vision slits on each side. Little else of significance was done until 1938 when the 3rd Engineers tested a machine-gun bunker designed to resist 155mm rounds. A secret report of May 6, 1939, from the commander of the 21st Brigade addressed to the commander of the Hawaiian Division recommended the creation of machine-gun emplacements.

On June 20, 1941, a UPI article in the *Honolulu Star Bulletin* announced that the army would use thousands of steel-plated "pillboxes" to defend its installations from Bermuda to the Far East. According to William Witheron, president of the Blaw-Knox Company in Pittsburgh, this type of pillbox was about 9 feet high and projected 4 feet above the ground. Its upper part was a rotating dome-like turret apparently able to resist rounds of 37mm. The hand-cranked turret was believed large enough for a .50-caliber machine gun or a 37mm gun and was supposed to include a periscope. The lower part was to include two holes to serve as passageways. However, the pillboxes that were completed and sent to Hawaii had only one hole and apparently were not intended to be linked to a tunnel system as the article indicated.

After the attack on Pearl Harbor, there is no evidence of any concrete bunkers or even emplacements of portable steel pillboxes on the West Coast, although the army made preparations to defend the coast against an invasion. A number of sandbagged weapons positions were added to coast artillery forts, including on top of gun casemates and other structures. In addition, the army built a number of simple, small, open concrete hexagonal positions with a steel center post for a .50-caliber machine gun most likely to serve as anti-aircraft positions. Several observation and

One of the few remaining examples of the portable steel-casted armored "pillboxes" that held a machine gun in a rotating turret. Photo courtesy of J. D. Bennett.

One of the mass-produced portable concrete bunkers built in Hawaii in 1942. The lifting rings can be seen on the side. Photo courtesy of William Gaines.

support positions of a non-standard design at Fort Stevens and Fort Columbia have been mistaken for combat bunkers.

On the Hawaiian Islands a greater effort was eventually made. An unknown number of the portable pillboxes with their rotating turrets were installed and hundreds of mass-produced concrete machine-gun bunkers were built by mid-1943. The latter were generally 8 feet by 8 feet and had thicker walls than the 1934 models. There were several types of these new bunkers with a number of variants. Unlike the older ones, their firing and observation position could be on any or all sides. The double-ended types were longer than the square ones and had rounded ends. It appears that the engineers mass-produced the square type, which could be assembled at a convenient location and hauled to the intended site. At least 150 of these concrete bunkers were built on Kauai and, according to some reports, up to two thousand on Oahu. But by the time these positions were completed, the threat had long passed.

A double bunker at Barber's Point, Oahu, with one-side facing inland and the other facing the sea. Photo courtesy of J. D. Bennett

Meanwhile, the government was greatly concerned about the security of the Hoover Dam. Since the end of August 1939, on the eve of the European War, various intelligence reports indicated that German saboteurs operating from Cuba and Mexico were planning to attack the dam. By 1940, the FBI became involved, and in January 1941 an MP battalion set up a camp nearby, but the army was not actively involved in the dam's protection. According to retired LTC Lincoln Clark, quoted by Julian Rhinehart in a 1995 article of the *Nevada Magazine*, several bunkers were built in the area of the dam by an MP battalion in 1942. As a first lieutenant he and his platoon maintained a squad on duty twenty-four hours a day, making sure that each bunker was always manned. The last remaining bunker today appears at a distance as a cubicle with a continuous observation slit on three sides. It is 24 feet in length and has six gun ports. The observation section of the bunker was 3 feet higher than the rear where it was protected by gun ports. The bunker is heavily camouflaged with rocks. The other bunkers have been removed.

In the northwest, a number of concrete sentry boxes, about 3 to 4 feet per side, were used at the Bonneville Dam. Although a marker today calls these structures bunkers, they are better defined as sentry boxes. Apparently they were mass-produced and included a ring on the roof for hauling them into position. It is possible that a number of these sentry boxes might have been used elsewhere including at coastal forts.

Two views of the last remaining bunker at Hoover Dam with a commanding view of the dam below. Photos courtesy of Patrick Paternostro.

Chapter 9

FROM GUNS TO THE MISSILE AGE

DURING WORLD WAR II, RADAR TOOK a leading role in defensive systems. As the war ended, only the 90mm AMTB batteries were manned in most coastal defenses of the United States while the Canadians retained their heavy gun batteries at Halifax and Victoria-Esquimalt until the early 1950s. By 1948, the army had deactivated virtually all American gun batteries from 6-inch to 16-inch guns, scrapping many of the weapons. In the early 1950s, Canada too abandoned its gun-bearing defenses. At FORT RODD HILL in the Victoria-Esquimalt Fortress, the last modern weapon, the deadly rapid-fire twin 6-pdrs installed in 1944, went out of service in 1956.

As the Cold War began, the American military became interested in developing missile and rocket technology to the point that it could provide the delivery system for a nuclear weapon. A rocket with an improved guidance system and a much greater range than the German V-2 could strike at any target, and if it carried a nuclear weapon, it could obliterate any existing target or fortification. This was the most important development in artillery since the breechloaded cannon was combined with the high-explosive shell. During the years following World War II and in the early 1950s, the main defenses of the United States consisted of open batteries of 90mm and 120mm antiaircraft guns. In the late-1950s, fortifications of reinforced concrete, many subterranean, reappeared when the missile became the new weapon requiring protection.

In 1949, the Soviets tested their first atomic bomb. However, since neither the United States nor the Soviet Union possessed a rocket capable of delivering an atomic bomb, antiaircraft guns and fighter aircraft remained the best defense against enemy bombers. The emphasis in coastal defenses shifted to air defenses. The role of fortifications was no longer to "defend and protect" by resisting the enemy, but to "detect and destroy" by finding and eliminating the enemy well before he could reach the target area. At the same time, the protection of surface-to-air missile (SAM) launch sites became a major preoccupation for the military. By the early 1960s, new defenses were built to protect the all-important long-range missiles needed to destroy bases in the enemy's homeland.

Spreading the Net

Homeland defense continued as the primary American concern, and to aid in this the United States teamed up with Canada to create an EARLY WARNING SYSTEM. Radar had become more effective since the beginning of World War II and further advances were made during the 1940s. By 1950, radar became the most important means of detecting and engaging enemy aircraft, but effective low altitude radars were lacking. The U. S. Air Force relied on the volunteer Ground Observers Corps for detecting low-flying aircraft. Deactivated at the end of World War II, the corps was called back into service in 1950. The volunteers manned eight thousand observation posts across the nation (the number doubled by 1952) and twenty-seven U.S. Air Force Filter Centers (this number nearly tripled by 1952) where observers called in to report their sightings. The Canadians formed a similar organization, but their volunteers had to build their own watchtowers. The corps was again deactivated at the end of the decade, as GAP FILLER RADARS for low altitude detection were set up at over 130 sites in the Continental United States. The Canadian Ground Observer Corps remained in operation until 1964.

In 1949, the United States began developing the PERMANENT SYSTEM, a radar-based aircraft control and warning system, and did not complete it until 1953. When it was finished, it proved only effective as a control system since any warning it could offer in the jet age would come too late. While the Permanent System was being perfected, the Air Force established a temporary system known as the LASHUP SYSTEM, which used the older AN/TPS 1B, 1C, and 1D long-range search radar. The AN/TPS 1B, with a range of about 120 miles, could detect bombers at 10,000 feet. The military also reactivated other World War II vintage radar units for the Lashup System. High costs caused a modification of the 1949 Permanent System plan. Only seventy-five radar stations (one-fifth of those originally planned) were throughout the continental United States and another ten were in Alaska. Actual

The Signal Corps had developed radar for the army and given each type the prefix SCR (Signal Corps Radio). In February 1943, the designations of new radars changed to avoid confusion. The prefix AN stood for Army/Navy and was followed by a three-letter code. The first letter indicated the type: F for fixed ground based, G for general ground use, M for mobile, T for ground transportable, etc. The second letter identified the type: P for radar, Q for sonar, and R for radio. The last letter stood for the function: G for fire control, R for passive detection, S for search, and T for transmitting.

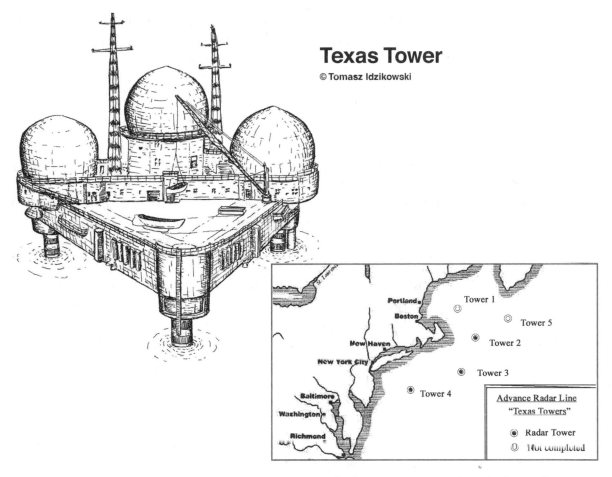

Texas Tower

© Tomasz Idzikowski

construction began in early 1950. However, even before it was completed, the military realized that the Permanent System had to be moved further north.

In the early 1950s, the government feared an attack upon the industrial and urban centers of the northeastern United States, with major sites from Boston to Washington as prime targets. To counter a surprise air assault, the U.S. Air Force established a radar chain at sea, on structures similar to the oil-drilling platforms now used in the Gulf of Mexico. The towers were named "TEXAS TOWERS." Of the five projected towers, only three were actually built. They were placed about one hundred miles from the coast, on the continental shelf in international waters. Each had three steel legs embedded in the sea floor. The superstructure included three decks on a triangular platform (210 feet per side). The radar equipment was on the upper level, which had a helicopter-landing pad. Two AN/FPS-6 long-range height finders and one AN/FPS-3A long-range search radar were located in specially built radomes (55 feet in diameter). The radar extended coverage between three hundred to five hundred miles eastward for advance warning of an enemy bomber attack. Initially, the crews were to consist of twenty-two men, but the number was more than doubled to ensure efficient operation of the facility. TEXAS

TOWER 2 (TT-2), the first to be moved into position in the summer of 1955, became operational the next year. It was placed on the Georges Shoal, one hundred miles off Cape Cod in waters 56 feet deep. Two other Texas Towers were built and put in operation by the spring of 1959. TT-3 was placed on Nantucket Shoal, one hundred miles southeast of Rhode Island in waters 85 feet deep, and TT-4 was erected on Unnamed Shoal eighty-four miles southeast of New York City in waters 185 feet deep. TT-1 and TT-5 were cancelled.

During the construction of the towers, Soviet submarines snooped around. In November 1955, a storm did some damage to TT-2. TT-4 was in the deepest waters and suffered from structural problems related to its location. In 1960, Hurricane Donna struck with fury and TT-4 suffered extensive damage. Luckily, the crew had evacuated before the storm. On January 15, 1961, another storm weakened the tower's legs, which collapsed, dropping the entire superstructure into the sea and killing everyone on board. The other two towers remained on duty, but their crews were ordered to withdraw before serious storms. Special escape capsules were placed in the towers in case the crew could not be evacuated in time. Frequent storms in 1962 and 1963 forced the crews to evacuate time and again. Finally, in early 1963, the Air Force deactivated both sites and sold them for scrap. Their effectiveness had been limited because their own power plants had caused excessive vibrations, not only making them uncomfortable, but also interfering with the operation of the electronic equipment. The towers were replaced with AWACS radar aircraft.

As fear of the spread of communism deepened, the countries of the newly formed North Atlantic Treaty Organization (NATO) strove to secure their frontiers. The Continental Air Command (CONAC), activated in 1948, working with the Royal Canadian Air Force (RCAF), drew up the PINETREE PLAN to establish a radar line across the continent (mainly in Canada) to guard the northern frontier from a Soviet air attack. The Pinetree Line was to include thirty-three radar stations, seventeen of which would be manned by Americans and the remainder by Canadians. The American-controlled Northeast Air Command was responsible for much of Labrador, Newfoundland, and Greenland. Ten of the new radar stations were located in its area with three in Greenland. About 40 percent of the Pinetree Line's radar stations were direction stations (for directing fighter interceptors to the threatened location) and 60 percent for early warning. The type of radar used was AN/CPS-5 or AN/TPS-1B for search radar and either AN/MPS-4 or AN/TPS-10 as a height finder. All of the buildings of the stations were above ground and none was blastproof. As segments of the line became operational, CONAC called up Air National Guard units to man these positions because the United States was involved in the Korean War. The line became fully operational by the end of 1954 and the last station was completed in the early 1960s. Only a half dozen of these stations were deactivated before 1965, while most remained active well past 1970.

Shortly after the Pinetree Line became operational, construction began on the MID-

Typical Installation of Radar Set AN/FPS-20A

© TOMASZ IDZIKOWSKI

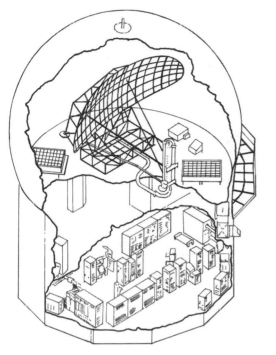

CANADA EARLY-WARNING LINE. This radar line generally followed the 55th Parallel and ran from Hopedale, Labrador, to Dawson Creek, British Columbia. It consisted of ninety doppler detection stations and eight section control stations. The radar sites were laid out in two lines about five to ten miles apart. The doppler sites were staggered in the two lines and placed about sixty-five miles apart. This allowed for more effective detection and determination of speed and direction. Construction of these stations was a major feat since much of the work was done in the trackless regions of the tundra in eastern Canada and the vast taiga of the Great Northern Forest west of Hudson's Bay. The subarctic conditions posed additional problems for equipment and personnel. Only the control stations were manned, but living facilities had to be provided at doppler sites for maintenance crews, who, in most cases, were flown in. The line was operational by early 1957. It was closed down in April 1965 because it was no longer effective in detecting modern aircraft.

Even as work began on the Mid-Canada Early Warning Line, the American and Canadian governments decided to create a more advanced line closer to the 69th Parallel called the DISTANT EARLY WARNING (DEW) LINE. It ran from Cape Lisburne, Alaska to Cape Dyer on Baffin Island, a distance of over three thousand miles and was located within the Arctic Circle. Begun in 1954, the DEW Line was completed in 1957. It was extended across Greenland in 1961, and was anchored in Scotland in the North East Air Command area. It included six main radar stations spaced at five hundred mile intervals, twenty-eight auxiliary stations about one hundred miles apart, and twenty-eight intermediate stations at fifty-mile intervals. The main and auxiliary stations were equipped with AN/FPS-19 search radar and AN/FPS-23 as Gap Filler units. The intermediate stations had only AN/FPS-23 transmitters. The DEW Line, built in the Arctic regions of tundra and even on the ice cap in Greenland, presented construction problems similar to, if not somewhat more difficult than, those of the Mid-Canada Line. Virtually all construction and maintenance material had to be flown in. During the winter, "cat trains" of tractors pulling sleds braved the Arctic night to bring in supplies.

Each manned station was completely self-sustained and included an airfield. The six main stations of the DEW Line were the largest. Generally, they consisted of modules,

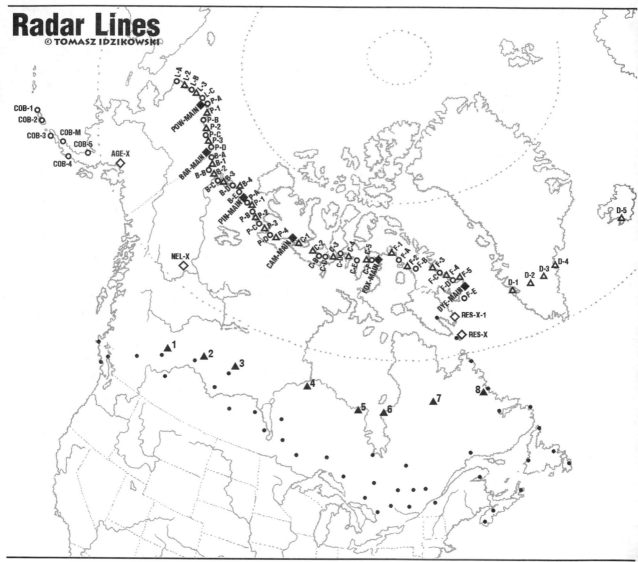

Radar Lines
© TOMASZ IDZIKOWSKI

- • Pine Tree Line radar stations
- ▲ Mid-Canada Line radar stations:
  1. Dawson Creek
  2. Stoney Mountain
  3. Cranberry Portage
  4. Bird
  5. Winisk
  6. Great Whale River
  7. Knob Lake
  8. Hopedale

- ◇ DEW Line rear area communications sites
- ◆ DEW Line main stations: AN/FPS-19 radar unit*
- △ DEW Line auxiliary stations: AN/FPS-19 radar unit
- ○ DEW Line intermediate stations: AN/FPS-23 radar transmitter unit **
  Abbreviations for DEW Line Stations (From West to East
  L - LIZ
  P - POW
  B - BAR
  P - PIN
  C - CAM
  F - FOX
  D - DYE

* The AN/FPS-19 was a long range radar which had a range of 200 miles, but normally used for a range of 160 miles.

** The main Auxiliary Stations included a receiver for the AN/FPS-23 radar transmitter to form a radar fence from sea level to 4,000'.

Right: View of DEW Line radar station FOX-Main on the Melville Peninsula of Canada in July 1961. The "trains" formed by components can be seen with the crossover and storage areas. Photo courtesy of Paul Kelly.

usually 16 feet by 28 feet each, put together to form two long buildings known as "trains" and linked by an overhead enclosed bridge. Each module had a function: power plant, transmitter room, receiving room, "commo" room, radar room, station offices, freezer room, storage, kitchen, dining room, recreation room, dorms, latrines (with septic tank), and so on. The main and auxiliary stations usually required several modules of each type: 3 or more power plant modules, 2 or more dorms modules, etc. All the key administrative, operations and living facilities, including plumbing, were contained within the buildings. The main and auxiliary sites also included garages, warehouses, hangars, and other facilities needed for independent operation. When the septic tank filled, a "honey wagon" hauled it away for disposal. The auxiliary sites consisted of about twenty-five modules and the main sites of many more. The smaller intermediate sites consisted of a small "train" of about five modules and a garage with a crew of only four (including a cook), only augmented by additional support and maintenance personnel in the summer months. In the tundra, the modules had to be placed on pilings to prevent the structure from "warming" the permafrost layer and thus causing it to melt during the summer, which would result in the structure sinking. The radome was about 30 feet above ground level and had a diameter of about 30 feet. During the six-month winter, the radio was the only link to the outside world. Each station was equipped with a single firearm, not to repel an enemy raid, but to ward off polar bears.

Once a station was completed, further changes were needed, including the introduction of SAGE, the SEMI-AUTOMATIC GROUND ENVIRONMENT computerized system to handle all the data coming in from the radar lines. SAGE was developed during the 1950s. It included twenty-two Direction Centers (numbered DC-1 through DC-22) and four Control Centers (numbered CC-1 through CC-4) located in the United States: CC-1 with

DC-3 at Hancock Field, New York; CC-2 with DC-7 at Truax Field, Wisconsin; CC-3 with DC-12 at McChord Air Force Base, Washington; and CC-4 with DC-19 at Minot Air Force Base, North Dakota. The Control Center occupied a blockhouse and was equipped with an AN/FSQ-7 and AN/FSQ-8. The Direction Centers had an AN/FSQ-7 known as Combat Direction Central. Both of these items were large-scale electronic digital computers built for the Air Force by IBM and constituted the main components of the SAGE system. [These computers had about the capacity of a personal desktop computer of the late 1990s.] The system was soon established throughout the United States, linking each Direction Center to all the radar sites in its sector. The Direction Center tied into the regional Control Center, which linked up to the other Control Centers. The Direction Centers also fed their information to the interceptor, antiaircraft, and guided missile units. The AN/FSQ-8, known as Combat Control Central, at the Control Center received the same data and performed the same type of coordinating functions, but it did not receive the raw radar data going to the Direction Centers whose 250-ton AN/FSQ-7 computers transmitted the processed data from the radars to the Control Center. In 1956, some news articles brought this new system to public attention. It pointed out that the United States was entering a push-button age of computers and missile defense.

The SAGE sites, consisting of square, four-level structures, 150 feet on each side, had one-level power plants and were protected from nuclear attack. The computers were in the basement. The buildings of reinforced concrete and steel were considered blastproof and were identified as blockhouses because they had no windows. Twenty-three SAGE sites were built, including one in Goosebay, Canada. In May 1958, General Curtis LeMay pronounced the system truly "revolutionary." The first structures and SAGE system went into operation by 1958, and the entire system was completed by 1963. But by that time, it had already become obsolete because it was inadequate to deal with the new INTER-CONTINENTAL BALLISTIC MISSILE (ICBM) threat. Additional modifications and changes in the radar warning system took place over the years. According to N. J. McCamely, author of *Cold War Secret Nuclear Bunkers*, the SAGE Direction Centers at Minot and Grand Forks air bases were replaced with underground Command and Control centers in 1963, taking SAGE off line.

SAGE was replaced by the BACK-UP INTERCEPTOR CONTROL (BUIC) CENTERS, originally designed to back it up. The BUIC centers were placed in better-protected facilities that included radiation protection. Most SAGE sites on SAC bases were situated in prime target areas, while the new underground Command and Control Centers with the BUIC equipment were less vulnerable.

With the three radar lines in operation, the United States and Canada established the North American Aerospace Defense Command (NORAD) in September 1957 to control the air defenses of both nations. The radar stations were able to identify any Soviet bombers taking the direct route to the United States over the Arctic regions, allowing up to five hours for the armed forces to react in the mid-1950s.

When ICBMs became a reality, major changes had to be made to the defense system. The missiles's speed and trajectory made them virtually undetectable as they streaked over the radar curtain, only to be detected shortly before they crashed on their targets with their deadly loads. Thus, work began on the BALLISTIC MISSILE EARLY WARNING SYSTEM (BMEWS) in the 1950s. Only thirty minutes elapsed between the time required for a Soviet missile launch in the U.S.S.R. to the time its warhead detonated on a target in the United States. The BMEWS was designed to scan the Arctic wasteland to detect Soviet missiles when they left their launch pads, and before they left the atmosphere, giving maximum warning time to North American Aerospace Defense Command (NORAD). Three BMEWS sites were setup at Thule, Greenland, in 1960; Clear, Alaska, in 1961; and Flyingdales, England, in 1963. These BMEWS radars were able to sound the alarm up to fifteen minutes in advance. The AN/FPS-50 detection radar had a range of three thousand miles and was able to detect missile launches in the U.S.S.R. Its antennas were 165 feet high and 400 feet long. In the mid-1960s, an AN/FPS-92 unit was added for tracking missiles and satellites. Improvements were made over the years, but these three bases remained as the centers of the primary warning system against ICBMs from the early 1960s until the time satellite systems took over the job.

An additional detection net was also set up to defend against a Soviet strike. It was an underwater network of microphones or hydrophones known as SOUND SURVEILLANCE SYSTEM (SOSUS). The navy began laying it down in the Atlantic and the Pacific in the 1960s. The network detected the movements of submarines, which meant that American attack submarines could be stationed wherever Soviet submarines lurked and if the war alert was given, they could move against the enemy before he could launch his ballistic missiles.

Antiaircraft Artillery

Between the 1950s and the 1960s, the only Cold War defense lines in North America consisted of the three radar lines with no means of defense from attack. Their mission was only to give warning, using their electronic equipment to probe beyond the northern frontier. The U.S. Air Force and the Royal Canadian Air Force (RCAF) provided the fighter interceptors to engage intruders. However, during the 1940s and 1950s, the last line of defense consisted of antiaircraft weapons protecting cities and bases.

In October 1946, the Air Defense Command (ADC) requested 140 antiaircraft (AA) battalions (half of them with AA guns and half with automatic weapons) for air defense. At the time, only two AA-gun battalions and two automatic weapons battalions were available for the defense of the United States and one of each was stationed at Fort Bliss (TX) and Orlando (FL) and were only at cadre strength. By 1948, there was a single provisional battalion at Fort Bliss, but it was not at full strength. In 1948, political tensions sparked fear of another major war in Europe, which led to an increased demand for an air defense system in the United States. The army began organizing twenty-six AA battalions, which were not ready until 1950. Their mission was to protect army units rather than serve in the ADC's air-defense plans.

In 1950, the army and air force worked out rules of engagement for GUN DEFENDED AREAS—areas with antiaircraft guns. The air defense system bore the burden of identifying all aircraft and notifying the AA-gun commanders, but this did not resolve interservice frictions and revealed a major weakness in America's home defense. However, the outbreak of the Korean War quickly resolved the dispute. The departments of the Army and Air Force jointly established the rules of engagement in order to insure coordination between interceptor aircraft and AA units and to avoid friendly fire accidents. They also selected the location for AA defenses.

The ARMY ANTIAIRCRAFT COMMAND was established and worked closely with the ADC to create an effective air defense system. Brigade-size AA units were created. They consisted of two to five groups, each of which included two to five battalions. The battalions had four batteries with four AA guns each. In 1954, the Eastern Army Antiaircraft Command had several brigades including the 56th AA Brigade manning the defenses of Boston, New York, and Niagara; the 53rd AA Brigade protecting Philadelphia and Pittsburgh; the 45th AA Brigade defending Chicago, Detroit, and the Sault Sainte Marie Locks; the 35th AA Brigade covering Baltimore, Washington, and Norfolk. The Central Army Antiaircraft Command had a single battalion located at Ellsworth Air Force Base in South Dakota. The Western Army Antiaircraft Command included: the 31st AA Brigade defending Seattle, the nuclear facility at Hanford under constant protection since the 1940s, and Fairchild Air Force Base; the 47th AA Brigade covered Los Angeles and March Air Force Base. Several battalions of 90mm guns and one or two of 120mm guns defended most major cities. In 1954, guided missiles replaced the first 120mm AA battalions in New York, Washington and Chicago. The Army Antiaircraft Command had sixty-two battalions at this time and ninety-one National Guard battalions could be activated in time of war.

The weapons employed in 1951 were .50-caliber quads (four machine guns mounted together), 40mm automatic weapons, and 90mm and 120mm guns. The 40mm weapon had a fire-control computer. The 90mm had a vertical range of 36,300 feet and the 120mm a range of 47,400 feet. The old computer systems of these two guns (M-9 and M-10) from World War II were replaced because they could not follow aircraft taking evasive action. The new M-33 computer, which had its own integrated radars (one for search and one for gun laying), replaced the older units by the end of 1953. The 75mm Skysweeper replaced the two automatic weapons systems beginning in March 1953. It had a vertical range of 18,600 feet and carried its own radar and fire-control system that could track enemy aircraft at twenty thousand yards. During 1953, the battalions received TPS-1D radar units that increased their effectiveness.

By 1957, the Army Antiaircraft Command prepared plans for the deployment of twenty-six gun, thirteen Skysweepers, and sixty-one Nike missile battalions. Soon gun units converted to missile units. During most of the 1950s, the Army Antiaircraft Command divided the United States into three regions, while the U.S. Air Force created its own Air Defense Divisions (the 25th, 26th, 27th, 28th, 29th, 30th, 31st, 32nd, 33rd, 34th, and 35th) in 1952. Several others were added later occupying their own regions of the United States. The creation of NORAD brought the antiaircraft units and tactical air units of both services and Canada into a more harmonious relationship for the sake of defense. Together they now assumed the responsibility once held by the Coast Artillery Corps (dissolved in January 1950) for almost half a century—the defense of the homeland.

The Soviet Threat and Missile Defense from 1950s to 1960s

In 1957, as missiles took on a more prominent role, the Army Antiaircraft Command (established July 1950) became the ARMY AIR DEFENSE COMMAND. This command no longer controled the early warning radar sites in the United States. The U.S. Air Force, on the other hand, held command control of all U.S. air defenses. In the past, the army anti-aircraft guns had served as the last line of defense, but by 1957 the gun units had converted to Nike missile units and the National Guard changed weapons in 1958. These surface-to-air missile (SAM) units had the ability to engage enemy aircraft that eluded air force fighter interceptors well before they reached the target area. By 1961, twenty-two population and industrial sites were defended by 250 army Nike missile batteries. The air force also maintained ten sites with its own BOMARC surface-to-air missile.

In January 1957, an additional item appeared in the arsenal of the U.S. Air Force: the GENIE. It was the first nuclear air-to-air non-guided missile, had a blast radius of 1000 feet, and used a 1.5-kiloton warhead and could seriously affect an enemy bomber formation. Only Alaska was vulnerable to Soviet medium-range bombers, but it offered little in the way of major targets. In October 1957, when an SS-6 "Sapwood" missile (SS for surface-to-surface) put Sputnik into orbit, the Soviets had their first ICBM. However, only about ten were deployed as ICBMs by 1959, but the Americans were convinced that there were hundreds waiting to strike undetected at American population and industrial centers. As a result of this erroneous intelligence, the military became convinced that there was a "Missile Gap" and urged a massive American buildup of strategic missiles. The Soviets finally developed the SS-7 "Saddler," a more effective ICBM with a range of over 6,500 miles, which was not deployed until 1961. The missile race had already begun in spite of the fact that the Soviets had only about two hundred ICBMs by the end of 1962. The Soviets would have just over 1,600 ICBMs by 1975, whereas the Americans had over 1,000, some of which carried multiple warheads.

The U.S. Army began developing a SURFACE-TO-AIR MISSILE (SAM) in the late 1940s for use with its antiaircraft defense. This program eventually became the NIKE

PROGRAM, which produced the NIKE-AJAX, and a little later, THE NIKE-HERCULES. The first Nike-Ajax unit, the 35th Antiaircraft Artillery (AAA) Battalion, became operational in December 1953 at Fort Meade (MD) after replacing its 120mm guns with missiles. By 1957, the 120mm and 90mm gun batteries would be replaced, even though the Nike SAM was originally only intended to supplement the gun units. The first gun batteries replaced by the Nike-Ajax were around Boston, Los Angeles, Chicago, Detroit, New York, and San Francisco. In 1955 the following thirty sites were given priority for Nike batteries: Washington/Baltimore area, New York metropolitan area, Chicago, Detroit, Philadelphia, Hanford nuclear facility in Washington state, San Francisco, Los Angeles, Seattle, Norfolk, Pittsburgh, and the Niagara/Buffalo area. Chicago officials were reluctant to have missile batteries in urban areas, while the mayor of St. Louis pleaded with the military to send batteries to his city. Between 1956 and 1958, longer-range Nike-Hercules batteries replaced two hundred Nike-Ajax batteries with the last Nike-Ajax retired for homeland service at Norfolk in 1963.

The NIKE-AJAX was a 34-foot-long, liquid-fuel missile with a range of from twenty-five to thirty miles reaching a height of up to 70,000 feet. It carried a conventional warhead capable of bringing down a bomber. The NIKE-HERCULES was a 41-foot-long solid-fuel rocket with a range of over seventy-five miles and could carry either a nuclear or conventional warhead for use against enemy aircraft at heights of up to 150,000 feet. Fear of a surprise attack and the possible effects of a nearby nuclear blast led officials to entrust the Corps of Engineers with the construction of relatively secure launch sites. A number of permanent sites were built for the SAM batteries in the late 1950s, but changes had to be made to accommodate the larger Nike-Hercules.

The NIKE MISSILE SITE was divided into three areas: Administrative, Integrated Fire Control (IFC), and Launch Area. The Launch and IFC areas were spaced from one thousand yards to over three miles apart, but within visual sight of each other. The guidance equipment could not function properly at distances of less than one thousand yards from the missile. The Administrative area was within the site and included flat-roofed structures of cinderblocks including a barracks, mess hall, motor pool, etc. The IFC had three tracking and acquisition radars, power plant, cables, etc. The battery control trailer with acquisition radarscope and controls, the guidance computer, and the telephone switchboard was placed in the IFC, along with the radar-control trailer.

The first Nike sites had above ground launchers. Soon, however, underground magazines of reinforced concrete had to be built. The underground magazine sheltered the ventilation equipment, a motor for powering the elevator, and quarters for the launch crew. Most sites had two to three magazines. An elevator lifted each missile into launching position on the surface. The crew pushed the missile off the elevator and along a rack to one of four launchers. Once in position the missile was raised to an almost vertical position. Not far from the launchers, an officer controlled the missile launchings from a trailer. A power supply was needed for these operations, and there was a nearby power plant housing three diesel generators. Additional buildings were used for missile assembly, maintenance, and other functions. The fuel storage area was behind a berm about 10 feet high to protect the launching site from an accidental explosion. The Nike-Ajax was first assembled, then fueled in the fueling area, and finally moved into the underground magazine. A few Nike accidents occurred, the most serious being an explosion of eight Nike-Ajax missiles at a base near Middleton, New Jersey that killed ten men in May 1958.

Another important element in the army's missile defense system was the establishment of the ARMY AIR DEFENSE COMMAND POST that coordinated a number of batteries. This command post was important because the guidance system of a Nike-Ajax site was able to handle only one enemy aircraft at a time whereas the command post could direct the firing of several missiles at several targets simultaneously. In 1957, these command posts were issued the AN/FSG-1 MISSILE MASTER, an integrated command and control system, which included its own radars and computers for target acquisition and tracking. It could coordinate twenty-four battery firings at twenty-four different targets for several batteries. The command post equipment occupied a blockhouse. Ten of these command post blockhouses that included protection against nuclear blast and fallout were built between 1957 and 1961. Battalions of SAM batteries not under their control received the less-expensive AN/GSG-5 system or BATTERY INTEGRATION AND RADAR DISPLAY EQUIPMENT (BIRDIE), which could handle four to sixteen sites. In the mid-1960s, the AN/TSQ-51 Missile Mentor system able to control twenty-four batteries, came into service.

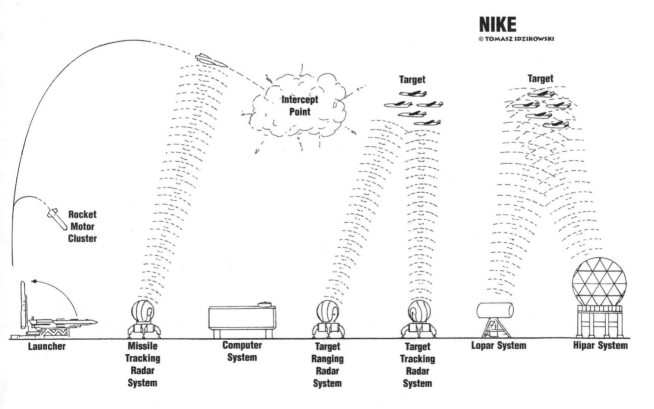

NIKE
© TOMASZ IDZIKOWSKI

Intercept Point

Target

Target

Rocket Motor Cluster

Launcher | Missile Tracking Radar System | Computer System | Target Ranging Radar System | Target Tracking Radar System | Lopar System | Hipar System

The deployment and control of the Ajax missile units changed little except for their equipment. Generally, the battalions's batteries encircled cities, and were usually located about twenty-five miles or more from the urban center. However, after the late 1950s, some units were assigned to the defense of SAC bases. The army engineers built thirty-five new installations for the Nike-Hercules between 1956 and 1958 and converted 110 Nike-Ajax sites for the larger solid-fuel missile that did not require a fueling area. The older magazines had room for only eight of the larger missiles. Racks, launchers and other equipment had to be modified. Except for locations where the terrain restricted their use, the Nike-Hercules employed the HIGH POWERED ACQUISITION RADAR (HIPAR) for tracking targets at a greater range to match the missiles's effectiveness. The ALTERNATE BATTERY RADAR (ABR) was also added to the IFC area as a backup for the HIPAR. A TARGET RANGING RADAR was also included to counter enemy jamming. The Nike sites included sentry posts and usually a double fence line, with barbed wire strung along the top of the chainlink fence, and dogs patrolling between the fences. (By 1970, the following Air Force Bases and cities were protected by the Nike system: Abilene (TX), Anchorage, Albany (GA), Austin, Baltimore, Barksdale AFB (LA), Boston, Buffalo/Niagara, Cincinnati/Dayton, Cleveland, Dallas, Detroit, Ellsworth AFB (SD), Fairbanks, Hanford Reservation (WA), Hartford, Kansas City (MO), Key West, Loring AFB (ME), Los Angeles, Homestead AFB (also covering Miami), Milwaukee, Minneapolis/St.Paul, Mountain Home AFB(ID), New Haven, New York City, Norfolk, Oahu, Omaha/Lincoln, Pittsburgh, Philadelphia, Providence (RI), Robbins AFB (GA), San Francisco, St. Louis, Seattle, Spokane, Walker AFB (NM), and Washington D.C.) The Nike-Hercules sites remained active through the 1960s and the last one was deactivated by 1975 except in Florida and Alaska, mainly because of the SALT I Treaty. The Army Air Defense Command was closed down. The army's smaller medium range Hawk batteries remained in service much longer, almost to the end of the century.

During the 1950s, the air force, in competition with the army, developed the BOMARC missile, its own version of the SAM. [The acronym BOMARC stands for the two organizations that designed it: Boeing and the University of Michigan's Aerospace Research Center.] The missile remained in service until the end of the decade. BOMARC was a 45-foot-long, solid-fuel rocket with two ramjet engines with a range of 440 miles. It operated differently than the army SAMs. It was launched and guided to the target by a ground station, but when it came within ten miles of the target, an on-board homing radar was activated. Since it was a long-range missile, it was used for area defense. In 1959, plans were made to build eighteen BOMARC sites, but in 1960 the number was reduced to ten sites, including two in Canada. The sites were located at Duluth and seven air bases between Duluth and the East Coast, in addition to the two in Canada. The BOMARC building had the appearance of a garage. Its roof consisted of two 10-ton leafs, 12 feet by 60 feet, which moved apart so the missile could be raised into the firing

BOMARC Model II shelter
based on Drawing from Defense and Deter

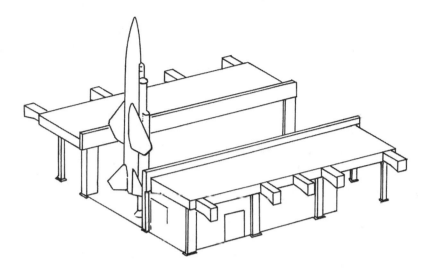

position. The associated operations equipment occupied an adjacent room. The number of launchers per site varied from as many as fifty-six launchers to as few as twenty-eight. All ten BOMARC sites were closed after the mid-1960s.

Defenses for the Offensive Weapons: The ICBMs

In the early 1950s, the army and air force competed to build offensive long-range missiles, but Secretary of Defense Charles Wilson ended the competition in 1956 by giving the air force control of missile systems with a range of over two hundred miles. The main purpose of ICBMs (Inter-Continental Ballistic Missiles) was the destruction of the Soviet Union in the event of war. During the arms race of the 1960s, it was assumed in the United States that the Soviet ICBMs and possibly some bombers would get through and destroy most of America's industrial and population targets, and possibly even some of the missile sites. The objective was to make certain that, if the early warning lines did not allow enough time for the United States to respond, enough of the ICBMs housed in hardened sites would survive a first strike to strike back at the U.S.S.R., ensuring that there would be no winners in World War III. Thus, the Corps of Engineers was assigned the task of fortifying the ICBM sites to resist all but direct hits from nuclear weapons. The first step was to build defensive radar lines with no protection against attack. The next step was to encase the missile launch sites in massive protection. The objective was not to defend the homeland or its people, but to defend the doomsday weapons.

Although the army was removed from the development and control of ICBM's, it was its Jupiter program that led to the development of the first American satellite in

Atlas E in its below-ground launcher
based on Drawing from Defense and Deter

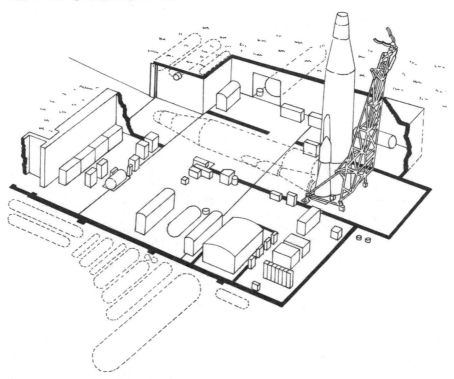

space. The first operational ICBM was the air force's ATLAS rocket, carrying a 1-megaton warhead, with ranges of 5,500 to 9,000 miles. The Atlas's great range allowed it to strike any target in the U.S.S.R. from bases in the continental U.S. The first squadron of six missiles were deployed at Warren Air Force Base (WY) in September 1960. The air force phased out its Atlas squadrons in 1965.

At the end of 1962, SAC deployed eleven squadrons of ATLAS D, ATLAS E, and ATLAS F models. Two squadrons were at Warren AFB (WY) and one at Offutt AFB (NE) with above ground launchers. Atlas-E squadrons were at Fairchild AFB (WA), Forbes AFB (KA), and Warren AFB deployed horizontally underground. The other six squadrons were Atlas F at Shilling AFB (KS), Lincoln AFB (NE), Altus AFB (OK), Dyess AFB (TX), Walker AFB (NM), and Plattsburg AFB (NY); all were stored vertically in underground silos.

The ability to resist the effect of a blast from a nuclear detonation within a few miles of the site was an important consideration. Three types of launch site were built: the standard above ground launcher, underground storage site with the missile in a horizontal position, and the underground silo for vertical storage. The surface launch site could withstand overpressure from a blast of five pounds per square inch (psi), the horizontal storage site twenty-five psi, and the silo one hundred psi. Only the silos that could withstand one hundred psi were considered hardened sites.

The horizontal storage could be above or below ground, but the underground site was a stronger position. The missile storage structure as well as the Launch Control Facility (LCF) was made of reinforced concrete below ground. The LCF was 50 feet by

94 feet and was linked to the launch area by a 150-foot underground tunnel. The missile's storage, service and launch structure was 105 feet by 100 feet. When the heavy roof retracted, the launch crew moved the Atlas E to the vertical launch position where it was fueled and fired.

The most secure positions were the silo and the LCF of reinforced concrete. The missile, which was 82 feet long, required a deep silo. The Atlas silo was one of the largest in America. It was 180 feet deep with a 65-foot diameter (sometimes the measurements of 174 feet and 55 feet are given, possibly accounting for the thickness of the walls). The standard construction procedure was to excavate the first 60 feet for the LCF and the silo. Next, the remainder of the silo was mined to help maintain strength without having to backfill the bottom portion. The six positions for a squadron required the removal of 2,700,000 cubic yards of earth, a steel framework, and 565,000 cubic yards of concrete. The amount of steel per silo was 100,000 tons. In the silo, the huge steel framework, known as the crib, supported the missile and the facilities, which were set on four sets of springs.

The silo consisted of eight levels: the bottom two, levels seven and eight, housed the fueling and storage tanks. The missile rested on an elevator at level six. Various tanks and pumps occupied most of the levels and most of the equipment for operating the 45-ton silo doors and elevator was on level one. Before launching, the Atlas had to be fueled and lifted to the surface with an elevator. The Atlas E and F were equipped with an all-inertial guidance system, removing the need for ground control and thus resulting in launch sites being twenty to thirty miles apart.

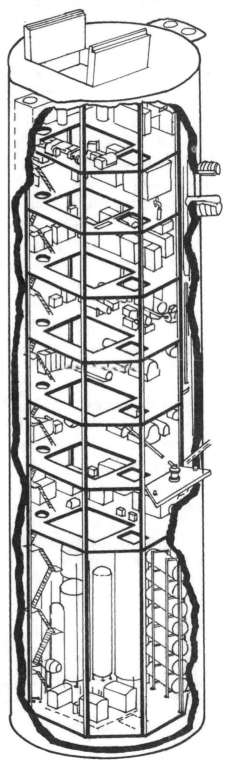

Atlas F silo
based on Drawing from Defense and Deter

The Launch Control Facility (LCF), 27 feet high with a 40-foot diameter, was linked to the silo by a 50-foot steel tunnel on its lower level that was sealed with two blast doors. The tunnel carried all the cable connections to the silo and served as access for the crew servicing the missile and silo. The LCF, which had a five-man crew, consisted of two levels with a stair access to the surface. The launch control room, commo room, and office were on the lower level. The upper level included the kitchen, toilets, and a ready room.

The TITAN PROGRAM, which produced the TITAN I and TITAN II, replaced the Atlas. These liquid-fuel rockets required huge underground silos. The TITAN I had a range of over six thousand miles and could strike at almost any Soviet target area. In April 1962, the first Titan missile squadron became operational at Lowry AFB (CO). Each squadron occupied three missile complexes spaced ten to twelve miles apart. Each of these sites comprised three silos and a launch control center. The Titan launch complexes with their associated underground facilities and silos proved to be the most costly of all the missile programs until 1970. The entire launch site, including the LCF and the silo were placed underground, creating a large subterranean complex. By the end of 1962, five more squadrons loaded their silos, making their missile complexes operational at Mountain Home AFB (ID), Beale AFB (CA), Larson AFB (WA), Ellsworth AFB (SD), and at Lowry AFB.

Although the Titan missile was 98 feet high, its silo was smaller than the Atlas's. It was160 feet deep and had a diameter of 44 feet with reinforced concrete walls 2 to 3 feet thick. Like the Atlas silo, the interior had an elevator to lift the Titan to the surface for launching after its two 125-ton doors opened. The supporting facilities and garrison area were underground and could be compared to some of the most advanced subterranean European forts of the 1930s, except for the fact that they only had guards with small arms and no defenses against a ground assault. The supporting facilities, all in circular structures, included propellant and equipment storage areas at depths of 24 feet below ground level, and adjacent to each missile silo, the control room (40 feet high and 100 feet in diameter) and a power plant (60 feet high and 127 feet in diameter). The lat-

Titan I launch complex
based on Drawing from Defense and Deter

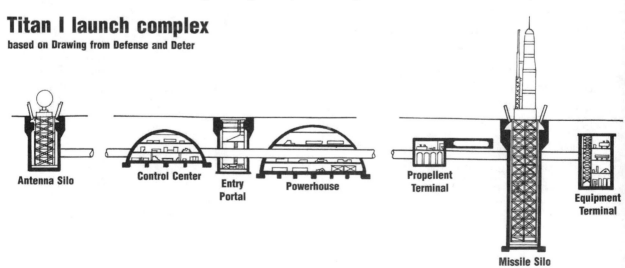

Antenna Silo   Control Center   Propellent   Equipment
                         Entry   Powerhouse   Terminal   Terminal
                         Portal

Missile Silo

Titan II silos and launch control facility

based on Drawing from Defense and Deter
© TOMASZ IDZIKOWSKI

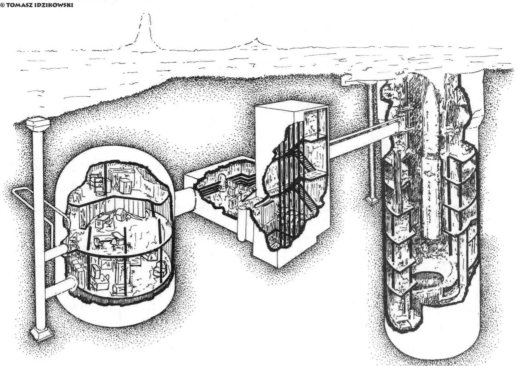

ter was usually about one hundred yards away and about 17 feet below ground. The power plant and control room, the largest structures at the site, were linked by a cylindrical steel tunnel 72 feet below the surface. Other smaller tunnels branched off this main passage toward the silos on one end. On the other end, the main tunnel ran toward the two small silos housing the radar antennae used for the missile guidance system. The antennae had to be sited at a distance of over 1,200 feet from the missiles. There were over 2,500 feet (about half a mile) of tunnels, including the small passages linking the positions to each other. The launch crew fueled the Titan I, then the elevator lifted it to the surface for launching, a process that took about fifteen minutes. At that time, the antennae for the ground guidance system extended out of their silos.

The TITAN II, like the Atlas E and F, had an all-inertial guidance system so its facilities did not need a ground guidance system like Titan I, so its silos were placed a minimum of seven miles apart. Unlike the Titan I, it required fewer subterranean facilities and a nearby SAC base served for support and garrison functions. The complex was super-hardened to withstand three hundred psi of over pressure. [According to James Gibson, author of *The History of the US Nuclear Arsenal*, these complexes could withstand a five-hundred kiloton blast at a distance of about 385 yards.) The silo was 147 feet deep and 55 feet in diameter. The Titan II was designed to be launched from within the silo, a procedure called "hot launch," and required a wider silo, a deflector at the base, and two exhaust ducts that ran up to the surface. A huge 740-ton door slid open for firing. When the missile was launched, the flame and smoke from inside the silo were vented through two exhausts, emitting a reddish plume on either side of the structure.

A 250-foot-long steel tunnel linked the silo to the Launch Control Center. Between the silo and launch center was a large blast lock that gave access to the surface, 35 feet above, and served as the crew's entrance. Each end of the blast lock had heavy steel doors that could withstand one thousand psi of pressure. The launch control center was 47 feet in diameter and all three floors were suspended from the ceiling. The top floor had quarters for the four-man crew and the two lower floors held all the communication and launch equipment. The first Titan II squadron became operational in June 1963 at Davis-Monthan AFB (AZ). Other squadrons were deployed at Little Rock AFB (AR) and McConnell AFB (KS). Each squadron had nine missile complexes, consisting of a silo and launch control center. The complexes were about ten miles apart. They went out of service in 1987.

The next development was the solid-fuel MINUTEMAN I with a range of about 6,300 miles followed by the MINUTEMAN II and MINUTEMAN III, whose range was almost one thousand miles over their predecessors. The first squadron of fifty missiles became operational in February 1963 at Malmstrom AFB. The air force maintained one thousand of these missiles between the 1960s and the mid-1980s. The first one thousand silos were completed between 1961 and 1966. The Minuteman's hardened sites were smaller and less expensive than the Atlas and the Titan sites. The silos, only 80 feet deep and 12 feet in diameter, were not manned. The prefabricated steel launch tube was suspended in the concrete silo with a system of shock absorbers on the floor. A two-level equipment room encircled the upper part of the silo that held all the tools and instruments needed for maintaining and launching the missile. The equipment support building was on the surface, until it was placed underground, next to the silo late in the 1960s. The Minuteman silos required only 15 percent of the concrete and 20 percent of the steel used for an Atlas F silo. About seventy Minuteman silos could be built for the same price as twelve Atlas silos.

The launch control center was 50 feet below ground at a distance of three and a half to seventeen miles from the silos. The capsule-like structure had 4-inch-thick walls of reinforced concrete lined with quarter-inch steel plate. It was 59 feet long and 29 feet in diameter and held a 28 foot by 12 foot suspended structure for a two-man crew who controlled ten silos. In its pale green interior were mounted the control consoles and communications equipment, giving it an "age of push-button warfare" look. After two officers turned their launch keys simultaneously, it took sixty seconds to launch the missile. If something happened to their control centers, the two officers were also able to launch the other forty missiles of their squadron. The Launch Control Facility included a large wood-frame support building with a garage. It had living quarters for the personnel who maintained the surface facilities, support equipment, and a place for the Air Police to guard access. Late in the 1960s, the support equipment of this structure was placed in an underground structure, next to the Launch Control Center. An elevator led down to the Launch Control Facility, past the guard station.

Minuteman Launch Facility – Minuteman III

based on Drawing from Defense and Deter

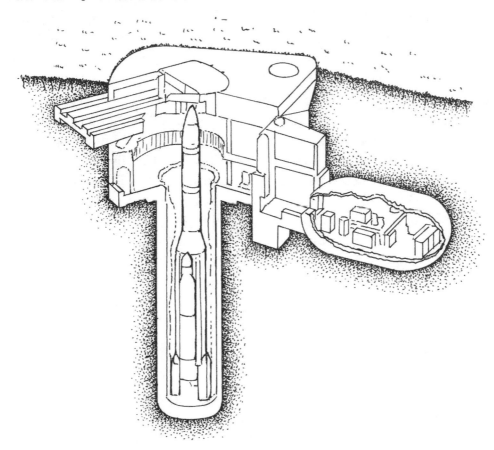

The Minuteman sites were fairly standards for all models. The first Minuteman II squadrons were activated in April 1966. Some were located in converted Minuteman I sites. The Minuteman III squadrons did not become operational until 1970. Minuteman IIIs were the first American missiles to carry two to three warheads apiece. The Minuteman sites were located near SAC bases and in lightly populated areas including Malmstrom AFB (MT), Ellsworth AFB (SD), Minot AFB (ND), Whiteman AFB (MO), Warren AFB (WY), and Grand Forts AFB (ND). The Minuteman sites formed the main offensive striking power by the end of the 1960s.

After the 1960s, the American-based missiles formed one part of a triad for retaliation against the Soviet Union. The other arm was also controlled by SAC, which maintained B-52 bombers on 24-hour alert, including in the air, to prevent a surprise attack from destroying them at their airfields in the United States. The third part of the triad was the Submarine Launched Ballistic Missile System (SLBM) carried on nuclear submarines, which remained on station underwater for months on end awaiting the signal to launch their missiles.

New Defense Against Missiles

Although the military believed that some of the SAMs could take out incoming missiles, they worked to create an effective ANTIBALLISTIC MISSILE (ABM) WEAPON. The ABM system began in the late 1950s under the army's Nike Zeus program and emerged as SAFEGUARD in 1969. The only site for this system was at Grand Forks (ND) at the STANLEY R. MICKELSEN SAFEGUARD COMPLEX. It included a Perimeter Acquisition Radar Building (PARB) near the town of Concrete and a Missile Site Control Building (MSCB) located twenty-five miles away, twelve miles south of Langdon. Four Remote Sprint Launch (RSL) sites were clustered within twenty miles. The Ballistic Missile Defense Center (BMDC) in Colorado integrated with Safeguard within NORAD. The MSCB site housed the short-range missile control radar and half of the Spartan and Sprint missile launchers. The other half of the missiles were at the four RSL sites (twelve to sixteen per site). They had an interception range of five hundred miles. In the mid-1960s, the army planned to create more of these sites near major cities, but President Richard Nixon cancelled those plans in an attempt to halt the arms race. Plans for two sites were reoriented to protect SAC bases, however, only one complex was eventually built in 1972.

The PERIMETER ACQUISITION RADAR BUILDING (PARB), the largest structure of the Safeguard system, measured 204 feet by 213 feet at the base and tapered off in a pyramidal shape as it rose 120 feet above the ground. It included five floors and required 58,000 cubic yards of concrete and 8,500 tons of steel to build. The radar was able to track incoming missiles at a range of two thousand miles. The structure's northern facade consisted of a 7-foot-thick reinforced concrete sloping wall mounting a massive array of antennae. The other three walls were 8 feet thick at the base and tapered off at the top. The entrance into the structure was through two blast locks. There was also a tunnel from the nearby power plant, also made of reinforced concrete with earthen cover and containing five diesel engines, a fuel supply, and cooling water system. An Army Surveillance Battalion of four hundred people operated this facility, working in three shifts around-the-clock. This site searched and acquired the targets at long range and alerted the MSCB.

The MISSILE SITE CONTROL BUILDING (MSCB) housed radar. Part of the four-sided structure was below ground. It had the shape of a truncated pyramid and its reinforced concrete walls were 3 feet thick. Each side of the structure mounted a large 400-ton circular antenna, 30 feet in diameter. Below the pyramidal structure, was a two-story structure 231 feet by 231 feet that housed the radar transmitting and receiving components, various systems, and the power plant with six diesel engines. The Army Safeguard Battalion of almost eight hundred men manned this position. After it was alerted by the PARB, this site acquired the target, launched the long-range Spartan missile, and guided it to the target before its re-entry into the atmosphere. Once near the target, the MSCB detonated the Spartan missile. It also launched the rapid-accelerating, short-range Sprints to destroy the remaining enemy targets.

Early in the 1970s, when the American ABM became a bargaining chip in arms reduction, most of the site's missile-launching positions were deactivated. The government accepted the fact that a mass of Soviet ICBMs using multiple warheads would be able to overwhelm this single complex.

Command, Communication, and Security

Command, communication, and security were a critical area for operating the radar lines and coordinating missile activities in defending the continent and launching offensive weapons. The sites on the radar warning lines were not designed to defend themselves against enemy attacks and their communications links were equally vulnerable. Equipment was not always located in blockhouses. At launch control facilities, many of the communications antennae were placed in hardened positions. On the DEW Line, most facilities were equipped with some form of small arms like rifles to protect against bears. The crews of the Minuteman Launch Control Facilities carried M-16 rifles and M-60 machine guns to protect the facilities from terrorists or surprise raids. Most command sites and missile launch and control facilities had protection against the Electro Magnetic Pulse (EMP) resulting from a nuclear detonation, which could disable all electronic equipment. Shock absorbers and various suspension methods only protected against blast effects. Shielding was needed against EMP, since the functioning of the electronics was mandatory for the site to operate.

The two most important COMMAND AND COMMUNICATION CENTERS (CCC) included one super site for the military and one for the government. The military site, built beneath the granite of Cheyenne Mountain, served as the headquarters for NORAD and other commands. After tunneling into the mountain between the summers of 1961 and 1962, massive subterranean facilities were carved out, but more work had to be done to secure the position. The site was occupied by 1966. It can withstand a 5-megaton blast detonated at a distance as close as one and a half miles from the site. The entrance is through the north portal, which leads to the main site about a third of a mile inside the mountain. The complex, protected by 2,000 feet of granite, occupies four and a half acres. Galleries branch off of it, including to the Command Center, which a 30-ton blast door seals off from the outside world. The complex includes fifteen steel-framed buildings, twelve of them three-stories high. Blast valves in reinforced concrete bulkheads in the air-intake and exhaust systems, water, sewer, and fuel lines are designed to handle the overpressure from an explosion. [These blast valves for protection against overpressure from a nuclear blast became standard features in most of the other large underground complexes mentioned here]. All of these steel buildings are mounted on large coil springs to protect sensitive equipment from a nuclear near-miss. Over a thousand military and civilian personnel work inside the complex.

Other CCC include the PENTAGON, completed in 1942, which is not expected to withstand nuclear attack, but is designed to resist most conventional weapons. The Pentagon's vulnerability led to the creation, between 1950 and 1953, of the ALTERNATE JOINT COMMUNICATIONS CENTER, located at the Raven Rock Mountain near Camp David in Pennsylvania. Known as SITE R, the large underground complex 650 feet beneath the 1,529-foot mountain peak is accessed through two sets of entrances. It includes several three-story structures (one news report claims six-story), a power plant, water and fuel supply, and everything else needed to survive a nuclear war. The army, navy, and air force operate communications facilities at the site.

In the mid-1950s, the Corps of Engineers was ordered to build another large tunnel complex at MOUNT WEATHER from where the government could operate in time of nuclear war. It occupies a 200,000-square-foot area 300 feet below the mountain summit, and includes a hospital, recreation areas, dormitories, power plant, radio and television studios, and reservoirs. It can accommodate two thousand members of the government and their staff. Today it is used as an emergency disaster operations center.

At White Sulphur Springs (WV), a massive two-level bunker was built beneath the Greenbrier Hotel and once served as the nuclear refuge for Congress and staff, accommodating up to twelve hundred people for thirty years. The government secretly built this hideout between 1959 and 1962. At Culpeper (VA), the MOUNT PONY FEDERAL RESERVE BUNKER was built to keep a secure supply of money available and protect business records during a nuclear war.

In Canada, the government created the DIEFENBUNKER (named for the leader of the government in 1957) for wartime security. It is located at Carp, Ontario. Begun in 1959 and completed in 1961, this four-story 100,000 square foot bunker was built with 32,000 cubic yards of concrete and 5,000 tons of steel. Diesel fuel was stored on the lower level with a vault for the Bank of Canada. The power plant was above that level. The communication facility was on the upper level.

In the United States as well as in Canada, Civil Defense played a rather limited role and lacked military support to create protective shelters for the masses. If the dreaded nuclear war ever materialized, the missiles would have left their silos for their targets, the SAC bombers would have flown toward their destinations, and the submarines would have launched their SLBMs from beneath the sea. The surviving bomber crews would have returned to non-operational airfields while the Titan and Minuteman missile crews would have no mission left with their silos empty. The submarines and other naval forces would have been left without naval bases to which they could return. The Soviet Union and the United States would have been transformed into giant wastelands, their major cities and military facilities a mass of rubble.

Fort	Nation	Location	Fort	Nation	Location
Quebec*	French	New France	Boston*	British	New England
Louisbourg*	French	New France	George	British	New England
Beausejour / Cumberland	French / British	New France / Nova Scotia	Dummer	British	New England
Chamby	French	New France	William Henry	British	New York
Frederic / Crown Point	French / British	New France / New York	Carillon / Ticonderoga	French / British	New France / New York
Frontenac	French	New France	Edward	British	New York
Levi	French	New France	Oswego**	British	New York
Niagara	French	Great Lakes	Cumberland	British	Maryland
Detriot	French	Great Lakes	Frederick	British	Maryland
St. Joseph	French	Great Lakes	Loudoun	British	Virginia
Michilimackinac	French	Great Lakes	Bedford	British	Pennsylvania
Presque Isle	French	Great Lakes	Ligioner	British	Pennsylvania
Le Boeuf	French	Ohio Valley	Augusta	British	Pennsylvania
Duquesne / Pitt	French / British	Ohio Valley	**Note**: *Fortress **Oswego consisted of three forts. Double box includes French & British fort on same site.		
Chartres	French	Mississippi	Prince George	British	South Carolina
Kaskaskia	French	Mississippi	Ninety-Six	British	South Carolina
Conde	French	Alabama	Loudoun	British	Tennessee
Toulouse	French	Alabama			

Important Forts of the French and Indian War

Battles of War of 1812 Involving Fortifications				
WAR of 1812 Battles & Campaigns	Year	Directly or Indirectly Involved		Victory
		Forts (US)	Forts (British)	
Fort Dearborn	1812	Ft. Dearborn		British
Detriot	1812	Ft. Lernoult	Ft.Malden	British
Queenston Heights	1812			--
Frenchtown	1813			British
Ft. Meigs	1813	Ft. Meigs		American
Sackets Harbor	1813	3 forts		American
Niagara	1813		Ft. George	American
Stony Creek	1813			British
Lake Erie	1813	Naval Battle - Detriot lost		American
Thames River	1813		Ft. Malden	American
Chateaugay River	1813			British
Chrysler's Farm	1813			British
Niagara	1813	Ft. Niagara		British
Chippewa River	1814		Ft. Erie	American
Lundy's Lane	1814	Ft. Erie		--
Ft. Erie	1814	Ft. Erie		American
Bladensburg	1814			British
Champlain	1814	Plattsburg		American
Ft. McHenry	1814	Ft.McHenry		American
New Orleans	1815			American
Ft. Bowyar	1815	Ft. Bowyer		British
NOTE: Grayed out battles - significant fortifications not involved				

Batt.= battery
Enclosed battery = either a small battery position surrounded by defenses or a small fort.
*Including a blockhouse
**Replaced by Fort Columbus
***Old fort from Revolutionary Era

1st and 2nd SYSTEM FORTS 1790–1812				
Name	Location	Built	# of Guns	Notes
MAINE				
Fort Sullivan	Moose Is.	1808-09	4	Circular stone batt.*
	Machias	1807-	4	Circular stone batt.*
	Penobscot	1807-	4	Small enclosed batt.
Fort George	Castine	1808-09	3	Small enclosed batt.
	Damariscotta	1807-	3	Small enclosed batt.*
	Edgecomb	1807-	6	Enclosed battery*
	Georgetown	1808	6	Enclosed battery
Fort Sumter	Portland	1794,1808	5	Enclosed battery
Fort Preble	Portland	1808	14	Star fort
Fort Scammel	Portland	1808	15	Circular battery*
NEW HAMPSHIRE				
Fort Constitution	Portsmouth	1794,1807	36	Irregular trace
Fort McClary	Portsmouth	1808	10	Circular battery
	Newbury	1808	5	Enclosed earth batt.
MASSACHUSETTS				
	Gloucester	1794,1798	7	Enclosed battery
Fort Pickering	Salem	1794,1808	6	Enclosed battery
Fort Sewall	Marblehead	1794,1808	8	Enclosed battery
Fort Independence	Boston	1800-03	54	Pentagonal trace
Fort Warren	Boston	1807-	12	Star fort
Governor's Island	Boston	1807-	20	2 circular batteries
	Charlestown	1808	8	Circular battery
	Plymouth	1808	5	Old fort
	New Bedford	1808	6	Enclosed battery
RHODE ISLAND				
Fort Adams	Newport	1798,1808	17	Irregular trace
Fort Wolcott	Goat Island	1798,1808	38	Small enclosed work
	Rose Island	1798	60	Not completed
CONNECTICUT				
Fort Trumbull	New London	1799,1808	18	Old fort***
Fort Hale	New Haven	1808-09	6	Enclosed battery

1st and 2nd SYSTEM FORTS 1790 – 1812 (continued)				
NEW YORK				
Fort Jay	Governors Is.	1794,1798		Razed 1806**
Fort Columbus	Governors Is.	1807-	60	On site of Ft. Jay
Castle Williams	Governors Is.	1808-12	52	Casemate Tower
Fort Wood	Bedloe's Is.	1809-10	24	Star fort
Fort Gibson	Ellis Is.	1809	14	Circular battery
Castle Clinton	New York	1809-	29	Circular battery
Humbert Battery	New York	1809	16	Circular battery
PENNSYLVANIA				
Fort Mifflin	Philadelphia	1798-00	38	Rebuilt old fort
MARYLAND				
Fort McHenry	Baltimore	1798-00	40	Pentagonal trace
Fort Madison	Annapolis	1809	13	Enclosed work
Fort Severn	Annapolis	1809	8	Circular battery
VIRGINIA				
Fort Washington	Potomac R.	1808-09	18	Irregular trace
Fort Powhatan	James R.	1808	25	Square trace
Fort Nelson	Norfolk	1794,1808	37	Irregular trace
Fort Norfolk	Norfolk	1794,1808	30	Irregular trace
NORTH CAROLINA				
Fort Johnston	Wilmington	1799-06	8	Battery***
Fort Hampton	Beaufort	1808-09	5	Small enclosed batt.
SOUTH CAROLINA				
Fort Wingaw	Georgetown	1809		Small battery*
Fort Johnson	Charleston	1794,1807	16	New batt.added***
Fort Moultrie	Sullivans Is.	1807-	40	Irregular Trace***
Castle Pinckney	Charleston	1807-	30	2 tiers of guns
Fort Marion	Beaufort	1809-	-	Not completed
GEORGIA				
Fort Jackson	Savannah	1808-	6	Enclosed work
LOUISIANA				
Fort St. Philip	Palaquemines	1793,1803	20	Acquired in 1803

Batt.= battery   **Replaced by Fort Columbus
*Including a blockhouse   ***Old fort from Revolutionary Era

FORTS OF THE BERNARD/TOTTEN THIRD SYSTEM —New England

Region/Fort's Name(location) 3rd System fort begun/completed++	Wartime Garrison 1851++ Estimate	Cannons 1851++ Estimate	Tiers Case. Arty.	Notes	Priority 1821/1826 Sides*#
Knox (Penobscot R., ME) 1843/1869	500	148 (137)	1		3/2 P
Popham (Kennebec R., ME) 1862/NC	500	150 (42)	2	Island Fort	3/2 C
Gorges (Portland, ME) 1859/1869		95 (195)	2	Island Fort	2/2 Six
Preble (Portland, ME) 1836 repairs. 184?/1847	200(2nd)* 300(3rd)	48 (2nd) 78 (3rd)	0 1	Island Fort	2/2 I
Scrammel (Portland, ME) 1836 repairs. 1845/1847	300 (2nd) 250 (3rd)	63 (2nd) 46 (3rd)	0	Comp.2 of 3 bastion	2/2 I
Constitution (Portsmouth, NH) 1836-1851 repairs. 1863/NC	250 (2nd)	58 (2nd) [149](3rd)	0 3#	Island Fort	1/2 P
McClary (Portsmouth, NH) 1836-1850 repairs. 1863/NC	80 (2nd) 750 (3rd)	15(2nd)** 150 (3rd)	0 1		0/3 P
Winthrop (Boston, MA) 1841 repairs. 1833/1850 (tower)	300(2nd)	68(2nd)	0	Island Fort Det. Bat.	0/3 P
Independence (Boston, MA) 1833 repairs. Rebuilt1837/1851	500	125 (225)	1	Island Fort	0/2 P
Warren (Boston, MA) 1833 (1837)/1861	1,500	334 (265)	2	Island Fort	1/1 P
Taber (Bedford, MA) 1857/NC	500	111 (70)	2		0/3 P
Adams (Newport, RI) 1822 (1825)/1857	2,440	464	2		1/1 I
Trumbull (New London, CT) 1838/1845	350	88 (62)	1	Old fort razed 1837	3/3 P

FORTS OF THE BERNARD/TOTTEN THIRD SYSTEM New York Harbor Area

Region/Fort's Name(location) 3rd System fort begun/completed++	Wartime Garrison 1851++ Estimate	Cannons 1851++ Estimate	Tiers Case. Arty.	Notes	Priority 1821/1826 Sides*
Schulyer (Throg's Neck) 1833/1845 (1856)	1,250	318(312)	3		1/1 P
Totten (Willet's Point) 1863/ NC		[68]	4#	Casemated Tower	1/1 P
Fort Columbus (Governor's Is.) 1831 repairs		105			
Castle Williams (Governor's Is.) 1831 repairs	700	78 (105)	3		
Gibson (Ellis Island) 1841-1844 repairs	80	15	0	Island Fort	
Wood (Bedlow's Island) 1841 repairs.	350	77	0	Island Fort	
Hamilton (Long Island) 1824 (1825)/1836 (1838)	800	118	1		1/1 T
Lafayette (The Narrows) 1812/1822	370	76	3	Island fort	T
Richmond (Staten Island) New fort 1847/1864	500	140 (116)	3		1/1 P
Tompkins (Staten Island) 1847/1868	500	64 (42)	0		1/1 P
Hancock (Sandy Hook) 1859/NC	1,000	291(208)	1		3/3 P

FORTS OF THE BERNARD/TOTTEN THIRD SYSTEM—East Coast

Region/Fort's Name(location) 3rd System fort begun/completed++	Wartime Garrison 1851++ Estimate	Cannons 1851++ Estimate	Tiers Case. Arty.	Notes	Priority 1821/1826 Sides*#
Delaware (Delaware R., DE) 1833 (1848)/1859	750	151 (175)	2	Island Fort	1/1 P
McHenry (Baltimore, MD) 1836-1840 repairs		53			
Madison (Annapolis, MD) 1846 repairs ? (see Notes)		31		Dismantled 1832 ?	
Severn (Annapolis, MD) 1841 repairs		14			
Carroll (Baltimore, MD) 1847/NC	800	159 (225)	4#	Island Fort Case.Tower	2/1 H
Washington (Potomac R., MD) Rebuilt 1816/1848	400	88	0		I
Monroe (Hampton Rds.,VA) 1817 (1819)/1837	2,450	371 (585)	1		1/1 I
Wool [Calhoun] (Hampton Rd) 1818 (1820)/NC	1,120	159 (216)	3#	Island Fort Case.Tower	1/1 I
Macon (Beaufort, NC) 1826/1834	300	61 (51)	0		2/3 I
Caswell (Cape Fear R., NC) 1826 (1827)/1836 (1838)	400	87 (64)	0	Citadel inc.	2/2 P
Moultrie (Charleston, SC) Modified 1841/1844	300	54	0		
Castle Pinckney (Charleston, SC) Rebuilt 1828-1831	100	25	0	Island Fort	
Sumter (Charleston, SC) 1829/1860	650	224 (135)	2	Island Fort Case.Tower	2/1 P
Pulaski (Savannah, GA) 1829/1847	800	150 (146)	1	Island Fort	2/1 P
Jackson (Savannah, GA) Modified 1842	70	14	0		2/2
Clinch (St. Mary's R., FL) 1850 (1846)/NC	550	146 (70)	0		3/2 P
Marion (St. Augustine, FL) Additions 1840/1844	100	25	0	Spanish fort	
Massachusetts (Ship Is., MI) 1858 (1859)/NC	400	89	1	Island Fort	

FORTS OF THE BERNARD/TOTTEN THIRD SYSTEM -- Gulf Coast

Region/Fort's Name(location) 3rd System fort begun/completed++	Wartime Garrison 1851++ Estimate	Cannons 1851++ Estimate	Tiers Case. Arty.	Notes	Priority 1821/1826 Sides*
Barrancas## (Pensacola, FL) 1839 (1840)/1846 (1844)	750	151 (175)	2	Island Fort	1/1 P
Advanced Redoubt (Pensacola, FL) 1845/1859		53			
Pickens (Pensacola, FL) 1828 (1829)/1844		31		Dismantled 1832 ?	
McRee (Pensacola, FL) 1833 (1834)/1837 (1844)		14			
Morgan (Mobile, AL) 1819/1834	800	159 (225)	4#	Island Fort Case.Tower	2/1 H
Gaines (Mobile, AL) 1819, 1846(1853)/1861	400	88	0		I
Pike (Rigolets, LA) 1819/1826	300	49 (40)	1	Citadel	1/1 C
Macomb (Chef Menteur, LA) 1822/1827	300	49	1	Citadel	1/1 C
Tower Dupre (Bayou Dupre) 1830/1848	50	7	2	Martello Tower	3/2
Proctor's Tower (Proctor Landing, LA)1853/NC	100	37	0	Island Fort	3/3
St. Philip (Plaquemine, LA) 1841 repairs	600	124	0		1/1 I
Jackson (Plaquemine, LA) 1822 (1824)/1832	600	150 (97)	1		1/1 P
Livingston (Grande Terre, LA) 1833 (1835)/NC	300	52	0	Island fort	3/1 T

FORTS OF THE BERNARD/TOTTEN THIRD SYSTEM --Miscellaneous

Region/Fort's Name(location) 3rd System fort begun/completed++	Wartime Garrison 1851++ Estimate	Cannons 1851++ Estimate	Tiers Case. Arty.	Notes	Priority 1821/1826 Sides*
Florida Keys					
E. & W. Martello Tower (Key West) 1861/1862###		14 each			
Taylor (Key West) 1845 (1846)/NC	1,000	185 (179)	2		T
Jefferson (Dry Tortuga) 1846/NC	1,500	298 (450)	2	Island Fort	H
San Francisco Bay					
Point 1853/1861		126	3	Casemated Tower	P
Alcatraz 1853/1867		108	0	Island Fort Citadel	I

NOTE: Those items noted as 2nd/3rd were basically 3rd System works built over the old 2nd System positions or added to them. NC = Not Completed, Comp. = completed, Det.Bat.= Includes detached battery, Case.Tower = Casemated Tower, Citadel = fort has a citadel, Island Fort = Fort occupies most of an island or is on an artificial island, Land Defense = Position only designed to defend landward approaches.

Estimate of Cannons represents number of cannons that the "planned" fort could mount. The number present was usually less.

Information on Fort Madison is contradictory. The 1851 Totten report claims it was repaired, but others sources claim it was dismantled before that.

+ New fort proposed in 1851 Report.

++ Numbers in brackets [ ] are from a later date. Numbers in parenthesis ( ) are other estimates from other sources.

* Numbers given for old fort (2nd) and new works (3rd), but these are not to be combined and only one is based on 1851 estimate.

** To be mounted in blockhouse & batteries.

Only 1 tier built.

Included old Spanish Water Battery

Each included seacoast wall with casemated guns.

*# 1821 and 1826 Priority for Construction were either 1st, 2nd or 3rd Priority (1, 2 or 3). They are shown for the two years as 1821/1826. Below is the number of sides the fort has. Most were 5-sided pentagons, including irregularly shaped, or 4-sided trapezoids. I = Irregular Trace , T = Trapezoidal Trace , P = Pentagonal Trace, C= Seacoast walls curved (form an arc).

Dates and Numbers: Completion dates are not given for many sites where work continued in the 1850s. The Executive Document for 1851 indicates they anticipated most work would be done by 1853, but that was not always the case and for that we give no date. Data derived from February 12, 1821, Report on Fortification for the House of Representatives, Executive Documents 1st Session 32nd Congress, 1851 to 1852, and *Legacy in Brick and Stone* by John Weaver.

WEAPONS OF THE ENDICOTT ERA for Coast Defense

Weapons Type	Range (yds)*	Muzzle Velocity FPS	Weight of Gun -Tons	Weight of Powder Charge lbs.	Weight of Projectile Lbs.
16-Inch BLR M-1895	15,558	2,150	127	612 Prop. / 46.1 AP-s / 139.3 AP-sh	2,400
12-Inch BLR M-1888	15,134	2,250	52	268 Prop. / 13 AP-s / 38.4 AP-sh	1,045
12-Inch BLR M-1895	11,636	2,250	52	268 Prop / 13 AP-s / 38.4 AP-sh	1,045
12-Inch BLR M-1900	13,513+	2,550++	59	325 Prop / 13 AP-s / 39.4 AP-sh	1,045
10-Inch BLR M-1888	12,259	2,250	30	155 Prop / 7.5 AP-s / 22.4 AP-sh	604
10-Inch BLR M-1895	14,062	2,250	30	155 Prop / 7.5 AP-s / 22.4 AP-sh	604
10-Inch BLR M-1900	14,162	2,250	34	205 Prop / 7.5 AP-s / 22.4 AP-sh	604
8-Inch BLR M-1888	11,019	2,200	14.5	80 Prop / 4 AP-s / 11.5 AP-sh	316
6-Inch QF Arm.	10,185	2,150	6.6	19 Prop / 4.3 BC	106
6-Inch Rapid Fire M-1897	11,799	2,600	7.25	29.75 Prop / 4.3 BC	106
6-Inch Rapid Fire M-1900	13,077	2,600	8.5	42 Prop / 4.3 BC	106
5-Inch Rapid Fire M-1897	10,431	2,600	3.8	16.5 Prop / 2.3 BC	58
4.72-Inch QF Arm.	11,211	2,600	2.9	8.2 Prop / 2 BC	45
4-Inch D.S. Rapid Fire	8,864	2,300	1.8	7.5 Prop / 4.5 BC	33

MORTARS	Minimum Range	Maximum Range	Weight of Weapon	Weight of Prop (lbs)	Weight of Round
12-Inch CI M-1886	65 deg elv 2,225	15 deg elv 9,557	14.25	Varies Prop / 33 Prop	1,046 / 824
12-Inch ST M-1890	65 deg elv 2,210	45 deg elv 12,019	13	Varies-Prop / Varies-Prop	1,046 / 824
10-Inch St M-1890		10,798	7.5		604

*At 15 degrees elevation
+Maximum elevation of 10 degrees
++ Reduce to 2,250 for longer barrel life
BLR - Breachloading Rifle
Prop. - Propelling Charge
AP-s. - Bursting charge for high-explosive Armor Piercing Shot
AP-sh -Bursting charge for Armor-Piercing Shell
Arm. - Armstrong (British)
D.S. - Driggs-Schroeder (produced in U.S.)
CI - Cast Iron
ST - Steel

Coastal and Harbor Defenses—1903-1944

Coastal Area Since 1903	Harbor Defense After 1925	Fort	Main Armament* 1903	1925	1944
Frenchman Bay (ME)	-	-		-	-
Penobscot River (ME)		Knox	-	-	-
		Baldwin	6"	3"	-
Kennebec River (ME)	HD of Kennebec	Popham	-	-	-
		Lyon	6"	3"	3"
		McKinley	12"	12"	12"
		Scammel	-	-	-
		Preble	6"	3"	3"
		Levett	12"	12"	12"
		Williams	12"	12"	12"
Portsmouth (NH)	HD of Portland	Foster	10"	10"	10"
		McClary	-	-	-
		Constitution	8"	3"	3"
		Stark	12"	12"	12"
		Dearborn	-	-	16"

continued on next page

Coastal and Harbor Defenses—1903-1944 (continued)					
Coastal areas Since 1903	**Harbor Defense after 1925**	**Fort**	**Main Armament***		
			1903	1925	1944
Boston (MA)	HD of Boston	Ruckman	-	12"	12"
		Heath	-	12"	12"
		Banks	12"	-	-
		Dawes	-	-	16"
		Strong	10"	10"	3"
		Standish	10"	10"	10"
		Warren	10"	12"	12"
		Andrews	6"	6"	6"
		Revere	12"	12"	12"
		Duvall			16"
New Bedford (MA)	HD of New Bedford	Rodman	8"	12"	12"
Narragansett Bay (RI)	HD of Narragansett Bay	Church			16"
		Adams		10"	10"
		Wetherill	10"	12"	12"
		Getty	12"	12"	6"
		Burnside	12"		16"
		Greble		10"	-
		Kearny	10"	6"	6"
		Varum			6"
		Greene			16"
Eastern Entrance To Long Island Sound (CT & NY)	HD of Long Island Sound	Mansfield	8"		
		H.G. Wright	12"	12"	12"
		Michie	10"	16"	16"
		Terry	12"	10"	6"
		Tyler			16"
		Hero	-	-	
New York East Entrance (NY)	HD of Eastern New York	Slocum	6"	-	-
		Schuyler	12"	12"	-
		Totten	12"	3"	3"
New York South Entrance (NY & NJ)	HD of Southern New York	Tilden	-		16"
		Hamilton	12"	16"	3"
		Wadsworth	12"	12"	12"
		Hancock	12"	12"	12"
		Highlands MR	-	12"	16"
Delaware River (NJ & DE)	HD of Delaware	Mott	12"	12"	
		Delaware	12"	12"	
		DuPont	12"	12"	
		Saulsbury		12"	12"
		Miles			16"
Baltimore (MD)	HD of Baltimore	Howard	12"	6"	-
		Carroll	12"		-
		Armistead	12"		-
		Smallwood	6"	12"	-

continued on next page

Coastal and Harbor Defenses—1903-1944 (continued)					
Coastal Area Since 1903	**Harbor Defense After 1925**	**Fort**	**Main Armament**		
			1903	1925	1944
Washington DC (MD & VA)	HD of Potomac	Washington Hunt	10" 8"	10"	- -
Hampton Roads (VA)	HD of Chesapeake Bay	Custis Monroe Wool Story	- 12" 6" -	- 12" 6" 16"	16" 12" 3" 16"
Cape Fear River (NC)	HD of Cape Fear River	Caswell	12"	12"	-
Charleston (SC)	HD of Charleston	Sullivan Is MR Moultrie Sumter	- 10" 12"	- 10" 12"	12" 10" 90-mm
Port Royal (SC)	HD of Port Royal Sound	Fremont Welles	10"	- -	- -
Savannah (SC)	HD of Savannah	Screven Pulaski	12" 3"		- -
St. Johns River (FL)	HD of Jacksonville	(site active during WWI)	4.7"	-	-
Key West (FL)	HD of Key West	Taylor W.Martello T. E.Martello T.	12"	12" 3"	12" 90-mm 6"
Tampa (FL)	HD of Tampa Bay	DeSoto Dade	3" 3"	6"	- -
Pensacola (FL)	HD of Pensacola	Pickens McRee Barrancas	12" 8" 2"	12" - -	12" 6" -

continued on next page

Coastal and Harbor Defenses—1903-1944 (continued)					
Coastal Area Since 1903	Harbor Defense After 1925	Fort	Main Armament*		
			1903	1925	1944
Mobile (AL)	HD of Mobile	Morgan	12"	12"	-
		Gaines	6"	6"	-
New Orleans (LA & TX)	HD of the Mississippi	St. Philip	10"		-
		Jackson			-
		(Sabine Pass)	8"		155-mm
Galveston (TX)	HD of Galveston	Travis	8"	12"	3"
		San Jacinto	10"	10"	6"
		Crockett	10"	12"	12"
		(Freeport)	-	-	6"
		(Port Aransas)	-	-	155-mm
San Diego (CA)	HD of San Diego	Emory	-	-	6"
		Pio Pico	3"		
		Rosecrans	10"	10"	16"
Los Angeles San Pedro (CA)	HD of Los Angeles	Bolsa Chica MR	-	-	6"
		White Pt. MR	-	-	16"
		Long Pt. MR	-	-	6"
		MacArthur	-	14"	14"
San Francisco	HD of San Francisco	Funston	-	5"	16"
		Miley	12"	12"	12"
		Scott	8"	12"	6"
		Mason	8"		
		McDowell	8"		
		Baker	12"	12"	90-mm
		Barry	12"	12"	12"
		Cronkhite	-	-	16"
Columbia River	HD of the Columbia	Stevens	10"	10"	10"
		Canby		6"	6"
		Columbia	8"	8"	6"
Puget Sound	HD of Puget Sound	Worden	12"	12"	12"
		Flagler	12"	12"	90-mm
		Casey	10"	10"	3"
		Ward	8"	5"	-
		Ebey	-	-	6"
		(Deception Pass)			
		(Camp Hayden)	-	-	16"
		Hayden	-	-	

*Only size of heaviest battery or batteries present identified, not including mortars.
- Fort did not exist yet, or taken out of service and no artillery in place
Sites listed with no weapons had positions under construction or planned, but not completed.

HARBOR ENTRANCE COMMAND POSTS 1941 to 1946			
Harbor Defense of:	Naval District	Location of HECP	Fort
Portland (ME)	1	Cape Cottage	Ft. Williams
Portsmouth (NH)	1	Coast Guard Station	Ft. Stark, Battery Kirk
Boston	1	Deer Island	Ft. Dawes
New Bedford	1	New Bedford	
Narragansett	1	Beavertail	Ft. Burnside
Long Island Sound	3	Fishers Island	Ft. H.G. Wright
New York	3	Staten Island	Ft. Wadsworth
Delaware	4	Cape Henlopen	Ft. Miles
Chesapeake	5	Norfolk	adjacent to Ft. Story
Charleston	6	Sullivan's Island	Ft. Moultrie
Key West	7	Key West	Ft. Taylor
Pensacola	8	Santa Rosa Island	Ft. Pickens, Battery Worth
Galveston	8	Fort Point	Ft. San Jacinto
San Diego	11	Point Loma	Ft. Rosecrans
Los Angeles	11	San Pedro	Ft. MacArthur, Batt.Merriam
San Francisco	12	Presidio	Ft. W. Scott, Dynamite Batt.
Columbia River	13	Point Adams	Ft. Stevens, Battery Mishler
Puget Sound	13	Point Wilson	Ft. Worden
PUERTO RICO			
San Juan	10	El Morro	Ft. Brooke, Battery Point
Vieques Sound	10	Punta Algodones	
PANAMA CANAL ZONE			
Cristobal	15	Toro Point	Ft. Sherman
Balboa	15	Balboa	Ft. Amador
HAWAII			
Pearl Harbor	14	Pearl Harbor	Navy Yard
Honolulu	14	Honolulu	
PHILIPPINES			
Manila & Subic Bay	16	Corregidor	Ft. Mills

MAJOR RADARS OF THE COLD WAR				
Radar Unit		**Range**	**Crew**	**Notes**
World War II Era				
AN/TPS-1		120 mi. at 10,000'	2	Used until 1948. Various models.
AN/CPS-6 ------- New component Added in 1954		100 mi. at 16,000' / 165 mi. at 45,000'	25	Required 85 freight cars to ship complete unit & components. Next component in 1954 extends range. Phased out in 1959.
AN/TPS-10		200 mi. at 10,000'		Effective at detecting bombers within 60 mi. at 10,000'.
Post World War II Radar				
AN/FPS-3		Over 200 mi. At 65,000'		Search radar first installed in 1950.
AN/FPS-6, 6A, and 6B				Main height finding radar of the 1950s.
AN/FPS-7		270 mi. at 100,000'		Used for air defense and at airports for air traffic control.
AN/FPS-8				Medium range search radar. Only 200 units produced between 1954-1958.
AN/FPS-14		Approx. 65 mi.		Gap Filler Radar (covers low altitudes)
AN/FPS-18				Medium search radar used 1950s-1960s.
AN/FPS-19				Gap Filler Radar(low altitude) for DEW Line
AN/FPS-20, 20A and 20B		Over 200 mi.		Main search radar for US air defense net in late 1950s.
AN/IFPS-27,27A		200 mi. at 150,000'		Search radar. First installed in 1963.
BALLISTIC MISSILE EARLY WARNING SYSTEM (BMEWS) Radars				
AN/FPS-49, 49A		3,000 mi.		Tracking radar, also used for satellite tracking. Deployed in BMEWS in 1960s.
AN/FPS-50				Two units installed in BMEWS in early 1960s in Alaska & Greenland. Determines trajectories and targets of missiles.
AN/FPS-85				Detects submarine launched missiles.

Other radars developed and put into use during the late 1960s and after.

Source: *Searching the Skies* by David Winkler

GLOSSARY

Abatis or Abattis—branches and trees cut and usually sharpened where possible, and laid out in a row or rows to form a barrier. One end is generally anchored to the ground.

Adobe—earth- or clay-like material made into sundried bricks. *See also* Tabby.

Banquette—the firing step behind the parapet on the rampart.

Bastion—a part of a fortification projecting out from the wall. Many of the first bastions were circular, but the angular ones were more effective for their main purpose of providing firing positions to cover the curtains. The angular bastions had two walls (left and right faces) meeting to form an angle and two additional walls (flanks) turned inward where they met the curtain. A demi-bastion or half-bastion had only one face and one flank.

Blockhouse—A stout wooden or masonry building, usually square, but not always. It consists of loopholes for defense and had one or more floors usually with the second floor wider than the first.

Caponier—a position which extends into the moat or ditch to defend it.

Carnot Wall—a high protective wall built in the moat in front of the curtain walls. It included firing positions for musketry while the ramparts behind it usually rose above it with positions for artillery. It was intended to mask the curtain wall from direct enemy fire and allow the defenders to control the counterscarp with small-arms fire. Conceived by a Frenchman and used in Europe, only Fort Gaines and Fort Clinch had this feature in the U.S.

Carronade—a large-caliber short-barrel cannon designed to deliver a heavy projectile at close range on ships; later used to cover the flanks of forts from bastions.

Casemate—usually refers to a bombproof room; many of these had vaulted roofs; usually designed with an embrasure for a weapon.

Cavalier—a platform or tower-like structure rising above the ramparts placed on the terreplein usually for mounting artillery.

Chevaux-de-frise—an obstacle known by various names, including "Spanish horse" and "knife rest." It includes a shaft from which are projected sharpened stakes (wooden or metal). They can be used to form a line or used individually to block roads or paths.

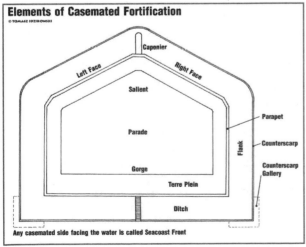

Elements of Casemated Fortification
© TOMASZ IDZIKOWSKI

Caponier

Left Face

Right Face

Salient

Parapet

Parade

Counterscarp

Flank

Gorge

Counterscarp Gallery

Terre Plein

Ditch

Any casemated side facing the water is called Seacoast Front

Citadel—a strongpoint in a fortification, usually a fort that formed part of the defenses of a walled city.

Counterguard or counter gard—a position with two faces like a ravelin, but the angle is not as acute. This type of position protects the flanks of a bastion or ravelin.

Counterscarp—the outer wall of the moat.

Covered Way—position on the counterscarp covered by the curtain walls behind it and allowing troops to defend the move to a firing position (the banquette) along the glacis in advance of the forts walls.

Cremaillere—in the American Civil War these were fieldworks with a saw tooth trace.

Crown work—an outwork with two demi-bastions on its corners and a bastion in the middle.

Cunette—a small ditch running in the center of a dry ditch or moat to serve as a drain.

Elements of Bastioned Fortification

© TOMASZ IDZIKOWSKI

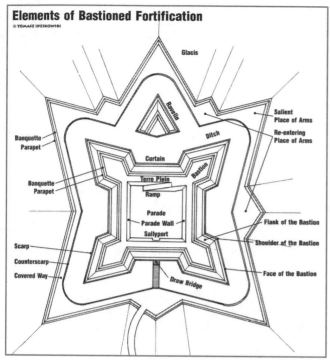

Curtain—usually refers to the walls of a fort or castle; in bastioned positions the walls between bastions.

Demi-bastion—*See* Bastion

Demi-Lune—*See* Ravelin

Enceinte—the enclosing positions (walls, bastions, etc.) of a fortified position, but not the outworks.

Embrasure—firing position in the parapet or walls of a fortification. Usually refers to an opening in a parapet or the casemate wall for artillery.

Epaulement—generally a work covering a side of a position which consists of fascines, gabions, sandbags, or even just a plain earthwork to provide protection against enemy flanking fire.

Esplanade—a cleared level area between a fortress and a town; also called a parade.

Fascines—bundles of sticks used to reinforce or revet an earthen fortification.

Flèche—a simple fieldwork, usually an earthen position, that has two faces forming a salient angle. The word is French and refers to an arrow which is also the arrow shape this type of position takes. (See half-redoubt)

Fougasses—a type of mine filled with explosives and covered.

Fraises—stakes inserted into the exterior of a rampart, the scarp or counterscarp as an obstacle to assaulting infantry.

Gabions—type of wicker basket-like work that can be used to reinforce earthen walls when filled with earth or also used by the besieger when building saps and parallels.

Glacis—usually a leveled and cleared area with a gentle slope down from the parapet above the covered way. It gave the defenders a clear field of fire from the outer parapet formed by the end of the glacis and also served to mask much of the fort, especially the curtains, from the direct view of the enemy.

Gorge—the rear face of a fortification. In many late-19th-century works includes the entrance, barracks, kitchen, etc.

Elements of fortification - profiles

© TOMASZ IDZIKOWSKI

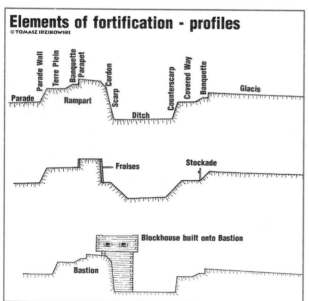

Haxo Casemate—developed be the Frenchman F. N. Haxo, these are found as a recommended type of position in many texts. It was basically a casemate built as part of the parapet and rising above the terreplein. In American fortifications it usually had thick earth covering for roof protection and and iron as part of its structure facing the enemy.

Hornwork—usually a position that included two half-bastions connected by a curtain.

Loophole—refers to an opening in the walls, usually for a rifle.

Lunette—in American fortifications this was a common individual position which had two fronts forming a salient angle and two parallel flanks. When part of a larger fortification it was placed with the ravelin.

Machicoulis—this was generally an extension added to the parapet which projected out from the parapet or was part of the parapet that projected beyond the wall so the defenders could fire down at anyone near the foot of the walls. Only used in some cases in America and usually not a complete machicoulis. It was a design mostly found on medieval castles.

Outwork—positions constructed outside the enceinte.

Palisade—a wall enclosure made of timbers set vertically in the ground. Usually a palisade (French term) by definition in English consisted of light timbers sunk into the ground which were loosely linked together in a vertical position (see stockade). The height of these timber walls was generally 15 to 18 feet and the tops of the wooden stakes were usually sharpened.

Parapet—the portion of wall or earthwork which rises above the rampart to give protection to the defenders on the banquette or terreplein.

Picket Fence—term sometimes used to refer to a palisade wall.

Priest Cap—Common term in the Civil War used for a field fortification that was shaped like a redan with two salient angles.

Presidio—a Roman Latin term usually referring to a small fort.

Rampart—the raised part of an earthwork or walls that forms the elevated part of the defenses.

Ravelin—an outwork, usually triangular shaped, used to mask either part of the curtain wall or cover the entrance. Also known as a demi-lune.

Rebar—term used to describe steel reinforcement bars used to strengthen concrete structures. The bars are of various thickness and are emplaced with a variety of methods before the concrete is poured.

Redan—a two faced outwork forming a salient known as a flèche and open at the rear, but in many cases not as simple a construction as a flèche. Generally it is an outwork, but the original French term referred to a jagged work which was linked to the curtain of the main work. When part of a curtain, many English sources refer to it as a salient rather than a redan.

Redoubt—a small, enclosed fortification that is often referred to as a fort. It does not include bastions and it could also be part of a fort.

Re-entering angle—an angle that projects inwards from the enemy.

Retrenchment—a line of defense constructed inside a fortification in the event part the outer section of the fort is taken.

Revetment—refers to the use of wood or masonry to maintain the shape of an earthwork.

Salient—part of a bastion projecting towards the enemy. Also used to refer to part of curtain or any feature that point outward toward the enemy.

Salient angle—an angle that projects toward the enemy.

Sap—a trench used by the besieger to advance his siege lines usually a zigzag type.

Scarp—the inner wall of the moat

Star Fort—has no bastions, only salient and re-entering angles that form a star shape.

Stockade—appears to be an English term generally used interchangeably with palisade (see palisade). Some English sources specify that a stockade had its timber stakes placed more tightly together and that usually they were thick.

Tabby—refers to a combination of mud mixed with oyster shells. It was poured into a wooden form to harden and then covered with lime, which acted as a cement. This was a type of construction that was used in areas too humid for adobe.

Tenon and Mortise—a method of construction using both logs and planks with small projections or tenons at the end of each plank or log and a mortise, an opening or groove in a vertical post, in which the tenon could fit. Usually the mortise was continuous so that the logs or planks could be placed horizontally between two vertical posts with the tenons fitting into the mortises.

Tenaille—a position placed in the moat or ditch protecting a length of curtains between two bastions from direct fire.

Terreplein—located behind the parapet, this was the broad level platform area for mounting the artillery and was also used as a passage.

Traverse—an earthen embankment placed to protect a position, usually an artillery position, from enfilade fire. Normally found in the interior.

BIBLIOGRAPHY

Key sources and other important books and reports on fortifications are in **bold**.

CDGS=Coast Defense Study Group, GPO=Government Printing Office, NPS=National Park Service

Ansel, William Jr. ***Frontier Forts Along the Potomac and Its Tributaries.*** Parsons (WV): McLain Printing Com., 1984 (1995 rep.).

Athearn, Robert G. *Forts of the Upper Missouri.* Lincoln (NB): University of Nebraska Press, 1967.

Azoy, LTC A.C.M. "A History of the Coast Artillery Corps (Part II)." *The Coast Artillery Journal,* Nov/Dec 1941, 573-78.

Barnard, Brev. Maj. Gen. J.G. ***A Report on the Defences of Washington to the Chief of Engineers.*** Professional Papers of The Corps of Engineers No. 20. Washington: U.S. GPO, 1871.

Barnard, Col. J.G., LTC H.G. Wright and Capt. P. Miche. ***Report on the Fabrication of Iron for Defense Purposes and Uses in Modern Fortifications Especially in Works of Coast Defence.*** Washington,GPO 1871.

Barnes, Frank. *Fort Sumter: National Monument South Carolina.* Washington, D.C.: NPS, 1952 (1962 rep.).

Barnes, LTC H.C. "A Regimental Organization for the Coast Artillery Corps." *The Coast Artillery Journal* 60, no. 4 (April 1924): 293-99.

Barry, James P. *Old Forts of the Great Lakes: Sentinels in the Wilderness.* Lansing (MI): Thunder Bay Press, 1994.

Bearss, Edwin C. "Unconditional Surrender: The Fall of Fort Donelson." *Tennessee Historical Quarterly* XXI, no. Nos 1 & 2 (1962).

_____. *The Fall of Fort Henry, Tennessee.* Eastern National Park and Monument Association, 1963.

Bearss, Edwin C. and Arrell M. Gibson. *Fort Smith: Little Gibraltar on the Arkansas.* Eastern National, 1969.

Berhow, Mark. "Alaska: A Brief Military History 1867-1945." *The Fort MacArthur ALERT 5,* no. 4 (Fall 1993).

Berhow, Mark A., ed. ***American Seacoast Defenses: A Reference Guide.*** Bel Air (MD): CDSG Press, 1999.

_____. "Caretaker Status in the Coast Artillery, 1912-1948." *CDSG Journal* 14, no. 4 (Nov 2000): 48-57.

Berhow, M.A. and T. McGovern. *American Defenses of Corregidor and Manila Bay.* Oxford: Osprey, 2003.

Board of Review of the War Department. ***Report of the Board of Review of the War Department on the Coast Defenses of the United States, the Panama Canal and the Insular Possessions.*** Washington: GPO, 1916.

Boatner, Mark M. III. *Encyclopedia of the American Revolution.* Mechanicsburg (PA): Stackpole Books, 1966.

Bogart, Charles H. ***Controlled Mine.*** Bennington (VT): Merriam Press, 1999.

Bradley, Dr. Chester. *Tales of Old Fort Monroe.* Fort Monroe (VA): Casemate Museum, 1965 c.

Branch, Paul. "The Confederate Defense of Fort Macon (Part I and Part II)." *Fort Macon Rampart,* Fall 2000 and Spring 2001. Http://www.clis.com/friends/default.htm.

Browning, Robert S. III. ***Two If by Sea: The Development of American Coastal Defense Policy.*** Westport (CT): Greenwood Press, 1983.

Brown, Roger D. *Sentinels from the Past: A Personal History of the Forts of Nova Scotia.* Windsor (Nova Scotia): Lancelot Press, 1977.

Buss, Lydus H. *U.S. Air Defense in the Northeast 1940-1957.* Historical Reference Paper Number 1. Colorado Springs (CO): Directorate of Command History, Office of Information Services, HQ Continental Air Defense Command, 1957.

Butler, Gerald W. *Military Annals of Nahant, Massachusetts.* Nahant (MA): Nahant Historical Society, 1996.

_____. *The Guns of Boston Harbor.* 1st Books, 2001.

Cagle, Mary T. *Development, Production, and Deployment of the Nike Ajax Guided Missile System 1945-1959.* Redstone Arsenal (AL): U.S. Army Missile Command, 1959.

Calhoun, John. *Letter from Sec. of War to Chairman of the Committee of Ways and Means on the Subject of the Appropriation for the Military Service of the Untied States, for the Year 1819.* Washington: Krafft, 1818.

Carter, Brig. General W.H. *Our Coast Defenses: General Staff Report.* Washington: GPO, 1903.

Charbonneau, André. *The Fortifications of Île Aux Noix: A Portrait of the Defensive Strategy on the Upper Richelieu Border in the 18th and 19th Centuries.* Ottawa: Department of Canadian Heritage, 1994.

Chartrand, René. *Louisbourg 1758: Wolfe's First Siege.* Oxford (UK): Osprey, 2000.

_____. *Ticonderoga 1758: Montcalm's Victory Against All Odds.* Oxford (UK): Osprey, 2000.

Chin, Brian B. ***Artillery at the Golden Gate: The Harbor Defenses of San Francisco in World War II.*** Missoula (MT): Pictorial Histories Publishing, 1994.

Clarke, Sir George Sydenham. ***Fortification: Its Past Achievements, Recent Developments, and Future Progress.*** Liphook (UK): Beaufort Publishing Ltd., 1907 (1995 reprint).

Clary, David A. ***Fortress America: The Corps of Engineers, Hampton Roads, and United States Coastal Defense.*** Charlottesville (VA): University Press of Virginia, 1990.

Coast Artillery Journal. *Gunner's Instruction, Submarine Mining, XII.* Harrisburg : Military Service Publ., 1933.

Coe, Major General F.W. "Annual Report of the Chief of Coast Artillery, 1924." *The Coast Artillery Journal* 61, no. 6 (December 1924): 481-505.

Coleman, James C. and Irene S. *Pensacola Fortifications, 1698-1980: Guardians of the Gulf.* Pensacola (FL): Pensacola Historical Society, 1982 (1995 revised).

Conn, Stetson, Rose Engelman and Bryon Fairchild. *Guarding the United States and Its Outposts.* Washington, D.C.: Center of Military History, US Army, 1962 (2000 reprint).

Coolidge, Richard H. (Asst. Surgeon U.S. Army). *Statistical Report on the Sickness and Mortality in the Army of the United States from January 1839 to January 1855.* Washington: A.O.P. Nicholson Printer, 1856.

Coolidge, Richard H. (Asst. Surgeon U.S. Army). *Statistical Report on the Sickness and Mortality in the Army of the United States Compiled from The Records of the Surgeon General's Office from Jan. 1855 to Jan. 1850.* Wash.: George W. Bowman, Printer, 1860.

Cooling, Benjamin Franklin III. **Symbol, Sword and Shield: Defending Washington During the Civil War.** Shippensburg (PA): White Mane Publishing Co., 1975 (1991 rep.).

Cooling, Benjamin Franklin III and Walton H. Owen II. *Mr. Lincoln's Forts: A Guide to the Civil War Defenses of Washington.* Shippensburg (PA): White Mane Publishing Company, 1988.

Corps of Engineers History Office. *Historical Vigneetes-Volume 2.* Washington, D.C.: U.S. Government Printing Office, 1979 May. Http://www.usace.army.mil/inet/usace-docs/eng-phamphlets/ep870-1-1/toc.htm.

Cross, Col. Matthew A. "Turrets and Casemates for Seacoast Batteries." *The Coast Artillery Journal*, July/Aug. 1937, 306-07.

Cunningham, Edward. *The Port Hudson Campaign, 1862-1863.* Baton Rouge (LA): LSU Press, 1963 (1991 rep.).

Cuthbertson, Brian. *The Halifax Citadel.* Halifax: Formac Publishing Company Ltd., 2001.

Davis, Major G.B., Leslie Perry, J.W. Kirkley and Capt C.D. Cowled. *The Official Military Atlas of the Civil War*, Washington: GPO, 1891-1895 (Fairfax Press 1978 rep.).

Dearborn, Henry. Letter from Secretary of War to Chairman of Committee. Estimate of the Annual Expenses of an Army of 32,800 men. City of Washington, 1807, 9 December.

_____. Letter from Secretary of War Enclosing his Report on State of Fortifications of the Respective Ports and Harbours of the United States with Statement of the Monies Appropriated for Fortifications. City of Washington, 1807, 8 December.

Dorrance, William H. **Fort Kamehameha: The Story of the Harbor Defenses of Pearl Harbor.** Shippensburg (PA): White Mane Publishing Co., 1993.

Duane, William. "Letter from Dr. Mitchill to Judge Spencer." *Aurorand General Advertiser* (Philadelphia), 21 October 1808.

Eggenberger, David. *A Dictionary of Battles.* Binghamton (NY): Thomas Crowell Company, 1967.

Ellison, Robet S. *Fort Bridger: A Brief History.* Cheyenne (WY): Wyoming State Archives, Museums and Hist. Dept., 1931 (1981 rep.).

Endicott, William C., et.al. **Report of the Board on Fortifications or Other Defenses.** GPO: Washington, 1886.

Everhart, William C. *Vicksburg and the Opening of the Mississippi River, 1862-63.* Washington, D.C.: NPS, 1986.

Faust, Patricia L., ed. *Historical Times Illustrated Encyclopedia of the Civil War.* New York: Harper & Row, 1986.

Fonvielle, Chris E. Jr. *Fort Anderson: Battle for Wilmington.* Mason City (Iowa): Savas Publishing Co., 1999.

"Fort Barrancas 1875." *Pensacola Historical Society Quarterly* (1974) Pensacola: The Pensacola Historical Society.

Frazer, Robert W. **Forts of the West: Military Forts and Presidios and Posts Commonly Called Forts West of the Mississippi River to 1898.** Norman (OK): University of Oklahoma Press, 1962 (1975 rep.).

_____. **Mansfield on the Condition of the Western Forts 1853-54.** Norman (OK): Univ. of Oklahoma Press, 1963.

Freeman, Douglas Southall. *R.E. Lee: A Biography.* New York: Charles Scribner's Sons, 1934.

Gaines, William. "Fort Schuyler and the Defenses of the Eastern Approaches to New York Harbor: A Historic Resource Study." *Coast Defense Study Group Journal* 10, no. 4 (Nov. 1996): 56-91.

_____. "The Defenses of Cumberland Sound, 1738-1900." *Coast Defense Journal* 17, no. 4 (Nov. 2003): 51-76.

Gannon, Michael. *Operation Drumbeat.* New York: Harper & Row Publishers, 1990.

Gardner, Fulton, Q.C. "The Coast Artillery School." *The Military Engineer* XXVIII, # 160 (July/Aug 1936): 278-81.

Gibbon, Brig. Gen. John. *The Artillerist's Manual (2nd Ed).* Dayton: Morningside House, 1863 (1991 rep.).

Gibson, James N. *The History of the U.S. Nuclear Arsenal.* Greenwich (CT): Brompton Books, 1989.

Gibson, Major R.T. "Organization and Operation of a Coast Artillery Maintenance Detachment." *The Coast Artillery Journal*, Sept./Oct. 1933, 371-73.

Grant, Bruce. *American Forts: Yesterday and Today.* New York: E. P. Dutton & Co., 1965.

Grau, Lester W. and Dr. Jacob W. Kipp. "Maintaining Friendly Skies: Rediscovering Theater Aerospace Defense." *Aerospace Power Journal*, Summer 2002.

Groene, Bertram H. *Pike: A Fortress in the Wetlands.* Hammond (LA): Southeastern Louisiana University Press.

Guay, Martin. *The Fortifications of Québec.* Quebec: Editions Continuite, 1998.

Gunston, Bill. *Illustrated Encyclopedia of the World's Rockets & Missiles.* New York: Crescent Books, 1979.

Halleck, Henry Wager. **Elements of Military Art and Science; or, Course of Instruction in Strategy, Fortification, Tactics of Battles & Etc.** Westport (CT): Greenwood Press, 1846 (1971 rep.).

Hanft, Marshall. *The Cape Forts: Guardians of the Columbia.* Portland (OR): Oregon Historical Society, 1973.

Hannon, Leslie F. **Forts of Canada.** Canada: McClellan and Stewart Ltd., 1969.

Hansen, David M. "Fortress Without Guns." *Coast Defense Study Group Journal* 9, no. 3 (Aug 1995): 4-16.

_____. "The Gun-Lift Battery in the Defenses of the United States." *CDSG Journal* 10, no. 4 (1996).

_____. "Zalinski's Dynamite Gun." *Coast Defense Study Group Journal* 11, no. 1 (Feb 1997): 4-22.

Hart, Herbert M. *Old Forts of the Northwest.* New York: Bonanza Books, 1963.

_____. *Old Forts of the Southwest.* New York: Bonanza Books, 1964.

_____. *Pioneer Forts of the West.* New York: Bonanza Books, 1967.

_____. ***Tour Guide to Old Western Forts: The Posts & Camps of the Army, Navy & Marines on the Western Frontier, 1804-1916.*** Boulder (CO): Pruett Publishing Co., 1980.

Herwig, Holger H. *The United States in German Naval Planning 1889-1941.* Boston: Little, Brown & Co., 1976.

Hickenlooper, A. "Our Volunteer Engineers." *Sketches of War History 1861-1865*, 301-18. Cincinnati: Robert Clarke & Co., 1890.

Hinds, J. R. and E. Fitzgerald. *Bulwark and Bastion.* Las Vegas (NV): Council on Abandoned Military Posts, 1981.

Hines, Frank T. and Franklin W. W. *The Service of Coast Artillery.* New York: Goodenough & Woglom Co., 1910.

Hitsman, J. Mackay. *The Incredible War of 1812: A Military History.* Toronto: Robin Brass Studio, 1965.

Howard, Robert West. *Thundergate: The Forts of Niagara.* Englewood Cliffs (NJ): Prentice Hall, 1968.

Hunt, Elvid Colonel. "History of Fort Leavenworth 1827-1937." Fort Leavenworth: C&GS School Press, 1937.

Hutslar, Donald A. "Campus Martius." *Timeline: A Publication of the Ohio Historical Society* 18, no. 1 (Jan./Feb. 2001): 2-13.

Institute of Strategic Studies. *The Military Balance 1969-1970.* London, 1969.

Jackson, Donald and Dorothy Twohig, eds. ***The Diaries of George Washington.*** Charlottesville (VA): University Press of Virginia, 1976-79. Http://memory.loc.gov/ammem/gwhtml/gwseries.html.

Johnson, Robert U. and Clarence Clough Buel, ed. ***Battles and Leaders of the Civil War.*** New York: Century, 1914.

Jones, Charles C. Jr. *The Siege of Savannah in December, 1864, and the Confederate Operations in Georgia.* Jonesboro (GA): Freedom Hill Press, 1874 (1988 rep.).

Jones, J. Norman. "America's First Vietnam: The Seminole Wars." *Command*, no. 41 (Jan. 1997): 66-79.

Kerrick, Captain Harrison S. *Military and Naval America.* Garden City (NY): Doubleday, Page & Company, 1916.

Kirchner, Cmdr. D.P. and Dr. E.R. Lewis. "The Oahu Turrets." *The Military Engineer*, Nov.-Dec. 1967, 430-33.

Lang, Walt. *United States Military Almanac.* London: Salamander Books Ltd., 1998.

Lattimore, Ralston B. *Fort Pulaski National Monument, Georgia.* Washington, D.C.: National Park Service, 1954.

Lavender, David. *Fort Laramie and the Changing Frontier.* National Park Service, 1983.

Lawson, Surgeon General Thomas. *Statistical Report on the Sickness and Mortality in the Army of the Untied States from January 1819 to January 1839.* Washington: Jacob Gideon Jr., 1840.

LeLauterel, General and John N. Richardson, trans. ***Manual of Military Reconnaissances, Temporary Fortifications and Partisan Warfare for Officers of Infantry and Cavalry.*** Atlanta: J. McPherson,1862.

Lewis, Emanuel Raymnd. ***Seacoast Fortifications of the United States: An Introductory History.*** Washington, D.C.: Smithsonian Institute Press, 1970.

Lonquist, John C. and David F. Winkler. ***To Defend and Deter: The Legacy of the United States Cold War Missile Program.*** USACERL Special Report 97/01. Rock Island (IL): Defense Publishing Service, 1996.

Lovatt, R. ***Shoot, Shoot, Shoot: A History of the Victoria-Esquimalt Coast Artillery Defences 1878-1956.*** Canada: Rodd Hill Friends Society, 1993.

Mahan, Dennis H. *A Treatise on Field Fortification.* New York: John Wiley, 1861 (Third Edition, Revised).

_____. *Summary of the Course of Permanent Fortification and of the Attack and Defence of Permanent Works, for the Use of the Cadets of the U.S. Military Academy.* Charleston (SC): Steam Power Presses of Evans and Cogswell, 1862 (Rep. of previous ed.).

Mahon, John K. *History of the Second Seminole War 1835-1842.* Gainesville: University of Florida Press, 1985.

Malone, Danny R. "Seacoast Artillery Radar 1938-1946." *American Seacoast Fortifications: A Reference Guide*, 398-415. Bel Air (MD): CDSG Press, 2004.

Manucy, Albert. *Artillery Through the Ages.* Washington, D.C.: NPS, 1949 (1985 reprint).

Manuel, Dale. "Characteristics of the Second System." *Coast Defense Journal* 15, no. 1 (Feb 2001): 84-99.

Martini, John A. *Fortress Alcatraz: Guardian of the Golden Gate.* Kalua (Hawaii): Pacific Monograph, 1990.

Martson, Daniel. *The French-Indian War 1754-1760.* Oxford (UK): Osprey, 2002.

Matloff, Maurice, ed. *American Military History.* Conshohoken (PA): Combined Books, 1996.

Mattison, Ray H. ***The Army Post on the Northern Plains 1865-1885.*** Gering (NE): Oregon Trail Museum Assoc., 1954 (1965 rep.).

McCamley, N.J. ***Cold War Secret Nuclear Bunkers.*** Barnsley (UK): Leo Cooper, 2002.

McGovern, Terrance. "The American Defences in Panama." *FORT 26* (1998): 3-120.

McLennan, J.S. *Louisbourg: From Its Foundation to Its Fall.* Toronto: The Bryant Press Ltd., 1918 (1917 rep.).

Mclure, Stanley W. ***The Defenses of Washington 1861-1865.*** NPS, n.d. (1961 rep.).

Michno, Gregoary F. *Encyclopedia of Indian War 1850-1890.* Missoula (MT): Mountain Press Publ. Co., 2003.

Milburn, Captain Bryan L. "The Relation of Harbor Defenses to Naval and Military Strategy." *The Coast Artillery Journal*, Sep./Oct. 1932, 343-46.

Miller, Charles Jr., Donald Lockey and Joseph Viconti Jr. *Highland Fortress: The Fortification of West Point During the American Revolution 1775-1783.* West Point (NY): United States Military Academy, 1979.

Moeller, Colonel Stephen P. "Vigilant and Invincible, United States Army Air Defense Command." *Air Defense Artillery Magazine,* May/June 1995, 2-42.

Mokler, A. J. *Fort Caspar (Platte Bridge Station).* Caspar (WY): The Prairie Publishing Co., 1939 (1983 rep.).

Monett, John R., Lester Cole and Jack C. Cleland. *Harbor Defenses of Los Angeles in World War II.* Los Angeles: Fort MacArthur Military Press, 1945 (1992 rep.).

Moore, David. *A Handbook of Military Terms Used in Connection with Fortifications of the Victorian Era.* The Palmerston Forts Society, 1996.

Moore, Jamie W. *The Fortifications Board 1816-1828 and the Definition of National Security.* Charleston: The Citadel: Military College of South Carolina, 1981.

Moorhead, Max L. *The Presidio: Bastion of the Spanish Borderlands.* Norman: Univ of Oklahoma Press, 1975.

Morton, James St. C. *Memoir on the Dangers and Defences of New York City: Addressed to the Hon. John B. Floyd, Secretary of War.* Washington: William A. Harris, 1858.

_____. *A New Plan for the Fortification of Certain Points of the Sea Coast of the United States.* Washington: William A. Harris, 1858.

_____. *Memoir on American Fortification Submitted to the Hon. John B. Floyd, Secretary of War.* Wash.: William A. Harris, Printer, 1859.

Muir, Thomas Jr. and David P. Ogden. *The Fort Pickens Story.* Pensacola (FL): Pensacola Historical Society, 1989.

Nebenzahl, Kenneth and Don Higginbotham. *Atlas of the American Revolution.* Chicago: Rand McNally, 1974.

Nelson, George. *The Alamo: An Illustrated History.* Uvalde (TX): Adline Press, 1998.

Niles, H. "Report on Fortifications, Department of War, 12 February 1821." *Niles Weekly Register* XX (23 June 1821): 263-69.

_____. "Fortifications of Canada, British House of Commons, July 7, 1828." *Nils Weekly Register* XXXV (6 Sept. 1828): 26-32.

Nimmo, Joseph. "Our Unprotected Seacoast." *Frank Leslie's Popular Monthly* XXIII, no. 3-17 (Mar 1887): 260 -72.

Office of History Staff. *The History of the U.S. Army Corps of Engineers.* Washington, D.C.: U.S. Government Printing Office, 1998. Http://www.hp.usace.army.mil/history/pubs.htm#on.

Office of the Chief of Ordnance. *American Coast Artillery Matériel.* Washington: U.S. GPO, 1922.

Ogden, David P. *The Fort Barrancas Story.* Eastern National, n.d.

Oliva, Leo E. *Fort Larned: Guardian of the Santa Fe Trail.* Topeka: Kansas State Historical Society, 1982.

_____. *Fort Scott: Courage and Conflict on the Border.* Topeka (KS): Kansas State Historical Society, 1984.

"Our Sea Coast Defense and Fortification System." *Putnam's Monthly Mag. of American Literature, Science and Art I,* no. 39 (Mar. 1856).

Page, Dave. *Ships Versus Shore.* Nashville: Rutledge Hill Press, 1994.

Parks, Virginia, Alan Rick and Norman Simons. *Pensacola in the Civil War.* Pensacola (FL): Pensacola Hist. Soc., 1978 (1997 rep.).

Pell, S.H.P., comp. *Fort Ticonderoga: A Short History.* Fort Ticonderoga Museum, 1966.

Peterson, Harold L. *Forts in America.* New York: Charles Scribner's Sons, 1964.

Poncelet, M. and Captain D.P. Woodbury. *Sustaining Walls: Geometrical Constructions to Determine Their Thickness Under Various Circumstances.* Papers on Practical Engineering No.3. Washington: Taylor and Maury, 1854 (2nd Ed.).

Porter, Charles III. *Fort Raleigh and the First English Settlement in the New World.* NPS, Div of Publications, 1985.

Purcell, Edward L. and Sarah J. Purcell. *Encyclopedia of Battles in North America: 1517 to 1916.* NY: Checkmark Books, 2000.

Quarstein, John V. and Dennis Mroczkowski. *Fort Monroe: The Key to the South.* Charleston (SC): Arcadia., 2000.

Ragan, Mark K. *Submarine Warfare in the Civil War.* Cambridge (MA): Da Capo Press, 1999 (2002 rep.).

Ray, Thomas W. *A History of Texas Towers in Air Defense 1952-1964.* U.S.A.F. Texas Tower Association.org. Http://www.texastower.com/a_history_in_texas_towers_air_defense.htm.

R. Christopher Goodwin & Associates, comp. *Historic Context for Department of Defense–World War II Permanent Construction.* Frederick (MD), 1997.

Reed, Rowena. *Combined Operations in the Civil War.* Annapolis (MD): Naval Institute Press, 1978.

Ripley, Warren. *Artillery and Ammunition of the Civil War.* New York: Promontory Press, 1970.

Robertson, R.G. *Competitive Struggle: America's Western Fur Trading Posts. 1764-1865.* Boise: Tamarack, 1999.

Roberts, Robert. *Encyclopedia of Historic Forts: The Military, Pioneer and Trading Posts of the United States.* New York: Macmillan Publishing Company, 1988.

Robinson, Willard B. *American Forts: Architectural Form and Function.* Chicago: Amon Carter Museum of Western Art, Fort Worth, 1977.

Sarty, Roger F. *Coast Artillery 1815-1914.* Bloomfield (Ontario): Museum Restoration Service, 1988.

Satterfield, Archie and David Lavender. *Fort Vancouver.* NPS, Division of Publications, n.d.

Scheliha, Viktor Ernst Karl Rudolf von. *Treatise on Coast Defence*. London: E. & F. N. Spon, 1868.

Schemmer, Benjamin et. al. *Almanac of Liberty: A Chronology of American Military Anniversaries from 1775 to the Present*. New York: Macmillan Publishing Co., 1974.

Schwartz, Seymour I. *The French and Indian War 1754-1763*. New York: Simon & Schuster, 1994.

Simmons, David A. "Military Architecture on the American Frontier." *Selected Papers from the 1983 and 1984 George Rogers Clark Trans-Appalachian Frontier History Conferences*, 81-99. Vincennes (IN), 1985.

Smith, Bolling. "The 16-Inch Batteries at San Francisco and the Evolution of the Casemated 16-Inch Battery." *Coast Defense Journal* 15, no. 1 (Feb. 2001): 16-83.

Smith, Bolling W. "Seacoast Weapons of the Rodman Period, 1866-1898."*CDSG Journal* 13, #2 (May 1999):4 -38.

Stern, Philip van Doren. *The Confederate Navy: A Pictorial History*. New York: Da Capo, 1962 (1992 rep.).

Stokeley, Jim. *Fort Moultrie: Constant Defender*. NPS, Division of Publications, 1985.

Swift, Joseph Gardner. *Report of General Joseph G. Swift of the Sums Required for the Several Fortifications and of the Buildings of West Point*. Washington, 1815 January.

Symonds, Craig L. *A Battlefield Atlas of the Civil War*. Baltimore: Nautical and Aviation Publishing Co., 1983.

_____. *A Battlefield Atlas of the American Revolution*. Baltimore: Nautical & Aviation Publishing Co., 1986.

Thompson, Enid et.al. *Bent's Old Fort*. State Historical Society of Colorado, 1997.

Thompson, Kenneth E. "Gun Houses in New England 1808." *CDSG Journal* 11, no. 3 (Aug. 1997).

Tilberg, Frederick. *Fort Necessity: National Battlefield Site, Pennsylvania*. Washington, D.C.: GPO, 1954.

Totten, Brevet Brig. General Joseph G. Totten. *Report Addressed to the Hon. Jefferson Davis, Secretary of War, on the Effects of Firing with Heavy Ordnance From Casemate Embrasures and the Effects of Firing Against The Same Embrasures with Various Kinds of Missiles at West Point*. Washington: Taylor and Maury, 1857.

Totten, Joseph G. *Report of the Chief Engineer*. Washington, 1853.

U.S. Army. *Army Antiaircraft in Air Defense 1946 to 1954*. Historical Study No.4. Colorado Springs (CO): Directorate of Historical Services, Headquarters ADC, 1954.

U.S. Congress. *Executive Documents in 1st Session, 32nd Congress*. Washington: U.S. Government, 1851-52.

_____. *Permanent Fortifications and Sea-Coast Defences*. Bel Air (MD): CDSG Press, 1862 (1998 rep.).

U.S. Missile and Munitions Center and School. *Nike Missile System Orientation*. Redstone Arsenal (AL), 1976.

Waddell, Louis M. and Bruce D. Bomberger. *The French and Indian War in Pennsylvania 1753-1763*. Harrisburg (PA): Pennsylvania Historical and Museum Commission, 1996.

Walker, Paul K. *Engineers of Independence: A Documentary History of the Army Engineers in the American Revolution, 1775-1783*. Washington, D.C.: GPO, 1985.

War Department. *The War of the Rebellion: A Compilation of the Official Records of the Union and Confederate Armies*. Washington: GPO, 1880-1901. Http://cdl.library.cornell.edu/moa/growse.mono-graphs/waro.html.

_____. *Coast Artillery Field Manual: Volume I: Seacoast Artillery*. Washington: GPO, 1933.

Washington, George. *The George Washington Papers at the Library of Congress 1741-1799*. Washington, D.C.: Manuscript Division, Library of Congress. Http://memory.loc.gov/ammem/gwhtml/gwhome.html.

Waters, K.L. "The Army Mine Planter Service." *Warship International*, no. 4 (1985): 400-11.

Weaver, John R. II. *A Legacy in Brick and Stone, 1816-1867*. Missoula (MT): Pictorial Histories, 2001.

Weigley, Russell F. *The American Way of War*. New York: Macmillan Publishing Co., 1973.

Weinert, Richard P. Jr. and Colonel Robert Arthur. *Defender of the Chesapeake: The Story of Fort Monroe*. Shippensburg (PA): White Mane Publishing Co., 1930 (1989 rep.).

Williams, Major C.F. *History of the Fortification of the Canal Zone*. Balboa Heights (C.Z.), 1931.

Williford, G. "Middle Ground of Chesapeake Bay–An Almost Fortress" *CDSG Journal* 14, no. 4 (Nov 2000): 39-47.

Winkler, David. *Searching the Skies: The Legacy of the United States Cold War Radar Defense Program*. Langley AFB (VA): HQ Air Combat Command, 1997.

Winslow, Col. Eben Eveleth. *Notes on Seacoast Fortification Construction*. Occasional Papers Engineer School, U.S. Army. Washington: GPO, 1920.

Wright, Horatio G. *Report of The Chief of Engineers, United States Army*. Washington: U.S. GPO, 1881.

INDEX